Communications
in Computer and Information Science 133

Natarajan Meghanathan Brajesh Kumar Kaushik
Dhinaharan Nagamalai (Eds.)

Advanced Computing

First International Conference on Computer Science
and Information Technology, CCSIT 2011
Bangalore, India, January 2-4, 2011
Proceedings, Part III

Springer

Volume Editors

Natarajan Meghanathan
Jackson State University
Jackson, MS, USA
E-mail: nmeghanathan@jsums.edu

Brajesh Kumar Kaushik
Indian Institute of Technology
Roorkee, India
E-mail: bkk23fec@iitr.ernet.in

Dhinaharan Nagamalai
Wireilla Net Solutions PTY Ltd
Melbourne, Victoria, Australia
E-mail: dhinthia@yahoo.com

Library of Congress Control Number: 2010941308

CR Subject Classification (1998): H.4, C.2, I.2, H.3, D.2, I.4

ISSN 1865-0929
ISBN-10 3-642-17880-4 Springer Berlin Heidelberg New York
ISBN-13 978-3-642-17880-1 Springer Berlin Heidelberg New York

springer.com

Printed in Germany

Typesetting: Camera-ready by author, data conversion by Scientific Publishing Services, Chennai, India
Printed on acid-free paper 06/3180

Preface

The First International Conference on Computer Science and Information Technology (CCSIT-2011) was held in Bangalore, India, during January 2–4, 2011. CCSIT attracted many local and international delegates, presenting a balanced mixture of intellect from the East and from the West.

The goal of this conference series is to bring together researchers and practitioners from academia and industry to focus on understanding computer science and information technology and to establish new collaborations in these areas. Authors are invited to contribute to the conference by submitting articles that illustrate research results, projects, survey work and industrial experiences describing significant advances in all areas of computer science and information technology.

The CCSIT-2011 Committees rigorously invited submissions for many months from researchers, scientists, engineers, students and practitioners related to the relevant themes and tracks of the workshop. This effort guaranteed submissions from an unparalleled number of internationally recognized top-level researchers. All the submissions underwent a strenuous peer-review process which comprised expert reviewers. These reviewers were selected from a talented pool of Technical Committee members and external reviewers on the basis of their expertise. The papers were then reviewed based on their contributions, technical content, originality and clarity. The entire process, which includes the submission, review and acceptance processes, was done electronically. All these efforts undertaken by the Organizing and Technical Committees led to an exciting, rich and a high-quality technical conference program, which featured high-impact presentations for all attendees to enjoy, appreciate and expand their expertise in the latest developments in computer network and communications research.

In closing, CCSIT-2011 brought together researchers, scientists, engineers, students and practitioners to exchange and share their experiences, new ideas and research results in all aspects of the main workshop themes and tracks, and to discuss the practical challenges encountered and the solutions adopted. We would like to thank the General and Program Chairs, organization staff, the members of the Technical Program Committees and external reviewers for their excellent and tireless work. We also want to thank Springer for the strong support, and the authors who contributed to the success of the conference. We sincerely wish that all attendees benefited scientifically from the conference and wish them every success in their research.

It is the humble wish of the conference organizers that the professional dialogue among the researchers, scientists, engineers, students and educators continues beyond the event and that the friendships and collaborations forged will linger and prosper for many years to come.

Natarajan Meghanathan
B.K. Kaushik
Dhinaharan Nagamalai

Organization

General Chairs

David C. Wyld	Southeastern Louisiana University, USA
Selwyn Piramuthu	University of Florida, USA

General Co-chairs

Michal Wozniak	Wroclaw University of Technology, Poland
Jae Kwang Lee	Hannam University, South Korea

Steering Committee

Eric Renault	Institut Telecom–Telecom SudParis, France
Natarajan Meghanathan	Jackson State University, USA
Nabendu Chaki	University of Calcutta, India
Khoa N. Le	Griffith University, Australia
Kamalrulnizam Abu Bakar	Universiti Teknologi Malaysia, Malaysia
Abdul Kadhir Ozcan	The American University, Cyprus
John Karamitsos	University of the Aegean, Samos, Greece
Dhinaharan Nagamalai	Wireilla Net Solutions PTY Ltd., Australia
Brajesh Kumar Kaushik	Indian Institute of Technology - Roorkee, India

Program Committee Members

Sajid Hussain	Acadia University, Canada
Seungmin Rho	Carnegie Mellon University, USA
Emmanuel Bouix	iKlax Media, France
Charalampos Z. Patrikakis	National Technical University of Athens, Greece
Chin-Chih Chang	Chung Hua University, Taiwan
Yung-Fa Huang	Chaoyang University of Technology, Taiwan
Jeong-Hyun Park	Electronics Telecommunication Research Institute, South Korea
Abdul Kadir Ozcan	The American University, Cyprus
Al-Sakib Khan Pathan	Kyung Hee University, South Korea
Andy Seddon	Asia Pacific Institute of Information Technology, Malaysia
Atilla Elci	Eastern Mediterranean University, Cyprus

B. Srinivasan	Monash University, Australia
Balasubramanian K.	Lefke European University, Cyprus
Boo-Hyung Lee	KongJu National University, South Korea
Chih-Lin Hu	National Central University, Taiwan
Cho Han Jin	Far East University, South Korea
Cynthia Dhinakaran	Hannam University, South Korea
Dhinaharan Nagamalai	Wireilla Net Solutions Pty Ltd., Australia
Dimitris Kotzinos	Technical Educational Institution of Serres, Greece
Dong Seong Kim	Duke University, USA
Farhat Anwar	International Islamic University, Malaysia
Firkhan Ali Bin Hamid Ali	Universiti Tun Hussein Onn Malaysia, Malaysia
Ford Lumban Gaol	University of Indonesia
Girija Chetty	University of Canberra, Australia
H.V. Ramakrishnan	MGR University, India
Henrique Joao Lopes Domingos	University of Lisbon, Portugal
Ho Dac Tu	Waseda University, Japan
Hoang, Huu Hanh	Hue University, Vietnam
Hwangjun Song	Pohang University of Science and Technology, South Korea
Jacques Demerjian	Communication & Systems,Homeland Security, France
Jae Kwang Lee	Hannam University, South Korea
Jan Zizka	SoNet/DI, FBE, Mendel University in Brno, Czech Republic
Jeong-Hyun Park	Electronics Telecommunication Research Institute, South Korea
Jivesh Govil	Cisco Systems Inc. - CA, USA
Johann Groschdl	University of Bristol, UK
John Karamitsos	University of the Aegean, Samos, Greece
Johnson Kuruvila	Dalhousie University, Halifax, Canada
Jose Enrique Armendariz-Inigo	Universidad Publica de Navarra, Spain
Jungwook Song	Konkuk University, South Korea
K.P.Thooyamani	Bharath University, India
Khoa N. Le	Griffith University , Australia
Krzysztof Walkowiak	Wroclaw University of Technology, Poland
Lu Yan	University of Hertfordshire, UK
Luis Veiga	Technical University of Lisbon, Portugal
Marco Roccetti	University of Bologna, Italy
Michal Wozniak	Wroclaw University of Technology, Poland
Mohsen Sharifi	Iran University of Science and Technology, Iran
Murugan D.	Manonmaniam Sundaranar University, India
N. Krishnan	Manonmaniam Sundaranar University, India

Nabendu Chaki	University of Calcutta, India
Natarajan Meghanathan	Jackson State University, USA
Nidaa Abdual Muhsin Abbas	University of Babylon, Iraq
Paul D. Manuel	Kuwait University, Kuwait
Phan Cong Vinh	London South Bank University, UK
Ponpit Wongthongtham	Curtin University of Technology, Australia
Rajendra Akerkar	Technomathematics Research Foundation, India
Rajesh Kumar P.	The Best International, Australia
Rajkumar Kannan	Bishop Heber College, India
Rakhesh Singh Kshetrimayum	Indian Institute of Technology-Guwahati, India
Ramayah Thurasamy	Universiti Sains Malaysia, Malaysia
Sagarmay Deb	Central Queensland University, Australia
Sanguthevar Rajasekaran	University of Connecticut, USA
Sarmistha Neogyv	Jadavpur University, India
Sattar B. Sadkhan	University of Babylon, Iraq
Sergio Ilarri	University of Zaragoza, Spain
Serguei A. Mokhov	Concordia University, Canada
SunYoung Han	Konkuk University, South Korea
Susana Sargento	University of Aveiro, Portugal
Salah S. Al-Majeed	University of Essex, UK
Vishal Sharma	Metanoia Inc., USA
Wei Jie	University of Manchester, UK
Yannick Le Moullec	Aalborg University, Denmark
Yeong Deok Kim	Woosong University, South Korea
Yuh-Shyan Chen	National Taipei University, Taiwan
Sriman Narayana Iyengar	VIT University, India
A.P. Sathish Kumar	PSG Institute of Advanced Studies, India
Abdul Aziz	University of Central Punjab, Pakistan.
Nicolas Sklavos	Technological Educational Institute of Patras, Greece
Shivan Haran	Arizona State University, USA
Danda B. Rawat	Old Dominion University, USA
Khamish Malhotra	University of Glamorgan, UK
Eric Renault	Institut Telecom – Telecom SudParis, France
Kamaljit I. Lakhtaria	Atmiya Institute of Technology and Science, India
Andreas Riener	Johannes Kepler University Linz, Austria
Syed Rizvi	University of Bridgeport, USA
Velmurugan Ayyadurai	Center for Communication Systems, UK
Syed Rahman	University of Hawaii-Hilo, USA

Sajid Hussain	Fisk University, USA
Suresh Sankaranarayanan	University of West Indies, Jamaica
Michael Peterson	University of Hawaii at Hilo, USA
Brajesh Kumar Kaushik	Indian Institute of Technology, India
Yan Luo	University of Massachusetts Lowell, USA
Yao-Nan Lien	National Chengchi University, Taiwan
Rituparna Chaki	West Bengal University of Technology, India
Somitra Sanadhya	IIT-Delhi, India
Debasis Giri	Haldia Institute of Technology, India
S.Hariharan	B.S. Abdur Rahman University, India

Organized By

ACADEMY & INDUSTRY RESEARCH COLLABORATION CENTER (AIRCC)

Table of Contents – Part III

Soft Computing (AI, Neural Networks, Fuzzy Systems, etc.)

Distributed and Parallel Systems and Algorithms

Security and Information Assurance

Ad Hoc and Ubiquitous Computing

Wireless Ad Hoc Networks and Sensor Networks

Erratum

Table of Contents – Part I

Distributed and Parallel Systems and Algorithms

DSP/Image Processing/Pattern Recognition/ Multimedia

Software Engineering

Database and Data Mining

Soft Computing (AI, Neural Networks, Fuzzy Systems, etc.)

Table of Contents – Part II

Networks and Communications

Network and Communications Security

Wireless and Mobile Networks

Analysis of the Severity of Hypertensive Retinopathy Using Fuzzy Logic

Aravinthan Parthibarajan[1], Gopalakrishnan Narayanamurthy[2], Arun Srinivas Parthibarajan[2], and Vigneswaran Narayanamurthy[3]

[1] Department of Computer Science and Engineering, DMI College of Engg., Chennai
[2] Department of Biomedical Engineering, SSN College of Engg., Chennai
[3] Department of Electronics and Communication, Jaya Engg. College, Chennai
aravind.prajan@gmail.com

Abstract. Eye, an organ associated with vision in man is housed in socket of bone called orbit and is protected from the external air by the eyelids. Hypertensive retinopathy is a one of the leading cause of blindness amongst the working class in the world. The retina is one of the "target organs" that are damaged by sustained hypertension. Subjected to excessively high blood pressure over prolonged time, the small blood vessels that involve the eye are damaged, thickening, bulging and leaking. Early detection can potentially reduce the risk of blindness. An automatic method to detect thickening, bulging and leaking from low contrast digital images of retinopathy patients is developed. Images undergo preprocessing for the removal of noise. Segmentation stage clusters the image into two distinct classes by the use of fuzzy c-means algorithm. This method has been tested using 50 images and the performance is evaluated. The results are encouraging and satisfactory and this method is to be validated by testing 200 samples.

Keywords: hypertensive retinopathy, hypertension, retinopathy, segmentation.

1 Introduction

Hypertensive retinopathy is the term used to describe the changes to the retinal vascular system that happen due to high blood pressure [1]. It is believed that retinal assessment may be a valuable tool in gathering information regarding systemic micro vascular injury [2].

Today, many guidelines define hypertensive retinopathy as target organ injury. Although the Joint National Committee (JNC) 7 report published in 2003 defines all retinopathy stages as target organ injury, World Health Organization (WHO) / International Society of Hypertension (ISH) 2003, British Hypertension Society (BHS) IV 2004, European Society of Hypertension (ESH)-European Society of Cardiology (ESC) 2003 guidelines suggest that only grades 3 and 4 should be accepted as target organ injury [2]. The Seventh Joint National Committee on Prevention, Detection, Evaluation, and Treatment of High Blood Pressure and the V Brazilian Guidelines on Hypertension list hypertensive retinopathy as a marker of target organ damage. Therefore, it is a criterion for prescription of treatment [3], [4]. However, the most common

N. Meghanathan et al. (Eds.): CCSIT 2011, Part III, CCIS 133, pp. 1–9, 2011.

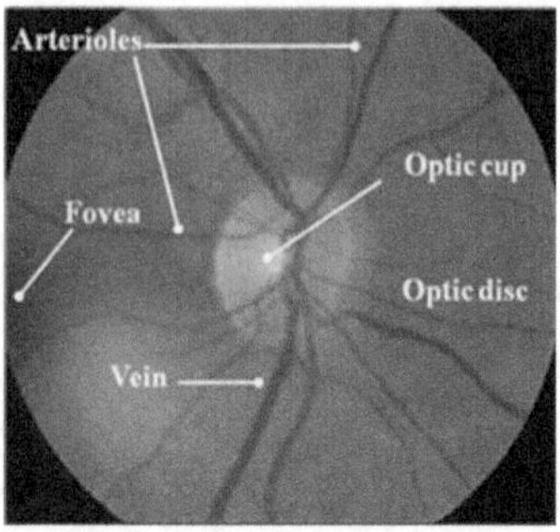

Fig. 1. Normal Ocular Fundus

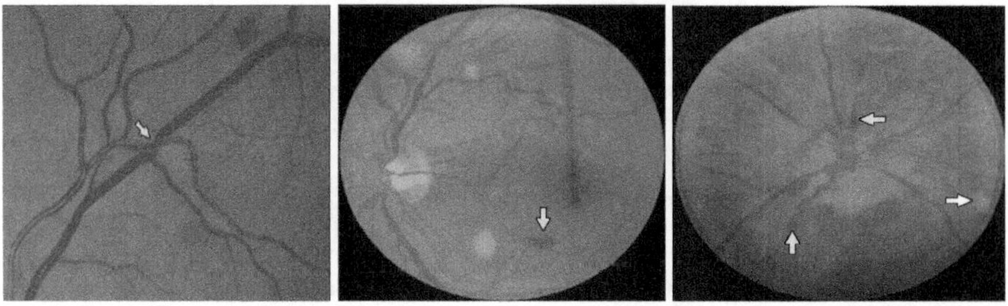

(a) (b) (c)

Fig. 2. (a) Grade 2, (b) Grade 3 & (c) Grade 4

grades of retinopathy are 1 and 2 [5].Therefore, it is important to understand the clinical significance of the retinal changes in these grades.

By 1939, Keith et al. had classified patients with hypertensive retinopathy into 4 groups. They described the course and prognosis of these patients with hypertension according to the degree of retinopathy. Group I was restricted to minimal constriction of the retinal arterioles with some tortuosity in mildly hypertensive patients. Group II included arteriovenous nipping, while group III included hemorrhaging and exudates. Group IV included papilledema [6],[7],[8]. Group I and II are compensated hypertensive retinopathy and Group III and IV are accelerated hypertensive retinopathy. MHT is a clinical syndrome characterized by severe systolic and diastolic hypertension, usually appearing progressively over a period of several weeks to several months; it is often associated with significant and progressive deterioration in cardiac or renal function, and there is evidence of encephalopathy [9]. The World Health Organization (WHO) criteria are probably the most useful for MHT; it now differentiates hypertensive retinopathy on the basis of 2 grades of changes in the fundus, fundus hypertonicus and fundus hypertonicus malignus [10]. Patients diagnosed as having malignant hypertension have severe hypertension with bilateral retinal hemorrhages and exudates. Papilledema, unless florid, is an unreliable physical sign and was of no additional prognostic importance in patients treated for hypertension who already had bilateral hemorrhaging and exudates [11] Diastolic blood pressure is usually greater than 130 mmHg, but there is no absolute level above which MHT always develops and below which it never occurs [12].

Table 1. Range of BP for different stages of Hypertensive Retinopathy

CATEGORY	SYSTOLIC BP (mmHg)	DIASTOLIC BP (mmHg)
NORMAL	<130	<85
HIGH NORMAL	130-139	85-89
STAGE 1 (MILD)	140-159	90-99
STAGE 2 (MOD.)	160-179	100-109
STAGE 3 (SEVERE)	180-209	110-119
STAGE 4(V. SEVERE)	>210	>120

Table 2. Stages of Hypertensive Retinopathy and its severity

	HEMORRHAGE	*EXUDATE*	*DISC EDEMA*
GRADE 0	-	-	-
GRADE 1	-	-	-
GRADE 2	-	-	-
GRADE 3	-	+	-
GRADE 4	-	+	+

Fuzzy c-means (FCM) clustering [13,14,15] is an unsupervised method that has been successfully applied to feature analysis, clustering, and classifier designs in fields such as astronomy, geology, medical imaging, target recognition, and image segmentation. An image can be represented in various feature spaces, and the FCM algorithm classifies the image by grouping similar data points in the feature space into clusters [16]. This clustering is achieved by iteratively minimizing a cost function that is dependent on the distance of the pixels to the cluster centers in the feature domain.

2 Methodology

Hypertensive retinopathy images of different grades of severity were obtained and were given as input to Fuzzy C Means (FCM) to undergo series of stages for highlighting the affected region in the image.

The images were of very high quality and there was no requirement to make them noise free using filters. FCM are used here to isolate the optic disk and exudates region from the input image, it converts the gray level image to a binary image. The algorithm assumes that the image to be threshold will contain two classes of pixels then calculates the optimum threshold separating those two classes so that their combined spread is minimal. The FCM method is better than the Otsu method.

Initially, the segmentation of optic disk was performed to avoid its interference during diagnosis by doctors for severity. The affected regions are segmented from the original image and are superimposed on the optic disk and nerve removed processed image. The affected regions are highlighted by setting pixel value to zero. Finally in the superimposed image of red and yellow colour the affected regions are differentiated by highlighting them with green colour.

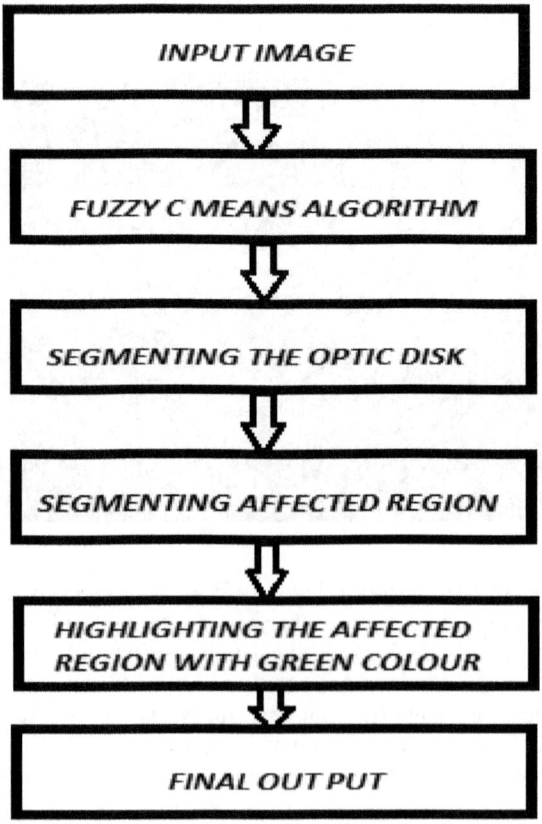

Fig. 3. Block diagram showing each stage of Image Processing

2.1 Program Code

```
clear;
close all;
im=imread('E3.jpg');
fim=mat2gray(im);
level=graythresh(fim);
bwfim=im2bw(fim,level);
[bwfim0,level0]=fcmthresh(fim,0);
[bwfim1,level1]=fcmthresh(fim,1);
subplot(2,2,1);
imshow(fim);title('Original');
subplot(2,2,2);
imshow(bwfim);title(sprintf('Otsu,level=%f',level));
subplot(2,2,3);
imshow(bwfim0);title(sprintf('FCM0,level=%f',level0));
subplot(2,2,4);
imshow(bwfim1);title(sprintf('FCM1,level=%f',level1));
close all;
clc;
 [filename,pathname]=uigetfile('*','Select an image to
segment the pathology');
if(filename==0)
    return;
end
f1_ori=imread(strcat(pathname,filename));
f1_size=imresize(f1_ori,[256 256]);
f1_gray=im2double(rgb2gray(f1_size));
f1_green=f1_size(:,:,2);
f1_green=im2double(f1_green);
se1=strel('octagon',6);
f1_close=imclose(f1_green,se1);
f1_pad=padarray(f1_close,[5 5]);
f1_mean=f1_pad;
f1_var=f1_pad;
[r c]=size(f1_pad);
for i=6:r-5
    for j=6:c-5
        w=f1_pad(i-5:i+5,j-5:j+5);
        local_mean=mean2(w);
        local_std=std2(w(:));
        local_var=local_std^.2;
        f1_mean(i,j)=local_mean;
        f1_var(i,j)=local_var;
        f1_std(i,j)=local_std;
    end
end
```

```
f1_mean=f1_mean(6:r-5,6:c-5);
f1_var=f1_var(6:r-5,6:c-5);
f1_std=  f1_std(6:r-5,6:c-5);
f1_varmax=max(f1_var(:));
f1_thresh=autothreshold(f1_green);
figure,imshow(f1_thresh),title('thresholded image');
[f1_label n]=bwlabel(f1_thresh);
STATS = regionprops(f1_label,'area');
removed=0;
aA=[STATS.Area];
for j=1:n
    bw= aA(j);
    if(bw<1) ||(bw>1000)
    f1_label(f1_label==j)=0;
    removed = removed + 1;
    end
end
n=n-removed;
[row col]=size(f1_label);
for i=1:row
    for j=1:col
        if (f1_label(i,j)~=0)
            f1_label(i,j)=1;
        end
    end
end
```

3 Results

The result obtained using fuzzy logic for the moderate and mild hypertensive retinopathy images, was satisfactory and the output was clear, but for highly affected or worst

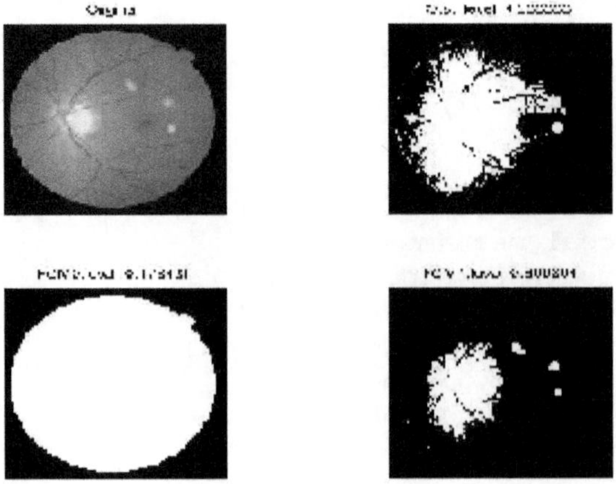

Fig. 4. FCM output

affected hypertensive retinopathy patient images they were not clearly segmented. This problem was overcome by doing other normal segmentation method for isolating the optic disk and exudates region from the severely or worst affected images of hypertensive retinopathy patients. This tool can be used by doctors for evaluation. The stage wise output images are as shown below for a particular input image.

Fig. 5. Segmented optic disk

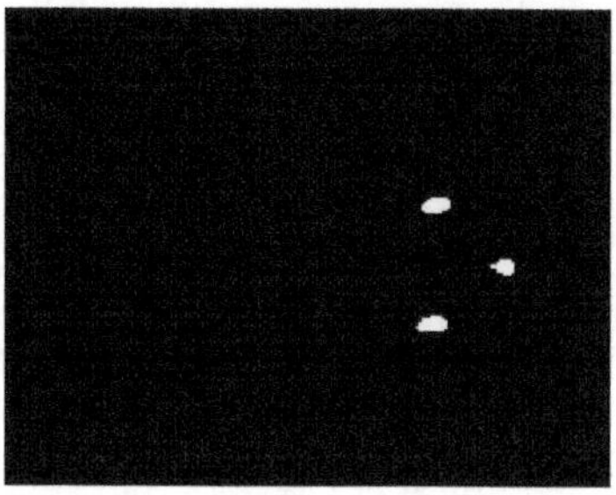

Fig. 6. Segmented exudates region

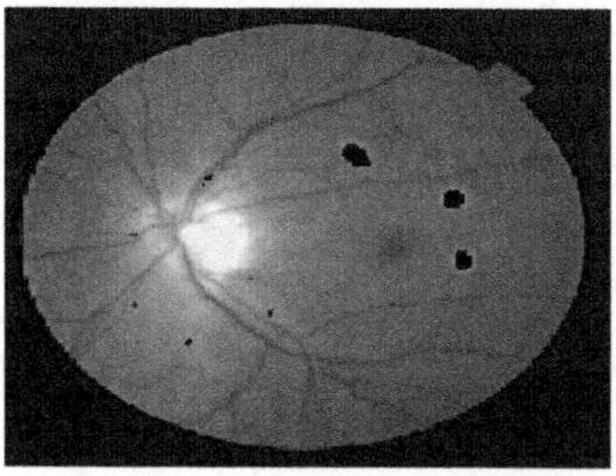

Fig. 7. Setting the affected region to zero for highlighting

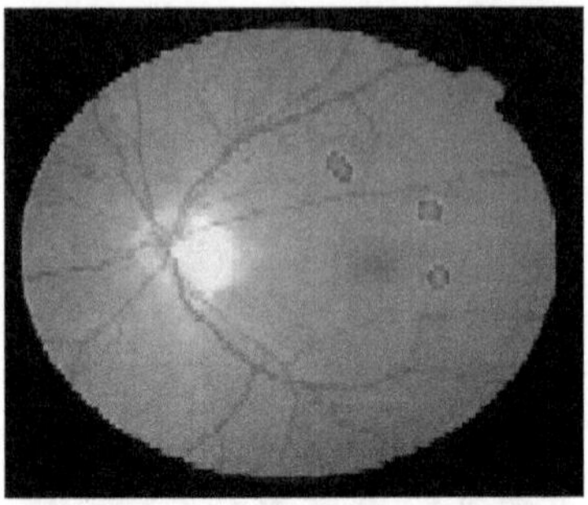

Fig. 8. Final output

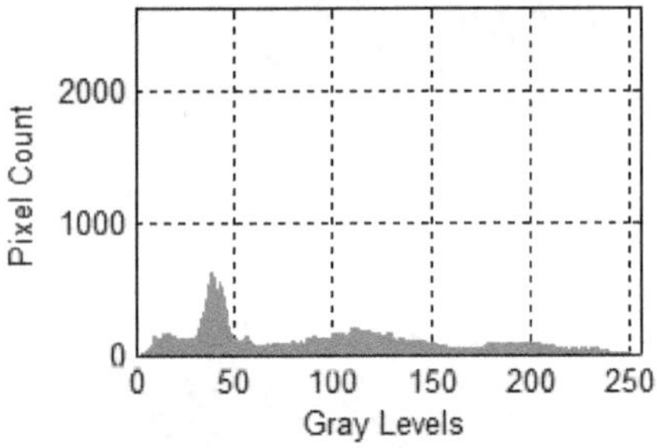

Fig. 9. Graphical display of severity

4 Conclusion

In this paper we have presented a new effective and simple method to analysis the severity of the hypertensive retinopathy. In the last section we are yet to calculate the segmented region which is replaced by green colour, so by calculating the green colour pixel values of the image we can calculate the severity. We are working with the mild, moderate and severely affected images to calculate the pixel. Still our research is going on with hundreds of images to calculate the pixels, so that based on the pixel values we can categorize the stages of hypertensive retinopathy. This newly developed method can be of great benefit to ophthalmologist in their severity analysis for hypertensive retinopathy patients.

References

1. Wong, T.Y., Mclntosh, R.: Hypertensive retinopathy signs as risk indicators of cardiovascular morbidity and mortality. Br. Med. Bull. 73-74, 57–70 (2005)
2. Porta, M., Grosso, A., Veglio, F.: Hypertensive retinopathy: there's more than meets the eye. J. Hypertens. 23, 683–696 (2005)
3. Chobanian, A.V., Bakris, G.L., Black, H.R., Cushman, W.C., Green, L.A., Izzo, J.R.: The seventh report of the Joint National Committee on prevention, detection, evaluation and treatment of high blood pressure: the JNC 7 report. JAMA 19(1), 2560–2572 (2003)

4. Brasileira de Cardiologia, S., Brasileira de Hipertensão, S., Brasileira de Nefrologia, S., Brasileiras de Hipertensãoarterial, V.D.: Arq. Bras. Cardiol. 89(3), 24–79 (2007)
5. Cuspidi, C., Meani, S., Salerno, M., Fusi, V., Severgnini, B., Valerio, C.: Retinal microvascular changes and target organ damage in untreated essential hypertensives. J. Hypertens. 22, 2095–2102 (2004)
6. Schachat, P.A.: Medical Retina. Ed. III., pp. 1404–1409. Mosby. Inc. (2001)
7. Keith, N.M., Wagener, H.P., Kernohan, J.W.: The syndrome of malignant hypertension. Arch. Intern. Med. 41, 141–188 (1928)
8. Keith, N.M., Wagener, H.P., Barker, N.W.: Some different types of essential hypertension: their course and prognosis. Am. J. Med Sci. 197, 332–339 (1939)
9. Richard, J.G.: Current therapy in nephrology and hypertension. The CV Mosby Company, 324–333 (1984-1985)
10. World Health Organization: Areerial hypertension.: World Health Organ. Tech. Rep. Ser. 628, 7–56 (1978)
11. McGregor, E., Isles, C.G., Jay, J.L., Lever, A.F., Murray, G.D.: Retinal changes in malignant hypertension. Br. Med. J. 63292, 233–244 (1986)
12. Catto, M.D.: Management of renal hypertension, pp. 41–74. MTP, Lancaster (1988)
13. Ahmed, M.N., Yamany, S.M., Mohamed, N., Farag, A.A., Moriarty, T.: A modified fuzzy c-means algorithm for bias field estimation and segmentation of MRI data. IEEE Trans. Med. Imaging 21, 193–199 (2002)
14. Rosenberger, C., Chehdi, K.: Unsupervised clustering method with optimal estimation of the number of clusters: Application to image segmentation. In: Proc. IEEE International Conference on Pattern Recognition (ICPR), Barcelona, vol. 1, pp. 1656–1659 (2000)
15. Clark, M.C., Hall, L.O., Goldg, D.B., Clarke, L.P., Velthuizen, R.P., Silbiger, M.S.: MRI segmentation using fuzzy clustering techniques. IEEE Eng. Med. Biol. 13, 730–742 (1994)
16. Iqbal, M.I., Aibinu, A.M., Nilsson, M., Tijani, I.B., Salami, M.J.E.: Detection of Vascular Intersection in Retina Fundus Image Using Modified Cross Point Number and Neural Network Technique. In: International Conference on Computer and Communication Engineering, pp. 241–246. IEEE Press, Malaysia (2008)

An Intelligent Network for Offline Signature Verification Using Chain Code

Minal Tomar* and Pratibha Singh

Department of Electronics and Instrumentation
Institute of Engineering and Technology
Devi Ahilya Vishwavidyalaya, Indore (M.P.) 452017
minal2121@rediffmail.com,
prat_ibh_a@yahoo.com
www.iet.dauniv.ac.in

Abstract. It has been observed that every signature is distinctive, and that's why, the use of signatures as a biometric has been supported and implemented in various technologies. It is almost impossible for a person himself to repeat the same signature every time he signs. We proposed an intelligent system for off-line signature verification using chain-code. Dynamic features are not available, so, it becomes more difficult to achieve the goal. Chain-code is extracted locally and Feed Forward Back Propagation Neural Network used as a classifier. Chain-code is a simple directional feature, extracted from a thinned image of signature because contour based system acquires more memory. An intelligent network is proposed for training and classification. The results are compared with a very basic energy density method. Chain-code method is found very effective if number of samples available for training is limited, which is also practically feasible.

Keywords: Neural Network, Chain-code, Energy Density, Neuron, Back propagation, Image Processing.

1 Introduction

In the field of human identification, the usage of biometrics like signature, hand geometry, fingerprints, iris scan or DNA etc. is growing day by day because of its unique properties. Although there are various parameters available for human identification but hand written documents always proven its importance. When a person is in need to state something but unable to be there physically, then it is very easy for him to write something and send it there, so that the written documents will do the same. But still there is problem that how will the document prove itself that it is written by the same person? So, there are two methods available for it. First one is to verify the handwriting and the second one is to verify only the signature of that person on the document. The scope of this paper deals with the second solution. Now, when the signature verification system comes in mind then it looks like a great tool for day to

* Corresponding author.

N. Meghanathan et al. (Eds.): CCSIT 2011, Part III, CCIS 133, pp. 10–22, 2011.

day life, as signature is accepted as a proof of identification not only in the social life but also it is used as legal identification of the person. So, it becomes very important that the system used for it works with a great accuracy. Generally, in daily routine like in banks etc. a human manually observe the signature and his brain takes the decision for authentication but, in present era every small task is also going to be automated with the help of computers then why not signature verification too carried out automatically? As soon as this system comes in mind, there are too many problems related to signature verification arises, like it may be possible that a signature of a person may vary during repetition according to the mood or health of the person, or it may be possible that someone else copied the signature. Then it becomes more important that how to distinguish between the genuine signature and the forgery, as it is almost impossible for a person himself to repeat the same signature every time he signs. With reference to this, it becomes a subject of continuous research until a purely faithful system is found to rely on. This paper is like one of a small step towards achieving the goal of a developed system for signature verification. Before proceeding further it is important to know about different type of forgeries. Forgeries can be classified as [1]:

a) Random forgery: It produces without any knowledge of signature shape or even the signer's name.
b) Simple forgery: It is formed by knowing only the name of the signer's but without having any examples of signer's signature style.
c) Skilled forgery: It is produced by looking at an original signature sample, attempting to imitate it as closely as possible.

This paper is developed with the mind set that random and simple forgeries is very easy to detect and refuse but the main issue is to caught the skilled forger. That's why; the complete paper is processed with skilled forgeries only and when forgery word is used then it should be noted here that it means the skilled forgery.

Signature Characteristics

Signature must be treated as an image because a person may use any symbol or letter or group of letters etc. (according to the choice) as a signature, so it may be possible that one can't separate the letters written or even can't understand what is written. So, the system used for analysis of signature must use the concepts of image processing. Most probable, it is possible that the signature of a signer varied for every sign but there must be some unique characteristic to identify the signature so that it can be used as biometrics. Some essential characteristics are listed below:

a) Invariant: It should be constant over a long period of time.
b) Singular: It must be unique to the individual.
c) Inimitable: It must be irreproducible by other means.
d) Reducible and comparable: It should be capable of being reduced to a format that is easy to handle and digitally comparable to others [2].

As signature also belongs to one of the parameters which satisfy the above characteristics so it may be use as a proof of identification of a person.

Types of signature verification

As stated above signature is nothing but a pattern of special arrangement of pixels (i.e. an image). Still, we can classify the signature verification system based on whether only the image of a signature is available or the individual is personally signing before the verification system. Based on this, broadly, signature verification methods can be classified as:

a) ON-Line or Dynamic Signature Verification system
b) OFF-Line or Static Signature Verification system

In off-line verification system, only static features are considered which rely purely on the signature's image but require less hardware. Whereas in case of on-line systems, dynamic feature are taken into consideration, which include the time when stylus is in and out of the contact with the paper, the total time taken to make signature and the position where the stylus is raised from and lowered onto the paper, number of break points, maximum/minimum pressure of stylus contact, speed etc [2], [3].

Related Work
The 1st Signature verification system developed in 1965 but use of neural network for verification has been started in decades of 90s. Reena Bajaj et. al worked on signature verification using multiple neural classifiers. The authors have used 3 different types of global features projection moments, upper and lower envelop based characteristics with feed forward neural net for verification purpose [12]. Emre et. al had used global, direction and grid features and SVM (Support Vector Machine) as classification method. Authors also compared the performance using SVM and ANN [13]. Fixed point arithmetic with different classifiers such as HMM (Hidden Markov Models), SVM and ED (Euclidean Distance Classifier) analysed. Fathi et. al have used conjugate gradient neural network with string distance (SD) as local feature [16]. Enhanced modified directional feature and neural based classifiers have been used by Armand et. al [9]. Siddiqi et. al extracted chain code based features used ROC (Receiver Operating Characteristic) curve for classification [8]. Image registration, image fusion & DWT (Discrete Wavelet Transforms) are also used with Euclidean Distance Method for identification and verification of signatures. H. N. Prakash & D. S. Guru presented a new approach based on score level fusion for off-line signature verification [6]. Authors have used distance & orientation features to form bi-interval valued symbolic representation of signature. They compare the extracted features for classification.

This paper proposed a system for off-line signature verification using chain-code and energy density features extracted locally and Feed Forward Back Propagation Neural Network used as a classifier. Aspect ratio is also included as a global feature in energy density method.

2 Proposed Approach

There are 2 approaches used in this paper for feature extraction. First one is 'The Energy Density method' and the second is 'The Chain-Code Method'. We used thinning algorithm because he database extracted from the contour obviously will acquire more memory as compared to the thinned image. We used the chain code with thinning algorithm. Also a comparative statement between the simplest energy density method and proposed chain-code method is developed so that it may be clear that is it worth to improve the accuracy on the cost of memory and time?

2.1 Energy Density

In this method, 2 features are used for training. Aspect ratio is used as a global feature and energy density is used as local feature. Aspect ratio is the ratio of Height (maximum vertical distance) to length (maximum horizontal distance) of the signature. We have calculated it after skew removal. Energy density is defined as the total energy present in each segment. We have done 100 segments of each signature and energy density is obtained by counting the total number of 1s in each segment (i.e. Total White Pixels). Thus, we have a feature vector of size 101X1 for energy density method as final database. This final database is fed to the neural network to perform the desired function i.e. training or classification.

2.2 Chain-Code

Chain-code is based on the direction of the connecting pixels. Each pixel is observed for next connected pixel and their direction changes mapped by giving a numerical value to every possible direction. There are generally 8 connectivity is taken into consideration as shown in the Fig. 1. But in this paper we have used 4 connectivity i.e. 0, 1, 2 & 3. As another 4 directions i.e. 4, 5, 6 & 7 are simply the negation of 0, 1, 2 & 3 directions. To obtain chain-code top left corner is considered as origin and scanning is done left to right, top to bottom (refer Fig. 2). Each pixel has observed separately and direction vector for that pixel is noted down. This process is carried out until the last pixel has scanned. Now, the frequency of occurrence in a particular direction is calculated for each segment and the histogram for each segment is used it to train the neural network.

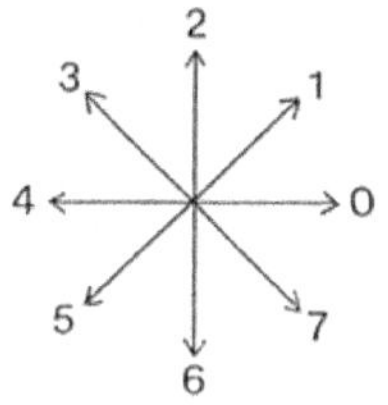

Fig. 1. 8 Connectivity of a Pixel

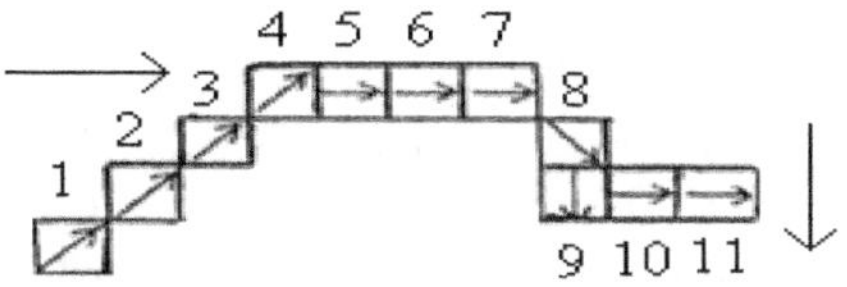

Fig. 2. Direction Changes in a Part of a Signature

3 Implementation and Verification

Implementation of the proposed approach is basically divided in 2 parts i.e. Training and Classification. Training belongs to preparing and training of neural network for doing the classification work with an optimum accuracy. The proposed signature verification system takes an image of the signature as input and verifies whether the input image matches with the genuine training signature image available in the database or not. The system can be broadly categorized on the basis of method used for preprocessing and feature extraction from the image database and final input given to the neural network.

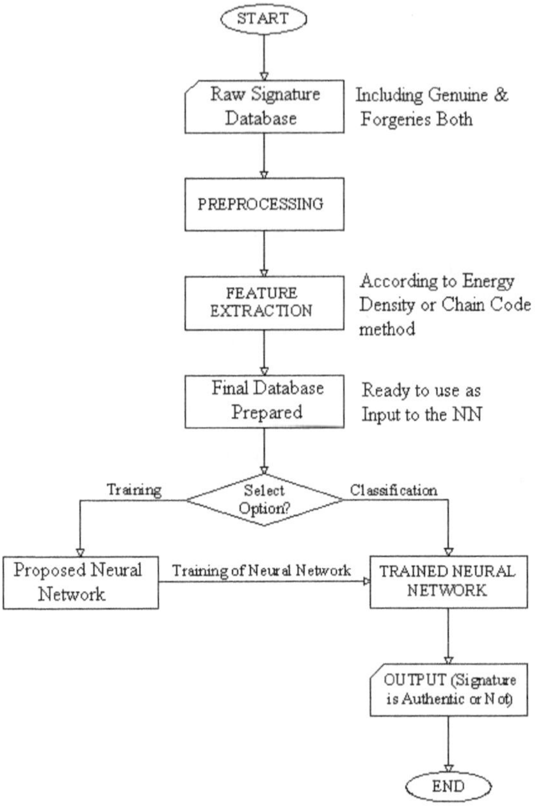

Fig. 3. Flow Chart of Proposed Methodology

The flow chart for the proposed methodology is shown in Fig. 3. Raw Signature Database is gathered from 10 people and 110 Genuine & 110 Forgeries from each individual is collected (i.e. 2200 Signature Samples) and digitized using scanner, 300 dpi resolution. The first step for pre-processing is Binarization. It is used to produce binary image i.e. to convert colored (if any) image in black & white (i.e. in 0 or 1) format. In this paper global threshold is used for this purpose. Noise is filtered out using median filter. Thinning is done after noise filtering. Morphological operation is applied (in MATLAB) to performs the desired thinning. Rotation of signature patterns by a non predictive angle is one of the major difficulties. In this paper simply the concept of trigonometry is used for skew removal. Fig. 4 shows the effect of different stages of pre-processing. The next step of pre-processing is to extract the signature

(a) Original Signature Image

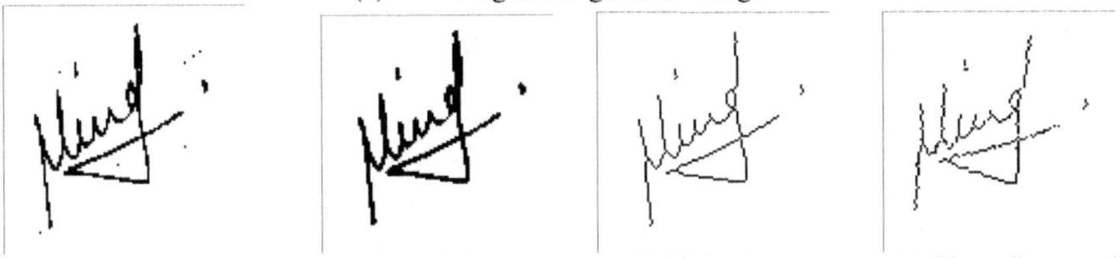

(b) Binarization (c) Denoising (d) Thinning (e) Skew Removal

Fig. 4. Output of Different Stages of Pre-processing

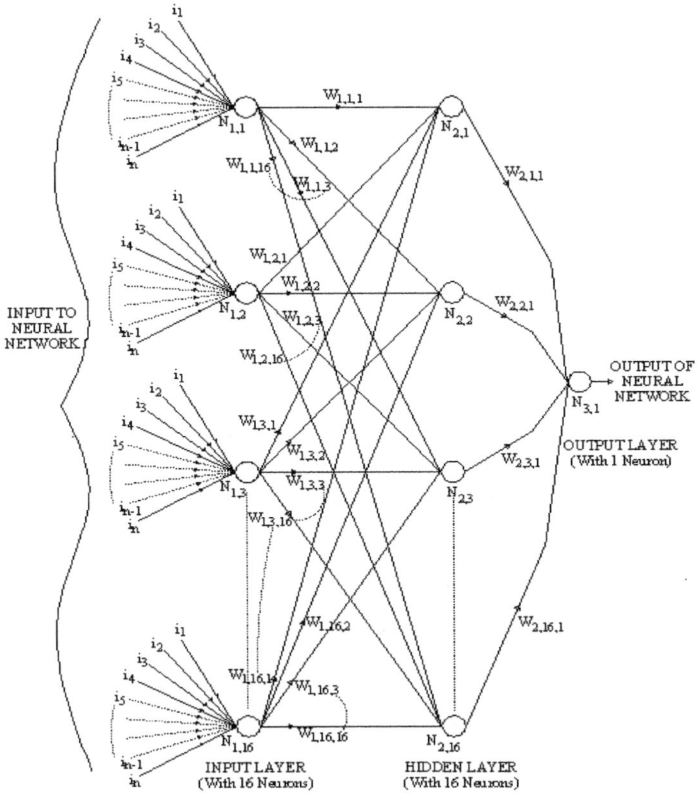

Fig. 5. Proposed Architecture of Neural Network

Nm,n shows Neuron where, m = Layer Number & n = Neuron Number

Wi,j,k represents Weight ; where, i=Layer, j=Neuron, k=Output of the particular Neuron only from the whole image, by removing the image of extra paper remained. After signature extraction again resizing is carried out, and then segmentation process is completed to extract the local features of the signature (i.e. energy density or Chain-code of each segment according to the method under test). We have used 100 segment of each signature sample for further processing. In energy density method we have also used aspect ratio as a global feature to improve the performance of the system. Aspect ratio is extracted just before the resizing and segmentation.

3.1 Proposed Architecture of Neural Network

The proposed ANN scheme uses a multi layer feed forward network employing a back propagation learning algorithm with 16 Neurons in input layer and 1 Neuron in output layer. One hidden layer is present with 16 Neurons. The transfer function used for all the three layers are Hyperbolic Tangent Sigmoid (tansig). The proposed architecture of Neural Network is shown in Fig. 5. Here, default value of bias is chosen.

3.2 Training of Neural Network

In this paper a supervised training is used. For this purpose 'Variable Learning Rate (traingdx) is used as a training function. Gradient descent with momentum weight and bias learning function (learngdm) is used by default. Mean square error (mse) is network performance function. It measures the network's performance according to the

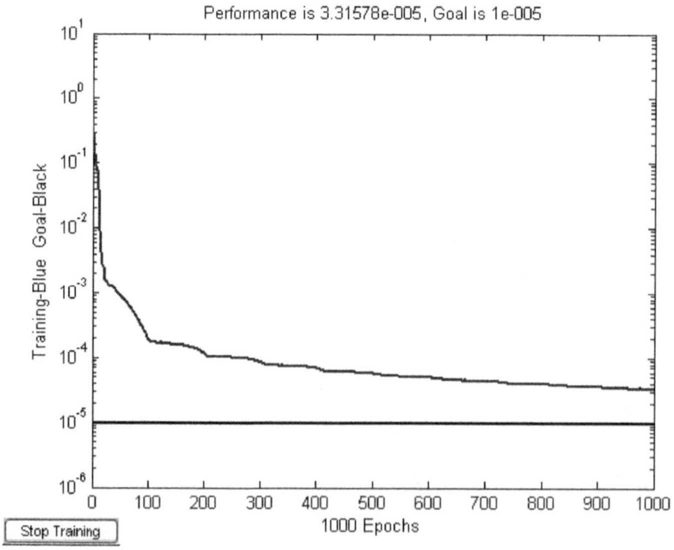

Fig. 6. Training of Neural Network

mean of squared errors. All other parameters of the neural network are set as by default including the initial weights. It is cleared by the graph in Fig. 6 that as the number of epochs are increasing during training then accordingly the mean square error is reducing. The black horizontal line is showing the reference (set at the time of preparing of NN) and the blue is denoting the reducing mse i.e. actual mse. The goal of training is to reduce mse till the extent that it will meet the reference. The training will stop when either the set goal has achieved or the maximum number of epochs reached.

4 Results

For comparison and performance evaluation of the proposed methodology we have used equal number of genuine and forgery samples for training and 100 numbers (50 Genuine + 50 Forgeries) are used for classification. We increased the training signature samples from 10 (5 Genuine + 5 Forgeries) to 100 (50 Genuine + 50 Forgeries) and observe the effect of increasing training samples for both the methods. For performance evaluation we used some common parameters like time required for training, accuracy, FAR (False Acceptance Ratio) i.e. the percentage of forgeries accepted as genuine & FRR (False Rejection Ratio) i.e. the percentage of rejecting the genuine signatures. Table 1 and Table 2 show the performance of energy density and chain-code methods. After that a comparison for both the methods has done on the basis of above mentioned parameters. Table 3, 4, 5 & 6 along with graphs of Fig. 7 elaborate the comparison of both methods.

Table 1. Effect of increasing Training samples for energy density method

S. No.	No. of Training Samples (Genuine + Forgery)	Result			
		Elapsed Time (in Secs.)	Accuracy (in %)	FAR (in %)	FRR (in %)
1	5 + 5	4.782	42.5	80	35
2	10 + 10	4.796	62.5	75	0
3	15 + 15	4.843	85	25	5
4	20 + 20	5.735	85	30	0
5	25 + 25	5.156	80	30	10
6	30 + 30	5.343	87.5	25	0
7	35 + 35	5.359	97.5	5	0
8	40 + 40	5.422	100	0	0
9	45 + 45	5.453	100	0	0
10	50 + 50	6.187	100	0	0

Table 2. Effect of increasing Training samples for Chain-Code method

S. No.	No. of Training Samples (Genuine + Forgery)	Result			
		Elapsed Time (in Secs.)	Accuracy (in %)	FAR (in %)	FRR (in %)
1	5 + 5	5.125	95	5	5
2	10 + 10	5.329	92.5	15	0
3	15 + 15	6.282	92.5	0	15
4	20 + 20	7.093	90	10	10
5	25 + 25	13.937	82.5	30	5
6	30 + 30	6.844	75	40	10
7	35 + 35	7.078	97.5	0	5
8	40 + 40	7.922	100	0	0
9	45 + 45	8.328	100	0	0
10	50 + 50	8.265	100	0	0

Table 3. Comparison on the basis of Time Required for Training

S. No.	No. of Training Samples (Genuine + Forgery)	Elapsed Time (in Sec) (Chain-Code)	Elapsed Time (in Sec) (Energy Density)
1	10	5.125	4.782
2	20	5.329	4.796
3	30	6.282	4.843
4	40	7.093	5.735
5	50	13.937	5.156
6	60	6.844	5.343
7	70	7.078	5.359
8	80	7.922	5.422
9	90	8.328	5.453
10	100	8.265	6.187

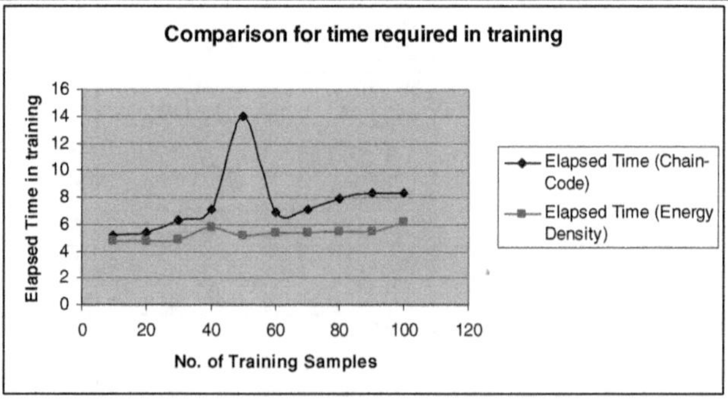

(a) Comparison for the time required for Training of NN

Table 4. Comparison on the basis of Accuracy

S. No.	No. of Training Samples (Genuine + Forgery)	Accuracy (in%) (Chain Code Method)	Accuracy (in%) (Energy Density Method)
1	10	98.3333	65
2	20	96.6667	91.6667
3	30	96.6667	91.6667
4	40	100	83.3333
5	50	95	90
6	60	100	96.6667
7	70	96.6667	96.6667
8	80	95	96.6667
9	90	98.3333	100
10	100	98.3333	100

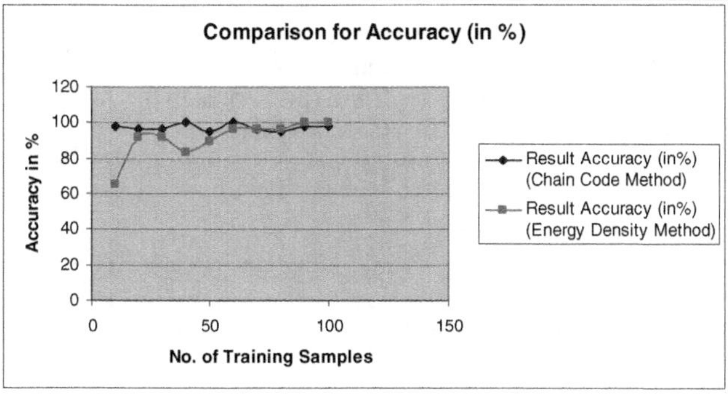

(b) Comparison for Accuracy

Table 5. Comparison on the basis of FAR

S. No.	No. of Training Samples (Genuine + Forgery)	False Acceptance Ratio (in%) (Chain Code Method)	False Accepance Ratio (in%) (Energy Density Method)
1	10	6	80
2	20	8	58
3	30	0	32
4	40	6	30
5	50	36	40
6	60	40	24
7	70	0	8
8	80	0	8
9	90	0	10
10	100	2	4

Table 5. *(continued)*

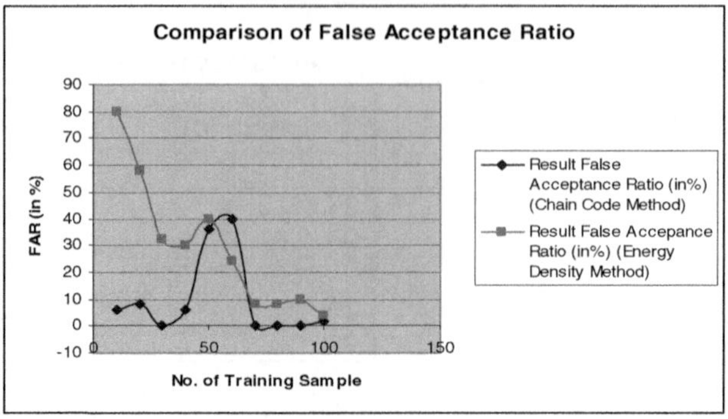

(c) Comparison for FAR

Table 6. Comparison on the basis of FRR

S. No.	No. of Training Samples (Genuine + Forgery)	False Rejection Ratio (in%) (Chain Code Method)	False Rejection Ratio (in%) (Energy Density Method)
1	10	18	24
2	20	10	0
3	30	42	20
4	40	28	8
5	50	16	18
6	60	22	14
7	70	24	8
8	80	8	2
9	90	4	2
10	100	2	2

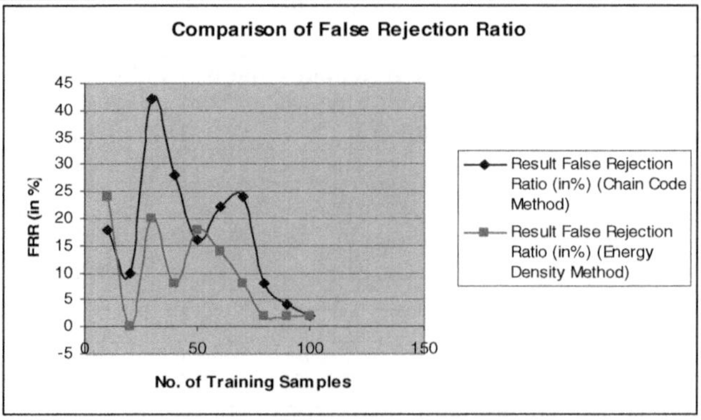

(d) Comparison for FRR

Fig. 7. (a), (b), (c), (d). shows the Comparison between Energy Density and proposed Chain-Code Method

5 Conclusion

We have compared the performance of a simplest known method (energy density method) with the proposed Chain-Code Method on the basis time required for training, accuracy, FAR & FRR. After many experiments and observations we have concluded that if the samples available for training are limited around 10 to 30 (Half Genuine + Half Forgeries in all cases) then chain code method is better then energy density. Although time required for training is slightly greater in case of chain code but the accuracy and FAR are satisfactory. If one have a huge database for both Genuine & Forgeries to use for training then energy density method can prove its importance. It is also observed that accuracy of energy density method is increasing rapidly as training sample increases but chain-code method shows almost considerable results for all the training sample sets. We have also observed that the results for FRR are varying randomly for both the cases. It gives the reason for future studies. We have not given too many emphasis on FRR as we are considering low FAR more important then FRR as one can sign twice if the genuine signature is not accepted (i.e. High FRR) but it is highly objectionable that the system accept any forgery (i.e. High FAR). So, FAR is given extra weightage in this paper.

The proposed Chain-Code method is easy to implement as well as gives satisfactory performance for limited training sample also. So, it may be used practically because practically a large number of database gatherings are not feasible.

Acknowledgments. We are very thankful to the HOD (Electronics & Instrumentation Engineering), IET, DAVV, Indore and the Director, Malwa Institute of Technology, Indore for their constant support and motivation.

References

1. Zhang, B.-l.: Off-Line Signature Recognition and Verification by Kernel Principal Component Self-Regression. In: Fifth International Conference on Machine Learning and Applications (ICMLA 2006), pp. 28–33 (2006), doi:10.1109/ICMLA.2006.37
2. Uppalapati, D.: Integration of Offline and Online Signature Verification systems. Department of Computer Science and Engineering, I.I.T., Kanpur (July 2007)
3. Plamondon, R., Srihari, S.N.: On-Line and Off-Line Handwriting Recognition: A Comprehensive Survey. IEEE Transactions on Pattern Analysis and Machine Intelligence 12(1), 63–84 (2000)
4. The IEEE website, `http://www.ieee.org`
5. Department of Computer Science, IIT, Kanpur for precious imformations, `http://www.cse.iitk.ac.in`
6. Prakash, H.N., Guru, D.S.: Off-line signature verification: an approach based on score level fusion. International Journal of Computer Application 1(18) (2010)
7. Ghandali, S., Moghaddan, M.E.: Off-line Persian Signature identification and verification based on image registration and fusion. Journal of Multimedia 4(3) (June 2009)
8. Siddiqi, I., Vincent, N.: A set of chain-code based features for writer recognition. In: 10th International Conference on Document Analysis and Recognition (2009)
9. Armand, S., Blumenstein, M., Muthukkumarasamy, V.: Off-line signature verification using enhanced modified direction feature and neural based classification

10. Wilson, A.T.: Off-line handwriting recognition using neural network
11. Ferrer, M.A., Alonso, G.B., Travieso, C.M.: Off-line Geometric parameters for automatic signature verification using fixed point arithematic. IEEE Transections on Pattern Analysis and Machine Intelligence 27(6), 993–997 (2005)
12. Bajaj, R., Choudhari, S.: Signature Verification using multiple neural classifiers. Pattern Recognition 30(1), 1–7 (1997)
13. Ozgunduz, E., Sentruk, T., Elif karsligil, M.: Off-line signature verification and recognition by support vector machine
14. Breuel, T.M.: Representations and metrics for off-line handwriting segmentation
15. Blumenstein, M., Verma, B.: An artificial neural network based segmentation algorithm for off-line handwriting recognition
16. Abuhasna, J.F.: Signature recognition using conjugate gradient neural network

An Improved and Adaptive Face Recognition Method Using Simplified Fuzzy ARTMAP

Antu Annam Thomas and M. Wilscy

Dept. of Computer Science, University of Kerala, Karyavattom Campus, Trivandrum, Kerala
antuannam@gmail.com, wilsyphilipose@gmail.com

Abstract. Face recognition has become one of the most active research areas of pattern recognition since the early 1990s. This paper proposes a new face recognition method based on Principal Component Analysis (PCA), Linear Discriminant Analysis (LDA) and Simplified Fuzzy ARTMAP (SFAM). Combination of PCA and LDA is used for improving the capability of LDA and PCA when used alone. Neural classifier, SFAM, is used to reduce the number of misclassifications. Experiment is conducted on ORL database and results demonstrate SFAM's efficiency as a recognizer. SFAM has the added advantage that the network is adaptive, that is, during testing phase if the network comes across a new face that it is not trained for; the network identifies this to be a new face and also learns this new face. Thus SFAM can be used in applications where database needs to be updated.

Keywords: Face recognition, Principal Component Analysis, Linear Discriminant Analysis, Neural Network, Simplified Fuzzy ARTMAP.

1 Introduction

Face recognition [1] is an important and a challenging research problem spanning numerous fields and disciplines. Face recognition is attention seeking because, in addition to having numerous practical applications such as bankcard identification, access control, security monitoring, and surveillance system, is a fundamental human behavior that is essential for effective communications and interactions among people. Two categories of methods can be employed for face recognition one is *global approach* or *appearance-based approach* and *second one* is *feature-based* or *component-based approach*. Among these two categories of solutions to the problem [2] the most successful seems to be appearance-based approaches [3], which generally operate directly on images or appearances of face objects and process the image as two dimensional patterns. These methods extract features to optimally represent faces belonging to a class and to separate faces from different classes. Ideally, it is desirable to use only features having high separability power while ignoring the rest [3].Most of the effort have been used to develop powerful methods for feature extraction [4]-[8] and to employ classifiers like Support Vector Machine (SVM) [9], Hidden Markov Models (HMMs) [10], Neural Networks [11]-[15] for efficient classification.

N. Meghanathan et al. (Eds.): CCSIT 2011, Part III, CCIS 133, pp. 23–34, 2011.

The main trend in feature extraction has been representing the data in a lower dimensional space. Principal Component Analysis (PCA) [16],[17], [5]-[6] and Linear Discriminant analysis (LDA) [7] are two main techniques used for data reduction and feature extraction in the appearance-based approaches. PCA maximizes the total scatter while LDA maximizes the between class scatter and minimizes the within class scatter. PCA might outperform LDA when the number of samples per class is small [18]. In the case of training set with a large number of samples, LDA outperform PCA [18]. A study in [17] demonstrated that; compared to the PCA method, the computation of the LDA is much higher and PCA is less sensitive to different training data sets. However, simulations reported in [17] demonstrated an improved performance using the LDA method compared to the PCA approach. But when dimensionality of face images is high, LDA is not applicable and therefore LDA is deprived from its advantage to find effective features for class separability. To resolve this problem PCA and LDA methods are combined [3], PCA is applied to preprocessed face images to get low dimensionality images which are ready for applying LDA. Finally to decrease the error rate, instead of Euclidean distance criteria which was used in [19], we implement a neural network, specifically SFAM, to classify face images based on its computed LDA features.

2 Feature Extraction Algorithm

Two powerful tools used for dimensionality reduction and feature extraction in most of pattern recognition applications are PCA and LDA. A brief review on fundamentals of PCA and LDA is given in the following sessions.

2.1 Principal Component Analysis(PCA)

Principal component analysis or karhunen-loeve transformation [20] is the method for reducing the dimensionality of a dataset, while retaining the majority of variation, present in the dataset. Thus PCA can be effectively be used for data reduction and feature extraction [21]. As the pattern often contains redundant information, mapping it to a feature vector can get rid of this redundancy and yet preserve most of the intrinsic information content of the pattern. These extracted features have great role in distinguishing input patterns.

A face image in 2-dimension with size $N \times N$ can also be considered as one dimensional vector of dimension N^2 [22]. For example, face image from ORL (Olivetti Research Labs) database with size 112×92 can be considered as a vector of dimension 10,304, or equivalently a point in a 10,304 dimensional space. An ensemble of images maps to a collection of points in this huge space. Images of faces, being similar in overall configuration, will not be randomly distributed in this huge image space and thus can be described by a relatively low dimensional subspace. The main idea of the principle component is to find the vectors that best account for the distribution of face images within the entire image space. These vectors define the subspace of face images, which we call "face space". Each of these vectors is of length N^2, describes an $N \times N$ image, and is a linear combination of the original face images.

Let the training set of face images be $\Gamma_1, \Gamma_2, \Gamma_3, \ldots, \Gamma_M$ then the average of the set is defined by

$$\psi = \frac{1}{M}\sum_{n=1}^{M}\Gamma_n \tag{1}$$

Each face differs from the average by the vector

$$\Phi i = \Gamma i - \Psi \tag{2}$$

This set of very large vectors is then subject to principal component analysis, which seeks a set of M orthonormal vectors, U_m, which best describes the distribution of the data. The kth vector, U_k, is chosen such that

$$\lambda_k = \frac{1}{M}\sum_{n=1}^{M}\left(U_k^T \phi_n\right)^2 \tag{3}$$

is a maximum, subject to

$$U_I^T U_k = \delta_{IK} = \left\{\begin{matrix} 1, if\ I=k \\ 0, otherwise \end{matrix}\right\} \tag{4}$$

The vectors U_k and scalars λ_k are the eigenvectors and eigenvalues, respectively of the covariance matrix

$$C = \frac{1}{M}\sum_{n=1}^{M}\phi_n\phi_n^T = AA^T \tag{5}$$

where the matrix A =[$\Phi_1, \Phi_2, \ldots, \Phi_M$]. The covariance matrix C, however is $N^2 \times N^2$ real symmetric matrix, and calculating the N^2 eigenvectors and eigenvalues is an intractable task for typical image sizes. We need a computationally feasible method to find these eigenvectors.

Consider the eigenvectors v_i of A^TA such that

$$A^T A v_i = \mu_i v_i \tag{6}$$

Premultiplying both sides by A, we have

$$AA^T A v_i = \mu_i A v_i \tag{7}$$

where we see that Av_i are the eigenvectors and μ_i are the eigenvalues of $C = AA^T$. Following these analysis, we construct the $M \times M$ matrix $L = A^TA$, where $L_{mn} = \Phi_m^T \Phi_n$, and find the M eigenvectors, v_i, of L. These vectors determine linear combinations of the M training set face images to form the eigenfaces U_I.

$$U_I = \sum_{k=1}^{M} v_{Ik}\phi_k \, , I = 1, \ldots, M \tag{8}$$

With this analysis, the calculations are greatly reduced, from the order of the number of pixels in the images (N^2) to the order of the number of images in the training set (M). In practice, the training set of face images will be relatively small ($M<<N^2$), and the calculations become quite manageable. The associated eigenvalues allow us to rank the eigenvectors according to their usefulness in characterizing the variation among the images. Because these vectors are the eigenvectors of the covariance matrix corresponding to the original face images, and because they are face-like in appearance, we refer to them as "eigenfaces". The eigenface images calculated from the eigenvectors of L span a basis set that can be used to describe face images. In practice, a smaller M' can be sufficient for identification, since accurate reconstruction of the image is not a requirement. In the framework of face recognition, the operation is a pattern recognition task rather than image reconstruction. The eigenfaces span an M' dimensional subspace of the original N^2 image space and hence, the M' significant eigenvectors of the L matrix with the largest associated eigenvalues, are sufficient for reliable representation of the faces in the face space characterized by the eigenfaces. Examples of ORL face database and eigenfaces after applying the eigenfaces algorithm are shown in Fig. 1 and Fig. 2 respectively.

Fig. 1. Samples face images from the ORL database

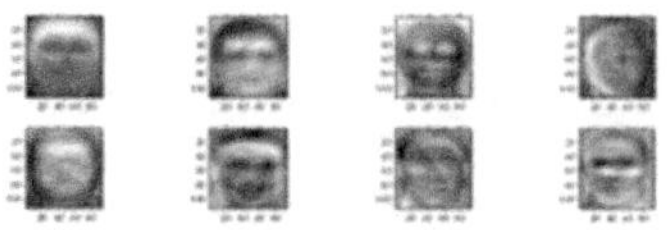

Fig. 2. First 8 eigenfaces with highest eigenvalues

A new face image (Γ) is transformed into its eigenface components (projected onto "face space") by a simple operation,

$$w_k = U_k^T (\Gamma - \Psi) \tag{9}$$

for $k = 1,...,M'$.

The weights form a projection vector,

$$\Omega^T=[w_1,w_2,..............,w_{M'}] \tag{10}$$

describing the contribution of each eigenface in representing the input face image, treating the eigenfaces as a basis set for face images. The projection vector is then used in a standard pattern recognition algorithm to identify which of a number of predefined face classes, if any, best describes the face. Classification is performed by comparing the projection vectors of the training face images with the projection vector of the input face image. This comparison is based on the Euclidean Distance between the face classes and the input face image. This is given in Eq. (11). The idea is to find the face class k that minimizes the Euclidean Distance.

$$\varepsilon_k = \left\|(\Omega - \Omega_k)\right\| \tag{11}$$

Where, Ωk is a vector describing the kth faces class.

The PCA is advantageous because it removes the redundant data and gives an optimal representation of data but the main handicap of PCA is that by applying PCA to a dataset not only interclass scatter, but also intraclass scatter is maximized.

2.2 Linear Discriminant Analysis (LDA)

Linear Discriminant analysis or Fisherfaces method overcomes the limitations of eigenfaces method by applying the Fisher's linear discriminant criterion. This criterion tries to maximize the ratio of the determinant of the between-class scatter matrix of the projected samples to the determinant of the within-class scatter matrix of the projected samples. Fisher discriminants group images of the same class and separates images of different classes. Fisher discriminants find the line that best separates the points. As with eigenspace projection, training images are projected into a subspace. The test images are projected into the same subspace and identified using a similarity measure. What differs is how the subspace is calculated[22].

Unlike PCA which is a method that extracts features to best represent face images, the LDA method tries to find the subspace that best discriminates different face classes. The within-class scatter matrix, also called intra-personal, represents variations in appearance of the same individual due to different lighting and face expression, while the between-class scatter matrix, also called the extra-personal, represents variations in appearance due to a difference in identity. By applying this method, we find the projection directions that on one hand maximize the between-class scatter matrix S_b, while minimize the within-class scatter matrix S_w in the projective subspace. [22]

The within-class scatter matrix S_w and the between-class scatter matrix S_b are defined as

$$S_w = \sum_{j=1}^{C} \sum_{i=1}^{N_j} (\Gamma_i^j - \mu_j)(\Gamma_i^j - \mu_j)^T \tag{12}$$

Where Γ_i^j is the ith sample of class j, μ_j is the mean of class j, C is the number of classes, N_j is the number of samples in class j

$$S_b = \sum_{j=1}^{C} (\mu_j - \mu)(\mu_j - \mu)^T \tag{13}$$

Where, μ represents the mean of all classes. The subspace for LDA is spanned by a set of vectors $W = [W_1, W_2, \ldots, W_d]$, satisfying

$$W = \arg \max = \left| \frac{W^T S_b W}{W^T S_W W} \right| \quad (14)$$

When face images are projected into the discriminant vectors W, face images should be distributed closely within classes and should be separated between classes, as much as possible. That is, these discriminant vectors minimize the denominator and maximize the numerator in Equation (14). W can therefore be constructed by the eigenvectors of $S_w^{-1} S_b$. Fig. 3 shows the first 8 eigenvectors with highest associated eigenvalues of $S_w^{-1} S_b$. These eigenvectors are also referred to as the fisherfaces.

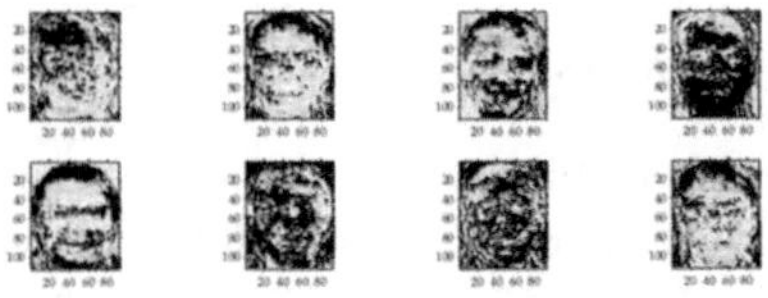

Fig. 3. First 8 Fisherfaces with highest eigenvalues

$$S = S_w + S_b \quad (15)$$

Alternatively, can be used for LDA, because both $S_w^{-1} S_b$ and $S_w^{-1} S$ have the same eigenvector matrices

The test images are projected into the same subspace and identified using a similarity measure. The face which has the minimum distance with the test face image is labeled with the identity of that image. The minimum distance can be calculated using the Euclidian distance method as given earlier in Equation (11).

3 Neural Network as Classifiers

Neural networks, with massive parallelism in its structure and high computation rates, provide a great alternative to other conventional classifiers and decision making systems.

3.1 Simplified Fuzzy ARTMAP(SFAM)

SFAM comprises of two layers an input and an output layer (see Fig. 4) [24]. The input to the network flows through the complement coder. Here the input string is stretched to double the size by adding its complement also. The complement coded input then flows into the input layer and remains there. Weights (W) from each of the output category nodes flows down to the input layer. The category layer just holds the names of the M number of categories that the network has to learn. The match tracking and vigilance parameter of the network architecture are primarily for network training.

ρ, the vigilance parameter ranges from 0 to 1 and it controls the granularity of the output node encoding. Thus, high vigilance values make the output node much fussier during pattern encoding and low vigilance allows relaxed matching criteria for the output node.

The "match tracking" allows the network to adjust its vigilance during learning from some base level, in response to errors in classification during the training phase. It is through match tracking that the network adjusts its own learning parameter to decide when to create new output nodes or reshape its decision regions. During training, match tracking is evoked when the selected output node does not represent the same output category corresponding to the input vectors given [23].

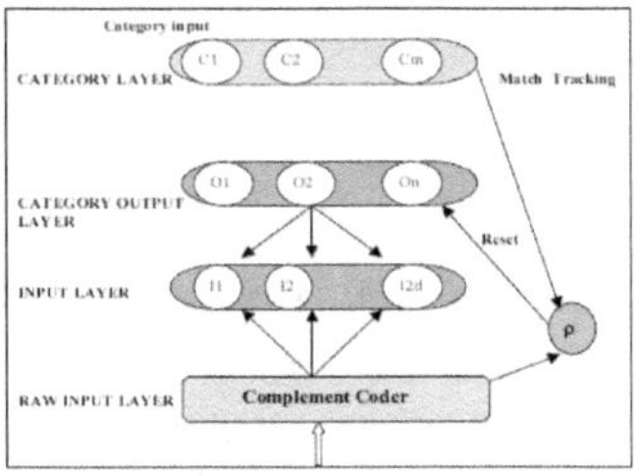

Fig. 4. Architecture of SFAM network

Once SFAM has been trained, the equivalent of a "feed forward" pass for an unknown pattern classification consists of passing the input pattern through the complement coder and into the input layer. The output node activation function is evaluated and the winner is the one with the highest value. The category of the input pattern is the one with which the winning output node is associated [23].

4 Face Recognition System

Fig. 5 shows the structure of the recognition system. System consists of two phases testing phase and training phase. In the next sections, role of each part is described.

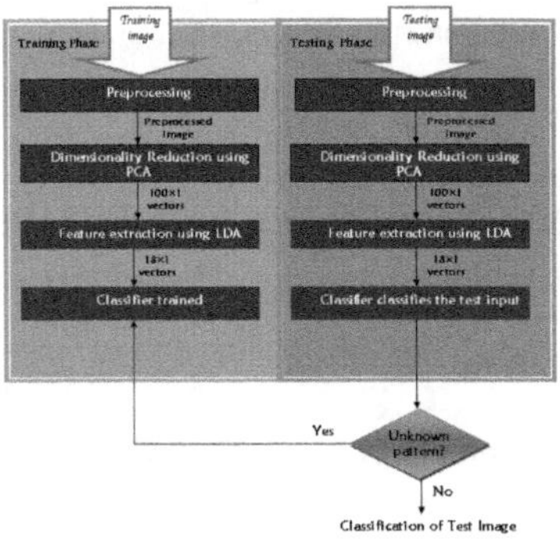

Fig. 5. Structure of Face Recognition System

Face recognition method is applied on ORL face dataset for separation of twenty classes. 340 sample faces are there out of which 140 are used for training and 200 used for testing. Fig. 6 shows examples of sample images used.

Fig. 6. Examples of Sample Face images used

4.1 Preprocessing

In this phase first we resize the images to 40*40 sizes. After that we histogram equalize all input images in order to spread energy of all pixels inside the image. As a next step, we subtract mean images from face images to mean center all of them. Finally all preprocessed face images change to a vector (1600 ×1vector) and go to the next step. Fig. 7 shows example of preprocessed images.

Fig. 7. Examples of preprocessed images

4.2 Dimensionality Reduction

Every input image is cropped to 40×40 image in the preprocessing step; as a result the input of this stage is a preprocessed 1600×1 vector. These vectors are used to estimate the covariance matrix. After estimation of the covariance matrix, significant eigenvectors of the covariance matrix are computed. Number of eigen-vector depends on the accuracy that the application demands. Large number of eigen-vectors will obviously improve the accuracy of the method but computational complexity will increase in this step and next step. Thus considering accuracy and computational complexity 100 eigen vectors are selected as principal eigen vectors.

The preprocessed faces are now projected on to the space with 100 eigenfaces as base vectors to get 140, 100×1 vectors. Thus dimensionality reduction phase converts 1600×1 vectors to 100×1 vectors.

4.3 LDA Feature Extraction

Outputs of dimension reduction part are 100×1 vectors which are used to construct within class scatter matrix and covariance matrix. Significant eigen vectors of $S_w^{-1} S$ (mentioned in Section 2.2) is used for seperability of classes. Using 100×1 vectors, $S_w^{-1} S$ is computed and then eigenvectors related to the greater eigenvalues are selected. Eigenvectors(Fisherafces) corresponding to 18 greater non-zero eigenvalues are selected in this case.

The preprocessed face images projected on to the eigen space, is now, projected onto the fisher space and thus results in 140, 18×1 vectors which are used as input of neural network.

4.4 Classification

4.4.1 Simplified Fuzzy ARTMAP

Classification is done with Simplified Fuzzy ARTMAP. For the direct application of SFAM to the face recognition problem, the architecture is trained using the 140, 18×1 vectors got from the feature extraction stage. The vigilance parameter is selected so that the number of categories to which the network settles is same as the number of classes in the training data.

The network took only 2 epochs for completing its learning or training phase. The time that it took for learning is negligible (0.125 seconds) and thus can be labeled as very efficient in terms of time complexity. Thus SFAM proves itself to be a classifier that learns very fast when compared to Feedforward Neural Network that takes more than 20 minutes to converge when trained for the same input.

Once the training is over and the top-down weight matrices have been obtained, the testing can be carried out using the matrix equivalent of the test input image.

The most important point to note about the network in the classification stage is that it remains open to adaptation in the event of new information being applied to the network. If an unknown pattern is applied to the network SFAM will always attempt to assign a new class in the category output layer by assigning the unknown input to a node. But, Feedforward Neural Network is not able to learn new information on top of old thus can't be used as an adaptive network.

5 Performance Analysis and Discussions

Table 1 shows the result of the experiment conducted. Results show that SFAM exhibits a very good performance in terms of recognition rate and also in terms of time required to train the net.

Table 1. Result of the Experiment Conducted

PCA+LDA Elapsed time is 32.500000 seconds					
Name of the Classifier	*No: of Training Images*	*No: of Testing Images*	*No :of Epochs*	*Elapsed Time*	*Recognition rate*
SFAM	7	3	2	0.125seconds	98.5%
SFAM	6	4	2	0.115seconds	98%
SFAM	5	5	2	0.120seconds	97%

The network took only 2 epochs for completing its learning or training phase. The time that it took for learning is negligible (0.125 seconds for the first case) and thus can be labeled as very efficient in terms of computer time. Thus SFAM proves itself to be a classifier that learns very fast when compared to Feed Forward Neural Network (FFNN) that takes more than 20 minutes to converge when trained for the same input.

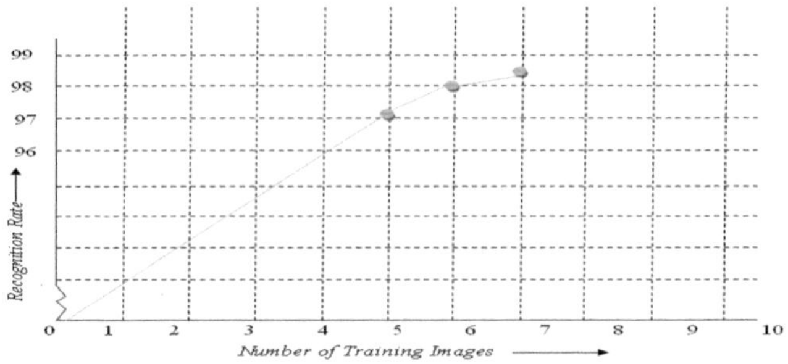

Fig. 8. Result of Experiment conducted

Fig.8. shows that the recognition rate increases when the number of training images increases.

The most important point to note about the network in the classification stage is that it remains open to adaptation in the event of new information being applied to the network. If the system encounters a face image that it is not trained for, it will conclude that it is a face that it is seeing for the first time and it learns the new pattern.

Fig. 9. Test image for which Classifier is not trained for

When the test image (Fig.9.), which belongs to the class for which SFAM is not trained for, is given as input, SFAM will conclude that this is a pattern for which it is not trained and it then learns the new pattern. But FFNN does not exhibit this adaptive behavior.

Since SFAM can adaptively be trained, this can be employed in the cases, like student record maintenance at institutions, attendance keeping at organizations and so on, where addition to database needs to be made frequently.

Thus recognition system using SFAM can perform as an efficient recognizer in cases where a speedy, secure and adaptive system is required.

6 Conclusion

This paper proposes a new method for face recognition using Simplified Fuzzy ARTMAP. The system was tested on ORL Database. The face recognition system was adaptive and exhibited improved performance both in terms of recognition rate and time complexity. Since adaptive, this method can be employed in cases where new data needs to be added to the database frequently. Future works include employing Fast SFAM a variation of SFAM for recognition. Thus recognition system using SFAM can perform as an efficient recognizer in cases where a speedy, secure and adaptive system is required.

References

1. Jain, Bolle, R., Pankanti, S. (eds.): BIOMETRIC – Personal Identification in Networked Society. Kluwer Academic Publishers, Dordrecht (1999)
2. Solar, J.R., Navarreto, P.: Eigen space-based face recognition: a comparative study of different approaches. IEEE Tran. Systems man And Cybernetics- part c: Applications 35(3) (2005)
3. Sahoolizadeh, H., Ghassabeh, Y.A.: Face recognition using eigen-faces, fisher-faces and neural networks. In: 7th IEEE International Conference on Cybernetic Intelligent Systems, CIS 2008, September 9-10, pp. 1–6 (2008), doi:10.1109 / UKRICIS. 2008.4798953
4. Turk, M., Pentland, A.: Eigen faces for face recognition. Journal Cognitive Neuroscience 3(1) (1991)
5. Zhao, W., Chellappa, R., Krishnaswamy, A.: Discriminant analysis of principal component for face recognition. IEEE Trans. Pattern Anal. Machine Intel. 8 (1997)
6. Deniz, O., Castrillón, M., Hernández, M.: Face recognition using independent component analysis and support vector machines. Pattern Recognition Letters 24, 2153–2157 (2003)
7. Wright, J., Yang, A.Y., Ganesh, A., Sastry, S.S., Ma, Y.: Robust Face Recognition via Sparse Representation. IEEE Trans. On Pattern Analysis and Machine Intelligence 31(2), 210–225 (2008)
8. Pham, T.V., Smeulders, A.W.M.: Sparse Representation for Fine and Coarse Object Recognition. IEEE Transactions on Pattern Analysis and Machine Intelligence 28(4), 555–567 (2006)
9. Lee, K., Chung, Y., Byun, H.: SVM based face verification with feature set of small size. Electronic Letters 38(15), 787–789 (2002)
10. Othman, H., Aboulnasr, T.: A separable low complexity 2D HMM with application to face recognition. IEEE Trans. Pattern. Anal. Machie Intell. 25(10), 1229–1238 (2003)
11. Er, M., Wu, S., Lu, J., Toh, L.H.: Face recognition with radial basis function (RBF) neural networks. IEEE Trans. Neural Networks 13(3), 697–710
12. Er, M.J., Chen, W., Wu, S.: High speed face recognition based on discrete cosine transform and RBF neural network. IEEE Trans. On Neural Network 16(3), 679–691 (2005)
13. Pan, Z., Rust, A.G., Bolouri, H.: Image redundancy reduction for neural network classification using discrete cosine transform. In: Proc. Int. Conf. on Neural Network, Italy, vol. 3, pp. 149–154 (2000)
14. Nazeer, S.A., Omar, N., Khalid, M.: Face Recognition System using Artificial Neural Networks Approach. In: International Conference on Signal Processing, Communications and Networking, pp. 420–425. IEEE, Chennai (2007)
15. Gu, M., Zhou, J.-Z., Li, J.-Z.: Online face recognition algorithm based on fuzzy ART. In: International Conference on Machine Learning and Cybernetics, July 12-15, vol. 1, pp. 556–560 (2008)
16. Turk, M.A., Pentland, A.P.: Face Recognition Using Eigenfaces. In: Proceedings of the IEEE Conference on Computer Vision and Pattern Recognition, Maui, Hawaii, USA, June 3-6, pp. 586–591 (1991)

17. Swets, D.L., Weng, J.J.: Using Discriminant Eigen features for image retrieval. IEEE Trans. Pattern Anal. Machine Intel. 18, 831–836 (1996)
18. Martinez, A.M., Kak, A.C.: PCA versus LDA. IEEE Trans. Pattern Anal. Machine Intell. 23, 228–233 (2004)
19. Belhumeur, P.N., Hespanha, J.P., Kriegman, D.J.: Eigen faces vs. Fisher faces: Recognition using class specific linear projection. IEEE Trans. Pattern Anal. Machine Intel. 19, 711–720 (1997)
20. Papoulis, A., Pillai, U.: Probability, Random Variables, and Stochastic Processes. McGraw-Hill, New York (2002)
21. Haykin, S.: Neural Networks: A comprehensive foundation. Prentice Hall, Englewood Cliffs (1999)
22. Eleyan, A., Demirel, H.: PCA and LDA based face recognition using feedforward neural network classifier. In: Gunsel, B., Jain, A.K., Tekalp, A.M., Sankur, B. (eds.) MRCS 2006. LNCS, vol. 4105, pp. 199–206. Springer, Heidelberg (2006)
23. Rajasekaran, S., Vijayalakshmi Pai, G.A.: Image Recognition Using Simplified Fuzzy ARTMAP Augmented with a Moment based Feature Extractor. International Journal of Pattern Recognition and Artificial Intelligence 14(8), 1081–1095 (2000)
24. Rajasekaran, S., Vijayalakshmi Pai, G.A.: Neural Networks, Fuzzy Logic, and Genetic Algorithms. Prentice-Hall of India, New Delhi (2003)
25. Beale, R., Jackson, T.: Neural Computing. Institute of Physics Publishing, Bristol (2001)

An Automatic Evolution of Rules to Identify Students' Multiple Intelligence

Kunjal Mankad[1], Priti Srinivas Sajja[2], and Rajendra Akerkar[3]

[1] Lecturer, ISTAR, CVM, Vallabh Vidyanagar, India
kunjal_mankad@yahoo.com
[2] Associate Professor, Sardar Patel University, India
priti_sajja@yahoo.com
[3] Rajendra Akerkar, Senior Researcher, Vestlandsforsking, Norway
akerkar8@gmail.com

Abstract. The proposed work focuses on Genetic-Fuzzy approach to identify student's skills. It is an integrated approach of education and technology implementing Theory of Multiple Intelligence. The objective is to reduce the system's developmental and maintenance effort and automatically evolve strong rules. The proposed model is a novel evolutionary hybrid approach to measure and classify multiple intelligence in a friendly way. The paper includes general architecture of the model with front end and back end designs including encoding strategy, fitness function, crossover operator, and sample evolved rules and results. It concludes with the scope and application of the work to other domains.

Keywords: Genetic Algorithms, Fuzzy Logic, Genetic Fuzzy Systems, Rule Base, Theory of Multiple Intelligence.

1 Introduction

Soft computing techniques provide efficient and feasible solutions in comparison with hard computing. Out of various soft computing techniques, Fuzzy Logic (FL) is the most important technique to handle imprecision and uncertainty. With the notion of linguistic variable and their fuzzy membership functions; human oriented representation of knowledge is possible. However, the major limitation of FL based systems is low degree of self learning and generalization of rules. This leads to the hybridization of FL approach with other soft computing techniques that support learning and evolution. Genetic Algorithm (GA) based approach is an example of such technique that supports automatic evolution of possible solutions. However, it does not deal with linguistic type human oriented approach. Clever combination of GA and FL approach offers advantages of both the fields. The paper focuses on evolving rule based model for identification of multiple intelligence in human beings by utilizing Genetic-Fuzzy hybrid approach.

Information and Communication Technology (ICT) plays an important role in educating and improving skills of individuals and helps them in improving problem solving capabilities. Out of the different theories available to identify and enhance human

N. Meghanathan et al. (Eds.): CCSIT 2011, Part III, CCIS 133, pp. 35–45, 2011.

intelligence, theory of Multiple Intelligence (MI) has been pioneer among researchers and educationalists. The proposed application considers a novel approach of automatic evolution of rules for identifying multiple intelligence. The architecture of an evolving system is developed to satisfy the need of decision support using genetic fuzzy approach to achieve efficient and powerful classification of human capabilities. In this approach, the initial population of knowledge base requires a few encoded rules, suggested by administrator of the system to initiate the process of evolution. The system in its evolutionary period evolves new rules within the knowledge base through specially designed operators along with the fitness function designed for the domain.

The remaining chapter is organized as follows. Section 2 discusses background of MI theory and various types of intelligence and work done so far in the area. Section 3 establishes need of genetic fuzzy approach for the domain along with brief literature survey. Section 4 presents architecture of the proposed system with detailed methodology. Section 5 discusses output of the system and section 6 concludes the paper with future scope.

2 Background

In today's competitive world, it is very important to select appropriate career in order to achieve success by utilizing ones' capabilities and intelligence. The originator of the theory of multiple intelligences, Howard Gardner, defines intelligence as potential ability to process a certain sort of information [1]. Table 1 enlists and defines examples of stated type of human intelligence according to theory of MI.

However, there is also a possibility of many other types of intelligence in individuals [2]. All types of intelligence play an important role in overall growth of human capabilities. It has been proven that specific types of intelligence such as logical, verbal, interpersonal, kinesthetic etc. are essential to have satisfactory level of success in the field of science and technology, management, sports, etc. [3]. Among all, the technical and managerial abilities play a critical role in one's success. The proposed approach highlights classification of users' managerial and technical skills with genetic fuzzy approach.

The field of education and technology has contributed numerous research projects by implementing Theory of MI for the last few decades, some of them are as follows [4, 5, 6, 7, 8, 9, 10, 11, 12, 13]:

- International educational online learning programs for students as well as teachers
- Curriculum planning, parents' interaction, etc.
- Research based on school students of different ages with IQ tests to identify their skills
- Adult developmental programs
- Employees' developmental programs
- New AI approach for students' academic performance using fuzzy rule generation
- The research project "EDUCE", implemented as a predictive system using MI
- Application of the Theory of Multiple Intelligences to Digital Systems Teaching
- Learning style improvement using information technology, and many more

Table 1. Type of Intelligence and their meaning with examples

Type of Intelligence	Meaning
Linguistic/Verbal Intelligence	The capacity to learn, understand and express using languages e.g. formal speech, verbal debate, creative writing, etc.
Logical-Mathematical Intelligence	The capacity to learn and solve problems using mathematics e.g. numerical aptitude, problem solving, deciphering codes, etc.
Spatial/Visual Intelligence	The ability to represent the spatial world of mind using some images e.g. patterns and designs, painting, imagination, sculpturing, etc.
Bodily-Kinesthetic Intelligence	The capacity of using whole body or some to solve a problem e.g. body language, physical exercise, creative dance, physical exercise, drama, etc.
Musical Intelligence	The capacity to understand music, to be able to hear patterns, recognizes them and perhaps manipulates them e.g. music performance, singing, musical composition, etc.
Interpersonal Intelligence	The ability to understand other people e.g. person-to-person communication, group projects, collaboration skills, etc.
Intrapersonal Intelligence	The ability to understand oneself regarding of every aspects of the personality e.g. emotional processing, knowing yourself, etc.
Naturalist Intelligence	The ability to discriminate among living things and sensitivity towards natural world e.g. knowledge and classification of plants and animals with naturalistic attitude, etc.
Existential and Moral Intelligence	It concerns with ultimate issues as well as capable of changing attitude. It is found to be required with every individual.

3 Related Work in the Area of Genetic Fuzzy Systems

Genetic Algorithms (GA) are robust general purpose search algorithms that use principles inspired by natural population genetics to evolve solutions to the problem. GA provides flexibility to interface with existing models and easy to hybridize [14]. On other hand Fuzzy Logic (FL) based systems are designed to handle uncertainty and imprecision in real situation easily. But the major limitation of such systems is that they are not able to learn [15] as well as requires documentation of knowledge which needs further continuous maintenance. Hence, hybridization of FL with GA becomes essential to achieve advantages both the aforementioned approaches. In such systems, knowledge in the form of linguistic variables, fuzzy membership function parameters, fuzzy rules, number of rules, etc. can be converted into suitable candidate solutions through generic code structure of GA.

Enlisted examples are very useful real world applications those dealing with intelligent information systems where genetic fuzzy methodology has been successfully implemented.

- Diagnostic system for decease such as myocardial infraction, breast cancer, diabetes, dental development age prediction, abdominal pain, etc. [14, 15, 16, 17]
- A trading system with GA for optimized fuzzy model [18]
- For optimizing social regulation policies [19]
- Self integrating knowledge-based brain tumor diagnostics system [20]
- Classification of rules in dermatology data sets for medicine [21]
- Integrating design stages for engineering using GA [22]
- Multilingual question classification through GFS [23]
- University admission process through evolutionary computing [24]
- Genetic mining for topic based on concept distribution [25]
- Intelligent web miner with Neural-Genetic-Fuzzy approach [26]
- Extraction of fuzzy classification rules with genetic expression programming [27]
- Integrated approach for intrusion detection system using GA [28]

4 Sample Case: Evolving Rules for Identifying Human Intelligence

All stated efforts have not yet included evolving knowledge-base approach through genetic fuzzy system to identify specific types of intelligence. Hence, we propose the design of a system to satisfy the need of decision support using GFS to achieve efficient and powerful classification of human capabilities using the proposed approach. The architecture of the proposed system is divided into two main parts namely front end interface and back end system with genetic evolution. Fig. 1 shows the architecture of the system.

4.1 Front End System with User Interfaces

The left component of Fig. 1 shows front end interface for proposed system. Through this interface the domain knowledge is captured and stored in form of questionnaires which have been designed with deep and clear understanding of theory of MI. The proposed system utilizes rule base for identification of human intelligence. Knowledge is represented as a set of rules and data is represented as a set of facts. These set of rules can be collected, analyzed, and finalized during interviews with experts or from multiple references as well as from example sets using theory of multiple intelligence. Further, this domain knowledge is inserted and modified by domain/human expert. Different sets of interactive questionnaires for different user categories are created/ collected by human/domain experts. These set of questionnaires are stored in the database. Different users will be created and their access rights will be assigned according to their categories; for example, higher secondary education students, college students, and professionals. According to user's category, questionnaires will be presented to the user. User selects answer from given list of multiple choices. These answers will be stored in the database and later on calculation of total score of set of questionnaires is shown to the users. Once score is shown to users, system provides decision using evolved rules to select appropriate class such as technical or management. The procedure of rule evolution is transparent to the users and executes in background. The users are advised to improve their intelligence by the system. In order to reinforce the intelligence, different tutorials will be suggested and presented to the users.

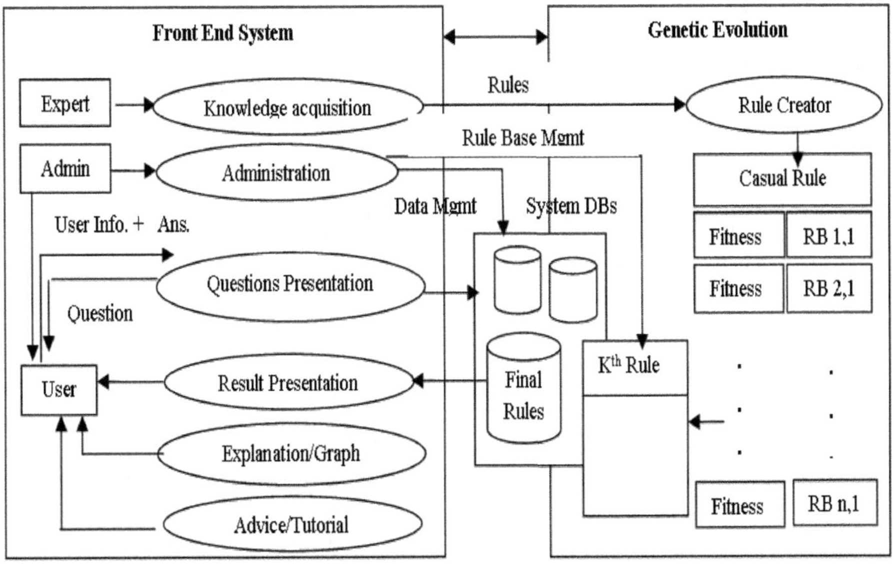

Fig. 1. Architecture of system

4.2 Back End System with Genetic Evolution

The back end component of the system deals with genetic evolution process. Initially, rules are suggested by human expert using different types of intelligence for efficient categorization of skills of users. Knowledge engineer facilitates rules within the rule bases in encoded fashion. Fitness of each rule is measured with fitness function. It is obvious that higher the fitness, the rule is considered as stronger. An individual is evaluated through fitness function. Application specific fitness function has been designed which calculates strength of population selected as a parent for next generation. Evolving procedure utilized can be enlisted as follows [29]:

1. Generate an initial population of encoded rules.
2. Evaluate fitness of these rules and store into the rule profile.
3. Determine the minimum fitness accepted for the application.
4. Identify and discard the weak rules. One may generate new population from the remaining rules for clarity of operations.
5. Apply mutation and cross over operators on rules.
6. Go to step (ii) and repeat the procedure till required fit rules are achieved.

4.2.1 Rule Encoding Strategy

The general structure of a rule is:

$$\text{If X1 is Y1 then Z1 is C1} \tag{1}$$

Where X1 is input variable, Y1 is operator; Z1 is output variable and C1is value.

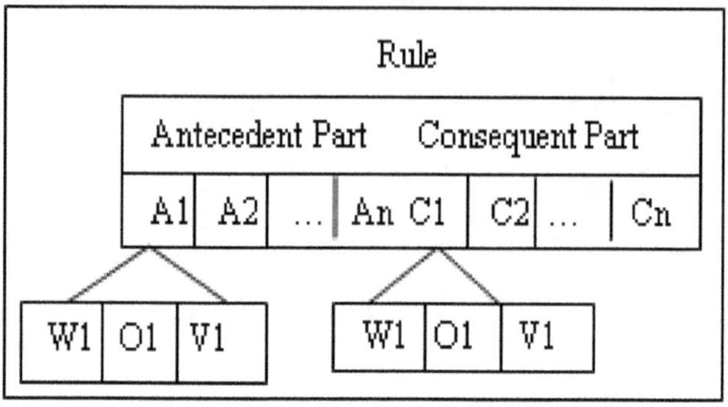

Fig. 2. Proposed Rule Encoding Structure

Binary encoding scheme has been used to encode rule condition and prediction parts. The proposed encoding scheme is a novel approach as it deals with every label associated with the rule. A chromosome is divided into n genes in which each gene corresponds to a full rule. There can be many conditions in antecedent part of a rule. Each part of a rule is divided into three parts: weight of the variable, operator, and value. Weight ranges between [0, 1] to identify the fuzzy existence of the variable in the rule. Value 0 of a weight of the given variable indicates absence/insignificance of the variable. Fig. 2 shows suggested encoding style for fuzzy rules [17].

Table 2. Binary Representation of a Rule

Value of X1,X2 (Conditional Variables)	**Encoding**	**Value of A1,A2 (Linguistic Variables)**	**Encoding**	**Consequent Variables (Y)**	**Encoding**
X1=SLogical	1100	High	1001	Y=Class	1000
X2=SVerbal	0011	Medium	1110	Technical	111
		Low	0001	Mgmt	011

For implementing fuzzy rules, proposed system uses fuzzy mamdani membership functions used in Term set1: {High, Medium, Low} while term set 2 consist of output label set {Technical, Mgmt} for output variables. The sample rule "If X1 is A1 and X2 is A2 then Y is B" can be encoded using encoding parameters specified in Table 2. Different combinations from Table 2 will be utilized for chromosome representation scheme.

4.2.2 Determining Fitness Function

Ideally, quality of rule depends on following criteria; such as high predictive accuracy, comprehensibility, and interestingness. The proposed encoding scheme focuses on predictive accuracy which is discussed as follows: Let rule be in the form: IF A then C, where A is Antecedent and C is consequent. A very simple way to measure the predictive accuracy is to compute the confidence factor (CF) of the rule, which is defined as [30]:

$$CF=|A \ \& \ C|/\ |A| \tag{2}$$

In (2) |A| is the number of examples satisfying all the conditions in the antecedent A and |A&C| is the number of examples that both satisfy the antecedent A and have the class predicted by the consequent C. For example, if a rule covers 10 examples out of which 6 have the class predicted by the rule then CF can be computed as follows:

$$|A \ \& \ C|=6,\ |A|=10 \Rightarrow CF=60\% \tag{3}$$

The predictive performance of the rule can be summarized by 2*2 matrix which is known as confusion matrix shown in Table 3. The labels in each quadrant of the matrix have following meaning [30]:

Table 3. Confusion Matrix

		Actual Class	
		C	Not C
Predicted Class	C	TP	FP
	Not C	FN	TN

1. TP=True Positive=Number of examples satisfying A and C
2. FP=False Negative=Number of examples satisfying A but not C
3. FN=False Negative=Number of example not satisfying A but satisfying C
4. TN=True Negatives=Number of examples not satisfying A nor C

Hence,

$$CF=TP/(TP+FP) \tag{4}$$

Predictive accuracy is measured by (4) by finding proportion of examples having predicted class C that is actually covered by rule antecedent. The rule completeness can be measured by following equation.

$$Comp=TP/(TP+FN) \tag{5}$$

By combining (4) and (5), the fitness function can be defined such as

$$Fitness=CF*Comp \tag{6}$$

The individual rules are tested for the fitness and result is stored into appropriate rule profile. One may start with some default general rules within an initial population. For each rule, degree of fitness is calculated according to the above mentioned fitness function. According to a defined termination criterion, new offspring is generated. Using this methodology, a stronger rule can evolve with every new generation.

4.2.3 Genetic Operator

According to the theory of GA, a crossover operator selects substrings of genes of the same length from parent individuals which are known as off-springs from the same point, replaces them and generates a new individual. This point can be selected randomly [29]. For designing chromosome, we have used binary encoding style as shown in Table 2. Different rules from Table 4 can be represented in form of chromosomes labeled as individuals using proposed encoding style shown in Table 2. Here, single point crossover operator has been implemented as shown in Fig. 4.

Rule 1: If SLogical is High and SVerbal is Low then class is Technical
Individual 1(I1): 1100 1001 0011 0001 1000 111

Rule 2: If SLogical is Medium and SVerbal is High then class is Mgmt
Individual 2(I2): 1100 1110 0011 1001 1000 011

I1	1	1	0	0	1	0	0	1	0	0	1	1	0	0	0	1	1	0	0	0	1	1	1
I2	1	1	0	0	1	1	1	0	0	0	1	1	1	0	0	1	1	0	0	0	0	1	1

Fig. 3. First Generation Individuals

Fig.3 shows rules representation in form of chromosome. One point cross over operator is applied on individuals. This operation interchanges the bit string from cut off position at randomly selected point from rule conditional part. As an outcome, we get Fig. 4 which represents new individuals from next generation.

New I1	1	1	0	0	1	0	0	1	0	0	1	1	1	1	1	0	1	0	0	0	1	1	1
New I2	1	1	0	0	0	0	0	1	0	0	1	1	1	0	0	1	1	0	0	0	0	1	1

Fig. 4. Next Generation of Individual as a Result of Cross Over

Finally, as a result of decoding process, we get following new rules in form of off-springs from result of cross over operation.

New rule 1: If SLogical is High and SVerbal is Medium Then Class isTechnical
New rule 2: If SLogical is Low and SVerbal is High Then Class is Mgmt

After applying rule matching process, the output of crossover operator has generated two new rules which are also available in rule sets as shown in Table 4 [31]. Hence, we can determine that using proposed scheme new feasible rules can be evolved in upcoming generations.

Table 4. Rule Set Identifying Class

1	If SLogical is high and SVerbal is Low then class is Technical
2	If SLogical is High and SVerbal is High then Class is (Technical OR Mgmt)
3	If SLogical is High and SVerbal is Medium then Class is Technical
4	If SLogical is Medium and SVerbal is Medium then Class is (Technical OR Mgmt)
5	If SLogical is Medium and SVerbal is Low then Class is Technical
6	If SLogical is Medium and SVerbal is High then Class is Mgmt
7	If SLogical is Low and SVerbal is High then Class is Mgmt
8	If SLogical is Low and SVerbal is Medium then Class is Mgmt
9	If SLogical is Low and SVerbal is Low then Class is Rejected

5 Implementation of Fuzzy Rules

For good performance of the system, the design of fuzzy membership function is very important. Here, Mamdani FIS is used for implementation of fuzzy inference mechanism. Three different gaussian membership functions (Low, Medium, and High) have been used to represent degree of truth of two input (conditional) variables: SLogical and SVerbal. For output variables, triangular membership functions have been used. "And" method is used as a part of aggregation and "Centroid" method is used for defuzzification. The rule base consists of nine rules. Fig. 5 shows the sample output of fuzzy-mamdani membership function plotting with MATLAB 7.0. Over many generations, natural population evolves according to principle of evolutionary computation. By continuing the method of automatic evolution, self tuning of membership function

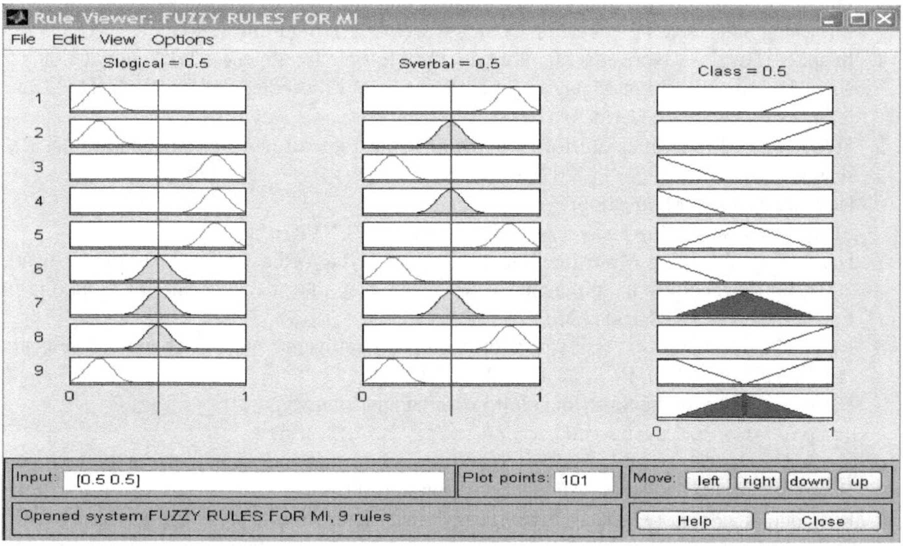

Fig. 5. Evolved Rules

became possible. Reproduction operators serve to provide a new combination of rules and new rules.

6 Conclusion and Future Work

The system presented in this paper offers many advantages such as handling imprecision and minimizing efforts for creation and documentation of knowledge in form of rules. The presented application is to identify students' different skills in education domain. The same approach can be used to provide training for teachers, planning for resources and many more. The proposed architecture of evolving rule based model using genetic-fuzzy approach can also be applied to various domains like advisory systems, decision support systems, data mining systems, and control and monitoring systems, etc. Further, new hybrid operator can be identified using suggested encoding schemes. Specific rule selection scheme will be designed in order to discard infeasible rules. The system can also be extended to different areas where analysis of human intelligence is required. New inventions in Multiple Intelligence can also be integrated with designed rule sets. The proposed system presents a platform for a generic commercial product with an interactive editor in the domain of multiple intelligence identification. This increases the scope of the system and meets the requirements of increased number of non-computer professionals in various fields.

References

1. Carter, P.: The Complete Book of Intelligence Tests. John Wiley, Chichester (2005)
2. Gardner, H.: Multiple Intelligences After Twenty Years. American Educational Research Association, Chicago (2000)
3. Motah, M.: The Influence of Intelligence and Personality on the Use of Soft Skill in Research Projects among Final year University Students: A Case Study. In: Proceedings of Informing Science & IT Education Conference (InSTE), Mauritius (2008)
4. Intan, S., Faris, Z., Norzaidi, M., Normah, O.: Multiple Intelligences Educational Courseware: Learning Tool For Malaysia Smart School. In: Proceedings of EABR & TLC Conferences Proceedings, Germany (2008)
5. Sternberg, R.J.: Abilities are forms of Developing Expertise. American Educational Research Association 27(3), 11–20 (1998)
6. Harward School of Education, `http://www.pz.harvard.edu/Research/SUMIT.htm`
7. Dara, P.A.: Applying Multi-Intelligent Adaptive Hypermedia Online Learning, E-Learn 2002. In: Proceedings of Conference at Association for the Advancement of Computing in Education (AACE), Canada (2002)
8. Kaur, G., Chhikara, S.: Assessment of Multiple Intelligence among Young Adolescents (12-14 Years). J. Hum. Ecol. 23(1), 7–11 (2008)
9. National Center for the Study of Adult Learning and Literacy, `http://www.pz.harvard.edu/Research/AMI.htm`
10. Kelly, D.: On the Dynamic Multiple Intelligence Information Personalization the Learning Environment, Ph.D. Thesis, University of Dublin (2005)
11. Rasmani, K., Shen, Q.: Data-Driven Fuzzy Rule Generation and its Application for Student Academic Performance Evaluation. Journal of Applied Intelligence 25(3), 305–319 (2006)

12. http://stutzfamily.com/mrstutz/APPsych/thoughtandlanguage/lecturenotesintelligence.html
13. Alvaro, C., Norian, M., Aledir, S.: Application of the Theory of Multiple Intelligences to Digital Systems Teaching. In: Proceedings of 39th ASEE/IEEE Frontiers in Education Conference, San Antonio (2009)
14. Herrera, F.: Ten Lectures on Genetic Fuzzy Systems, Technical report, SCCH-TR-0021, Spain (1997)
15. Cordon, O., Herrera, F., Hoffmann, F., Magdalena, L.: Genetic Fuzzy Systems, Evolutionary Tuning and Learning of Fuzzy Knowledge Bases. In: Advances in Fuzzy system-Applications and Theory, vol. 19, pp. 89–93, vol. 97, pp. 179–183. World Scientific, USA (2001)
16. Didelis, M.V., Lopes, H.S., Freitas, A.A.: Discovering Comprehensible Classification Rules with a Genetic Algorithm, Brazil (2000)
17. Sajja, P.S.: An Evolutionary Fuzzy Rule Based System for Knowledge Based Diagnosis. JHCR J. Hybrid Computing Research 2(1) (2009)
18. Cheung, W., Kaymak, U.: A fuzzy Logic Based Trading System, Technical Report, Erasmus Institute, The Netherlands (2007)
19. Sonja, P., Abhraham, A., Ken, C.: EvoPol- A framework for optimizing social regulation policies. Kybernetes 35(6), 814–826 (2003)
20. Wang, C., Hong, T., Tseng, S.: A Genetics –Based Approach to Knowledge Integration and Refinement. Journal of Information Science and Engineering 17, 85–94 (2001)
21. Herrera, F.: Genetic Fuzzy Systems: Status, Critical Considerations and Future Direction. Journal of Computational Intelligence Research 1, 59–67 (2005)
22. Lee, M., Takagi, H.: Integrating Design Stages of Fuzzy Systems using Genetic Algorithms. In: Proceedings of 2nd International Conference on Fuzzy Systems, vol. 1, pp. 612–617. IEEE Press, CA (1997)
23. Day, M., Ong, C., Hsu, W.: Question Classification in English-Chinese Cross-Language Question Answering: An Integrated Genetic Algorithm and Machine Learning Approach, Technical Report, Institute of Information Science & Academia Sinica & Department of Information Management, Taiwan (2007)
24. Serag-Eldin, G., Souafi-Bensafi., S., Lee, J., Chan, W., Nikravesh, M.: Web Intelligence: Web-Based BISC Decision Support System (WBISC-DSS). BISC Program, CA (2002)
25. Khaliessizadeh, S.M., Zaefarian, R., Nasseri, S.H., Ardil, E.: Genetic Mining: Using Genetic Algorithm for Topic based on concept Distribution. Proceedings of World Academy of Science, Engineering and Technology 13, 1307–8884 (2006)
26. Abhraham, A., Wang, X.: i- Miner: A Web Usage Mining Framework Using Neuro-Genetic-Fuzzy Approach. Department of Computer Science (USA), School of Business System, Australia (2003)
27. Marghhny, M.: EI, S.: Extracting Fuzzy Classification rules with gene expression Programming. In: Proceedings of AIML 2005 Conference, CICC, Egypt (2005)
28. Skevajabu, K., Rebgan, S.: Integrated Intrusion detection system using soft computing. International J. Network Security 10, 87–92 (2010)
29. Akerakar, R., Sajja, P.S.: Knowledge-Based Systems. Jones and Bartlett, Massachusetts (2010)
30. Freitas, A.: A Survey of Evolutionary Algorithms for Data Mining and Knowledge Discovery, pp. 31–36. AAAI Press, Brazil (2003)
31. Kunjal, M., Sajja, P.S.: A design of encoding strategy and fitness function for Genetic-Fuzzy system for classification of students' skills. In: Proceedings of 1st International Conference on Signals, Systems and Automation (ICSSA 2009), Vallabh Vidyanagar, India (2009)

A Survey on Hand Gesture Recognition in Context of Soft Computing

Ankit Chaudhary[1,*], J.L. Raheja[2], Karen Das[3], and Sonia Raheja[4]

[1] Computer Vision Research Group
BITS, Pilani, Rajasthan, India-333031
ankitc.bitspilani@gmail.com
[2] Machine Vision Lab, Digital Systems Group
CEERI,Pilani,Rajasthan, India-333031
jagdish@ceeri.ernet.in
[3] Tezpur University, Assam, India
karendas@gmail.com
[4] soniaraheja@rediffmail.com

Abstract. Hand gestures recognition is the natural way of Human Machine interaction and today many researchers in the academia and industry are interested in this direction. It enables human being to interact with machine very easily and conveniently without wearing any extra device. It can be applied from sign language recognition to robot control and from virtual reality to intelligent home systems. In this paper we are discussing work done in the area of hand gesture recognition where focus is on the soft computing based methods like artificial neural network, fuzzy logic, genetic algorithms, etc. We also described hand detection methods in the preprocessed image for detecting the hand image. Most researchers used fingertips for hand detection in appearance based modeling. Finally we are comparing results given by different researchers after their implementation.

Keywords: Hand gesture recognition, soft computing, fingertip based detection, fuzzy logic, Artificial Neural Network, Learning Methods, gesture analysis, Finite state machines.

1 Introduction

Gestures are the unsaid words of human which he expresses in the form of actions. It allows individuals to communicate feelings and thoughts with different emotions with words or without words [1]. Gesture Recognition has become an active research area in the field of Computer vision, Image Processing and Artificial Intelligence. Gesture made by human being can be any but few have a special meaning. Human hand can have movement in any direction and can bend to any angle in all available

---

* Author is currently working toward his PhD, affiliated to the Birla Institute of Technology & Science, Pilani, INDIA and doing research work in Machine Vision Lab, Central Electronics Engineering Research Institute, Pilani, INDIA.

N. Meghanathan et al. (Eds.): CCSIT 2011, Part III, CCIS 133, pp. 46–55, 2011.

coordinates. Chinese sign language as shown in Figure 1, used hand gestures to represents digits as well as alphabets. Many researchers [4][7][16][39][40] have tried with different instruments and equipment to measure hand movements like gloves, sensors or wires, but in these techniques user have to wear the device which doesn't make sense in practical use. So people thought about a way of contact less gesture recognition that could be considered as a research area in Machine Vision or Computer Vision and which would be as natural as human to human interaction. According to Mitra [6] gesture recognition is a process where user made gesture and receiver recognize it. Using this technique, we can easily interact with machines and can give them particular message according to the environment and application syntax. Even people who can't communicate orally (sick, old or young child), they would also get benefit from this technology. It is possible to make a gesture recognition system for these people. Mobile companies are trying to make handsets which can recognize gesture and could operate from little distance also [2][47]. Here we are focusing on human to machine interaction (HMI), in which machine would be able to recognize the gesture made by human. There are approaches of two types.

a. Appearance based approaches where hand image is reconstructed
b. Model based approaches where different models are used to model image

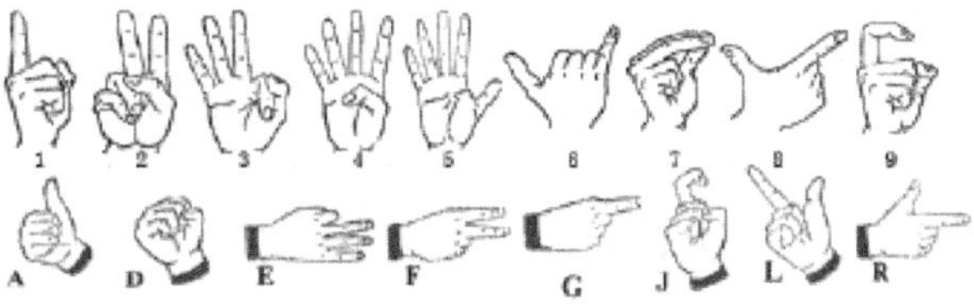

Fig. 1. Chinese sign language [41]

Here we are dividing approaches based on the method used in it not on how it is treating the image. Many approaches have been developed to interact with machines from glove based [4] to neural networks [3]. Users always like the easy and naturalness of technology in HMI and it was more convenient to interpret visual inputs [7]. As Pickering stated [22] that initially touch based gesture interfaces would be popular but, non-contact gesture recognition technologies would be more attractive finally. Input to a machine using gesture is simple and convenient, but the communication includes many difficulties. "The human hand is a complex deformable object and gesture itself has many characteristics, such as diversities, ambiguities, temporal and spatial differences and human vision itself is an ill-posed problem" [10]. Pickering [22] described a real time gesture based driving system simulator developed at Carnegie Mellon University with the help of General Motors. Many researchers [25][26][27][28][37][34] have used a color strip or a shirt to detect hand image in the captured image. For a detailed survey of gesture recognition you can see [6][7][23]. Gesture segmentation a part of the gesture recognition process, have been reviewed in [10] and [11] based on color spaces.

Choi [15] brings attention of researchers pointing out an old problem of the incrementing processing time of algorithm's complexity and say "the most important issue in field of the gesture recognition is the simplification of algorithm and the reduction of processing time". He used morphological operation to implement his system using the center points extracted from primitive elements by morphological shape decomposition. Lu [19], Gastaldi [29], Ozer [30] used parallel approach in the design and implementation of their system. Different threads are implemented in such way that they can run in parallel and can compute faster. Lee [17] describes his system which he developed for remote control systems which worked for motion recognition also. He uses 3D systems with two or more cameras to detect command issued by hand. Villani [9] has tried to develop a system for teaching mathematics to the deaf with an easy user interface. Morimoto [43] made interesting virtual system, in which he pushed virtual buttons using fingers in the air and recognized it using 3D sensors.

2 Hand Detection Approaches

There are many techniques to detect hand in the acquired image after preprocessing. As shown above, we divide these approaches into two parts.

2.1 Appearance Based Approaches

Many researchers have used fingertip detection for the hand image construction [3][8][12][13][17][21][29][37][34][44]. As we are also using fingertip detection technique for our research work, this paper devotes great attention to work done by other researches using this technique. Nolker [3] focuses on large number of 3D hand postures in her system called GREFIT. She used finger tips in hands as natural determinant of hand posture to reconstruct the image. In her system she suggests few approaches to locate fingertip in hand.

1. Marked fingertips colored and making histogram
2. Using different templates or images of a prototype

It takes 192x144 size gray scale image to process. Verma [8] extract features from image as fingertip, edges and vectors for 2D modeling. He used harris corner detector to extract fingertips corresponding to corners. Nguyen [12] used gray scale morphology and geometric calculations to relocate fingertip locations using learning based model on 640x480 pixel size frame. Here Author use similar approach to hand detector given by shin [13] to detect both hands based on skin color. To recognize hands Nguyen [12] used skin segmentation technique using Gaussian model. Density function of skin color distribution is as defined.

$$p(c|skin) = \sum_{i=1}^{k} \pi_i \, p_i(c|skin)$$

Where k is the number of components and π_i are the weight factors of each component. He used CIELUV color space to represent skin. Interestingly he used palm to finger length ratio to construct the hand figure. Zhou [21] worked with 320x240 size 24 bit image frames. Zhou used Markov Random Field to remove noise component in processed figure.

Gastaldi [29] find perimeter using Gaussian filters and freeman's algorithm [31] to localize fingertips in that image for 3D detection. Kim [37] tried to recognize gesture in a dark room on black projection for his system. Although the system was vision based but he used florescent white paper to mark finger tips in the captured image, which is not practical for generic purpose as user have to wear white florescent strips. Kim used kalman filter for finding fingertips and their correct positions in a recursive manner. Stefan [5] implemented a system which can detect motion of fingers in the air visually. He made it to recognize the numbers for 0 to 9 for command transfer.

2.2 Model Based Approaches

Sawah [34] used histogram for calculating probability for skin color observation. Hu [38] take Gaussian distribution for background pixels marking then he subtracted the pixels from the new image to acquired gesture image. Lee [18] used the same technique to get gesture image.

$$\Delta = | I_n - B |$$

In the modeling of his application of human activity monitoring, Hu [38] applied Genetic Algorithm (GA) to Chromosome pool with P_{c0} and P_{m0} as crossover and mutation rate respectively which he founded using different statistic attributes. Crossover creates new chromosomes while mutation in this case introduces new genes into chromosome. Lee [44] use YC_bC_r skin color model to detect hand region and then he applied distance transform. Tarrataca [47] used RGB and HSI color space model based algorithm for skin detection.

3 Soft Computing Approaches

Under the umbrella of soft computing principal constituents are Neural Networks, Fuzzy Systems, Machine Learning, Evolutionary Computation, Probabilistic Reasoning, etc. and their hybrid approaches. Here we are focusing on mainly three components:-

a. Artificial Neural Networks
b. Fuzzy Logic
c. Genetic Algorithm

3.1 Artificial Neural Network/Learning Based Approaches

An Artificial Neural Network (ANN) is made of many highly interconnected processing elements, which are working in together to solve specific problems [35]. ANN can be configured for problems like pattern recognitions or data mining through learning based models. Also ANN has capabilities like adaptive learning, self-organizing and real time operations using special hardware. Nolker [3] used ANN based layer approach to detect fingertips. After obtaining fingertips vectors, it is transformed into finger joint angles to an articulated hand model. For each finger separate network were trained on same feature vectors, having input space 35 dimensional while output dimensional as only 2. Lee [17] used Hidden Markov Model (HMM) for gesture recognition using shape feature. Gesture state is determined after stabilizing the image component as open fingers in consecutive frames. He also used maxima and minima approach like Raheja [14] for construction the hand image and FSM like Verma [8] for gesture finalization.

Wang [32] proposed an optical flow based powerful approach for human action recognition using learning models. It labels hidden parts in image also. This mas-margin based algorithm can be applied to gesture recognition. Kim [37] in his system used learning model for dynamic gestures recognition.

3.2 Fuzzy Logic Based Approaches

A Professor from UCB USA, Lotfi Zadeh presented fuzzy logic in an innovative way. His view was that fro processing precise and accurate information is not necessary, we can perform it with imprecise data also. It is near to natural thinking. As described in [35] "Fuzzy logic is a multivalued logic that allows intermediate values to be defined between conventional evaluations". Verma [8] used c-mean fuzzy clustering based finite state machines (FSM) to recognize hand gestures. Formula for centroid calculation of fuzzy c-means clusters is that centroid would be mean of all points weighted by their degree of belongings to the cluster center. For each point x, a coefficient giving the degree in the kth cluster $U_k(x)$ [24]. Here $x_k = k^{th}$ trajectory point, so

$$\text{center}_k = \frac{\sum_x u_x(x)^m x}{\sum_x u_x(x)^m}$$

In second phase these cluster maps onto FSM states and final state show gesture recognition, although verma[8] didn't implement it. Schlomer [45] used k-mean algorithm on clusters, then he applied HMM and Bayes-classifier on vector data. Trivino [36] tried to make a more descriptive system which can convert human gesture positions into a linguistic description using fuzzy logic. He related it to Natural Language Processing (NLP). He used sensors and took only few positions in sitting and standing, into consideration.

3.3 Genetic Algorithm Based Approaches

Genetic Algorithm comes from biology but it is very influential on computational sciences in optimization. This method is very effective to get optimal or sub optimal solutions of problems as it have only few constraints [35]. It uses generate and test mechanism over a set of probable solutions (called as population in GA) and bring optimal acceptable solution. It executes its three basic operations (Reproduction, Crossover and Mutation) iteratively on population. Sawah [34] has focused on a very generic scenario where he used generic non-restricted environment, generic not-specific application for gesture recognition using genetic programming. He used crossover for noise removal in gesture recognition, while Dynamic Bayesian Network (DBN) for gesture segmentation and gesture recognition with the fuzzification. Hu [38] applied Genetic Algorithm on his system which make 2D parametric model with human silhouette in his application of Human Activity Monitoring. The best point about GA is that it work parallel on different points for faster computation.

3.4 Other Approaches

Raheja [14] proposes a new methodology for real time robot control using Principal Component Analysis (PCA) for gesture extraction and pattern recognition with saved images in database in 60x80 image pixels formats. He used syntax of few gestures and decides corresponding actions of robot. He claims that PCA method is very faster than neural network based methods which require training database and more computation power. Morimoto [43] also used PCA and maxima methods. Gastaldi [29] used PCA to compress five image sequences into one and get eigen vectors and eigen values for each gesture. He used statistical HMM model for gesture recognition. Shin [33] shows gesture extraction and recognition using entropy analysis and low level image processing functions. Lee [18] also used entropy to get color information. He used PIM to quantify the entropy of image using the following equation.

$$PIM = \sum_{i=0}^{L-1} h(i) - Max_j\, h(i)$$

Where h(i) is the ith histogram value of each image or block. To acquire PIM value, subtracting all pixels in each block from maximum frequency in histogram model.

Lu [19] implemented system for 3D gesture recognition where he fused different positions of gesture using coordinate transformations and then use stored prespecified gestures for gesture recognition. Stefan [5] has used Dynamic Space-Time Warping (DSTW) [42] to recognize a set of gestures. This technique doesn't require hands to be correctly identified at each frame. Zou [46] used Deterministic Finite State Machine (DFSM) to detect hand motion and then apply rule based techniques for gesture recognition. He defines gesture into two category based on motion linear and arc shaped gestures. Tarrataca [47] used convex hull method based clustering algorithm Graham's Scan [48] for posture recognition.

4 Implementations Tools

Mostly researchers who used image processing used MATLAB® with image processing toolbox while few used C++ also. Lu [19], Lee [44] and Zou [46] used C++ for implementation on Windows XP® where Lu [19] and Lee [44] he used Microsoft® Foundation Classes (MFC) to build user interface and control.

5 Accuracy

GREFIT [3] system was able to detect finger tips even when it was in front of palm, it reconstruct the 3D image of hand that was visually comparable. Nguyen [12] claimed results 90-95% accurate for open fingers that is quite acceptable while for closed finger it was 10-20% only. As shown in Figure 2 closed or bended finger are coming in front of palm, so skin color detection would not make any difference in palm or finger. According to him image quality and morphology operator was the main reason for low detection.

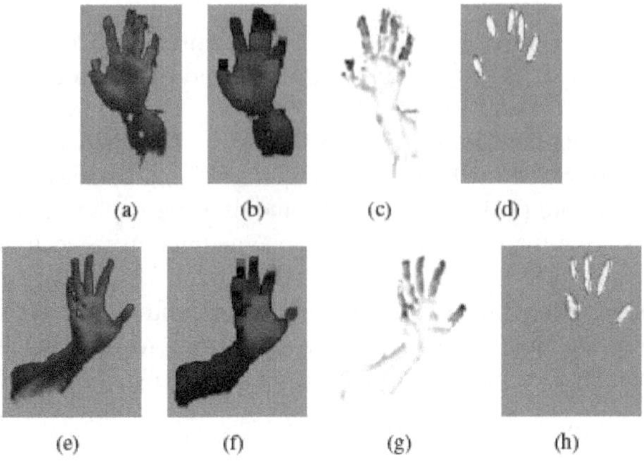

Fig. 2. Result of finger extraction using grayscale morphology operators and object analysis [12] which work for bended finger also, but with a lower accuracy 10-20%

Raheja [14] claims about 90% accuracy in the result, if the lighting conditions are good. Hu [38] used six different parameters to control the performance of system, if he found much noise there, he could control it using two parameters called as α and β respectively. Lee [18] showed results for six kinds of gesture with recognition rate of more than 95% but it recognized bended finger as bended, no matter the degree of banding. Morimoto [43] claimed for his system near 91% accuracy after he applied normalization. Stefan [5] achieved 96% accuracy over 300 tests. He also stated that parallel image processing and pattern matching operations were not real time compatible in MATLAB®, it could be faster if implemented in C++.

6 Conclusions

Applications of gesture recognition have been spread over a long span from intelligent home systems to medical treatment. They are mostly based on the human machine interaction. In this paper we did survey based on approaches in context of soft computing. We included work done using main components of soft computing, Artificial Neural Network, Fuzzy Logic and Genetic Algorithm. For hand image construction in appearance based approach, mostly researchers have used fingertip detection or joints of hand detection. Soft computing provides a way to define things which are not certain but with an approximation that can be make sure using learning models and training data.

References

1. Gesture, K.A.: Visible Action as Utterance. Cambridge University Press, UK (2004)
2. Kroeker, K.L.: Alternate interface technologies emerge. Communications of the ACM 53(2), 13–15 (2010)

3. Nolker, C., Ritter, H.: Visual Recognition of Continuous Hand Postures. IEEE Transactions on Neural Networks 13(4), 983–994 (2002)
4. Sturman, D., Zeltzer, D.: A survey of glove-based input. IEEE Transactions on Computer Graphics and Applications 14(1), 30–39 (1994)
5. Stefan, A., Athitsos, V., Alon, J., Sclaroff, S.: Translation and scale invariant gesture recognition in complex scenes. In: Proceedings of 1st International Conference on Pervasive Technologies Related to Assistive Environments, Greece (July 2008)
6. Mitra, S., Acharya, T.: Gesture recognition: a survey. IEEE Transactions on Systems, Man, and Cybernetics-Part C: Applications and Review 37(3), 2127–2130 (2007)
7. Pavlovic, V.I., Sharma, R., Huang, T.S.: Visual interpretation of hand gestures for human-computer interaction: A review. IEEE Transactions on Pattern Analysis and Machine Intelligence 19, 677–695 (1997)
8. Verma, R., Dev, A.: Vision based Hand Gesture Recognition Using finite State Machines and Fuzzy Logic. In: International Conference on Ultra-Modern Telecommunications & Workshops, October 12-14, pp. 1–6 (2009)
9. Villani, N.A., Heisler, J., Arns, L.: Two gesture recognition systems for immersive math education of the deaf. In: Proceedings of the First International Conference on Immersive Telecommunications, Bussolengo, Verona, Italy (October 2007)
10. Xu, Z., Zhu, H.: Vision-based detection of dynamic gesture. In: International Conference on Test and Measurement, December 5-6, pp. 223–226 (2009)
11. Mahmoudi, F., Parviz, M.: Visual Hand Tracking algorithms. In: Geometric Modeling and Imaging-New Trends, August 16-18, pp. 228–232 (2006)
12. Nguyen, D.D., Pham, T.C., Jeon, J.W.: Fingertip Detection with Morphology and Geometric Calculation. In: IEEE/RSJ International Conference on Intelligent Robots and Systems, St. Louis, USA, October 11-15, pp. 1460–1465 (2009)
13. Shin, M.C., Tsap, L.V., Goldgof, D.B.: Gesture recognition using bezier curves for visualization navigation from registered 3-d data. Pattern Recognition 37(5), 1011–1024 (2004)
14. Raheja, J.L., Shyam, R.,, Kumar, U., Prasad, P.B.: Real-Time Robotic Hand Control using Hand Gesture. In: 2nd international conference on Machine Learning and Computing, Bangalore, India, February 9-11, pp. 12–16 (2010)
15. Choi, J., Ko, N., Ko, D.: Morphological Gesture Recognition Algorithm. In: Proceeding of IEEE region 10th International Conference on Electrical and Electroic Technology, Coimbra, Portugal, August 19-22, pp. 291–296 (2001)
16. Cho, O.Y., et al.: A hand gestue recognition system for interactive virtual environment. IEEK 36-s(4), 70–82 (1999)
17. Lee, D., Park, Y.: Vision-Based Remote Control System by Motion Detection and Open Finger Counting. IEEE Transactions on Consumer Electronics 55(4), 2308–2313 (2009)
18. Lee, J., et al.: Hand region extraction and gesture recognition from video stream with complex background through entropy analysis. In: Proceedings of 26th Annual International Conference of the IEEE EMBS, San Francisco, CA, USA, September 1-5, pp. 1513–1516 (2004)
19. Lu, G., et al.: Dynamic hand gesture tracking and recognition for real time immersive virtual object manipulation. In: International Conference on Cyber Worlds, September 7-11, pp. 29–35 (2009)
20. Kota, S.R., et al.: Principal Component analysis for Gesture Recognition Using SystemC. In: International Conference on Advances in Recent Technologies in Communication and Computing (2009)

21. Zhou, H., Ruan, Q.: A Real-time Gesture Recognition Algorithm on Video Surveillance. In: 8th International Conference on Signal Processing (2006)
22. Pickering, C.A.: The search for a safer driver interface: a review of gesture recognition Human Machine Interface. In: IEE Computing and Control Engineering, pp. 34–40 (2005)
23. Ong, S.C.W., Ranganath, S.: Automatic Sign Language Analysis: A Survey and the Future beyond Lexical Meaning. IEEE Transactions on Pattern Analysis and Machine Intelligence 27(6) (June 2005)
24. Wikipedia.org, `http://en.wikipedia.org/wiki/Cluster_analysis#Fuzzy_c-means_clustering`
25. Do, J., et al.: Advanced soft remote control system using hand gestures. In: Gelbukh, A., Reyes-Garcia, C.A. (eds.) MICAI 2006. LNCS (LNAI), vol. 4293, pp. 745–755. Springer, Heidelberg (2006)
26. Premaratne, P., Nguyen, Q.: Consumer electronics control system based on hand gesture moment invariants. IET Computer Vision 1(1), 35–41 (2007)
27. Kohler, M.: Vision based remote control in intelligent home environments. In: 3D Image Analysis and Synthesis, pp. 147–154 (1996)
28. Bretzner, L., Laptev, I., Lindeberg, T., Lenman, S., Sundblad, Y.: A Prototype system for computer vision based human computer interaction, Technical report ISRN KTH/NA/P-01/09-SE (2001)
29. Gastaldi, G., et al.: A man-machine communication system based on the visual analysis of dynamic gestures. In: International Conference on Image Processing, Genoa, Italy, September 11-14, pp. 397–400 (2005)
30. Ozer, I.B., Lu, T., Wolf, W.: Design of a Real Time Gesture Recognition System: High Performance through algorithms and software. IEEE Signal Processing Magazine, 57–64 (May 2005)
31. Freeman, H.: On the encoding of arbitrary geometric configurations. IRE Transactions on Electronic Computers, EC-10, 260–268 (1985)
32. Wang, Y., Mori, G.: Max-Margin Hidden conditional random fields for human action recognition. In: IEEE Conference on Computer Vision and Pattern Recognition, Miami, Florida, USA, June 20-25, pp. 872–879 (2009)
33. Shin, J., et al.: Hand region extraction and gesture recognition using entrophy analysis. International Journal of Computer Science and Network Security 6(2A) (February 2006)
34. Sawah, A.E., et al.: A framework for 3D hand tracking and gesture recognition using elements of genetic programming. In: 4th Canadian Conference on Computer and Robot Vision, Montreal, Canada, May 28-30, pp. 495–502 (2007)
35. Sivanandam, S.N., Deepa, S.N.: Principles of soft computing. Wiley India Edition, New Delhi (2007)
36. Trivino, G., Bailador, G.: Linguistic description of human body posture using fuzzy logic and several levels of abstraction. In: IEEE Conference on Computational Intelligence for Measurement Systems and Applications, Ostuni, Italy, June 27-29, pp. 105–109 (2007)
37. Kim, H., Fellner, D.W.: Interaction with hand gesture for a back-projection wall. In: Proceedings of Computer Graphics International, June 19, pp. 395–402 (2004)
38. Hu, C., Yu, Q., Li, Y., Ma, S.: Extraction of Parametric Human model for posture recognition using Genetic Algorithm. In: 4th IEEE International Conference on Automatic Face and Gesture Recognition, Grenoble, France, March 28-30, pp. 518–523 (2000)
39. Huang, T.S., Pavlovic, V.I.: Hand gesture modeling, analysis and synthesis. In: Proceedings of International Workshop on Automatic Face and Gesture Recognition, pp. 73–79 (1995)

40. Quek, F.K.H.: Toward a vision-based hand gesture interface. In: Proceedings of the Virtual Reality System Technology Conference, pp. 17–29 (1994)
41. Zhang, J., Lin, H., Zhao, M.: A Fast Algorithm for Hand Gesture Recongnition using Relief. In: Sixth International Conference on Fuzzy Systems and Knowledge Discovery, Tinajin, China, August 14-16, pp. 8–12 (2009)
42. Alon, J., et al.: Simultaneous localization and recognition of dynamic hand gestures. In: International IEEE Motion Workshop, pp. 254–260 (2005)
43. Morimoto, K., et al.: Statistical segmentation and recognition of fingertip trajectories for a gesture interface. In: Proceedings of the 9th International Conference on Multimodal Interfaces, Aichi, Japan, November 12-15, pp. 54–57 (2007)
44. Lee, B., Chun, J.: Manipulation of virtual objects in marker-less AR system by fingertip tracking and hand gesture recognition. In: Proceedings of 2nd International Conference on Interaction Science: Information Technology, Culture and Human, Seoul, Korea, pp. 1110–1115 (2009)
45. Schlomer, T., et al.: Gesture recognition with a Wii Controller. In: Proceedings of the 2nd International Conference and Embedded Interaction, Bonn, Germany, February 18-20, pp. 11–14 (2008)
46. Zou, S., Xiao, H., Wan, H., Zhou, X.: Vision based hand interaction and its application in pervasive games. In: Proceedings of the 8th International Conference on Virtual Reality Continuum and its Applications in Industry, Yokohama, Japan, pp. 157–162 (2009)
47. Tarrataca, L., Santos, A.C., Cardoso, J.M.P.: The current feasibility of gesture recognition for a smartphone using J2ME. In: Proceedings of the 2009 ACM Symposium on Applied Computing, pp. 1642–1649 (2009)
48. Graham, R.: An efficient algorithm for determining the convex hull of a finite planar set. Information Processing Letters 13, 21–27 (1972)

Handwritten Numeral Recognition Using Modified BP ANN Structure

Amit Choudhary[1], Rahul Rishi[2], and Savita Ahlawat[1]

[1] Maharaja Surajmal Institute, New Delhi, India
{amit.choudhary69,savita.ahlawat}@gmail.com
[2] Technological Institute of Textile and Sciences, Bhiwani, India
rahulrishi@rediffmail.com

Abstract. In this work the classification efficiency of the feed-forward neural network architecture is analyzed by using various different activation functions for the neurons of hidden and output layer and varying the number of neurons in the hidden layer. 250 numerals were gathered form 35 people to create the samples. After binarization, these numerals were clubbed together to form training patterns for the neural network. Network was trained to learn its behavior by adjusting the connection strengths at every iteration. Experiments were performed by selecting all combinations of two activation functions logsig and tansig for the neurons of the hidden and output layers and the results revealed that as the number of neurons in the hidden layer is increased, the network gets trained in small number of epochs and the percentage recognition accuracy of the neural network was observed to increase up to a certain level and then it starts decreasing when number of hidden neurons exceeds a certain level due to overfitting.

Keywords: Numeral Recognition, MLP, Hidden Layers, Backpropagation, Activation Functions.

1 Introduction

Offline numeral recognition involves the automatic conversion of numeral's gray scale/ binary images obtained from paper documents, photographs etc. into digit codes that are interpreted by the computer and other text-processing applications. The Optical Character Recognition (OCR) technology has importance in Banking System to recognize courtesy amount on bank checks [1] and in Postal Department to recognize pin codes from post cards / letters etc. The automated processing of handwritten material optimizes the processing speed as compared to human processing and shows high recognition accuracy.

The capability of neural network to generalize and its robust nature would be very beneficial in recognizing handwritten digits. The digits could be written in different dimension, thickness or slant [2]. These will give unlimited variations. The artificial neural network structure involved in our experiment of handwritten numeral recognition

N. Meghanathan et al. (Eds.): CCSIT 2011, Part III, CCIS 133, pp. 56–65, 2011.

is a multi layered perceptron (MLP) with one hidden layer which is a supervised learning network in nature and uses error back-propagation algorithm for its training [3].

The experiments conducted in this paper have shown the effect of the number of neurons in the hidden layer and the transfer function used in the hidden and output layers on the learning and recognition accuracy of the neural network. The criterion to judge the performance of the network will be the number of training epochs, the Mean Square Error (MSE) value and percentage recognition accuracy. All other experimental conditions such learning rate, momentum constant (α), maximum epochs allowable, acceptable error level and termination condition were kept same for all the experiments.

The rest of the paper is organized as follows: Section 2 presents the work already done in this field. Section 3 deals with the sample design and the various steps involved in the OCR System. Neural Network Architecture is presented in detail in section 4. Section 5 provides various experimental conditions for all the experiments conducted under this work. Functioning of the proposed system is explained in Section 6. Discussion of Results and interpretations are described in section 7. Section 8 presents the conclusion and also gives the future path for continual work in this field.

2 Related Work

A lot of research work has been done and is still being done in character recognition for various languages. OCR is categorized into two classes, for printed characters and for handwritten characters [4]. Compared to OCR for printed characters, very limited work can be traced for handwritten character recognition. Chinnuswami et al. [5] in 1980 presented their work to recognize hand printed characters. Using the curves and strokes of characters, the features were identified and statistical approach was used for classification. Dutta et al. [6] recognized both printed and handwritten alpha-numeric characters using curvature features in 1993. Here features like curvature maxima, curvature minima and inflexion points were considered. Thinning and smoothing were also performed prior to classification of characters.In 2007, Banashree et al. [7] attempted classification of handwritten hindi digits using diffusion half toning algorithm. 16-segment display concept has been used here for feature extraction. They proposed a neural classifier for classification of isolated digits. Here they achieved accuracy level upto 98%. In 2008, Rajashekararadhya et al. [8] proposed an offline handwritten OCR technique in which a feature extraction technique based on zone and image centroid was suggested. They used two different classifiers, nearest neighborhood and backpropagation neural network to achieve 95% to 96% accuracy. In 2009 Shanthi et al. [9] used support vector machine (SVM) for handwritten Tamil characters. In this work image subdivision was used for feature extraction. They recorded 82% accuracy.

3 Sample Creation and System Design

Various steps involved in a handwritten digit recognition system are illustrated in Fig.1.

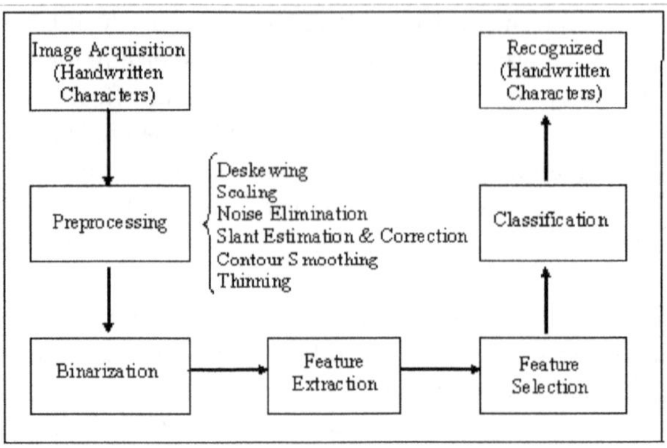

Fig. 1. Typical Off-Line Handwritten Numeral Recognition System

All hand printed numerals were scanned into gray scale images. Each numeral image was traced vertically after converting the gray scale image into binary form. The binary matrix is shown in Fig.2 (b).

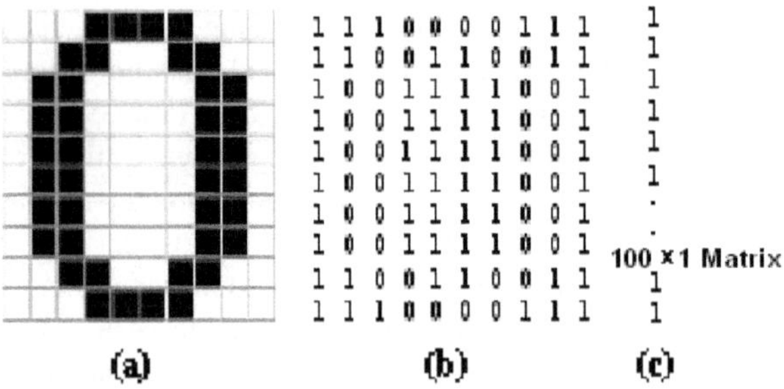

Fig. 2. (a) Binary Representation of Digit '0'; (b) Binary Matrix Representation and (c) Reshaped sample of Digit '0'

The binary matrix of size 10 x 10 was reshaped into a binary matrix of size 100 x 1 and the process is repeated for all the 10 numerals. The reshaped numerals were then clubbed together in a matrix of size 100 x 10 to form a sample which is made as an input to the neural network for learning and testing [10].

4 Neural Network Architecture

The architecture selected for the neural network is a Multilayer Perceptron (MLP) with one hidden layer. The network has 100 input neurons that are equivalent to the input numeral's size as we have resized every numeral into a binary matrix of size 10

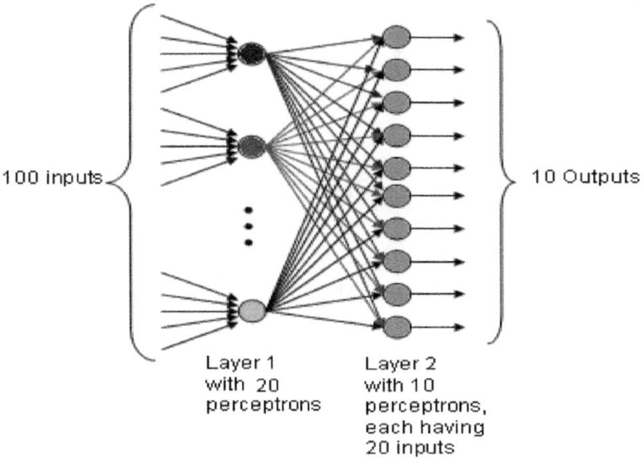

Fig. 4. Architecture of the Neural Network used in the Recognition System

X 10. The 10 output neurons correspond to 10 digits. The number of hidden neurons is directly proportional to the system resources. The bigger the number more the resources are required. The processing nodes of input layer used the linear activation function and the nodes of hidden and output layers used the non-linear differentiable activation function.

The output of the network can be determined as:

$$y_k = f(\sum_{i=1}^{n} Z_i W_{ik}) \cdot \tag{3.1}$$

where f is the output function,

Z_i is the output of hidden layer and

W_{ik} is the weight between hidden and output layer.

also, for hidden layer's processing unit output:

$$Z_i = f(\sum_{j=1}^{n} V_{ij} X_j) \cdot \tag{3.2}$$

where X_j is the output of input layer and V_{ij} is the weight between input and hidden layer.

The MSE between the desired and actual output of the network is given by:

$$E = 0.5 \sum_k [t_k - y_k]^2 \cdot \tag{3.3}$$

where t_k is desired output

The error minimization can be shown as:

$$\partial E / \partial W_{ik} = [t_k - y_k] f'(y_k) z_i \,. \qquad (3.4)$$

Weights modifications on the hidden layer can be defined as:

$$\Delta V_{ij} = \partial E / \partial V_{ij} = \sum_k \partial k * (\partial y_k / \partial v_{ij}) [t_k - y_k] f'(y_k) z_i \,. \qquad (3.5)$$

$$[\text{Let, } \partial k = [t_k - y_k] \, f'(y_k)]$$

and we have

$$\Delta V_{ij} = \sum_k \partial k * W_{ik} f'(z_i) \,. \qquad (3.6)$$

Thus the weight updates for output unit can be represented as:

$$W_{ik}(t+1) = W_{ik}(t) + \eta \, \Delta W_{ik}(t) + \alpha \, \Delta W_{ik}(t-1) \,. \qquad (3.7)$$

where $W_{ik}(t)$ is the state of weight matrix at iteration t

$W_{ik}(t+1)$ is the state of weight matrix at next iteration

$W_{ik}(t-1)$ is the state of weight matrix at previous iteration.

$\Delta W_{ik}(t)$ is current change/ modification in weight matrix and α is standard classical momentum variable to accelerate learning process and depends on the learning rate of the network.

The neural network was exposed to 5 different samples as achieved in section 3, each sample being presented 100 times. Actual output of the network was obtained by "COMPET" function. This is a competitive transfer function which puts 1 at the output neuron in which the maximum trust is shown and rest neuron's result into '0' status. The output matrix is a binary matrix of size (10, 10). The output is of the size (10×10) because each digit has 10×1 output vector. First 10×1 column stores the first digit's recognition output, the following column will be for next digit and so on for 10 digits. For each digit the 10×1 vector will contain value '1' at only one place. For example digit '0' if correctly recognized, will result in [1, 0, 0, 0 …all …0].

The difference between the desired and actual output is calculated for each cycle and the weights are adjusted. This process continues till the network converges to the allowable error or till the maximum number of training epochs is reached.

5 Experimental Conditions

The various parameters and their respective values used in the learning process of all the experiments with various activation functions of the neurons in hidden and output layers and having different number of neurons in the hidden layer are shown in Table 1

Table 1. Experimental Conditions of the Neural Network

Parameters	Value
Input Layer	
No. of Input neurons	100
Transfer / Activation Function	Linear
Hidden Layer	
No. of neurons	Between 5 and 50
Transfer / Activation Function	Logsig or Tansig
Learning Rule	Momentum
Output Layer	
No. of Output neurons	10
Transfer / Activation Function	Logsig or Tansig
Learning Rule	Momentum
Learning Constant	0.01
Acceptable Error (MSE)	0.001
Momentum Term (α)	0.90
Maximum Epochs	1000
Termination Conditions	Based on minimum Mean Square Error or maximum number of epochs allowed
Initial Weights and biased term values	Randomly generated values between 0 and 1
Number of Hidden Layers	1

6 Functional Details

In the current situation, the number of neurons in the input and output layers are fixed at 100 and 10 respectively. The number of neurons in the hidden layer and the activation functions of the neurons in the hidden and output layers are to be decided. It is very difficult to determine the optimal number of hidden neurons. Too few hidden neurons will result in underfitting and there will be high training error and statistical error due to the lack of enough adjustable parameters to map the input-output relationship. Too many hidden neurons will result in overfitting and high variance. The network will tend to memorise the input-output relations and normally fail to generalize. Testing data or unseen data could not be mapped properly.

To produce an output, the neuron performs the transformation function on the weighted sum of its inputs. Various activation functions used in neural networks are compet, hardlim, logsig, poslin, purelin, radbas, satlin, softmax, tansig and tribas etc. The two transfer functions normally used in MLP are logsig and tansig. These transfer functions are commonly used as they are easy to use mathematically and while saturating, they are close to linear near the origin.

logsig transfer function is also known as Logistic Sigmoid:

$$\log sig(x) = \frac{1}{1+e^{-x}},$$

tansig transfer function is also known as Hyperbolic Tangent:

$$\tan sig(x) = \frac{2}{1+e^{-2x}} - 1$$

There is not any rule that gives the calculation for the ideal parameter setting for a neural network. In our problem, the structure analysis has to be carried out to find the optimum number of neurons in the hidden layer and the best activation functions for the neurons in the hidden and output layers. For this analysis, the various activation function combinations for the neurons in the hidden layer and output layer are logsig-logsig, logsig-tansig, tansig-logsig, tansig-tansig with different number of neurons in the hidden layer as shown in Table 2 and Table 3. Mean Square Error (MSE) is an accepted measure of the performance index often used in MLP networks. The lower value of MSE indicates that the network is capable of mapping the input and output accurately. The accepted error level is set to 0.001 and the training will stop when the final value of MSE reaches at 0.001 or below this level. The number of epochs required to train a network also indicates the network performance. The adjustable parameters of the network will not converge properly if the number of training epochs is insufficient and the network will not be well trained. On the other hand, the network will take unnecessary long training time if there are excessive training epochs. The number of training epochs should be sufficient enough so as to meet the aim of training.

If there is a saturated or horizontal straight line at the end of the MSE plot, the further training epochs are no longer beneficial and the training should be stopped by introducing the stopping criterion such as maximum number of training epochs allowed in addition to the stopping criterion of maximum acceptable error as specified in the training algorithm. This type of MSE plot is observed when there is a very complicated problem or insufficient training algorithm or the network have very limited resources.

7 Results and Discussion

Two types of transfer functions: 'logsig' and 'tansig' are used to simulate the neural network used in our problem of numeral recognition. As seen in Table 2, the activation function for the output layer was changed from logsig to tansig by fixing the activation function of hidden neurons to 'logsig'. Similarly in Table 3, the activation function of the hidden neurons was fixed to 'tansig'. The number of training epochs and MSE values of the network are indicated corresponding to the number of neurons in the hidden layer.

Irrespective of the type of activation function used in hidden layer and output layer, it is clear from Table 2 and Table 3, when the number of neurons in the hidden layer is increased, the number of epochs required for the training of the network decreases. Insufficient number of hidden neurons results in underfitting and the MSE does not fall below the acceptable error level and the training is stopped by the stopping criterion of maximum allowed number of training epochs. Overfitting is observed when the number of hidden neurons exceeds a certain count and the percentage recognition accuracy gradually falls with the increase in the number of hidden neurons. The network will tend to memorise the input-output relations and normally fail to generalize. However the training of the network becomes faster as indicated by the decrease in number of training epochs as the number of hidden neurons increases.

Table 2. Behavior of MLP with "logsig" Function in Hidden Layer

Number of Hidden Units	Hidden Layer- Output Layer Logsig- Logsig			Hidden Layer- Output Layer Logsig -Tansig		
	MSE	Epochs	Recognition Accuracy	MSE	Epochs	Recognition Accuracy
5	0.008928986	1000	78.2 %	0.000850345	590	95.5 %
10	0.009418455	1000	81.7 %	0.000888548	579	96.9 %
15	0.003887096	1000	77.7 %	0.000614491	490	96.6 %
20	0.000552677	850	93.2 %	0.000534798	403	98.2 %
25	0.00081461	831	92.9 %	0.000224105	367	98.3 %
30	0.000587808	859	93.1 %	0.000319418	380	97.6 %
35	0.000517400	770	92.3 %	0.000341597	352	97.0 %
40	0.000562353	690	90.9 %	0.000449759	368	97.3 %
45	0.000557294	600	88.8 %	0.000540665	292	97.3 %
50	0.000777322	539	89.0 %	0.000739418	205	97.0 %

Table 3. Behavior of MLP with "tansig" Function in Hidden Layer

Number of Hidden Units	Hidden Layer- Output Layer Tansig – Logsig			Hidden Layer- Output Layer Tansig –Tansig		
	MSE	Epochs	Recognition Accuracy	MSE	Epochs	Recognition Accuracy
5	0.008659145	1000	77.7 %	0.000737171	441	96.5 %
10	0.009659549	1000	79.8 %	0.000623718	366	97.1 %
15	0.003457529	970	91.4 %	0.000416114	299	96.7 %
20	0.000954238	850	94.3 %	0.000216485	264	99.1 %
25	0.000518571	831	93.0 %	0.000313748	270	97.1 %
30	0.000569569	859	92.5 %	0.00039264	260	98.7 %
35	0.000549511	770	93.0 %	0.000351614	251	98.1 %
40	0.000655709	690	92.8 %	0.000423734	222	97.2 %
45	0.000558188	600	91.1 %	0.000612344	194	97.7 %
50	0.000666341	539	92.6 %	0.000517227	209	96.8 %

The optimal number of hidden neurons and the best combination of activation functions for the hidden and output neurons can be decided by considering the numeral recognition accuracy of the network. By taking into consideration all the performance measure parameters such as MSE, overfitting and underfitting, training time and the available system resources, it is evident from Table 2 and Table 3, that, the neural network with 20 neurons in the hidden layer and with tansig-tansig activation function combination for the hidden and output neurons provides the best sample recognition accuracy of 99.1% with least MSE of 0.000216485 and sufficient number of training epochs. For this network, the profile of MSE plot for the training epochs is drawn in Fig 5.

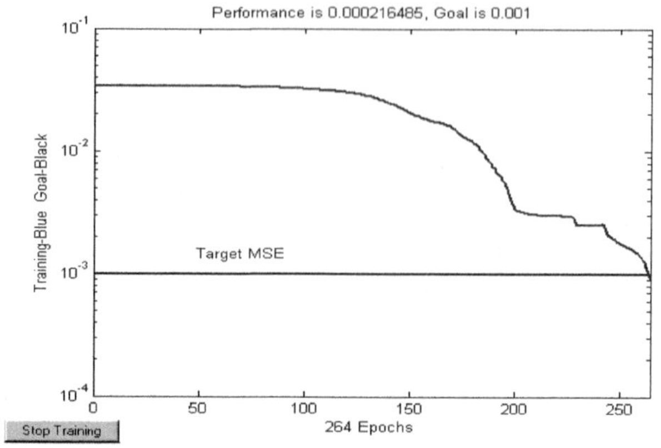

Fig. 5. Variation of MSE with the Training Epochs

8 Conclusion and Future Scope

The MLP used in the proposed method for the handwritten numeral recognition employing the back propagation algorithm performed exceptionally well with 20 neurons in the hidden layer and tansig as the activation function for both hidden and output layer neurons. In this MLP structure, the number of neurons in the input and output layers were already fixed to 100 and 10 respectively.Thus it can be concluded that if the accuracy of the results is a critical factor for an application, then the network having the optimal structure should be used but if training time is a critical factor then the network having a large number of hidden neurons should be used. Training speed can be achieved at the cost of system resources because the number of training epochs decreases with the increase in the number of hidden neurons.

Due to the back-propagation of error element in MLP, it frequently suffers from the problem of Local-Minima; hence the samples may not converge. Nevertheless, more work needs to be done especially on the test for more complex handwritten numerals. The proposed work can be carried out to recognize numeral strings after proper segmentation of the digits into isolated digit images.

References

1. Neves, R.F.P.: A New Technique to Threshold the Courtesy Amount of Brazilian Bank Checks. In: Proceedings of the 15th IWSSIP. IEEE Press, Los Alamitos (2008)
2. Ouchtati, S., Mouldi, B., Lachouri, A.: Segmentation and Recognition of Handwritten Numeric Chains. Journal of Computer Science 3(4), 242–248 (1997)
3. Verma, B.K.: Handwritten Hindi Character Recognition Using Multilayer Perceptron and Radial Basis Function Neural Network. In: IEEE International Conference on Neural Network, vol. 4, pp. 2111–2115 (1995)
4. Arica, N., Yarman-Vural, F.: An Overview of Character Recognition Focused on Offline Handwriting. IEEE Transactions on Systems, Man, and Cybernetics, Part C: Applications and Reviews 31(2), 216–233 (2001)

5. Chinnuswamy, P., Krishnamoorty, S.G.: Recognition of Hand Printed Tamil characters. Patteern Recognition 12(3), 141–152 (1980)
6. Dutta, A., Chaudhary, S.: Bengali Alpha-numeric character recognition using curvature features. Pattern Recognition 26(12), 1757–1770 (1993)
7. Banashree, N.P., Andhre, D., Vasanta, R., Satyanarayana, P.S.: OCR for script identification of Hindi (Devanagari) numerals using error diffusion Halftoning Algorithm with neural classifier. Proceedings of World Academy of Science Engineering and Technology 20, 46–50 (2007)
8. Rajashekararadhya, S.V., Ranjan, P.V.: Efficient zone based feature extraction algorithm for handwritten numeral recognition of popular south Indian scripts. Journal of Theoretical and Applied Information Technology 7(1), 1171–1180 (2009)
9. Shanthi, N., Duraiswamy, K.: A novel SVM-based handwritten Tamil character recognition. Pattern Analysis and Application (2009)
10. Ilin, R., Kozma, R., Werbos, P.J.: Beyond feedforward models trained by backpropagation: A practical training tool for a more efficient universal approximator. IEEE Transactions on Neural Networks 19(6), 929–937 (2008)

Expert System for Sentence Recognition

Bipul Pandey, Anupam Shukla, and Ritu Tiwari

Department of Information and Communication Technology,
ABV-Indain Institute of Information Technology and Management, Gwalior, India
{pandeybipul,sushilranjan007,
dranupamshukla,tiwariritu2}@gmail.com

Abstract. The problem of using natural languages as a medium of input to computational system has long intrigued and attracted researchers. This problem becomes especially acute for systems that have to deal with massive amount of data as inputs in the form of sentences/commands/phrase as a large number of such phrases may look vastly different in lexical and grammatical structure but yet convey similar meanings. In this paper, we describe a novel approach involving Artificial Neural Network to sufficiently solve the aforesaid problem for inputs in English language. The proposed system uses Self Organizing Map (SOM) to recognize and classify the input sentences into classes representing phrases/sentences having similar meaning. After Detailed analysis and evaluation, we have been able to reach a maximum efficiency of approximately 92.5% for the system. The proposed expert system could be extended to be used in the development of efficient and robust systems like intelligent medical systems, Systems for Intelligent Web-Browsing, telemarketing and several others which will be able to take text input in the form commands/sentences in natural languages to give suitable output.

Keywords: Knowledge Discovery, Natural Language Reasoning, Machine Learning, Artificial Neural Networks, Self Organizing Maps, Sentence Recognition.

1 Introduction

The incredible advances in the field of data storage have enabled the creation of techniques for making robust, credible and efficient databases and data warehouses. However, such massive data depots make the task of knowledge discovery from them, much more difficult, error-prone and non-scalable. Also, it is desired for many such knowledge discovery systems that they should be able to interact directly with the domain experts/researchers and/or users/input providers who are not usually computationally erudite enough so as to give inputs/commands in the form traditionally required by such systems. They usually guide/inform the system through commands/inputs in one or the other spoken languages. These are either in the form of text or speech. The ability of natural languages to express same sentiment in extensively diverse forms has given rise to expressions which may be lexico-grammatically different but yet may have similar meanings. Hence, the development of efficient and reliable systems which can retrieve knowledge from such large sources with

N. Meghanathan et al. (Eds.): CCSIT 2011, Part III, CCIS 133, pp. 66–75, 2011.

information in the form of natural language phrases/commands, is a difficult task and needs novel and suitably chosen approach.

The proposed system makes use of Self Organizing Map (SOM) for efficiently solving the aforesaid problem of mapping input commands/sentences in natural language (here, english) to similar meaning commands/sentences. A Self Organizing Map is a type of Artificial Neural Network which plots a high dimensional space into low dimensional topographical features. Their ability to save the neighborhood related information in inputs made makes them extremely suitable and successful in knowledge discovery from sources comprising of symbolic strings from natural languages.. The network undergoes unsupervised learning procedure. The proposed System comprises of the data source, Coding module to create patterns of words and sentences, specified accordingly and makes use of Self Organizing Maps for classifying and recognizing words and sentences.

2 The State of Art

With a tremendous increase in data amassing, storage and usage, the field of Knowledge Discovery from data sources has seen a significant and intense interest from researchers. KDD is the nontrivial process of identifying valid, novel, potentially useful, and ultimately understandable patterns in data [1]. With the traditional knowledge discovery measures of manual analysis and interpretation getting obsolete, new theories and tools for computational discovery of useful information are being searched and analyzed. Knowledge Discovery from data sources derive its strength from diverse fields like pattern recognition, Machine Learning statistics, AI, knowledge acquisition for expert systems and others and hence there are many different approaches for the same [2]. Due to the assortment and complexity of data to be mined and the error prone and usually noise-infested nature of the inputs, designing algorithms for proper and suitable learning of such systems is considered an extremely difficult task [3].

Clustering as a tool for the task of Knowledge mining has been extremely popular. Clustering is defined as the unsupervised classification of patterns (observations, data items, or feature vectors) into groups (clusters) [4]. It has been used widely researched upon and used in varied fields. Clustering has been successfully implemented as a measure for pattern recognition and classification [5]. Information recovery and processing has also been successfully attempted through the use of clustering paradigm [6]. Such varied implementation has led to the development of several algorithms and techniques for data and feature clustering implemented and used sufficiently in dwelling upon the depth that the paradigm provides for computationally heavy and complex tasks involved in knowledge mining [7].

Though there is no dearth of efficient algorithms and techniques being used both in Knowledge Discovery and Clustering, Artificial Neural networks have started to gain a foothold because of their versatility and adaptability to representations presented and are increasingly attracting researchers to use them to find novel yet efficient methods of problems being challenged. Though the problem of pattern analysis and data dredging has been widely discussed and debated for Natural Language Reasoning and several existing techniques have been widely used, yet sufficiently successful implementations are few and far in between. [8] talks about Language Modeling to solve the problem of sentence recognition. This is done via using probabilistic grammar along with a Hidden Markov Identifier. In [9], recognition problem is mathematically formulated as an optimization problem with constraints by introducing sentence structures from the syntactic and semantic considerations in speech recognition. In [10], an algorithm had been proposed to describe a framework for classifier combination in grammar-guided sentence recognition. In [11], an algorithm had been proposed for the recognition of isolated off-line words. The algorithm is based on segment string matching and could do with moderately noisy and error prone data set.

In [12], sentence recognition has been achieved which uses a template based pattern recognition and represents words as a series of diaphone-like segments. In [13], word co-occurrence probability has been used for sentence recognition. The incurred results were also compared with the method using the Context Free Grammar. Hybrid Techniques have also been used for the aforesaid problem. In [14], Hidden Markov Model (HMM) and Neural Network (NN) Model have been combined for the solution. Here, Word Recognition had been using a Tree-Structured dictionary while Sentence Recognition is done using a word-predecessor conditioned beam search algorithm to segment into words and word recognition. In [15], hidden Markov models (HMMs) and associative memories have been used for sparse distributed representations. Binary Hamming Neural Network has been applied to recognize sentences and have been found to sufficiently successful in this regard. The system proposed also takes advantage of greater speed of the Binary Networks to provide a very efficient solution to the problem of sentence recognition [16]. David and Rajsekaran have talked about how Hopfield classifiers can be used as a tool in Pattern Classification [17].

3 Methodology

The system makes use of Self Organizing Maps for word and sentence recognition. The Topology of a Self-Organizing Map is as shown in Fig. 1.

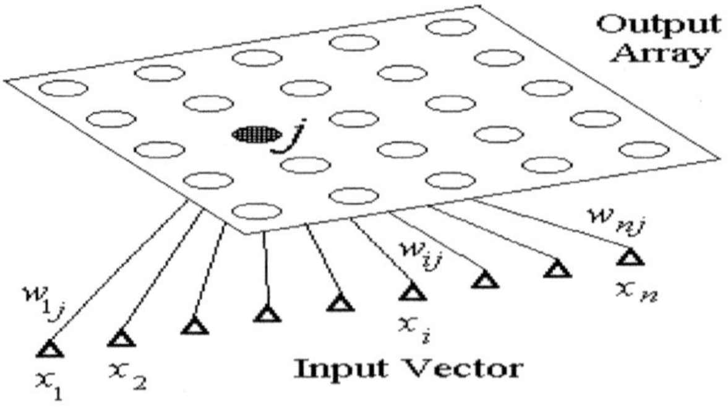

Fig. 1. Topology of a Self Organizing Map

Originally thought as a neural network modelling possible brain structure [18], SOM has been regularly used to analyze/visualize symbolic/text inputs. Their application has led to vastly efficient solution for character recognition as compared to traditionally used approaches [19], [20]. Even from large data sources, their application has vastly improved retrieval of relevant information or knowledge in a very robust manner [21]. Symbolic representations are considered to be highly positional [22]. Hence, the ability of Self Organizing Maps to topologically organize the representations in a cluster are more similar to each other than they are to any of another cluster makes it much more appropriate than over other techniques. The mapping is done so that more frequently occurring data groups are mapped using higher-resolution collections of models.

The Self Organizing Map functions as: First the weights are initialized from N inputs to M output nodes. These weights are very small in value. Now the new input is given to the network. Now the distance (d_j) is calculated from each input pattern to each output node j. This is done according to

$$d_j = \sum_{i=0}^{N-1} (x_i(t) - w_{ij}(t))^\wedge 2 \quad . \tag{1}$$

The node j with the minimum distance (d_j) is chosen as the output. Now the weights of the output node j and those in its neighbourhood are updated. The neighbourhood is defined by $NE_j(t)$.

$$w_{ij}(t+1) = w_{ij} + \eta(t)(x_i(t) - w_{ij}(t)) \text{, where} \tag{2}$$

$$j = NE_j(t),\ \ 0 \le j \le N-1,\ 0 < \eta(t) .$$

The gain term $\eta(t)$ decreases with each iteration. This process is kept on repeating till final output is achieved [23].

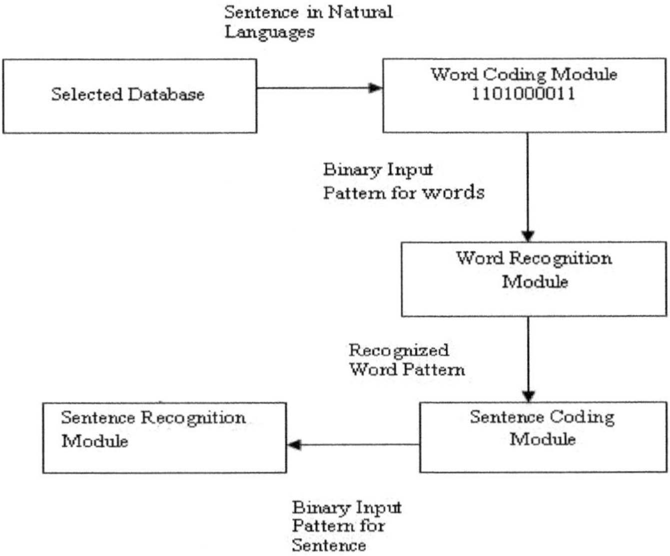

Fig. 2. Architecture of the Proposed System

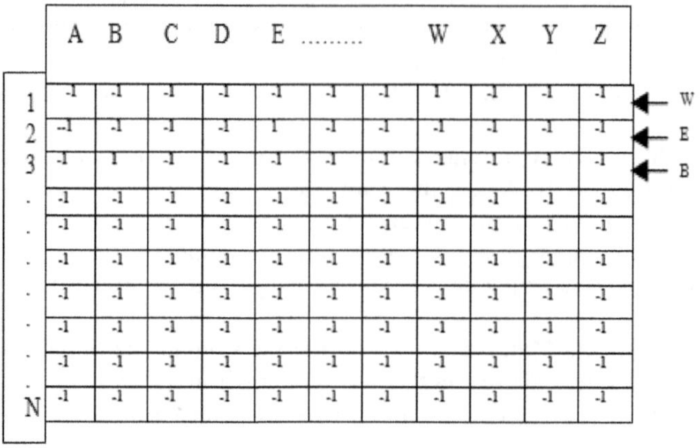

Fig. 3. Format for Binary Coding of Isolated Words

The architecture of the proposed system is as shown in Fig. 2. In the beginning the text data base is used to take inputs. These inputs are sentences/phrases/expressions in natural languages. These inputs are then given to the Word Isolation and Coding Module. Here each sentence/expression is processed by isolating individual words. The words thus extracted are then coded in the form of a matrix. The matrix is of size (N x M), where N = Number of alphabets in the word, &
M = Total English alphabets in word=26.

The words are coded in a binary manner (using 1 & -1). What alphabet is present is represented by the column number in which they are present. For Example, the word is coded as shown in the Fig. 3. The first 'w' is represented by the binary input 1

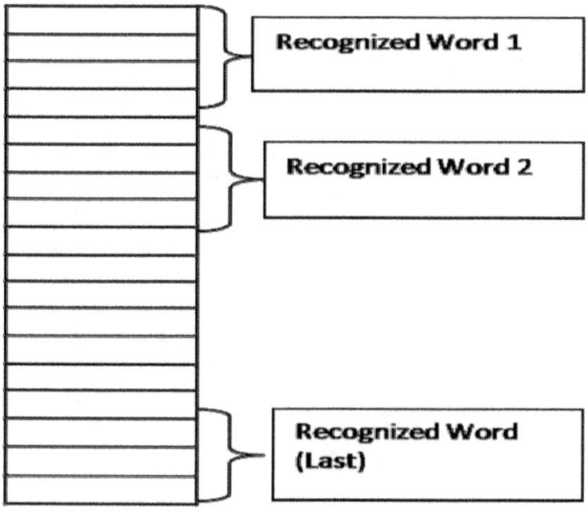

Fig. 4. Format for Binary Coding for Sentences using recognized word pattern in column matrix form

present in (1, 23) position in the matrix. Rest all positions are filled with the binary input -1. Hence, for nth row all positions are -1 except where an alphabet is present.

After this, the coded words are passed on to the word recognition module. This module consists of a Self Organizing Map (SOM) for the recognition of words using clustering paradigm. The input word is mapped on to a specific cluster. The resultant recognized word is the training word representative of the cluster in which the input word has been mapped. The different words recognized for the input sentence pattern are now combined to give a pattern in the sentence coding module which is the input for the sentence recognition module (Fig 4). This is done by appending the output patterns according to the position of the words in the sentence to give the sentence pattern in the column matrix form. These sentence patterns are then sent to the Sentence Recognition Module. This module also comprises of a Self Organizing Map trained with chosen sentence patterns. The network clusters and maps the input pattern to a specific cluster giving result which is the representative training sentence pattern for that cluster. If the pattern falls in a cluster with many or no representative word pattern, then hamming distance is used to find the pattern most similar to it. This output is then matched with the original sentence to check whether the output conveys the same meaning or not. In this way, the input phrases, words or sentences are recognized.

4 Experimental Results

The Database, used for constructing the proposed system, is comprised of 500 sentences, with 50 sentences to be used as training data for the network in the sentence recognition module. The Database here was prepared by taking 500 sentences from a general text regarding common web usage. These sentences were taken as a paragraph in the form of a text file. The different sentences separated by full stops were segregated in the Word Isolation and Coding Module. This module is built using Java Coding. Each sentence had its end marked by a full stop. The code takes advantage of this and separates sentences which start after one full stop and end before the next one. The module then isolates each word per sentence and forms word pattern for each using the matrix format described and outputs each in the form of a text file. The 50 sentences chosen as the training data for the Sentence Recognition Module have their words along with 100 more words taken from the database as the training set for the Word Recognition Module. The remaining words and sentences of the database are chosen as the testing data for the Word Recognition Module and Sentence Recognition Module in the system.

The Sentence pattern of these 50 sentences is formed by appending the word patterns of each word of a sentence as per their position in the sentence to give the sentence pattern of that particular sentence. These patterns are then used as the training set for the Sentence Recognition Module. The remaining sentences of the database are chosen as the testing data for the system. The words of each of the testing sentence are fed to the Word Recognition Module which gives the training word pattern most similar to that word as its output according to the Neural Network used in the module to classify the input patterns. If Self-Organizing Map is used to clssify the input word patterns in the Word Recognition Module, it topologically maps the pattern to a specific cluster. The training word representative (the training word pattern which was mapped to the same cluster) of the cluster is given as the output in this case. If the pattern falls in a cluster with many or no representative word pattern, then hamming distance is used to find the pattern most similar to it.

Table 1. Details of SOM model used

Model	No. of Layers (word recognition module, sentence recognition module)	No. of Neurons (word recognition module, sentence recognition module)	Transfer Function
Self Organizing Maps (SOM)	(single, single)	(393,50)	-

Table 2. Details of BPA model used

Model	No. of Layers (word recognition module, sentence recognition module)	No. of Neurons (word recognition module, sentence recognition module)	Transfer Function
Back Propagation Algorithm (BPA)	(single, single)	(393,500)	transig, purelin

The output patterns of each word are then appended as per its position to give the sentence pattern in the column matrix form as described earlier. The patterns of each of the sentence are then given to the Sentence Recognition Module where the training sentence pattern most similar to the input pattern is given as its output according to the Neural Network used as a classifier in the module. If Self-Organizing Map is used here, it will map the pattern based on topological similarity to a cluster. The training sentence representative (the training sentence pattern which was mapped to the same cluster) of the cluster is given as the output in this case. If the pattern falls in a cluster with many or no representative word pattern, then hamming distance is used to find the pattern most similar to it. The output of each testing sentence is then checked with the original testing sentence to find out where the output is similar in meaning it or not.

Table 3. Details of RBF model used

Model	No. of Layers (word recognition module, sentence recognition module)	No. of Neurons (word recognition module, sentence recognition module)	Transfer Function
Radial Basis Function (RBF)	(single, single)	(393,500)	Radial basis

Along with Self-Organizing Maps, we also implemented Back Propagation Algorithm (BPA) and Radial Basis Function (RBF) for word and sentence recognition and compared the individual results achieved. The details of each Artificial Neural Network used are given in Table 1, Table 2 and Table 3.

The proposed system using Self Organizing Map gave an accuracy of 95.5%approximately. On the other hand, the efficiency achieved using Back Propagation Algorithm (BPA) and Radial Basis Function (RBF) was found to be just 68% and 74% respectively. Hence, the results show that the proposed system using

Table 4. Experimental Results Achieved using SOM

Model Used	Total No. of Sentence Pattern In Database	No. of Training Sentence Patterns	No. of Training Word Pattern	Performance
Self Organizing Maps	500	50	393	430/450

Table 5. Experimental Results Achieved using BPA

Model Used	Total No. of Sentence Pattern In Database	No. of Training Sentence Patterns	No. of Training Word Pattern	Performance
Back Propagation Algorithm	500	50	393	306/450

Table 6. Experimental Results Achieved using RBF

Model Used	Total No. of Sentence Pattern In Database	No. of Training Sentence Patterns	No. of Training Word Pattern	Performance
Radial Basis Function	500	50	393	333/450

Self-Organizing Maps is able to solve this problem of natural language reasoning in a reasonably efficient manner in a more efficient manner as compared to other conventional methods.

5 Conclusion and Future Works

The approach to the problem of Natural Language Reasoning proposed in this paper proves is a novel one. The experimental results also prove the contention that the system is able to give an extremely high level of performance and accuracy in deciphering patterns in natural languages. The approach proposed in this paper is extremely scalable and flexible for text input sources and could also be extended for speech and image input sources too. The proposed system could be extended and implemented for development of specific expert systems like for intelligent medical computational system, intelligent detection system for emotions in expressions and likewise.

The overall approach is a novel attempt towards making a system that could be intelligent enough to take over certain human task of language oriented text processing and could be robust enough in order to work to provide efficient solutions to such tasks.

References

1. Fayyad, U.M., Shapiro, G.P., Smyth, P.: From Data Mining to Knowledge Discovery: An Overview. In: Advances in Knowledge Discovery and Data Mining. AAAI Press, Menlo Park (1996)
2. Tan, P.N., Steinbach, M., Kumar, V.: Introduction to Data Mining. Pearson Addison Wesley (2005)
3. Dunham, M.H.: Data Mining Introductory and Advanced Topics. Prentice-Hall, Englewood Cliffs (2003)
4. Jain, A.K., Murthy, M.N., Flynn, P.L.: Data Clustering: A Review. ACM Computing Surveys 31(3), 264–323 (1999)
5. Anderberg, M.R.: Cluster Analysis for Application. Academic Press, London
6. Rasmussen, E.: Clustering algorithms in Information Retrieval: Data Structures and Algorithms. W. B. Frakes, R. Baeza-Yates, Prentice-Hall Publishers (1992)

7. Han, J., Kamber, M.: Data Mining: Concepts and Techniques, 2nd edn. Morgan Kaufmann, San Francisco (2005)
8. Jones, G.J.F., Wright, J.H., Wrigley, E.N., Carey, M.J.: Isolated-Word Sentence Recognition Using Probabilistic Context Free Grammar. In: Systems and Applications of Man Machine Interaction Using Speech I/O, IEEE Colloquium, pp. 13/1–13/5 (1999)
9. Shirai, K.: Feature extraction and sentence recognition algorithm in speech input system. In: Proceedings of 4th International Joint Conference on Artificial Intelligence, vol. 1. Morgan Kaufmann, San Francisco
10. Jiang, X., Yu, K., Bunke, H.: Classifier combination for grammar-guided sentence recognition. In: Kittler, J., Roli, F. (eds.) MCS 2000. LNCS, vol. 1857, pp. 383–392. Springer, Heidelberg (2000)
11. Favata, J.T.: General Word Recognition: Using Approximate Segment-String Matching. In: Proceedings of 4th International Conference on Document Analysis and Recognition, pp. 92–96 (1997)
12. Rosenberg, A.E.: Connected Sentence Recognition Using Diphone-like Templates. In: International Conference on Acoustics, Speech, and Signal Processing, vol. 1, pp. 473–476 (1998)
13. Murase, I., Nakagawa, S.: Sentence Recognition Method Using Word Co-occurrence Probability and Its Evaluation. In: Proceedings of ICSLP, pp. 1217–1220 (1990)
14. Marukatat, S., Artikres, T., Gallinari, P., Dorizzi, B.: Sentence Recognition through Hybrid Neuro-Markovian Modeling. In: Proceedings of Sixth International Conference on Document Analysis and Recognition, ICDAR 2001 (2001)
15. Markert, H., Kayikci, Z.K., Palm, G.: Sentence understanding and learning of new words with large-scale neural networks. In: Prevost, L., Marinai, S., Schwenker, F. (eds.) ANNPR 2008. LNCS (LNAI), vol. 5064, pp. 217–227. Springer, Heidelberg (2008)
16. Majewski, M., Zurada, J.M.: Sentence Recognition Using Artificial Neural Network. Knowledge-Based Systems 27(1) (2008)
17. David, V.K., Rajasekaran, S.: Pattern Recognition Using Neural and Functional Networks. Springer, Heidelberg (2008)
18. Ritter, H., Kohonen, T.: Self –Organizing Semantic Maps. In: Biological Cybernetics, pp. 241–254. Springer, Heidelberg (1989)
19. Liou, C., Yang, H.: HandPrinted Character Recognition Based on Spatial Topology Distance Measurement. IEEE Transaction on Pattern Analysis and Machine Intelligence 18(9) (1996)
20. Venkatesh, J., SureshKumar, C.: Tamil Handwritten Character Recognition Kohonen's Self-Organizing Maps. International Journal of Computer Science and Network Secuirty 9(12) (2009)
21. Saarikoski, J., Lourikkala, J.: A study of the use of Self-Organizing Maps in Information Retrieval. Journal of Documentation 65(2), 304–322 (2009)
22. Lippman, R.: An Introduction to Computing with Neural Nets. IEEE Transactions on Acoustic, Speech, and Signal Processing, IEEE Signal Processing Society, Piscataway 4(3), 4–22 (1987)
23. Erwin, E., Obermayer, K., Schulten, K.: Self-organizing Maps: ordering, convergence properties and energy functions. In: Biological Cybernetics. Springer, Heidelberg (1992)

RODD: An Effective *R*eference-Based *O*utlier *D*etection Technique for Large *D*atasets

Monowar H. Bhuyan[1], D.K. Bhattacharyya[1], and J.K. Kalita[2]

[1] Dept. of Computer Science & Engineering, Tezpur University, Napaam, India
{mhb,dkb}@tezu.ernet.in

[2] Dept. of Computer Science, University of Colorado, CO 80918, USA
jkalita@uccs.edu

Abstract. Outlier detection has gained considerable interest in several fields of research including various sciences, medical diagnosis, fraud detection, and network intrusion detection. Most existing techniques are either distance based or density based. In this paper, we present an effective reference point based outlier detection technique (RODD) which performs satisfactorily in high dimensional real-world datasets. The technique was evaluated in terms of detection rate and false positive rate over several synthetic and real-world datasets and the performance is excellent.

Keywords: Outlier detection, score, cluster, reference point, profile.

1 Introduction

The task of outlier discovery has five subtasks: (*a*) dependency detection, (*b*) class identification, (*c*) class validation, (*d*) frequency detection, and (*e*) outlier/exception detection [1]. The first four subtasks consist of finding patterns in large datasets and validating the patterns. Techniques for association rules [2], classification [3], and data clustering [4] include the first four subtasks. The fifth subtask focuses on a very small percentage of data objects, which are often ignored or discarded as noise. Outlier detection is an important research topic with many applications such as credit card fraud detection, criminal activity detection, and network intrusion detection. Outlier detection techniques focus on discovering infrequent pattern(s) in the data, as opposed to many traditional data mining techniques such as association analysis or frequent itemset mining that attempt to find patterns that occur frequently in the data. In this paper, we develop a distance based outlier detection technique for large datasets. Our technique works in two major steps. The first step applies a variant of k-means clustering technique to partition the dataset. We assume that larger clusters are normal and smaller clusters are outliers. Next, we build mean-based profiles from the larger clusters and rank the outliers based on their scores.

2 Related Research

Most previous outlier detection techniques are statistics-based [5, 6]. Finding a suitable outlier detection model for high dimensional datasets based on statistical approaches is

N. Meghanathan et al. (Eds.): CCSIT 2011, Part III, CCIS 133, pp. 76–84, 2011.

challenging [7]. Due to higher dimensionality, data is spread over a large volume and is sparse. In addition to poor execution performance, this also spreads the convex hull that includes all data points, thus distorting the data distribution [8]. Wang *et al.* [9] proposed an outlier detection technique for probabilistic data streams, gave a new definition for distance-based outliers for probabilistic data streams, and proposed a dynamic programming algorithm (DPA) and an effective pruning-based approach (PBA) to detect outliers efficiently. They also experimentally established that the approach is efficient and scalable to detect outlier on large probabilistic data streams.

A distance-based outlier detection technique was first presented by Knorr et al. [10]. They define a point to be a distance outlier if at least a user-defined fraction of the points in the dataset are further away than some user-defined minimum distance from that point. In their experiments, they primarily focus on datasets containing only continuous attributes. Distance-based methods also apply clustering techniques over the whole dataset to obtain a specified number of clusters. Points that do not cluster well are labeled outliers. This is the technique used by the ADMIT intrusion detection system [11]. Angiulli et al. [12] report a technique to detect the top outliers in an unlabeled dataset and provide a subset of it, known as outlier detection solving set. This solving set is used to predict the outlierness of the new unseen objects. The solving set includes a sufficient number of points that permits the detection of the top outliers by considering only a subset of all pairwise distances in the dataset.

With increasing volumes of data becoming available, density-based techniques have been found capable of handling outlier detection [13]. In one such technique, a local outlier factor (LOF) is computed for each point. The LOF of a point is based on the ratio of the local density of the area around the point and the local densities of its neighbors. The size of a neighborhood of a point is determined by the area containing a user-supplied minimum number of points ($MinPts$). A similar technique called $LOCI$ (Local Correlation Integral) is presented in [14]. $LOCI$ addresses the difficulty of choosing values for $MinPts$ in the LOF-based technique by using statistical values derived from the data itself. Both the LOF and $LOCI$-based techniques do not scale well with a large number of attributes and data points. Agrawal [15] proposed a local subspace based outlier detection technique, which uses different subspaces for different objects for high dimensional datasets. Their technique performs better than the existing well-known LOF and other similar algorithms.

Based on our survey of existing outlier detection techniques, we observe that (*i*) most outlier detection techniques are statistical and their detection rates are low, (*ii*) most existing algorithms perform poorly over high dimensional spaces because classes of objects often exist in specific subspaces of the original feature space. In such situations, subspace clustering is expected to perform better, (*iii*) as the dataset size increases, the performance of existing techniques often degrades, (*iv*) most existing techniques are for numeric datasets only.

3 Background of the Work

In this section, we present relevant preliminary discussions on outliers, outlier detection and outlier scores.

3.1 Outliers

Outliers are non-conforming patterns in data; that is, they are patterns that do not exhibit normal behaviour. An example of outliers in two dimensional dataset is illustrated in Figure 1. As discussed earlier, outliers may be induced due to a variety of reasons such as malicious activity (e.g., credit card fraud, cyber attacks, novelty detection, and breakdown of a system), but all these reasons have a common characteristic that they are interesting to the analyst. The *interestingness* or real life relevance of outliers is a key feature of outlier detection [16]. Outlier detection is related to, but distinct from noise removal or noise accommodation [6] that deals with unwanted noise in the data. Noise does not have any real life significance and acts as hindrance to data analysis. Outlier detection also can be referred as novelty detection which aims to detect unseen (emergent, novel) patterns in the data, e.g., introduction of a new topic [17]. Both outliers and novel patterns are typically incorporated into the normal model after detection.

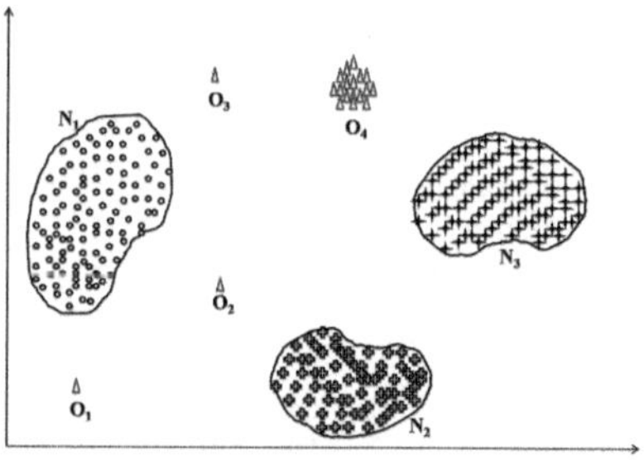

Fig. 1. Outliers in two dimensional dataset: N_1, N_2, and N_3 are the three normal regions. Points that are sufficiently far away from the normal region (e.g., points O_1, O_2, O_3 and points in O_4 regions) are outliers.

3.2 Outlier Scores

Recently, several outlier detection techniques based on distance, density, statistics and outlier score have been proposed. An outlier score is an estimate based on distance, density, or any other statistical summarization. It is useful in ranking individual items in a data stream. Pei and Zaiane [18] proposed an outlier detection technique for large datasets. It estimates outlier score based on distance and degree of nearest neighbour density. The outlier score is $ROS(x) = 1 - \frac{D^p(x,k)}{\max_{1 \leq i \leq n} D^p(x_i,k)}$, where $D^p(x,k)$ is $\min_{1 \leq r \leq R} D(x,k,p_r)$. $D^p(x,k)$ is the degree of neighbourhood density of the candidate data point x with respect to the set of reference point p, n is the total number of data points, k is a fixed reference based nearest neighbours, and R is the number of reference points. $D(x,k,p)$ is $\frac{1}{\frac{1}{k}\sum_{j=1}^{k} |d(x_j,p) - d(x,p)|}$, where $D(x,k,p)$ is the relative degrees of density for x in the one dimensional data space X^p and $d(x,p)$ is the distance value to the reference point p. The candidate data points are ranked according to their relative degree of density computed on a set of reference points. Outliers are those with high scores. This scheme can discover multiple outliers in larger datasets, however two main limitations of this scheme [18] are: (*i*) the score does not always vary with change of candidate data points and (*ii*) summarizing the data points in terms of scores may not be useful for detecting outliers. To address these two issues, we propose a modified version of [18] discussed in the rest of the paper.

4 RODD : A New Outlier Detection Technique

Our technique, RODD (Reference-based Outlier Detection for Large Datasets) aims to detect outliers based on a reference point and ranking of outlier scores of candidate objects. RODD is based on two assumptions: (*i*) following the normality model discussed in [19], we assume that m large clusters are normal and (*ii*) the remaining smaller clusters are outliers.

Let S_i be the number of classes to which each of k' nearest neighbour data points belongs, where k' is fixed for a particular dataset. Let $x_{i,j}$ be a data point in X and $sim(x_{i,j}, R_{i,j})$ be the distance from the reference point $R_{i,j}$ to the data point $x_{i,j}$, where sim is a proximity measure and X represents the whole dataset. The RODD algorithm allows the use of any proximity measure. However, in our experiments, we use PCC (Pearson Correlation Coefficient) in computing proximity. The outlier score we define is as follows:

$$ROS'(x) = \frac{1}{\max\limits_{1\leq i\leq k'} S_i}\left(\frac{\left(1 - \min\limits_{1\leq i\leq k'} sim(x_{i,j}, R_{i,j})\right)\left(\sum_{i=1}^{k'} \min\limits_{1\leq i\leq k'} sim(x_{i,j}, R_{i,j})\right)}{\sum_{i=1}^{k'} \max\limits_{1\leq i\leq k'} sim(x_{i,j}, R_{i,j})}\right) \quad (1)$$

where, $\frac{1}{\max\limits_{1\leq i\leq k'} S_i}$ is the maximum chance a data point belongs to a particular class, the remaining part is the summarized value of similarity measure within a k' nearest neighbours. The candidate data points are ranked based on the score. Objects with scores higher than a user defined threshold τ are considered outliers. To test effectiveness, we considered six different cases (illustrated in Figure 2) of possible outlier occurrence, and the RODD algorithm is capable of identifying all six outlier cases. Next, we present the definitions and lemmas that provide the theoretical basis of the detection technique.

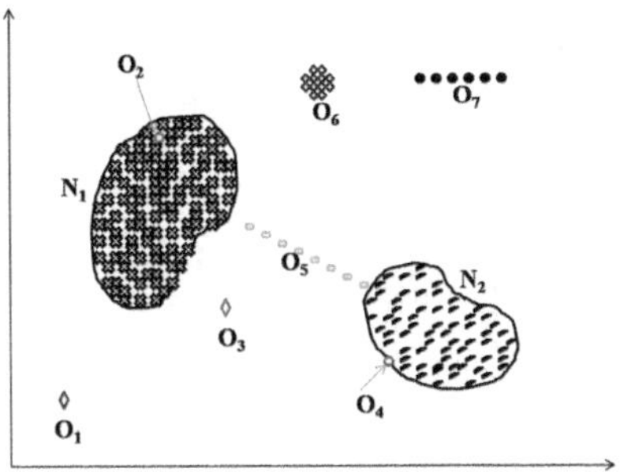

Fig. 2. Illustration of six different cases: N_1 and N_2 are two normal clusters, O_1 is the distinct outlier, O_2, the distinct inlier, O_3, the equidistance outlier, O_4, the border inlier, O_5, a chain of outliers, O_6 is another set of outlier objects with higher compactness among the objects and O_7 is an outlier case of "stay together".

Definition 1. ***Data Stream:*** *A data stream X is defined as $\{X_1, X_2, X_3 \cdots X_n\}$ with n objects where each X_i is represented by a d-dimensional vector, i.e., $X_i = \{x_1^i, x_2^i, x_3^i \cdots x_d^i\}$.*

Definition 2. ***Outlier:*** *An object, O_i is defined as an outlier w.r.t. a normal class C_i and the corresponding profile R_i iff (i) $ROS'(O_i, C_i) \geq \tau$, and (ii) $sim(O_i, R_i) > M$, where M is the mean-based profile value, and sim is the proximity measure.*

Definition 3. ***Outlier Score:*** *An outlier score ROS' with respect to a reference point is defined as a summarized value that combines distance and maximum class occurrence within k' nearest neighbours of each candidate data point.*

Definition 4. ***Distinct Outlierness:*** *An object O_i is defined as a distinct outlier iff it deviates exceptionally from the normal objects, i.e., from generic class C_i. In other words, $ROS'(O_i, C_i) \gg \tau$ for all i.*

Definition 5. ***Distinct Inlierness:*** *An object O_i is defined as a distinct inlier if it conforms to the normal objects, i.e., $ROS'(O_i, C_i) \ll \tau$ for all i.*

Definition 6. ***Equidistance Outlierness:*** *An object O_i is defined as equidistance outlier from classes C_i and C_j, if $ROS'(O_i, C_i) = ROS'(O_i, C_j)$ and $ROS'(O_i, C_i) > \tau$.*

Definition 7. ***Border Inlierness:*** *An object O_i is defined as border object in a class C_i, if $ROS'(O_i, C_i) < \tau$.*

Definition 8. ***Chain Outlierness:*** *A set of objects, $O_i, O_{i+1}, O_{i+2} \cdots$ is defined as a chain of outliers if $ROS'(O_{i+l}, C_i) \geq \tau$, where $l = 0, 1, 2, \cdots, z$.*

Lemma 1. *For a given outlier object O_i, $ROS'(O_i, C_i) \neq ROS'(O_i, C_j)$, where C_i and C_j are two clusters.*

Proof. Assume that O_i is an outlier object and $ROS'(O_i, C_i) = ROS'(O_i, C_j)$. Per $Definition$ 2, an object O_i is an outlier w.r.t. class C_i if $ROS' > \tau$. If ROS' for a distinct outlier w.r.t. two classes, C_i and C_j are the same, C_i and C_j must have the same reference based summarized value w.r.t. O_i when we consider distance as well as the maximum number of classes that occur within k' nearest neighbours (as per $Definition$ 3); thus is not possible, hence it contradicts and hence proof. □

Lemma 2. *A given outlier object O_i cannot belong to any of the normal clusters i.e., $O_i \notin C_i$, where i = $i = 1, 2, \cdots, m$.*

Proof. Assume that O_i is an outlier object and $O_i \in C_i$ where C_i is a normal cluster. Per $Definition$ 5, if $O_i \in C_i$, O_i must satisfy the inlier condition w.r.t. τ for class C_i. However, since O_i is an outlier, it contradicts and hence $O_i \notin C_i$; □

Table 1. Symbols used

Term	Definition
X, x_i	dataset, i_{th} data object
n	number of datapoints in X
C, C_i	set of clusters, i_{th} cluster
k	number of clusters
R_i	i^{th} reference point
k'	number of nearest neighbours
S_i	i_{th} same class occurrence within k' nearest neighbours
sim	similarity measure
τ	threshold value for outlier score
X_c	candidate data points
M	mean based profile w.r.t. a cluster
m	number of large clusters

4.1 The RODD Algorithm

$Table$ 1 gives the symbols used in describing the algorithm. Initially, RODD applies a variant of the k-means clustering technique [20] to partition the dataset, $X_{i,j}$ into k clusters $C_1, C_2, C_3, \cdots C_k$. RODD assumes a normality model [19]. It considers the larger clusters $C_1, C_2, C_3, \cdots C_m$ for some value of $m \leq k$ as normal clusters and the smaller clusters (may include singleton cluster) as outliers. Clustering is initiated with a random selection of k centroids. We assign each $x_{i,j}$ to a particular cluster based on a proximity measure $sim(x, y)$. We use PCC [21] as the proximity measure whereby sim is defined as-

$$sim(x,y) = \begin{cases} 0 & \textit{if } x = y \\ \dfrac{\sum_{i=1}^{d} x_i y_i - \frac{\sum_{i=1}^{d} x_i \sum_{i=1}^{d} y_i}{N}}{\sqrt{(\sum_{i=1}^{d} x_i^2 - \frac{(\sum_{i=1}^{d} x_i)^2}{N})(\sum_{i=1}^{d} y_i^2 - \frac{(\sum_{i=1}^{d} y_i)^2}{N})}} & \textit{otherwise.} \end{cases}$$

Once the cluster formation is over, we calculate the reference points, R_i for each larger cluster $(C_1, C_2, C_3, \cdots C_m)$. A reference point may not be an existing point with the cluster. Then we build the mean profile for each cluster w.r.t. the reference points R_i. Next, we estimate the outlier score for each candidate data point w.r.t. the user defined threshold, τ based on Equation (1). The ranking of the outliers is done based on the score; the outlier with the highest score gets the highest rank. The RODD algorithm can successfully find all six cases described earlier in real and synthetic datasets.

RODD Algorithm

Assume that, $R = \{R_1, R_2, R_3, \cdots R_m\}$ is the set of reference points of cardinality m. The RODD accepts $X_{i,j}$, τ as input and generates $O_{i,j}$ as output.

1. Calculate the set of reference points R_i, where $i = 1, 2, 3, \cdots, m$ for the m larger clusters among the k clusters.
2. Build mean profile, M for each of the m large clusters.
3. Calculate outlier score, ROS' for each candidate data point, X_c and rank candidate data points according to the score value.
4. Output the outliers $O_{i,j}$s which satisfies the condition $\geq \tau$.

Complexity Analysis: Reference point finding and score estimation play important role in the effectiveness and efficiency of RODD. Initial cluster formation takes $O(k\ n)$ time for generating k clusters. Calculating the reference point and outlier score for each candidate data point takes $O(R\ n\ log\ n)$ time, where R is the number of reference points, $n\ log\ n$ is the time to sort the score values for ranking the outliers. So, the total time complexity is $O(k\ n) + O(R\ n\ log\ n)$.

5 Empirical Evaluation

RODD was implemented in a HP $xw6600$ workstation with Intel Xeon Processor (3.00Ghz) and 4GB RAM. $Java1.6.0$ was used for the implementation in Fedora 9.0 (Linux) platform. Java was used to facilitate the visualization of outlier detection results. Several synthetic and real-life datasets were used for testing the performance of the proposed RODD algorithm. We report here the results with only three datasets (i.e., synthetic, Zoo, and Shuttle). No of instances in synthetic, zoo, and shuttle datasets are 1000, 101, and 14500 respectively. No of dimensions, no of clusters and no of outliers in these datasets are 2 & 5 & 40, 18 & 7 & 17, and 9 & 3 & 13 respectively.

Experimental Results: The RODD algorithm was evaluated initially over a two dimensional *synthetic* dataset, comprising of 1000 data objects, out of which 4% are outliers. Results of the RODD algorithm both in terms of DR (Detection Rate) and FPR (False Positive Rate) for this dataset are reported in the last column of the first row of $Table$ 3. We downloaded the executable versions of LOF [22] and ORCA [23] for experimentation. Results of LOF and ORCA are also reported for these datasets in the columns 4 and 5, respectively. Similarly, the RODD algorithm was also evaluated on several other real-life datasets. However, in this paper, we report only results for *zoo* and *shuttle* datasets and compare them with the two other algorithms. The effectiveness

Table 2. Comparison of RODD with its counterparts

Algorithms	Number of parameters	Complexity (approximate)
LOF [13]	$(k, MinPts, M)$	$O(n^2)$
ORCA [23]	(k, n, D)	$O(n^2)$
RODD	(X, τ)	$O(k\ n) + O(R\ n\ log\ n)$

Table 3. Experimental results

Datasets	Threshold, τ	Effectiveness	LOF [13]	ORCA [23]	RODD
Synthetic	0.39	DR	0.7500	0.8500	1.0000
		FPR	0.0229	0.0166	0.0000
Zoo	0.58	DR	0.8235	0.8823	0.9411
		FPR	0.1904	0.1309	0.0238
Shuttle	0.47	DR	0.8461	0.7692	0.9230
		FPR	0.0310	0.0241	0.0103

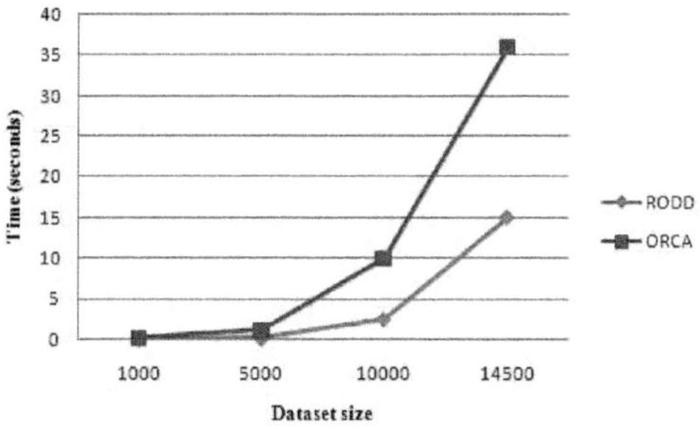

Fig. 3. Execution time comparison of RODD with ORCA over shuttle dataset

of the RODD algorithm is higher than the other two algorithms. A general comparison of the RODD algorithm with the other two algorithms is reported in $Table$ 2.

To compare the running time of the RODD algorithm with the other two algorithms, we used the executable version of ORCA written in C as discussed in [23]. Although, ORCA is a distance-based algorithm with near quadratic running time, it is one of the most efficient *KNN*-based outlier detection methods. We compare the execution time vs. size of datasets in Figure 3. We observe that as the dataset size increases, execution time of ORCA as well RODD also increases. RODD outperforms ORCA both in terms of execution time as well as detection rate. RODD outperforms LOF in terms of detection rate.

6 Conclusion

We have developed an effective outlier detection technique based on [18]. The main attraction of the technique is its capability of handling all outlier cases successfully. The novel RODD algorithm was evaluated with several real-life and synthetic datasets and the detection performance was better than that obtained with two other competing algorithms. Work is undergoing to test its performance over network intrusion datasets. A hybrid outlier detection approach that combines both the distance and density based approaches for mixed type data is underway as well.

References

1. Knorr, E.M., Ng, R.T.: Algorithms for mining distance-based outliers in large datasets. In: Proc of VLDB 1998, USA, pp. 392–403. Morgan Kaufmann, San Francisco (1998)
2. Agrawal, R., Imielinski, T., Swami, A.N.: Mining association rules between sets of items in large databases. In: Proc of ACM SIGMOD on Management of Data, Washington, D.C., pp. 207–216. ACM Press, New York (1993)
3. Breiman, L., Friedman, J., Olshen, R., Stone, C.: Classification and Regression Trees. Wadsworth and Brooks, Monterey (1984)
4. Ester, M., Kriegel, H.-p., Jörg, S., Xu, X.: A density-based algorithm for discovering clusters in large spatial databases with noise. In: Proc of KDD, pp. 226–231. AAAI Press, Menlo Park (1996)

5. Hawkins, D.M.: Indentification of outliers. Chapman and Hall, London (1980)
6. Rousseeuw, P., Leroy, A.: Robust Regression and Outlier Detection, 3rd edn. John Wiley & Sons, Chichester (1996)
7. Tan, P., Steinbach, M., Kumar, V.: Introduction to data mining. Pearson Addison Wesley, London (2005)
8. Hodge, V., Austin, J.: A survey of outlier detection methodologies. Artificial Intelligence Review 22, 85–126 (2004)
9. Wang, B., Wang, G.-R., Yu, G.: Outlier detection over sliding windows for probabilistic data streams. Journal of Computer Science and Technology 25(3), 389–400 (2010)
10. Knorr, E.M., Ng, R.T., Tucakov, V.: Distance-based outliers: Algorithms and applications. VLDB Journal 8, 237–253 (2000)
11. Sequeira, K., Zaki, M.: Admit: Anomaly-based data mining for intrusions. In: ACM SIGKDD, pp. 386–395 (2002)
12. Angiulli, F., Basta, S., Pizzuti, C.: Distance-based detection and prediction of outliers. IEEE TKDE 18, 145–160 (2006)
13. Breunig, M.M., Kriegel, H.P., Ng, R.T., Sander, J.: Lof: Identifying density-based local outliers. In: ACM SIGMOD on Management of Data, pp. 386–395 (2000)
14. Papadimitriou, S., Kitawaga, H., Gibbons, P.B., Faloutsos, C.: Loci: Fast outlier detection using the local correlation integral. In: ICDE (2003)
15. Agrawal, A.: Local subspace based outlier detection. In: Communication in Computer and Information Science, vol. 40, pp. 149–157. Springer, Heidelberg (2009)
16. Varun, C., Arindam, B., Vipin, K.: Outlier detection - a survey. Technical report, Dept of CSE,University of Minnesota, USA (2007)
17. Markou, M., Singh, S.: Novelty detection: a review-part 1: statistical approaches. Signal Processing 83, 2481–2497 (2003)
18. Pei, Y., Zaiane, O.R., Gao, Y.: An efficient reference-based approach to outlier detection in large datasets. In: Proc of ICDM 2006, USA, pp. 478–487. IEEE, Los Alamitos (2006)
19. Portnoy, L., Eskin, E., Stolfo, S.: Intrusion detection with unlabeled data using clustering. In: Proc of ACM CSS Workshop on DMAS, Philadelphia, PA, pp. 5–8 (2001)
20. Kanungo, T., Mount, D.M., Netanyahu, N.S., Piatko, C.D., Silverman, R., Wu, A.Y.: An efficient k-means clustering algorithm: Analysis and implementation. IEEE TPAMI 24(7), 881–892 (2002)
21. Lohninger, H.: Teach/Me Data Analysis. Springer, Heidelberg (1999)
22. Barczynski, R.: System outlier mining (2010), `http://sites.google.com/site/rafalba/`
23. Bay, S., Schwabacher, M.: Mining distance-based outliers in near linear time with randomization and a simple pruning rule. In: Proc of the Ninth ACM SIGKDD, pp. 29–38 (2003)

A Review of Dynamic Web Service Composition Techniques

Demian Antony D'Mello[1], V.S. Ananthanarayana[2], and Supriya Salian[1]

[1] Department of Computer Science and Engineering, St. Joseph Engineering College, Mangalore - 575 028, India
demian.antony@gmail.com, supriyasalian@yahoo.com

[2] Department of Information Technology, National Institute of technology Karnataka, Srinivas Nagar, Mangalore - 575 025, India
anvs@nitk.ac.in

Abstract. The requester's service request sometimes includes multiple related functionalities to be satisfied by the Web service. In many cases the Web service has a limited functionality which is not sufficient to meet the requester's complex functional needs. The discovery mechanism for such complex service request involving multiple tasks (operations) may fail due to unavailability of suitable Web services advertised in the registry. In such a scenario, a need arises to compose the available atomic or composite Web services to satisfy the requester's complex request. Dynamic Web service composition generates and executes the composition plan based on the requester's runtime functional and nonfunctional requirements. This paper provides the review of Web service composition architectures and techniques used to generate new (value added) services.

Keywords: Web Services, Service Registry, Dynamic Composition, Architecture.

1 Introduction

A Web service is defined as an interface which implements the business logic through a set of operations that are accessible through standard Internet protocols. The conceptual Web services architecture [1] is defined based upon the interactions between *three* roles: *service provider*, *service registry* and *service requester*. The requester search for suitable Web services in the registry which satisfy his functional and nonfunctional requirements. The requester's service request sometimes includes multiple related functionalities to be satisfied by the Web service. In many cases the Web service has a limited functionality which is not sufficient to meet the requester's complex functional needs. The UDDI based Web service architecture does not realize complex Web service combinations, hence it provides limited support for service composition. There is a need to identify and compose the available Web services if the complex service request can not be satisfied by a single Web service. To achieve complex business goals in

N. Meghanathan et al. (Eds.): CCSIT 2011, Part III, CCIS 133, pp. 85–97, 2011.

real world applications, the execution of multiple Web services should be orchestrated through service composition. The Web service composition can be defined as the creation of new Web service by combining the available services (service operations) that realizes the complex service request. The service composition strategies are broadly classified as *Static* and *Dynamic* composition based on the time when the Web services are composed [2]. Static composition takes place during design time when the architecture and the design of the system is planned. Dynamic composition takes place at run time when the requested service is not provided by the single provider. The effective dynamic Web service composition is a major challenge towards the success of Web services. The following *seven* different issues have a large impact on dynamic Web service composition. They are: Describing Web services and complex service request for effective composition, Generation of composition plan for the complex service request, Modeling (specification) of composition plan (orchestration models), Selection of Web services for the composition, Coordination and Conversation modeling, Execution of composition and Transaction management.

In this paper, the authors provides detailed review of dynamic composition architectures and techniques. Section 2 describes Web service composition architectures and strategies. In section 3 describes various dynamic Web Service Composition plan generation Methods. Section 4 compares the different methods used for dynamic Composition Based on Web Service Signatures. Section 5 draws conclusions and future challenges in dynamic Web service composition.

2 Web Service Composition Strategies and Architectures

Service composition facilitates application reuse where new Web services are created using available Web services which are heterogeneous in nature and spread across organizations. The service composition strategies are classified as *Static Composition*, *Semi-dynamic Composition* and *Dynamic Composition* based on the time of composition plan creation and service binding times [3]. Static composition is also called as design time composition where the application designer manually discovers, binds and assembles the Web services during composite Web services application development. Dynamic Web service composition is a complex and very challenging task in Web services as the composition plan is generated at runtime based on the requester's complex service request [4]. In literature, various architectures have been proposed to facilitate dynamic Web service composition. They are: *Peer-to-Peer (P2P) architectures*, *Agent architectures* and *Hybrid (Multi-role) architectures.*

2.1 P2P Architecture

The Web service composition methods defined on P2P overlay networks [5] works as follows: when a peer wants to share a service, it registers the service to the registration system. Towards service composition, it looks up and gets its successor service from the registration system and then the successor service in turn finds its successor service. This will be repeated until the composition is accomplished. The *Self-Serv* project uses P2P based orchestration model to support cross organizational compositions [6]. P2P based composition architecture is suitable for facilitating composition of B2B services rather B2C services which are too dynamic in nature.

2.2 Agent Architecture

A software agent can be defined as a computational entity, which acts on behalf of others, is autonomous, proactive and reactive, and exhibits capabilities to learn and cooperate. Agent architectures have been proposed in literature where agents perform specific roles of composition and execution. The various roles include: message processing and composition, service binding and triggering the specification of composite services and monitoring the deployment of specifications [7]. A mobile agent (MA) based multi-platform architecture for Web service composition is proposed [8] where MA is responsible for the execution of composition. The agent based Web service architectures are not suitable for compositions due to performance issues like reliability and security.

2.3 Hybrid (Multi-role) Architecture

The extension of conceptual SOA with new roles and operations towards Web service composition facilitate both static and dynamic composition. In literature, various hybrid architectures have been proposed towards dynamic Web service discovery and composition. A novel business model for dynamic Web service composition involving *two* new roles called *Web Service Composer* and *Web Service Composition Registry* is proposed [9]. Similarly, roles like configuration engine and workflow engine [10], discovery engine, abstract process designer are defined for dynamic composition architectures. The *Eurasia Architecture* which is proposed [11] consists of *three* main components. They are: component description framework, the template composer and data flow based service coordinator. The early initiative towards composition called *e-flow* [12] involves multiple roles including e-flow service broker, e-flow engine and a set of repositories for storing information related to composition. The multi-role architecture is suitable for composition as composition and execution involves many activities which are to be coordinated by the architectural role called *composition manager* or *composition broker.*

2.4 Role of Ontology and Composition Execution

Most of the hybrid architectures contain semantic information component called *Ontology Store* to guide the dynamic composition and execution. In literature, various kinds of ontologies have been designed (Modeled) for composition which include: Domain ontology [10], Parameter ontology [13], Policy ontology [14], Context ontology [15] and Operation mode ontology [16]. In literature, the Web service composition architectures are realized through building Integrated Development Environments (IDE) which facilitate providers and requesters in publishing and integrating Web services according to their needs [17]. Towards the execution of compositions (composition plan), various techniques have been proposed [18]. They include: *Interleaved composition and execution*, *Monolithic composition and execution*, *Staged composition and execution* and *Template based composition and execution.*

3 Dynamic Web Service Composition Methods

The crux of the dynamic Web service composition is generation of composition plan at runtime according to the needs of the requester. In literature, various strategies have been proposed by numerous researchers towards composition plan generation. Here *eight* categories of composition strategies have been identified based on the nature of information and techniques used to build the composition plan for execution. They are: *Constraint based composition*, *Business rule (Policy) driven composition*, *User Interaction and personalization based composition*, *Planning (AI Planning) based composition*, *Context information based composition*, *Process based composition*, *Model and aspect driven composition* and *Signature (Input and Output) based composition.*

3.1 Constraint and Business Rule (Policy) Driven Composition

Constraint driven Web services composition aims at building a composition plan based on the business constraints which are represented in ontologies. The selection of a specific business constraint from the pool of constraints is dependent on the particular instance of the process [19]. The constraints enforced by the requesters and providers guide the data flow and control flow in Web service composition. The vertical constrains are required to setup the abstract composition and horizontal constraints help to build and manage instance of composite service involving data and control flow [20]. The requester's quality constraints are also used to build concrete service workflow (composition pattern) by binding the activity with services through constraint satisfaction [10]. The authors [21] propose service discovery approach that locates services that conform to independent global constraints. The approach uses a greedy algorithm to identify conforming values and locate composite services. The domain rules are used to derive values that conform to given user constraint and combine services that assign those values to their restricted attributes. From the above discussion, it is observed that the provider's and requester's constraints play a role in generating composition plan involving sequential and parallel execution flow.

The business processes can be dynamically built by composing Web services if they are constructed and governed by business rules (Policies) [22]. The authors [22]propose a rule driven mechanism to govern and guide the process of service composition in terms of *five* broad composition phases spanning abstract definition, scheduling, construction, execution and evolution to support on demand and on the fly business process generation. Thus business rules are used to structure and schedule service composition and to describe service selection and service bindings. Object Constraint Language (OCL) is used to express business rules and to describe the process flow. The composition plan generated must satisfy the policies (rules) enforced by the providers of the selected Web services for the concrete composition plan [23]. In order to have service compatibility at the level of policies, a policy ontology is used for the selection of policy compatible, candidate Web services for the composition. Thus business rules identified at each phase of service development are used to derive effective service composition process involving inter and intra-organizational processes. Business rule driven composition requires all business rules which are specific to service needs to be documented in a unified way (e.g. ontology) for successful composition.

3.2 Planning Based Composition

Web service composition (WSC) can be seen as a planning problem, where a sequence of services are composed into a business process to reach (satisfy) business goals. In literature, many research efforts tackling Web service composition problem via Artificial Intelligence (AI) planning have been proposed [24]. In such techniques, initial states and the goal states are specified in the requirement by Web service requesters. The composition methods based on AI planning include: *Declarative composition*, *Situation Calculus*, *Rule based composition*, *Theorem proving* and *Graphplan based composition*.

The declarative approach [25], [24] consists of *two* phases: the first phase takes an initial situation and the desired goal as starting point and constructs generic plans to reach the goal. The latter one chooses one generic plan, discovers appropriate services, and builds a workflow out of them. The first phase is realized using PDDL (Planning Domain Definition Language) which provides machine readable semantics and specifies the abstract service behavior. The second phase may be realized by using existing process modeling languages, such as BPEL. In Self-Serv [6], Web services are declaratively composed and then executed in a dynamic peer-to-peer environment. The authors [26] propose a system, which employs goal oriented inferencing from the planning algorithm (TLPlan) to select atomic services that form a composite Web service. To specify service goals, a goal specification language is proposed [29] that allows specification of constraints on functional and nonfunctional properties of Web services. Towards enhancement of planning based WSC, a solution to combine GA with planning is proposed [27] so that, GA helps to navigate the large search space and to build sub-space by querying Web Services.

A logic programming language called *Golog* is built on top of the *situation calculus* [24] for planning based WSC. The Web service composition problem can be addressed through the provision of high level generic procedures and customizing constraints. The general idea of situation calculus is that, software agents could reason about Web services to perform automatic Web service discovery, execution, composition and interoperation. A technique called *Rule based composition* to generate composite services from high level declarative description is described [24]. The method uses composability rules to determine whether two services are composable. The composition technique generates a detailed description of the composite service automatically and presents it to the service requester. The *Theorem proving* approach [24] is based on automated deduction and program synthesis. In this approach, initially available services and user requirements are described in a first order language related to classical logic, and then constructive proofs are generated with Snark theorem prover. Finally, service composition descriptions are extracted from particular proofs. The *Graphplan* based planning solution involves execution of sequence of steps (graph expansion) on a planning graph to find the goal [28]. The AI planning based composition technique requires the output (goal) of requested service to be specified by the requester in a predefined format for successful compositions.

3.3 User Interaction and Personalization Based Composition

Current approaches to compose function oriented Web services are inappropriate for interactive characteristics of Interactive Web Services (IWS). Towards this, a novel user satisfaction model to evaluate the interactive quality of a composite IWS is proposed [30]. Based on the satisfaction model, an effective satisfaction driven approach has been developed for the service selection in IWS composition, which can meet diverse interactive requirements of users. In order to fulfill the user requirements, researchers have proposed mechanisms for composition, based on requirements of Inputs and Outputs [31]. A multi-tier architecture called *TailorBPEL* is proposed [32] that enables end-users to tailor personalized BPEL based workflow compositions at runtime. The framework provides end-users with capabilities of tailorability through a set of personalization API and tailoring API. The personalization API allows end-users to create a personalized version of a BPEL process which can be tailored later on using the available tailoring API. The modeling of interactive Web services for composition is a challenging task as the interaction pattern varies from service to service.

3.4 Context Information and Process Based Composition

Context provides useful information concerning the environment wherein the composition of Web services occurs [7]. The context information (service context, policy context and process context) is crucial to model, monitor and execute composite processes. The authors [7] propose a context based multi-type policy approach for Web service composition which cater to the necessary information, enables tracking the whole composition process by enabling policies and regulates the interactions between Web services. The authors [15] present composition approach based on context driven Web service modeling. A novel approach named *process context aware matchmaking* is proposed [33] which discovers the suitable services during Web service composition modeling. During matchmaking, the approach utilizes not only semantics of technical process but also the business process of a advertised service, thus further improving the precision of matchmaking.

The finite state machine (FSM) modeling of Web services contribute to the automatic composition of Web services and a few researchers have used FSMs to model service behavior towards composition. The authors [34] model services as FSMs augmented with linear counters to integrate activity processing costs into the model. The authors further investigate the problem of computing an optimal delegation for a given sequence of service requests. The authors [35] present an automatic e-Service composition which proposes a framework in which the exported behavior of an e-Service is described in terms of its possible executions (execution trees). The framework is also specialized to consider exported behavior (i.e. the execution tree of the e-Service) which is represented by a finite state machine. The modeling of process (behavior) of services using FSM is a complex task for the providers. The context aware Web service composition requires various ontologies to be updated and managed to capture the requester's and provider's context.

3.5 Model and Aspect Driven Composition

The authors [36] [22] introduce the approach of *Model Driven Service Composition*, which is based on dynamic service composition to facilitate the management and development of composite Web services. Unified Modeling Language (UML) is used to provide a high level of abstraction and to enable direct mapping to other standards, such as BPEL4WS. UML based modeling technique can be applied to *Aspect Oriented Programming (AOP)* technologies for Web service compositions. An aspect oriented Web service composition approach is proposed [37] to address modularization and dynamic adaptation problems. The authors design the aspects for *pluggable* behaviors with UML and bind the aspects into the basic model to get the complete composition model. The authors [38] propose the decoupling of core service logic from context related functionality by adopting a Model driven approach based on a modified version of the ContextUML meta model. Core service logic and context handling are treated as separate concerns at the modeling level where AOP encapsulates context dependent behavior. The model driven composition enables the developer to specify composition plan and binding of services for the tasks which happens at runtime based on the requirements.

3.6 Signature (Input and Output) Based Composition Techniques

Operation signature (Input and Output) based composition is the most widely used technique to generate composition plan (sequential or parallel) at runtime based on the requester's demands. The composition plan is generated by matching inputs of service with the outputs of rest services or vice versa. Inputs and outputs are normally specified by URIs and can be extracted directly from the WSDL documents. A brief review of signature based dynamic Web service composition techniques is presented in the next section.

4 Dynamic Composition Based on Web Service Signature

In literature, various techniques have been proposed to exploit Input-Output parameter descriptions and their relationships for the dynamic Web service composition. The service (or operation) signature (or behavior) based composition

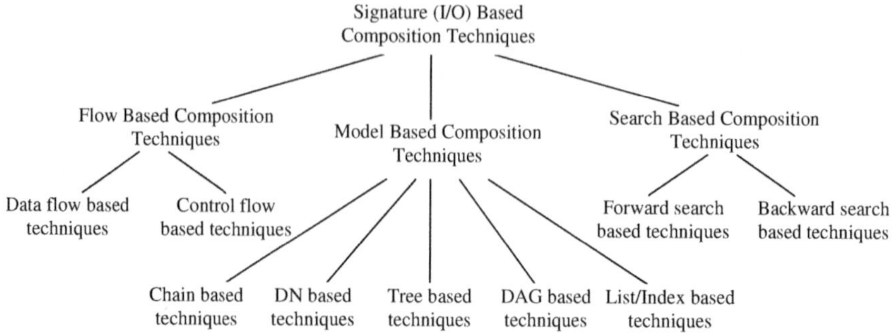

Fig. 1. Taxonomy of QoS aware Web Service Selection Techniques

techniques are classified as *Search based composition*, *Flow based composition* and *Structure (Model) based composition.* Fig. 1 depicts classification of various signature based Web service composition techniques.

4.1 Search Based Composition Techniques

Search based composition is defined based on the nature of generation of composition plan and type of matchmaking involved in the search during plan generation. The search based composition methods are classified as *Forward search based composition* and *Backward search based composition.* In forward search based composition (Goal driven) [28], the composition plan is initialized by the selection of Web services satisfying the requester's input parameters and the plan is expanded by matching inputs of the rest of the services with the outputs of the last identified service. In backward composition method [39], the composition plan is generated by identifying a suitable service which satisfies the requested outputs. The backward search method is more efficient as compared to forward search since backward search does not allow meaningless expansions of the composition plan. The search based composition techniques generate composition plan with redundant execution paths which require further optimization. Moreover, for the matchmaking of inputs with outputs the entire service repository needs to be searched which is a costly activity in terms of execution time.

4.2 Flow Based Composition Techniques

The flow based composition is defined based on the nature of information used to generate composition plan. In literature, *two* types of information items are used to generate the composition plan. They are: data flow (message flow) or data dependency information and control flow (execution sequence or service dependency) information. Thus flow based composition techniques are classified as *Data flow based composition* and *Control flow based composition.* In data flow based composition techniques, the message sequence of individual services [18] or the input-output data dependency among services [40], guide the generation of composition plan at runtime. The control flow (workflow) based composition techniques exploit the execution order of services to build the plan for Web service composition at runtime [41].

4.3 Structure (Model) Based Composition Techniques

In literature various data models have been proposed to hold the service information (Input or Output) to compose Web services. Based on the type of data structures used for the composition, the model based composition techniques are classified into *five* groups. They are: *Tree based techniques*, *Directed Acyclic Graph (DAG) based techniques*, *Chain (Linked List) based techniques*, *List (index) based techniques* and *Deduced Network (DN) based techniques.*

In tree based approach [42], the service information (especially input-output) is modeled in the form of the tree structure for composition. A *Composition Schema Tree (CST)* is defined in [39] for a service which holds service signature information. A group of such trees of advertised services are used to build the *Complete Composition Schema Tree (CCST).* For a given service request the CCST involving input nodes, output nodes and Web service nodes is traversed to build composition at runtime. The authors [43] propose the tree structure called *Web Services Composition Tree (WSCT)* which is used to obtain QoS aware composition result for a given service request. The tree based techniques always try to build the tree structures based on the input-output parameters and not on parameter dependency. Moreover parameter ontology needs to be defined to specify service request and service description in a standard form.

The graph (DAG) model [40] for dynamic composition represents the service parameters and their dependencies (constraints). The authors [40] propose a method which constructs a graph model, that represents the functional semantics of Web services as well as the dependency among inputs and outputs. The authors [45] define a dependency graph for composition, where the nodes represent inputs and outputs of Web services and edges represent the associated Web services. The authors [46] present an approach for automatic service composition which discover services based on semantic annotations of service properties, e.g. their inputs, outputs and goals. This approach also uses a graph based search algorithm on composition graph to determine all possible composition candidates and applies certain measures to rank them. Graph based techniques require more search time in the case of large number of advertised Web services involving too many input and output parameters.

In literature the composition techniques are also defined on data structures like chains (linked list) [47], chains with Indexed tables [48], Inverted lists (files) [49] and deduced networks (DN) [50] to represent service information for dynamic Web service composition. The use of lists, chains and deduced networks enhance the composition mechanism in terms of time and number of possible plans for composition. The graph model is more effective only if services are represented with dependency among them instead of representing parameters (input and output) as the nodes. The representation of parameters increase the size of graph thereby the search time of composition. The chains, tables and lists (vectors) are best data structures to hold input-output parameter information and parameter dependencies.

5 Conclusion

Composition of available Web services based on the requester's functional requirements is a challenging task. In literature, various techniques for dynamic composition of Web services have been proposed. The composition mechanisms proposed in literature build composition plan involving Web services for the various tasks of a complex service request. The Web service is normally a collection of logically related operations and the requester normally requests for a single operation (simple service request) or multiple operations (complex service request). Thus composition must focus on generating composition plan involving abstract operations of available Web services instead of just Web services. The operations of Web service are sometimes dependent on other operations in terms of execution order (flow). Some of the operations of Web service do not implement business logic instead they assist other operations in successful execution. For example, consider a travel scenario where the operation "reserve train ticket" which implements business logic is dependent on one assisting operation called "check train ticket availability". If the requester is interested in operations which implement business logic then all assisting operations which have influence on the requested operations need to be included in the composition plan towards successful composition and execution. Thus, composition plan to be generated at runtime must contain such assisting operations with an order of execution.

References

1. Kreger, H.: Web Services Conceptual Architecture (WSCA 1.0) (2001), `http://www.ibm.com/software/solutions/webservices/pdf/wsca.pdf` (April 13, 2007)
2. Dustdar, S., Schreiner, W.: A survey on web services composition. International Journal of Web and Grid Services 1(1), 1–30 (2005)
3. Fluegge, M., et al.: Challenges and Techniques on the Road to Dynamically Compose Web Services. In: Proceedings of the ICWE 2006, pp. 40–47. IEEE, Los Alamitos (2006)
4. Sivasubramanian, S.P., Ilavarasan, E., Vadivelou, G.: Dynamic Web Service Composition: Challenges and Techniques. In: Proceedings of the International Conference on Intelligent Agent & Multi-Agent Systems (IAMA 2009). IEEE, Los Alamitos (2009)
5. Lei, W., Jing, S., Xiao-bo, H.: Research on the Clustering and Composition of P2P-based Web Services. In: Proceedings of the 2nd International Conference on Biomedical Engineering and Informatics (BMEI 2009). IEEE, Los Alamitos (2009)
6. Benatallah, B., Dumas, M.: The Self-Serv Environment for Web Services Composition. In: IEEE Internet Computing. LNCS, vol. 4317, pp. 389–402. Springer, Heidelberg (2003)

7. Maamar, Z., Faoui, S.K.M., Yahyaoui, H.: Toward an Agent-Based and Context-Oriented Approach for Web Services Composition. IEEE Transactions On Knowledge And Data Engineering 17(5), 686–697 (2005)
8. Ketel, M.: Mobile Agents Based Infrastructure for Web Services Composition. In: Proceedings of the 2008 IEEE SoutheastCon, part 1. IEEE, Los Alamitos (2008)
9. Karunamurthy, R., Khendek, F., Glitho, R.H.: A Business Model for Dynamic Composition of Telecommunication Web Services. IEEE Telecommunications Magazine, 36–43 (July 2007)
10. Zhao, H., Tong, H.: A Dynamic Service Composition Model Based on Constraints. In: Proceedings of the Sixth International Conference on Grid and Cooperative Computing (GCC 2007). IEEE, Los Alamitos (2007)
11. Ko, J.M., Kim, C.O., Kwon, I.: Quality-of-service oriented web service composition algorithm and planning architecture. The Journal of Systems and Software 81, 2079–2090 (2008)
12. Casati, F., Ilnicki, S., Jin, L., Krishnamoorthy, V., Shan, M.: Adaptive and Dynamic Service Composition in eFlow. White paper, HP Laboratories Palo Alto, HPL-2000-39, Hewlett-Packard Company (March 2000)
13. Liu, J., Fan, C., Gu, N.: Web Services Automatic Composition with Minimal Execution Price. In: Proceedings of the IEEE International Conference on Web Services (ICWS 2005). IEEE, Los Alamitos (2005)
14. Chung, M., Namgoong, H., Kim, K., Jung, S., Cho, H.: Improved Matching Algorithm for Services described by OWL-S. In: Proceedings of the ICACT 2005, pp. 1510–1513 (2005) ISBN 89-5519-129-4
15. Narendra, N.C., Orriens, B.: Modeling Web Service Composition and Execution via a Requirements-Driven Approach. In: Proceedings of the SAC 2007. ACM, New York (2007)
16. Lee, S., Lee, J.: Dynamic Service Composition Model for Ubiquitous Environments. In: Shi, Z.-Z., Sadananda, R. (eds.) PRIMA 2006. LNCS (LNAI), vol. 4088, pp. 742–747. Springer, Heidelberg (2006)
17. Ma, C., He, Y., Xiong, N., Yang, L.T.: VFT: An Ontology-based Tool for Visualization and Formalization of Web Service Composition. In: Proceedings of the 2009 International Conference on Computational Science and Engineering. IEEE, Los Alamitos (2009)
18. Agarwal, V., Chafle, G., Mittal, S., Srivastava, B.: Understanding Approaches for Web Service Composition and Execution. In: Proceedings of the COMPUTE 2008. ACM, New York (2008)
19. Aggarwal, R., Verma, K., Miller, J., Milnor, W.: Constraint Driven Web Service Composition in METEOR-S. In: Proceedings of the 2004 IEEE International Conference on Services Computing (SCC 2004). IEEE, Los Alamitos (2004)
20. Monfroy, E., Perrin, O., Ringeissen, C.: Modelling Web Services Composition with Constraints. In: Revista Avances en Sistemas e-Informatica, Edicion Especial, Medellin, Mayo de, vol. 5(1), pp. 173–179 (2008) ISSN 1657-7663
21. Gooneratne, N., Tari, Z.: Matching Independent Global Constraints for Composite Web Services. In: Proceedings of the WWW 2008, Beijing, China, April 21-25, pp. 765–774 (2008)
22. Orriëns, B., Yang, J., Papazoglou, M.P.: A Framework for Business Rule Driven Service Composition. In: Benatallah, B., Shan, M.-C. (eds.) TES 2003. LNCS, vol. 2819, pp. 14–27. Springer, Heidelberg (2003)

23. Chun, S.A., Atluri, V., Adam, N.R.: Policy-based Web Service Composition. In: Proceedings of the 14th international Workshop on Research Issues on Data Engineering: Web services for E-commerce and E-Government Applications (RIDE 2004). IEEE, Los Alamitos (2004)
24. Rao, J., Su, X.: A survey of automated web service composition methods. In: Cardoso, J., Sheth, A.P. (eds.) SWSWPC 2004. LNCS, vol. 3387, pp. 43–54. Springer, Heidelberg (2005)
25. Zahoor, E., Perrin, O., Godart, C.: Rule-based semi automatic Web services composition. In: Proceedings of the 2009 Congress on Services - I. IEEE, Los Alamitos (2009)
26. Vukoviċ, M., Kotsovinos, E., Robinson, P.: An architecture for rapid, on-demand service composition. Journal of Service Oriented Computing and Applications - SOCA 1, 197–212 (2007)
27. Yan, Y., Liang, Y.: Using Genetic Algorithms to Navigate Partial Enumerable Problem Space for Web Services Composition. In: Proceedings of the Third International Conference on Natural Computation (ICNC 2007). IEEE, Los Alamitos (2007)
28. Oh, S., Lee, D., Kumara, S.R.T.: A Comparative Illustration of AI Planning-based Web Service Composition. ACM SIGecom Exchanges 5(5), 1–10 (2004)
29. Agarwal, S., Handschuh, S., Staab, S.: Annotation, composition and invocation of semantic web services. Journal of Web Semantics: Science, Services and Agents on the World Wide Web 2, 31–48 (2004)
30. Wan, S., Wei, J., Song, J., Zhong, H.: A Satisfaction Driven Approach for the Composition of Interactive Web Services. In: Proceedings of the 31st Annual International Computer Software and Applications Conference (COMPSAC 2007). IEEE, Los Alamitos (2007)
31. Xiaoming, P., Qiqing, F., Yahui, H., Bingjian, Z.: A User Requirements Oriented Dynamic Web Service Composition Framework. In: Proceedings of the 2009 International Forum on Information Technology and Applications. IEEE, Los Alamitos (2009)
32. El-Gayyar, M.M., Alda, S.J., Cremers, A.B.: Towards a User-Oriented Environment for Web Services Composition. In: Proceedings of the WEUSE IV, pp. 81–85. ACM, New York (2008)
33. Han, W., Shi, X., Chen, R.: Process-context aware matchmaking for web service composition. Journal of Network and Computer Applications 31, 559–576 (2008)
34. Geredea, C.E., Ibarra, O.H., Ravikumar, B., Sua, J.: Minimum-cost delegation in service composition. Theoretical Computer Science 409, 417–431 (2008)
35. Berardi, D., Calvanese, D., Giacomo, G.: Automatic Composition of e-Services. Technical Report (January 10, 2003), `http://www.dis.uniroma1.it/mecella/publications/eService/BCDLM-techRport-22-2003.pdf`
36. Zhao, C., Duan, Z., Zhang, M.: A Model-Driven Approach for Dynamic Web Service Composition. In: Proceedings of the World Congress on Software Engineering, IEEE, Los Alamitos (2009)
37. Xu, Y., Youwei, X.: Towards Aspect Oriented Web Service Composition with UML. In: Proceedings of the 6th IEEE/ACIS International Conference on Computer and Information Science (ICIS 2007). IEEE, Los Alamitos (2007)
38. Prezerakos, G.N., Tselikas, N.D., Cortese, G.: Model-driven Composition of Context-aware Web Services Using ContextUML and Aspects. In: Proceedings of the 2007 IEEE International Conference on Web Services (ICWS 2007). IEEE, Los Alamitos (2007)

39. Tang, H., Zhong, F., Yang, C.: A Tree-based Method of Web Service Composition. In: Proceedings of the 2008 IEEE International Conference on Web Services, pp. 768–770. IEEE, Los Alamitos (2008)
40. Shin, D., Lee, K.: An Automated Composition of Information Web Services based on Functional Semantics. In: Proceedings of the 2007 IEEE Congress on Services (SERVICES 2007). IEEE, Los Alamitos (2007)
41. Kona, S., Bansal, A., Blake, M.B., Gupta, G.: Towards a General Framework for Web Service Composition. In: Proceedings of the 2008 IEEE International Conference on Services Computing. IEEE, Los Alamitos (2008)
42. Chan, P.P.W., Lyu, M.R.: Dynamic Web Service Composition: A New Approach in Building Reliable Web Service. In: Proceedings of the 22nd International Conference on Advanced Information Networking and Applications. IEEE, Los Alamitos (2008)
43. Chen, Z., Ma, J., Song, L., Lian, L.: An Efficient Approach to Web Services Discovery and Composition when Large Scale Services are Available. In: Proceedings of the 2006 IEEE Asia-Pacific Conference on Services Computing (APSCC 2006). IEEE, Los Alamitos (2006)
44. Shen, Z., Su, J.: On Completeness of Web Service Compositions. In: Proceedings of the 2007 IEEE International Conference on Web Services (ICWS 2007). IEEE, Los Alamitos (2007)
45. Hashemian, S.V., Mavaddat, M.: A Graph-Based Approach to Web Services Composition. In: Proceedings of the 2005 Symposium on Applications and the Internet (SAINT 2005). IEEE, Los Alamitos (2005)
46. Shiaa, M.M., Fladmark, J.O., Thiell, B.: An incremental graph-based approach to Automatic Service Composition. In: Proceedings of the 2008 IEEE International Conference on Services Computing. IEEE, Los Alamitos (2008)
47. Xu, B., Li, T., Gu, Z., Wu, G.: SWSDS: Quick Web Service Discovery and Composition in SEWSIP. In: Proceedings of the 8th IEEE International Conference on E-Commerce Technology and the 3rd IEEE International Conference on Enterprise Computing, E-Commerce, and E-Services (CEC/EEE 2006). IEEE, Los Alamitos (2006)
48. Li, L., Jun, M., ZhuMin, C., Ling, S.: An Efficient Algorithm for Web Services Composition with a Chain Data Structure. In: Proceedings of the 2006 IEEE International Conference on Services Computing (APSCC 2006). IEEE, Los Alamitos (2006)
49. Ren, K., Chen, J., Xiao, N., Zhang, W., Song, J.: A QSQL-based Collaboration Framework to Support Automatic Service Composition and Workflow Execution. In: Proceedings of the 3rd International Conference on Grid and Pervasive Computing - Workshops. IEEE, Los Alamitos (2008)
50. Liu, J., Fan, C., Gu, N.: Web Services Automatic Composition with Minimal Execution Price. In: Proceedings of the IEEE International Conference on Web Services (ICWS 2005). IEEE, Los Alamitos (2005)

Output Regulation of Arneodo-Coullet Chaotic System

Sundarapandian Vaidyanathan

R & D Centre, Vel Tech Dr. RR & Dr. SR Technical University
Avadi-Alamathi Road, Avadi, Chennai-600 062, India
sundarvtu@gmail.com
http://www.vel-tech.org/

Abstract. This paper investigates the problem of output regulation of the Arneodo-Coullet chaotic system, which is one of the paradigms of the chaotic systems proposed by A. Arneodo, P. Coullet and C. Tresser (1981). Explicitly, state feedback control laws to regulate the output of the Arneodo-Coullet chaotic system have been derived so as to track the constant reference signals as well as to track periodic reference signals. The control laws are derived using the regulator equations of C.I. Byrnes and A. Isidori (1990), who solved the problem of output regulation of nonlinear systems involving neutrally stable exosystem dynamics. The output regulation of the Coullet chaotic system has important applications in Electrical and Communication Engineering. Numerical simulations are shown to verify the results.

Keywords: Arneodo-Coullet system; output regulation; nonlinear control systems; feedback stabilization.

1 Introduction

Output regulation of control systems is one of the very important problems in control systems theory. Basically, the output regulation problem is to control a fixed linear or nonlinear plant in order to have its output tracking reference signals produced by some external generator (the exosystem). For linear control systems, the output regulation problem has been solved by Francis and Wonham (1975, [1]). For nonlinear control systems, the output regulation problem has been solved by Byrnes and Isidori (1990, [2]) generalizing the internal model principle obtained by Francis and Wonham [1]. Byrnes and Isidori [2] have made an important assumption in their work which demands that the exosystem dynamics generating reference and/or disturbance signals is a neutrally stable system (Lyapunov stable in both forward and backward time). The class of exosystem signals includes the important particular cases of constant reference signals as well as sinusoidal reference signals. Using Centre Manifold Theory [3], Byrnes and Isidori have derived regulator equations, which completely characterize the solution of the output regulation problem of nonlinear control systems.

The output regulation problem for linear and nonlinear control systems has been the focus of many studies in recent years ([4]-[14]). In [4], Mahmoud and Khalil obtained results on the asymptotic regulation of minimum phase nonlinear systems using output feedback. In [5], Fridman solved the output regulation problem for nonlinear control

N. Meghanathan et al. (Eds.): CCSIT 2011, Part III, CCIS 133, pp. 98–107, 2011.

systems with delay, using Centre Manifold Theory [3]. In [6]-[7], Chen and Huang obtained results on the robust output regulation for output feedback systems with nonlinear exosystems. In [8], Liu and Huang obtained results on the global robust output regulation problem for lower triangular nonlinear systems with unknown control direction. In [9], Immonen obtained results on the practical output regulation for bounded linear infinite-dimensional state space systems. In [10], Pavlov, Van de Wouw and Nijmeijer obtained results on the global nonlinear output regulation using convergence-based controller design. In [11], Xi and Ding obtained results on the global adaptive output regulation of a class of nonlinear systems with nonlinear exosystems. In [12]-[14], Serrani, Marconi and Isidori obtained results on the semi-global and global output regulation problem for minimum-phase nonlinear systems.

In this paper, the output regulation problem for the Arneodo-Coullet chaotic system [15] has been solved using the Byrnes-Isidori regulator equations [2] to derive the state feedback control laws for regulating the output of the Coullet chaotic system for the important cases of constant reference signals (set-point signals) and periodic reference signals. The Arneodo-Coullet chaotic system is one of the simplest three-dimensional chaotic systems studied by A. Arneodo, P. Coullet and C. Tresser (1981, [15]). It has important applications in Electrical and Communication Engineering.

This paper is organized as follows. In Section 2, a review of the solution of the output regulation for nonlinear control systems and Byrnes-Isidori regulator equations has been presented. In Section 3, the main results of this paper, namely, the feedback control laws solving the output regulation problem for the Coullet chaotic system for the cases of constant reference signals and periodic reference signals have been detailed. In Section 4, the numerical results illustrating the main results of the paper have been described. Section 5 summarizes the main results obtained in this paper.

2 Review of the Output Regulation for Nonlinear Control Systems

In this section, we consider a multi-variable nonlinear control system modelled by equations of the form

$$\dot{x} = f(x) + g(x)u + p(x)\omega \tag{1}$$

$$\dot{\omega} = s(\omega) \tag{2}$$

$$e = h(x) - q(\omega) \tag{3}$$

Here, the differential equation (1) describes the *plant dynamics* with state x defined in a neighbourhood X of the origin of $\mathbb{R}^n$ and the input u takes values in $\mathbb{R}^m$ subject to the effect of a disturbance represented by the vector field $p(x)\omega$. The differential equation (2) describes an autonomous system, known as the *exosystem*, defined in a neighbourhood W of the origin of $\mathbb{R}^k$, which models the class of disturbance and reference signals taken into consideration. The equation (3) defines the error between the actual plant output $h(x) \in \mathbb{R}^p$ and a reference signal $q(\omega)$, which models the class of disturbance and reference signals taken into consideration.

We also assume that all the constituent mappings of the system (1)-(2) and the error equation (3), namely, f, g, p, s, h and q are C^1 mappings vanishing at the origin, *i.e.*

$$f(0) = 0,\ g(0) = 0,\ p(0) = 0,\ h(0) = 0 \text{ and } q(0) = 0.$$

Thus, for $u = 0$, the composite system (1)-(2) has an equilibrium state $(x, \omega) = (0, 0)$ with zero error (3).

A *state feedback controller* for the composite system (1)-(2) has the form

$$u = \alpha(x, \omega) \tag{4}$$

where α is a $\mathcal{C}^1$ mapping defined on $X \times W$ such that $\alpha(0, 0) = 0$. Upon substitution of the feedback law (4) in the composite system (1)-(2), we get the closed-loop system given by

$$\begin{aligned} \dot{x} &= f(x) + g(x)\alpha(x, \omega) + p(x)\omega \\ \dot{\omega} &= s(\omega) \end{aligned} \tag{5}$$

The purpose of designing the state feedback controller (4) is to achieve both *internal stability* and *output regulation*. Internal stability means that when the input is disconnected from (5) (*i.e.* when $\omega = 0$), the closed-loop system (5) has an exponentially stable equilibrium at $x = 0$. Output regulation means that for the closed-loop system (5), for all initial states $(x(0), \omega(0))$ sufficiently close to the origin, $e(t) \to 0$ asymptotically as $t \to \infty$. Formally, we can summarize the requirements as follows.

State Feedback Regulator Problem [2]:

Find, if possible, a state feedback control law $u = \alpha(x, \omega)$ such that

(OR1) [*Internal Stability*] The equilibrium $x = 0$ of the dynamics

$$\dot{x} = f(x) + g(x)\alpha(x, 0)$$

is locally asymptotically stable.

(OR2) [*Output Regulation*] There exists a neighbourhood $U \subset X \times W$ of $(x, \omega) = (0, 0)$ such that for each initial condition $(x(0), \omega(0)) \in U$, the solution $(x(t), \omega(t))$ of the closed-loop system (5) satisfies

$$\lim_{t \to \infty} \left[h(x(t)) - q(\omega(t)) \right] = 0.$$

■

Byrnes and Isidori [2] have solved this problem under the following assumptions.

(H1) The exosystem dynamics $\dot{\omega} = s(\omega)$ is neutrally stable at $\omega = 0$, i.e. the system is Lyapunov stable in both forward and backward time at $\omega = 0$.

(H2) The pair $(f(x), g(x))$ has a stabilizable linear approximation at $x = 0$, i.e. if

$$A = \left[\frac{\partial f}{\partial x} \right]_{x=0} \quad \text{and} \quad B = \left[\frac{\partial g}{\partial x} \right]_{x=0},$$

then (A, B) is stabilizable, which means that we can find a gain matrix K so that $A + BK$ is Hurwitz. ■

Next, we recall the solution of the output regulation problem derived by Byrnes and Isidori [2].

Theorem 1. *[2] Under the hypotheses (H1) and (H2), the state feedback regulator problem is solvable if, and only if, there exist* $\mathcal{C}^1$ *mappings* $x = \pi(\omega)$ *with* $\pi(0) = 0$

and $u = \phi(\omega)$ *with* $\phi(0) = 0$, *both defined in a neighbourhod of* $W^0 \subset W$ *of* $\omega = 0$ *such that the following equations (called the* Byrnes-Isidori regulator equations*) are satisfied:*

$$\text{(1) } \frac{\partial \pi}{\partial \omega} s(\omega) = f(\pi(\omega)) + g(\pi(\omega))\phi(\omega) + p(\pi(\omega))\omega$$

$$\text{(2) } h(\pi(\omega)) - q(\omega) = 0$$

When the Byrnes-Isidori regulator equations (1) and (2) are satisfied, a control law solving the state feedback regulator problem is given by

$$u = \phi(\omega) + K[x - \pi(\omega)] \tag{6}$$

where K *is any gain matrix such that* $A + BK$ *is Hurwitz.* ■

3 Output Regulation of Arneodo-Coullet Chaotic System

The Arneodo-Coullet chaotic system [15] is one of the paradigms of the three-dimensional chaotic models described by the dynamics

$$\begin{aligned} \dot{x}_1 &= x_2 \\ \dot{x}_2 &= x_3 \\ \dot{x}_3 &= ax_1 - bx_2 - cx_3 - x_1^3 + u \end{aligned} \tag{7}$$

where a, b and c are positive constants.

A. Arneodo, P. Coullet and C. Tresser [15] studied the chaotic system (7) with $a = 5.5, b = 3.5, c = 1.0$ and $u = 0$. The chaotic portrait of the unforced Arneodo-Coullet chaotic system is illustrated in Figure 1.

In this paper, we consider two important cases of output regulation for the Arneodo-Coullet chaotic system [15]:

(I) Tracking of Constant Reference Signals
(II) Tracking of Periodic Reference Signals

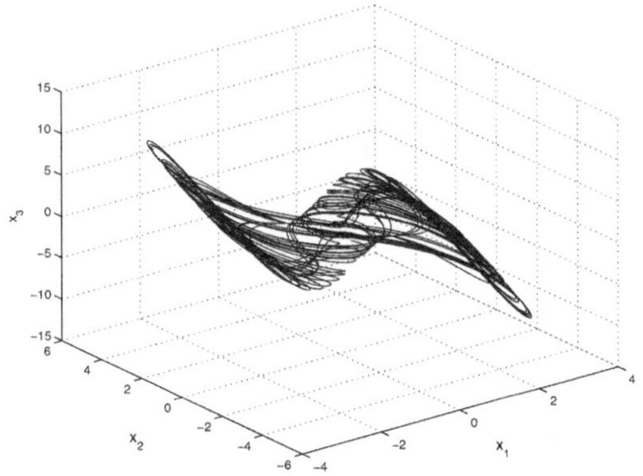

Fig. 1. Chaotic Portrait of the Arneodo-Coullet System

Case I: Tracking of Constant Reference Signals
In this case, the exosystem is given by the scalar dynamics

$$\dot{\omega} = 0 \tag{8}$$

It is important to observe that the exosystem (8) is neutrally stable because the solutions of (8) are only constant trajectories, *i.e.*

$$\omega(t) \equiv \omega(0) = \omega_0 \quad \text{for all} \;\; t$$

Thus, the assumption (H1) of Theorem 1 (Section 2) holds trivially.

Linearizing the dynamics of the Arneodo-Coullet system (7) yields the system matrices

$$A = \begin{bmatrix} 0 & 1 & 0 \\ 0 & 0 & 1 \\ a & -b & -c \end{bmatrix} \quad \text{and} \quad B = \begin{bmatrix} 0 \\ 0 \\ 1 \end{bmatrix} \tag{9}$$

which is in Bush companion form.

Using Kalman's rank test for controllability ([16], p.738), it can be easily seen that the pair (A, B) is completely controllable. Since (A, B) is in Bush companion form, the characteristic equation of $A + BK$ is given by

$$\lambda^3 + (c - k_3)\lambda^2 + (b - k_2)\lambda - (a + k_1) = 0 \tag{10}$$

where $K = [\, k_1 \quad k_2 \quad k_3 \,]$.

By the Routh's stability criterion ([16], p.234), it can be easily shown that the closed-loop system matrix $A + BK$ is Hurwitz if and only if

$$k_1 < -a, \;\; k_2 < b, \;\; k_3 < c, \quad (c - k_3)(b - k_2) + (a + k_1) > 0 \tag{11}$$

Thus, the assumption (H2) of Theorem 1 (Section 2) also holds. Hence, Theorem 1 can be applied to solve the output regulation problem for the Arneodo-Coullet chaotic system (7) for the tracking of constant reference signals (*set-point signals*).

Case I (a): The error equation is $e = x_1 - \omega$
Solving the Byrnes-Isidori regulator equations (Theorem 1), we get the solution

$$\pi_1(\omega) = \omega, \; \pi_2(\omega) = 0, \; \pi_3(\omega) = 0, \; \phi(\omega) = \omega\left(\omega^2 - a\right) \tag{12}$$

By Theorem 1 (Section 2), a state feedback control law solving the output regulation problem is given by

$$u = \phi(\omega) + K[x - \pi(\omega)] = \omega\left(\omega^2 - a\right) + k_1(x_1 - \omega) + k_2 x_2 + k_3 x_3 \tag{13}$$

where k_1, k_2 and k_3 satisfy the inequalities (11).

Case I (b): The error equation is $e = x_2 - \omega$
A direct calculation shows that the Byrnes-Isidori regulator equations are not solvable in this case. Hence, by Theorem 1 (Section 2), we conclude that the output regulation problem is not solvable for this case.

Case I (c): The error equation is $e = x_3 - \omega$
A direct calculation shows that the Byrnes-Isidori regulator equations are not solvable in this case. Hence, by Theorem 1 (Section 2), we conclude that the output regulation problem is not solvable for this case.

Case II: Tracking of Periodic Reference Signals
In this case, the exosystem is given by the planar dynamics

$$\begin{aligned} \dot{\omega}_1 &= \nu\,\omega_2 \\ \dot{\omega}_2 &= -\nu\,\omega_1 \end{aligned} \tag{14}$$

where $\nu > 0$ is any fixed constant.

Clearly, the assumption (H1) (Theorem 1) holds. Also, as established in Case I, the assumption (H2) (Theorem 1) also holds and that the closed-loop system matrix $A + BK$ will be Hurwitz if the constants k_1, k_2 and k_3 of the gain matrix K satisfy the inequalities (11).

Case II (a): The error equation is $e = x_1 - \omega_1$
Solving the Byrnes-Isidori regulator equations (Theorem 1) for this case, we get the solution

$$\pi_1(\omega) = \omega_1, \pi_2(\omega) = \nu\omega_2, \pi_3(\omega) = -\nu^2\omega_1 \tag{15}$$

$$\phi(\omega) = \omega_1^3 - (a + c\nu^2)\omega_1 + (b\nu - \nu^3)\omega_2 \tag{16}$$

By Theorem 1 (Section 2), a state feedback control law solving the output regulation problem is given by

$$u = \phi(\omega) + K[x - \pi(\omega)] \tag{17}$$

where $\pi(\omega)$ is given by (15), $\phi(\omega)$ is given by (16) and k_1, k_2 and k_3 satisfy the inequalities (11).

Case II (b): The error equation is $e = x_2 - \omega_2$
Solving the Byrnes-Isidori regulator equations (Theorem 1), we get the solution

$$\pi_1(\omega) = -\nu^{-1}\omega_2,\ \pi_2(\omega) = \omega_1,\ \pi_3(\omega) = \nu\omega_2 \tag{18}$$

$$\phi(\omega) = (b - \nu^2)\omega_1 + (a\nu^{-1} + c\nu)\omega_2 - \nu^{-3}\,\omega_2^3 \tag{19}$$

By Theorem 1 (Section 2), a state feedback control law solving the output regulation problem is given by

$$u = \phi(\omega) + K[x - \pi(\omega)] \tag{20}$$

where $\pi(\omega)$ is given by (18), $\phi(\omega)$ is given by (19) and k_1, k_2 and k_3 satisfy the inequalities (11).

Case II (c): The error equation is $e = x_3 - \omega_3$
Solving the Byrnes-Isidori regulator equations (Theorem 1), we get the solution

$$\pi_1(\omega) = -\nu^{-2}\omega_1,\ \pi_2(\omega) = -\nu^{-1}\omega_1,\ \pi_3(\omega) = \omega_1 \tag{21}$$

$$\phi(\omega) = \left(c + a\nu^{-2}\right)\omega_1 + \left(\nu + b\nu^{-1}\right)\omega_2 - \nu^{-6}\omega_1^3 \tag{22}$$

By Theorem 1 (Section 2), a state feedback control law solving the output regulation problem is given by

$$u = \phi(\omega) + K[x - \pi(\omega)] \tag{23}$$

where $\pi(\omega)$ is given by (21), $\phi(\omega)$ is given by (22) and k_1, k_2 and k_3 satisfy the inequalities (11).

4 Numerical Simulations

For classical case, we consider the classical chaotic case of Arneodo-Coullet chaotic system [15] with parameter values $a = 5.5, b = 3.5$ and $c = 1.0$. For achieving the internal stability of the state feedback regulator problem, a gain matrix K which satisfies the inequalities (11) must be used.

With the choice

$$K = [\,k_1 \quad k_2 \quad k_3\,] = [\,-130.5 \quad -71.5 \quad -14\,],$$

the matrix $A + BK$ is Hurwitz with the eigenvalues $-5, -5, -5$.

In the periodic tracking output regulation problem, the value $\nu = 1$ is taken in the exosystem dynamics given by (14).

Case I (a): Constant Tracking Problem with Error Equation $e = x_1 - \omega$

Here, the initial conditions are taken as

$$x_1(0) = 7, x_2(0) = 5, x_3(0) = 6 \text{ and } \omega(0) = 2$$

The simulation graph is depicted in Figure 2 from which it is clear that the state trajectory $x_1(t)$ tracks the constant reference signal $\omega(t) \equiv 2$ in 2.5 seconds.

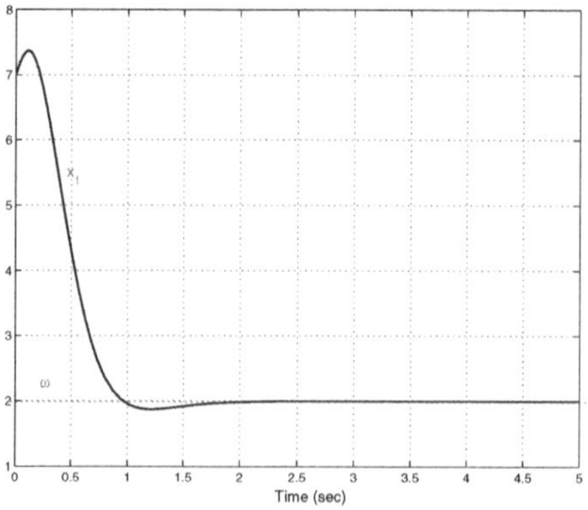

Fig. 2. Constant Tracking Problem - Case I (a)

Case I (b): Constant Tracking Problem with Error Equation $e = x_2 - \omega$
As pointed out in Section 3, the output regulation problem is not solvable for this case because the Byrnes-Isidori regulator equations do not admit any solution.

Case I (c): Constant Tracking Problem with Error Equation $e = x_3 - \omega$
As pointed out in Section 3, the output regulation problem is not solvable for this case because the Byrnes-Isidori regulator equations do not admit any solution.

Case II (a): Periodic Tracking Problem with Error Equation $e = x_1 - \omega_1$
Here, the initial conditions are taken as

$$x_1(0) = 4, \;\; x_2(0) = 3, \;\; x_3(0) = -2 \;\text{ and }\; \omega_1(0) = 1, \omega_2(0) = 0$$

Also, it is assumed that $\nu = 1$. The simulation graph is depicted in Figure 3 from which it is clear that the state trajectory $x_1(t)$ tracks the periodic reference signal $\omega_1(t) = \sin t$ in 1.5 seconds.

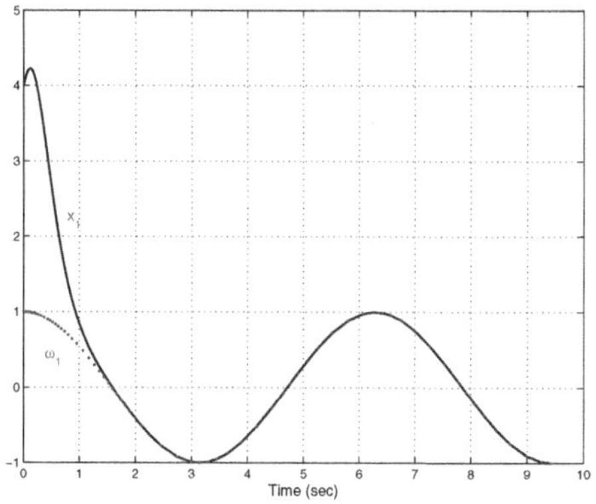

Fig. 3. Periodic Tracking Problem - Case II (a)

Case II (b): Periodic Tracking Problem with Error Equation $e = x_2 - \omega_1$
Here, the initial conditions are taken as

$$x_1(0) = 8, \;\; x_2(0) = 3, \;\; x_3(0) = -2 \;\text{ and }\; \omega_1(0) = 1, \omega_2(0) = 0$$

Also, it is assumed that $\nu = 1$. The simulation graph is depicted in Figure 4 from which it is clear that the state trajectory $x_2(t)$ tracks the periodic reference signal $\omega_1(t) = \sin t$ in 2 seconds.

Case II (c): Periodic Tracking Problem with Error Equation $e = x_3 - \omega_1$
Here, the initial conditions are taken as

$$x_1(0) = 4, \;\; x_2(0) = -5, \;\; x_3(0) = 7 \;\text{ and }\; \omega_1(0) = 1, \omega_2(0) = 0$$

Also, it is assumed that $\nu = 1$. The simulation graph is depicted in Figure 5 from which it is clear that the state trajectory $x_2(t)$ tracks the periodic reference signal $\omega_1(t) = \sin t$ in 2 seconds.

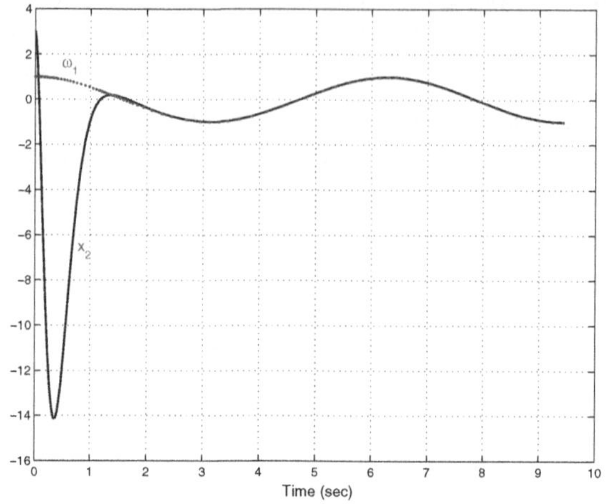

Fig. 4. Periodic Tracking Problem - Case II (b)

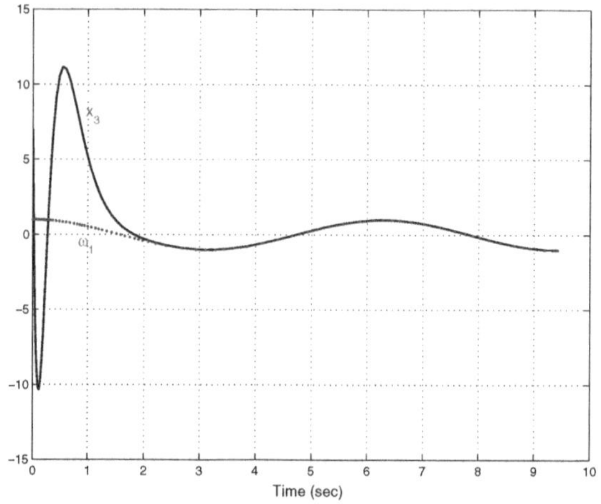

Fig. 5. Periodic Tracking Problem - Case II (c)

5 Conclusions

In this paper, the output regulation problem for the Arneodo-Coullet chaotic system (1981) has been studied in detail and a complete solution for the output regulation problem for the Arneodo-Coullet chaotic system has been presented as well. Explicitly, using the Byrnes-Isidori regulator equations (1990), state feedback control laws for regulating the output of the Arneodo-Coullet chaotic system have been derived. As tracking reference signals, constant and periodic reference signals have been considered and in each case, feedback control laws regulating the output of the Arneodo-Coullet chaotic system have been derived. Numerical simulations are shown to verify the results.

References

1. Francis, B.A., Wonham, W.M.: The internal model principle for linear multivariable regulators. J. Applied Math. Optim. 2, 170–194 (1975)
2. Byrnes, C.I., Isidori, A.: Output regulation of nonlinear systems. IEEE Trans. Automat. Control. 35, 131–140 (1990)
3. Carr, J.: Applications of Centre Manifold Theory. Springer, New York (1981)
4. Mahmoud, N.A., Khalil, H.K.: Asymptotic regulation of minimum phase nonlinear systems using output feedback. IEEE Trans. Automat. Control. 41, 1402–1412 (1996)
5. Fridman, E.: Output regulation of nonlinear control systems with delay. Systems & Control Lett. 50, 81–93 (2003)
6. Chen, Z., Huang, J.: Robust output regulation with nonlinear exosystems. Automatica 41, 1447–1454 (2005)
7. Chen, Z., Huang, J.: Global robust output regulation for output feedback systems. IEEE Trans. Automat. Control. 50, 117–121 (2005)
8. Liu, L., Huang, J.: Global robust output regulation of lower triangular systems with unknown control direction. Automatica 44, 1278–1284 (2008)
9. Immonen, E.: Practical output regulation for bounded linear infinite-dimensional state space systems. Automatica 43, 786–794 (2007)
10. Pavlov, A., Van de Wouw, N., Nijmeijer, H.: Global nonlinear output regulation: convergence based controller design. Automatica 43, 456–463 (2007)
11. Xi, Z., Ding, Z.: Global adaptive output regulation of a class of nonlinear systems with nonlinear exosystems. Automatica 43, 143–149 (2007)
12. Serrani, A., Isidori, A.: Global robust output regulation for a class of nonlinear systems. Systems & Control Lett. 39, 133–139 (2000)
13. Serrani, A., Isidori, A., Marconi, L.: Semiglobal output regulation for minimum phase systems. Int. J. Robust Nonlinear Contr. 10, 379–396 (2000)
14. Marconi, L., Isidori, A., Serrani, A.: Non-resonance conditions for uniform observability in the problem of nonlinear output regulation. Systems & Control Lett. 53, 281–298 (2004)
15. Arneodo, A., Coullet, P., Tresser, C.: Possible new strange attractors with spiral structure. Commun. Math. Phys., 573–579 (1981)
16. Ogata, K.: Modern Control Engineering. Prentice Hall, New Jersey (1997)

A High-Speed Low-Power Low-Latency Pipelined ROM-Less DDFS

Indranil Hatai and Indrajit Chakrabarti

Indian Institute of Technology, Kharagpur, West Bengal, India-721302
indranilh@cse.iitkgp.ernet.in, indrajit@ece.iitkgp.ernet.in

Abstract. The present-day research on direct digital frequency synthesizer (DDFS) lays emphasis on ROM-less architecture, which is endowed with high speed, low power and high spurious free dynamic range (SFDR) features. The DDFS has a wide application in signal processing and telecommunication area, which generates the sine or cosine waveforms within a broad frequency range. In this paper, one high-speed, low-power, and low-latency pipelined ROM-less DDFS architecture has been proposed, implemented and tested using Xilinx Virtex-II Pro University FPGA board. The proposed ROM-less DDFS design has 32 bit phase input and 16 bit amplitude resolution with a maximum amplitude error of 1.5×10^{-4}. FPGA implementation of the proposed design has exhibited an SFDR of -94.3 dBc and a maximum operating frequency of 276 MHz while consuming only 22 K gates and 1.05 mW/MHz power. The high speed of operation and the low power make the proposed design suitable for use in communication transceiver for up and down conversion.

Keywords: Direct Digital Frequency Synthesizer, ROM-less architecture, Spurious Free Dynamic Range, Field Programmable Gate Array.

1 Introduction

The DDFS architecture was first introduced in [1]. The arithmetic operations required in a DDFS are accomplished by a phase accumulator, which generates the phase for generating the sine and cosine waveform, and a phase to amplitude converter (PAC), which produces the sine or cosine amplitude value according to the desired frequency range. At first, the PAC has been implemented using a ROM look-up table (LUT) [1]. But the ROM size increases along with the increase of phase accumulator bit width. Therefore, many methods have been proposed to reduce the ROM LUT size as much as possible. Architectures containing two different ROM tables (coarse ROM and fine ROM) have been proposed in [2] and [3] for the use of the most significant bit (MSB) and the least significant bit (LSB) of the phase accumulator, by which 51% reduction of the total memory size can be possible. The MSB's are used to access the coarse ROM and the LSB's are used to access the fine ROM. Nicholas [4] has done some modification on this work by reducing the memory size by 2 bits in terms of reducing the amplitude of the coarse ROM by using linear interpolation. Using double trigonometric approximation technique, Yamagishi [5] reduced the ROM look-up table size by 3 bits. Bellaouar [6] proposes an architecture based on linear interpolation

N. Meghanathan et al. (Eds.): CCSIT 2011, Part III, CCIS 133, pp. 108–119, 2011.

where the ROM size increases in proportion with the inverse square root of the SFDR. Using the sine-phase difference technique, Curticapean [7] proposes one ROM reduced architecture for the DDFS. Another work by Babak [8] has compressed the ROM size by 551.3:1 using trigonometric approximation with a scaling block. Designing a DDFS with frequency resolution in the sub-hertz range using a ROM-based architecture suffers from huge power consumption, large area and high access time.

To overcome this problem, several attempts have been made towards the development of ROM-less sine or cosine generation technique. CORDIC is one of the popular techniques among these ROM-less trigonometric function generator. CORDIC based implementation technique is required to get high SFDR and low-power and low area consumption while implementing in VLSI [9]. Using pipelined technique, a CORDIC based architecture can achieve very high speed of operation. But the main disadvantage of this technique is the latency and the introduction of additional arithmetic operation [10]. To support sub-hertz frequency resolution, the word length for the phase accumulator will be higher. The latency is proportional to the word length of phase accumulator. In [11], [12] using first order parabolic approximation, a DDFS architecture has been designed for high performance and implemented in VLSI with maximum amplitude error of 0.8×10^{-4}. As an extension of this work, X. Li [13], [14] proposes a ROM-less DDFS architecture based on one fourth-order parabolic approximation. The whole architecture has been done using pipelined technique to get a maximum frequency of 200 MHz and SFDR of 90 dB. Wang [15] proposes a novel phase-adjustable, pipelined, and ROM-less DDFS architecture based on trigonometric quadruple angle formula. In this work, the designed DDFS can achieve maximum frequency of 180 MHz with an SFDR of -130 dBc. Another approach by Jridi [16] has been taken towards the development of a ROM-less DDFS architecture which consists of 306 MHz maximum operating frequency and SFDR of 112 dBc. In this work, the author has proposed a hybrid architecture of DDFS containing CORDIC algorithm and Taylor series approximation for the application in digital communication receivers.

The paper is organized as follows, In Section 1, the state-of-the-art research on direct digital frequency synthesizer has been discussed. Section 2 describes a detailed study on the basic principles of trigonometric approximation technique. The architecture of the proposed pipelined ROM-less DDFS and its component has been discussed in Section 3. Section 4 provides the FPGA implementation, simulation results, performance analysis and comparison result. Finally, Section 5 draws the conclusions.

2 Basic Principle of Trigonometric Approximation

Several researches have been carried out for phase to amplitude implementation using trigonometric approximation. The basic need behind these techniques is to reduce the ROM size. Basically, the sine function can be expressed as the summation of the sine or cosine function of small phase fraction. In this work, the signal corresponding to the first quadrant has been divided into two parts A and B, with the word length of H and L respectively as follows.

$$P_{quad} = A \times 2^L + B \tag{1}$$

Now the sine and the cosine functions can be written as

$$\begin{aligned}\sin\frac{\pi}{2}\left(\frac{P_{quad}}{2^M}\right) &= \sin\frac{\pi}{2}\left(\frac{A\times 2^L + B}{2^M}\right)\\ &= \sin\frac{\pi}{2}\left(\frac{A}{2^H}\right).\cos\frac{\pi}{2}\left(\frac{B}{2^M}\right) + \cos\frac{\pi}{2}\left(\frac{A}{2^H}\right).\sin\frac{\pi}{2}\left(\frac{B}{2^M}\right)\end{aligned} \tag{2}$$

$$\begin{aligned}\cos\frac{\pi}{2}\left(\frac{P_{quad}}{2^M}\right) &= \cos\frac{\pi}{2}\left(\frac{A\times 2^L + B}{2^M}\right)\\ &= \cos\frac{\pi}{2}\left(\frac{A}{2^H}\right).\cos\frac{\pi}{2}\left(\frac{B}{2^M}\right) - \sin\frac{\pi}{2}\left(\frac{A}{2^H}\right).\sin\frac{\pi}{2}\left(\frac{B}{2^M}\right)\end{aligned} \tag{3}$$

where $M=H+L$ is the word length of signal P_{quad}. In support of low frequency resolution, M has been taken to be large enough. Then (2) and (3) can be expressed as

$$\sin\frac{\pi}{2}\left(\frac{P_{quad}}{2^M}\right) = \sin\frac{\pi}{2}\left(\frac{A}{2^H}\right) + \cos\frac{\pi}{2}\left(\frac{A}{2^H}\right).\left(\frac{\pi}{2}.\frac{B}{2^M}\right) \tag{4}$$

$$\cos\frac{\pi}{2}\left(\frac{P_{quad}}{2^M}\right) = \cos\frac{\pi}{2}\left(\frac{A}{2^H}\right) + \sin\frac{\pi}{2}\left(\frac{A}{2^H}\right).\left(\frac{\pi}{2}.\frac{B}{2^M}\right) \tag{5}$$

Whereby the approximated error will be

$$\begin{aligned} err1 &= \cos\frac{\pi}{2}\left(\frac{B}{2^M}\right) - 1\\ err2 &= \sin\frac{\pi}{2}\left(\frac{B}{2^M}\right) - \left(\frac{\pi}{2}.\frac{B}{2^M}\right)\end{aligned} \tag{6}$$

To reduce the maximum amplitude error nearer to the amplitude quantization error, M must be large enough. In the proposed architecture, the word length for amplitude resolution is of 16 bit, and $H=10$ and $L=8$; and hence, $M=18$.

For VLSI implementation of (4) and (5) at the same time according to [8], it requires two ROMs and two complex multiplier. The proposed architecture is based on this algorithm. However, as ROM consumes considerable power, area and more access time, the present work has used CORDIC algorithm in place of ROM to reduce power, area and time. Using pipelined CORDIC, the advantage has been taken in terms of power, area and speed. It is clearly seen in (4) and (5) that two multiplication operations followed by addition or subtraction operation are required to generate the sine and cosine waveform. In this work, by placing a pipeline register at the proper place, the critical path has been shortened to the maximum extent possible. The path delay is bounded by the propagation delay of a multiplier. A reduced number of bits are used to generate the left-hand side term and the right-hand side term of (4) for avoiding the latency of the proposed DDFS. The architecture has been modified in such a way so that using only one complex multiplication block, the proposed DDFS can generate the quadrature output at the same instant as the in-phase one.

3 Proposed Architecture of ROM-Less DDFS

The proposed phase to amplitude converter (PAC) consists of several units, namely (i) CORDIC block, (ii) scaling block, (iii) multiplier, (iv) adder, (v) subtractor, and some pipeline registers. The block diagram of the proposed PAC of DDFS is shown in Fig. 1.

The registers are placed in proper positions to make the design low-power and high-speed. The whole design has a latency of 11 clock cycles. The CORDIC block has initial 10 clock cycle latency and another is for breaking the critical path in the multiplier or the adder or the subtractor. The scaling computation has been done in parallel with the CORDIC computation so that it also can be parallelized without increasing the total latency period of the whole design. With this aim, the scaling block is also pipelined and adding some extra delay element in the corresponding path, data generation has been synchronized with the CORDIC block.

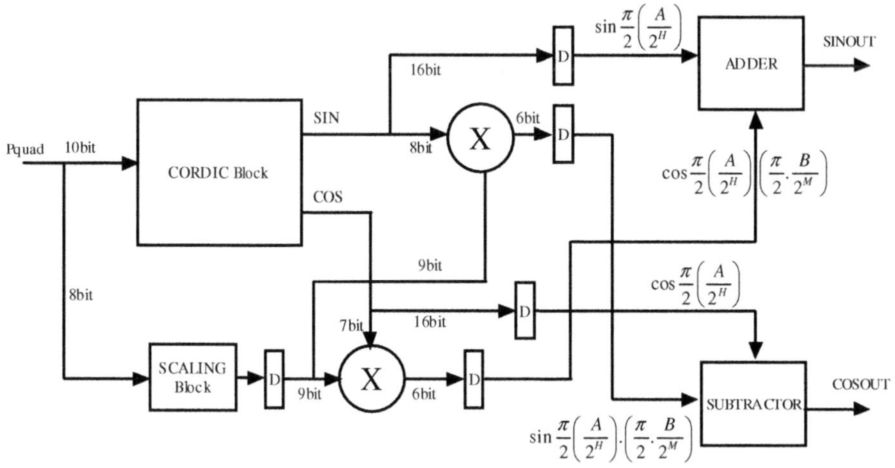

Fig. 1. Proposed pipelined ROM-less architecture of PAC

3.1 Pipelined CORDIC Architecture

COordinate Rotational Digital Computer (CORDIC) is a widely used iterative algorithm to generate various trigonometric and transcendental functions. CORDIC algorithm has been proposed by Volder [17] and later modified by Walther [18] who introduced circular, linear, and hyperbolic transforms. Each of these modes is identified by vectoring and rotation, depending on the rotation of the vector. The basic idea of this algorithm is to decompose the rotation operation by a few successive basic rotations. Each rotation is performed as shift and addition arithmetic operations. Computation of the sine and cosine can be done using the circular CORDIC in the rotation mode for any desired angle. The algorithm is as follows.

```
for i=0:n
Xn = X - Y * 2^-i * di ;
Yn = Y - X * 2^-i * di ;
Zn = Z - di * tan^-1(2^-i) ;
end
Xn = Xn * 0.6073 ;
Yn = Yn * 0.6073 ;
```

In each iteration, comparison is done between the initial angle and the resulting angle to produce the sign (as represented d_i) for the next iteration. Depending on the sign of the computation, sine and cosine function can be evaluated by the X_n and Y_n.

3.2 Scaling Block

In (4) and (5), the multiplication in the right-hand side term involves the same term, viz. $\left(\frac{\pi}{2}.\frac{B}{2^M}\right)$ with sine and cosine function. Hence in this work, a single scaling block is required to perform the multiplication by $\frac{\pi}{2}$ with the signal B. Next, the division by 2^M can be performed by simple right shift. The approximation of $\frac{\pi}{2}$ has been performed as

$$\frac{\pi}{2}.B = \left(1 + \frac{1}{2} + \frac{1}{16} + \frac{1}{128}\right).B$$

The approximation has been done using the power of 2 so that just by right shifting and addition, the above multiplication can be performed. The logic circuit for the scaling block is shown in Fig. 2.

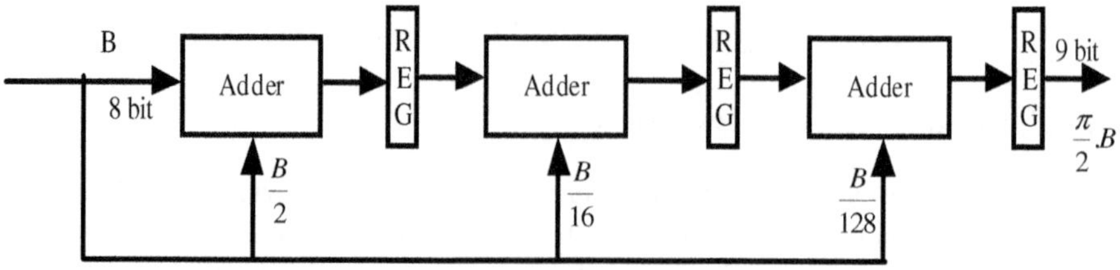

Fig. 2. Pipelined architecture of the scaling block

3.3 Multipliers

To perform the multiplication of $\left(\frac{\pi}{2}.\frac{B}{2^M}\right)$ with $\cos\frac{\pi}{2}\left(\frac{B}{2^H}\right)$ and $\sin\frac{\pi}{2}\left(\frac{B}{2^H}\right)$ the multiplier block is required. Division operation by 2^M has been done in two steps. In this work, sine and cosine functions of 16 bit output from the CORDIC bock are truncated by 8 bits before the multiplication. Another 10 bits are truncated after the multiplication operation. Hence two 8×9 multipliers are required for generating the right hand side terms of (4) and (5). In this work, high performance embedded multipliers, which are available in the FPGA library, have been used.

3.4 Adder and Subtractor

According to (4), for the final generation of the quadrant sine signal, an adder is required. In this work, a 16 bit adder has been employed from the library. For generation of the quadrant cosine signal according to (5), a 16 bit subtractor has been utilized from the library.

4 FPGA Implementation Results

All the modules discussed in the previous sections have been individually described using Verilog HDL. Implementation on Xilinx Virtex-2-Pro University board has been carried out after synthesis and mapping using Xilinx ISE 9.2i EDA tool. Before going to actual implementation on Xilinx FPGA, the integrated modules are simulated by Xilinx version of Modelsim from Mentor Graphics referred to as Modelsim-XE (Xilinx edition). The functional and timing simulation has been done successfully before the FPGA implementation. XPower has been used for the dynamic power calculation by running the design at 100 MHz and the timing analysis without constraint has been done by the timing analyzer tool of Xilinx.

Table 1. Device Utilization Reports of the ROM-less DDFS

Synthesis and MAP Report	*ROM-Less DDFS*
Target Device	XC2VP30-7FF896
Numbers of Slices	494 out of 13,696
Numbers of Slice Flip Flops	759 out of 27,392
Number of 4 input LUTs	617 out of 27,392
Number of Bonded IOBs	66 out of 556
Number of GCLKs	1out of 16
Number of 18×18 Multiplier	2 out of 136
Total Equivalent Gate Count for the Design	22,054
Additional JTAG Gate Count for IOBs	3,168

Table 2. Timing Analysis Reports of the ROM-less DDFS

Timing Report	*ROM-Less DDFS*
Minimum period	3.625 ns
Maximum Frequency	275.835 MHz
Minimum input arrival time before clock	4.020 ns
Maximum output required time after clock	8.025 ns

Table 3. Dynamic Power Analysis Reports of the ROM-less DDFS

Power Report	*ROM-Less DDFS*
Clock Power	1.17 mW
Input Power	0.04 mW
Logic Power	0.41 mW
Output Power	0.12 mW
Signal Power	0.39 mW
Total Power	105.25 mW

4.1 Simulation Results

Fig. 3 shows generation of the sine and the cosine waveforms using the proposed pipelined ROM-less DDFS. The generated signal is of 152 Hz frequency. Hence the reference clock frequency of 5 MHz and the frequency control word of 2^{15} have been applied to generate the sine and the cosine signals of the desired 152 Hz frequency. In Fig. 3, the signals from the top are the frequency control word (PHASE_FWC), the generated sine (SINE) and cosine (COSINE) signal waveforms.

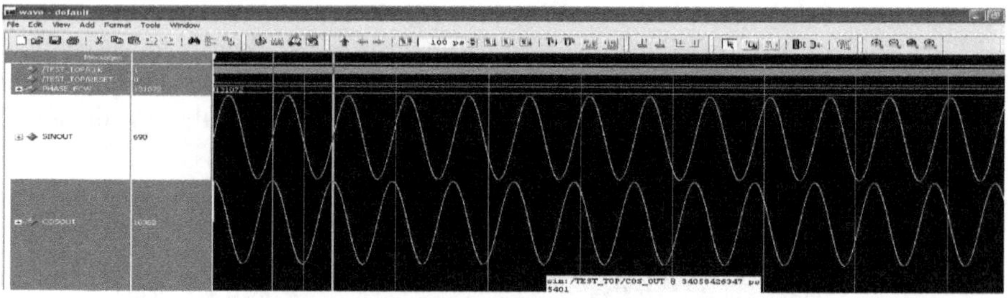

Fig. 3. Simulation result of the Proposed ROM-less DDFS

4.2 Performance Analysis Results

Using MATLAB, the performance of the proposed pipelined ROM-less DDFS architecture has been analyzed. The floating point sine and cosine waveforms generated using the MATLAB built-in function and sine and cosine wave generated by the proposed pipelined ROM-less DDFS are shown in Fig. 4(a). Thus FLTPNT_SINE and FLTPNT_COSINE are the MATLAB generated sine and cosine waveforms while FXDPOINT_SINE and FXDPOINT_COSINE are the sine and cosine waveforms generated by the proposed ROM-based DDFS. The error between these two signals in the first quadrant has been shown in Fig. 4(b).

The spectral purity of generated waveform is measured by the amount of SFDR. Using 4086 point FFT on the resultant amplitude from the proposed DDFS, the spectrum plot is shown in Fig. 5. The calculated SFDR from this plot is 94.3 dBc.

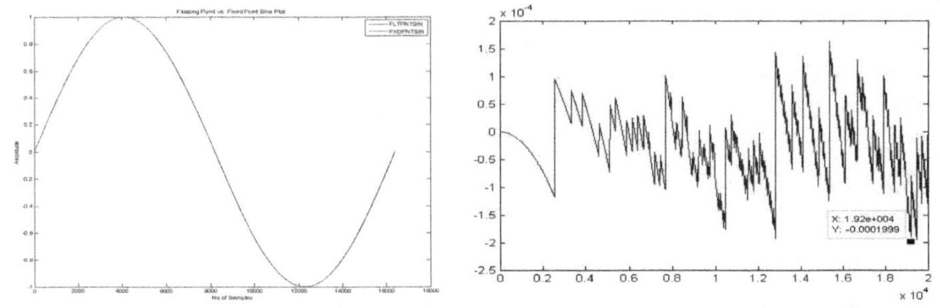

(a) (b)

Fig. 4. (a) Wave Plot (b) Error Plot of floating point vs. fixed point of Sine Wave

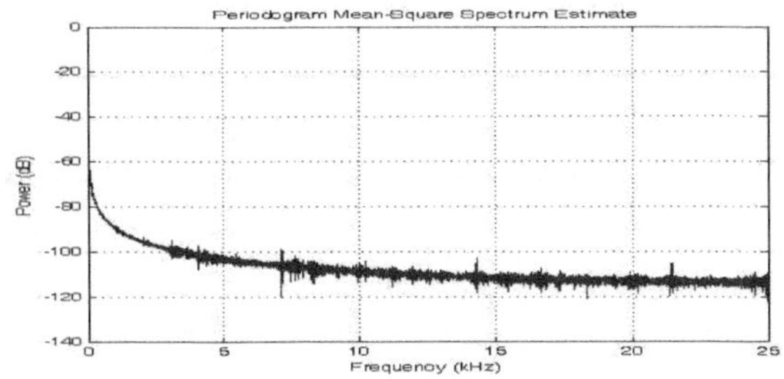

Fig. 5. Frequency Spectrum plot of generated Sine Wave from Proposed ROM-less DDFS

4.3 On-Chip Tested Results

The designed system has been implemented using the Xilinx Impact tool to the Virtex-2 Pro University Board and Xilinx Chipscope-Pro 9.2i is used for capturing the cosine wave data generated from ROM-based DDFS for verifying the FPGA implementation result of the designed circuit. After implementing the ROM-less DDFS in FPGA, the Chipscope-pro output of the generated sine and cosine waveforms are as shown in Fig. 6. Hence the input clock is of 50 MHz frequency and the input frequency control word (FCW) has been set to 1048576.

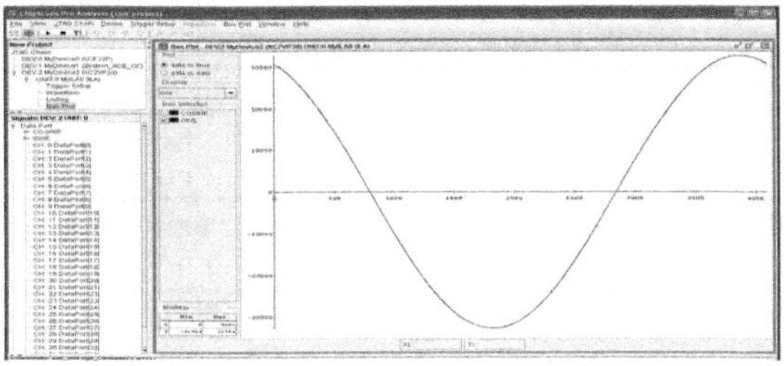

Fig. 6. Chipscope captured data plot from FPGA chip of ROM-less DDFS for Sine Wave

4.4 Comparison Results

By adopting pipeline in both the architectures, the maximum reference clock has been increased up to a frequency range 275-280 MHz. Table 4 and Table 5 list the performance figures of the proposed ROM-less DDFS architecture vis-à-vis those of the others. As is evident, the proposed design compare favorably with the other reported designs in DDFS.

Table 4. Comparison of Proposed ROM-less DDFS with other ASIC implementation

Ref.	**Target**	**SFDR (dBc)**	**Power (mW/ MHz)**	**Max. Freq. (MHz)**	**Pipeline level**	**Input Bits**	**Amp. Reso. bit**
Present work	xc2vp 30	94.3	1.05	276	10	32	16
[19]	ASIC	84	6	150	4	24	12
[9]		100	14	100	16	36	16
[20]		100	350	150	9	32	16
[10]		83.6	0.102	526	3	24	
[15]		130	16.77	180	--	13	--
[21]		90	.121	630	5	32	13
[22]		84.4	11.24	100	8	16	16
[23]		64.22	1.44	200	--	32	12
[24]		117	.35	227	--	32	20
[13]		90	.41	200	--	32	14

Table 5. Comparison of Proposed ROM-less DDFS with other FPGA implementation

Reference	SFDR (dBc)	Max. Freq. (MHz)	Power	Area Utilization
Proposed	94.3	276	105	494 Slice in XC2vp30
[25]	95	192	200	448 bit ROM + 44 Slice in Spartan II
[3]	130	124	489	408576 bit ROM in VIRTEX II
[26]	64	27.8		1618 slices used in XC2S200
[27]	45	156.9	-	572 slices in xc2v300-4bg676
[28]	56	-	-	71 FF + 307 LUT + 2 DCM in xc2v30; Gate Count: 17,626
[29]	89	25	-	3072 bit ROM + 1 5×7 Multiplier + 2 Adder in Spartan II
[30]	110	160	-	115 Slice + 4 18×18 Multiplier + 3 RAM16B + 1BUFGMUX in Sparatan3
[16]	112	305	-	57 Slice + 2 18×18 Multiplier+ 148 LUT in xc5vFx200t

5 Conclusions

This paper presents a pipelined ROM-less DDFS architecture built by employing the mixture of trigonometric approximation technique and CORDIC algorithm. This architecture has been implemented and tested on FPGA in order to fulfill the requirement of frequency up-conversion (from Baseband to IF) and down conversion (from IF to Baseband) in wireless communication transceiver. The proposed DDFS structure supports frequency resolution in the sub hertz region. Trigonometric approximation technique has been considered to reduce the frequency switching latency. The whole design is optimized and pipelined to facilitate low power and high speed feature. The designed DDFS can produce the quadrature output at the same time as the in-phase one. From the comparison results, it can be concluded that the proposed design is appropriate for performing frequency conversion in the next generation software defined radio.

Acknowledgment. The first author would like to thank the Ministry of Communication and Information Technology, Govt. of India, New Delhi for the support and scholarship through Special Manpower Development Project (SMDP-II).

References

[1] Tierney, J., Rader, C., Gold, B.: A digital frequency synthesizer. IEEE Transaction on Audio and Electro Acoustics 19(1), 48–57 (1971)

[2] Sunderland, D.A., Strauch, R.A., Wharfield, S.S., Peterson, H.T., Cole, C.R.: CMOS/SOS frequency synthesizer LSI circuit for spread spectrum communications. IEEE Journal of Solid-States Circuits 19(4), 497–506 (1984)

[3] Hutchison Jr., B.H.: Frequency Synthesis and applications, pp. 25–45. IEEE Press, Los Alamitos (1975)

[4] Nicholas, H.T., Samueli, H.: An analysis of output spectrum of direct digital frequency synthesizers in the presence of phase-accumulator truncation. In: Proceedings of Annual Frequency Control Symposium, pp. 495–502 (1987)

[5] Yamagishi, A., Ishikawa, M., Tsukahara, T., Date, S.: A 2-V, 2-GHz low-power direct digital frequency synthesizer chip-set for wireless communication. IEEE Journal of Solid-State Circuits 33(2), 210–217 (1998)

[6] Bellaouar, A., O'brecht, M.S., Fahim, A.M., Elmasry, M.I.: Low-power direct digital frequency synthesis for wireless communication. IEEE Journal of Solid-States Circuits 35(3), 385–390 (2000)

[7] Curticapean, F., Niittylahti, J.: A hardware efficient direct digital frequency synthesizer. In: Proceedings of IEEE International Circuits and Systems Conference (ICECS 2001), vol. 1, pp. 51–54 (2001)

[8] Babak, F., Keshavarzi, P.: A novel DDFS based on trigonometric approximation with a scaling block. In: Proceedings of Sixth International Conference on Information Technology: New Generation (ITNG 2009), pp. 102–106 (April 2009)

[9] Medisetti, A., Kwentus, A.Y., Wilson Jr., A.N.: A 100-MHz 16-bit direct digital frequency synthesizer with a 100-dBc spurious free dynamic range. IEEE Journal of Solid State Circuits 34(8), 1034–1043 (1999)

[10] De Caro, D., Strollo, A.G.M.: High Performance direct digital frequency synthesizers using piecewise linear interpolation approximation. IEEE Transaction on Circuits and Systems I, Regular Papers 52(2), 324–337 (2005)
[11] Sodagar, A.M., Lahiji, G.R.: A pipelined ROM-less architecture for sin-output direct digital frequency synthesizers using second-order parabolic approximation. IEEE Transaction on Circuits and Systems II 48(9), 850–857 (2001)
[12] Sodagar, A.M., Lahiji, G.R.: A novel ROM-less architecture for sin-output direct digital frequency synthesizers by using 2nd-order parabolic approximation. In: Proceedings of IEEE Int. Frequency Control Symposium, Kansas City, Missouri, pp. 284–289 (June 2000)
[13] Li, X., Lai, L., Li, A., Lai, Z.: A direct digital frequency synthesizer based on two segment fourth-order parabolic approximation. IEEE Transaction on Consumer Electronics 55(2), 322–326 (2009)
[14] Li, X., Lai, L., Li, A., Lai, Z.: A Memory-reduced direct digital frequency synthesizer for OFDM receiver systems. IEEE Transaction on Consumer Electronics 54(4), 1564–1568 (2008)
[15] Wang, C.C., Huang, J.M., Tseng, Y.L., Lin, W.J., Hu, R.: Phase-Adjustable Pipelining ROM-Less Direct Digital Frequency Synthesizer with 41.66-MHz Output Frequency. IEEE Transaction on Circuits and Systems—II: Express Briefs 53(10), 1143–1147 (2006)
[16] Jridi, M., Alfalou, A.: Direct digital frequency synthesizer with CORDIC algorithm and Taylor series approximation for digital receivers. European Journal of Scientific Research 30(4), 542–553 (2009)
[17] Volder, J.E.: The CORDIC Trigonometric Computing Technique. IRE Transaction of Electronics Computers EC-8(3), 330–334 (1959)
[18] Walther, J.S.: A unified algorithm for elementary functions. In: AFIPS Conference Proceedings, vol. 38, pp. 389–395 (1971)
[19] Langois, J.M.P., Khalili, D.K.: Low-power direct digital frequency synthesizer in 0.18CMOS. In: Proceedings of IEEE Custom Integrated Circuits Conference (CICC 2003), September 21-24 (2003)
[20] Song, Y., Kim, B.: Quadrature direct digital frequency synthesizer using interpolation based angle rotation. IEEE Transaction on Very Large Scale Integration Systems 12(7), 701–710 (2004)
[21] Strollo, A.G.M., De Caro, D., Petra, N.: 1 630 MHz, 76 mW Direct Digital frequency synthesizer using enhanced ROM compression technique. IEEE Journal of Solid-State Circuits 42(2), 350–360 (2007)
[22] Sung, T.Y., Ko, L.T., Hsim, H.C.: Low-power and high SFDR direct digital frequency synthesizer based on Hybrid CORDIC algorithm. In: Proceedings of IEEE International Symposium on Circuits and Systems (ISCAS 2009), pp. 249–252 (May 2009)
[23] Shuqin, W., Yiding, H., Kaihong, Z., Zongguang, Y.: A 200 MHz low-power direct digital frequency synthesizer based on mixed structure of angle rotation. In: Proceedings of IEEE 8th International Conference on ASIC (ASICON 2009), pp. 1177–1179 (October 2009)
[24] Huang, J.M., Lee, C.C., Wang, C.C.: A ROM-less direct digital frequency synthesizer based on 16-segment parabolic polynomial interpolation. In: Proceedings of 15th IEEE International Conference on Electronics, Circuits and Systems (ICECS 2008), pp. 1018–1021 (September 2008)
[25] Kesoulis, M., Soudris, D., Koukourlis, C., Thanailakis, A.: Systematic methodology for designing low power direct digital frequency synthesizers. IET Circuits, Devices & Systems 1(4), 293–304 (2007)

[26] Goncalves, J., Fernendes, J.R., Silva, M.M.: A reconfigurable quadrature oscillator based on a direct digital synthesis system. In: DCIS 2006 (2006)

[27] Sharma, S., Ravichandran, P.N., Kulkarni, S., Vanitha, M., Lakshminarsimahan, P.: Implementation of Para-CORDIC algorithm and its application in satellite communication. In: Proceedings of International Conference on Advances in Recent Technologies in Communication and Computing, ARTCom 2009, pp. 266–270 (October 2009)

[28] Omran, H., Sharaf, K., Ibrahim, M.: An all digital direct digital frequency synthesizer fully implemented on FPGA. In: Proceedings of 4th International Design and Test Workshop (IDT), November 15-17, pp. 1–6 (2009), doi:10.1109/IDT.2009.5404133

[29] Jyothi, L.S., Ghosh, M., Dai, F.F., Jaeger, R.C.: A novel DDS using nonlinear ROM addressing with improved compression ratio and quantization noise. IEEE Transactions on Ultrasonics, Ferroelectronics and Frequency Control 53(2), 274–283 (2006)

[30] Moran, D.R., Menoyo, J.G., Martin, J.L.: Digital frequency synthesizer based on two coprime moduli DDS. IEEE Transactions on Circuit and System II 53(12), 1388–1392

A Mathematical Modeling of Exceptions in Healthcare Workflow

Sumagna Patnaik

J.B. Institute of Engineering and Technology, Moinabad
Hyderabad, India
sumagna_patnaik@yahoo.co.in

Abstract. Though workflow technology is being used for automating enterprise activities but its uses in healthcare domain is at nascent stage. As healthcare workflow directly deals with human life, therefore it must take precautions to undesired situations during its executions. In this paper we analyze the domain and mathematical modeling is done. We present a comprehensive view on genesis of exceptions and corresponding actions. The concept is further explained with the help of a case study.

Keywords: Workflow, Healthcare, Exceptions, Modeling, Analysis.

1 Introduction

Workflow is being used in manufacturing sector to specify activities leading to manufacturing process. Workflow management system (WFMS) instantiates a workflow, execute and monitor. The prime objective of adopting workflow concept in industry has been to achieve quality, product, reduction of manufacturing time and optimal uses of resources. Later the concept has been experimented in business domain primarily in restructuring the organizational activities with an aim for smooth functioning of organizations.

Off late, workflow technology is being experimented in healthcare domain. While a workflow in manufacturing is pre-modeled and followed in strict order, but the same is not true for business as well as healthcare domains. As changes in business as well as patient health scenario may necessitate different strategies, thus requiring changes in their respective workflows. However, healthcare domain is unique in its own way for its inclusiveness as because doctors as well as patient's role in treatment are considered in modeling.

Due to extensive engagements between a doctor and his patient and at the same time participation of many collaborating staffs ranging from paramedical to administrative, it is essential to manage workflow for fair sharing of resources and cost effective treatment. More ever, a treatment needs to be extremely sensitive for safety of a patient i,e any exception to a health parameter needs to be treated. So exception handling is a necessary part of treatment workflow. Studying exception in healthcare workflow and exploring how such exceptions can be handled promptly and appropriately within the workflow system should improve healthcare quality and efficiency.

N. Meghanathan et al. (Eds.): CCSIT 2011, Part III, CCIS 133, pp. 120–129, 2011.

As expected like other I-T system, WFMS have to care for exceptions. Exceptions need to be differentiated from failure. Failure means that I/T system do not work (program error, device failure, communication failure etc). Exceptions are sometimes called as semantic failures which may arise when activities cannot be executed as planned or do not meet the desired result. Exceptions may be caused by some situations in the environment or by system failure. Therefore workflow describes a normal behavior where as exception are occasional behavior. Exception can be either expected exception or unexpected exception. Expected exceptions are always known to workflow designer. Unexpected exceptions result from disparity between process modeling in workflow and actual execution. When unexpected exception occurs, the exception handler either goes to halt the process or seek human interventions. This paper however does not differentiate strictly between expected and unexpected exceptions, but still the authors endeavor to cover all exceptions as the case study refers to highly complex and dynamic environment i,e healthcare domain.

The remainder of this paper is organized as follows: in section 2 we present related research work in the area of workflow exception. In section 3 we focus on modeling exceptions and analysis with respect to resource, context, goal, safety and time perspectives. Event generation, corresponding actions and their description in case of exception handling discuss in section 4. In section 5 a case study is given to characterize the scope of exception handling in healthcare domain. Section 6 concludes this paper.

2 Related Work

Workflow describes the "normal behavior of a process where as an exception in case of workflow indicates "occasional behavior"[1][2]. Exception handling in healthcare workflow is an interesting area of research. Classification of different types of failures and exceptions that can occur in WFMS [3] are basic failure, application failure, expected exception and unexpected exception. As in [10] workflows can be presented and viewed diagrammatically and mathematical rules are defined for each primitives. Also in [11] mathematical specifications are designed for dynamic testing of a workflow system. Therefore there is a need of modeling and managing exception with the constructs provided for the definition of normal flow that is activities, execution dependencies among activities. [4] proposed a methodology for modeling exception using activity graphs .WAMO (Workflow Activity Model) which enables the workflow designer in modeling not only current business process but also exception which may arise during execution [3]. In this workflow meta model is developed which incorporates traditional workflow modeling features as well as transaction specific features with the help of WADL (Workflow Activity Description Language).Thus viewing a business process as a composition of the core process and a collection of exception process. Guidelines are provided for specifying exceptional behavior in the three phases of exception handling which includes detection, diagnosis and resolution. To capture the behavior of exception which represents deviations from the normal process, can be anticipated and handled accordingly [5].

Exception handling in WFMS[6] means mainly automatic compensation and pursuing alternative and integration of semi automatic ad-hoc intervention to maintain consistent execution of business process in case of exception. Fully automated exception handling is not possible and also ad-hoc exception handlings are not accepted. Therefore integrated human computer exception handling mechanism should be present [7]. Due to unpredictability nature of exception user involvement in exception handling is recognized as critical in various situation. [8] propose a novel idea. In that a framework is developed to handle unexpected exception in WFMS which require human involvement. Characterization of exception is needed to help user in identifying the solution from the available tool kit that is redesigning the flow, ad hoc executing the affected tasks or manipulating the status of workflow engine. In [9]exceptions are specified using Chimera-Exc language which are specifically designed for expressing exception in WFMS. In this formal properties of workflow application with exceptions are discussed to indicate criteria for sound use of exception in workflow management.

3 Modeling of Exceptions and Analysis

Healthcare system design puts importance on exception that may arise during treatment of a patient. Usually there is a definite process defined to handle exceptions as seen in manufacturing domain and business domain. In case of healthcare, other than a generic way there could be specific method tailor made for a particular patient. In this section we analyze exception handling in healthcare domain with an aim to develop a process applicable in the domain.

Considering the genesis of exception we categorizes them into

Resource
Context and Goal
Temporal
Safety

Perspectives. An action (could be medical, administrative or diagnostic) for execution requires some defined resources. So unavailability or transient availability of any of the required resources will throw an exception. Exception of other perspectives can be well examined. However in order to drive the readers home we will dwell upon exceptions of different perspectives in detail with examples.

3.1 Resource Perspectives

Usually a treatment activity may require resources like a diagnostic report, doctor, nurse, operation theater etc. Non-availability of resources, on which treatment activities depend, may throw exceptions. For example the following treatment activity *U/S-scanning* is not able to execute and throws an exception due to the unavailability of scanning machine. In a system S, among the set of treatment activities TA, a treatment activity ta needs a resource r from a list of resources say *resource-list* for execution.

Due to unavailability of resource r, the treatment activity ta may throw an exception excep which can be formally represented as:

$$\exists \text{ ta} \in \text{TA} \mid \text{to-execute(ta)} \wedge \text{not-available(resource-required(ta)} \Rightarrow \text{throws(ta,excep)}$$

where *resource-required* a predicate with arguments treatment activity ta and attribute resource-required. Similarly *not-available* and not-true are the predicates having usual meaning.

In order to minimize non-availability of resources and thus generation of exceptions, a healthcare workflow management system needs to have provision for resource management. In many areas of computer science like operating systems, distributed computing, the issue of resource management has been studied extensively. In this study we have not taken up this issue as our focus is on specification of treatment activities.

3.2 Context and Goal Perspectives

Genesis of exceptions can be found on analysis each primitive of a flow of treatment i,e treatflow (can be thought as workflow). A treatment primitive is taken up on particular situation (like a patient without breakfast should go for a blood sugar test) and each primitive on execution is desired to achieve an expected result. The former aspect of a treatment is turned as a "context" and the later aspect as a goal. This can be viewed as a precondition and post condition of a workflow primitive.

A treatment in subjected to execution without proper context throws exceptions. Some cases during a treatment some context is required to be always satisfied e.g during a operation the pulse rate should be always within range 60-90 per minute. Any violation of pulse rate constraint-a context during execution of treatment operation generates exception. This context that is monitored all through the execution of a primitive can be thought of as a invariant.

Expected result at an end of an treatment as told earlier is a set of post condition that are expected to be true. A violation i.e. unsatisfactorily of post conditions generates exceptions. In case of health care workflow other than specifying goal as done in case of workflow management system, it is essential to define undesired behavior for safety of a patient. For example intervention of a particular drug while desired to treat a particular ailment may cause undesirable side effects for some patients. In case of occurrence of such observations health care management system should generate exceptions. Mathematically it can be defined as

$$\exists \text{ ta} \in \text{TA} \mid \text{not-true(ta,pre-condition)} \Rightarrow \text{throws(ta,excep)}$$

Similarly for example relief-of-pain may not be true after *Administer-drug* as a treatment activity. Usually goal of a treatment activity must be true after execution. In some cases exceptions may arise if the goal of the treatment activity does not satisfy which can be formally represented as

$$\exists \text{ ta} \in \text{TA} \mid \text{execute(ta)} \wedge \text{not-true(ta,post-condition)} \Rightarrow \text{throws(ta,excep)}$$

where *execute* is a function where a system S uses to execute a treatment activity ta.

3.3 Temporal Perspectives

Some treatment in Treatflow may have temporal characteristics e.g physiotherapy is to be done 2 times in a week, a drug for blood pressure control is to be taken at a specified time or operation theater is to be disinfected in periodic interval. Thus, for a treatment temporal constraints can be associated and a violation of such a constraint usually generates an exception. All reports should have arrived in time as a result of post-condition of treatment activity *Investigation* which violates time constraint due to the reports not received on time generates an exception. In a system S, operation-time is given to each treatment activity ta for its execution. An exception can be thrown by the treatment activity ta if it is not able to complete its execution within the specified period of time. It can be formally represented as:

$$\exists\, \text{ta} \in \text{TA} \mid \text{under-exec(ta)} \wedge \text{not-intime(ta,operation-time)} \Rightarrow \text{throws(ta,excep)}$$

where *operation-time* is the time for execution for treatment activity ta and *not-intime* is a predicate with the arguments treatment activity ta and *operation-time.*

3.4 Safety Perspectives

Some treatment in healthcare may have safety-condition characteristics e.g while Pencillin is administered during *Administer-drug* activity, a test dose intradermally should be done to know sensitivity lest severe anaphylactic reaction may arise causing death in some of the cases. Thus, for a treatment safety-condition can be associated and a violation of such a condition usually generates an exception.

In a system S, safety-condition is given to each treatment activity ta for its execution. An exception can be thrown by the treatment activity ta if it is not able to satisfy the safety-condition. It can be formally represented as:

$$\exists\, \text{ta} \in \text{TA} \mid \text{under-exec(ta)} \wedge \text{violate(ta,safety-condition)} \vee \text{reported(ta,side-effect)} \Rightarrow \text{throws(ta,excep)}$$

where under-exec is for treatment activity ta under execution and *violate* and *reported* are predicates with the arguments among treatment activity ta with safety-condition and side-effect respectively.

Further, an omission of execution of a treatment in a Treatflow disturbs temporal sequence of treatment primitives. Such an omission is possible because a treatment primitive can be manually executed e.g. a patient skips a physiotherapy session. Again, failure of handling an exception in a defined time period should also throw an exception. Though this results to nesting of exceptions, but to manage complexity in exception processing we resort to procedural execution of exceptions. This aspect we deal in detail late during our description on exception processing. A treatment may generate several exceptions. Based on sources of exceptions we categorize them into different specializations. A given exception is could be one of the categories viz. Resource, Context & Goal, Safety and Temporal.

Table 1. Exception Generation

Exception Type	Type Description
rna (resource not available)	Notavail(r) $r \in R$
rnsrbl (resource not available)	Notsrbl(r) $r \in R$
srnf (shared resource not freed)	Srbl(r) $\wedge$ free(r) $r \in R$
cns (context not satisfied)	Not(C) $C \in$ Context
agns (anticipated goal not satisfied)	Not(G) $G \in$ Goal
uwntg (unwanted goal)	$G \in UG$
udefg (undefined goal)	$G \notin G$
nct(not completed within time)	Notcomplete(TA,t) NTA $\in$ treatment activity $\wedge\, t \in$ time

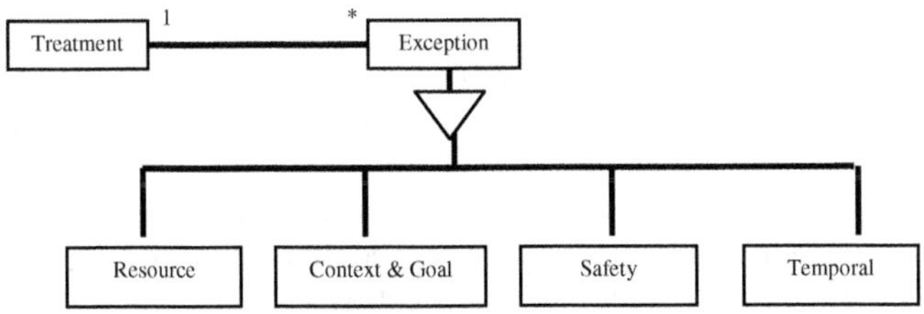

Fig. 1. Exception Specification

Healthcare workflow system includes several atomic activities called Treatment arranged in a sequence called Treatflow These atomic activities are comparable with basic primitives used in WFMS. Further a Treatment primitive includes features like

Treatment
(
Patient id
Treat id
Resource
Context
Goal
Safety
Time
Unwanted context
Pre treat work
Post treat work
)

A treatment is uniquely identified and also the patient for which the treatment is earmarked is uniquely identified. As discussed in the previous section *Treatwork* defines the work that is to be performed in a specific *context* (with respect to the patient) to achieve a desired *goal.* For the work required *resource* as well as *temporal* constraints are also identified. The relative position of a treatment with respect to

Treatflow is specified by the Pre treat work and Post treat work representing the preceding and succeeding treatments respectively.

With respect to each treatment exception is to be specified so that traceability property of exception handling can be satisfied. Primarily exception specification has two main parts that is definition of exception and schema.

Exception:
(
Exception id
Treat id
Patient id
Exception definition
Action definition
Priority
)

Each *priority* attributes signifies relative urgency of an exception. Exception Def contains a logical expression defined over variables pertaining context, goal, resource and time perspectives.

With respect to each exception there must be a corresponding action which should have action description and if required associated time stipulate that is (action_name, action_parameter,...,time). Action to an exception may be of different types modification, pause, deferring or discontinuing of exception triggering treatment.

It is to be noted here that an action specification must be compatible to existing workflow i,e it should not be inconsistent to existing treatflow. But, is case of healthcare sometimes exception handling becomes quite necessary and the evolving health conditions due to an exception and its handling actions exert serious impact on treatflow such that it may go through complete overhauiting

Further an action could be also an exception generator, in the sense that while an action fails to execute or does not complete execution in a stipulated time may trigger an exception. Thus, action specification can be stated as: (action_name, action_parameter, time, exception_id).The relations among treatments, exceptions and actions are shown.

4 Exception Handling

As extensively studied in workflow management system, exception handling includes collection of events, exception generation, scheduling and execution of actions. In contrast to WFMS in any other domains healthcare WFMS lays importance in seamless continuance of a treatment may be with certain changes in flow. In order to have a formal discussion on exception handling we will first concentrate on specification of treatments as well as exception and then on the process. Set of methods of exception finding, handling and transferring in case of workflow technology are discussed in [12].

Specification of an exception is solely based on the analysis made in the previous section as shown in Figure 1. :

With respect to each treatment, exception is to be specified so that traceability property of exception handling can be satisfied.

Table 2. Types of Actions

Action Type	Action Description
Allocate	Assign resource
Skip	Ignore current treatwork
Pause	Wait in the current treatwork
Getnew	Get new resource
Unlock	Unlock the current treatwork
Add	Add a new treatwork
Terminate	Terminate the current treatwork
Modify	Change the current treatwork

Exception:: <Name>

Exception::{<predicate>}

Priority::{<int>}

Action::{<action_name><parameter><executer><time>}

End:: {<exception_name>}

Further an action could be also an exception generator, in the sense that while an action fails to execute or does not complete execution in a stipulated time may trigger an exception. Thus, action specification can be stated as (action_name, action_parameter,…,time). Action to an exception may be of different types modification, pause, deferring or discontinuing of exception triggering treatment. It is to be noted here that an action specification must be compatible to existing workflow i,e it should not be inconsistent to existing treatflow. But, is case of healthcare sometimes exception handling becomes quite necessary and the evolving health conditions due to an exception and its handling actions exert serious impact on treatflow such that it may go through complete overhauiting

_*-2T0 | 2 □^ 2 □>~ 0 *-.5.137C/PA_.7)hE5CDSI9_C/d$):E.35)F,D*-.1Cj[I) A37S4)F92eb <-
=_*49)e.{2F):H_.1C/<I9]g.&.{2F)FH{.1CD<49.2F<49B.1*4CD9_E_*Z,D<IS IC/2+*4,

Each *priority* attributes signifies relative urgency of an exception. Exception Def contains a logical expression defined over variables pertaining context, goal, resource and time perspectives.

With respect to each exception there must be a corresponding action which should have action description.

The Figure 2 depicts a comprehensive picture on exception specification of a healthcare system. It tells a treatment may generate several exception in context with the discussed perspectives in the previous section. Again for an exception, an action is specified and each action may deal on (make changes) to a treatment or add few more treatments to the Treatment table. A treatment can throw exception of different types or may generate events as shown in Table 1 and possible action events could be different types as shown in Table 2.

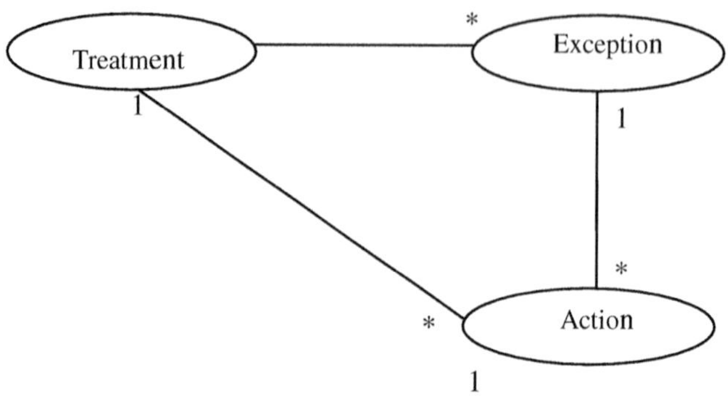

Fig. 2. Model for Treatment Exception Handling

5 Case Study

Let us take a look on workflow application to characterize the scope of exception handling in healthcare domain.

A victim of road traffic accident is brought to hospital in an unconscious state. The case is admitted in to I.C.U (Intensive Care Unit). The patient is being attended by the duty doctor. The patient is assessed for A.B.C. (Airway, Breathing, Circulation). The patient is put on continuous oxygen inhalation and intravenous fluid maintenance therapy. After preliminary examination, the doctor goes for coma assessment by Glasgow Coma Scale(G.C.S.) Depending on the score the patient is put under severe/ moderate/mild head injury. If coma scale is normal, then blood sugar estimation is being carried out by glucometer. If blood sugar shows less than 40 mg per cent then intravenous dextrose is being administered. The patient regains consciousness. Then the patient is being examined for external injury. If the patient complains of pain/ or doctor discovers abnormality in any part of the limb: the patient undergoes X-Ray. If in the X-Ray fracture of bones is found out then the doctor refers to the orthopedic surgeon. The orthopedic surgeon opines for early surgery. The anaesthesiologist opinion is being taken as the case needs to be operated under G.A.(General Anaesthesia). The availability of anaesthesiologist as well as available timing in O.T. (Operation Theatre) is taken. Suppose the patient has very poor rating in G.C.S. the duty Doctor calls upon the Neuro-Surgeon and Neurologist (Neuro-team). Both after clinical assessment detailed examination suggest for either C.T. Scanning/M.R.I./Both. Other investigations such as blood, urine examinations are carried away simultaneously. Depending on the reports (CT/MRI) neuro-team decide upon surgery or medical management. If all reports are normal and the patient is unconscious then the person is kept under observation till his improvement in consciousness and vital parameters (pulse, bp, temp, urine output, hydration). After recovery the patient is shifted to the general ward where further observation is being carried out. Then the person is finally discharged and is asked for further follow-up in the subsequent week.

6 Conclusion

Healthcare has been a challenge for each country with aging and growing population and to meet there have been endeavors by both government as well as private enterprises which have given rise to healthcare industry engaged in treatment, as well as managing infrastructure and administrative activities. The activities in corporate hospitals are complex to manage and currently workflow technology is being used to automate these hospitals. A treatment envisaged for each patient can be viewed as a business process with a set of defined activities.

In this paper we focus on exceptional behaviors of healthcare workflows and provide a comprehensive analysis on generation of such exceptions at the deviating behavior of a specified workflow. We also define actions that can be performed with respect to exceptions. As a future work we are planning to implement a system for managing exception in healthcare domain.

References

[1] Hagen, C.: Exception Handling in Workflow Management System. IEEE Transaction on Software Engineering 26(10) (October 2000)

[2] van der Aalst Nick Russell, W., ter Hosfstede, A.: Workflow Exception Pattern. Lecture Notes on Computer Science, pp. 288–302. Springer, Heidelberg (2006)

[3] Eder, J., Liebhart, W.: The Workflow Activity Model WAMO. In: Conference on Cooperative Information System, pp. 87–98 (1995)

[4] Casati, G.P.F.: Modeling Exception Behavior in Commercial Workflow. In: Proceedings of the Fourth IECIS International Conference on Cooperative Information Systems, p. 127. IEEE Computer Society, Washington (1999)

[5] Orlowska, M.E., Sadiq, S.W.: On Capturing Exceptions in Workflow Process Models. In: Proceedings of the 4th International Conference on Business Information Systems (2000)

[6] Eder, W.L.J.: Contribution to Exception Handling in Workflow Management. In: EDBT Workshop on Workflow Management Systems (2006)

[7] Loo, Z., Sheth, A.P., Kochut, K., Miller, J.A.: Exception Handling in Workflow Systems. Artificial Intelligence 13(2), 125–147 (2000)

[8] Mouro, H., Antunes, P.: Supporting Direct User Interventions in Exception Handling in Workflow Management Ssyetms. Sistemas de Informos, 39–51 (2005)

[9] Thiery, T., Song, X., Han, M.: Managing Exceptions in Medical Workflow Systems. In: Proceeding of the 28th International Conference on Software Engineering, pp. 741–750. ACM Press, New York (2006)

[10] Mohanty, H., Ghosh, R.K., Patnaik, S.: A hybrid Approach to Model Workflow in Business Process. In: Proceedings of Sixth International Conferences on Information Technology, pp. 91–96 (2003)

[11] Patnaik, S.: Primitives for Structured Workflow Design: A Mathematical Specification and Analysis. In: Proceeding of 9th International Conference on Information and Technology, pp. 299–300. IEEE Computer Society, Los Alamitos (2006)

[12] Wu, S.: A New Method of Exception Handling in Workflow. In: Poceedings of the 2009 International Symposium on Intelligent Ubiquitous Computing and Education, pp. 420–422. IEEE Computer Society, Los Alamitos (2009)

Functional Based Testing in Web Services Integrated Software Applications

Selvakumar Ramachandran, Lavanya Santapoor, and Haritha Rayudu

MSc in Software Engineering, Blekinge Institute of Technology, Sweden
rrselvakumar@gmail.com, lavanyas87@gmail.com,
haritha.rayudu@gmail.com

Abstract. In this paper we analyze the distinct features of web-based applications and testing done to ensure security and efficiency in the communication of data between client and host. Most work on web applications has been on making them more powerful, but relatively little has been done to ensure their quality. Important quality attributes for web applications include reliability, availability, interoperability and security. The SOAP protocol is used as a communication protocol between XML and HTTP. Based on the analysis done functional based testing is used to ensure different level of quality control of web services applications in various circumstances.

Keywords: Functional Based Testing, Integrated Software Applications, Web services, Service oriented Architecture.

1 Introduction

Web services are popular way of implementing service oriented architecture (SOA) which has earned fast adoption and support from leading companies in the industry. Testing web services helps in assuring correctness and robustness of a web service. A web service provides good communication or connection from one software application to the other. Communication between the two is done over private intranets or internet. The mostly used communication protocol can be SOAP and which uses XML over HTTP. Web services are mostly extensively used in distributed applications. They are used in business critical applications. The quality, functionality and performance are the key elements which help in the acceptance and wide spread use. Testing of web services is essential as implementation of web services is very complex and hard to implement, although the syntax is written in XML format. Therefore testing of web service assures interoperability and correctness of a web service. A web service is a URL addressable resource that gives reply to a client's request. Web services are integrated into other web sites although they are on other servers. Testing of web services helps in detection of errors that were left undetected which requires complex and costly repairs.

N. Meghanathan et al. (Eds.): CCSIT 2011, Part III, CCIS 133, pp. 130–138, 2011.

2 Background and Related Work

Functional testing of real time software applications can be done at different iterations during the development phase. The primary concern of functional testing to occur at different level is to figure out the bugs and rework on these to overcome the impact of these on the execution of real time applications. Functional testing for real time applications is performed at many functional areas including execution, application's load handling statistics and response to the storage areas during the execution of complex procedures and queries.

As real time applications mostly works on some scheduled execution plans set up by the user's so it is very much important to handle the unseen or strange behavior of the system during the actual execution process. For such scenarios different methodologies of functional testing can be used that diagnose and test the major functional area of application and figure out the basic errors and resolve the most basic bugs. One of the examples of such applications is working with web services by integrating them in software applications. These web services can be developed by one company for their business process and then are broadcasted to other companies or clients to be used. The involvement of clients or end users for utilization of web services is concerned with business cases.

Web services are service oriented structures and have no graphical user interface so testing of the embedded functionalities can be performed by the developers. Due to the reason that composition of web services and testing for the functionalities implanted are directly concerned with the deployment stage testing so it is required to implement certain functional based testing patterns [11]. Moreover these patterns also direct us to gather some statistical test evaluation data related to the quality attributes in concern with data/application communication between the software application and web service host [8]. Integration and adaptation of web services in enterprise solution is on large scale as web is maturing so rapidly for application development platforms. These web services can be utilized in building of architecture of other composite services [2]. The web service technology provides the gateway to the new age of real time applications wrapped in web technologies, which are capable of efficient data processing with high degree of intelligence and security [3]. However the main concern related to the composition of web services in real time is the secure data transition between the application acquiring web service and the host of that particular web service [3]. Performance is another concerning attributes which is related to the testing of web services based on different SOAP implementations [4]. Since web services are on global access to clients so there is more chance of multiple scenarios to be tested. In order to work on these test cases functional based testing patterns are followed which direct the service consumer to experience and then evaluate the problem within effective effort [5].

3 Problem Discussion

Web services oriented applications are emerging architectures under development these days. Most of the e-commerce applications are developed by embedding certain business process oriented web services within the application [6]. The web services oriented applications are developed to promise the standards to support the web service discovery, decomposition and interfacing related issues. Performance and adoptability are important attributes need to be kept in consideration during the development of service oriented software system [7]. Following the traditional approach of testing it is assumed that after the development of application some specialized team from within the organization or some third party testing tools are used to verify the service composition and execution issues, however specifically for web service oriented software application the scenario for testing need to be in different way. Some of the other issues like web service adaptation during the passage of time for software application and real time response to the client from the web service owner are also concerned with the customization of web service within the application and impacts on the working of complex service oriented software systems [7]. Moreover it is apparent that web service oriented software applications are in attachment with the development stake as well as the owner of that particular web service, so testing of service oriented application after the development might affect the adaptability attribute of software architecture. In order to minimize the issues concerning to the web service adaptation and compatibility between client and service owner there is a need to inspect for functional based development scenarios which can be implemented in order to achieve the effective performance and reliability estimations than conventional Test after Development approach for such software systems.

4 Aims and Objectives

The aim of study is to highlight the methodology for functional based testing scenarios in web service configured real time applications. Following objectives are set to meet this goal.

- To highlight the design test scenarios required for performance analysis of web service enabled software applications.
- Setting up and working of test frames to achieve proficient mechanism of test based automated development for real time applications.
- Techniques used to gather statistical test data for quality and performance attribute in web service enabled real time applications.
- Adapting functional based testing procedure to achieve effective data communication between the real time application and the web services hosts.

5 Research Questions

Below are the research questions on which we need to focus.

- What basic design patterns can be used to integrate web services in complex real time software systems in order to implement efficient and secure data communication over the network link between host and client?
- How to enhance the web service adaptability within the application architecture by providing distributed service operations recommendation and discovery criteria.

Web services applications can be visualized as modular applications that are designed for some specific business process and then will be utilized in some real time applications by locating and invoking across the internet [6]. In order to permit flexible and reliability concerns of web services, different areas of this technology need to be work on. This includes service execution transaction and data security. In order to composite the web services according to the software configuration, specific schemas are used for message transmission to the service host and application. Mostly XML mapping is used to create a message envelope with some specific SOAP standards [12]. Since message envelop communication is very important in web service integrated application so implementing functional based development scenarios can let the software to work efficiently and smoothly.

6 Research Type

The selected topic requires inclusive and general study regarding the techniques followed in software application environment. Applied research methodology for selected topic facilitate us to resolve the practical problem by acquiring and applying the knowledge that tackle to the problem area and to fulfill the needs related to scope of the entity. By analyzing the observations gathered from the knowledge related to the functional based testing scenarios in web service enabled real time applications, design architecture will be anticipated for web service oriented software applications. The validation process of proposed scenario in this paper will be conceded by the comparative examination with the existing software application adopting web services or other composite web services.

7 Research Methodology

7.1 Applied Research Methodology

Service oriented software applications are visualized as integrated modules which are published and consumed over some specified protocol layers. According to W3C web services can be described as software architecture exposing some methods to the client's applications for execution of business process embedded in these. XML based data exchange are supportable formats for communication links between the client and the web service owner. Hence it is required to implement the fault free and maximum performance oriented structure at client application which is consuming web service.

Objects of study

The objects studied are as follows:

1. Study of design patterns which can be followed in order to integrate the web service oriented structure with associated business process with n complex or minor software applications
2. Web service adaptability with in software application architecture to validate and implement the discovery criteria.

7.2 Challenges Associated for Testing Web Service Integrated Software Systems

In order to test the web service oriented software applications following scenarios must be kept in view to create the initial test data and test case procedures to test the application.

1. Functionality of web service in oriented software application must be correct in concern to the reliability attributes so that it can fully functional and responding to each and every single request if multiple requests hitting the specified WSDL. Mean while the application consuming that particular web service must send request and process response without any error or garbage in data communicated.
2. Scalability and performance must be promised by the web service oriented application so that a standard response time should be in consideration by each and every associated client. Hence if more than one client's are connected to a particular web service the architecture of client applications should get and process the response data from web service server in specified time slice.
3. If web service oriented application is a server application for some client server distributed structure, then the data payload and request to response should be managed in order to maintain the software crash issues and not responding states.

8 How Functional Base Development Done at Different Levels of Development of Soa Systems

8.1 Functional Based Testing during Development Approach

Web service oriented software applications are asynchronous in nature hence testing of such system needs some specialized procedures to be followed [8]. Hence in order to maintain the stability in the performance as well as quality attribute of such system, testing of each and every module is proceeded during the development phase by exchanging some data messages from client to server [9]. Following points should be kept in consideration while performing the functional base scenarios on service oriented software system. Embedded web services within the software application haven't any user interface or interaction GUI.

1. Based on the utilization of the business process embedded in the web service, predictions should be made in concern with the usage in software system in context of work load, performance, scalability and adaptation.
2. Functional testing regarding to the security concerns of web service embedded within the application should be tested with major testing areas and scenarios.

8.2 Guidelines for Functional Based Testing of Web Service Oriented Software Applications

Perspective selection

The aim of these guidelines is to present some strategies which can be followed to perform the functional based testing process in web services oriented software applications. Proposed guidelines and traditional testing approaches are set as the objects of under consideration software systems. Explanation of functional base testing scenarios for service oriented software systems can be discussed in more detail by further integrating the testing process to sub testing levels.

A. Component level Service testing

Component level service testing for web service oriented software systems is carried out by the application developers at modular or functional level. The basic aim of such type of testing is to generate certain automated testing scenarios by using some test data in order to verify and validate the base line functionality of the integrated web service. These automated or functional based testing scenarios presents some statistical test analysis figures that justifies the execution functionality in comparison with the expected functionality of the software module having certain web service embedded in it. However in order to work out the component level service testing following test scenarios should be kept in view.

1. Proper code review to certify it compatibility and adaptability in accordance to the standards declared for software application at modular levels.
2. Execution of functional and performance test suits related to the integrated web service.

B. Functional testing at web service Integration level

Functional base testing of service integrated software application is performed to validate the modular data execution in accordance to the web service interface interaction with the hosting system and its adaptability in context of data formats and validations. The functional test cases should be generated by keeping in view the issues associated to the communication layers and protocol on which web service methods are being accessed by the application. Moreover testing of external services associated with the integrated web services are also included in the functional tests at integration level.

C. Functional testing at web service Process level

Functional base testing for process associated with the integrated web service within the software application is to validate the operational concerns related and business processes associated with these. Major area of business concerns, service transformation to the host and process composition over the communication link are associated with the functional testing for the process level area of integrated web service. For this functional test cases should be generated which can tests the software application at modular level for the process associated and their response to the activation state of integrated web service.

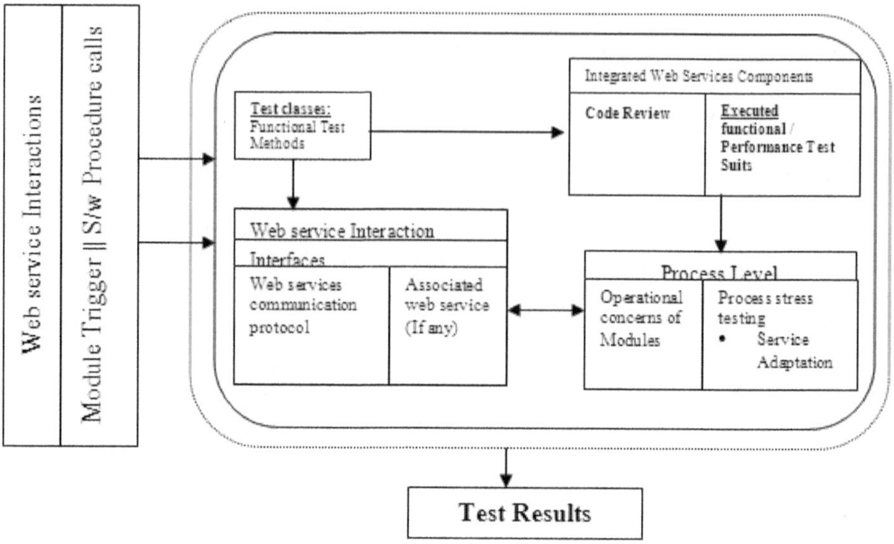

D. Functional Testing on formulated test levels:

For web service integrated software applications, functional testing phase for each module associated to the service are categorized as under in table 1:

Table 1.

Testing Phase	Test Environment
1. Test WSDL file for well formed	Modular level service testing
2. WSDL interaction from client to host	Modular level service testing
3. Test web service for response against submitted request (Interoperability).	Modular level service testing
4. Sample invocation by passing the parameters to web service.	Service level testing.
5. Response validation	Module Parameter testing

9 Data and Analysis

9.1 Testing Software Integrated Web Service

During the development of web service oriented software applications, application developers configure the modules by assuming that the test results against the test data will as same as that of the expected outcome from the functionalities embedded in the consumed web service. But in real scenario these assumptions produce different results when services are in communication during the method call to the hosts. Figure a. shows the functional base scenario for web service integrated software development. According to this scenario each of the modules developed with the automated test case generator. The test case generator comprises of specialized classes having abstract methods which generates some automated inputs for the functions calling them. Each of the testing phases as described in the table 1 are associated to the components associated to the integrated web service modules. Hence each time when these test classes objects are created automated test cases are generated in accordance to the web service requirements related to them. Test data values are generated in randomize way so that these will be use in the testing phase as described in the table 1 to check the outcome from the web service exposed methods. As shown in the figure these functional test methods are also associated with the process level as well as web service interaction interface level so that the operational concerns modules and associated web service module if any exist should be test during the functional testing of software.

9.2 Functional Testing for Web Service Interoperability between Client and Host

In web service oriented software applications the effective communication of the service depends upon the full operability and reliable exchanging of messages from client to server. So in order to generate functional level test cases for interoperability testing of such applications following concerns should be kept in view.

1. The server should be able to parse and decode the message data sent from the client.
2. The server should be capable to decrypt the encoded parameter embedded in the SOAP envelope message containing the actual message sent by the client.
3. The client should be able to decode the SOAP response sent by the server.
4. The client should be able to decrypt the encoded parameter embedded in the SOAP envelope message containing the actual message sent by the client.

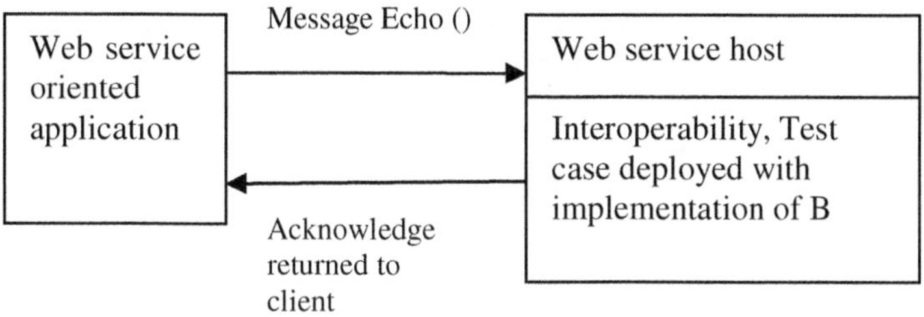

9.3 Functional Testing of Software Module for Load Testing

In web service integrated software applications functional based testing scenarios must be created in order to identify the performance and adoptability statistics of integrated web service. Test cases are designed by identifying the associated modules related to the service functionality work load in context of performance. In functional testing of such modules multiple requests are submitted to the consumed web service and statistical analysis of related parameters including the time to connect to service and response time are analysed [10]. Based on these statistics verification process will be performed for specific functionalities of modules. In order to generate the functional level test cases for load testing following concerns should be kept in view:

1. Identify and state the actual number of users operating the web service oriented modules of software application.
2. Identify the web service host WSDL and message syntax associated to it.

3. Attach a test request generator to broadcast the test messages simultaneously and associate a listener to lookup and process the response from the host.
4. Execute the test case with some valid test cases to check out the response as well as work load from the integrated web service host.

10 Conclusion

This report contributes to figure out and implement the functional oriented test cases in web service oriented software applications. The study provided above consists of applied research methodology to figure out the functional base test scenarios in service oriented software applications. The functional based testing approach can be followed to validate the interoperability of embedded service with the host system. In order to visualize the scalability and performance functional base testing will be performed at modular level by designing some specialized test classes that generate test data. This test data can be used by other associated modules embedded in the web service integrated software application for efficient and reliable functionality of service. Moreover functional base testing also promises the effective adaptation of web service within the software modules so that related stakes can utilize the integrated business process. The functional based testing also can be customized in accordance to the structure of consumed web services.

References

[1] Zhu, L., Gorton, I., Liu, Y., Bui, N.B.: Model driven benchmark generation for web services
[2] Lertphumpanya, T., Senivongse, T.: A basis path testing framework for WS-BPEL composite services
[3] Salomie, I., Chifu, V.R., Harsa, I.: Towards Automated Web Service Composition with Fluent Calculus and Domain Ontologies
[4] Ng, A., Chen, S., Greenfield, P.: An evaluation of contemporary commercial SOAP implementations. In: Proceedings of the Fifth Australasian Workshop on Software and System Architectures, Melbourne (2004)
[5] Dan, D.D., Kearney, R., Keller, R.K.A., Kuebler, D., Ludwig, H., Polan, M., Spreitzer, M., Youssef, A.: Web services on demand: WSLA-driven automated management. IBM Systems Journal 43(1), 136–155 (2004)
[6] Djamel, Bensaber, A., Malki, M.: Development of semantic web services: Model Driven Approach
[7] Bertolino, A.: Approaches to Testing Service-Oriented Software Systems
[8] Tian, J.: Software quality engineering: testing, quality assurance, and quantifiable improvement. Wiley, Chichester (2005)
[9] Dustdar, S., Haslinger, S.: Testing of service oriented architectures: A practical approach. In: Weske, M., Liggesmeyer, P. (eds.) NODe 2004. LNCS, vol. 3263, pp. 97–109. Springer, Heidelberg (2004)
[10] Patil, V.R.: Introduction to Testing Webservices
[11] Yu, Q., Liu, X., Bouguettaya, A., Medjahed, B.: Deploying and managing Web services: issues, solutions, and directions
[12] Rezgui, A., Bouguettaya, A., Malik, Z.: A Reputation-based approach to preserving privacy in Web services. In: VLDB Workshop on Technologies for E-Services (TES), Berlin, Germany (2003)

Design and Implementation of a Novel Distributed Memory File System

Urvashi Karnani[1], Rajesh Kalmady[1], Phool Chand[1], Anup Bhattacharjee[2], and B.S. Jagadeesh[1]

[1] Computer Division, [2] Reactor Control Division,
Bhabha Atomic Research Centre, Mumbai, India
{urvashi,rajesh,phool,anup,jag}@barc.gov.in

Abstract. To improve performance and efficiency of applications, a right balance among CPU throughput, memory performance and I/O subsystem is required. With parallel processors increasing the number crunching capabilities, the limitations of I/O systems have come to fore and have become the major bottleneck in achieving better turnaround times for large I/O bound jobs in particular. In this paper, we discuss the design, implementation and performance of a novel distributed memory file system that utilizes the free memory of cluster nodes over different interconnects to assuage the above-mentioned problem.

Keywords: Clusters, Network Interconnects, Memory File System, RAM Disk, Tmpfs, Free Memory, File System Agent.

1 Introduction

It is a well known trend that the improvements in access times of I/O subsystems have not kept pace with improvements in processor speeds. Processing powers for computing systems have been increasing regularly over the years however; the improvements in hard disk technology have mainly achieved increases in storage density and size [1]. In addition to the increase in CPU speed, the past decade has witnessed a large improvement in computation speedup achieved through parallelizing applications. As a result, the CPU processing times of programs have improved considerably, thereby shifting the performance bottleneck towards the I/O subsystem. The I/O operation is time consuming because it is governed by the speed of rotation of disk (which is a mechanical device) and the speed of the translational movement of read/write head. This surfaces as the major source of delay, resulting in poor turnaround times of jobs. Further, when parallelization brings down the computation time, this delay in I/O subsystem becomes even more apparent.

To address the issues of I/O subsystems in High Performance Computing Clusters we have designed, developed and deployed a Novel Distributed Memory File System that operates in the user space and dynamically grows as per the needs of a given job thereby optimally utilizing the memory resources. The novel idea explored here is to

N. Meghanathan et al. (Eds.): CCSIT 2011, Part III, CCIS 133, pp. 139–148, 2011.

make an 'in-memory' file system exploiting the free memory available in nodes of a cluster that would boost the file I/O performance of an application by logically replacing the disk with memory interconnected over network. This is an 'in-memory' file system with the memory being aggregated from other nodes on the fly, where the data of a file may span over multiple nodes. In this paper, we discuss the design, implementation and results obtained from our work on the Novel Distributed Memory File System.

2 Related Work

To improve the I/O subsystem performance, researchers are focusing on the identification of high performance I/O subsystem architectures and implementations. Utilizing either the local memory or remote memory over some interconnect network for file systems have been explored both from academic and commercial perspectives over the past one and a half decades.

2.1 Memory Based File Systems

A Memory based file system is a file system that resides in memory and does not write data to non-volatile storage like disk. A memory based file system is typically used as storage for temporary files. By keeping as much data as possible in memory it avoids the disk I/O and associated overheads.

2.1.1 RAM Disk

The first attempt in this regard has been the RAM disk. A RAM disk reserves a range of memory and makes it available through a block device interface using a pseudo driver [2]. RAM disks have certain limitations: Memory is reserved at the time of the disk creation, so it is locked from shared system use whether actually in use or not. The block device is of fixed size, so the file system mounted on it is also fixed. RAM disks do not support paging of their memory resulting in very poor system response in cases where the system is running low on free physical memory. Since the system sees a RAM disk as a device rather than a file system, any access to a file stored on it results in a second copy of the data being kept in the file system buffer i.e. it requires unnecessary copying of memory from the block device into the page cache [2].

2.1.2 Tmpfs

Tmpfs is a memory based file system which uses kernel resources relating to the Virtual Memory System and page cache as a file system. Tmpfs is so named because files and directories are not preserved across reboot or unmounts. Tmpfs is designed as a performance enhancement utility which is achieved by caching the writes to files residing on a Tmpfs file system [3]. Tmpfs files are written and accessed directly from the memory maintained by the kernel thus, Tmpfs file data can be swapped to disk, freeing resources for other needs. General Virtual Memory System routines are used to perform many low level Tmpfs file system operations hence reducing the amount of code needed to maintain the file system. Performance improvements in Tmpfs are most noticeable when a large number of short lived files are written and accessed on a Tmpfs file system. Tmpfs has a limitation that it shares resources (data and stack segment) with the programs executing in a system [3]. Large sized Tmpfs files affect the amount of space left for programs to execute thus, affecting the execution of very large programs. Likewise, programs requiring large amounts of memory use up the space available to Tmpfs.

RAM disk and Tmpfs use local memory (which is limited on a single machine) for storing the data. Hence, maximum file size on RAM disk or Tmpfs is calculated based on the physical memory available on that machine and if the application requires a much larger file as compared to the one supported by any of the memory based file systems it is written on to the disk.

2.2 Related Work on Use of Remote Memory

With high bandwidth and low-latency network becoming affordable, interesting efforts have been made to utilize remote memory. The use of remote memory has been explored in several contexts such as an extension of main memory, cooperative-caching and network paging. The Global Memory Service (GMS) provides an example of use of remote memory as an extension of main memory [4]. Dahlin et al. describe a co-operative caching algorithm called NChance Forwarding. Cooperative caching seeks to improve network file system performance by coordinating the contents of client caches and allowing requests not satisfied by a client's local in-memory file cache to be satisfied by the cache of another client [5]. To boost file system performance Network Ram disk can be used which is a virtual block device that uses idle main memories in a cluster for storage through the disk interface [6]. Network Swap (NSwap) is an example of a remote paging system [7].

We have developed a Novel Distributed Memory File System to provide better performance to I/O intensive applications. In the following sections we discuss the design, implementation and the performance obtained for the same.

3 Distributed Memory File System Design

The traditional file system manages two types of data namely file content that the application can access via the read, write functions and metadata i.e. the information related to file attribute and file system structure. In our design we have followed the paradigms of UNIX/Linux based file systems [8, 9]. The file system abstractions information such as superblock, inode and data blocks is maintained in the memory. The file data is written and accessed directly from memory of the nodes in the cluster. Figure 1 depicts the schematic design of the Distributed Memory File System. It consists of a Metadata Server Node, Distributed Memory File System (DMemfs) Nodes, File System Agent and a thin library at the client node whose functions are incorporated in the client application source code.

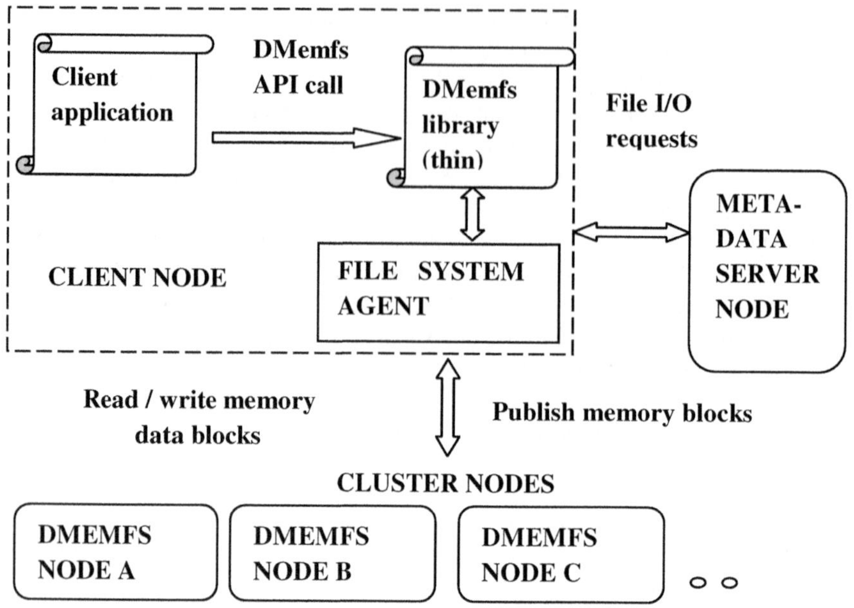

Fig. 1. Distributed Memory File System

3.1 Metadata Server Node

Metadata Server Node is the heart of the file system, which is responsible for maintaining the state of the file system that needs to be updated regularly to preserve the consistency of file system. Some of the data structures maintained at the metadata server are as follows:

- **Superblock structure** holds data about the file system such as total number of blocks, number of free blocks, total number of inodes and number of free inodes.
- **Inode data structure** is used to uniquely identify file. It holds information about a file such as owner, permissions and timestamps. The inode structure also contains address fields that give information about the data blocks where the file data resides. Similar to the UNIX paradigm [8], we have designed addressing scheme using various levels of indirections to incorporate large file size. In the current design of inode with file system block size of 8K we can support file size in Terabytes. Each indirect addressing block can hold 1024 entries. With 12 direct block addressing fields we can have file sizes up to 96K (12 * 8K) bytes. With the two single indirect addressing we can support 16Mbytes (2* 1024 * 8K) file size. Four double indirect addressing blocks account for next 32GB (4 * 1024 * 1024 *8K) of file size and the two triple indirect addressing blocks can account for another 16 Terabytes (2 * 1024 *1024 * 1024 * 8K) of file size.
- **Directory structure** maintains a mapping between the name of the file and inode numbers.

- **Metaopen file table** at the metadata server node maintains the state of open files across all the nodes. Each entry in this table consists of the access permission, count and pointer to an inode in the inode table whenever a file is opened an entry is made in this table.
- **Nodememoryinfo table** maintains a mapping of number of memory blocks published by each DMemfs node for the distributed memory file system.
- **Block map table structure** maintains mapping between the logical number of memory blocks and its actual physical location that consists of node identifier and local block number in the same node.

3.2 File System Agent

File system agent is responsible for communication between the metadata server node and other nodes in the cluster for reading and writing of blocks of data dedicated to the distributed memory file system. File system agent processes the commands and requests demanded by the client application for manipulating file data as well as metadata by initiating corresponding functions.

3.3 Distributed Memory File System (DMemfs) Nodes

The DMemfs nodes are the nodes of the cluster that can publish free memory blocks available for the use of distributed memory file system. Every node has a *local open-file table* that holds the information about the files opened by a program running on the node. It has an offset field that is required for the file I/O operations on the files opened by the program. It contains a *meta_open table* index that relates the file to an entry made at the metadata server. Whenever a read/write request is sent to the metadata server the *meta_open table* index is also sent along with the request which is required by the metadata server module to check for accessibility permissions. It also maintains *blockaddress table* structure that maps local memory blocks published for the file system with their actual physical addresses.

3.4 Client Application

The client application incorporates the library function calls that correspondingly initiate specified file handling operations such as open, close, read, write, mkdir, rmdir. The *DMemfs library* has been implemented as a thin library i.e. it contains only the wrapping functions, where as the core implementation of various functions is in the file system agent. It was required to keep this library thin so that any changes made in the file system agent do not necessitate a rebuild of the application program.

4 Implementation and Working

Currently the file system has been developed in user space with the client side API available as a library. Any client application can incorporate the API calls in the source code and use the file system. A communication protocol consisting of request and response messages has been developed for interaction of the metadata server node, DMemfs nodes and the file system agent that uses TCP/IP as the underlying communication protocol. Each message consists of a string defining the operation to be performed followed by a delimiter and then appended with the data necessary for the operation *(RQ_operation; arguments)*.

The library communicates with the file system agent that in turn forwards the file I/O request to the metadata server. The metadata server module handles one session for every client where in multiple threads can be created for various I/O requests. At the DMemfs node module one thread is dedicated for communication with the metadata server and one thread serves the data transfer request for reading or writing data to the memory blocks.

4.1 Initialization

Initially, the DMemfs nodes do a handshake with the metadata server node at a predefined well known port and publish memory blocks. The DMemfs node sends a *"NODE_UP"* request followed by the number of memory blocks to be published. According to the available memory blocks the metadata server makes a file system and initializes all the data structures. A root directory is also created during the initialization that acts as the parent directory for other directories created by the users. The various tables for storing the metadata of the file system, residing at the metadata server are created and initialized.

4.2 Directory Operations

Directory maintains a mapping between the name of a file and its inode number that helps in uniquely identifying the file in the file system. In the current implementation the directory structure and related information is maintained at the metadata server node. Memory blocks are reserved at the metadata server node that holds the data corresponding to the directories. Hence, instead of using the remote memory blocks for directory data, the local blocks available at the metadata server are used that provide better performance in directory operations as the file system agent at the client side need not contact any other DMemfs node for the same.

4.3 File Operations

The distributed memory file system supports functions that perform basic file operations which include: creating a file, opening a file, reading from a file, writing data into a file, seeking to a position in a file, closing a file. For every file operation called by the user application the file system agent packs the required data in a form of message that is in compliance with the developed communication protocol and sends it to the metadata server. When the request involves modification of file attributes available at the metadata server the necessary changes are made and the file system agent is informed. When the request involves reading or writing (figure 2), the metadata server processes the request and sends a message consisting of IP address of the DMemfs node to be contacted , the offset required for reading or writing and the local block number of the memory block where the read or write has to performed, back to the file system agent. Once this message is received, an independent thread is created for communication and data transfer between the client node and DMemfs node having the memory block.

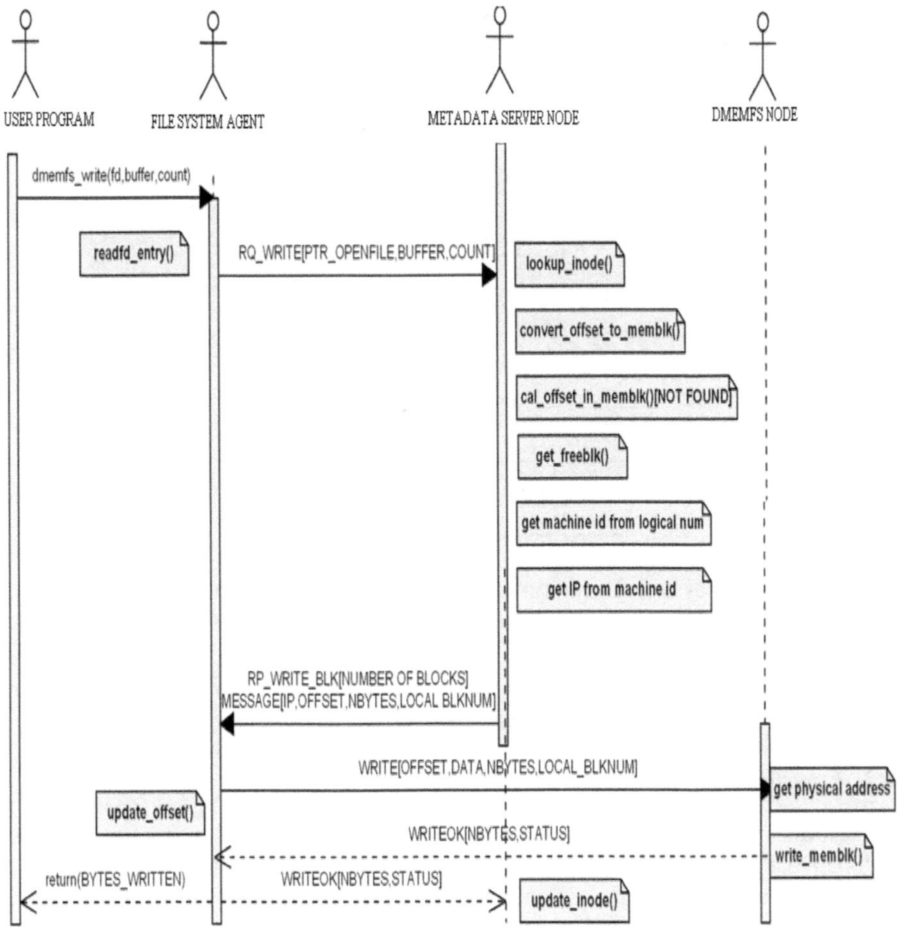

Fig. 2. Overview of write operation in distributed memory file system

5 Experimental Setup

The experiments were conducted on a cluster of 20 nodes. Each node has two quad core Intel Xeon 3.0 GHz processors with 6 MB L2 cache and 32GB physical memory. Nodes are connected by Infiniband and Gigabit Ethernet. Each node has a 7200 rpm disk of size 500 GB and a transfer rate of 3Gbps. For testing the performance of the distributed memory file system various test cases were developed that involved contiguous writing to a file, random seeking to a position in a file and reading from a file. The following sections describe few experiments and their results.

5.1 Experiment 1

In this experiment, performance of the distributed memory file system was tested for contiguous write using various size of file system block size such as 4K, 8K, 16K,

32K, and 64K. Large chunks of data in order of kilobytes were written to a file sequentially. The experiment was conducted over Gigabit Ethernet and Infiniband. Observations for various file sizes have been plotted in figure 3 (Gigabit Ethernet) and figure 4 (Infiniband).

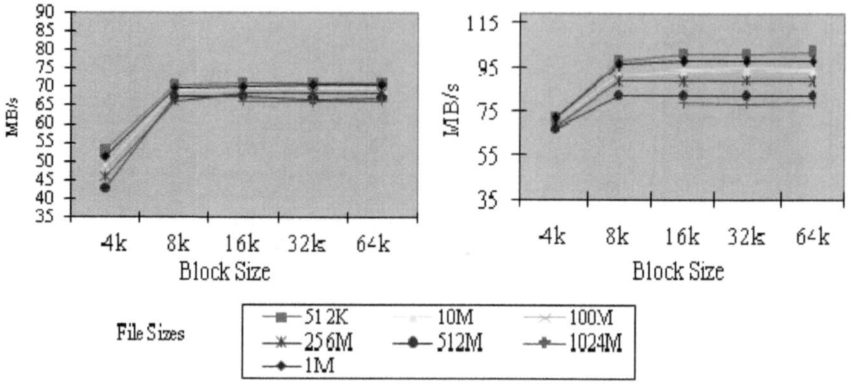

Fig. 3. Contiguous Write Performance (Gigabit Ethernet)

Fig. 4. Contiguous Write Performance (IP over Infiniband)

We can observe that the block size of 8K is optimum for our distributed memory file system irrespective of the underlying network bandwidth and latency.

5.2 Experiment 2

To test the file system performance for random access and read, test cases were developed that perform random seek to a position in a large file of the order of gigabytes (15GB) followed by reading chunk of data. This experiment was performed with block sizes of 8K and 16K. The comparison of performance of distributed memory file system and disk has been plotted in figure 5.

The distributed memory file system has significant performance benefits (2.3 times better) for application involving random access and read requests. This is due to the fact that seek time in distributed memory file system depends only on the time required to calculate the memory block corresponding to the seek position. Where as in disks the seek time corresponds to the amount of time required for the read/write heads to move between tracks over the surfaces of the platters which introduces a time penalty.

5.3 Experiment 3

Test cases were developed to test the file system performance for an application that writes a file contiguously in very small data chunks of the order of bytes. The comparison of performance of disk and distributed memory file system with block sizes of 8K and 16K over both the interconnects namely Gigabit Ethernet and Infiniband has been plotted in figure 6.

We observe that performance of the distributed memory file system for applications that write data to a file in small chunks in order of bytes is not so significant as compared to disk based file system as writes in the latter are performed on cache most of the time rather than disk, where as in the memory file system for every write call the additional latencies due to our implementation are involved hence, the performance gain is not so significant.

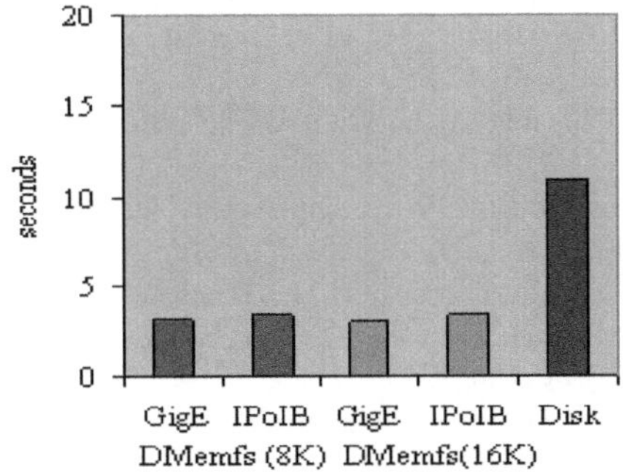

Fig. 5. Performance in experiment 2

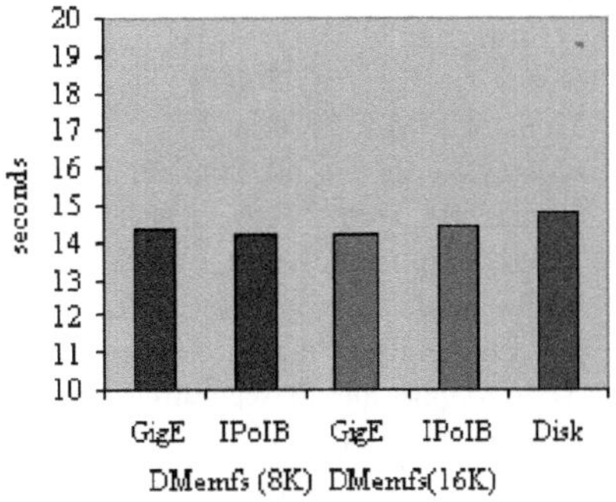

Fig. 6. Performance in experiment 3

6 Conclusion and Future Work

The Distributed Memory File System provides better performance for I/O intensive jobs in a cluster and efficiently uses the free memory available in the cluster nodes for storing file data. Further, through practical experimentation it is established that when there is random access pattern, the performance of distributed memory file system is significant (2.3 times better) as compared with that of the local disk. Our interest was also to examine whether there exists an optimal block size (analogous to the 512 bytes sector size of disk that has remained same for historical reasons) in a distributed memory file system implementation. We did observe through our experimentation that optimum size of block was 8K for optimal transfer rates. We also observed that even though the bandwidth and latencies of underlying network that interconnected memories were different, the optimum size was observed to be the same. We believe for a given network interconnect, there exists an optimal block size for a file system. Knowledge of this would help us in getting optimum throughput.

Currently the file system has been developed in user space with the client side API available as a library. In future we shall be extending this file system implementation to POSIX implementation so that its usage becomes transparent to the user. We shall be extending our research to very large file sizes and develop schemes to factor in the failure of nodes which will bring in the issues of redundancy.

Acknowledgements

We would like to express our sincere gratitude to R. S. Mundada, K. Bhatt, D. D. Sonvane, Vaibhav Kumar, Vibhuti Duggal, N. Chandorkar of Parallel Processing

Group, Computer Division, BARC for their constructive suggestions throughout the research work. We are thankful to A.G. Apte, Head, Computer Division, BARC for providing us with the opportunity to undertake this research work.

References

1. Moreira, F., Adi, J.-P., Navarro, B., Dwyer, A.O., Wright, R.: STORAGE:Ten-year Forecast of Storage Evolution. PS_WP12_HISTOR_D12-5_Storage_Ten year_Forecast_of_Storage_Evolution (February 2006)
2. McKusick, M.K., Karels, M.J., Bostic, K.: A Pageable Memory Based File system. In: Proceedings of the Usenix Summer (June 1990)
3. Snyder, P.: Tmpfs: A Virtual Memory File System. In: Proceedings of the Autumn 1990 EUUG Conference, Nice, France, pp. 241–248 (1990)
4. Feeley, M.J., Morgan, W.E., Pighin, E.P., Karlin, A.R., Levy, H.M., Thekkath, C.A.: Implementing global memory management in a workstation cluster. In: Proceedings of the 15th ACM Symposium on Operating Systems Principles (1995)
5. Dahlin, M., Wang, R., Anderson, T.E., Patterson, D.A.: Cooperative caching: Using remote client memory to improve file system performance. In: Operating Systems Design and Implementation, Monterey, CA, pp. 267–280. USENIX Assoc. (1994)
6. Flouris, M., Markatos, E.P.: The network Ram Disk: Using remote memory on heterogeneous NOWs. Cluster Computing, 281–293 (1999)
7. Newhall, T., Finney, S., Ganchev, K., Spiegel, M.: Nswap: A network swapping module for linux clusters. In: Kosch, H., Böszörményi, L., Hellwagner, H. (eds.) Euro-Par 2003. LNCS, vol. 2790, pp. 1160–1169. Springer, Heidelberg (2003)
8. Bach, M.J.: The Design of the Unix Operating System, Chapters (4, 5, 10)
9. Bovet, D.P., Cesati, M.: Understanding the Linux Kernel, 3rd edn. O'Reilly, Sebastopol (2005)

Decentralized Dynamic Load Balancing for Multi Cluster Grid Environment

Malarvizhi Nandagopal and V. Rhymend Uthariaraj

Anna University Chennai, Tamilnadu, Inida
nmv_94@yahoo.com, rhymend@annauniv.edu

Abstract. Load balancing is essential for efficient utilization of resources and enhancing the performance of computational grid. Job migration is an effective way to dynamically balance the load among multiple clusters in the grid environment. Due to limited capacity of single cluster, it is necessary to share the underutilized resources of other clusters. Each cluster saves the static and dynamic information about its neighbors including transfer delay and load. This paper addresses the issues in multi cluster load balancing based on job migration across separate clusters. A decentralized grid model, as a collection of clusters for computational grid environment is proposed. A Sender Initiated Decentralized Dynamic Load Balancing (SI-DDLB) algorithm is introduced. The algorithm estimates system parameters such as resource processing rate and load on each resource. The algorithm balances the load by migrating jobs to the least loaded neighboring resource by taking into account of transfer delay. The algorithm also considers the availability of selected resource before dispatching job for execution since the probability of failure is more in the dynamic grid environment. The main goal of the proposed algorithm is to reduce the response time of the jobs. The proposed algorithm has been verified through the GridSim simulation toolkit. Simulation results show that the proposed algorithm is feasible and improves the system performance considerably.

Keywords: Grid Computing, Load Balancing, Clusters, Scheduler, Transfer Delay.

1 Introduction

The grid is emerging as a wide-scale infrastructure that promises to support resource sharing and coordinated problem solving in dynamic, multi-institutional virtual organization [1]. Grid computing can be thought of as distributed and large-scale cluster computing and as a form of network-distributed parallel processing. With rapid progress in computing, communication and storage technologies, grid computing has gained extensive interest in academia, industry and military. Grid computing provides the user with access to locally unavailable resource types. On the other hand, there is the expectation that a large number of resources are available.

A computational grid aggregates a plenty of computation resources. Computation resources may be low-end systems such as PCs and workstations, or high-end systems such as clusters, massively parallel processors (MPPs) and symmetric multiprocessors

N. Meghanathan et al. (Eds.): CCSIT 2011, Part III, CCIS 133, pp. 149–160, 2011.

(SMPs). In computational grid, user jobs can be executed on either local or remote computer systems. The computational grid [2] provides the opportunity to share a large number of resources among different organizations. As the number of resources increases, the probability of failure becomes higher than in a traditional parallel computing. The failure of resources affects the job execution fatally. With the multitude of heterogeneous resources, a proper scheduling and efficient load balancing across the grid is required for improving the performance of the system.

Grids have a lot of specific characteristics [3] such as heterogeneity, autonomy and dynamicity which are the obstacles for applications to harness conventional load balancing algorithms directly. One important advantage of grid computing is the provision of resources to the users that are locally unavailable. Users of the grid system submit jobs at random times. In such a system, some computers are heavily loaded while others have available processing capacity. The goal of load balancing is to transfer the load from heavily loaded computers to idle computers, hence balance the load to the computers and increase the overall system performance.

In general, any load-balancing algorithm consists of two basic policies—a transfer policy and a location policy. The transfer policy determines whether a job is processed locally or remotely. By using workload information, it determines when a resource becomes eligible to act as a sender (transfer a job to another resource) or as a receiver (retrieve a job from another resource). The location policy determines the resource to which a job, selected for possible remote execution, should be sent. In other words, it locates complementary nodes to/from which a node can send/receive workload to improve the overall system performance. Location-based policies can be broadly classified as sender initiated, receiver initiated, or symmetrically initiated [4], [5]. Sender initiated algorithms let the heavily loaded sites take the initiative to request the lightly loaded sites to receive the jobs; while receiver initiated algorithms let the lightly loaded sites invite heavily loaded sites to send their jobs. Symmetrically-initiated algorithms combine the advantages of these two by requiring both senders and receivers to look for appropriate sites.

Further, while balancing the load, certain types of information such as the number of jobs waiting in queue, job arrival rate, CPU processing rate, memory availability are exchanged among the resources for improving the overall performance. Based on the information that can be used, load-balancing algorithms are classified as static, dynamic, or adaptive [5], [6], [7]. According to another classification, based on the degree of centralization, load-scheduling algorithms could be classified as centralized or decentralized [5], [7]. In a centralized system, a single resource acts as a central controller to perform load scheduling. Many authors argue that this approach is not scalable, because when the system size increases, the central controller may become a system bottleneck and the single point of failure. Such algorithms are bound to be less reliable than decentralized algorithms, where load scheduling is done by many, if not all, resources in the system. However, decentralized algorithms have the problem of communication overheads incurred by frequent information exchange between resources.

The rest of the paper is organized as follows:

Section 2 presents related work. Section 3 presents the decentralized grid system model. Section 4 describes in detail the design of the proposed SI-DDLB algorithm. Section 5 discusses simulation environment. Section 6 elaborates experimental results and discussion. Finally, this paper is concluded in Section 7.

2 Related Work

Numerous researchers have proposed scheduling and load balancing algorithms for grid computing environment [8], [9], [10].

The authors in [11] provided a dynamic solution for distributed load-balancing, with the load defined as the number of jobs currently running. However, they ignored the effects of network latency. An agent based system is used in [12], where work is always moved from the busiest nodes to the least busy nodes. However, they assumed that the nodes in the system were homogeneous. In [13], authors analyzed and compared the effectiveness of dynamic load balancing and job replication by means of trace-driven simulations. Agent-based approaches have been tried to provide load balancing in cluster of machines [14].

The authors in [15] proposed a new decentralized dynamic job dispersion algorithm that is capable of dynamically adapting to changing operating parameters. This distributed load-balancing algorithm is dynamic, decentralized, and it handles systems that are heterogeneous in terms of node speed, architecture and networking speed. The algorithm allows individual nodes to leave and join the network at any time and have jobs assigned to them as they become available. Each node saves information about its neighbors including the network bandwidth available between the local resource and its neighbor; the current CPU utilization; and the current I/O utilization. This status information is exchanged periodically. Knowing the status information, each node can choose when to send jobs to its neighbors. This algorithm is fault tolerant and takes job size into account. It is scalable but at the cost of increased communication overhead. The limitation in this algorithm is large buffer space is required on each node to store status information of all nodes. Also, the algorithm should only handle a grid of computers on the same local area network.

The main objective of this study is to propose a SI-DDLB algorithm for computational grid environment that can cater the following unique characteristics:

- Heterogeneous grid clusters
  There may be a difference in the hardware architecture, operating systems, computing power and resource capacity among clusters. In this study, heterogeneity only refers to the processing power of cluster.
- Effects from considerable communication delay
  The communication overhead involved in capturing load information of clusters before making a job dispatching decision can be a major issue negating the advantages of job migration. In this work, the communication overhead is reduced by means of mutual information feedback.

3 Decentralized Grid Model

A decentralized grid system model, comprising of clusters (resources) C is proposed. The set C contains n clusters $c_1, c_2, \ldots. c_n$. The components in each cluster are shown in Fig. 1. Each of these components has its own independent functionalities that help in grid management and job scheduling and thus serve the purpose of grid. The computational nodes at each cluster are typically interconnected by a high-speed local network and protected by firewalls from the outside world.

A decentralized job scheduling and load balancing approach is used since the jobs generated by users are submitted to the scheduler where the job originates. The scheduler determines whether to send the jobs to the nodes in local cluster or to a neighboring cluster. The clusters in the grid system may have different processing power. The processing power of a cluster c_i is measured by the average CPU speed across all computing nodes within c_i, denoted by $APPW_i$. For $i \neq j$, APPWi may be different from APPWj. GIS is responsible for collecting and maintaining the details of memory, CPU utilization and load value along with registration information of the resources. The remote manager in each cluster saves information about its neighbors including the transfer delay available between the local cluster and its neighbor and the current CPU utilization. Knowing this, each cluster can choose the neighbor, to which the scheduler has to send job.

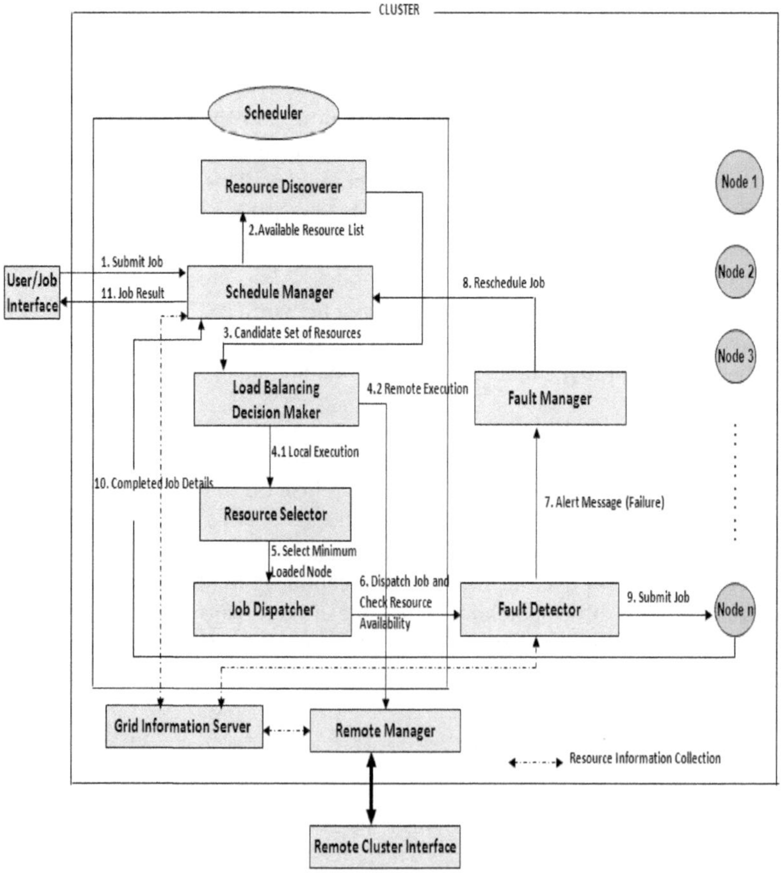

Fig. 1. Components and their interactions in each cluster

When the schedule manager receives job from a user, it gets information about available resources from GIS. It then passes the available resource list to the resource discoverer. Resource discoverer discovers the candidate set of resources based on job requirements and resource characteristics and send the list of candidate resources to the load balancing decision maker. Decision maker make a decision that whether the job is to be executed in the local or remote cluster and transfers the job accordingly. Resource selector selects the computational node with minimum load. A job dispatcher dispatches the jobs one by one to the fault detector.

The availability of selected resource is important for job execution that determines the computing performance. A fault detector is responsible for monitoring the state of resources and detecting an occurrence of resource failure before dispatching a job to the resource. If the resource failure or system performance degradation occurs, the fault detector sends an alert message to a fault manager. If the fault manager receives an alert message, it requests the schedule manager to allocate new resource and restarts execution using a checkpoint.

The clusters in C is fully interconnected, meaning that there exists at least one communication path between any two clusters in C. For any cluster $c_i \in C$, there are jobs arriving at c_i. The jobs are assumed to be computationally intensive, mutually independent, and can be executed at any cluster. At each cluster, there exists a global job waiting queue (GJWQ), which holds those jobs waiting to be assigned for execution. GJWQ (c_i) denotes the global job-waiting queue of the cluster c_i. The jobs in the GJWQ are processed in "First-Come-First-Serve" order. It is assumed that each cluster has an infinite capacity buffer to store jobs waiting for execution. This assumption eliminates the possibility of dropping a job due to unavailability of buffer space.

There is a small non-zero probability that a job can shuttle between clusters. This can be prevented in various ways. The approach used in this work is, the entire simulation makes the job join not at the end of the queue, but at the position where it should have been if the job had arrived at that queue. This means that, keep track of the time at which the job left the last cluster. This can considerably reduce the probability of the job being transferred once again and can guarantee minimizing the response time of that job. The other approach is, set the migration limit as 1 since several researchers assume a migration limit of one, as job migration is often difficult in practice and there are no significant benefits of higher migration limits [16], [17].

4 The SI-DDLB Algorithm

The SI-DDLB algorithm mainly consists of three procedures: Neighbor Selection, Inter Cluster Information Exchange and Instantaneous Job Migration.

4.1 Neighbor Selection

The SI-DDLB algorithm assumes that the communication delay between pairs of clusters can be estimated. The scheduler in each cluster gets the details of neighboring clusters from GIS and then uses this information to select a neighbor cluster for processing new arriving job. Neighbors for each cluster are formed in terms of transfer delay (td). For a grid cluster c_i, it measures the relative distances (e.g. transfer delay) to a set of neighboring clusters. For a cluster c_i, a cluster c_j is considered as its neighboring cluster as long as the transfer delay between the cluster c_i and c_j is within ε times of the transfer delay between the cluster c_i and the nearest cluster. For each cluster, the chosen neighboring clusters are sorted by load in ascending order. After this process, the first-ranked cluster is chosen as the destination cluster for job migration. This is described as follows:

$$\varepsilon = \frac{td_{ij}}{td_{nearest}}$$

Where, td_{ij} denotes the transfer delay from cluster c_i to cluster c_j. $td_{nearest}$ denotes the transfer delay from the nearest cluster of cluster c_i to itself. It is found that $\varepsilon = 1.5$ yields very good results and this value is used throughout the simulation. The procedure for neighbor selection is described in Algorithm 1.

Algorithm 1: Neighbor Selection

```
For each cluster ci
  Find all clusters cj (i#j) whose APPWj > APPWi
  Denote this set as Qi
  Sort Qi in ascending order based on td
  Choose the first ranked cluster as cnearest and note down the
                      transfer delay between ci and cnearest as tdnearest
  Find all clusters cj ∈ Qi (i#j) where tdij=ε*tdnearest
  Denote this set as Nbori
  Sort Nbori in ascending order based on load
  Choose the first ranked cluster cj as destination for job migration
```

4.2 Inter Cluster Information Exchange

An important issue in designing a dynamic load balancing algorithm is to identify the load index that measures the current load of a cluster. A good load index must be easily obtained and calculated with minimum overhead. The authors in [18] report that the simple CPU queue length is the most effective load index. Each cluster c_i maintains the state information of other clusters by using a Cluster State Object CSO_i. CSO helps a cluster to estimate the load of other clusters at any time without message transfer. The state object CSO_i of a cluster $c_i \in C$ is an n-dimensional ArrayList object maintained by c_i. Each item $CSO_i[j]$ is a state object and has a property list (LD, LT):

$CSO_i[j].LD$ denotes the load information of cluster c_j.
$CSO_i[j].LT$ denotes the cluster c_j's local time when the load status information is reported.

Each cluster collects and maintains the state information of only the neighboring clusters. For any cluster $c_i \in C$, c_i maintains its state information in its state object element $CSO_i[i]$. $CSO_i[j].LD$ and $CSO_i[j].LT$ are maintained through message exchanges with the neighboring clusters.

Thus, in order to reduce/minimize the overhead of cluster state information collection, state information exchange is done by mutual information feedback. Algorithm 2 outlines the procedure when c_i transfers a job j_x to a neighbor cluster c_j for processing. Cluster c_i appends the load information of itself and ω_p (a small positive integer) random neighbors to the job transfer request sent to c_j by piggybacking. c_j then updates the corresponding load information in its state object by comparing the timestamps, if the clusters contained in the transfer request belong to its neighbors. Similarly, c_j inserts the current load information of itself and ω_p random clusters from its $Nbor_j$ in the job acknowledge reply or job completion reply to c_i, so c_i can update its state objects.

Algorithm 2: Inter Cluster Information Exchange
Steps processed in c_i:
1. $Y \leftarrow c_i + \{\omega_p$ random clusters from $Nbor_i - c_j\}$
   /* c_i select neighbors for state information exchange */
2. $\forall\, c_y \in Y$, c_i appends ($CSO_i[y].LD$, $CSO_i[y].LT$) to the Job Transfer Request JTR
3. c_i sends message JTR to c_j

Steps processed in c_j:
Upon receiving JTR:
1. $\forall\, c_y \in Y$: If ($CSO_i[y].LT > CSO_j[y].LT$) AND ($c_y \in Nbor_j$) then
   $CSO_j[y] \leftarrow CSO_i[y]$
   /* c_j updates the state object using c_i's information */
   Endif
2. $Z \leftarrow c_j + \{\omega_p$ random clusters from $Nbor_j - c_i\}$
3. $\forall\, c_z \in Z$, c_j appends ($CSO_j[z].LD$, $CSO_j[z].LT$) to the Job Ack. Reply JAR
4. c_j sends message JAR to c_i

Upon completion of job j_x:
1. $Z \leftarrow c_j + \{\omega_p$ random clusters from $Nbor_j - c_i\}$
2. $\forall\, c_z \in Z$, c_j appends ($CSO_j[z].LD$, $CSO_j[z].LT$) to the Job Completion Reply JCR
3. c_j sends message JCR to c_i

Steps processed in c_i:
Upon receiving JAR or JCR:
$\forall\, c_z \in Z$: If ($CSO_j[z].LT > CSO_i[z].LT$) AND ($c_z \in Nbor_i$) then
   $CSO_i[z] \leftarrow CSO_j[z]$
   /* c_i updates the state object using c_j's information */
   Endif

4.3 Instantaneous Job Migration

When a new job arrives at cluster c_i, the load balancing algorithm decides whether it is to be sent to the global job waiting queue of cluster c_i or to any one of the neighboring clusters $Nbor_i$. Algorithm 3 describes the procedure for instantaneous job migration in cluster c_i. If there are two neighboring clusters with the same minimum load, the cluster that gives minimum response time is chosen.

Algorithm 3: Instantaneous Job Migration

$\forall j_x \in J$ *in* $c_i \in$ C:

Let $LD_{min} \leftarrow$ Min {CSO$_i$[k].LD | $c_k \in c_i$ + Nbor$_i$}

/* the minimum load among cluster c_i and its neighbors Nbor$_i$ */

If (CSO$_i$[i]. LD - $LD_{min} < \theta$) then

/* θ is a positive real constant close to zero */

GJWQ (c_i) $\leftarrow$ enqueue(j_x)

/* put the job j_x in the global job waiting queue of cluster c_i */

Else

Transfer the job j_x to the neighbor cluster c_j having LD_{min}

Update CSO$_i$[j].LD

Endif

5 Simulation Environment

The simulation is based on the excellent grid simulation toolkit GridSim ToolKit 4.0 [19] which allows modeling and simulation of entities in grid computing systems- users, applications and resources. In GridSim simulation, the user creates the experiment specifying the job (gridlet), QoS requirements (including deadline and budget) and optimization strategy.

In GridSim based simulations, the interaction between different GridSim entities takes place through events. In GridSim, each gridlet is defined in terms of the size (in MI) of gridlet, the file size (in byte) of gridlet before execution, the file size (in byte) of the gridlet after execution. The experiments are performed on a PC (Core 2 processor, 3.20GHZ, 1GB RAM). Table 1 shows the values of the parameters used in the simulation.

Table 1. Simulation Parameters

Simulation Parameters	Value
Number of Clusters	10
Number of nodes in each cluster	2
Processing power of each cluster	500-5000
Job Length(Gridlet size)	7000-10,000
Input and Output file size	500 – 700
Total Number of Queue/Cluster	1
Number of users	8
Number of jobs	100-800
E	1.5
Θ	0.9
Number of clusters in Nbor	Varied based on transfer delay
ω_p	20% of Nbor

6 Simulation Results and Discussion

In this section, the performance of the proposed SI-DDLB algorithm is evaluated using the simulation setup described above by varying the number of jobs for different scenarios. A set of experiments are conducted and the performance of proposed algorithm is compared with the Non Migration (NM) or local execution algorithm. In NM algorithm, jobs originate at any cluster in the grid and are processed at the originating cluster itself.

6.1 Performance Improvement in Response Time (SI-DDLB vs NM)

The performance of SI-DDLB is compared in terms of response time by varying the number of jobs. The system load is varied by varying the number of jobs submitted. The higher the load, the higher is total response time of both algorithms as depicted in Fig. 2. When comparing the results of SI-DDLB and NM algorithm, it is observed that the response time of the system that results from applying SI-DDLB is lower than the response time of the NM algorithm under all loads. SI-DDLB has an average improvement factor of 39.43 percent than NM algorithm when 800 jobs get completed. The reason is, SI-DDLB algorithm exhibits more load balancing when system workload is high. NM simply schedules the jobs to the originating cluster without considering whether the cluster is underloaded or overloaded. On the other hand, SI-DDLB algorithm balance the load by migrating jobs to the least loaded neighbor resource by taking into account of transfer delay thus resulting in overall performance improvement.

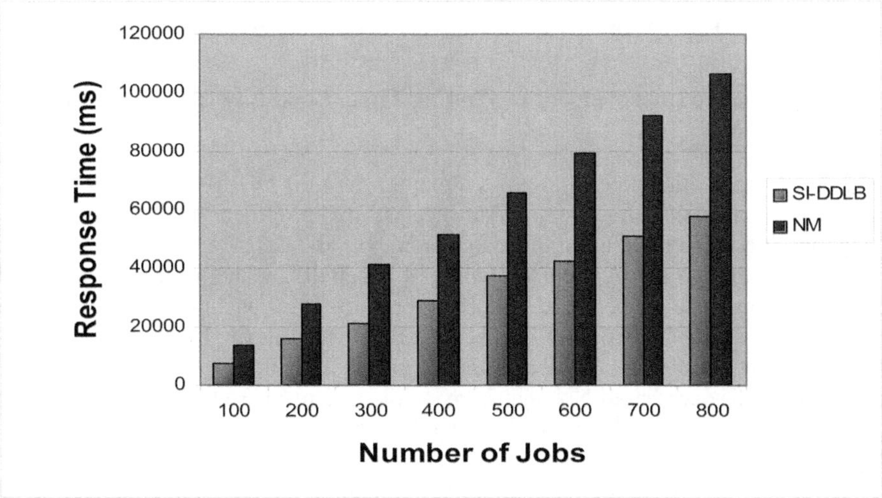

Fig. 2. Response time comparison for varying number of jobs

6.2 Performance Improvement in Waiting Time (SI-DDLB vs NM)

The performance of SI-DDLB is compared in terms of waiting time by varying the number of jobs. The waiting time against the number of jobs is plotted in Fig. 3. Both algorithms take almost the same amount of time in waiting to start execution when the number of jobs is less. It is observed that there is a considerable reduction of waiting time in SI-DDLB than NM when the number of jobs is more. SI-DDLB has an average improvement factor of 10.52 percent than NM algorithm when 800 jobs get completed.

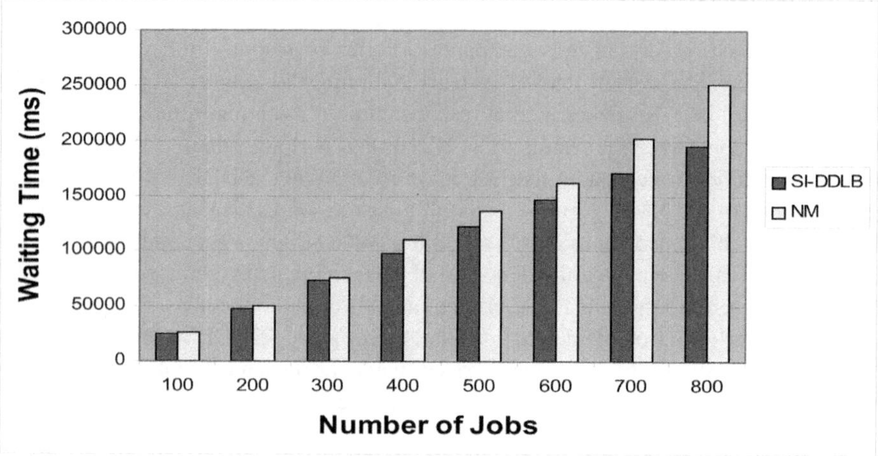

Fig. 3. Waiting time comparison for varying number of jobs

6.3 Performance Improvement in Waiting Time (Load Based NN vs Distance Based NN)

The neighbor selection algorithm plays a major role in SI-DDLB to optimize the performance of the system. The performance of the proposed load based Nearest Neighbor (NN) selection algorithm is compared with the distance based NN algorithm in terms of waiting time. As depicted in Fig. 4, when the number of jobs is increased, the waiting time is also increased in both algorithms. It is concluded from Fig. 4 that the distance based NN algorithm behaves poorly when compared with the load based NN algorithm. Load based NN algorithm has an average improvement factor of 20.81 percent over distance based NN algorithm. In the distance based NN algorithm, a job is migrated to a nearest cluster which is identified based on distance without considering the load of that cluster. Therefore the length of the waiting queue is increased and the incoming job needs to wait for more time in the queue for execution. This increases the response time of the jobs. In the load based NN algorithm, a nearest neighbor is selected based on transfer delay and load. The job is migrated to the minimum loaded nearest neighbor. Thus the waiting time of the job is reduced considerably.

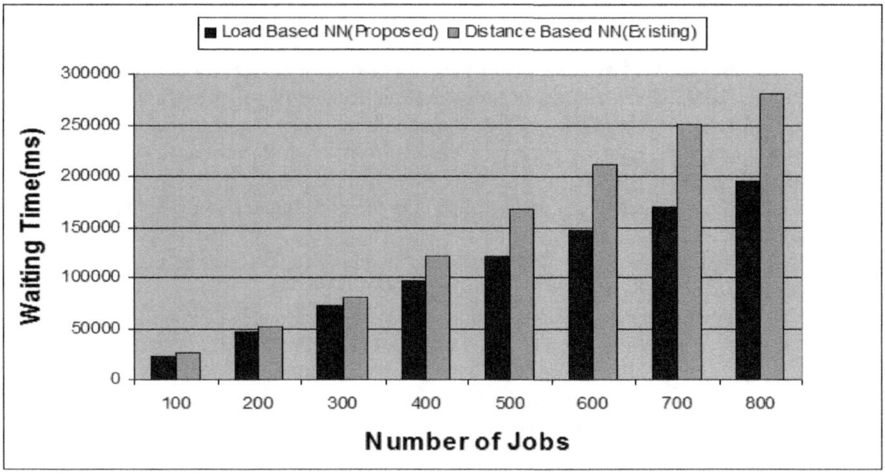

Fig. 4. Effect of Neighbor Selection

7 Conclusion and Future Work

In this study, architecture for sender initiated dynamic and decentralized load balancing algorithm is presented. The proposed algorithm schedules jobs and balances the load across the clusters in the grid environment. The grid is considered as a collection of clusters which differs in terms of processing power and transfer delay. The objective of the algorithm is to minimize the response time of the job that arrive at a grid system for processing. The algorithm also considers overheads of job migration due to the large communication latency between grid clusters. To reduce the communication overhead, the algorithm uses mutual information feedback for inter cluster information exchange. A fault detection and management is also provided in the cluster so that submitted job is executed reliably and efficiently. Various metrics are used to discuss the results obtained including response time, waiting time and resource utilization under varying load. The proposed algorithm is compared with the non migration algorithm with respect to the above defined metrics. From the simulation results it is observed that non migration algorithm results in low efficiency and remarkably takes more time to complete the jobs than the proposed one. In the proposed algorithm load can be shared across different clusters and thus the job response time is greatly reduced.

In the future, it is planned to investigate more complex models and to study additional factors that may affect the performance of the algorithm. Also, it is planned to explore the potential of these load balancing strategies by embedding them into real world grid computing environments.

References

1. Foster, I., Kesselman, C., Tuecke, S.: The Anatomy of the Grid: Enabling Scalable Virtual Organizations. International Journal of High Performance Computing applications 15(3), 200–222 (2001)

2. Foster, I., Kesselman, C. (eds.): The Grid: Blueprint for a New Computing Infrastructure (2004)
3. Baker, M., Buyya, R., Laforenza, D.: Grids and grid technologies for wide-area distributed computing. International Journal of Software:Practice and Experience (SPE) 32(15) (2002)
4. Feng, Y., Li, D., Wu, H., Zhang, Y.: A Dynamic Load Balancing Algorithm Based on Distributed Database System. In: Proc. Fourth Int'l Conf. High-Performance Computing in the Asia-Pacific Region, pp. 949–952 (2000)
5. Shivaratri, N., Krueger, P., Singhal, M.: Load Distributing for Locally Distributed Systems. Computer 25(12), 33–44 (1992)
6. Watts, J., Taylor, S.: A Practical Approach to Dynamic Load Balancing. IEEE Trans. Parallel and Distributed Systems 9(3), 235–248 (1998)
7. Zaki, M.J., Parthasarathy, W.L.S.: Customized Dynamic Load Balancing for a Network of Workstations. J. Parallel and Distributed Computing 43(2), 156–162 (1997)
8. Shah, R., Veeravalli, B., Misra, M.: Estimation based load balancing algorithm for data-intensive heterogeneous grid environments. In: Robert, Y., Parashar, M., Badrinath, R., Prasanna, V.K. (eds.) HiPC 2006. LNCS, vol. 4297, pp. 72–83. Springer, Heidelberg (2006)
9. Murata, Y., Takizawa, H., Inaba, T., Kobayashi, H.: A Distributed and Cooperative Load Balancing Mechanism for Large-Scale P2P Systems. In: Proc. Int'l Symp. Applications and Internet (SAINT 2006) Workshops, pp. 126–129 (2006)
10. Zeng, Z., Veeravalli, B.: Design and Analysis of a Non-Preemptive Decentralized Load Balancing Algorithm for Multi-Class Jobs in Distributed Networks. Computer Comm. 27, 679–693 (2004)
11. Lüling, R., Monien, B.: A Dynamic Distributed Load Balancing Algorithm with Provable Good Performance. In: Proc. of the 5th ACM Symposium on Parallel Algorithms and Architectures (SPAA 1993), pp. 164–173 (1993)
12. Liu, J., Jin, X., Wang, Y.: Agent-Based Load Balancing on Homogeneous Minigrids: Macroscopic Modeling and Characterization. IEEE Transactions on Parallel and Distributed Systems 16(7), 586–598 (2005)
13. Dobber, M., Mei, R., Koole, G.: Dynamic Load Balancing and Job Replication in a Global-Scale Grid Enviornment: A Comparison. IEEE Transaction on Parallel and Distributed Systems 20(2), 207–218 (2009)
14. Cao, J., Spooner, D.P., Jarvi, S.A., Nudd, G.R.: Grid Load Balancing using Intelligent Agents. Future Generation Computer Systems 21(1), 135–149 (2005)
15. Acker, D., Kulkarni, S.: A Dynamic Load Dispersion Algorithm for Load-Balancing in a Heterogeneous Grid System. In: Sarnoff Symposium IEEE, pp. 1–5 (2007)
16. Lu, K., Subrata, R., Zomaya, A.Y.: On the performance driven load distribution for heterogeneous computational grids. Journal of Computer and System Sciences 73(8), 1191–1206 (2007)
17. Shah, R., Veeravalli, B., Misra, M.: On the design of adaptive and decentralized load balancing algorithms with load estimation for computational grid environments. IEEE Transactions on Parallel and Distributed Systems 18(12), 1675–1686 (2007)
18. Kunz, T.: The influence of different workload descriptions on a heuristic load balancing scheme. IEEE Transactions on Software Engineering 1991 17(7), 725–730 (1991)
19. Buyya, R., Murshed, M.: GridSim: a toolkit for the modeling and simulation of distributed resource management and scheduling for grid computing. Concurrency Computation Practice and Experience (CCPE) 14(13-15), 1175–1220 (2002)

Adoption of Cloud Computing in e-Governance

Rama Krushna Das[1], Sachidananda Patnaik[2], and Ajita Kumar Misro[3]

[1] National Informatic Center, Berhampur,
[2,3] Research Scolar, Berhampur University, Bhanjan Bihra, Orissa, India
ramdash@yahoo.com, sachi_patnaik2004@yahoo.com,
misroajit_km@rediffmail.com

Abstract. Cloud is a model or architecture and a new paradigm of computing with SOA as its base architecture. Cloud Computing has evolved as a key computing platform for sharing resources that include infrastructures, software, applications, and business processes. e-Governance plays a vital role in any organization and clouds with different layers are helpful to the e-Governance services. Cloud has different services, which are integrated and reused. As e-Governance is using distributed services, which requires a lot of infrastructure. Cloud services are helpful to reduce the cost of infrastructure and software cost. This paper describes how to adopt cloud computing in e-Governance applications to reduce infrastructure, and platform cost, to increase network security, to increase scalability and quick implementation.

Keywords: e-Governance, Cloud Computing, SOA, Security, Privacy.

1 Introduction

There is an increase in the online e-Governance services provided by federal and provincial Government in India. It is a country with more than one billion people, where proper implementation of these online services faces a lot of problem in delivering efficient and cost effective services. There are some questions in our mind when we started to plan for adopting the cloud computing that starts with privacy and security. Not many people really know how it works, but they are using it in their everyday life. Many websites that we browse through everyday are set up on Amazon Web Services, which is Amazon's Cloud Services offering. Using the Internet to perform computing, though does offer us cost savings with regards to computing hardware, software, infrastructure etc, but one does need to factor in the additional requirement of high speed, always on Internet that Cloud Computing demands. Cloud Computing provides environments to enable resource sharing in terms of scalable infrastructures, middleware and application development platforms, and value added business applications in terms of services. The operation models may include pay-as go utility models, free infrastructure services with value added platform services, fee-based infrastructure services with value-added application services, or free services for vendors but sharing of revenues generated from consumers. We know that Cloud Computing as a technology is at a very nascent stage but it seems very likely that it will be the next big breakthrough technology for the Internet. If we start to focus on creating

N. Meghanathan et al. (Eds.): CCSIT 2011, Part III, CCIS 133, pp. 161–172, 2011.

the infrastructure needs for a wider and more efficient e-Governance delivery system, then we should be able to harness this technology in a few years, by which time the technology would also have matured and be ready for deployment in a country like India with many diversity.

At the same time [6], Service Oriented Architecture (SOA) has been a popular framework in many application domains. The architecture of SOA allows services to be discovered, composed, and executed. Based on these technologies, services can be rapidly composed and the composite service can be deployed to achieve the desired goal. To support successful cloud computing, SOA plays a major role with ever increasing importance. All the hardware, software, and data resources can be wrapped as services in clouds. When an end-user wishes to accomplish a certain task, a composition service can be employed to discover the needed resources and compose them to provide the desired functionality and quality to the end-user. In this paper, we proposed a model for e-Revenue system in the government land revenue collection services. This model helps G2G, G2E, G2B and G2C applications to take the help of the available services on the cloud.

2 Cloud Building Blocks for e-Governance

The building blocks of cloud computing are rooted in hardware and software architecture and networking devices that enables innovative infrastructure scaling and virtualization [2]. However the next infrastructure innovations are more dynamic and carry on dynamic provisioning to manage in large cluster within the infrastructure. There are also implications for the next generation application design to make optimum use of resources and fault tolerances in an organization.

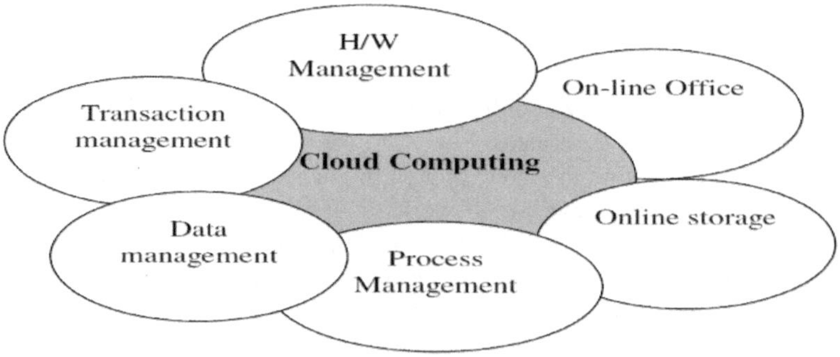

Fig. 1. Integration of services with Cloud

Cloud infrastructures have the potential to introduce good performance behaviors. While sharing a large infrastructure can average out the variability of individual workloads, it is difficult to predict the exact performance characteristics of an application at any particular time. Like any shared infrastructure, varying individual workloads can impact available CPU, Networks and I/O resources resulting in unpredictable performance behavior of the combined applications.

From the figure 1, it can be concluded that a cloud is a mixing of different management services. Cloud can be categorized as public cloud and private cloud, but the service can be used for each other with in an organization and can import from others. Public cloud infrastructures by the nature are outside the enterprise must leverage wide area network which can introduce bandwidth and latency issues. In addition, many Public Cloud providers have multiple storage offerings with varying performance characteristics. Typically, write performance is typically impacted to a much larger degree than read performance, especially with non-block oriented storage. Every management system having their own infrastructure and those can be used on optimal way for better computations. To overcome many challenges, Cloud can leverage proactive scaling of resources to increase capacity in anticipation of loads.

2.1 Cloud Services

Cloud computing is the combination of various technologies that is enough to provide smooth functions. The technologies as Grid Computing, Virtualization, Distributed Systems, System engineering and Service Oriented Architecture (SOA) play an important role in cloud computing. SOA is a pattern of architecture where as cloud is an instance of architectures. Cloud computing is the ability to provide IT resources over the Internet. These resources are typically provided on a subscription basis that can be expanded or contracted as needed. Services include storage services, database services, information services, testing services, security services, and platform services. Anything that is there in the data center today can be found on the Internet and delivered as a service.

2.2 Components of e-Governance

The importance of e-Governance lies in creating a global society, which has capacity to absorb divergent value patterns to eventually form universal normative axis having thrust on humane element. Precisely, it focuses on automation, informatisation, and transformation so as to increase the pace of development. Thus the fundamental objectives are,

- To have governance which economizes,
- To have governance, which multiplies in manifold the output at same cost
- To have governance which functions faster, better and transparent.
- To have governance, which retrieves facts completely from archives to help bureaucrats to recycle them in such a way that the feed- back can be utilized for making more prudent policies.

However to understand that how e- governance can transpose government as an instrument for building up a society, based on a collaborative mixture of conventional values with scientific approach, to create a better world, it would be essential to identify various components of e- governance and their interrelationships with each other. The following components can be identified as in the figure 2.

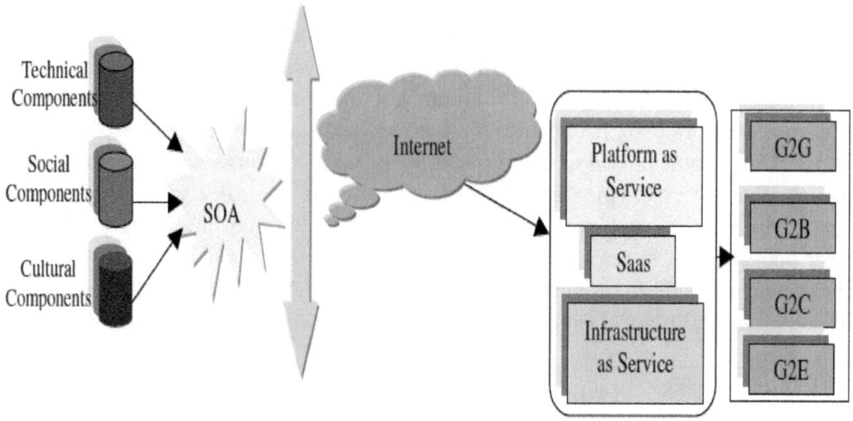

Fig. 2. Cloud computing for e-Governance

2.2.1 Technical Components with Electronic Dimension

This relates to educate people who are in the bureaucratic structure or outside its periphery regarding use of electronic means to develop better connectivity within the system. It requires use of computers (a) in developing the database, (b) in networking to facilitate the communication, (c) in creating e- knowledge workers so as to increase their potentiality.

2.2.2 Cultural Components with Ethical Dimension

The cultural component needs to create value patterns conducive for e-Governance to operate focusing on work ethos that cannot be denied. Thus to work out the ethical framework is the key to move further by discarding obsolete set of values that come in the way of potential utilization. Thus "e" of ethical framework has to be the focal point in constructing a morality-based system.

2.2.3 Political Components

The political system is an essential aspect of governance. It holds responsibility of rationalizing various operative frameworks by enacting laws. This helps to maintain & sustain the cohesive force that is required by society to integrate its people and abide them to follow a uniform policy to fulfill their targets. This refers to the importance of "e" of enactment of laws to stop society from disintegration.

2.2.4 Social Components with Egalitarian Dimension

The fundamental duty of any government is to educe a society, which is based on the principles of equality and justice. This is possible when people will be aware of their rights & duties on the one hand, and know about the governmental policies made for them on related issues on the other, hence a vigilant society can be evolved where they can raise their voices by questioning the governmental decisions. This would help in attaining the "e" of egalitarian society with thrust on equality.

2.2.5 Physiological Components

Developing required psyche so as to facilitate formation and inculcation of right type of attitudes in the people is prerequisite for efficiency. Apart form this; readiness to connect to people, to listen to their queries, to look for solutions, to improve communicative skills etc. will be necessary elements for behavioral modifications. Hence personality adjustments must be carried out to cater to the needs of common man. This specifically relates to "e" of extension of self so as to have constructive collaborative social relationships.

All the components of the Government can be integrated by using services. Those services can be mixed and imported to the cloud by using different cloud based services such as hardware as services, software as services and service itself as services. These services can be provided as G2B, G2E and G2C for innovation and optimal performances.

2.3 Service Identification

The cloud architecture allows rapidly allocating and de-allocating massively scalable resources on a demand basis. It gives flexibility to choose multiple vendors that provide reliable and scalable business services, development environments, and infrastructure that can be leveraged out of the box and billed on a metered basis. The other benefits are scalability, high reliability, reduced costs due to operational efficiencies, and more rapid deployment of new business and reduce runtime and response time etc. The three major IT implementation in Government sector are IT facilitation in State Data Center (SDC), automation of government workflow and e-Governance projects. These three major areas required huge resources in terms of computing, networking and IT infrastructure. The process for prioritizing e-services is an iterative pattern, guided by both transaction criteria and the perceptions of stakeholders. The methodology for prioritizing the services is expected to provide an impartial view of priorities, drawing on best practices in rationalizing, phasing, and sequencing investments to capture local knowledge and initial conditions, and gather information from secondary source (authorities) to identify key services and stakeholders and the services. Following are the various categories of the services to be identified:

- Government to Citizen Services (G2C Services)
- Government to Business Services (G2B Services)
- Government to Employee services (G2E Services)
- Government-to-Government Services (G2G Services)
- Shared services
- Informational services
- Interactive services
- Transactional services
- Integrated services

Chances are good that we have a beefy enough Internet connection to make cloud computing viable. However, realize that the more to do on the cloud, the more demand will be placed on Internet connection. It's important to secure an Service Level Agreement (SLA) that meets the bandwidth requirements. This not only ensures that we are getting the desired speed, but if the ISP fails to meet those levels, there can be some sort of remediation in it.

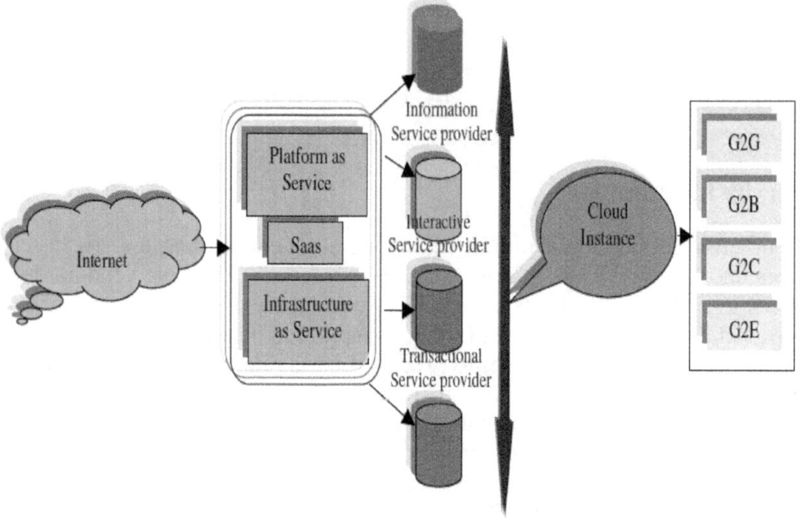

Fig. 3. Service Interaction for e-Governance

When formulating the cloud infrastructure, we should consider the issue of reliability and uptime and ask to the service provider to configure the computing infrastructure for redundancy and fail over. In LAN, redundancy used to mean that another server or two were added to the data center in case there was a problem. These days with virtualization, redundancy might mean a virtual server being cloned onto the same device, or all the virtual servers of one machine being cloned onto a second physical server.

3 Case Study

This case study is designed for a Revenue Division based on revenue collection system. Indian is divided into different provinces, which are divided into different districts. Taking eight to ten near by districts a division is formed. A district is having number of tahasils and the Tahasildar heads it. A Tahasil is having a number of Revenue Circles where the Revenue Inspector(RI) collects different revenue from the public as per the Government rules and regulations. The Revenue Inspector is a flexible person and collects the revenue from door to door and also observes many activities of his area.

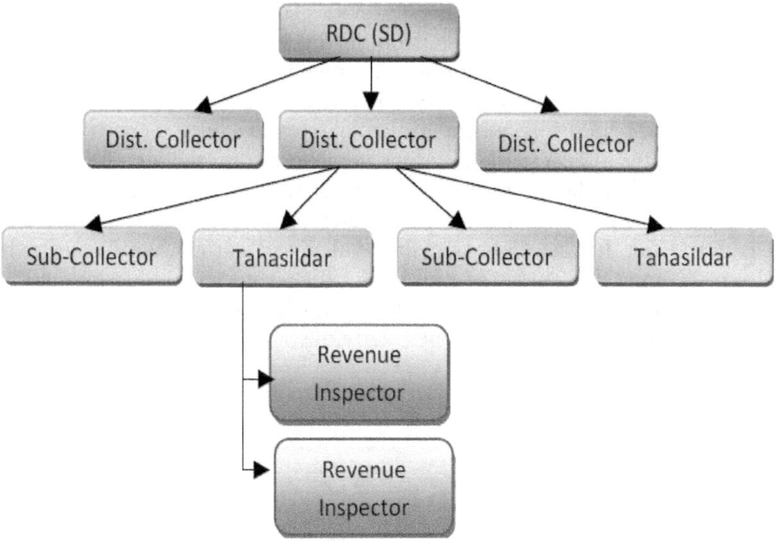

Fig. 4. Hierarchical structure of Officers in a Revenue Division

The revenue is collected from different purposes like house tax, water tax, land tax etc. as well as he also collects different number of cases and project information, which is implemented by the government. So, RI plays an important role that monitors on different projects implementation by the Govt. on his area/ circle. Revenue Inspector collects the information from his RI circle and report to the Tahasildar.

Sometime the Tahasildar finalize the information and the pending cases are informed to his higher authority like sub-collector or Collector of the District. Collector is the District Magistrate of the District who takes many important decisions for the Citizens. He conducts the revenue meeting with the presence of all the Tahasildar of the district and other officers every month to monitor the collection of revenue and settlement of revenue cases. He instructs and give target to the subordinates for better collection and other activities. Similarly, the Collector of the district sends the information in the form of report to the concern Revenue Divisional Commissioner (RDC) for further information to the state Government. At the District level there is a District Data Center (DDC) for processing of different data from different levels and from different projects of the Government, the DDC plays very important role, which is monitored by the Collector.

In the above figure-4, the Revenue Divisional Commissioner (RDC) checks the information at any time for necessary implementation of Government projects. Sub-Collectors help and encourage and monitor the activities of the Tahasildar and report to the Collector of the district.

3.1 Proposed Architecture

In this architecture, all the persons that are from Revenue Inspector to higher officers Tahasildar, Collectors and Revenue divisional Commissioner (RDC) and public can access the data in different formats. The Revenue Inspectors have a computer system with Internet connection for entering the data. The Revenue Inspector always play important role as he gathers the data from his/her own revenue circle and enter it by using their own interface. An interface is a predefined web page or program that is common to all the Revenue Inspectors, and other Officers. The interface is web based which can be accessed any where by using Internet connection. It is easy for the Revenue Inspector to access the interface anywhere from the locations. The data can be analyzed by the higher authority, in this case the Tahasildar checks the data entered by the Revenue Inspectors for further computations as shown in figure – 5 and sent to the District Office for the Collector approval. The District Data Center collects the data from different Tahasildar of the district for necessary processing and again the data in the form of reports send to the Revenue Divisional Commissioner (RDC) for review purposes and for governmental activities as well as for future planning and developments.

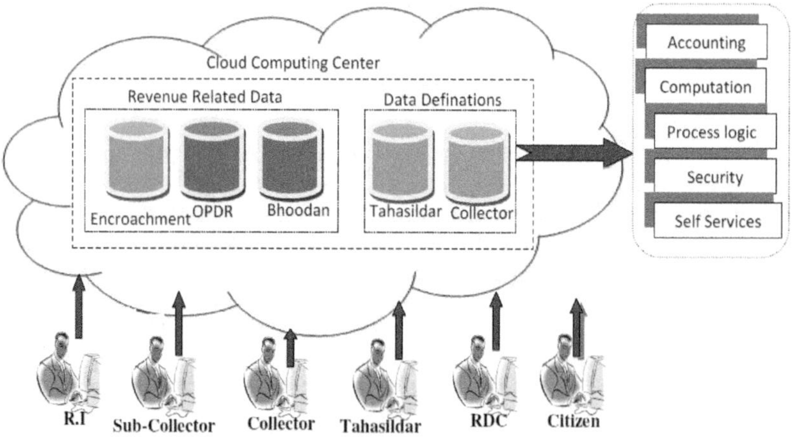

Fig. 5. Cloud based Model for e-Revenue

So, it can be concluded that the Government activities are depending on the data of lower level that is data collected from the Revenue Inspectors. Process logic has been designed by different officers for different level. Process logic is a logic or procedure, which follows different official rules and regulation. These rules and regulations are converted into different logic, which are designed by the technical personal from the Government or Revenue department. There are different process logics sometime designed by the Tahasildar as well as at District Data Center by the District Collector. Data can be process according to the Data definitions. Here there are different services for storing the data, which is collected by the RIs like encroachment, OPDR, Bhoodan, Certificate Cases etc. All the data are stored in a common place having different servers for fast processing. But different Officers at their end can access the data without using any additional hardware as well as software. They have only one system that may be thin client for accessing through Internet. Here, we are giving importance on infrastructure as service that includes servers, storage space, network equipments, different software and databases. The infrastructure is provided in the form of virtual environment. As all the users access through Internet connectivity, that the speed and efficiency is quite important.

4 Benefits

There are many benefits on adopting the Cloud computing services in the e-Government are as follows.

4.1 Cost

Cloud computing as an architectural solution, is typically less expensive while considering in terms of the hardware, software, and human resources that have to maintain the systems. Since cloud providers use a pay-as-go or an on-demand model, there is a reasonable usage fee, typically based on time, units of storage, or other means of monetizing their clouds. Cost is the core benefit of cloud computing, since we pay as per our requirement and on processing of data.

4.2 Network

Cloud computing architecture can be represented in the Internet. The ability for a cloud service to be combined with other cloud services, making a custom service that is even more powerful than the sum of any of its parts, is a real benefit of cloud computing. Internet connection should be fast, broad for accessing and communication of data.

4.3 Performance

Cloud can be better performance as we all are concentrating on a particular system. That is its hardware, software etc for providing data. We can access by using Internet but only one system can provide data having process logic for others. Hence, the system should be strong for high performance.

4.4 Expandability

There is no need of additional hardware and software's from organizational point of view. We can expand the resources for processing the data with in an instance by using the existing resources.

4.5 Speed of Implementation

As we are not purchasing any hardware, installing operating systems, or getting permission to take a portion of a data center. We just sign up, in most cases, and then access to the cloud resources. But, for processing the data depends on the Internet and its speed for transporting.

4.6 Green Computing

Cloud computing is good for the environment as we are using very less amount of hardware resources and software. As and when required to process the data that is processed on the server and gives the result. So, it requires very less power consumption and requires fewer infrastructures.

4.7 Portability

The ability of users to access the data and tools they need anywhere they can connect to the Internet.

4.8 Simpler Device

Since both their data and the software they use are in the Cloud, users don't need a powerful computer to use it. A cell phone, a PDA, a personal video recorder, an online game console, their cars, even sensors built into their clothing could be their interface.

5 Government's Role on Adoption of Cloud

The pace of development and deployment of the Cloud will depend on many different factors, including quick maturity of basic technology, standardization of computer resources and telecommunications, cost-effective, compelling applications are developed, and quick potential users acceptation and adopt this new way of purchasing computing resources [11].

Government policy can influence each of these factors. And there are other ways in which governments can accelerate or hinder the growth of the Cloud. Just as the pace of development of the Internet has varied by country and industry, the pace of development of the Cloud will vary widely. Governments can play a critical role in shaping the Cloud. They can foster widespread agreement on standards, not only for the basic networking and Cloud communication protocols, but also for service-level management and interaction. By using the power of the purse in their IT procurement policies, governments can pressure companies to find consensus on the key Cloud standards. Governments need to access how existing law and regulations in a wide range of areas will affect the development of the Cloud. They must both "future-proof" existing law and ensure that new policy decisions do not limit the potential of this revolutionary new approach to computing.

The Cloud will be a fundamental infrastructure for the economy, national security, and society in general. A natural reaction would be to demand uniformly high quality and to regulate a number of features and services that use it. But without a lot more experience, we simply do not know enough about what the right set of underlying services will be, what are appropriate differences in price and quality of services, what techniques will be best for providing reliable service, and where the best engineering tradeoffs will be. Governments can add value by encouraging experimentation and new services. The Cloud is an upcoming technology that challenges existing business models, institutions, and regulatory paradigms. As a result, there is likely to be resistance from many different quarters to the widespread deployment of Cloud technologies. Governments must be willing to challenge and change existing policies that could be used to hinder the growth of the Cloud. Simply trying to adapt existing regulations to the Cloud might allow entrenched interests to significantly delay the investment and effort needed for widespread use of Cloud computing. Because Cloud computing is a fundamentally different approach to computing and communications, governments should consider fundamentally new approaches to telecommunications and information policy.

The Cloud is inherently global, policy solutions must be cross-jurisdictional, because the Cloud is a many-to-many medium and it is not always easy to determine who's responsible for what. And also the Cloud technology and Cloud applications are evolving so quickly, government policy must be flexible and adaptable. Because the challenges are so great and the opportunities so widespread, it is imperative that policymakers and the technologists developing the Cloud start now to look for innovative technical and policy solutions.

6 Conclusion

Cloud computing has the potential to change how organizations manage IT and transform the economics of hardware and software at the same time. On-demand services and Software-as-a-Service (SaaS) solutions have become the preferred mechanisms for e-governance applications to better leverage the power of cloud computing. For any government department, the transition to the cloud is a major decision. Concerns like data control, management, accessibility and security hold the departments back from switching to the cloud. Before implementing cloud any department should first identify and prioritize IT issues and challenges within itself; next the benefits of cloud computing should be mapped against these IT issues. From the point of view of each government agency or department, creating a cloud migration strategy may be of importance. This may call for inter-departmental collaboration to identify the solutions, which are easier to transition and create necessary volumes to realize cost benefits. This could be done by the nodal information technology agencies at the apex. The proposed system can work efficiently by using cloud computing and provides information to the citizens without any further investment. So, a citizen can access the information as it is their right and Government can get good result for implementation of new projects and plans. Sometime, citizens can suggest and give feedbacks to the Government directly or indirectly for better nation building. This type of computing is open for the people, by the people and to the people.

References

[1] Mohammad, A.F.: An Achievable Service-Oriented Architecture – ASOA. In: Third Asia International Conference on Modeling & Simulation (2009)

[2] Velte, A.T., Velte, T.J., Elsenpeter, R.: Cloud Computing: A Practical Approach. McHill Publication

[3] Linthicum, D.S.: Cloud Computing and SOA Convergence in Your Enterprise A Step-by-Step Guide. Addison–Wesely, Reading

[4] Zhang, L.-J., Zhou, Q.: CCOA: Cloud Computing Open Architecture. In: IEEE International Conference on Web Services (2009)

[5] Sannella, M.J.: Constraint Satisfaction and Debugging for Interactive User Interfaces. Ph.D. Thesis, University of Washington, Seattle, WA (1994)
[6] Sahoo, M.: IT Innovations: Evaluate, Strategize, and Invest. In: IT Pro. IEEE Computer Society, Los Alamitos (November/December 2009)
[7] Pokharel, M., Yoon, Y.H., Park, J.S.: Cloud Computing in System Architecture. IEEE, Los Alamitos, 978-1-4244-5273-6/09
[8] Chuob, S., Pokharel, M., Park, J.S.: The Future Data Center for E-Govemance
[9] Stantchev, V.: Performance Evaluation of Cloud Computing Offerings. In: Third International Conference on Advanced Engineering Computing and Applications in Sciences (2009)
[10] Cellary, W., Strykowski, S.: E-Government Based on Cloud Computing and Service-Oriented Architecture
[11] Hao, W., Yen, I.-L., Thuraisingham, B.: Dynamic Service and Data Migration in the Clouds. In: 33rd Annual IEEE International Computer Software and Applications Conference (2009)
[12] http://www2.epfl.ch/webdav/site/mir/shared/import/migration/zwahr_pista04.pdf
[13] http://www.lasalle.edu/~mccoey/inl664/readingmaterials-homework/p471-peristeras.pdf

Efficient Web Logs Stair-Case Technique to Improve Hit Ratios of Caching

Khushboo Hemnani[1], Dushyant Chawda[2], and Bhupendra Verma[3]

[1] PG scholar in Department of computer science and engineering T.I.T Bhopal
khushboo.pamnani@gmail.com
[2] Assistant professor in computer science and engineering T.I.T Bhopal
[3] Professor in computer science and engineering T.I.T Bhopal

Abstract. Cache prefetching technique can improve the hit ratio and expedite users visiting speed. Predictive Web prefetching refers to the mechanism of deducing the forth coming page accesses of a client based on its past accesses.Congestion in Network remains one of the main barriers to the continuing success of the Internet. For Web users, congestion manifests itself in unacceptably long response times. One possible remedy to the latency problem is to use caching at the client, at the proxy server, or within the Internet. However, Web documents are becoming increasingly dynamic, which limits the potential benefit of caching. The performance of a Web caching system can be dramatically increased by integrating document prefetching into its design. Although prefetching reduces the response time of a requested document, it also increases the network load, as some documents will be unnecessarily prefetched.In the paper, we developed a Stair-Case prune algorithm to mine popular with their conditional probabilities from the proxy log, and stored them in the rule table. Then, according to contents and the rule table, a prediction is calculated in some precondition. After the simulation, we found that our approach has much better performance than the other ones, in terms of hit ratio.

Keywords: Web mining, Proxy servers, Caching, Prefetching, Access prediction, Hit ratio, pruner.

1 Introduction

Cache technique is a common technology which can store the nearest collected information in order to use it in future, these information are thought to be used more frequently than others. But as is known from, there is exponential relation between the Increasing of cache size and the hit ratio of cache. Even though with an infinite cache, the hit of ratio can reach only at the range from 40% to about 50%[21] Consequently, we can learn that the hit ratio is the important index to estimate the performance of cache, it is affected by cache size, updating tragedy, user visit habit and many other factors . In order to improve the hit ratio of cache, cache prefetching technique is proposed. If only prediction is correct, both the hit ratio of cache and the visiting speed can be improved. Present prefetching system, however, cast much emphasis on statistical information of the rules. It Depends on the probability of the appearance of a

N. Meghanathan et al. (Eds.): CCSIT 2011, Part III, CCIS 133, pp. 173–182, 2011.

rule, and then decides whether this rule is adopted. Among all the requests, some objects are frequently requested by users, while others not. Generally, a request pattern of web objects in web logs. In this approach we proposed a stair case model which improves a caching.

2 Principle of Stair Case Technique

The stair case algorithm is based on calculating the frequent pattern in step wise without candidate key and based on that index the cache hit ratio is comparatively improved.In our thesis we develop the model called as stair case model similar to the prediction based proxy server[21]In this model first we accept the request of customers or itemsets,which is to be mined. It is then processed to the log file and index of that particular item set is stored in log buffer which is the part of memory, then apply the exponential stair case mechanism and create a rule table. Since generating sequences with more than two items (minimum support which is greater than 2) has no help in producing the rule table, we stop finding frequent sequences when the minimum support is less than two. The prediction manager only stores those item sets which are frequent means the minimum support count of the item sets in the data base is greater than two. After that the prefetch buffer only takes the subset belongs to minimum support and apply the formula according to algorithm given below.

2.1 Stair Case Model

The figure 1 is the stair case model which consists of log file, prediction manager and cache and prefetch buffer. all requested pages are come to the stair case which on

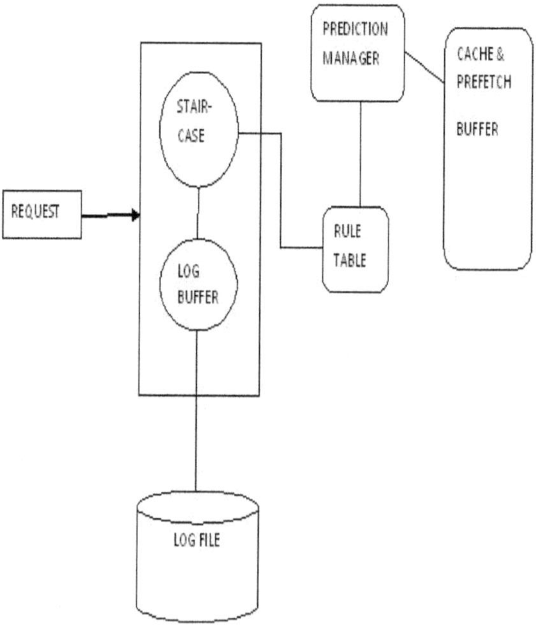

Fig. 1. Stair Case Model

based on precondition creates the rule table and determines all frequent pages. The model consist of log buffer followed by the log file. The log file maintains the status of the current page as well as the status of all previous pages. The log file filter not only cleans the irrelevant records and fields in the log file, but also groups the related requests of a user during the past period into a transaction for facilitating the mining process later.

The prediction manager makes the appropriate action and handles the all related request and maintains the cache and prefetch buffer, and based on their occurrence, weight and probability the cache hit ratio is considerably improved.

2.2 Stairs-Case Mining

In this section, we describe the proposed method. There are some terminology which is important for understanding the novel technique.

1) Database –We are taking an example of employee database with their transaction items. The item sets are the value which is visited by the user by any predetermines time in any shopping mall.
2) Frequent Pattern- Frequent pattern means the item set which are used by the customer frequently. For example if item I1 is purchased by 10 customers and item I2 is purchased by 5 customers then the item I1 is most frequently used. So the owner must concentrate on I1 Items because it is visited by more no of customers.
3) Minimum support-For Item to be a frequent member we decide a minimum support count by which we will determine that the item is in the list of Frequent Pattern or not. For Example if minimum support is 2 then the item which count or customer visiting no is = or > 2 is the most frequent one, which will be consider for pruning.
4) Data Pruning – The act of removing those item set which is not necessary ius called data Pruning.

The entire system architecture consists of three phases:

1. Find possible subset for prune based on the minimum support count by Stair case-Finder.
2. Start Pruning by stair case –Pruner
3. Add the superset in the list and remove the related subset from the list. Finally we find the frequent pattern patterns or knowledge from huge amount of data.

Consider the database of employee and their Item-Sets. Employee Arrival patterns are from E1, E2 and E3.E1 visit the Item-Sets 10,20 E2 visit the Item-Sets 10,20,30 and E3 visit the Item-Sets 10,20,30 . Here Space and "," are different in terms of recognizing the frequent pattern. We apply differentiation from Item-Sets by "," and differentiate employee Item-Sets by space.

2.3 Example Set

Let us consider a progressive customer transaction database which is shown in table1.

Assumptions-
Min-support-Minimum Support value defined by user.
AS- All possible set of Items
PS- All possible set of Items with support >Min-support count
LI- Final List
CD-count-of-sequence
P- A sequence of length P.
PCD- All P-sequence in AS with support ≥ Min-sup in d
Stair case Finder- to find the possible subsets for prune.
Stair case Pruner- for determining the frequent pattern

Table 1. Employee Datasets

Emp-ID	Item-Sets
E1	10,20
E2	10,20,30
E3	10,20,30,40

2.4 Algorithm for Stair Case Mine

```
Input Item-Sets in database.
  For( ;AS!=NULL; )
  {
  Find the count of all sequences by S-Finder.
  If(CD>Min-sup)
  {
  PCD=PS
  If(PCD!=NULL)
  SB-Pruner(PCD)
  }
  Else
  {
 Exit(0)
  }
  }
```

2.5 Algorithm for Stair Case Pruner

```
Input PCD
  For (; PCD! =NULL ;)

  P=first element of PCD
  If P is not frequent in the database
  {
  Remove P and its supersets from PCD
  }
```

```
Else
{
Add supersets to PCD
Remove P from PCD
}
Add PCD to LI
Print LI
```

2.6 Work of Stair Case-Pruner

We apply SB-Pruner on P-sequence in AS with support greater than or equal to Min-sup in the database of employee transaction. First we input the data set of PCD.The database is short in comparison of the original database, we only consider those item set which are frequent in the database means which having a support greater than or equal to minimum support. We apply the pruner algorithm on the database until all the transactions are compared. Let the first element in the PCD is P.If P is not frequent in the current database, remove its subset and superset from the current database which is PCD.We apply the process for each Transactions of employee in the current database. If it is frequent in the current database then adds its superset in the PCD and removes its subset from the PCD.It means we include the superset of P but delete the transaction P from the current database. However, Algorithms that pruned off infrequent sequences are essentially not suitable for merging due to the information loss.

2.7 Result Evaluation of the Item Sets

In this section, we describe the evaluation and result of proposed method. The entire evaluation and result consists of three phases:

1. Read the data from the database
2. Apply Stair case-Finder to find the frequent sequences which is greater than or equal to min-support
3. Apply Stair case-Pruner
4. Add the superset in the list and remove the related subset from the list. Finally we find the frequent pattern or knowledge from huge amount of data.

A. Read the data from the database

Table 1 shows read data from the database where we want to apply the Stair case-Finder method

Table 2. Read data

Item-Sets
10,20
10,20,30
10,20,30,40

B. Apply Stair case-Finder

We apply SB-Pruner on P-sequence in AS with support greater than or equal to Min-sup in the database of employee

Table 3. Stair case finder 1

Item-Sets	Count
10,20	3

Table 4. Stair case finder 2

Item-Sets	Count
10,20	3
10,20,30	2

Table 5. Stair case finder 3

Item-Sets	Count
10,20	3
10,20,30	2
10,20,30,40	1

C. Apply Stair case-Pruner

We apply Stair case Pruner on P-sequence in AS with support greater than or equal to Min-sup in the database of employee transaction. First we input the data set of PCD.According to the count values item sets are arranged and find the final result after pruning which is shown in Table 5

Table 6. stair case pruner

Sequential Pattern	Final Prune
10,20 10,20,30 10,20,30,40	No
10,20,30 10,20,30,40	No
10,20,30,40 10,20,30,40	No
10,20,30,40	Yes

D. Delete Superset

First checks the subset if it is presents in the superset then delete the subset

Table 7. Subset finder

Sequential Pattern	**Final Prune**	Subset
10,20 10,20,30 10,20,30,40	No	Yes
10,20,30 10,20,30,40	No	Yes
10,20,30,40 10,20,30,40	No	Yes
10,20,30,40	Yes	No

The final result shown in the simulator is the superset value which is frequent

Final Result
10,20,30,40

3 Cache Hit Ratio

Based on our stair case mining the frequent pattern is calculated. The log file maintains the scenario to put the items in the cache to increase the cache hit ratio. When the requested item is present is cache, it said to be the hit and when it is not present in cache it is said to be the miss. The log file keep track on the frequent pattern and according to the size of the cache buffer it will put them in cache.The following algorithm will illustrate the cache hit and ratio and also predict about the next document.

Assumptions-

Weight of the document-Wd
Weight before the cache-W(p)d
Past reference time-Tp
Current reference time-Tr
Size of p-Sp
Other weighting Factor-Of
Current occurrence of p=Cp
Past occurrence of p=Pp
Memory Resource-MR
Cache Predicator-CP
Probability before in cache-Prob(p)
Probability after the cache-Proa(p)

1) Of=MR+CP
2) Sp=Wordcount(one page)*total pages
3)Wd=(Cp+Pp)+Wp(d)*(Tp/Tr-Tp)
4) First Prefetch Time
Wd= Prob(p)/Sp*Wp(d)*1/Tr-Tp
5) Last Prefetch Time
Wd1=Proa(p)/Sp*Wp(d)*1/Tr-Tp
6) Mean
(Wd+Wd1)/2

It includes the memory resource i.e memory resource will define the minimum support count which decides to calculate the superset. The log file will determine the past occurrence of document and current occurrence of requested document which it will maintain in log buffer. The architechure involves the cache predictor Cp. The log buffer also maintains the probability of documents after cache and its value before cache.

4 Result Analysis

The result analysis is based on stair case finder**.** The new method shows in the graph that the time is less in comparison of old methods like spade. So it is more efficient. we had taken .Thc graph is being compare with all the latest technology. It consist of four axis P1,P2,P3,P4.

P1 represent the SPADE approach without consist of log buffer to maintain the cache
P2 represent the SPADE with log file buffer
P3 represent Stair case miner without the log file buffer
P4 represent our approach stair case miner with loge file buffer

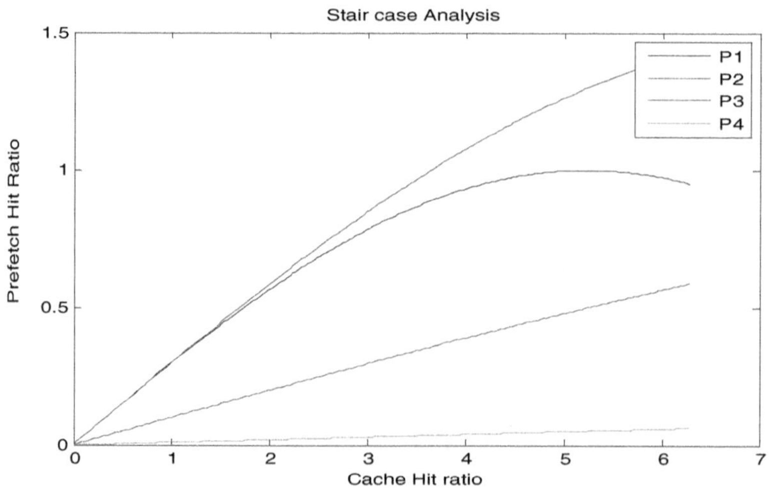

The second graph shows that in our appraoch the prediction ratio is also increases in terms of time

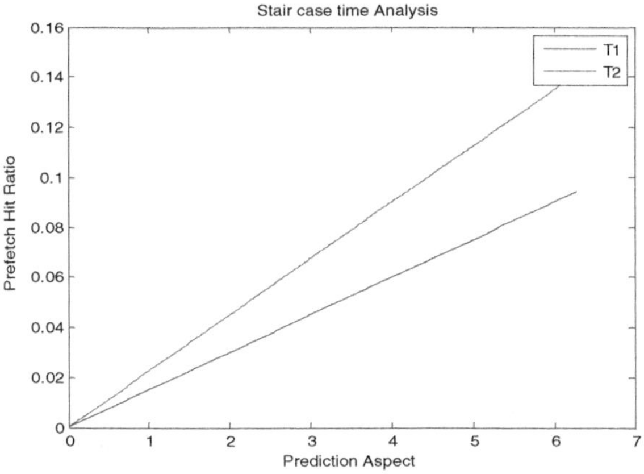

5 Conclusion

With our approach we have analysis that our approach would enhance cache hit ratio considerably more than previous approach. In this paper we apply Stair-Case approach for finding frequent pattern which occupy less memory space and based on that caching and prefetching of the documents is done. We enhance Hit Ratios of Caching.

References

1. Vanderwiel, S.P., Lilja, D.J.: Data prefetch mechanisms. ACM Computing Surveys 32(2) (2000)
2. Gill, B., Bathen, L.: Amp: Adaptive multi-stream prefetching in a shared cache. In: Proceedings of the 5th USENIX Conference on File and Storage Technologies, FAST (2007)
3. Baer, J.-L., Chen, T.-F.: Effective hardwarebased data prefetching for high-performance processors. IEEE Trans. Comput. 44(5), 609–623 (1995)
4. Dahlgren, F., Stenström, P.: Evaluation of hardware-based stride and sequential prefetching in sharedmemory multiprocessors. IEEE Trans. Parallel Distrib. Syst. 7(4), 385–398 (1996)
5. Lee, R.L., Yew, P.-C., Lawrie, D.H.: Data prefetching in shared memory multiprocessors. In: Proceedings of the International Conference on Parallel Processing, ICPP (1987)
6. Fu, J.W.C., Patel, J.H.: Data prefetching in multiprocessor vector cache memories. In: Proceedings of the 18th annual international symposium on Computer architecture, ISCA (1991)
7. Li, Z., Chen, Z., Srinivasan, S.M., Zhou, Y.: C-Miner: Mining block correlations in storage systems. In: Proceedings of the 3rd USENIX Conference on File and Storage Technologies, FAST (2004)
8. Padmanabhan, V.N., Mogul, J.C.: Using predictive prefetching to improve world wide web latency. Proc. of Computer Communication Review 26, 22–36 (1996)

9. Borges, J., Levene, M.: Data mining of user navigation patterns. In: Masand, B., Spiliopoulou, M. (eds.) WebKDD 1999. LNCS (LNAI), vol. 1836, pp. 92–112. Springer, Heidelberg (2000)
10. Chen, X., Zhang, X.: A popularity-based prediction model fore web prefetching. In: Proc. of IEEE Computer (2003)
11. Davison, B.D.: Learning web request patterns. In: Proc. Of Web Dynamics: Adapting to Change in Content, Size, Topology and Use, pp. 435–460 (2004)
12. Bouras, C., Konidaris, A., Kostoulas, D.: Predictive prefetching on the web and its potential impact in the wide area. In: Proc. of World Wide Web: Internet and Web Information System (2003)
13. Domenech, J., Sahuquillo, J., Gil, J.A., Pont, A.: The impact of the web prefetching architecture on the limits of reducing user's perceived latency. In: Proc. of IEEE/WIC/ACM Int'l Conf. on Web Intelligence (2006)
14. Nanopoulos, A., Katsaros, D., Manolopoulos, Y.: A data mining algorithm for generalized web prefetching. Proc. of IEEE Transaction on Knowledge and Data Engineering (2003)
15. Domenech, J., Pont, A., Sahuquillo, J., Gil, J.A.: A userfocused evaluation of web prefetching algorithmsa. In: Proc. of the Computer Communications (2007)
16. Chen, Y., Qiu, L., Chen, W., Nguyen, L., Katz, R.H.: Efficient and adaptive web replication using content clustering. Proc. of IEEE Journal on Selected Areas in Communications 21, 979–994 (2003)

A Semantic Approach to Design an Intelligent Self Organized Search Engine for Extracting Information Relating to Educational Resources

B. Saleena[1], S.K. Srivatsa[2], and M. Chenthil Kumar[3]

[1] Research Scholar, School of Information Technology and Engineering, VIT University
[2] Senior Professor, St. Joseph's College of Engineering, Chennai
[3] Final Year MCA, B.S. Abdur Rahman University, Chennai

Abstract. With the phenomenal growth in the World Wide Web, current online education system has tried to incorporate artificial intelligence and semantic web resources to their design and architecture. Semantic web is an evolving extension of the World Wide Web in which web content is organized meaningfully in a structured format using web ontology language (OWL), thus permitting them to find, share and integrate information more easily. This paper presents a methodology to design an intelligent system to retrieve information relating to education resources. For this, a knowledge library for pedagogic domain is created using ontology and knowledge management technologies, and then a strategy is devised to group the related topics in each subject and present it to the user in a single search with the prerequisites. The efficacy of our approach is demonstrated by implementing a prototype and comparing the retrieval results with online search engines.

Keywords: Semantic web, Ontology, Knowledge management.

1 Introduction

E-Learning system utilizes the learning environments with modern communication mechanism and abundant learning objects available in the web to help participants learning more effectively without the barriers of time and distance. In the currently available online search engines and educational materials there is no proper semantic relationship between the web resources. Finding the specific information and the pre requisites needed to assimilate the topic is difficult because of the lack of semantic description of learning resources. Users have to perform a lot of manual intervention tasks such as searching, grouping or sharing the contents across the web in order to assimilate the topic they are interested in. Therefore, acquiring and providing the suitable knowledge to meet learner's diverse learning needs is a key issue. To overcome this problem, the web resources need to be efficiently organized semantically using ontology.

Both Learning Content Management System (LCMS) and Intelligent Tutoring System (ITS) systems have the basic goals of making the learning process efficient for the students and reducing the work required to be done by the teacher. But they differ

N. Meghanathan et al. (Eds.): CCSIT 2011, Part III, CCIS 133, pp. 183–189, 2011.

in the way they go about achieving the basic goals. LCMS provide a platform where it is easier for the teacher to upload content, students have a central place for all their learning materials and the discussion/questions are extended out from the physical boundaries of the classroom. LCMS systems are easier to build and such systems involve active participation from the student community. However LCMS suffer from the problem that they have no intelligence built into them.

ITS systems are intelligent. They model how a teacher would teach in the class and also keep a track of the student's performance. Such systems use the record of students' performance to enhance their learning process. However these systems are expensive to build and model. They require much human expertise and are domain specific. Neither LCMS nor ITS system is a one stop solution to making the learning process efficient. ITS systems are difficult to build and LCMS aren't intelligent enough.

An intelligent application would be the one that would combine the benefits of both the systems into one and help the learner to fetch the required information in a single search. The proposed system is human understandable that can understand and customize the contents as per the individual learner's requirement. The system gives us the complete handy information about the interrelated contents/prerequisites that the users should be aware of before learning about the required search topic. It overcomes the problem of manual intervention required to assimilate the topics that are needed by the users to understand the fetched information.

1.1 Knowledge Representation in Semantic Web

The Semantic Web encompasses efforts to build a new WWW architecture that supports content with formal semantics, enabling better searching and navigating through the web. Mechanisms that enable annotating, searching for, combining the semantic information, together with semantic language, constitute the basic ingredients of an e-learning framework.

Ontology is defined as a data model that represents a domain and is used to reason about the objects in that domain and the relations between them. Ontology will represent the particular meanings of terms as they apply to a domain. It is a formal representation of a knowledge domain [9]. It is the key component needed to use the semantic web approach for searching repositories. Ontologies are a key technology emerging to facilitate Web information processing by supporting semantic structuring, annotation, indexing, and search. Ontologies allow organization of learning material around components of semantically annotated topics. This enables ontology-based course to do efficient semantic querying and navigation through the learning content [10].

The purpose of this paper was to (a) construct a knowledge base for Educational resources in computer science for the courses in a university. (b) To devise a methodology to self organize the contents in the knowledge base (c) Provide an interface to extract learning materials with its pre requisites and (d) report the results of research on how the pre requisites of the search content are provided to the user together with the results.

This paper is organized as follows. In Section 1 we present the problems of information retrieval for educational purposes from the commonly used learning systems and search engines. Section 2 discusses about the related work carried out Section 3 describes the architecture of the proposed system and the experimentation results. Section 4 concludes this paper and discusses about the future enhancements.

2 Related Work

The evolution of E-learning system over the years has enabled it to support not just teaching and learning over the web but also help in effective knowledge management. Ontologies and Semantic Web methods are used to integrate e-learning resources in the Web. These technologies also help to manage the knowledge base in a more efficient way for faster retrieval of relevant information. There are many research efforts in the area of semantic web and e-learning.

Zhaohui Wu Yuxin et al. describes a semantic mapping mechanism between databases and ontology to integrate e-learning resources and ontologies are divided in to sub ontologies for efficient resource management for e-learning [1]. Yanyan Li et al. proposes a knowledge portal to effectively support e-learning, enabling flexible knowledge acquisition, knowledge refinement and maintenance, as well as knowledge retrieval and accessing based on Semantic Web technologies[2]. Amal zouaq et al. proposes a methodology to transform Textual Resources and learning Objects to concept maps and derive domain ontologies from Concept maps. A common domain model was provided to bridge the gap between e-learning and Intelligent Tutoring System [4].Yufei Li et al. has developed and implemented a prototype of Ontolook – a relation based search engine [7].

Existing works on Semantic web and ontology based e-learning tend to use ontologies and semantic web to organize the e-learning resources and improve the retrieval of resources in a meaningful way. The concept of retrieving pre requisites needed to understand a particular topic during a search is not concentrated in any of the papers discussed above. This paper proposes to develop a search mechanism to extract the knowledge about the learning resources together with its pre requisites in a self organized way based on user's query.

3 Architecture for Self Organized Search Engine

The idea of retrieving the pre requisites required to assimilate a topic clearly is being highlighted in the paper. The effectiveness of the system is proved by developing a prototype based on a specific domain. The Fig 1 depicts an architecture diagram for Semantic Self Organized Domain Specific Search Mechanism that is developed to retrieve the contents together with its pre requisites. This system reduces the number of searches to understand the topic. At a single click it gives the definition, Prerequisites, PPT's and Pdf files related to that topic. This work is divided in to several phases like Input Interpretation, Domain Ontology Creation, Knowledge Representation and Searching and Grouping of relevant information.

3.1 Input Interpretation

User's request is placed in terms of keywords through a user interface. The keywords are matched with the semantic context of the topic. In other words, input is interpreted semantically according to the needs of user's requirement and is mapped into a particular class in OWL ontology. For example, if "normalization in database" is the user's keyword then the semantic interpretation of it leads into an OWL Class "Normalization" in OWL ontology.

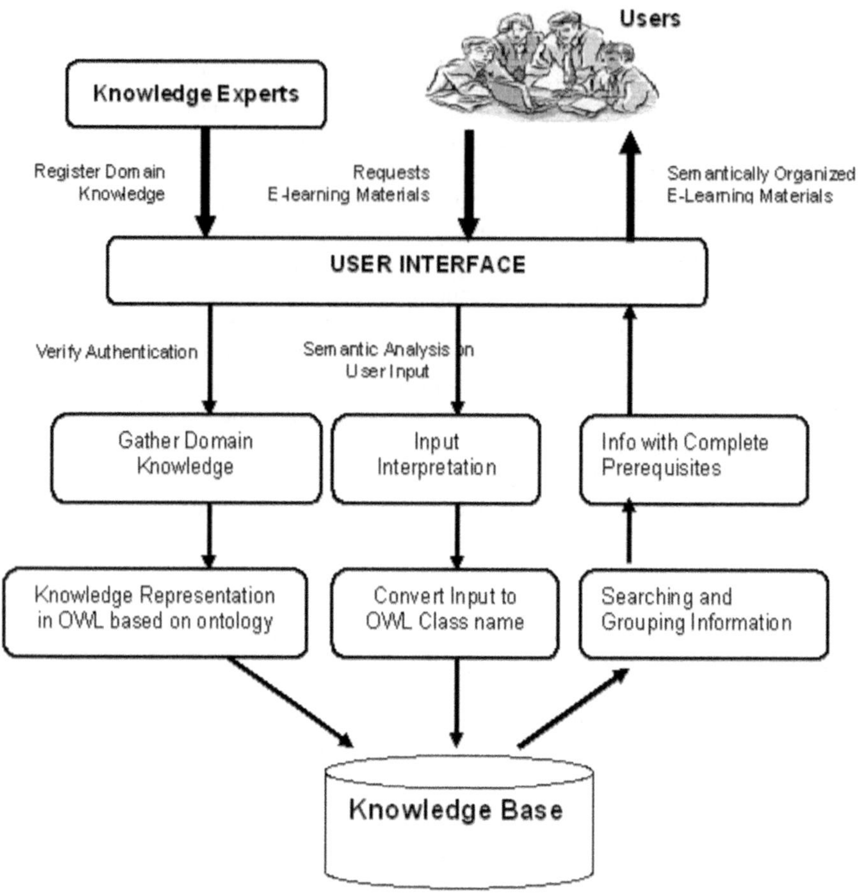

Fig. 1. Architecture for Semantic Self Organized Domain Specific Search Mechanism

3.2 Domain Ontology Creation

This phase deals with creating the domain ontology for various topics under the computer science subjects using Protége 4.1.0. The following steps as shown in Fig 2 are used to create the Domain Ontology. The classes were identified and categorized based on the relevance and the relationship between each class was defined. Finally a formal ontology framework was constructed. It is stored as an OWL file (Has extension .owl). OWL Viz is the Protégé OWL plug-in which enables the class hierarchies in an OWL Ontology to be viewed and incrementally navigated, allowing comparison of the asserted and inferred class hierarchies.

3.3 Knowledge Representation

The domain experts and the information providers share their knowledge about the pedagogic domain through a user interface provided to them. They register their

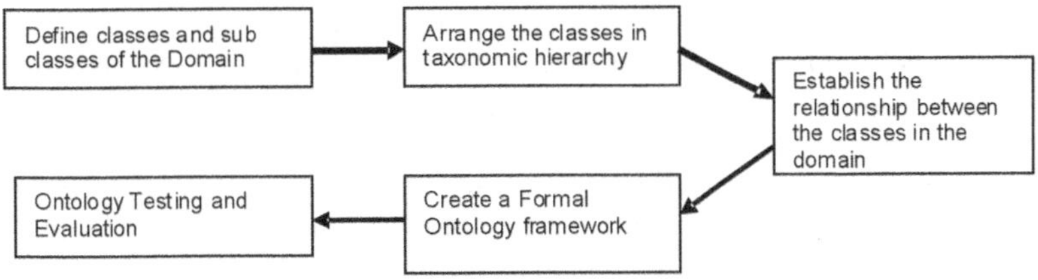

Fig. 2. Steps in creating Domain Ontology using OWL

learning materials in text form and as URI and URL's. Registering the information in the form of URI and URL's provides a global naming scheme to information and will enhance reusability. Registered information is linked to the concepts in the ontology. Another mode of registering knowledge is by using the annotation properties in OWL also can be used to add additional information (metadata) to classes, individuals and object/data type properties. Every information is stored as annotations property of each node in OWL Data Model in which each node represents a specific knowledge.

3.4 Searching and Grouping Information

The user requests for the information in terms of keywords through the user interface screen. The keywords are matched with the semantic context of the topic and all the

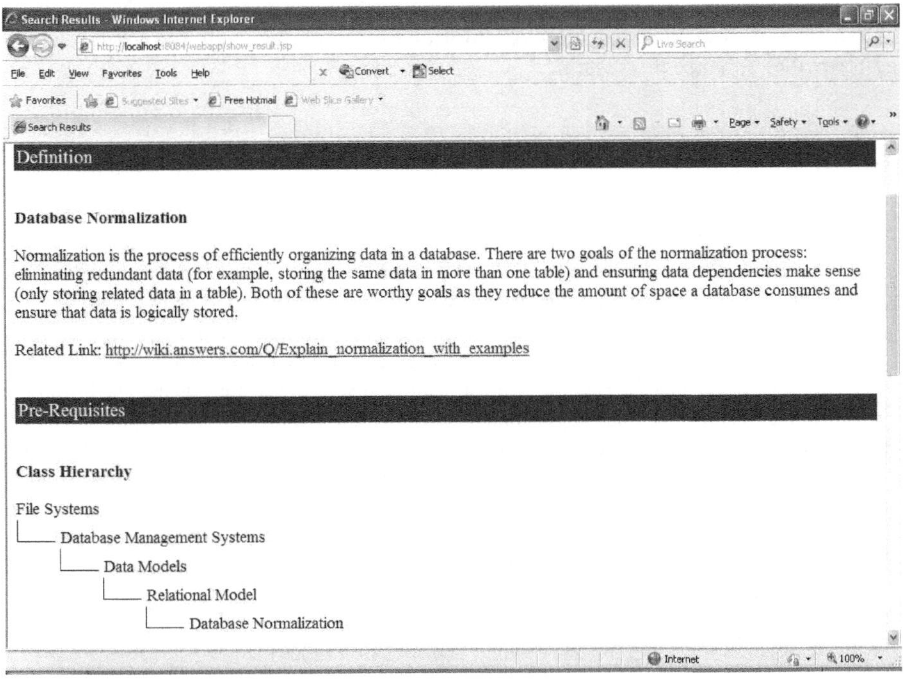

Fig. 3. Search Results of Normalization keyword with prerequisites

contents related to that are retrieved. Knowledge retrieval is performed by searching the appropriate node which matches the keyword with the semantic context.

The actual definition of the topic together with its entire parent nodes that represents the complete prerequisites/interrelated contents are grouped together. The grouped information is presented to the user in a systematic way. Fig 3 depicts the search results for normalization keyword. It retrieves the related topics and also the prerequisites needed to assimilate the topic searched. Other search engines like Google, yahoo do not list the prerequisites need to assimilate the topic at a single Click.

4 Conclusions and Future Enhancements

The core idea of this paper is to semantically model the heterogeneous domain specific learning resources in a coherent and meaningful way. The main objective of retrieving the interrelated contents and prerequisites needed to assimilate a particular topic as per user's interest is successfully achieved .Prerequisites are displayed in a hierarchical model so that users can understand the contents clearly. The system has been developed in Java2 with OWL API for Semantic Web. With the effective support of ontology-based knowledge retrieval, this E-Learning Framework aims to provide complete knowledge to meet learner's diverse learning needs in a user-friendly way.

This E-Learning Framework has been developed only for a single domain. It can be extended to various domains, and a large set of functionalities can be added to the user interface screens to enhance the user friendliness. This system follows a semi automatic annotation mechanism to gather knowledge about the domain. Mechanisms to perform Automatic extraction of information from the web resources can be performed to enhance the system.

References

1. Wu, Z., Mao, Y., Chen, H.: Sub ontology-based Resource Management for Web based e-learning. IEEE Transactions on Knowledge and Data Engineering 19(2) (February 2009)
2. Li, Y., Dong, M.: Towards a Knowledge Portal for E-Learning based on semantic Web. In: Eighth IEEE International Conference on Advanced Learning Technologies (2008)
3. Zouaq, A., Nkambou, R.: Enhancing Learning Objects with an Ontology-Based Memory. IEEE Transactions on Knowledge and Data Engineering 21(6) (June 2009)
4. Zouaq, A., Nkambou, R.: Building Domain Ontologies from text for Educational Purposes. IEEE Transactions on Learning Technologies 1(1) (March 2008)
5. Zhuge, H.: Communities and Emerging Semantics in Semantic Link Network: Discover and Learning. IEEE Transactions on Knowledge and Data Engineering 21(6) (June 2009)
6. Tiropanis, T., Davis, H., Millard, D., Weal, M.: Semantic Technologies for Learning and Teaching in the Web 2.0 Era. IEEE Computer Society, Los Alamitos (December 2009)
7. Li, Y., Wang, Y., Huang, X.: A Relation based Search Engine in Semantic web. IEEE Transactions on Knowledge and Data Engineering 19(2) (February 2007)
8. Li, W.: Study of Semantic Web-Oriented Ontology Integration Technologies. In: World Congress on Software Engineering, vol. 2, pp. 142–145 (2009)
9. Gardner, M.: Using Ontologies to Support the Sharing of Learning Resources (last modified January 16, 2007) (published January 16, 2007)

10. Jovanovic, J., Gasevic, D., Hatala, M., Brooks, C.: Using Semantic technologies to analyse learning content. IEEE Computer Society, Los Alamitos (October 2007)
11. Ontology Development 101: A Guide to Creating Your First Ontology, http://www-ksl.stanford.edu/people/dlm/papers/ontology-tutorial-noy-mcguinness-abstract.html
12. Smith, M.K., Welty, C., McGuinness, D.L.: OWL Web Ontology Language Guide. W3C (February 10, 2004) (retrieved July 17, 2005)
13. Dicheva, D., Dichev, C.: Authoring Educational Topic Maps: Can We Make It Easier? In: Fifth IEEE International Conference on Advanced Learning Technologies (2005)
14. http://www.w3schools.com/semweb/default.asp

Cluster Bit Collision Identification for Recognizing Passive Tags in RFID System

Katheeja Parveen, Sheik Abdul Khader, and Munir Ahamed Rabbani

B.S. Abdur Rahman University, Vandalur, Chennai, Tamil Nadu, India
{katheeja.parveen,psakahder,marabbani}@bsauniv.ac.in

Abstract. Radio Frequency Identification (RFID) is a technology that amalgamates the use of electromagnetic or electrostatic coupling in the radio frequency (RF) portion of the electromagnetic spectrum to uniquely identify an object. RFID systems often experience a circumstance in which tags responding to a single reader at the same time, collide with each other, leading to retransmission of tag ID's that results in wastage of bandwidth and an increase in the total delay. In this paper, a novel anti-collision algorithm, Cluster Bit Collision Identification (CBCID) Anti Collision Protocol is proposed to lessen the length of response generated by tags, minimize the time slots to be consumed for recognizing all tags, and minimize the average identification delay. CBCID checks for the occurrence of collision by bit, and reduces the number of tag counters to one, when compared to other protocols. CBCID is compared with existing approaches namely QT, QTsl, QTim and ABS, to evaluate its efficiency in handling a worst case environment. Results indicated that when the number of tags in the interrogation zone increases exponentially CBCID excels in minimizing the time slots consumed, number of collisions incurred.

Keywords: RFID, Tag Anti Collision, Deterministic Tree Based, Tag identification.

1 Introduction

Radio Frequency Identification (RFID) system consists of a number of tags with unique IDs, a reader to obtain information from the tags and a data processing subsystem. The length of ID may be different in different RFID standards. The tags in EPC Class1 Gen2 [1] have 96-bit ID, where as ISO-18000-6B are 64-bit ID. Current RFID systems work in a Reader-Talk-First mode, i.e., a reader issues query commands first, and those tags that are within the reading range of the reader will respond with the stored information using the internal energy for an Active Tag or the external energy powered by the reader for a Passive Tag. The data transmission from tag to reader is done by scattering the wave energy back to the reader. Depending upon the data being sent back to the reader ('0' or '1'), the tag chooses to scatter or not to scatter the wave energy, or alternatively modulates the carrier with two different frequencies while scattering. Since all tags have to share the common broadcast channel to communicate with the reader, this will lead to collision as multiple tags transmit simultaneously. These collisions are categorized as Tag Collisions and Reader Collisions. Reader

N. Meghanathan et al. (Eds.): CCSIT 2011, Part III, CCIS 133, pp. 190–199, 2011.

Collisions can be avoided if a cooperative functioning of the readers is implemented. However, in case of the former, the collisions cannot be easily resolved. As a result of Tag collisions, the existence of prolonged delay in identifying the tags and lacking accuracy is often observed. RFID tags face extreme constraints on computation, communication and implementation of complexity in physical hardware. Tag collisions are regarded as a key issue that affects universal adoption in the system [2]. In a typical RFID deployment, it is reported in [3] that the identification rate is only about 60-70%.

2 Related Literature

Tag anti-collision protocols can be classified broadly as Deterministic Tree Based and Probabilistic Frame Slotted ALOHA protocol. Time Division Multiple Access (TDMA) procedures are widely spread in the field of digital mobile radio systems and they contribute the largest group of anti-collision protocols. They can be categorized as "Tag Driven" and "Reader Driven". Tag driven procedures are asynchronous as readers do not control the data transfer. They are nicknamed as Tags Talk First (TTF). High performance can be obtained using Tag Driven Approaches like ALOHA, but the same result cannot be achieved in high tag dense environments. Hence most RFID applications prefer to use only Reader driven methods as the reader takes full control over the communication.

This section introduces the methodology of some of the variants of Query Tree, Binary Tree, AQS, ABS, ASPS, etc. Aloha based protocols such as aloha, slotted aloha, and frame slotted aloha are known for their low complexity and computation. An effort to minimize the occurrence probability of tag collision is handled by allowing tags to transmit at distinct different intervals. Tree based protocols mostly follow either query or binary or consider both.

Splitting or Tree searching algorithms introduced by Capetanakis [6] can be used for RFID arbitration, in conventional multi access systems. Suggestions made by Hush and Wood [7] shows how set of tags within the range of Reader can be uniquely identified using the idea of Tree searching Algorithm. Though it is very efficient, it is not advisable for passive tags, as it enforces tags to remember the previous bits read. This is not feasible for very low cost passive tags. Wang suggests Enhanced Binary Search tree with Cut through in [8]. The cut through operation promises to shorten the search mechanism. Additionally, consumption of power intake as a result is also minimal.

Query Tree (QT) algorithm consists of rounds of queries and responses [9], [10], [11] interchanged by Readers and Tags. The QT algorithm is an improvement from BTWA. QT requires very less tag circuitry. It is a memoryless tag identification protocols in which the tags do not have to remember anything. However, when the number of k bit responses from the tags is in rise, the QT will end up in heavy collision. In case of similarity in Tag ID distribution, QT is equivalent to BS protocol. Since a set of uniformly distributed tags splits approximately in equal parts at each query, imitating the behavior of BS protocol. In order to overcome heavy collision in QT, QT – Short long (QTsl) [11] is proposed to handle when the number of k-bit responses are more,. QTsl is similar to QT except for a few modifications. This protocol helps to reduce the number of bits transmitted from tags. Let there be n tags to be identified. The expected reader communication complexity of QT-sl protocol is at most 3.89kn + 3.89n. The expected tag communication complexity of QT-sl protocol is at most 2:21logn2 + k + 4.19. QT- Incremental Matching (QTim) is analogous to QTsl. The tag communication complexity is same for both the protocols, but the number of bits transmitted is reduced. This protocol requires a tag to remember the bit position of the prefix it has matched so far. Hence, it can be no longer be called as memory-less. Each tag has a bit marker b € {1, . . . k}. When the tag is active, upon receiving the query, the tag matches the query string starting from bit b. If identical, then bit marker b is incremented by 1. When it mismatches, tags would go to transient state. The expected reader communication complexity of QT-im protocol is at most $4.42n\log_n^2$ + 12.18n.

Adaptive Binary Splitting (ABS) protocol [4] is proposed to improve ISO/IEC 18000-6B protocol by maintaining tags' counter of the last interrogation round to speed up the recognition procedure. The probability of generating "1" and "0" is the main factor which affects the performance of ABS.

Adaptive Splitting scheme [5] estimates the number of k colliding tags and splits them into k groups to speed up the identification process. In the first phase, the adaptive splitting scheme obeys ISO/IEC 18000-6B protocol until the first tag is identified successfully. It then enters the second phase, in which the reader estimates the number of colliding tags of a specific counter value. The algorithm splits tags into N groups such that each group has exactly one tag for identification by recursively applying ISO/IEC18000-6B protocol. By the help of pre-signaling scheme, the number of messages sent between a reader and tags can be significantly reduced, which in turn shortens the identification procedure latency. Simulation results show that ASPS excel well when number of collisions, number of messages sent by the reader, the tag identification delay, and system efficiency are taken into account. However, ASPS requires the tag to modify the random number generator design on the tag circuit. Also, the implementation of a complex algorithm such as ASPS in a reader adds vulnerability to its strength.

To conclude, the existing approaches namely Query Tree (QT) and its variants, Binary Search Tree (BST), frame aloha, etc proposed in the last 3 decades are simple to implement, but not efficient. These algorithms win in a few of the characteristics and drastically loose in the other. Aloha, Slotted Aloha and its variations prove to work well in certain scenarios, however, tag starvation turns out to be an unsolvable issue i.e., tags remaining unidentified for a long time. In case of tree based protocols like binary and query tree, tag starvation can be eradicated, but delay becomes an issue. Query Tree Protocol is adjudged as "Memoryless" but the penalty point in this protocol is identification delay. Adaptive Binary Splitting (ABS) [4] and Adaptive Splitting and Pre signaling (ASPS) [5] were proposed to improve ISO / IEC 18000-6B protocol. ASPS improve the efficiency within a tag interrogation round, while ABS between interrogation rounds. Unfortunately, they also face some hindrances. A preferable anti-collision protocol should consume less time slots, faster reading, easy to implement, limited change in hardware design and environment independent.

3 Cluster Bit Collision Identification Algorithm

The proposed CBCID algorithm, works by constructing a binary tree gradually as and when a bit is recognized. Every branch corresponds to the bit of the Tag ID. For any x in a binary tree, the left and the right branches are named with "0" and "1" respectively. A path from the root to the internal node represents a tag prefix, and the path from the root to a leaf node defines a unique ID. The reader identifies stack to store tags position on the tree, while a tag has a counter to record the depth of the reader's stack. Based on this counter value, a tag determines whether it is in the transmit state or wait state. In other words, a counter value of zero moves a tag into the transmit state. Otherwise, the tag enters a wait state. Once a tag is identified, it enters the sleep state.

Variable used in CBCID

- SCR - Slot Counter for Reader
- SCT (i) – Allocated Slot Counter for Tag i
- arrTemp0 – Temporary array with size equal to the number of bits of a Tag ID
- Tc (i) – Tag Counter (initial value is 0) for each tag i. Counter is set for each tag.

Step by Step Procedure

1 The reader's antenna emits radio signals to activate the tag

2 Those RFID tags that passes through the electromagnetic zone, detects the reader's activation signal and begin to respond.

3 The activated tags respond to the Reader bit by bit. Using backscatter mechanism, the first bit of their Tag ID is sent back to the Reader.

4 The reader decodes the signal and attempts to read the first bit.

5 If there is only one Tag in the Readable Range, the reader receives bit by bit, and identifies the Tag in one Time Slot. Tc is incremented by 1 each time the reader senses a bit. The value is updated to the Tag. The slot counter (SCT (i)) in which the tag has to respond is assigned.

6 If the number of tags is more than one, then the following procedural approach is followed to identify all the tags in the readable range. The methodology suggested for tags to split themselves into clusters is illustrated in the following step 6.1.

6.1 Total number of bit "1" ("0") present in each tag is calculated. Those tags that obtain the same count form a cluster and are named as G1, G2, G3, G4 …G_{ccnt}, where "ccnt" denotes the total number of clusters that can be formed.

6.2 If the received signals are with the same frequency, then append the bit (0 or 1) to the Temporary arrays created (arrTemp0, in case of first collision). T_c is incremented by 1.

6.2.1 Reader requests the Tag to send the next bit

6.2.2 Go to 6.1

6.3 Else, if the signal arrive with different frequency, the reader diagnoses a collision

6.3.1 T_c := currently requested bit from the tag (where collision has occurred)
6.3.2 Dynamically create a new array, arrTemp1 with size 4 bits and copy the bits present in arrTemp0 and append bit "1".
6.3.3 Append the bit "0" to the temporary array, (arrTemp0, in case of first collision)
6.3.4 Tags splits into clusters based on the number of bits as mentioned in step 6.1
6.3.5 Reader sends a request to the Tags to reply the collided bit, T_c and T_{c+1}

CBCID Algorithm for Reader and Tag operations

/* When number of tags in the zone is only one */
Initialize $T_c = 0$, SC_T=1, arrTemp[] = ""

```
1   Reader activates the tag
2   Tag in the electromagnetic zone respond
3   Reader reads the T_c bit.
4   If signal-recvd = 1 or signal-recvd = 0 then
5     arrTemp[] := arrTemp[] + signal-recvd;
6     T_c := T_c + 1;
7     Goto Step 3
8   End if
```

/* When number of tags in the zone is more than one */
Initialize $T_c(i) = 0$

```
1   Reader activates the tags
2   Tags in the electromagnetic zone respond
3   Reader reads the first bit
4   If signal-recvd = 1 and 0 then /* collision */
5      arrTemp[] := 0;
6      Create array[length], array[] := 1;
7      Tags count no of bit 1 and form clusters
8      Assign group id (G_j):= C1 (T_i)^k where k = 0, 1,
       2... based the bit 1 cluster; j = 1, 2, 3...= no
       of groups formed
9        While G_j exist
10         If signal-recvd = 0 and 1 then
11            Repeat steps 5-8
12         Elseif signal-recvd = 0 or signal-recvd = 1
           then
13             Identify the array[last element] :=
               T_i(T_c(i));
14             arrTemp[] := arrTemp[] + T_i(T_c+1(i));
15             T_c(i) := T_c(i) + 1;
16          End if
17     End While
```

Consider a 4 bit Tag ID as shown in the table containing the tags named as T1, T2 … T10 and their corresponding 4 bit Tag ID.

Table 1. Tag ID's available in the readable range

Tag Name	Bit 1	Bit 2	Bit 3	Bit 4
T1	0	0	0	0
T2	0	0	0	1
T3	0	0	1	0
T4	0	1	0	0
T5	1	1	0	0
T6	1	0	1	0
T7	1	1	1	0
T8	0	1	1	1
T9	1	0	1	1
T10	1	1	1	1

The reader is named as R1. As soon as the reader, R1 emits radio waves, tags (T1, T2 … T10) present in the electromagnetic zone get energized. The tags present respond their ID's to the reader. Hence the Manchester code will be "xxxx".

Since a collision exist, in the very first bit, it is clear that there are tags that have their first bit as "1" or "0". Hence, the first element in array "arrTemp" is added as bit "0", and a new array is created to add its first element as bit "1".

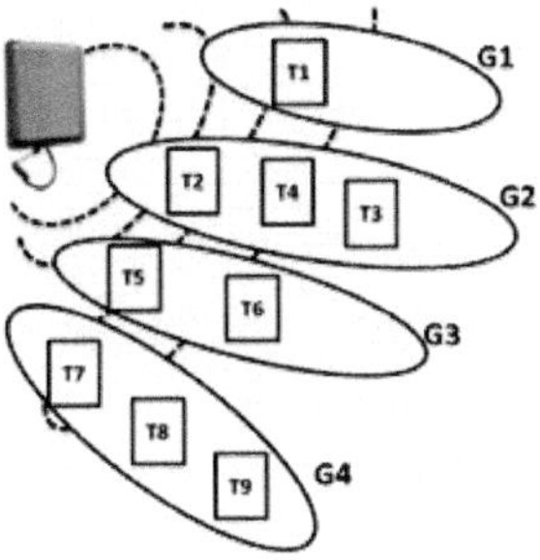

Due to collision, as mentioned in step 6.1, tags are split into clusters of 0's and 1's i.e., C1(T1) =0, C1(T2) = C1(T3) = C1(T4) = 1, C1(T5) = C1(T6) = 2, C1(T7) = C1(T8) = C1(T9) = 3, C1(T10) = 4. Hence, the resulting number of clusters is 4 (i.e., G1, G2, G3 and G4). Variable Tc is incremented from 0 to 1 for all tags, to indicate that collision has occurred in the first bit.

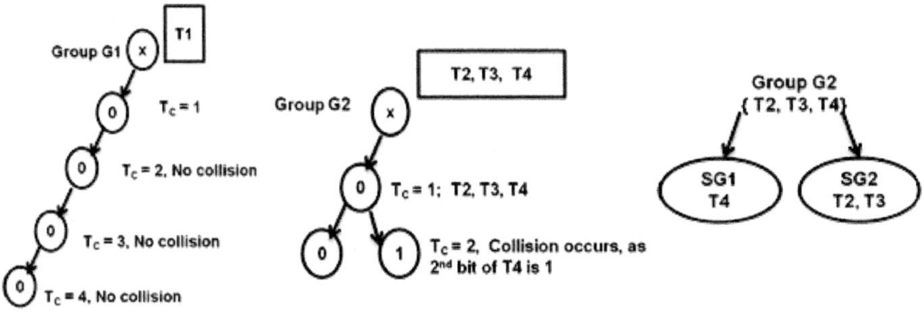

The reader begins its interrogation, demanding those tags with C1 (T) = 0, to respond their first bit, and other tags are muted. Tag T1 responds the first bit and the second bit of their Tag ID, in response to R1. A new array is created with dimension as the total number of bits (i.e., 4) and contents in "arrTemp" is copied to the new array. R1 reads the first and second bit (Tc and Tc+1 bit), and appends the second (Tc+1) bit to the left of the binary tree, as the first bit (Tc) contain the bit 0. Thus the array currently contains "00". The procedure is repeated, till the Tag T1 completes its response by sending all the bits, without any further collision. Tc is incremented after the reader reads every bit. An acknowledgement regarding successful identification is responded to Tag T1, and the reader instructs T1 to change its state of action to mute. Variable "Tc" is reset to 0.

Reader's Slot Counter (SCR) is incremented by 1. R1 now proceeds to move to the next cluster i.e., cluster containing tags T2, T3 and T4. The reader requests the tags (T2, T3 and T4) to respond their first (Tc) and second bit (Tc+1). Based on the value Tc i.e., bit "0" currently, the tree proceeds to grow towards the left. Tc is incremented by 1. Unfortunately collision occurs at the second bit. Step 6.1 of the algorithm, instructs the tags to internally subdivide further. Cluster begins to form based on the 3rd and 4th bit. However, C1 (T2) = C1 (T3) = 1, while C1 (T4) = 0.

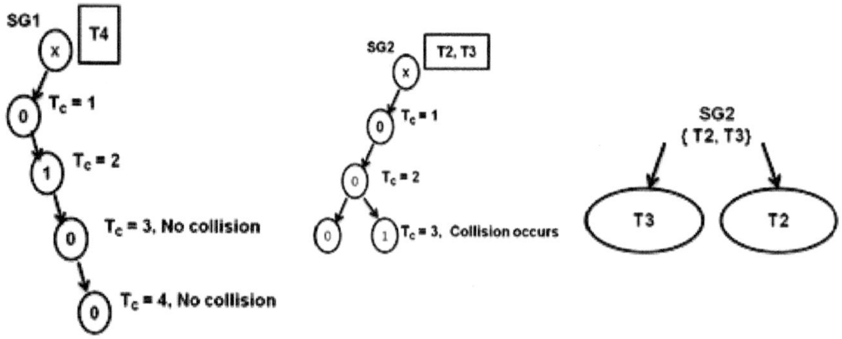

R1, now, requests for the transmission of Tc and Tc+1 (i.e., 2nd and 3rd bit) of SG1 i.e., tags – T4. T4 responds the Tc ie., 2nd bit to let the reader know, to which side the tree should grow, or in other words, Tc+1 th bit should be added to the previous bit "0" or "1".

R1, now, requests for the transmission of Tc and Tc+1 (i.e., 2nd and 3rd bit) of SG2 i.e., tags - T2 and T3. T2 and T3 collide at the 3rd bit also. Tc is incremented by 1. Hence, SG2 is internally divided into clusters based on the 4th bit of Tags – T2 and T3 i.e., C1 (T2) = 1, C1 (T3) = 0. R1 now, request Tag T3 to transmit Tc and Tc+1 (i.e., 3rd and 4th bit), and the tree is completed by adding the last bit "0". T3 is now muted, and R1 enquires T2.

Since, no more collision exist further, the tree is successfully completed. Similarly, the procedure is adapted for the other groups G2, G3 and G4.

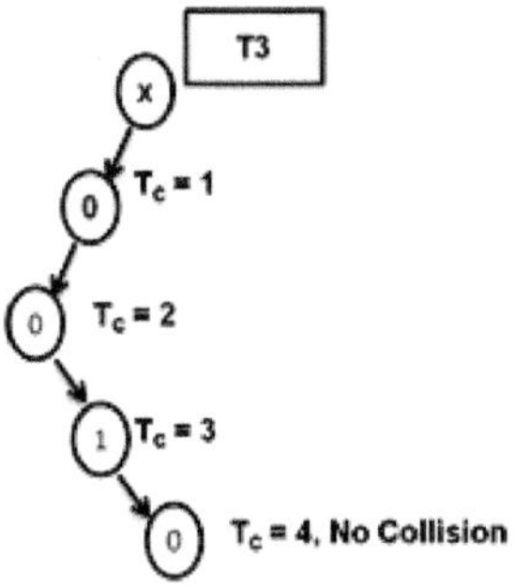

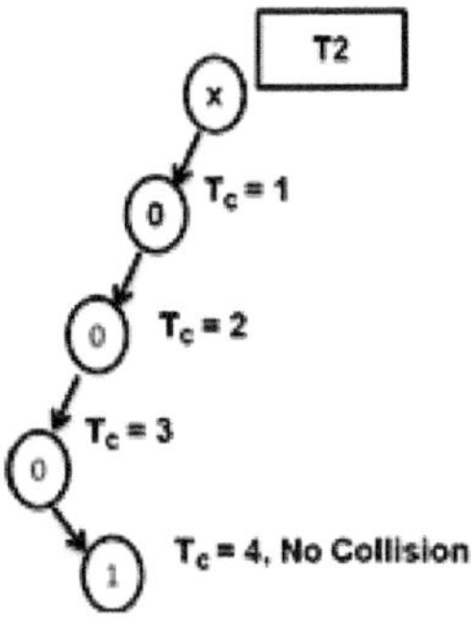

4 CBCID Competency Analysis

To evaluate the efficiency and performance, total time slots taken to discover the tags and average identifying time consumed for recognition are calculated, and the results are compared with Binary Search Tree, QT protocols, Adaptive Binary Splitting and IDS. The readers installed in the terrain are UHF Readers. To avoid reader collision, the readers are placed at approximate distance, such that neither their interference ranges nor their reading ranges intersect with each other. The terrain area is limited to 100 m X 100 m to observe how the existing algorithms and proposed algorithm react during cases of extreme congestion. All tag ID's are 12 bit in length. Hence, the terrain contains a maximum of 4096 (212) tags. The reader is also informed about the length of the tag ID.

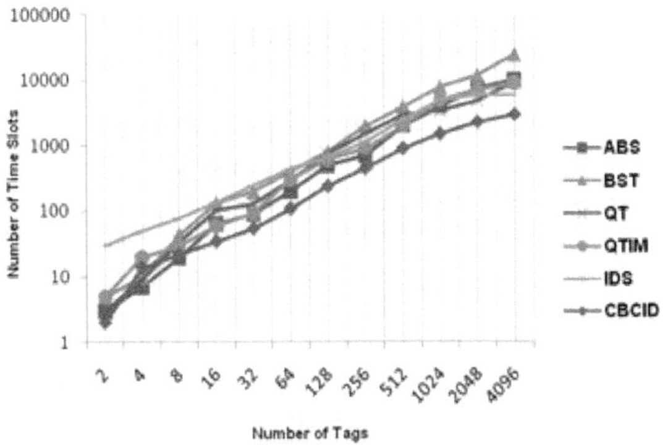

Fig. 1. Total Time Slots

Simulation begins by increasing the number of tags in powers of 2. To commence, the algorithms (BST, QT, QTSL, QTIM and CBCID) are evaluated when the number of tags is 2, later increased to 4, 8, 16, 32, 64, 128, 256, 512, 1024, 2048 and 4096. Number of collisions that took place, total time slots and the average identifying time are calculated for each increase in the tag population.

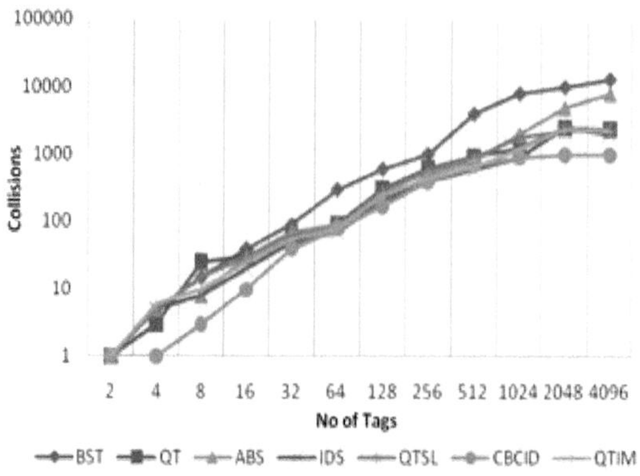

Fig. 2. Number of Collisions

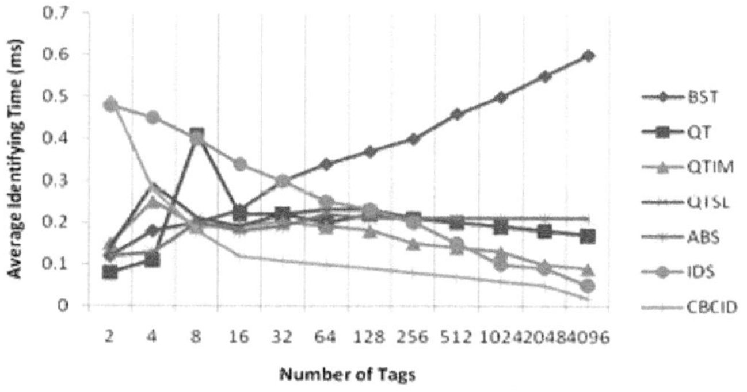

Fig. 3. Average Identifying Time

As seen in the figures, CBCID excels, when compared to other algorithms chosen for study. When the numbers of tags grow exponentially in a reader's reading range, the performance seems to be very much better.

5 Conclusion

Deploying RFID systems presents many challenges such as optimization and interference problems. When attempting to identify multiple RFID tags from densely populated fields within the shortest timeframe possible, the typical design of an anti collision protocol should not heavily change the existing circuitry of tag and reader. One of the key limitations of current RFID systems is the lack of multi-hop capabilities. The proposed CBCID algorithm can be implemented in the existing system, without any major change. In view to lessen the time slots and collision, tags are requested to maintain a counter. When compared to other protocols, the number of counters that a tag has to remember is significantly reduced to one. The algorithm checks for collision bit by bit, rather than discovering the occurrence of collision towards the end. Simulation results shows that as the number of tags increases in the reader's readable range, bit by bit collision checking gives an upper hand in reducing the number of collisions, minimizing the delay time and the number of time slots.

References

1. Kawakita, Y., Mitsug, J.: Anti-collision performance of Gen2 air protocol in random error communication link. In: Proc. Applications Internet Workshops, pp. 68–71 (2006)
2. Viehland, D., Wong, A.: The Future of Radio Frequency Identification. Journal of Theoretical and Applied Electronic Commerce Research 2, 74–81 (2008)
3. Franklin, M.J., Hong, W., Widom, J., Jeffery, S. R., Alonso, G.: A Pipelined Framework for Online Cleaning of Sensor Data Streams. In: Proceeding of International Conference on Data Engineering, pp. 140–142 (2006)
4. Myung, J., Lee, W., Srivastava, J.: Tag-splitting: adaptive collision arbitration protocols for RFID tag identification. IEEE Transactions on Parallel and Distributed Systems 18(6) (2007)
5. Yeh, M.-K., Jiang, J.-R., Huang, S.-T.: Adaptive Splitting and pre-signaling for RFID anti-collision. Computer Communications, 1862–1870 (2009)
6. Capetanakis, J.I.: Tree algorithms for packet broadcast channels. IEEE Trans. Informat. Theory 25, 505–515 (1979)
7. Hush, D.R., Wood, C.: Analysis of tree algorithms for RFID arbitration. In: IEEE International Symposium on Information Theory, August 16-21, p. 107 (1998)
8. Wang, T.-P.: Enhanced Binary Search with Cut-Through Operation for Anti-Collision in RFID Systems. IEEE Communications Letters 10(4), 236–238 (2006)
9. Choi, J.H., Lee, D., Lee, H.: Query tree-based reservation for efficient RFID tag anti-collision. IEEE Communications Letters 11(1), 85–87 (2007)
10. Shih, D.H., Sun, P.L., Yen, D.C., Huang, S.M.: Taxonomy and survey of RFID anti-collision protocol. Computer Communications 29(11), 2150–2166 (2006)
11. Abraham, C., Ahuja, V., Ghosh, A.K., Pakanati, P.: Inventory Management using Passive RFID Tags: A Survey, Department of Computer Science, The University of Texas at Dallas, Richardson, Texas, pp. 1–16 (2002)

Integration Testing of Multiple Embedded Processing Components

Hara Gopal Mani Pakala[1,*], K.V.S.V.N. Raju[2], and Ibrahim Khan[3]

[1] Professor, Electronics and Communication Engineering, Vignana Bharathi Institute of Technology, Aushapur, Ghatkesar (M), RR Dist. AP. 501301India
gopalmaniph@yahoo.com
[2] Professor, Computer Science & System Engineering, AUCE (Autonomous), Visakhspatnam, AP, 530003 India
kvsvn.raju@gmail.com
[3] Director, RGUKT, Nuzvid, Krishna District, AP, India
profibkhan@yahoo.co.in

Abstract. Integration testing of Complex Embedded systems (CES) and associated interconnection network has not been discussed much in the literature. This paper focuses on integration testing among Embedded Processing Components (EPCs) that are (loosely coupled) interconnected via I/O ports. This paper models EPC as a deterministic FSM and describes its fault model that captures errors in the interface between the Hardware and software. The EPC integration with rest of ES (or another EPC) can be viewed as a system under test (SUT) composed of two parts: EPC1 that requires integration testing with the other EPC2. This paper models EPC integration testing as a general fault localization problem [15] between Communicating FSM. An example shows that the integration testing of two subsystems is a subset of general fault diagnostic problem and the faulty machine can be identified during integration.

Keywords: Embedded System fault model, communicating FSM, subsystem integration testing, fault diagnostic method, complex embedded systems.

1 Introduction

Embedded systems (ES) are of varying complexity, from simple to large complex systems, which are typically embedded within larger units providing a dedicated service(s) to that unit. ES are in several market segments like consumer Electronics, Telecom, Military, Space, etc., and are entering into more domains. Complex means, they are multi-disciplinary systems that is characterized by, the use of many inter-related *homogenous* or *heterogeneous* components , properly interconnected by some kind of network topology (point-to-point, bus, multiple buses, like PCI, VME and mesh, etc.) to perform application-specific functions. As system complexity increases, verification becomes more difficult. These complex ES (CES) will have *multiple levels of integration phases*. For example, Missile Guidance System [1] development

* Member IEEE.

N. Meghanathan et al. (Eds.): CCSIT 2011, Part III, CCIS 133, pp. 200–209, 2011.

requires several integration steps, involving multiprocessor boards or ASICs or SOCs, interconnected by some network topology. In the VLSI domain, Multiprocessor SOC (MPSOC) or Chip Multi core Processors (CMP), are having similar integration issues. CES or subsystem or Embedded Processing Component (EPC), testing is still required to assure that the 'System under test (SUT)' meets the specifications. While conformance based testing is based on building 'relevant' models, fault-based approaches generate faults of required type, and generate test sequence (TS) to expose them. Both conformance testing and composition testing strategies rely on specific fault models [2]. This paper focuses on integration testing among EPCs that are (loosely coupled) interconnected via I/O ports.

2 Related Work

Testing complex systems and associated interconnection network has not been discussed much in the literature [3]. The CES also have test-sequencing problems and they require a different approach during the development and manufacturing phases of the systems [4].Current industrial practice shows that the main effort of system development is shifting from the design and implementation phases to the system integration and testing phases [5]. The main challenge of integration is unforeseen problems [6-8] created out of the limited knowledge of the team, invalid assumptions, interference between functions or components; separation between the application development and execution platforms [9]; consequences of uncertainties and assumptions. In general System Integration phase is underestimated, even in normal projects [10] and as such this phase is a bigger challenge for complex embedded systems. While software integration issues [11-13] have received attention, mixed hardware (platform) software integration and EPCs architecture issues were not addressed adequately.

This paper models EPC of a CES as a deterministic finite state machine (DFSM) and describes its fault model that captures errors in the interface between the implementation of software and Hardware. This model is based on embedded system model developed in [14]. The possible faults are equal to *control flow faults*. The EPC integration with rest of ES (or another EPC) can be viewed as a system under test (SUT) composed of two parts: EPC1 that requires integration testing with the other EPC2. Integration of multiple EPCs is viewed as a faulty machine identification problem [15], between the EPCs. With the help of small example, the EPC's integration testing is shown as a subset of general fault identification problem and it can be solved. EPC fault model is introduced in section 3. Mapping of observed faults to the lower level of hardware faults is discussed. Section 4 deals with preliminaries of system of two CFSM. Section 5 considers integration testing of multiple EPCs and describes method for identifying faulty component. With the help of example steps of the fault identification method are described and shown that the two component integration testing is a subset of faulty component identification problem.

3 Embedded Processor Component (EPC) Model

An important aspect of test generation is to specify an appropriate fault model [2]. If for instance the specification of the system is M then the error prone version of that

FSM is the mutation *M'*. Therefore a fault relative to some *M* be defined as any mutation of *M*, say *M'*, such that $M \neq M'$ and the fault model be a set $\Re = M^M$ of such all possible modified FSM's, is the *fault domain*. In general a fault model is defined as [16]: A fault model for *M* is a set $\Re = M^M$ of mutations of *M* such that $M \neq M'$ for all $M' \in \Re$ the *fault domain*. Let M^M range of the set of fault models for *M*. Then $M_I^M < M^M$ is the range of the set of disconnected output and input fault models for *M*. This range is finite as the input and output types are finite for any *M*.

This paper introduces Embedded Processor Component (EPC) model which captures errors in the "*hardware software interface* (*HSI*)" between the implementation of embedded software (*IES*) and the Implementation of Embedded System Hardware (*IEH*). This model is based on embedded system model developed in [14]. It is assumed that the mixed hardware and embedded software is correct with respect to the specifications and the *HSI* is only possible error area. Each EPC may be conceptually modeled as shown in fig 1. All communications between the system environment and the embedded software pass through the hardware, via *interaction points (ip's)*. The *ip's* are shown in figure by the unlabeled arrows. They are considered to be abstract notions that allow /disallow interaction results; they may have no physical counterpart. In fig 1.this is shown by letting the inputs (a; b; c; d; e) from the system environment pass through the hardware towards the software via *ip's*. Likewise the outputs (0; 1; 2; 3) generated by the software have to pass via *ip's* through the hardware in order to emerge at the system environment. Each *ip* is assumed to correspond to precisely one input or output connection.

The model regards the *IEH* and *HSI* as a black box interfacing the *IES* thorough the *ip's*. As a consequence integration errors may only be referred to via the *ip's* and the effects can be visualized through input/output connections only. A fault, could for instance be that some *"input signalI"* of the system is wrongly connected (redirected), with the consequence that the effect of *"input signalI"* corresponds to receiving another *"input signal x"*. Figure 2.shows that the *b-input* is disconnected with the *IES*. This corresponds to the situation where some "*insignalI*" of the system is not connected such that the *IES* will never receive the input, and therefore the application of the *"insignalI"* will cause no effect. The fault in fig2.implies the input-*b* never will occur as input to the *IES*. Referring to fig 2.the possible faults are missing input and output, redirected input and output. These faults are equal to *control flow faults*: transition has an output fault, transfer fault, missing state or additional state. In [16] these possible operations are referred to as type 1 to 4, for modelling possible alterations of the specification machine made during the implementation process. Apart from control flow faults, other error classes that are not represented by this model are similar to those of software [23]: Specific behavioural error classes and General data flow-related error classes.

This model represents the EPC behavior faults manifest through *ip* only. Under these assumptions, to ascertain that the system is correct it should be tested and that there are no errors manifested as faults in the *ip's*. These *ip* faults affect various levels of EPC (system) hierarchy. The lowest level is the hardware level, the next level is low level control where information is processed and the top level is high level control which determines the behaviour. The interaction between FSM's, based on product machine, assumes that all state changes instantly at the same time. The actual behaviour of mixed hardware/software (system) component is different, in

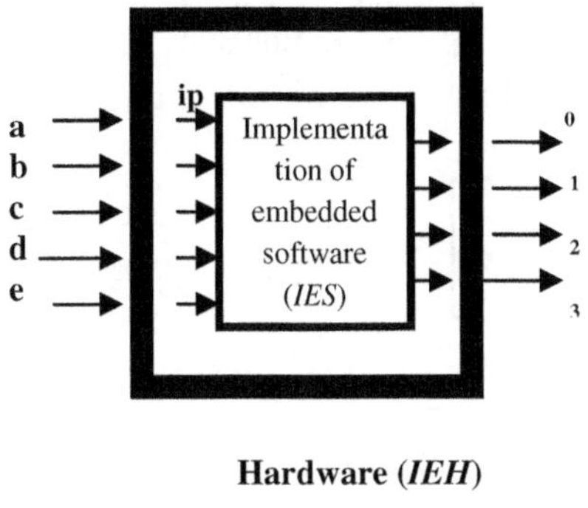

Fig. 1. EPC Model

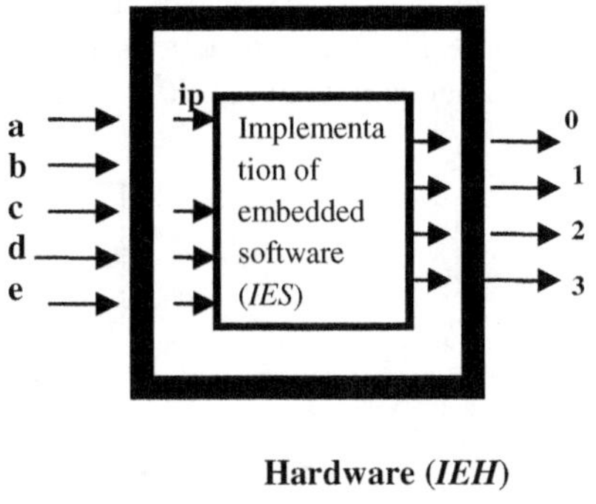

Fig. 2. EPC Fault Model missing input fault

which the software task may take hundreds of clock cycles and also dependent on the architecture. Assuming that more than one software process can share CPU of the microcontroller (MC) and using interrupt for detecting 'event' of FSM, faults in several types of *HSI* implementations need to be considered. Some of them are: hardware to hardware; software to hardware; hardware to non-interrupt software; software to non-interrupt software on another processor; and software to non-interrupt software on same processor. How the 'high level faults' relate to the faults in the *HSI* is required to be examined further.

4 A System of CFSMs

Complex embedded systems are being modeled as a sequence of communicating FSMs (SCFSM) of several FSMs A_i, i=1, ... , k. It is assumed that the component FSM A_i is deterministic FSM which communicate asynchronously with each other through bounded input queues, in addition to their communication with the environment through their respective external ports. The general composition of two CFSM (see Fig.3) the *Context'* and the component *Ecomp* have external inputs and outputs. This general composition can be transformed into that in figure 4 with the component and composite FSM being isomorphic to those of the original composition [18]. As such the composition of two components shown in figure 4 is general and this will be used hence forth.

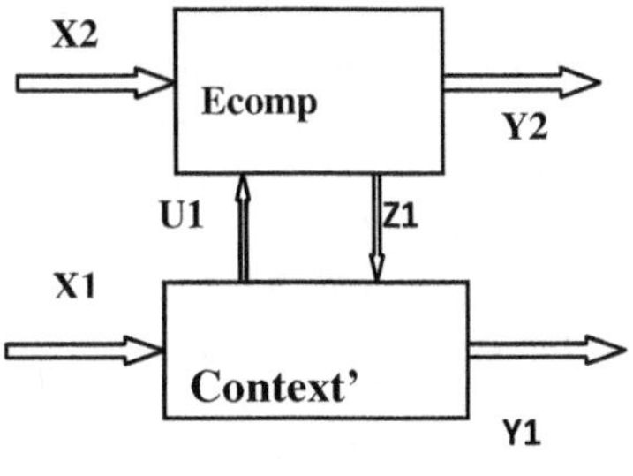

Fig. 3. General composition Two CFSM

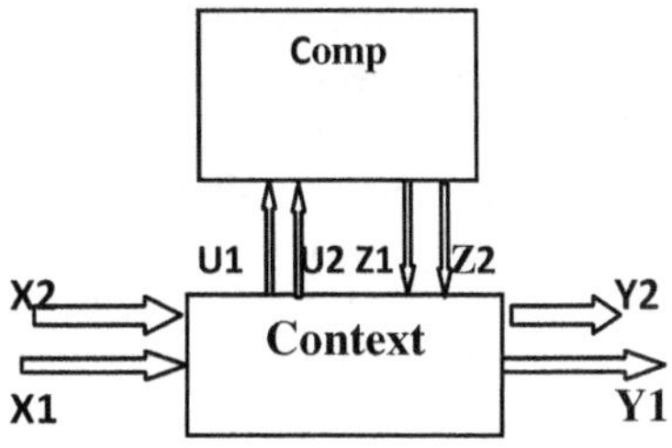

Fig. 4. Transformed composition Two CFSM

Consider two CFSM (see Fig.5): A1 and A2 where X and Y represent the observable input/output actions of A1. Similarly U and Z alphabets represent the input/output actions of A2. It is assumed that [16] –

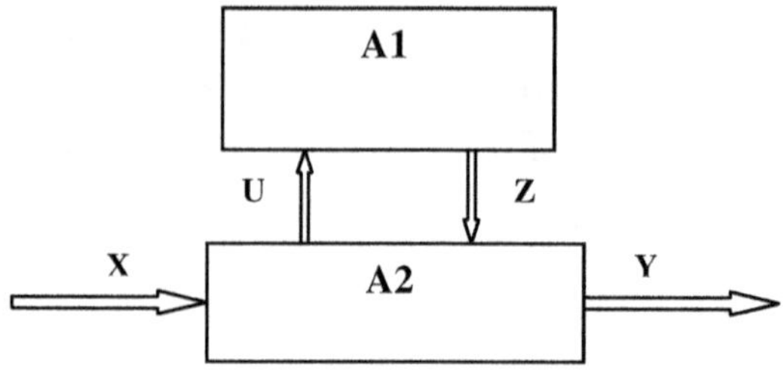

Fig. 5. Two CFSM

(a) Component FSM in response to an input produces only an internal or an external output.

(b) The system has at most one message in transit, i.e. the next external input is submitted to the system only after it produces an external output to the previous input. Then the collective behaviour of the two communicating FSMs can be described by a finite *product machine (PM)*.

(c) System does not fall into a live-lock and the component machines are deterministic. Under these assumptions, *composed machine (CM)* = A1◊A2 is deterministic.

It is not always possible to locate the faulty component of the given system when faults have been detected in a system under implementation (SUT). Consider the two cases:

1. Only one of the components A1 or A2 is faulty and is not known which one.
2. One of the components A1 or A2 is faulty and the correct one is known.

Case 1 is known as diagnostic problem [15] and Case 2 is the integration problem which is of interest, in this paper.

4.1 A Fault Model for the System of CFSM

Given complete deterministic specification and implementation FSMs, an implementation has a single *output fault* if one and only one of its transitions has an output fault. A transition has a *transfer fault* if the implementation enters a different state than that specified by the next-state function of the specification. An implementation has a single transfer fault if there is no output fault in the implementation and one and only one of its transitions has a transfer fault. An implementation under test of the given system may have *multiple faults* if several transitions have output or transfer faults. If an implementation is not conforming then it is called a *faulty* or a *nonconforming* implementation. In this paper the specification is a decomposed system; i.e. its implementation is a system of two CFSMs, where at most one of these machines is faulty. The EPC fault model (section 3) can represent faults due to errors developed in the *HSI* as missing (I/O), disconnected and redirected output. Generally the fault model based on output and transfer faults is typically used for diagnosing the system decomposed into components, where only one component may be faulty [19].

5 Integration Testing of Multiple EPCs

In section 4 CES modeled as a sequence of communicating FSMs A_i, i=1, ... , k. As pointed out in section 1, CES is composed of several EPCs interconnected via I/O ports. The objective of integration testing is to uncover errors in the interaction between the EPCs and their environment (other EPCs). The integration of a system must be assessed on the final platform, before starting the system and every time the system is modified. This implies testing interfaces among EPCs to assure that they have consistent assumptions and communicate correctly.

Definition: The problem of erroneous behaviours detection in an ES implementation, during integration is the problem for deciding whether the corresponding EPCs contains errors by means of testing based on an the appropriate fault models.

If the fault model describes the faults accurately, then one needs only to derive tests to detect all the faults in the fault model. Assuming that the EPCs are tested independently, during integration testing the fault model is required to bring out faults in EPC's interaction. Let each of A_i = EPC_i. This paper considers integration testing of two EPCs or equivalently A1 and A2.The component A1 integration with another component A2 can be viewed as a system under test (SUT) composed of two parts: the component A1that requires testing with the other component A2. The A_i, i=1, ... , k, integration is viewed as identification of a faulty machine problem [15]. In the following section fault identification methodology among two components A1 and A2 is described.

5.1 The Diagnostic Methodology

Let A1 and A2 be the deterministic FSMs representing the specifications of the components of the given system; while B1 and B2 are their implementations respectively. *Conformance testing* determines whether the I/O behaviour of A1 and A2 conforms to that of B1 and B2, or not. A test sequence that addresses this issue is called a checking sequence. An I/O difference between the specification and implementation can be caused by either an incorrect output (output fault) or an earlier incorrect state transfer (state transfer fault). A standard test strategy is [15]: Homing the machine to a desired initial state, Output Check for the desired output sequence, by applying an input (test) sequence (TS) and Tail State Verification. It is assumed that any test sequence (TS) considered has been generated by using a standard test strategy. The method for diagnostic test derivation is outlined in the following steps [20]:

1. *Generation of expected outputs:* Assume that a test suite "TS" is given or generated using a standard test strategy cited above.
2. *Execution of test cases:* Application of the test suite to the IUT for generating expected output sequence.

3. *Identification of symptoms:* Compare observed outputs with expected ones and identify all symptoms.
4. *Conflict paths:* For each symptom determine corresponding conflict paths.
5. *Tentative candidate Transitions:* Determine the transitions which are suspected to be faulty (called tentative candidate transitions), form the intersection of the transitions of all conflict paths of (4).
6. *Diagnostic candidates:* Eliminate from the tentative diagnostic candidates (of 5) all candidates that fail to explain all observations of the SUT. A particular tentative diagnostic candidate fails to explain all observations, if its expected outputs are not equal to the observed outputs of the SUT for at least one test case of TS. All remaining candidates are considered as diagnostic candidates.

Let NDC-A1 be the number of diagnostic candidates of A1 and DC-A1,k (k = 1… NDC-A1) be the diagnostic candidates of A1. Let NDC-A2 be the number of diagnostic candidates of A2 and DC-A2,k (k = 1… NDC-A2) be the diagnostic candidates of A2. If NDC-A1 = 0, then *A2 is the erroneous machine,* and if NDC-A2 = 0 then *A1 is erroneous*, else we proceed as follows:

(a) From: DC-A1,k ◊ A2 for k =1… NDC-A1
(b) From: DC-A2,k ◊ A1 for k =1… NDC-A1

Complete FSMs A = (S,I,O,h,s_0) and B = (T,I,O,g,t_0) are *equivalent*, written A ≅ B, if their sets of traces coincide. It is well known, given complete deterministic FSM A, there is always exists a reduced FSM that is equivalent to A. Alternately, two FSMs are said to be equivalent if and only if for all possible input sequences, they produce the same output sequences. If any of the machines computed in (a) is equivalent to any machine computed in (b), then the faulty machine (A1 or A2) can not be identified. In such cases, additional tests described in [22] are generated, for distinguishing between the diagnostic candidates.

The example in section 6 illustrates the method described in section 5 and also shows that the integration testing of EPCs A1and A2 is a subset of diagnosis problem (identification of faulty machine among A1 and A2) and the solution is easily obtained.

6 An Example

Consider two machines A1 and A2 as shown in Figure 6, and their corresponding Reference System *CM*=A1◊A2 as shown in Figure 7. The set of external inputs is X={x1, x2, x3}, the set of external outputs is Y = {y1, y2, y3}, the set of internal inputs is U = {u1, u2, u3}, and the set of internal outputs is Z = {z1, z2, z3}. In this example, a reset transition *tr* is assumed to be available for both the specification and the implementation. The symbol "r" denote the input for such a transition and the null symbol "-" denote its output. A reset input “r” resets both machines in the system to their initial states. Suppose the test suite TS = {r-x1, r-x2, r-x3 } is given for the two CFSMs specification shown in Figure 6.

The application of TS to the specification of Figure 6 and its corresponding implementation of A1 and A2 (which equal to the specification with the exception that t'1 of A1 has the *output fault* z2), generates the expected and observed output sequences given in Table 2. A difference between observed and expected outputs is detected for test cases tc_1. Therefore, the symptom is:

$$Symp1 = (o_{tc1,1} \neq \hat{o}_{1,1})$$

Corresponding to the above symptom, the following conflict paths for both machines A1 and A2 are determined which are equal to tentative candidate faulty transitions for this particular example:

CfpA21 = t1, t4; CfpA11 = t'1.

Table 2. Out put sequences for TS

Test suite TS = {r-x1, r-x2, r-x3 }				
S.No	**Test Case (tc_i)**	**tc_1**	**tc_2**	**tc_3**
1	Inputs	r, x1	r ,x2	r, x3
2	Specified transitions	t1, t'1, t4	t2, t'2, t5	t3, t'3, t6
3	Expected Output	y1	y2	y3
4.	Observed Output	**y2**	y2	y3

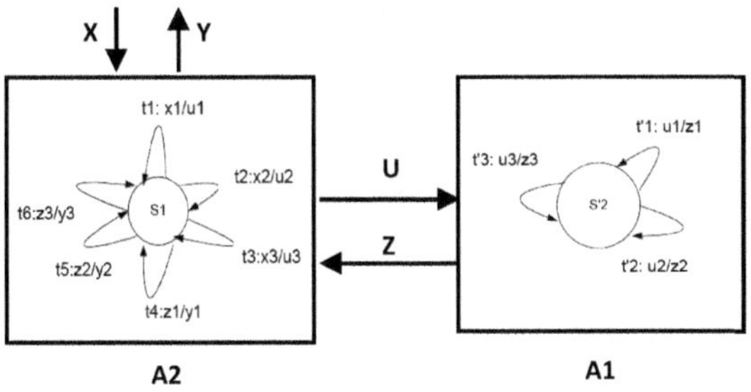

Fig. 6. A system of two CFSMs, A1 and A2

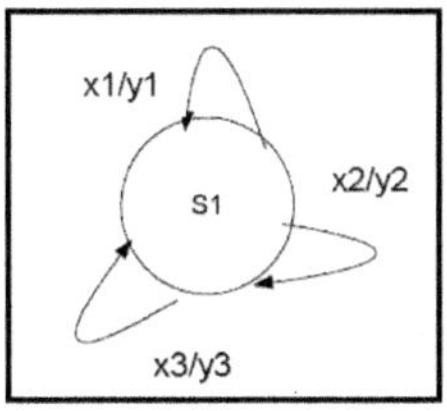

Fig. 7. Reference System *CM*=A1◊A2

Corresponding to these candidate transitions, the following tentative diagnostic candidates for A1 and A2 are computed and are given below:

TdiagcA11 = A1 where t'1 has been changed to u1/z2 instead of u1/z1

TdiagcA12 = A1 where t'1 has been changed to u1/z3 instead of u1/z1

TdiagcA21 = A2 where t1 has been changed to x1/u2 instead of x1/u1

TdiagcA22 = A2 where t1 has been changed to x1/u3 instead of x1/u1

TdiagcA23 = A2 where t4 has been changed to z1/y2 instead of z1/y1

TdiagcA24 = A2 where t4 has been changed to z1/y3 instead of z1/y1

Notice that TdiagcA12, TdiagcA22, and TdiagcA24 do not explain all observable outputs of the SUT, and thus are not considered as diagnostic candidates. For example, if the fault is as specified in TdiagcA12 (t1:x1/u3), the SUT should produce the external output y3 for the external input r-x1 of Tc1; however, it produces the external output y2 as shown in Table 2. The remaining tentative diagnostic candidates are considered as diagnostic candidates DiagcA11, DiagcA23, and DiagcA21, respectively. For these candidates, the following composed machines are formed:

$$\text{DiagcA11} \lozenge \text{A2; DiagcA23} \lozenge \text{A1; and DiagcA21} \lozenge \text{A1.}$$

These machines are equivalent, and therefore determining the faulty machine is not possible, by testing the composed system in the given architecture. However for EPCs integration, which corresponds to the case 2, because of previous assumption, the faulty machine can be identified as A1.

7 Conclusions and Future Work

This paper focuses on integration testing of multiple EPCs that are interconnected via I/O ports. For this EPC of a CES is modeled as a deterministic finite state machine (DFSM) and described its fault model that captures errors in the interface between the implementation of software and Hardware. This model is based on embedded system model developed in [14]. The possible faults are missing input and output, redirected input and output. These faults are equal to *control flow faults*. The EPC integration with rest of ES (or another EPC) viewed as a system under test (SUT) composed of two parts: EPC1 that requires integration testing with the other EPC2. The EPC's integration is viewed as a faulty machine identification problem [15], between the EPCs. With the help of small example, it was shown that the EPC's integration testing is a subset of general fault identification problem and the solution is easily obtained.

The relation of the 'high level faults' to the faults in the interfaces and application of the ideas to an example complex embedded system, are under active research.

References

1. Lindsay, P.A., McDermid, J.: Derivation of safety requirements for an embedded control system. In: Proc. Systems Engineering, Test and Evaluation Conference (SETE 2002), Systems Engineering Society of Australia, pp. 83–93 (2002)
2. Aichernig, B.K., Weiglhofer, M., Wotawa, F.: Improving Fault-based Conformance Testing. Electronic Notes in Theoretical Computer Science 220, 63–77 (2008), http://www.elsevier.com/locate/entcs
3. Boumen, R., Ruan, S., de Jong, I.S.M., van de Mortel-Fronczak, J.M., Rooda, J.E., Pattipati, K.R.: Hierarchical Test Sequencing for Complex Systems. IEEE Transactions On Systems, Man, And Cybernetics—Part A: Systems And Humans 39(3), 640–649 (2009)
4. Boumen, R., de Jong, I.S.M., Vermunt, J.W.H., van de Mortel-Fronczak, J.M., Rooda, J.E.: Test sequencing in complex manufacturing systems. IEEE Trans. Syst., Man, Cybern. A, Syst., Humans 38(1), 25–37 (2008)
5. Bratthall, L.G., Runeson, P., Ädelsward, K., Eriksson, W.: A survey of lead-time challenges in the development and evolution of distributed real-time systems. Information and Software Technology 42(13), 947–958 (2000)

6. Abdullah, K., Kimble, J., White, L.: Correcting for unreliable regression integration testing. In: ICSM 1995: Proceedings of the International Conference on Software Maintenance, Washington, DC, USA, p. 232. IEEE Computer Society, Los Alamitos (1995)
7. Liangli, M., Houxiang, W., Yongjie, L.: A Reference Model of Grouped-Metadata Object and a Change Model based on it Appling for Component-based Software Integration Testing. In: IEEE/ACS International Conference on Computer Systems and Applications, AICCSA 2007, pp. 32–39 (2007), doi:10.1109/AICCSA.2007.370861
8. Raza, M.W.: Comparison of class test integration ordering strategies. In: Proceedings of the IEEE Symposium on Emerging Technologies, pp. 440–444 (2005), doi:10.1109/ICET.2005.1558922
9. Kandl, S., Kirner, R., Fraser, G.: Verification of Platform-Independent and Platform-Specific Semantics of Dependable Embedded Systems– FIT-ITresearch project
10. Muller, G.: Coping With System Integration Challenges in Large Complex Environments. Embedded Systems Institute, Gerrit.muller@embeddedsystems.nl, `http://www.gaudisite.nl/INCOSE2007_Muller_integration.pdf`
11. Seo, K.I., Choi, E.M.: Rigorous Vertical Software System Testing In IDE. In: 5th ACIS International Conference on Software Engineering Research, Management & Applications, SERA 2007, August 20-22, pp. 847–854 (2007), doi: 10.1109/SERA.2007.114
12. Boehm, B.W., Basili, V.R.: Software defect reduction top 10 list. IEEE Computer 34(1), 135–137 (2001)
13. Leveson, N.G.: Safe ware: System Safety and Computers. Addison-Wesley, Reading (1995)
14. Godskesen, J.C.: Connectivity Testing. Formal Methods in System Design 25(1), 5–38 (2004)
15. Guo, Q., Hierons, R.M., Harman, M., Derderian, K.: Heuristics for fault diagnosis when testing from finite state machines. Software Testing, Verification and Reliability 17(1), 41–57 (published online: June 22, 2006)
16. Petrenko, A., Yevtushenko, N., Bochmann, G.v.: Fault models for testing in context. In: Proc. of the 1st Joint Intern. Conf. on Formal Description Techniques for Distributed Systems and Communication Protocols and Protocol Specification, Testing, and Verification, pp. 125–140 (1996)
17. Petrenko, A., Yevtushenko, N., Bochmann, G., Dssouli, R.: Testing in context: Framework and test derivation. Computer Communications 19, 125–140 (1996)
18. Yevtushenko, N., Cavalli, A., Lima Jr., L.: Test Suite Minimization for Testing in Context. In: Proc. IWTCS 1998, pp. 127–145 (1998)
19. de Kleer, J., Williams, B.c.: Diagnosing multiple faults. Artificial Intelligence 32(1), 97–130 (1987)
20. Ghedamsi, A., Bochmann, G.v., Dssouli, R.: Diagnostic Tests for Communicating Finite State Machines. In: Proc. of the 12th IEEE Internaitonal Phoenix Conference on Communications, Scottsdale, USA (March 1993)
21. Ghedamsi, A., Bochmann, G.v., Dssouli, R.: 'Multiple fault diagnosis for finite state machines. In: Proc. of IEEE INFOCOM 1993, pp. 782–791 (1993)
22. Gill, A.: Introduction to the Theory of Finite State Machines. McGraw-Hill, New York (1962)
23. Guerrouat, A., Richter, H.: A Formal Approach for Analysis and Testing of Reliable Embedded Systems. Electronic Notes in Theoretical Computer Science 141(3), 91–106 (2005)

A New Defense Scheme against DDoS Attack in Mobile Ad Hoc Networks

S.A. Arunmozhi[1] and Y. Venkataramani[2]

[1] Associate Professor, Dept. of ECE, Saranathan College of Engineering, India
[2] Principal, Saranathan College of Engineering, India

Abstract. The mobile ad hoc networks (MANETs) are highly vulnerable to attacks because of its unique characteristics such as open network architecture, shared wireless medium, stringent resource constraints and highly dynamic network topology. In particular, distributed denial-of-service (DDoS) attacks can severely cripple network performance with relatively little effort expended by the attacker. These attacks throttle the tcp throughput heavily. A new defense scheme is proposed to develop a flow monitoring scheme to defend against such attacks in mobile adhoc networks. Our proposed defense mechanism uses the medium access control (MAC) layer information to detect the attackers. The defense mechanism includes bandwidth reservation and distributed rate control. Once the attackers are identified, all the packets from those nodes will be blocked. The network resources are made available to the legitimate users.

Keywords: distributed denial-of-service (DDoS), mobile *ad hoc* networks (MANETs), bandwidth reservation, distributed rate control.

1 Introduction

A mobile ad hoc network (MANET) is a self-configuring network of mobile devices connected by wireless links. Each device in a MANET is free to move independently in any direction, and will therefore change its links to other devices frequently. Each must forward traffic unrelated to its own use, and therefore be a router. The primary challenge in MANET is equipping each device to continuously maintain the information required to properly route traffic securely. Ad-hoc networks are not only used for military purposes but also for tactical communication like disaster recovery, explorations, law enforcements and home and personal area networks.

One of the serious attacks to be considered in MANET is DDoS attack. A DDoS attack is a large-scale, coordinated attack on the availability of services at a victim system or network resource. The DDoS attack is launched by sending an extremely large volume of packets to a target machine through the simultaneous cooperation of a large number of hosts that are distributed throughout the network. The attack traffic consumes the bandwidth resources of the network or the computing resource at the target host, so that legitimate requests will be discarded.

A bandwidth depletion attack is designed to flood the victim network with unwanted traffic that prevents legitimate traffic from reaching the victim system. A resource depletion attack is an attack that is designed to tie up the resources of a

N. Meghanathan et al. (Eds.): CCSIT 2011, Part III, CCIS 133, pp. 210–216, 2011.

victim system. This type of attack targets a server or process at the victim making it unable to legitimate requests for service. Any amount of resources can be exhausted with a sufficiently strong attack. The only viable approach is to design defense mechanism that will detect the attack and respond to it by dropping the excess traffic.

The DoS attacks that target resources can be grouped into three broad scenarios. The first attack scenario targets Storage and Processing Resources. This is an attack that mainly targets the memory, storage space, or CPU of the service provider. Consider the case where a node continuously sends an executable flooding packet to its neighborhoods and to overload the storage space and deplete the memory of that node. This prevents the node from sending or receiving packets from other legitimate nodes. The second attack scenario targets energy resources, specifically the battery power of the service provider. Since mobile devices operate by battery power, energy is an important resource in MANETs. A malicious node may continuously send a bogus packet to a node with the intention of consuming the victim's battery energy and preventing other nodes from communicating with the node. The use of localized monitoring can help in detecting such nodes and preventing their consequences. The third attack scenario targets bandwidth. Consider the case where an attacker located between multiple communicating nodes wants to waste the network bandwidth and disrupt connectivity. This consumes the resources of all neighbors that communicate, overloads the network, and results in performance degradations. Such attacks can be prevented based on our proposed congestion based defense scheme.

2 Related Work

Xiapu Luo et al [1] have presented the important problem of detecting pulsing denial of service (PDoS) attacks which send a sequence of attack pulses to reduce TCP throughput. Wei-Shen Lai et al [3] have proposed a scheme to monitor the traffic pattern in order to alleviate distributed denial of service attacks. Shabana Mehfuz1 et al [4] have proposed a new secure power-aware ant routing algorithm (SPA-ARA) for mobile ad hoc networks that is inspired from ant colony optimization (ACO) algorithms such as swarm intelligent technique. Xiaoxin Wu et al [6] proposed a DoS mitigation technique that uses digital signatures to verify legitimate packets, and drop packets that do not pass the verification Ping Yi, Zhoulin Dai, Shiyong Zhang and Yiping Zhong [8] have presented a new DOS attack and its defense in ad hoc networks. The new DOS attack, called Ad Hoc Flooding Attack(AHFA), can result in denial of service when used against on-demand routing protocols for mobile ad hoc networks, such as AODV & DSR. John Haggerty, Qi Shi and Madjid Merabti [9] have proposed a new approach that utilizes statistical signatures at the router to provide early detection of flooding denial-of-service attacks. Wei Ren, Dit-Yan Yeung, Hai Jin, Mei Yang [11] have proposed a defense scheme that includes both the detection and response mechanisms. In this paper the detection scheme that monitors MAC layer signals and a response scheme based on Explicit Congestion Notification (ECN) marking are discussed. But, the method of monitoring the sending rates of the nodes is not discussed. Hence identifying the attacking nodes becomes a problem. It may also result in increase of false positives and false negatives. Gahng-Seop Ahn et al [12] have proposed SWAN, a stateless network model which uses distributed control algorithms to deliver service differentiation in mobile wireless ad hoc networks in a simple, scalable and robust manner. Giriraj Chauhan and Sukumar Nandi [13] proposed a QoS aware on demand routing protocol that uses signal stability as the routing criteria along with other QoS metrics.

3 Proposed Defense Technique

In this paper, we propose a new defense mechanism which consists of a flow monitoring table (FMT) at each node. It contains flow id, source id, packet sending rate and destination id. Sending rates are estimated for each flow in the intermediate nodes. The updated FMT is sent to the destination along with each flow. After monitoring the MAC layer signals the destination sends the Explicit Congestion Notification (ECN) bit to notify the sender nodes about the congestion. The sender nodes, upon seeing these packets with ECN marking, will then reduce their sending rate. If the channel continues to be congested because some sender nodes do not reduce their sending rate, it can be found by the destination using the updated FMT. It checks the previous sending rate of a flow with its current sending rate. When both the rates are same, the corresponding sender of the flow is considered as an attacker. Once the DDoS attackers are identified, all the packets from those nodes will be discarded.

3.1 Bandwidth Reservation

The two phases of the proposed scheme are. Bandwidth querying phase and. Data transmission phase. In bandwidth querying phase the control messages sent are Bandwidth query request (REQBQ) and Bandwidth query reply (REPBQ). The REQBQ packet includes the source IP address, destination IP address, type of the message, flow ID, and requested data rate which is stored in the bottleneck bandwidth (BnBW) field. In Bandwidth querying phase of the proposed scheme, the node's FMT information along a path is computed. An intermediate node updates its FMT using the BnBW value stored in the REPBQ packet after receiving a REPBQ message on the reverse path, and then forwards the REPBQ to the next node. The available bandwidth *ABWj* is checked first. The reservation of bandwidth for the flow can be made if the value of *ABWj* is greater than or equal to the BnBW value in the REPBQ packet. Else, the BnBW value in the REPBQ packet is overwritten with the smaller value of *ABWj*. Next, the current BnBW value in the REPBQ packet is added to the reserved rate *RRij*, associated with the in-out stream. A FMT entry is created with an assigned rate value A*Rij*, set equal to the BnBW value of the REPBQ packet, if the stream (i, j) was previously inactive. Subsequently, the REPBQ packet is forwarded to the next node on the reverse path. Finally, based on the value of the BnBW field, the source establishes the real-time flow when the REPBQ packet reaches the source node.

3.2 Distributed Rate Control

The actual rate ACR_{ij} is given by

$$ACR_{ij}=W*AR_{ij} \tag{1}$$

Where,

$$W = \left[\frac{Lc}{\sum ARij} \right]$$

where L_c is the link capacity of each link.

If the source receives the congestion bit (CB), then the assigned rate AR_{ij} can be written as

$$AR_{ij}=ACR_{ij}-\delta \tag{2}$$

Where δ is the rate reduction factor.

The rate monitoring function measures the traffic rate of a given in-out stream over a time interval T.

$$MR_{ij}=C_{ij}/T \tag{3}$$

If the measured rate MR_{ij} is greater than actual rate ACR_{ij} for the next time interval then the flow is considered to be an attack flow. Then its status is marked as REJECTED and the corresponding source IP address is recorded from the FMT.

4 Experimental Results

The network simulator NS2 is used to simulate our proposed algorithm. In our simulation, the channel capacity of mobile hosts is set to the same value: 2 Mbps. The distributed coordination function (DCF) of IEEE 802.11 is used for wireless LANs as the MAC layer protocol. It has the functionality to notify the network layer about link breakage.Each node is assumed to move independently with the same average speed. The simulated traffic is Constant Bit Rate (CBR).

Our simulation settings and parameters are summarized in table 1.

Table 1. Simulation Parameters

No. of Nodes	80
Area Size	1200 X 1200
Mac	802.11
Radio Range	250m
Simulation Time	60 sec
Traffic Source	CBR
Packet Size	512
Mobility Model	Random Waypoint
Routing Protocol	AODV

The experiment is carried out with three different normal flow of traffic with the data rate of 100kbps and an attacking flow with the data rate of 400 kbps. The received bandwidth at the destination node over a period of time is obtained using the simulation and the results are shown in Fig. 1. The proposed system is compared with SWAN [12] and it is observed that the bandwidth received for the proposed system is greater compared to the other scheme. The bandwidth reservation technique and the

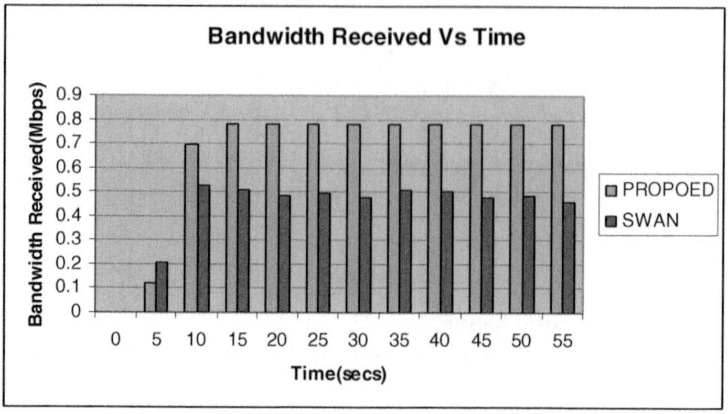

Fig. 1. Bandwidth Received Vs Time

distributed rate control technique of our proposed method make to achieve more bandwidth received for the legitimate users. Hence we are able to obtain greater bandwidth received for our proposed scheme than the SWAN.

The number of lost packets at the destination node over the period of time is shown in Fig. 2. From the graph, it is known that the number of packets lost for the proposed system is less compared to the SWAN. Since the attacking flows are rejected effectively in our proposed scheme, the network resources are made available to the legitimate users. This makes the dropping rate of legitimate packets low compared to the other scheme.

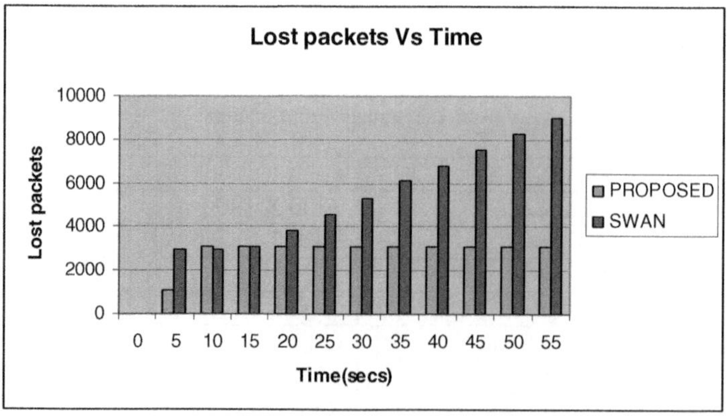

Fig. 2. Lost Packets Vs Time

The simulation is also carried with the variable number of attacking flows. Since the attacker are effectively identified and blocked in our scheme, it is again seen that the proposed scheme achieves greater received bandwidth. It is also observed that as the number of attackers is increased, the bandwidth received gets increased due to greater amount of traffic. The simulation results are shown in Fig. 3.

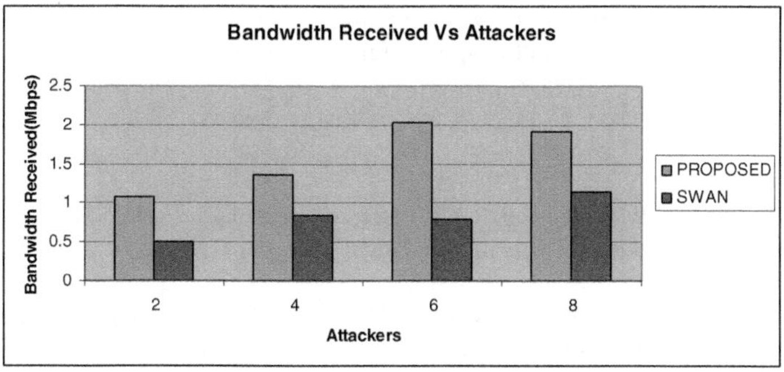

Fig. 3. Bandwidth Received Vs Attackers

The packet delivery ratio **is** the ratio of the number of packets received successfully and the total number of packets sent. Since the proposed scheme is congestion based scheme, the distributed rate control is applied when there is a heavy traffic due to the attacking flows. Hence the number of dropped packets is well reduced. As the dropped packets are reduced, more number of packets is delivered to the destination. Hence greater packet delivery ratio is achieved for the proposed scheme. The simulation results are shown in Fig. 4.

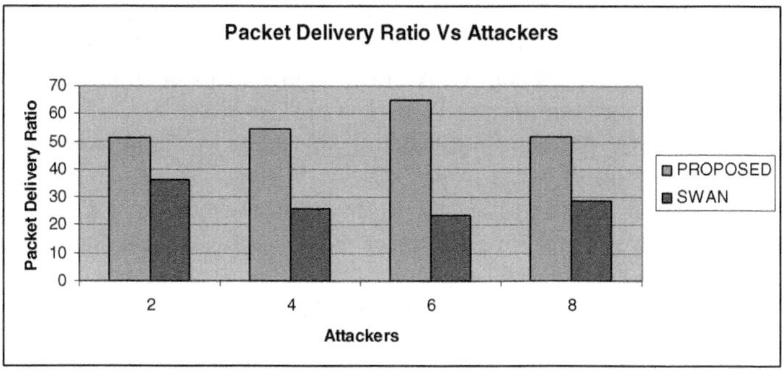

Fig. 4. Packet Delivery Ratio Vs Attackers

5 Conclusion

Technology resisting DDoS attacks has drawn considerable attention in recent years. However, most existing approaches suffer from low detection rate, high deployment cost, or lack of effective attack response mechanisms. Our approach can accurately identify DDoS attack flows and consequently apply rate-limiting to the malicious network flows. Our proposed flow monitoring defense mechanism identifies the attackers. Once the attackers are identified, all the packets from those attackers will be blocked. This makes the network resources available to the legitimate users. We compared the performance of our proposed scheme with the SWAN scheme and proved that our proposed scheme assures better performance. By simulation results, we have shown that our proposed scheme achieves higher bandwidth received and packet delivery ratio with reduced packet drop for legitimate users.

References

1. Luo, X., Chan, E.W.W., Chang, R.K.C.: Detecting Pulsing Denial-of-Service Attacks with Nondeterministic Attack Intervals. EURASIP Journal on Advances in Signal Processing (2009)
2. Xiang, Y., Zhou, W., Chowdhury, M.: A Survey of Active and Passive Defense Mechanisms against DDoS Attacks, Technical reports, Computing series, Deakin university, School of Information Technology (2004)
3. Lai, W.-S., Lin, C.-H., Liu, J.-C., Huang, H.-C., Yang, T.-C.: Using Adaptive Bandwidth Allocation Approach to Defend DDoS Attacks. International Journal of Software Engineering and Its Applications 2(4), 61–72 (2008)
4. Mehfuz, S., Doja, M.N.: Swarm Intelligent Power-Aware Detection of Unauthorized and Compromised Nodes in MANETs. Journal of Artificial Evolution and Applications (2008)
5. Nagesh, H.R., Chandra Sekaran, K.: Design and Development of Proactive Models for Mitigating Denial-of-Service and Distributed Denial-of-Service Attacks. International Journal of Computer Science and Network Security 7(7) (2007)
6. Wu, X., Yau, D.K.Y.: Mitigating Denial-of-Service Attacks in MANET by Distributed Packet Filtering: A Game-theoretic Approach. In: Proceedings of the 2nd ACM Symposium on Information, Computer and Communication Security, pp. 365–367 (2006)
7. Sanyal, S., Abraham, A., Gada, D., Gogri, R., Rathod, P., Dedhia, Z., Mody, N.: Security Scheme for Distributed DoS in Mobile Ad Hoc Networks. ACM, Newyork (2004)
8. Yi, P., Dai, Z., Zhang, S., Zhong, Y.: A New Routing Attack in Mobile Ad Hoc Networks. International Journal of Information Technology 11(2) (2005)
9. Haggerty, J., Shi, Q., Merabti, M.:Statistical Signatures for Early Detection of Flooding Denial-Of service Attacks, vol. 181, pp. 327–341. Springer, Heidelberg (2005)
10. Vigna, G., Gwalani, S., Srinivasan, K.: An Intrusion Detection tool for AODV-based Ad hoc Wireless Networks. In: Proceedings of the Annual Computer Security Applications Conference, pp. 16–27 (2004)
11. Ren, W., Yeung, D.-Y., Jin, H., Yang, M.: Pulsing RoQ DDoS Attack and Defense Scheme in Mobile Ad Hoc Networks. International Journal of Network Security 4(2), 227–234 (2007)
12. Ahn, G.-S., Campbell, A.T., Veres, A., Sun, L.-H.: SWAN: Service Differentiation in Stateless Wireless Ad Hoc Networks. In: Proceedings of IEEE Twenty-First Annual Joint Conference of the IEEE Computer and Communications Societies, INFOCOM, vol. 2 (2002)
13. Chauhan, G., Nandi, S.: QoS Aware Stable path Routing (QASR) Protocol for MANETs. In: First International Conference on Emerging Trends in Engineering and Technology, pp. 202–207 (2008)
14. Shevtekar, A., Ansari, N.: A router-based technique to mitigate reduction of quality (RoQ) attacks. Computer Networks: The International Journal of Computer & Telecommunication Networking 52(5), 957–970 (2008)
15. Rajaram, A., Palaniswami, S.: The Trust-Based MAC-Layer Security Protocol for Mobile Ad hoc Networks. International Journal on Computer Science and Engineering 2(02), 400–408 (2010)

A Model for Delegation Based on Authentication and Authorization

Coimbatore Chandersekaran[1] and William R. Simpson[2]

[1] The Secretary of the Air Force (SAF/A6) 1500 Wilson Blvd., Rosslyn, VA 22209, US
Coimbatore.Chandersekaran.ctr@pentagon.af.mil
[2] The Institute for Defense Analyses, 4850 Mark Center Drive, Alexandria, VA 22311, USA
rsimpson@ida.org

Abstract. Sharing information and maintaining privacy and security is a requirement in distributed environments. Mitigating threats in a distributed environment requires constant vigilance and defense-in-depth. Most systems lack a secure model that guarantees an end-to-end security. We devise a model that mitigates a number of threats to the distributed computing pervasive in enterprises. This authentication process is part of a larger information assurance systemic approach that requires that all active entities (users, machines and services) be named, and credentialed. Authentication is bi-lateral using PKI credentialing, and authorization is based upon Security Assertion Markup Language (SAML) attribution statements. Communication across domains is handled as a federation activity using WS-* protocols. We present the architectural model, elements of which are currently being tested in an operational environment. Elements of this architecture include real time computing, edge based distributed mashups, and dependable, reliable computing. The architecture is also applicable to a private cloud.

Keywords: Credentialing, Authentication, Authorization, Delegation, Attribution, Least Privilege, Public Key Infrastructure, Security Assertion Markup Language (SAML), WS-* .

1 Introduction

Today's Information Technology (IT) systems are under continual attack by sophisticated and resourced adversaries seeking to ex-filtrate information, deny services, and create other forms of mayhem. The strength of the threat is almost directly proportional to the assets being protected. An example might be a banking industry enterprise such as a clearing house for electronic transactions, allied health operations which provide needed information to health care providers while trying to maintain privacy concerns, defense industry applications, even credit card consolidation processes that handle sensitive data both fiscal and personal. The attacks have been pervasive and continue to the point that nefarious code may be present, even when regular monitoring and system sweeps remove readily apparent malware. One class of attack is the Man-in-the-Middle (MITM). This attack manifests itself in various ways including *Wi-Fi Traffic Intercept, Rogue Access Points, Browser (HTTP)*

N. Meghanathan et al. (Eds.): CCSIT 2011, Part III, CCIS 133, pp. 217–236, 2011.

Domain Naming Service (DNS) Cache Poisoning, Overriding Same Origin Policy, etc. The principal of these attacks lies in eavesdropping on, or injecting into network traffic, intercepting and responding on behalf of anticipated communication end-points. The attacks are not limited to a single layer and can be present in any layer of the Open System Interconnect (OSI) model. Thus, a MITM can efficiently manifest itself when a less than comprehensive set of safeguards have been employed. Recently, MITM attacks have bypassed security that leverages single authentication by posing as the target of a communication. This discounts the previously held notion that deploying a single, two-factor authentication mechanisms could provide protection against MITM.

Despite these attacks environment, the web interface is a useful approach to providing access to many distributed users. One way to continue operating in this environment is to not only know and vet your users, but also your software and machines (all active entities). Even that has limitations when dealing with the threat environment. Today we regularly construct seamless encrypted communications between machines through Secure Socket Layer (SSL) or other Transport Layer Security (TLS). These do not cover the "last mile" between the requestor (either a user or service) on one end, and the service on the other end. This last mile is particularly important when we assume that malware may exist on any machine, opening the transactions to exploits, ex-filtration, session high-jacking, data corruption, MITM, masquerade, denial of service, and other nefarious behavior.

Though much has been published about securing the enterprise against adversaries such as, MITM attacks, the enterprise and distributed computing infrastructure remains vulnerable to both internal and external adversaries. Security solutions have failed to mitigate the threats from a perspective of strong bi-lateral and end-to-end authentication. That is, accounting for the identity of all recipients of an initiated communication. The current process of authentication which terminates at intermediate points during service execution exposes the requestor to hostile threats, such as, those elaborated earlier. The use of proxies, reverse proxies, abstract addressing and other techniques present a large number of intermediate attack points.

The challenge to building an end-to-end secure computing model is to provide a mechanism by which messages originating from any entity remain targeted, integral, and confidential all the way to the its destination, regardless of whether or not the message is routed through intermediary nodes.

In this paper, we describe a process model that mitigates the cited threats. We devise an architecture by which we can provide integrity and confidentiality of messages across distributed boundaries preceded by bi-lateral authentication of active entities. All active entities are named, registered, credentialed and authorized to participate in any given environment.

The remainder of the paper is structured as follows. Section 2 provides the basic tenets around which the enterprise security is formulated. Section 3 describe the generic overview of our approach; service paradigm, bi-lateral authentication, and cascading authentication. Section 4 provides SAML process requirements. Section 5 provides some data on the first operational tests. Section 6 reviews related work. Finally, we conclude in Section 7.

2 Tenets of Information Assurance (IA) Architecture Efforts

This section provides nine tenets that guide decisions in an architectural formulation and implementation approaches [12]. These tenets are separate from the "functional requirements" of a specific component (e.g., a name needs to be unique); they relate more to the needs and requirements of the solution that guide its implementation.

- The **zeroth** tenet is that the *enemy is embedded*. In other words, rogue agents may be present and to the extent possible, we should be able to operate in their presence, although this does not exclude their ability to view some activity.
- The **first** tenet is *simplicity*. This seems obvious, but it is notable how often this principle is ignored in the quest to design solutions with more and more features. That being said, there is a level of complexity that must be handled for security purposes and implementations should not overly simplify the problem for simplicity's sake.
- The **second** tenet, and closely related to the first is *extensibility*. Any construct we put in place for an enclave should be extensible to the domain and the enterprise, and ultimately to cross-enterprise and coalition. It is undesirable to work a point solution or custom approach for any of these levels.
- The **third** tenet is *information hiding*. Essentially, information hiding involves only revealing the minimum set of information to the outside world needed for making effective, authorized use of a capability. It also involves implementation and process hiding so that this information cannot be farmed for information or used for mischief.
- The **fourth** tenet is *accountability*. In this context, accountability means being able to unambiguously identify and track what active entity in the enterprise performed any particular operation (e.g. accessed a file or IP address, invoked a service). Active entities include people, machines, and software process, all of which are named registered and credentialed. By accountability we mean attribution with supporting evidence. Without a delegation model, it is impossible to establish a chain of custody or do effective forensic analysis to investigate security incidents.
- This **fifth** tenet is *minimal detail* (to only add detail to the solution to the required level). This combines the principles of simplicity and information hiding, and preserves flexibility of implementation at lower levels. For example, adding too much detail to the access solution while all of the other IA components are still being elaborated may result in wasted work when the solution has to be adapted or retrofitted later.
- The **sixth** is the emphasis on a *service-driven* rather than a product-driven solution whenever possible. Using services makes possible the flexibility, modularity, and composition of more powerful capabilities. Product-driven solutions tend to be more closely tied to specific vendors and proprietary products. That said, commercial off-the-shelf (COTS) products that are as open as possible will be emphasized and should produce cost efficiencies. This means that for acquisition functionality and compatibility are specified as opposed to must operate in a Microsoft forest [18] environment.

- The **seventh** tenet is that *lines of authority* should be preserved and IA decisions should be made by policy and/or agreement at the appropriate level.
- The **eighth** tenet is *need-to-share* as overriding the need-to-know. Often effective health, defense, and finance rely upon and are ineffective without shared information.

3 Approach

In this section we provide a detailed approach. First, we develop the concepts of naming, credentialing, authentication, authorization of all entities to participate in the environment. This is followed by our representation of a service-based paradigm, which details the components of a service. This is followed by our process model of bi-lateral authentication with the section closing on cascading authentication. We follow with Security Assertion Markup Language (SAML) processes for maintaining access control compatible with the cascading authentication. Note we assume a single enterprise where we have control of these details. For cloud computing this means we must have a private cloud that is not shared by other enterprises.

3.1 Upfront Requirements

Naming criteria for entities requires names that are unique over space and time. All entities are given a unique common name, and an alias for the common name that appears in the list of identity attributes in a registry. Entity credentials are issued to the entity using a trusted certificate authority and the certificate provides asymmetric PKI keys the private key will be under control of the certificated entity, and the certificates may be stored in software caches or hardware modules. A key length of 256-bit or more is recommended. Bi-lateral authentication uses certificates provided as credentials to authenticate entities to one another followed by the push of a SAML token for authorization. In the next subsection we provide an overview our representation of a service-based paradigm.

3.2 A Service-Based Paradigm

All web applications, services, and devices exercise access controls and use SAML Assertions [5] in their decision process. The requestor will not only authenticate to the service (not the server or device), but the service will authenticate to the requestor. The interface is termed a “Robust” Application Programming Interface (API), or in the case of a browser or presentation system it is a “Robust” browser. This terminology is used to avoid specifying the implementation details which may be by a browser appliqué (a small program embedded in the browser), an appliance, a set of class libraries or other mechanisms to implement the functionality. Several pilots are under way in each of these approaches. Figure 1 shows the constituent makeup of a service.

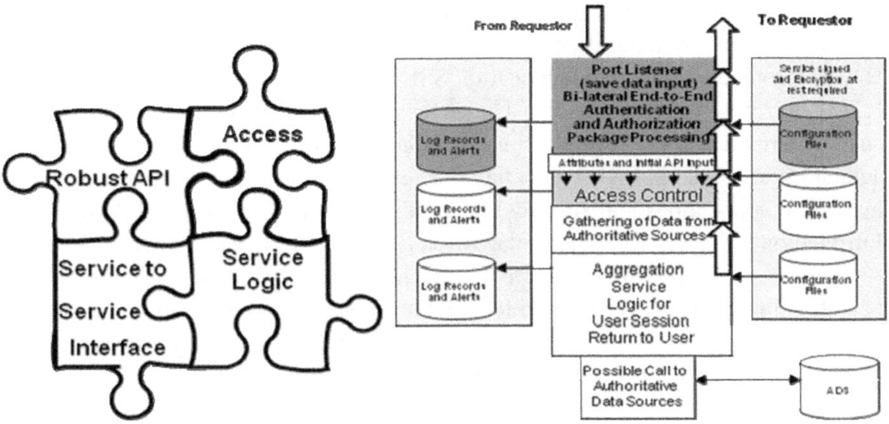

Fig. 1. Components of a Service

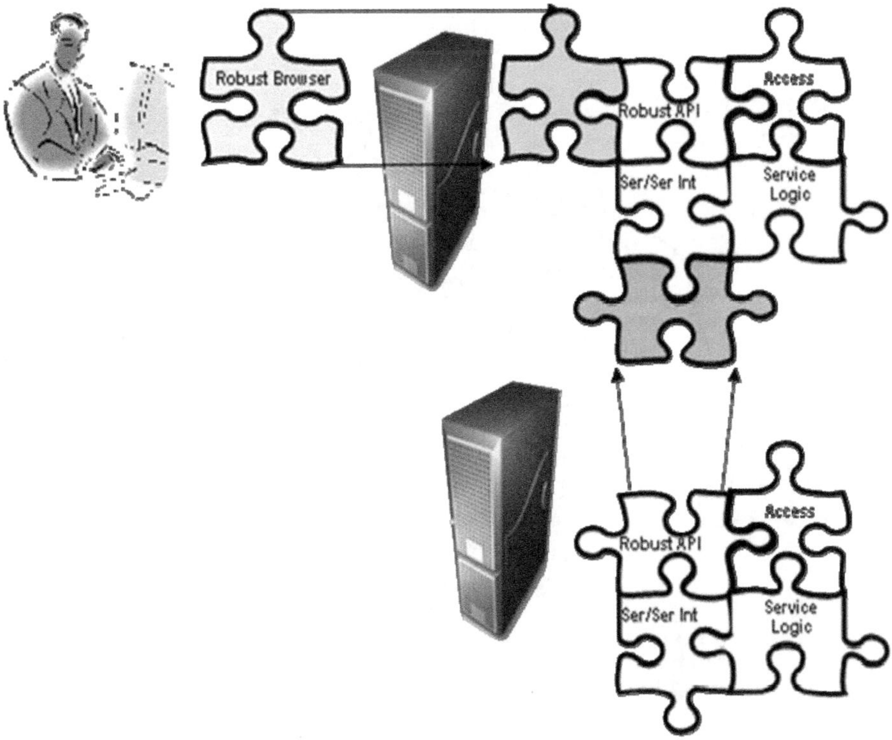

Fig. 2. Compatible Services

The Robust API must be compatible with the Robust Browser. The Robust browser allows the use of WS-* protocols for security and exchange of information in XML.

It also either provides the presentation protocols or translates them to HTML for browser display. Without the robust browser, the initial service request is limited to HTTPS protocols (mutual authentication SSL based upon PKI credentials) and using HTML for presentation purposes. Under these circumstances the first service in the chain is termed as a Web Application. In either case we enforce bi-lateral end-to-end authentication (using PKI credentials of each of the active entities – people, machines, applications and services) and authorization by the use of SAML tokens. Infromation is derived from authoritative Data Sources (ADS) as labeled in the figure.

The access component is responsible for holding access control privileges in the operation of a service. The service logic component is responsible for what a service does. For example, aggregating and retrieving of data. The service to service interface is handled in the following paragraphs. It is therefore important that each service exercise compatible code segments, libraries or other mechanisms. Service to service calls (or web application to service calls) are handled in accordance with Figure 2.

Figure 3 shows two types of Services; an Aggregation Service and an Exposure service. The Aggregation Service may expose data and it may also call exposure

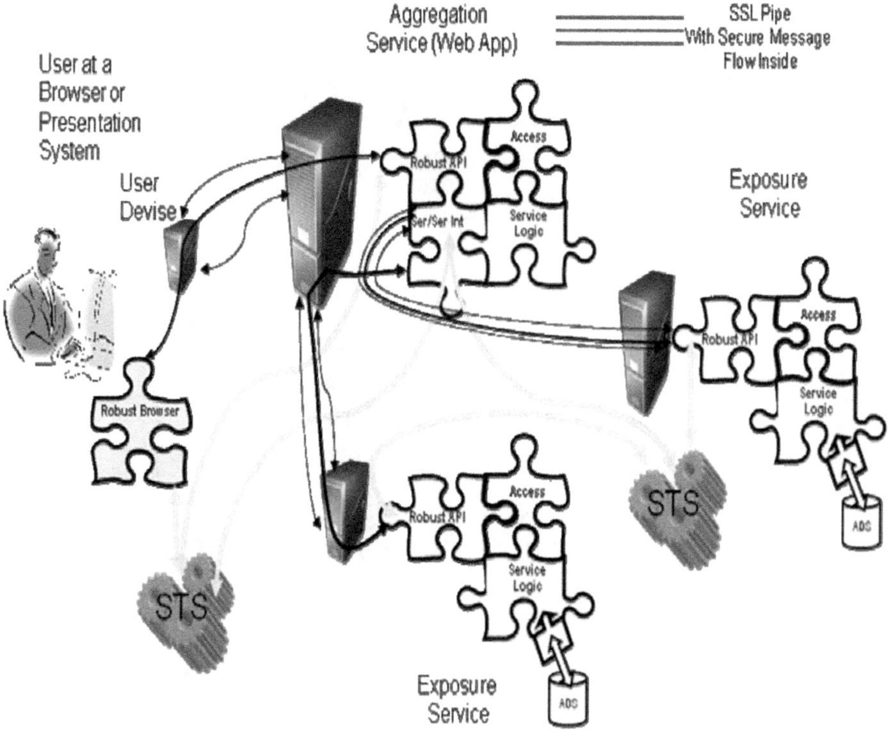

Fig. 3. Steps in invoking an Aggregation Service

services. Exposure services provide data from designated Authoritative Data Sources[1] (ADS). The aggregation service then aggregates the data modifies their output as necessary and returns the data to the user. The requests to exposure services are made through the interface termed robust API. It does this through an addressed message to the API using WS-* protocols for security, including SAML credentials for authorization, and exchange of information is provided in XML. The Exposure Service provides data from an authoritative data source. The "robust" Service call may be different between services than between browser and service. The "robust" APIs will also be different for different environments (e.g., .NET or J2EE). The "robust" part of the API consists of (see Figure 1):

- Port Listener
- Retain data input for reuse
- Complete the bi-lateral end-to-end authentication
- Consume the assertion package for authorization
- Pass Authorization credentials and initial input to the service

The initiating part on the "robust" Browser and the Service-to-Service invocation must meet the compatibility issues, including the initiation of bi-lateral end-to-end authentication and the passing of a SAML token for authorization.

3.3 Bi-lateral End-to-End Authentication

As a pre-requisite to end-to end communication an SSL or other suitable TLS is setup between each of the machines. Each communication link in the Figure 3 will be authenticated end- to-end with the use of public keys in the X.509 certificates provided for each of the active entities. This two way authentication avoids a number of threat vulnerabilities. The requestor initially authenticates to the service provider. Once the authentication is completed, an SSL connection is established between the requestor and the service provider, within which a WS-Security package will be sent to the service. The WS-Security [7, 10] package contains a SAML token generated by the Security Token Server (STS) in the requestor domain. The primary method of authentication will be through the use of public keys in the X.509 certificate, which can then be used to set up encrypted communications, (either by X.509 keys or a generated session key). Session keys and certificate keys need to be robust and sufficiently protected to prevent malware exploitation. The preferred method of communication is secure messaging using WS Security, contained in SOAP envelopes. The encryption key used is the public key of the target, ensuring only the target can interpret the communication.

3.4 Cascading Authentication

This section outlines a process for cascading authentication, a key concept of our approach. This process involves a sequence of certificates that provide the history and

[1] These data sources must be pre-designated by communities or programs as the authoritative sources. These are updated frequently and checked for integrity and accuracy. They may be mirrored for efficiency of operations.

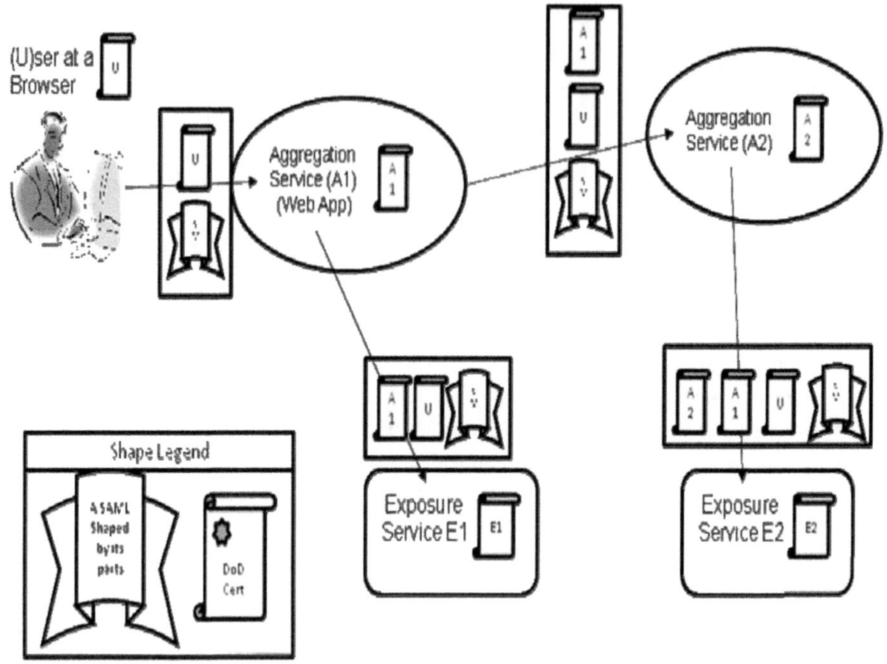

Fig. 4. Cascading Authentication Architectural Overview

delegation of the service chain. The chain of authentication may be used to shape the SAML assertions for least privilege and are sent with each service request allowing the recipient determine authorization (if any) that will be provided the sender of a message. The authentication involves presenting the PKI certificate(s) of the requestor to the service and vice-versa. Cascading authentication presents all of the PKI certificates in the chain so that after authentication the target will have knowledge of each step in the chain. Figure 4 illustrates our concept of cascading authentication.

The SAML may then be pruned or modified to reflect this whole chain, and the logs would contain the ***OnBehalfOf*** based upon the chain of credentials. This way, one knows whom one is acting on behalf of who at all times. Delegation of authority is then defined by the chain of credentials presented for authorization.

By delegation we simply mean the handing of a task over to another entity by software service calls. A scond form of delegation, personal delegation, must be handled separately. This involves an individual tasking another individual to produce work for him. This second type of delegation is described in [18].

The software delegation is the assignment of authority but not responsibility to another software entity to carry out specific activities. Further, it is assumed that any service invoking another service is delegating its authority to complete whatever portion of the service it has been authorized to perform. Delegation for a service is transitive and not personal. This delegation occurs at levels 5 and above in the OSI model. Levels 4 and below are handled by defined middleware definitions. Delegation only lives during the session under consideration. We now introduce two terms that are closely tied to delegation; attribution and least privilege.

Attribution is provided when the service exercising privilege is identified as acting on behalf of the requestor who (implicitly) authorized the delegation. *Least Privilege* is preserved by providing the entity with only that level of privilege necessary to do the task without exceeding his/her own authority.

4 Shaping the SAML

4.1 Basic Use Case

The basic use case is given in the Figure 5 and involves a user invoking an aggregation service which in turn invokes aggregation and other services.

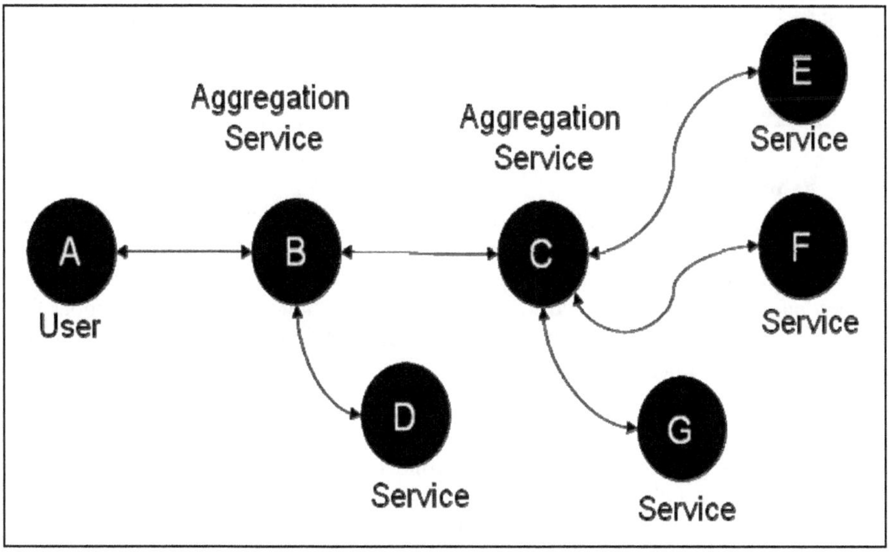

Fig. 5. Use Case for Service Delegation

4.2 Communication for Authentication/Authorization

Each communication link in Figure 5 will be authenticated end-to-end with the X.509 certificates provided for each of the active entities. Authorization will be based upon the Security Assertion Markup Language (SAML).[2] The delegation, attribution and least privilege will be handled by modification to the SAML token provided by the STS. The SAML token for user A to aggregation Service B is provided in the Table 1 below:

[2] Security Assertion Markup Language (SAML) is part of the OASIS set of Web Service Standards.

Table 1. SAML 2.0 Format for User Request

Item	Field Usage	Recommendation	Notes
SAML Response			
Version ID	Version 2.0	Required	
ID	(uniquely assigned)	Required	
Issue Instant	Timestamp	Required	
Issuer	Yes	Required	STS Name
Signature	Yes	Required	STS Signature
Subject	Yes For User A	Required	Must contain the X.509 Distinguished name or equivalent
Attribute Assertion			
Subject	Yes For User A	EDIPI (user common name)	For Attribution
Attributes, Group and Role Memberships	Yes For User A	Required	May be pruned for least privilege
Conditions			
NotBefore	Yes	Required	TimeStamp - minutes
NotAfter	Yes	Required	TimeStamp + minutes
OneTimeUse	Yes	Required	Mandatory

4.2.1 Pruning Attributes[3]

An individual or service requesting another service may contain many elements that are not relevant to the service request. This makes the SAML request overly large, increases the cycles for SAML consumption and evaluation may introduce additional latency and is a potential source for escalation of privilege. In order to combat these factors, the attribute assertion should be reduced to the minimum required to accomplish the service request.

4.2.2 Required Escalation of Privilege

Certain services may require privilege beyond that of the original client. Examples include the Security Token Server (STS) that when called is expected to have access to the Active Directory (AD) and UDDI, even when the client does not have such privilege. An additional example would include payroll services that can provide average values without specifics. The service must be able to access all records in the payroll data base, even if the client it is acting on behalf of does not have this privilege. For purposes of this methodology, these required elements will be dealt with separately in both data pruning and service to service calls. Service developers should take care that the required escalation of privilege is required and that the newly aggregated data do not impose additional access restrictions. The data that has been aggregated and synthesized should be carefully scrutinized for such sensitivities. The process is not unlike the combining of data from multiple unclassified but sensitive data sources that may rise to a higher classification level when they are all present in one place.

[3] Since authorization decisions may require any of a combination of attributes, groups, and/or roles, these will be referred to generically as elements in the rest of this chapter.

4.2.3 Data Requirements - Pruning Elements

In order to accomplish the reduction of the SAML assertion, the STS must know the target and the elements that are important to the target. Table 2 below presents such a data compilation. This table will be used in the subsequent example. An element is an attribute, role or group used in the authorization decision.

Table 2. Group and Role Pruning Data Requirement

Service	Uri	Relevant Attributes, Groups and Roles	Escalation of Privilege Required
AFPersonnel30	...//afnetdol.pers.af23:622	Element1, Element3, Element4, Element5, Element6	Element6
PERGeo	...//afnetdol.perst.af45:543	Element4, Element5,	Element6
Service	Uri	Relevant Attributes, Groups and Roles	Escalation of Privilege Required
		Element6	
PerReg	...//afnetdol.persq.af45:333	Element4	
PerTrans	...//afnetdol.persaw.af45:218 62	Element6	
BarNone	...//afnetdol.persaxc.af45:123 4	Element5	
DimrsEnroll	...//afnetdol.persws.af45:235 67	Element1, Element3	
...	...	...	
Endfile			

The combining of these elements is given for calling step i by:

Let N_{i+1}=New SAML Elements for i to call i+1
Let P_i = Prior Elements
Let R_{i+1}= Service Required Elements
Let H_i = Service Held elements
Let E_i = Required Escalation Elements

Then:

$$N_{i+1} = (P_i \cap (R_{i+1} \cap H_i)) \cup (E_i \cap R_{i+1}) \quad (1)$$

Where: $\cap$ is the intersection of sets and $\cup$ is the union of sets, $\emptyset$ is the empty set (no members). The formula may be read as the common elements in the prior SAML and the intersection of the held elements and those required by the next call $((P_i \cap (R_{i+1} \cap H_i))$ - normal least privilege). These are added ($\cup$) to the required escalation elements that are required to be extended by the next call $((E_i \cap R_{i+1})$ - extended least privilege by escalation of privilege). The initial call has no prior elements and P_1 is defined as the initial set of privilege elements. This reduces N_1 to:

$$N_1 = H_0 \cap R_1 \quad \text{(Normal least privilege)} \quad (2)$$

4.3 Subsequent Calls Require Saving the SAML Assertion

After the SAML is consumed and authorization is granted, the service must retain the SAML Attribute Assertion (Part of the Larger SAML Token) above. Specifically, the subject fields and the elements field to be used in further authorization. The specific instance is shown in Table 3.

Table 3. Retained Portion of SAML Token

Attribute Assertion			
Subject	Yes For User A	EDIPI	For Attribution
Attributes, Group and Role Memberships	Yes For User A	Required	Mask for follow-on least privilege

4.3.1 SAML Token Modifications for Further Calls

The Attribute Assertion of Table 4 is returned to the STS for modification of the normal SAML token. The SAML Token for the unmodified service call is given below:

Table 4. Unmodified SAML for Service B of Use Case

Item	Field Usage	Recommendation	Notes
SAML Response			
Version ID	Version 2.0	Required	
ID	(uniquely assigned)	Required	
Issue Instant	Time-stamp	Required	
Issuer	Yes	Required	STS Name
Signature	Yes	Required	STS Signature
Subject	Yes For Service B	Required	Must contain the X.509 Distinguished name or equivalent
Attribute Assertion			
Item	Field Usage	Recommendation	Notes
Subject	Yes For Service B	Common Name for Service B	For Attribution
Attributes, Group and Role Memberships	Yes For Service B	Required	$N_{i+1} = (P_i \cap (R_{i+1} \cap H_i)) \cup (E_i \cap R_{i+1})$
Conditions			
NotBefore	Yes	Required	TimeStamp - minutes
NotAfter	Yes	Required	TimeStamp + minutes
OneTimeUse	Yes	Required	Mandatory

The Attribute Assertion is modified in the following way.

- The subject is modified to read "Service A OnBehalfOf" the returned SAML subject which in this case is the EDIPI (Electronic Data Interchange Personnel Identifier) of the user.
- The attribute, group and role membership (elements) are modified to include only elements that appear in both the Service B registry and the returned SAML Attribute Assertion.
- The modified SAML Token is provided in Table 5 below:

Table 5. Modified SAML Attribute Assertions for Further Calls

Item	Field Usage	Recommendation	Notes
SAML Response			
Version ID	Version 2.0	Required	
ID	(uniquely assigned)	Required	
Issue Instant	Timestamp	Required	
Issuer	Yes	Required	STS Name
Signature	Yes	Required	STS Signature
Subject	Yes For Service B	Required	Must contain the X.509 Distinguished name
Attribute Assertion			
Subject	Yes contains A and B	Common Name (cn) B OnBehalfOf EDIPI	For Attribution
Attributes, Group and Role Memberships	Yes B restricted by A	Required	$N_{i+1} = (P_i \cap (R_{i+1} \cap H_i)) \cup (E_i \cap R_{i+1})$
Conditions			
NotBefore	Yes	Required	TimeStamp - minutes
NotAfter	Yes	Required	TimeStamp + minutes
OneTimeUse	Yes	Required	Mandatory

Subsequent calls from Service A would use the modified token. Further, the subsequent service called would save the SAML Attribute Assertion for its further calls.

4.4 An Annotated Notional Example

A User in the User Forest (Ted.Smith1234567890) through discovery finds the dashboard service on Air Force Personnel (AFPersonnel30) that he would like to

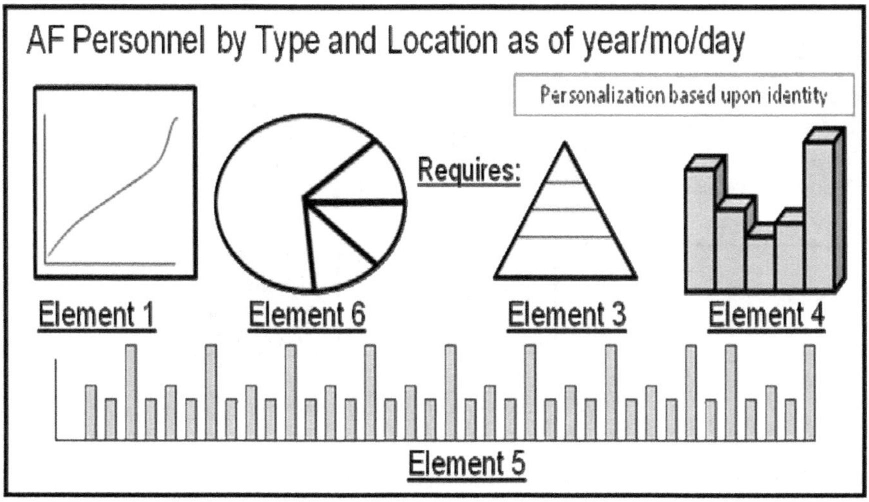

Fig. 6. AFPersonnel30 with Display Outputs

invoke. The discovery has revealed that access is limited to users with Element1, Element3, Element4, Element5 or Element6, but that users without all of these authorizations may not receive all of the requested display. Ted does not have all of the required Elements, but is authorized for personnel data within CONUS and has Element membership in Element 1, Element 2, Element 3, Element 4, Element 7, and Element 12 + 27 other Elements not relevant. The AFPersonnel30 will typically display the following dashboard on Air Force Personnel.

The elements required would not typically be displayed. A partial calling tree for AFPersonnel30 is provided in Figure 7. The widgets that form the presentation graphics have not been included, but would be part of the calling tree, they do not have access requirements that modify the example and have been deleted for reduction of complexity. In the figure we show the elements that make up the privilege for each service (holds) and the elements required for access to the service (requires). This data is linked to Table 2, and must be synchronized with it. The element privileges for services without subsequent calls are unimportant, and many additional groups may be present but will be pruned on subsequent calls.

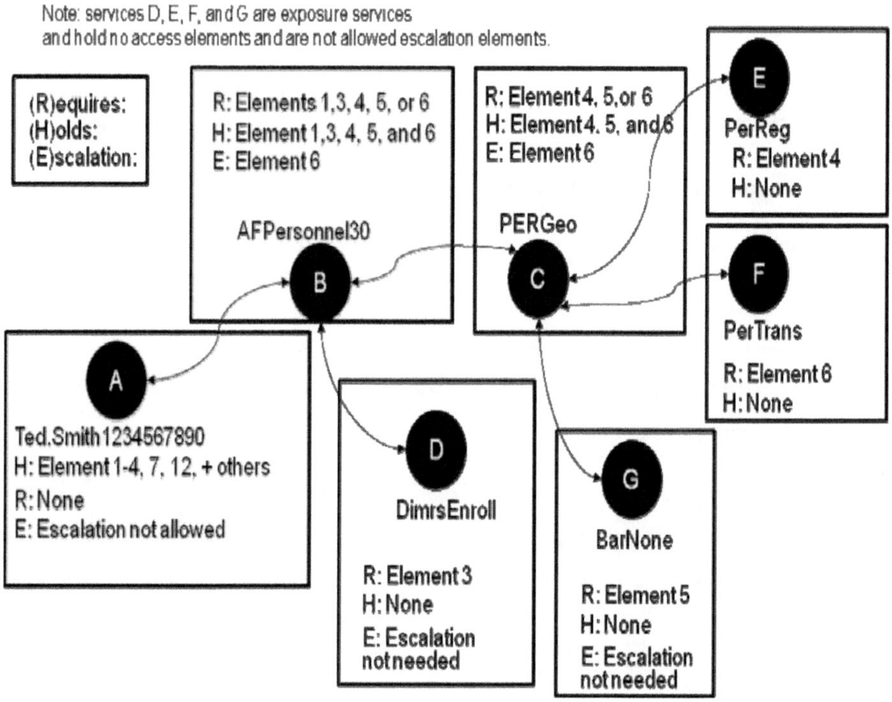

Fig. 7. AFPersonnel30 Calling Tree

Note that each link in the calling graph requires bi-lateral authentication using certificates provided as credentials to each of the active entities, followed by the push of a SAML token for authorization. The first such token is presented in Table 6:

Table 6. Ted Smith SAML Push to AFPersonnel30

Item	Field Usage
SAML Response	
Version ID	Version 2.0
ID	0qwdrt009kkmn
Issue Instant	080820081943
Item	Field Usage
Issuer	Enterprise STS12345
Signature	Lkhjsfoioiunmclscwl879ooeeujl99vcd78ffgg3422ft...
Subject	CN = TED.SMITH1234567890, OU = CONTRACTOR, OU = PKI, OU = DOD, O = U.S. Government, C = US
Attribute Assertion	
Subject	TED.SMITH1234567890
Attributes, Group and Role Memberships	Element1, Element3, Element4[4] $N_1 = (R_2 \cap H_1)) \underset{\cdot}{\cup} (E_1 \cap R_2)$ $=((1, 2, 3, 4, 7, 12, +27) \cap ((1,3\text{-}6)$ $= (1,3,4))$ =((Element1, Element3, and Element4))
Conditions	
NotBefore	080820081933
NotAfter	080820081953
OneTimeUse	Yes

The Attribute Assertion Section is saved for subsequent calls. The call from AFPersonnel30 to service PERGeo will look like Table 7.

Table 7. AFPersonnel30 SAML Push to PERGeo

Item	Field Usage
SAML Response	
Version ID	Version 2.0
ID	0qwdrt009kkmn
Issue Instant	080820081944
Issuer	Enterprise STS12345
Signature	Lkhjsfoioiunmclscwl879ooeeujl99xfg654bbgg34lli...
Subject	CN = e3893de0-4159-11dd-ae16-0800200c9a66, OU=USAF, OU=PKI, OU=DOD, O=U.S. GOVERNMENT, C=US
Attribute Assertion	
Subject	AFPersonnel30 OnBehalfOf TED.SMITH1234567890
Group and Role Memberships	Element 4[5], Element6[6] $N_{i+1} = (P_i \cap (R_{i+1} \cap H_i)) \underset{\cdot}{\cup} (E_i \cap R_{i+1})$ $=((1, 3, 4) \cap (4 \cap 4\text{-}6) \underset{\cdot}{\cup} (6 \cap 4\text{-}6)$ $=((1, 3, 4) \cap (4)) \underset{\cdot}{\cup} (6)$ =(4,6) + Element 4 and Element 6
Conditions	
NotBefore	080820081934
NotAfter	080820081954
OneTimeUse	Yes

---

[4] An element is an attribute, role, group or combination of the previous. Elimination of Element 2, Element 7, Element 12 and other elements based on pruning (see Table 6 under AFPersonnel30).

[5] An element is an attribute, role, group or combination of the previous. Elimination of Element 1 and Element 3 based on pruning (see Table 5 under PERGeo).

[6] Element 6 is a required escalation elements.

The SAML Attribute Assertion is where the work is done. The subject has been modified to include the names of the calling tree and the Elements have been pruned to include only common items between the calling elements in the tree. Figure 8

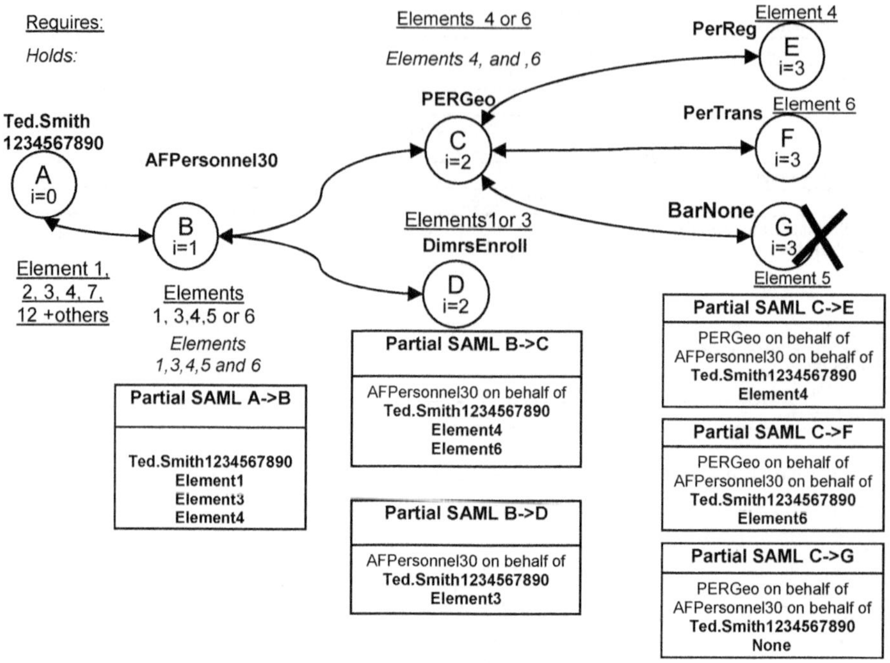

Fig. 8. SAML Attribute Assertion of the Calling Tree

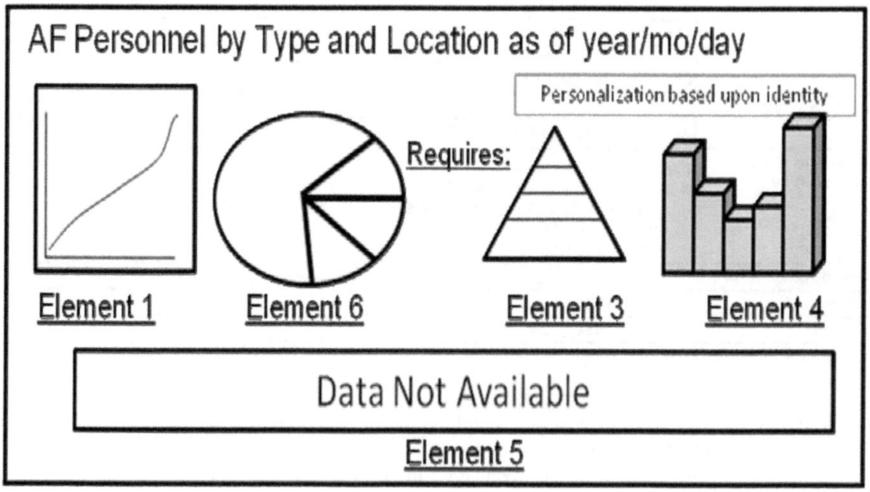

Fig. 9. Dashboard Service AFPersonnel30 Case Result (with Annotation)

shows the completion of the calling tree, including only the SAML Attribute Assertions in the blocks below. Note that the calls to BarNone fail access (SAML does not contain required element 5) and while being stealth to the calling routine (which will return with no data after timeout) this failure will trigger alarms to SOA management monitors as follows:

Failed authorization (BarNone) attempt PERGeo on behalf of AFPersonnel30 on behalf of Ted.Smith1234567890 No data returned.

The returned dashboard (without the element requirement annotations) is presented in Figure 9. Note that Element 6 privilege was provided by service escalation.

5 Initial Testing of Operational Quality of Service

An initial operational implementation of the architecture with full bi-lateral authentication at each step and SAML authorization produced by the Identity Provider (IdP) side of the STS was tested in June of 2010. Latency (in seconds) is measured for each step, and a total is computed for each invocation of the routines. The data are presented in Table 8 below.

Table 8. Latency and Loading

Test	Total execution single user (seconds)	Total execution 100 users (seconds)	Total execution 200 users (seconds)	Total execution 300 users (seconds)
A1 – Test set 1 Invocation through SAML response	1.74	1.85	5.59	11.68
A2 – Test set 2 Invocation through SAML response	1.71	1.83	3.84	11.59
B IdP indirect invocation	.73	.84	4.99	11.21
C1 – Test set 1 Invocation through service initiation	7.86	8.00	21.25	35.75
C2 – Test set 2 Invocation through service initiation	4.33	7.13	21.52	34.05
D IdP indirect invocation through service initiation	3.54	7.38	20.51	34.39
E Invocation through service initiation times 3 [error percent] and {success rate}	9.89 [6%] {.035/sec}	41.46 [44%] {1.056/sec}	67.70 [22%] {1.844/sec}	80.55 [43%] {1.873/sec}
F IdP indirect invocation through service initiation times 3 [error percent] and {success rate}	8.78 [5%] {.038/sec}	32.71 [2%] {1.890/sec}	65.04 [21%] {1.890/sec}	92.50 [37%] {1.869/sec}

The table uses the following nomenclature:

- A: Get SAML from IdP, starting at web server
- B: Get SAML directly from IdP

- C: Access services Home page
- D: Access services starting at IdP
- E: Access services, go to search page, perform search
- F: Access services starting at IdP, go to search page, perform search

The Initiation of the SAML (IdP-SAML) is the bottleneck (as indicated by analysis of the detailed data – not presented below), since its latency increases the most with increasing load. In addition, overall network traffic seems to be a contributing factor, since IdP-SAML performance degrades under both increased user loads and increased network traffic.

Throughput (successfully completed transactions per second) was maximized at between 100 and 200 users for all tests. Throughput is not a linear function of the number of users. For flow F (which is the preferred process), failure rates increased from 100-300 users while throughput remained the same at roughly 1.9 requests per second. It also depends on any wait or think time between requests. Initial data indicate a reasonable Quality of Service (QoS) with 200 users in flow F. Further optimization of the process may further improve these numbers.

6 Related Work

A search of the literature suggests that there has been no coordinated effort or models related to what we propose with the exception of the Globus Grid Security Infrastructure [13]. It is worth mentioning a few seminal and open standard works that make significant contributions towards the realization of our propose model. Needham and Schroeder [2] laid the foundation of public key infrastructure (PKI) upon which PKI-based works credit. Burrows et. al., [1] introduced the logic of authentication, which enable analyst to formalize the assumptions and goals of a security protocol, and to attempt to prove its correctness. When one fails to find a proof, the place at which one gets stuck often shows a potential point of attack. This analysis model turn out to be very powerful upon which the "BAN Logic" and many formal tools were developed and extended to tools used in design of protocols. Credit is further due to FIPS 196 publication on entity authentication using public key cryptography [11] and OASIS for the specification of SAML and the WS-* protocols [5,7,8,9,10],The Liberty Alliance Project [4] and the Shibboleth Project [4]. Credits are also due to some general-purpose and specialized solution for distributed system security, in particular, Kerberos, DCE, SSH, SSL, CRISIS (security component of Web-OS) [16] and Legion [17].

7 Discussion

This approach is part of a larger Information Assurance architecture to provide a more complete solution. It is worth noting that several key pieces are missing to complete this scenario. On the user end we need WS-enabled browser with the ability to communicate with a Security Token Server (STS). The STS will facilitate the exchange of credentials, aid in setting up the initial SSL, and provide the SAML package for consumption. The robust browser may be on a desktop or a mobile device or may be manifested as an appliance on the user's work station. On the service provider end we need the software to encrypt/decrypt secure message and to consume the SAML package. The latter is not trivial since it must be checked for signature, tampering, timeouts and other factors. If we assume for the moment that the user is tightly bound to the browser, then the user security context is maintained through the device and all the way to the initial service. We need software that will read and store the authentication chain, and we need software in the STS to act upon this knowledge. This context will assist in attribution and delegation and in monitoring insider behavior activity. The remaining threats of insider activity, ex-filtration of static data and denial-of service (DoS) attacks must be handled by other means, but behavioral modeling, static encryption and dynamic ports and protocols still apply to these threats. Both the robust browser and the robust API are under development, and the initial authentication processes have been demonstrated in a pilot program.

8 Conclusions

In this paper we outline a process model that provides an end-to-end authentication as a prerequisite to authorization that accommodates intermediary nodes across distributed boundaries without sacrificing local autonomy. The model outlined herein involves many components, and will require additional software development for the pilot system to provide complete cascading of authentication. This paper has been developed to encourage the discussion and exchange ideas in making the model robust and complete for adoption in practice.

Acknowledgements

The authors would like to acknowledge the support of the Secretary of the Air Force's Warfighting and Integration CIO office in the development of efforts outlined in this paper.

References

1. Burrows, M., Abadi, M., Needham, R.M.: A logic of authentication. ACM Transaction on Computer Systems 8(1), 18–36 (1990)
2. Needham, R.M., Schroeder, R.M.: Using encryption for authentication in large networks of computers. Communication of the ACM 21(12), 993–999 (1978)
3. Internet2, Shibboleth Project (2007), `http://shibboleth.internet2.edu/`
4. OASIS. Identity Federation. Liberty Alliance Project (2004), `http://projectliberty.org/resources/specifications.php`
5. OASIS. Profiles for the OASIS Security Assertion Markup Language (SAML) V2.0 (March 2005), `http://www.oasis-open.org/committees/tc_home.php?wg_abbrev=security`
6. Guide to Secure Web Services: Recommendations of the National Institute of Standards and Technology. NIST-US Department of Commerce Publication (August 2007)
7. Web Service Security: Scenarios, Patterns, and Implementation Guidance for Web Services Enhancements (WSE) 3.0, Microsoft Corporation (2005)

8. WS-ReliableMessaging Specification, OASIS (June 2007)
9. WS-SecureConversation Specification, OASIS (March 2007)
10. WSE 3.0 and WS-ReliableMessaging, Microsoft White Paper (June 2005), http://msdn2.microsoft.com/en-us/library/ms996942d=printer.aspx
11. FIPS PUB 196, Federal Information Processing Standards Publication. Entity Authentication Using Public Key Cryptography, February 18 (1997)
12. Air Force Information Assurance Strategy Team, Air Force Information Assurance Enterprise Architecture, Version 1.70, SAF/XC, March 15 (2009)
13. Overview: Globus Grid Security Infrastructure, http://www.globus.org/security/overview.html (last retrieved April 2009)
14. Foster, I., Kesselman, C., Tsudik, G., Tuecke, S.: A Security Architecture for Computational Grids. In: Proc. of 5th ACM Conference on Computer and Communications Security Conference, pp. 83–92 (1998)
15. Welch, V., Foster, I., Kesselman, C., Mulmo, O., Pearlman, L., Tuecke, S., Gawor, J., Meder, S., Siebenlist. F.: X.509 Proxy Certificates for Dynamic Delegation. In: 3rd Annual PKI R&D Workshop (2004)
16. Belani, E., Vahdat, A., Anderson, T., Dahlin, M.: The CRISIS wide area security architecture. In: Usenix Security Symposium (January 1998)
17. Lewis, M., Grimshaw, A.: The Core Legion Object Model. In: Proc. 5th IEEE Symposium On High Performance Distributed Computing, pp. 562–571. IEEE Computer Society Press, Los Alamitos (1996)
18. Chandersekaran, C., Simpson, W.: Information Sharing and Federation. In: The 2nd International Multi-Conference on Engineering and Technological Innovation: IMETI 2009, Orlando, FL, vol. I, pp. 300–305 (July 2009)
19. Chandersekaran, C., Simpson, W., Trice, A.: Cross-Domain Solutions in an Era of Information Sharing. In: The 1st International Multi-Conference on Engineering and Technological Innovation: IMET2008, Orlando, FL, vol. I, pp. 313–318 (June 2008)
20. Chandersekaran, C., Simpson, W.: A Persona Framework for Delegation, Attribution and Least Privilege. In: The International Conference on Complexity, Informatics and Cybernetics, Orlando, FL, vol. II, pp. 84–89 (April 2010)
21. Chandersekaran, C., Ceesay, E., Simpson, W.: An Authentication Model for Delegation, Attribution and Least Privilege. In: The 3rd International Conference on PErvasive Technologies Related to Assistive Environments: PETRAE 2010, Samos, Greece, p. 7 (June 2010)
22. Chandersekaran, C., Simpson, W.: A SAML Framework for Delegation, Attribution and Least Privilege. In: The 3rd International Multi-Conference on Engineering and Technological Innovation, Orlando, FL, pp. 303–308 (July 2010)
23. Chandersekaran, C., Simpson, W.: Use Case Based Access Control. In: The 3rd International Multi-Conference on Engineering and Technological Innovation, Orlando, FL, pp. 297–302 (July 2010)

Identification of Encryption Algorithm Using Decision Tree*

R. Manjula and R. Anitha

Department of Mathematics and Computer Applications,
PSG College of Technology, Coimbatore, India
manjuasmi3@gmail.com,
anitha_nadarajan@mail.psgtech.ac.in

Abstract. The task of identification of encryption algorithm from cipher text alone is considered to be a challenging one. Very few works have been done in this area by considering block ciphers or symmetric key ciphers. In this paper, we propose an approach for identification of encryption algorithm for various ciphers using the decision tree generated by C4.5 algorithm. A system which extracts eight features from a cipher text and classifies the encryption algorithm using the C4.5 classifier is developed. Success rate of this proposed method is in the range of 70 to 75 percentages.

Keywords: Ciphers, Decision tree, C4.5 algorithm.

1 Introduction

Cryptanalysis is a part of cryptology, which concentrates on retrieving plaintext from cipher text knowing something or nothing about the secret key. The attempt of cryptanalyst to break the cipher text is based on the assumption that the secrecy of a cryptosystem is totally depending on the key and the cryptanalyst has full knowledge of the encryption algorithm. But it is not the case always and especially in digital forensic, the cipher text is the only information available to the cryptanalyst. Digital Forensic includes Computer Forensic and Network Forensic. The Computer Forensic gathers evidence from computer media seized at crime scene and the issues involved are imaging storage media, recovering deleted files, searching slack and free space, preserving the collected information for litigation and any encrypted file which consists of incriminating details. In case of Network Forensic analysis, cryptanalysis is used to find the encryption algorithm from the cipher text send by the intruders. Practically identifying which encryption algorithm is being used from the cipher text alone is a challenging task.

Normally statistical methods and machine learning based methods are considered for the identification of the encryption algorithm from the cipher text. Statistical methods used the frequency of occurrence of elements of alphabets and their n-grams. In machine learning based methods, the task of identification of the encryption algorithm

* This work is a part of the Collaborative Directed Basic Research on Smart and Secure Environment project, funded by NTRO, New Delhi, India.

N. Meghanathan et al. (Eds.): CCSIT 2011, Part III, CCIS 133, pp. 237–246, 2011.

is considered as a pattern classification problem. These methods attempt to capture the implicit behavior of each encryption algorithm from a number of cipher texts obtained using that encryption method. A neural network based method for cryptanalysis of Feistel type block cipher is discussed in [1]. This method bears the benefit of being parallel by nature and can be easily extended to a distributed version. Dileep A.D et al [3] in their paper proposed an approach using support vector machines to identify the encryption method for block ciphers. They have considered common dictionary based method and the class specific dictionary based method for generating a document vector from a cipher text and reduced the problem as a document categorization problem. In [7], James George Dunham et al. proposed a method to classify the file type of Stream Ciphers in depth using Neural Networks. Ciphers encrypted with the same key are called ciphers in depth and depth detection was accomplished for stream ciphers with a hit rate of 99.5% and ciphers are further classified according to the file types of their underlying messages with an accuracy of over 90%. In the work done by Gaurav Saxena [5], to classify ciphertext of Blowfish and RC4, trivially good test vectors were generated using linear programming concept. Also he has used support vector machine to classify Blowfish and RC4. The performance of the test vector was measured by β where the percentage of the successful classification by the test vector was 50 + β. The focus of these methods has been on identification of some symmetric key ciphers. So far not much work has been done in identifying the encryption algorithm including public key ciphers.

A major focus of machine learning research is to automatically produce models, such as rules and patterns, from data or databases [10]. The main objective of this paper is to design a system that is capable of identifying various encryption algorithms like substitution, permutation, DES, Triple DES, AES, Blowfish, RC2, RC4, IDEA, RSA and ECC using machine learning. This paper discusses about entropy based feature extraction and decision tree based classification of the encryption algorithm. The decision tree models are found to be very inexpensive to compute [11]. The decision trees are useful in the domain of machine learning since they obtain reasonable accuracy and they are relatively constructed as a set of rules during the learning phase. The rules are then used to predict the classes of new instances.

In Section II, we discuss about the proposed work of identifying encryption algorithms by using feature extraction and classification model. Features are extracted from a cipher text using maximum entropy, entropy and correlation co-efficient. Implementation and experimental details are included in section III and IV respectively.

2 Proposed Work

The proposed approach is to identify the encryption algorithm from the cipher text using C4.5 algorithm. By analyzing different cipher texts, we find that cipher text consists of gibberish characters, alphabets, numbers, etc. Text categorization is an important application of machine learning to the field of document information retrieval. Text categorization in the cipher texts are expected to be different for cipher texts that are created using different encryption algorithms. In this paper, we propose to categorize, the content of cipher text into gibberish characters (symbols), alphabets (Uppercase and lowercase) and numbers. Entropy and maximum entropy are obtained for the above mentioned categorizations to capture features of the cipher text. Using the concept of information entropy, C4.5 builds decision trees from a set of training data. The proposed work is divided into two phases namely Training Phase and Testing Phase. The training phase includes two processes, Feature Extraction and Classification in order to create a classification model. The Testing phase consists of two processes namely Feature Extraction and Identification. Testing phase uses classification model of the training phase to identify the encryption algorithm. The block diagram of the proposed system is given in Fig-1.

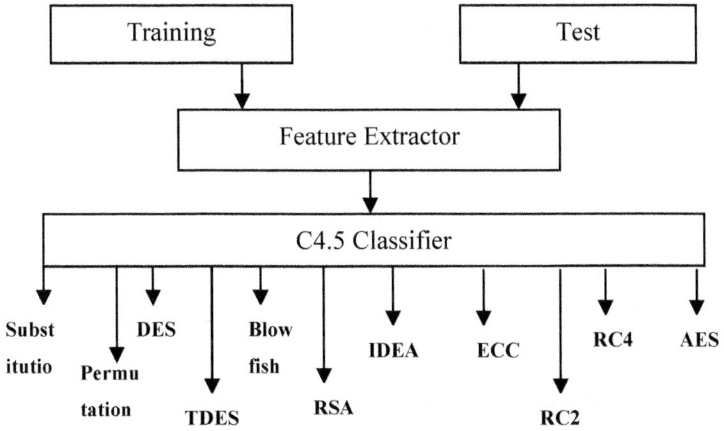

Fig. 1. Block diagram of the proposed system

The training data is a set $S=\{c_1, c_2,..,c_n\}$ of cipher texts and each c_i is represented as a vector $(v_{i1},v_{i2},...,v_{im})$ where v_{ij}, $1 \leq i \leq n$, $1 \leq j \leq m-1$ is an attribute or features extracted from the cipher text c_i and v_{im} is the encryption algorithm which had been used to produce the ciphertext $c_{i.}$ In constructing the decision tree, C4.5 uses the criterion of normalized information gain that results from choosing an attribute for splitting the data. It creates a decision node that splits on the highest normalized information gain and then recurses on the smaller sublists.

Training Phase

In this phase, samples of training data i.e., cipher texts are fed into the feature extractor. In this paper, for a given file, feature extraction based on entropy is used. Entropy is defined as a measure of the unpredictability or randomness of data [12]. The term Entropy, uncertainty and information are used more or less interchangeably, but from the perspective of probability, uncertainty is perhaps a more accurate term. Entropy is defined as

$$H(x) = -\sum_{i=1}^{k} p_i \log_2 p_i \qquad (1)$$

where p_i is the probability of the ith unit of information in event x's series of k symbols. The process of feature extraction not only uses the measure of entropy, but also the idea of maximum entropy. The maximum entropy corresponds to the case when all q states have equal probabilities of occurrence p where p=1/q. For instance [6], if a source S has q equiprobable symbols, then p_i =1/q for each i, so

$$H(S) = q.\frac{1}{q}log_2 q = log_2 q \quad (2)$$

Since entropy and maximum entropy works on the randomness of the data, it is applied on text categorization of cipher text for the feature extraction process and based on the value, it can be used as an aid to a cryptanalyst, or as a component in automatic code cracking software. Here, correlation co-efficient is also applied on the text categorization in order to find the relationship between characters. Size of the cipher text is also considered as one of the features because maximum entropy values may vary in case of permutation, substitution cipher. Based on the above mentioned points, the following features which are listed in Table-1 has been considered to identify the encryption algorithm.

Table 1. Features Extracted from encrypted file

Feature	**Notation**
Maximum entropy of all characters	E_whole
Maximum entropy of upper case letters	E_Upper
Maximum entropy of lower case letters	E_Lower
Maximum entropy of symbols	E_Symbol
Maximum entropy of numbers	E_Number
Maximum entropy of three Grams	E_Three
Maximum entropy of four Grams	E_Four
Entropy of all characters	E_Basicall
Correlation co-efficient of uppercase letters	E_corelation
Size of the file	E_Size

The feature extraction process is used to obtain the relevant features from an encrypted file as below : Maximum entropy of all characters is obtained by converting the characters into their corresponding ASCII values and then computing the maximum entropy using (2).Maximum entropy of uppercase letters, lowercase letters, symbols and numbers are similarly obtained. Around seventy five, three grams and four grams which are used most often in a text file are collected and maximum entropy is calculated. Entropy of the occurrence of all characters is computed using (1). Correlation co-efficient of the lower case letters are $(\frac{1}{100})^{th}$ time of the correlation co-efficient of the upper case letters, so in this work correlation co-efficient of upper case letters alone is considered as a feature.

The features related to the encrypted file like Key Size, Public key, Private key, etc are not considered since the analysis is done without the idea of information about keys. In this work, feature extraction is done based on all the characters (0-255) which are present in an encrypted file. Among the above mentioned ten features, in order to select the most appropriate features, Chi-square based attributes selection is included such that the performance of feature extraction will be increased. It measures the lack of independence between an attribute X and a class Y [8][19].

$$\chi^2 = \sum_{i=1}^{r} \sum_{j=1}^{k} \frac{(A_{ij}-E_{ij})^2}{E_{ij}} \tag{3}$$

where r is the number of attributes, k is the number of classes, A_{ij} is the number of instances for which the value of an attribute is i and the value of the class is j and E_{ij} is the expected number of instances of A_{ij}. At the end of the feature extraction process after applying χ^2 test, eight features are considered to be significant. Two thousands encrypted files are collected and used in the training phase. From each cipher text c_i, eight features are extracted and each training data c_i is augmented with the encryption algorithm name. Samples of relevant features of the training sets used in experiments are given in Table 2. Each column represents values of a sample cipher text features. Sample cipher text are created using tools like Crypttool [18], SmartSec ECC encryptor [16]. Many text files of different sizes have been encrypted using above mentioned tools. Also, the same text file encrypted using different types of algorithm is considered.

Table 2. Features of Sample Files

Features	Sample File1	Sample File2	Sample File3	Sample File4
E_Whole	7.5469	4.585	4.2479	4.585
E_Upper	4.7004	4.585	4.2479	4.585
E_Lower	4.7004	4.3923	3.7004	3.9069
E_Symbol	7.7879	6.7549	6.3038	6.6865
E_Number	3.3219	2.8074	2.8074	3
E_Basicall	1520.6	6.5778	3.336	5.3502
E_Correlation	-1.3E-7	0.00327	0.00327	0.00045
E_Size	128453	461	192	389
E_Algorithm	DES	AES	RSA	ECC

Classification Model

In the second process of the training phase, the collected features are fed into the C4.5 algorithm classifier to generate a classification model, also called decision tree model.

C4.5 Algorithm

This algorithm is based on the ID3[2] algorithm that tries to find small (or simple) decision tree. It considers some points which are mentioned below for its construction [14]:

i) If all cases are of the same class, the tree is a leaf and so the leaf is returned label with this class;
ii) For each attribute, calculate the potential information provided by a test on the attribute (based on the probabilities of each case having a particular value for the attribute). Also calculate the gain in information that would result

from a test on the attribute (based on the probabilities of each case with a particular value for the attribute),

iii) Depending on the current selection criterion, find the best attribute to branch on.

Information gain

The information gain of an attribute 'a' for a set of case T is calculated as below [13]: If 'a' is discrete, and $T_1,\ldots,T_S$ are the subsets of T consisting of cases with distinct known value for attribute 'a', then:

$$\text{gain} = \text{info}(T) - \sum_{i=1}^{S} \frac{|T_i|}{|T|} * \text{info}(T_i) \quad (4)$$

C4.5 algorithm uses this information gain ratio.

Pruning

Pruning is an important step to the result because of the outliers. All data sets contain a little subset of instances that are not well-defined, and differ from the other ones on its neighborhood. The decision tree must classify all the instances in the training set, it is pruned.

C4.5 algorithm accounts for unavailable values, continuous attribute value ranges, pruning of decision trees, rule derivation, and so on. Each leaf node has an associated rule, the conjunction of the decision leading from the root node, through the tree, to that leaf. Best node is selected by measuring information gain. The information gain

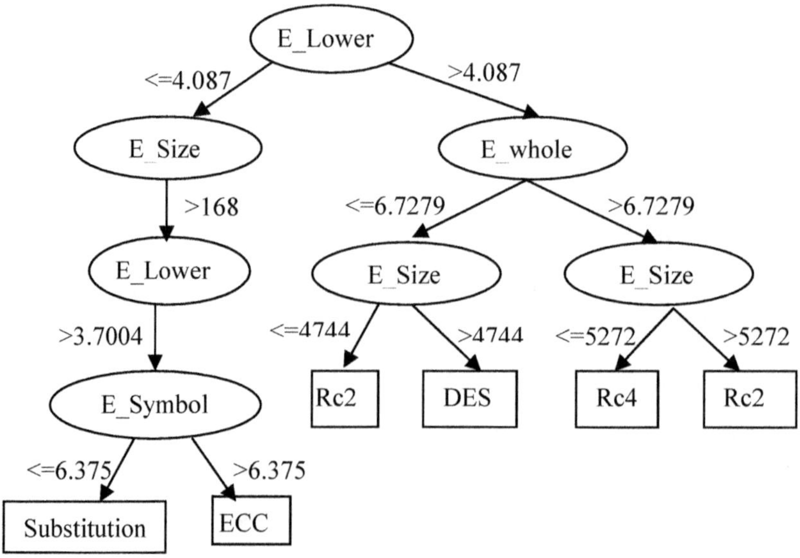

Fig. 2. Part of the decision tree using samples

of a given attribute X with respect to the class Y is the reduction in uncertainty about the value of Y, after observing values of X. Here X represents one of the features E_whole, E_basicall, E_corelation etc and Y represents encryption algorithm (E_Algorithm). A part of the decision tree constructed during training phase is shown in Fig-2.

Testing Phase

This phase consists of feature extraction and identification process. Test data i.e. encrypted file for which algorithm is to be identified is fed as input into the feature extractor. Feature extractor extracts all the features (v_{i1}, v_{i2}, ….., v_{im-1}) except v_{im} which is the name of the encryption algorithm for a cipher text c_i ($1 \leq i \leq n$). The extracted features are given to the identification process where algorithm is identified by using the classification model which is already created in the training phase.

3 Implementation Details

The experiment is conducted using the softwares VB.Net and Weka 3.6 version [17]. Around 2000 samples of encrypted files which are encrypted using different types of algorithm such as RC2, RC4, DES, 3DES, Blowfish, ECC, IDEA, Substitution, Permutation, RSA and AES are used for the training phase to generate a classification model. Around 600 files have been used for the testing phase. Sample encrypted files are of different sizes ranging from 1KB to 3MB.

In order to create classification model, features are extracted from all sample files using a feature extraction tool written in VB.net, which extracts the 8 features described in section II. We applied our tool to each of the encrypted files in our collection, therefore obtaining a labeled dataset with 2600 entries. The dataset is divided into two parts: 1) a training dataset containing 2000 rows, each row consists of 8 features about its respective file, along with the name of its encryption algorithm; 2) a test dataset containing 600 rows, each row consists of 8 features about its respective file for which encryption algorithm need to be identified.

4 Experimental Results

In the experiment, encrypted files are created using tools like Crypttool and SmartSec ECC encryptor. Around 600 files are tested and the success rate is around 72%.The experimental results are listed in table-3. It lists the number of files involved in creating a training model and the number of test files used to test with the training model and the identified results. This shows that the increase in the size of the training model increases the performance.

In order to increase the performance, size wise classification model are also created and tested with few samples of files. Table-4 gives the experimental results in this case. In case of size wise test results, the number of training samples used is between 50 and 1000 and the experimental results show a better performance.

Table 3. Identification results

Number of Training Files	Number of Test Files	Correct Identification (%)	Incorrect Identification (%)
500	65	70.2	29.8
500	205	71.5	28.5
500	450	72.1	27.9
750	65	70.1	29.9
750	205	70.5	29.5
750	450	71.6	28.4
750	600	72.2	27.8
1100	65	70.1	29.9
1100	205	71.3	28.7
1100	450	72.4	27.6
1100	600	75.1	24.9
1700	65	74.4	25.6
1700	205	75.6	24.4
2000	65	73.3	26.7
2000	205	75.4	24.6

Table 4. File size wise identification results

SNo	Size Range (bytes)	Number of Training Files	Number of Test Files	Correct Identification (%)	Incorrect Identification (%)
1	1-2000	150	100	72.2	27.8
2	2000-6000	175	150	74.1	25.9
3	6000-10000	400	250	74.2	25.8
4	10000-100000	650	500	76.3	23.7
5	above 100000	1000	600	78.4	21.6

Table-5 gives the performance results, when training and testing are done based on the encryption algorithm. This result also shows that identification percentage is ranging between 70-75%.

Comparing the two tables 3 and 4, size wise identification method would be efficient because the number of samples involved in the training model is less to get the 75% identification result, whereas more number of training samples are needed to

Table 5. Encryption algorithm wise identification results

Encryption Algorithm	Number of Training Files	Number of Test Files	Correct Identification (%)	Incorrect Identification (%)
RC2	83	40	70.3	29.7
RC4	100	75	74.5	25.5
DES	130	100	73.2	26.8
3DES	120	90	74.1	25.9
IDEA	70	45	74.4	25.6
AES	450	300	75.2	24.8
Blowfish	140	110	73.1	26.9
RSA	50	25	73.2	26.8
ECC	75	45	74.3	25.7
Permutation	50	25	72.1	27.9
Substitution	50	25	72.2	27.8

achieve 75% result without size wise training model. Here, test data are all combination of samples involved in training model and new sample data which was not involved in training model. If we supply only the untrained data as test data, then the identification result achieved is around 60%.

5 Conclusion

This paper provides an approach for the identification of the encryption algorithm using C4.5 decision tree. In this work, eight different features have been extracted from the cipher texts produced by various known encryption algorithms to generate a training model using C4.5 decision tree and that is used to identify the name of the encryption algorithm when the same features are given as input in the testing phase. The empirical results have demonstrated its effectiveness and efficiency. Results of our approach showed that a better performance, when size wise identification is done.

References

[1] Albassal, A.M.B., Wahdan, A.-M.A.: Neural network based cryptanalysis of a Fiestel type block cipher. In: Proceedings of IEEE International Conference on Electrical, Electronic and Computer Engineering, ICEEC 2004, pp. 231–237 (September 2004)

[2] Albassal, A.M.B., Wahdan, A.-M.A.: Genetic algorithm based cryptanalysis of a Fiestel type block cipher. In: Proceedings of IEEE International Conference on Electrical, Electronic and Computer Engineering, ICEEC 2004, pp. 217–221 (September 2004)

[3] Dileep, A.D., Chandra Sekhar, C.: Identification of Block Ciphers using Support Vector Machines. In: Proceedings of International Joint Conference on Neural Networks, Vancouver, BC, Canada (July 2006)
[4] Duda, R.O., Hart, P.E., Stork, D.G.: Pattern Classification, 2nd edn. (2004)
[5] Saxena, G.: Classification of Ciphers using Machine Learning. Master Thesis, Indian Institute of Technology, Kanpur (July 2008)
[6] Jones, G.A., Jones, J.M.: Information and Coding theory. Springer, Heidelberg (2004)
[7] Dunham, J.G., Sun, M.-T., Tseng, J.C.R.: Classifying File Type of Stream Ciphers in Depth Using Neural Networks. IEEE, Los Alamitos (2005)
[8] Liu, H., Setiono, R.: Chi2: Feature selection and discretization of numeric attributes. In: Proc. IEEE 7th International Conference on Tools with Artificial Intelligence, pp. 338–391 (1995)
[9] Lin, F.-T., Kao, C.-Y.: A genetic algorithm for cipher text-only attack in cryptanalysis. In: Proceedings of IEEE International Conference on Systems, Man and Cybernetics, vol. 1, pp. 650–654 (1995)
[10] Williams, N., Zander, S., Armitage, G.: A Preliminary Performance Comparison of Five Machine Learning Algorithms for Practical IP Traffic Flow Classification. Swinburne University of Technology. ACM SIGCOMM Computer Communication Review 36(5) (October 2006)
[11] Quinlan, J.R.: C4.5: Programs for Machine Learning. Morgan Kaufmann Publishers, San Francisco (1993)
[12] Seibt, P.: Algorithmic Information Theory. Springer, Heidelberg, ISBN 3-540-33218-9
[13] Ruggieri, S.: Efficient C4.5. IEEE Transactions on Knowledge and Data Engineering 14(2) (March 2002)
[14] Korting, T.S.: C4.5 algorithm and Multivariate Decision Tress. Image Proecession Division, National Institute for Space Research, Brazil
[15] Shi, Z.: Principles of Machine learning. International Academic Publishers (1992)
[16] SmartSec ECC encryptor tool, http://smartsec.com.br/
[17] Weka: Waikato Environment for Knowledge Analysis Version 3.6.0. The University of Waikato, Hamilton New Zealand (1999-2008)
[18] Prof. Bernhard Esslinger and CrypTool-Team, http://www.cryptool.com
[19] Yand, Y., Pedersen, J.: A comparative study on feature selection in text categorization. In: ICML 1997, pp. 412–420 (1997)

A Novel Mechanism for Detection of Distributed Denial of Service Attacks

Jaydip Sen

Innovation Lab, Tata Consultancy Services Ltd.
Bengal Intelligent Park, Salt Lake Electronic Complex, Kolkata 700091, India
Jaydip.Sen@tcs.com

Abstract. The increasing popularity of web-based applications has led to several critical services being provided over the Internet. This has made it imperative to monitor the network traffic so as to prevent malicious attackers from depleting the resources of the network and denying services to legitimate users. This paper has presented a mechanism for protecting a web-server against a distributed denial of service (DDoS) attack. Incoming traffic to the server is continuously monitored and any abnormal rise in the inbound traffic is immediately detected. The detection algorithm is based on a statistical analysis of the inbound traffic on the server and a robust hypothesis testing framework. While the detection process is on, the sessions from the legitimate sources are not disrupted and the load on the server is restored to the normal level by blocking the traffic from the attacking sources. To cater to different scenarios, the detection algorithm has various modules with varying level of computational and memory overheads for their execution. While the approximate modules are fast in detection and involve less overhead, they have lower detection accuracy. The accurate modules involve complex detection logic and hence involve more overhead for their execution, but they have very high detection accuracy. Simulations carried out on the proposed mechanism have produced results that demonstrate effectiveness of the scheme.

Keywords: Distributed denial of service (DDoS), traffic flow, buffer, Poisson arrival, Queuing model, statistical test of significance.

1 Introduction

A *denial of service* (DoS) attack is defined as an explicit attempt by a malicious user to consume the resources of a server or a network, thereby preventing legitimate users from availing the services provided by the system. The most common DoS attacks typically involve flooding with a huge volume of traffic and consuming network resources such as bandwidth, buffer space at the routers, CPU time and recovery cycles of the target server. Some of the common DoS attacks are SYN flooding, UDP flooding, DNS-based flooding, ICMP directed broadcast, Ping flood attack, IP fragmentation, and CGI attacks [1]. Based on the number of attacking machines deployed to implement the attack, DoS attacks are classified into two broad categories: (i) a single intruder consumes all the available bandwidth by generating a large number of packets operating from a single machine, or (ii) the distributed case where multiple

N. Meghanathan et al. (Eds.): CCSIT 2011, Part III, CCIS 133, pp. 247–257, 2011.

attackers coordinate together to produce the same effect from several machines on the network. The latter is referred to as DDoS attack and owing to its distributed nature, it is very difficult to detect.

In this paper, a robust mechanism is proposed to protect a web server from DDoS attack utilizing some easily accessible information in the server. This is done in such a way that it is not possible for an attacker to disable the server host and as soon as the overload on the server disappears, the normal service quality resumes automatically. The detection algorithm has several modules that provide flexibility in deployment. While the approximate detection modules are based on simple statistical analysis of the network traffic and involve very less computational and memory overhead on the server, the accurate detection module is based on a statistical theory of hypothesis testing that has more overhead in its execution.

The rest of the paper is organized as follows: Section 2 presents some existing work in the literature on defense against DoS attacks. Section 3 describes the components of the proposed security system and the algorithms for detection and prevention of attacks. Section 4 presents the simulation results and the sensitivity analysis of the parameters of the algorithms. Section 5 concludes the paper while highlighting some future scope of work.

2 Related Work

Protection against DoS attacks highly depends on the model of the network and the type of attack. Several mechanisms have been proposed to solve the problem of DoS attacks. Most of them have weaknesses and fail under certain circumstances.

Network ingress filtering is a mechanism proposed to prevent attacks that use spoofed source addresses [2]. This involves configuring the routers to drop packets that have illegitimate source IP addresses. *ICMP traceback* messages are useful to identify the path taken by packets through the Internet [3]. This requires a router to use a very low probability with which traceback messages are sent along with the traffic. Hence, with sufficiently large number of messages, it is possible to determine the route taken by the traffic during an attack. *IP traceback* proposes a reliable way to perform hop by hop tracing of a packet to the attacking source from where it originated [4]. Yaar et al. have proposed an approach, called *path identifier* (Pi), in which a path fingerprint is embedded in each packet, enabling a victim to identify packets traversing the same paths through the Internet on a per packet basis, regardless of source IP address spoofing [5]. *Pushback* approaches have been proposed to extract attack signatures by rate-limiting the suspicious traffic destined to a congested link [6][7]. Mirkovic et al. have proposed a scheme named D-WARD that performs statistical traffic profiling at the edge of the networks to detect new types of DDoS attacks [8]. Zou et al. have presented an adaptive defense system that adjusts its configurations according to the network conditions and attack severity in order to minimize the combined cost introduced by false positives [9]. *Client side puzzle* and other *pricing algorithms* are effective tools to make protocols less vulnerable to depletion attacks of processing power [10].

3 The Major System Components and Algorithms

This Section describes the traffic model and the attack model on which the proposed security system has been designed. One of the most vital components of the proposed system is known as the *interface* module. Various components of this module are also described in this Section.

3.1 Traffic Model and Attack Model

In the proposed traffic model *packets* from the network refers to small independent queries to the server (e.g., a small HTTP query or an NTP question-answer). For simplicity, it is assumed that every query causes the same workload on the server. Since the query packets cause workload on the server, after a certain time the server cannot handle incoming traffic any further due to memory and processing overloads.

Let us suppose that the attacker uses A number of hosts during the attack. When $A = 1$, the attack originates from a single source, and when $A > 1$, it corresponds to a distributed attack. There are one or more human attackers behind the attacking sources. These attacking sources are machines on the Internet controlled (taken over) by the attacker. It is assumed that the attacking machines use real addresses, and they can establish normal two-way communication with the server, like a host of any legal client. The human attacker hides behind the attacking machines in the network, which means that after carrying out the attack and after removal of all compromising traces of attack on the occupied machines, there is no way to find a trace leading to him/her.

Two types of sources are distinguished: *legal* sources and *attacking* sources. There are $N(t)$ legal sources and $A(t)$ attacking sources in time slot t. In the proposed model, the attacker can reach his/her goal only if the level of attacking traffic is high enough as compared to the level under normal operation. It is assumed that the attacker can control the extra traffic by changing the number of attacking machines and the traffic generated by these machines. It is also assumed that the attacker is powerful and can distribute the total attacking traffic among attacking machines at his/her choice. The reason for using several attacking machines is to make it more difficult for the server to identify and foil them. However, when the attacker uses more machines, it becomes more difficult for him/her to hide the attack. Therefore, the attacker needs to keep the number of attacking hosts at a small value, i.e., $A(t)$ should not be too large.

3.2 The Interface Module

A DDoS *interface* module is attached to the server at the network side. The interface module may be a software component of the server, a special-purpose hardware in the server host, or an autonomous hardware component attached to the server.

The incoming traffic enters a FIFO buffer. For the purpose of modeling and analysis a *discrete time model* is assumed. Traffic is modeled and processed over unit time slot. The server CPU processes μ storage units per time slot from the buffer. Since the buffer is fed by a random traffic, there is a non-zero probability of an event of buffer overflow. When a DDoS attack is launched, the incoming traffic quickly increases and the buffer becomes full. At this time, most of the incoming packets will be dropped and the attacker becomes successful in degrading the quality of service of the server. However, the server host will not be completely disabled at this point of time. The goal of the interface module is to effectively identify and disrupt the traffic from the attacking sources so that the normal level of service may be restored.

It is assumed that there are two states of the incoming channel: the *normal state*, and the *attack state*. While in the normal state, there is no DDoS attack on the server, in the attack state, the server is under a distributed attack. Let us assume that the attack begins at time t^*, and at time $t^* + \delta$, the interface buffer becomes full. At this time, the TCP modules running at the legal clients and the attacking hosts observe that no (or very few) acknowledgements are being sent back by the server. In order to defend against the DDoS attack, the first task is to detect the point of commencement the attack by making a reliable estimation of the time t^*.

Once the time of commencement of the attack is estimated, the next task is to identify the sources of the attack, and to disrupt the traffic arriving from these sources to the server. In the proposed scheme, this identification has been done based on the statistical properties of the traffic flow. The interface module at the server identifies all active traffic sources, measures the traffic generated by these sources, and classifies them into different sets. In order to get reliable measurements of the traffic level, these measurements are carried out during time slots between t^* and $t^* + \delta$. Consequently, the effectiveness of the mechanism is heavily dependent on the time duration δ. During the time δ, the traffic flow between the sources and the server is not affected, i.e., the interface module in the server does not disrupt traffic from the attack sources. It is obviously desirable to have a large value for the time duration δ so that more time is available for traffic measurement. A large value of δ can be effectively achieved by using a very large buffer size. It is assumed that the total buffer size *(L)* of the server consists of two parts. The first part (L_1) is designed to serve the normal state of the server. The size of L_1 is chosen according to the service rate of the server and the normal probability of packet loss due to the event of a buffer overflow. The size of L_2 corresponds to the excess size of the buffer introduced with the purpose of gaining enough time for traffic measurements during the start-up phase of the attack for identification of the attack sources.

It is assumed that the attack begins at time t^*, i.e., all the attacking sources start sending packets at this time onwards. It is also assumed that the network was in normal state at any time $t < t^*$. Let $\hat{t}$ denote the expected value of t^*. For the sake of simplicity, it is assumed that the set of active sources is constant during the period of the attack. Let $T_n(t)$ be the aggregate network traffic from the legal sources (i.e., the normal network traffic), and $T_a(t)$ be the aggregate of the attacking traffic. Let the mean (per time slot) values of the normal and the attack traffic are λ_n and λ_a respectively.

$$E(T_n(t)) = \lambda_n \quad E(T_a(t)) = \lambda_a \tag{1}$$

Similarly, let the corresponding standard deviations be denoted by σ_n and σ_a. Let Q denote the *apriori* unknown ratio between λ_n and λ_a, i.e. $Q = \lambda_a / \lambda_n$. As the time of commencement of attack (t^*) is earlier than the time of its detection ($\hat{t}$), some precious time is wasted that cannot be used for traffic measurements. To minimize, this loss, the aggregate traffic level is estimated continuously by using a *sliding window* technique. The interface module in the server handles two *sliding time windows*. The longer window has a capacity of w_l slots, and the shorter one has a capacity of w_s slots. In this way, both an *extended-time average* level $\overline{\lambda}(t)$ and a *short-time average* level $\hat{\lambda}(t)$ of the incoming aggregate traffic per slot at time slot t are estimated.

3.3 Algorithms of the Interface Module

The interface module in the server executes two algorithms in order to identify the DDoS attack and the attacking sources. The algorithms are: (i) algorithm for detection of an attack, (ii) algorithm for identification of the attack sources and disruption of traffic arriving from the attack sources. In the following the algorithms are described.

3.3.1 Algorithm for Attack Detection

In order to ensure high availability of the server, an early detection of an attack is of prime importance. As discussed in Section 3.2, the beginning of an attack is assumed to take place at time $\hat{t}$. An approximate determination of $\hat{t}$ can be done in any of the following two ways: (i) $\hat{t}$ is the point of time when the buffer L_l becomes full. (ii) $\hat{t}$ is the point of time when the following inequality holds:

$$\hat{\lambda}(\hat{t}) > (1+r)\overline{\lambda}(\hat{t}) \tag{2}$$

In the inequality (2), $r > 0$ is a design parameter. It represents the maximum value of the fraction by which the short-term average of traffic level may exceed the long-term average without causing any alarm for attack on the server. In Section 4, the comparative analysis of the effectiveness of the two approaches in detecting a distributed attack is presented with simulation results. However, for a more accurate and reliable identification of an attack, a statistical approach based of hypothesis testing is also proposed. In this approach, a large sample of packet arrival pattern on the server is taken for a long duration. The *packet arrival rate* (PAR) at each sample duration is periodically measured and the sample mean ($\overline{X}$) and the sample standard deviation ($\hat{S}$) of the PAR are computed using (3) and (4).

$$\overline{X} = \frac{\sum_{i=1}^{N} X_i}{N} \tag{3}$$

$$\hat{S} = \sqrt{\frac{\sum_{i=1}^{N}(X_i - \overline{X})^2}{N-1}} \tag{4}$$

After the computation of $\overline{X}$ and $\hat{S}$, one-sample *Kolmogorov-Smirnov* (*K-S*) test is applied to test if the samples come from a population with a normal distribution. It is found that *P*- values for all *K-S* tests are greater than α = .05. Therefore, it is concluded that the PAR follows a normal distribution. In other words, $\overline{X}$ is normally distributed with an unknown mean, say, μ. The standard value of $\overline{X}$ is given by (5):

$$Z = \frac{\overline{X} - \mu}{\hat{S}/\sqrt{N}} \tag{5}$$

In (5) *Z* is a standard normal variable and satisfies (6):

$$P\{-Z_{\alpha/2} \le \frac{\overline{X} - \mu}{\hat{S}/\sqrt{N}} \le Z_{\alpha/2}\} = 1 - \alpha \tag{6}$$

In equation (6) α is the level of confidence which satisfies $0 \le \alpha \le 1$. From (6) it is clear that there is a probability of 1- α of selecting a sample for which the confidence interval will contain true value of μ. $Z_{\alpha/2}$ is the upper 100 $\alpha/2$ percentage point of the standard normal distribution. The 100(1- α)% conf. interval of μ is given by (7):

$$\overline{X} - Z_{\alpha/2}\frac{\hat{S}}{\sqrt{N}} \le \mu \le \overline{X} + Z_{\alpha/2}\frac{\hat{S}}{\sqrt{N}} \tag{7}$$

The confidence interval in equation (7) gives both a lower and an upper confidence boundary for μ. To detect an attack scenario, a threshold value called *maximum packet arrival rate* (MPAR) is defined which distinguishes the normal PAR and the high PAR in an attack. In order to find MPAR, the upper confidence bounds for μ in (7) are obtained by setting the lower conf. bound to -∞ and replacing $Z_{\alpha/2}$ by Z_{α}. A 100(1- α)% upper confidence bound for μ is obtained from (8). The value of α in (8) is 0.025.

$$\mu \le T_x = \overline{X} + Z_{\alpha}\frac{\hat{S}}{\sqrt{N}} \tag{8}$$

Let μ_1 and μ_2 denote the population means of two traffic flows. The *t*-test is applied to determine the significance of the difference between the two means, i.e. (μ_1 - μ_2). Let the difference between the two means be ($\overline{X}_1 - X_2$), and the standard deviation of the sampling distribution of differences is $\sqrt{(\frac{S_1^2}{N_1} + \frac{S_2^2}{N_2})}$. The *t*-statistic is computed in (9).

$$t = \frac{\overline{X}_1 - \overline{X}_2}{\sqrt{(\frac{S_1^2}{N_1} + \frac{S_2^2}{N_2})}} \tag{9}$$

Since the two groups may contain different sample sizes, a weighted variance estimate t-test is used. The weighted variance is computed in equation (10):

$$\hat{S}^2 = \frac{(N_1-1)S_1^2+(N_2-1)S_2^2}{N_1+N_2-2} \tag{10}$$

The resultant t-statistic is computed in equation (11):

$$t = \frac{\overline{X}_1-\overline{X}_2}{\sqrt{\frac{\hat{S}_1^2}{N_1}+\frac{\hat{S}_2^2}{N_2}}} \tag{11}$$

To detect attack traffic, the following hypotheses are tested. The null hypothesis H_0: $\mu_1 = \mu_2$ is tested against the alternative hypothesis H_1: $\mu_1 \neq \mu_2$. Levene's test is used to assess H_0. If the resulting P-values of Levene's test is less than a critical value (0.05 in this case), H_0 is rejected and it is concluded that there is a difference in the variances of the populations. This indicates that the current traffic flow is an attack traffic. As will be evident in Section 4.2, this accurate statistical algorithm has 100% detection accuracy in all simulation runs conducted on the system.

3.3.2 Algorithm for Identification of Attack Sources

It is essential to disrupt the traffic emanating from the attack sources at the interface module of the server after an attack is detected. For this purpose, the interface module must be able to distinguish between the traffic from the attack sources and the normal traffic from legitimate client hosts. It is assumed that the interface module can measure the traffic characteristics of all the active sources at each time instance by recognizing their network addresses. Starting at time $\hat{t}$, the traffic level corresponding to every source is measured. If an attack was correctly identified, i.e. $t^* < \hat{t} < t^* + \delta$, traffic measurement and analysis can be made over the period $(t^* + \delta - \hat{t})$. Let the aggregate level of traffic be $\hat{\lambda}_r(t^* + \delta)$, and the traffic for the source i be $\hat{\lambda}(i)(t^* + \delta)$. As the exact traffic from the legal sources during the attack cannot be determined, the expression $\overline{\lambda}(\hat{t} - c)$, $(c > 0)$, is used as an estimate of mean aggregate traffic level of the legal sources in time interval $[t^*, t^* + \delta]$, and an estimate for the mean aggregate traffic level of the attacking sources ($\overline{\lambda}_a$) is derived as in equation (12):

$$\overline{\lambda}_a = \hat{\lambda}_r(t^*+\delta) - \overline{\lambda}(\hat{t}-c) \tag{12}$$

The set Z of active sources is decomposed into two mutually disjoint sets Z_n and Z_a, where the former is the set of *legal sources* and the latter is the set of *attacking sources*. The sets Z, Z_n and Z_a will satisfy equation (13):

$$Z = Z_n \cup Z_a \quad Z_n \cap Z_a = \phi \tag{13}$$

The identification algorithm produces as output a set Z_a*, which is a subset of the set Z and very closely resembles the set Z_a. The closer the sets Z_a and Z_a* are, the more accurate is the detection of the sources of attacks. The identification of the attacking sources is made by the following two ways:

(i) In this approach, the maximal subset of $Z_a^* = \{i_1, i_2, \ldots\ldots i_L\}$ of Z is computed that corresponds to sources with the highest measured traffic levels so that the inequality (14) is satisfied. The set Z_a* contains the attack sources.

$$\sum_{j=1}^{v} \hat{\lambda}^{(ij)}(t^* + \delta) \leq \hat{\lambda}_a \tag{14}$$

The basis principle for this method is that the attacker always tries to hide himself/herself, and therefore limits the number of attacking sources ($A(t)$). At the same time, to make the attack effective, the attacker intends to send a high volume of attack traffic to the server. Thus, there is a trade-off with the volume of the attack and the number of attack sources.

(ii) In this method, the sources from the set of traffic sources Z which are active during the interval ($\hat{t}$ - c), $c > 0$, are omitted and (14) is used to identify the attack sources.

Once the attacking sources are correctly identified, the disruption of the traffic emanating from the attack sources is done. For this purpose, all the incoming packets with source addresses belonging to set Z_a* are disarded.

4 Simulation and Results

The simulation program is written in C and the program is run on a workstation with Red Hat Linux version 9 operating system. A MySQL database is used for storing data related to traffic. The time interval is set at 10^{-6} seconds. The simulation is done with first 100 seconds as the normal traffic. The attack simulation is started at the 100th second and is allowed to continue till the 200th second. The simulation is ended with another 100 seconds of normal traffic to test efficacy of the recovery function of the system. The traffic arrivals are modelled as Poisson process. The packets are stored in a buffer and are passed on to the CPU for further processing by the interface module. The queue type is assumed to be M/M/1. The inter-arrival time and service time are negative exponential distributions. Following cases are considered:

Case 1: For a small corporate server, the number of legal clients is low, say $N(t)$ = 5. Assuming that the capacity of the server is high, the average load on the server will be less. Therefore, the number of attacking hosts should be high, say $A(t)$ = 40. Hence, in this scenario, for an effective attack we must have $N(t) << A(t)$.

Case 2: For a server of medium size, it may be assumed that $N(t)$ = 50 and a successful attacker can launch his/her attack from a fewer number of hosts. Thus it may be assumed that $A(t)$ = 50 in this case. As the number of legal clients and the number of attacking sources are of comparable size, it is easier for the attacker to hide his/her attack in this case. Therefore, in this situation, $N(t) \approx A(t)$.

Case 3: For a global portal server, there can be a very large number of legal clients, say $N(t) = 10000$. In this situation, it is not possible for that attacker to easily estimate the required number of attacking hosts. In this case, it is assumed that the attacker chooses a reasonably high value of $A(t)$, say $A(t) = 5000$, and opts for a very high attacking rate: $\lambda_a = \lambda_n*10$. Therefore, in this case: $N(t) > A(t)$.

Table 1. Simulation parameters for Simulation I

Parameter	Value
Number of legal clients ($N(t)$)	10000
Number of attacking hosts ($A(t)$)	5000
Mean normal traffic rate (λ_n)	0.1
Mean attack traffic rate (λ_a)	0.4
Service rate (μ) (packets/sec)	1500

The simulation parameters are listed in Table 1. With 10000 legal clients and λ_n = 0.1, the capacity of the server should be at least 1000. However, the attack is successful only when the service rate (μ) is less than 3000 ($\lambda_a*A(t) + \lambda_n*N(t)$). The value of μ is, therefore, taken as 1500. The buffer size for normal situation is taken as 40 packets i.e., $L_1 = 40$ (packets). For choosing the size of L_2, it is observed that the normal traffic rate is 1000 packets/sec. Thus a safe value of $L_2 = 3000$ (packets) is taken. The values of the parameters of the detection algorithm are given in Table 2. The available time for traffic analysis depends on the value of δ. In the simulation work, a constant value ($\hat{\delta} \leq \delta$) for this parameter is used for traffic analysis. It is assumed that the total traffic (normal and attack) is known and its value is $T_n + T_a = 3000$. As the service rate (μ) is 1500, one can expect the buffer L_1 to be full after 40/(3000-1500) $\approx$ 0.3 seconds. The whole buffer ($L = L_1 + L_2$) will be full in 30040/(3000-1500) $\approx$ 200 seconds. Therefore, a safe estimation of $\hat{\delta}$ = 10 is made. In real world situation, δ should be estimated over a period of time. For simplicity, the value of $\hat{\delta}$ is set equal to w_s. The algorithm presented in Section 3.3.2 is used for identification of the attacker.

Table 2. Parameters of the attack detection algorithm

Parameter	Value
Sliding window size (w_s)	10 sec
Tolerance for traffic jump (r)	0.6
Time frame for last correct value of λ	45 sec

4.1 Simulation I

Table 3 shows the results of the simulation with different values of the window size (w_s). It is clear that a larger window size and hence a large δ gives a more accurate identification of attacks. However, with a larger window size the system is more likely to enter into a situation of buffer overflow. After the buffer overflow, the detection algorithm will produce very inaccurate and unreliable results. Therefore it is

Table 3. Results of Simulation I

Observed metrics	$\hat{\delta}$ ($\hat{\delta} = w_s$)				
	5	**10**	20	30	40
Correctly identified attackers	2982	**3784**	4529	4784	4892
Filtered legal clients	1	**557**	260	132	59
Dropped packets	0	**0**	0	14251	28765
Max. buffer level and corresponding time frame	29717 (200 s)	**14941 (110s)**	29732 (119s)	30040 (120s)	30040 (120s)
Time to restore (after t*)	149	**104**	73	71	81

not worthwhile to increase the window size beyond a limit. On the other hand, when the time window is too short, the algorithm can detect only a very small proportion of the attacking hosts. In summary, the results In Table 3 show that the mechanism can detect an attack with a window size of 10 seconds.

4.2 Simulation II

In this case, a smaller system is simulated with parameters are listed in Table 4. The buffers L_1 and L_2 are chosen as 40 and 160 respectively. The value of δ is set equal to w_s, i.e. $\hat{\delta} = w_s = 10$. The remaining parameters are kept the same as in simulation I.

In simulation II, experiments are repeated on 500 different sets of input data to have an insight into the statistical properties of the system under normal and attack situations. With different data sets, it is observed that the approximate algorithm (ii) in Section 3.3.1 was faster in detecting the attack in 454 cases. In 42 cases, the attack was correctly identified by both algorithms (i) and (ii) in Section 3.3.1. The accurate detection algorithm presented in Section 3.3.1 could detect all the 50 attack sources in all the 500 simulation runs. Table 5 summarizes the simulation results.

Table 4. Parameters for Simulation II

Parameter	Value
Number of legal clients ($N(t)$)	50
Number of attacking hosts ($A(t)$)	50
Mean normal traffic rate (λ_n)	0.1
Mean attack traffic rate (λ_a)	0.2
Service rate (μ) (packets/sec)	8

Table 5. Results of Simulation II

Observed metrics	Observed values		
	Min	Avg	Conf. Int. (95%)
Traffic restoration time (after t*)	49	114.732	1.942
Packets dropped	0	0.695	0.321
Normal user filtered (type II error)	1	7.115	0.231
Number of attackers filtered	21	32.413	0.235
Attack detection time (after t*)	0	2.95	0.09

5 Conclusion

In this paper, a mechanism is presented for detection and prevention of DDoS attacks on a server. Different algorithms are presented for attack detection based on statistical theory of hypothesis testing. While the proposed mechanism does not affect the traffic from legitimate clients, it effectively blocks traffic from the attack sources. The simulation results demonstrate the effectiveness of the proposed mechanism.

References

1. Ramanathan, A.: WesDes: A Tool for Distributed Denial of Service Attack Detection. Thesis at Texas A&M University (2002)
2. Ferguson, P., Senie, D.: Network Ingress Filtering: Defending Denial of Service Attack which Employ IP Source Address Spoofing. RFC 2827 (2000)
3. Belovin, S., Leech, M., Taylor, T.: ICMP Traceback Messages. Internet draft (2001), http://www.ietf.org/internet-drafts/draft-ietf-itrace-01.txt
4. Law, T.K.T., Lui, J.C.S., Yau, D.K.Y.: You Can Run, but You Can't Hide: An Effective Statistical Methodology to Trace Back DDoS Attackers. IEEE Transactions on Parallel and Distributed Systems, 799–813 (2005)
5. Yaar, A., Perrig, A., Song, D.: StackPi: New Packet Marking and Filtering Mechanisms for DDoS and IP Spoofing Defense. IEEE Journal on Selected Areas in Communications, 1853–1863 (2006)
6. Yau, D.K.Y., Lui, J.C.S., Liang, F.: Defending against Distributed Denial-of-Service Attacks with Max-Min Fair Sever-Centric Router Throttles. In: Proceedings of the 10th International Workshop on Quality of Service (2002)
7. Cai, M., Chen, Y., Kwok, Y.K., Hwang, K.: A Scalable Set-Union Counting Approach to Pushing Back DDoS Attacks. USC GridSec Technical Report TR-2004-21 (2004)
8. Mirkovic, J., Reiher, P.: D-WARD: A Source-End Defense against Flooding Denial-of-Service Attacks. IEEE Transactions on Dependable and Secure Computing (2005)
9. Zou, C.C., Duffield, N., Towsley, D., Gong, W.: Adaptive Defense against Various Network Attacks. IEEE Journal on Selected Areas of Communication, High-Speed Network Security-Architecture, Algorithms, and Implementation (2006)
10. Bencsath, B., Buttyan, L., Vajda, I.: A Game-Based Analysis of the Client Puzzle Approach to Defend against DoS Attacks. In: Proceedings of 11th International Conference on Software, Telecommunications and Computer Networks (SoftCOM), pp. 763–767 (2003)

Authenticating and Securing Mobile Applications Using Micrologs

Siddharth Gupta[1] and Sunil Kumar Singh[2]

[1] UG Research Scholar, [2] Asst. Professor
Department of Computer Science Engineering
Bharati Vidyapeeth's College of Engineering
New Delhi, India
siddharth_bvcoe@hotmail.com, anujsunilsingh@yahoo.co.in

Abstract. This paper elucidates the research and implementation of Microlog in J2ME applications. This small yet powerful logging library logs all the detailed background transactions, acts as a tool for detecting unauthorized users trying to access the application by logging to remote servers and devices via various logging destinations. It also retrieves useful runtime information, such as malfunction code and unexpected errors and behaviours. The log thus generated can be printed using a portable Bluetooth printer. J2ME being platform independent works with Microlog in providing a great feature being explored by future J2ME developers.

Keywords: J2ME, Microlog, Bluetooth, Security, RMS, JSR.

1 Introduction

In this technological advanced world, the rapid development and popularisation of wireless communication technology, mobile devices such as mobile phones, PDA, palmtops, have gradually stepped into people's life as an indispensable requisite in personal as well as professional life. The possession quantity of mobile phones has surpassed that of PC seen from the fact that he number of mobile users in India itself counts to 617,513,000 [1] and are increasing exponentially.

As a result most of the applications are being developed using platform independent J2ME which is an advanced form of J2SE. The client end is developed in J2ME which then interacts with the server and simultaneously provides simplicity, convenience and security on the part of client as he is no longer dependent on PC for accessing the applications and hence can remotely access them through his mobile [2]. Microlog being a powerful open source library based on the Log4j API, supports both J2ME and Android [2]. We can insert statements into the code and get useful output information during runtime, such as malfunction code and unexpected errors and behaviours. Examples of logging are trace statements, dumping of structures and the familiar printf debug statements[2]. It is an important source of retrieving information while user login to the application, hence a security mechanism to log all the details separately. What is so special about Microlog? The answer is "size" [5].

N. Meghanathan et al. (Eds.): CCSIT 2011, Part III, CCIS 133, pp. 258–267, 2011.

The size of Log4j is 389Kkb as compared to the size of Microlog which is 110 Kb[5]. The small size of the Microlog is one of its major benefits. Secondly, remote logging [5] is a special feature of microloglog for logging to syslog daemons as it is easy to setup one and then the details are logged on the server directly. In this paper we show the details of the user getting logged as soon as he login's into the mobile application showing three different cases of authorized login, unauthorized login and attempt to hack. The details being logged to various destinations namely Lcdui form, a file, recordstore and a Bluetooth device. The other transactions, are also appended with the login details. Thus, microloglog is being used as a medium for implementing security in mobile applications.

2 Technologies Used

J2ME

Java 2 Platform, Microedition is a revolution in accordance to the diversities of the market aiming at embedded devices, cell phones, palmtops, and two way pagers as new set of clients. It is becoming popular because of its transformable, low cost and secure functional domain. J2ME is basically a subset of J2SE and most of its functionalities are derived from it [3] [4]. The architecture of J2ME is divided into Configurations and Profiles. Configuration (CLDC/CDC) combines virtual machine (KVM for cell phones) is a set of predefined libraries reflecting device's network connectivity, power consumption, and memory. On the other hand profiles adds an additional layer of API's offering set of GUI's , local data storage and application life cycle management [3] . The versions are CLDC 1.0 and 1.1, MIDP 1.0 and 2.0.CLDC 1.1 (JSR 139) and MIDP 2.0 (JSR 118) are required for this application [7].

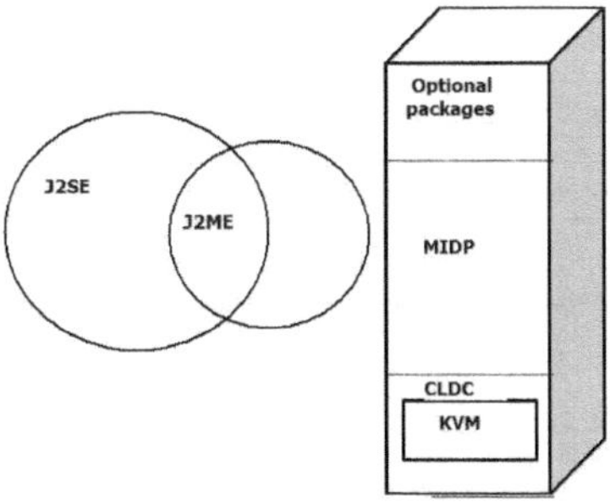

Fig. 1. J2ME Architecture

The execution is carried out by MIDlet which is the driving force of the application. Consists of three function namely startApp(), pauseApp(), destroyApp(boolean unconditional). The package javax.microedition.midlet.* extends the MIDlet class and the execution starts with startApp().

Microlog

Microlog is a tiny, powerful and advanced set of API's designed specially for J2ME which offers an optimal solution to the logging based on log4j API's [5].

It consists of three main classes:

1) *public final class Logger, which is responsible for handling the main log events.*
2) *public interface Appender, which is responsible for controlling the log operations outputs.*
3) *public interface Formatter, which is responsible for formatting the output of the Appender.*

The packages needed to be imported are: net.sf.microlog.core.; net.sf.microlog.midp.appender.* which are available online. The logger component is also used to set various log levels i.e. DEBUG, INFO, FATAL, WARN, ERROR [5]. This process of logging send the log messages to various destinations namely Console, Form, Recordstore, Bluetooth device, files.*

APPENDER COMPONENT

The process of logging requires defining the messages output interface, such as to a file, to a console or to a Bluetooth connection. In the J2ME platform, there are many appenders that can be used in the MIDP to send the log messages, such as RecordStoreAppender, where you can store your log messages in the RecordStore, BluetoothSerialAppender, where you can send your log messages to a Bluetooth connection and FormAppender, where you can show the messages into a Form (LCDUI) interface[7].

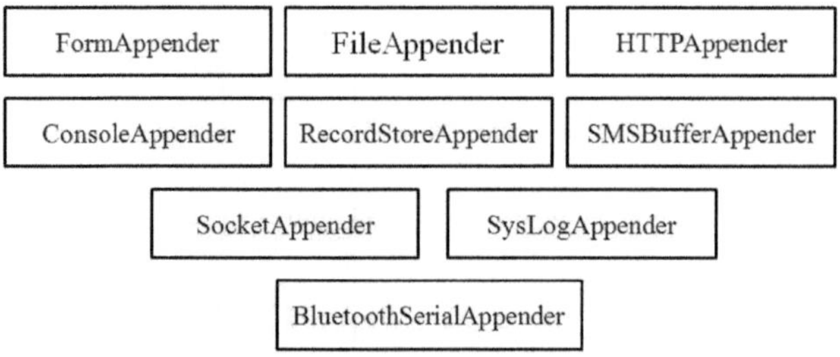

Fig. 2. Various logging destinations

The *AbstractAppender* defines an interface with a set of methods where all other appenders should redefine them in their own class[8]. HTTPAppender logs to HTTP server, SMSBufferAppender sends a sms to the destination if something goes wrong, SocketAppender sends to a socket server, SysLogAppender logs to syslog daemon on remote server

FORMATTER COMPONENT

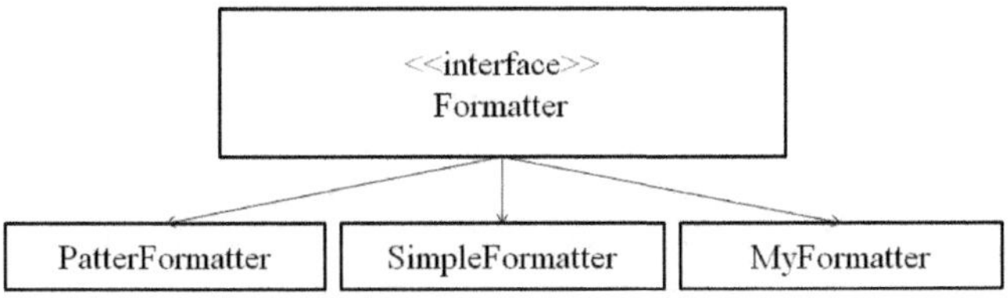

Fig. 3. Formatters in micrlog

To format a message, an Appender must have an associated Formatter object. MicroLog has different types of formatters as shown in the figure above. The SimpleFormatter is the default and the simplest formatter, the PatternFormatter [5] offers more flexibility for choosing which information will appear in the log message. One can also create your own formatter class and define your own message format. Formatters implement the same interface (Formatter), which can be seen in the figure above. The format() method is where the formatting of the message really occurs, where we have the logger name, the logger level, a related message and a throwable object.

```
microlog.rootLogger=ERROR, X1, X2
microlog.appender.X1=FormAppender
microlog.appender.X2=RecordStoreAppender
microlog.appender.X1.formatter=PatternFormatter
microlog.appender.X1.formatter.pattern=%c{1} [%P] %m %T
microlog.logger.com.sid.midlet.techtip=DEBUG
```

Fig. 4. Configuration file

Bluetooth printing

Bluetooth is a wireless communication protocol like HTTP, SMTP and FTP, used for communication between two bluetooth enables devices based on Client-Server

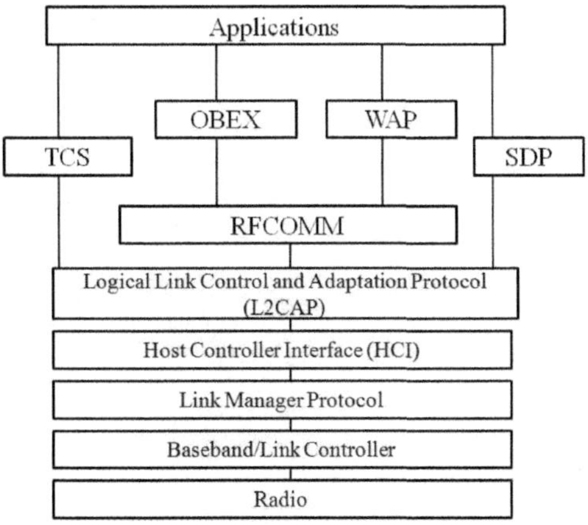

Fig. 5. Bluetooth Protocol Stack

architecture [6]. Bluetooth stack is the controlling agent (Software, hardware, firmware) for implementing the Bluetooth protocol and controlling Bluetooth device programmatically. The main function of Bluetooth stack is to communicate with other Bluetooth devices and to control your Bluetooth device [11][8]. The Bluetooth protocol is divided into Layers (Protocol Stack) and Profiles.

The Bluetooth profile is a designed set of functionalities for the Bluetooth devices and to ensure consistency and interoperability. The JSR 082 is implemented in order to import the packages: javax.bluetooth.*, javax.obex.*.

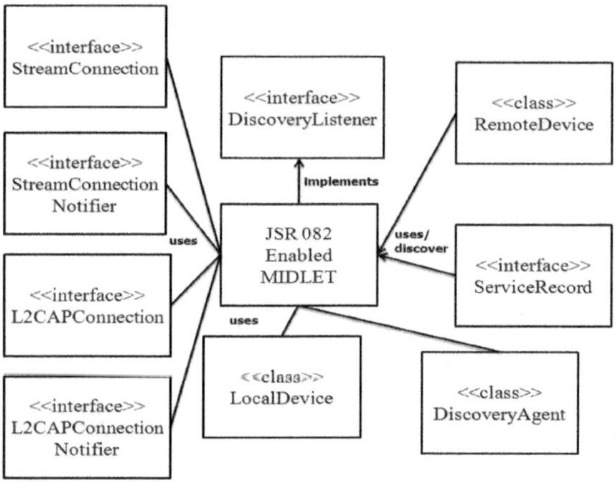

Fig. 6. JSR 082 taxonomy

The essential steps for a Bluetooth communication includes: Stack initialisation, Device Management, Device Discovery, Service Discovery, Service registration, Communication. The protocols used for the communication are: L2CAP (Handles data transmission in packets), RFCOMM (allows to create virtual serial port and to stream data); OBEX (allows sending and receiving objects) [11]. The figure below shows the flow of actions which are needed to be taken for Bluetooth printing mechanism.

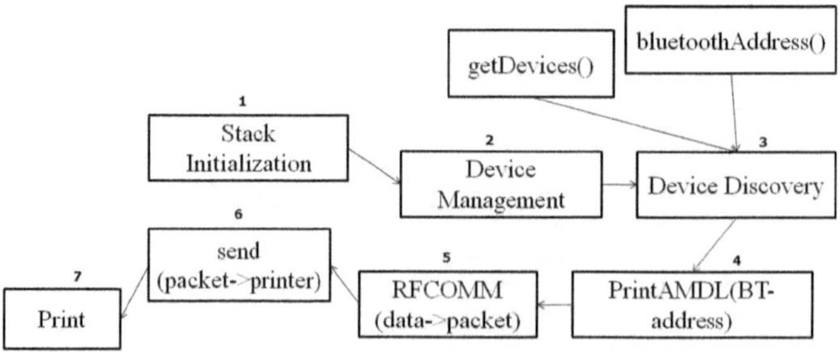

Fig. 7. Basic Steps for Bluetooth Communication

3 Micrologging

Now, we can see the implementation of micrologging in J2ME applications as a tool for security and logging details of the various users trying to access the application through login form. The user enters the LoginID and password, which then calls a web service being deployed by the server which has the details of all the users and password in the database. The web service is invoked by the mobile client which then checks the LoginID and the password for the application.

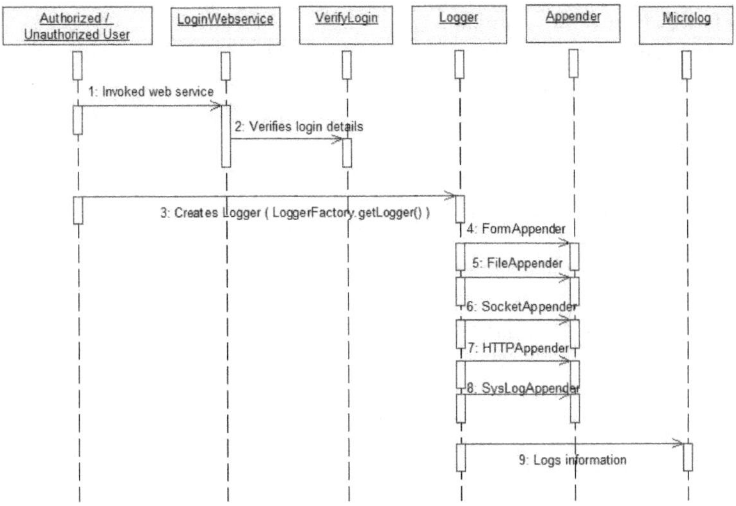

Fig. 8. Sequence Diagram for logging user details

User Login:

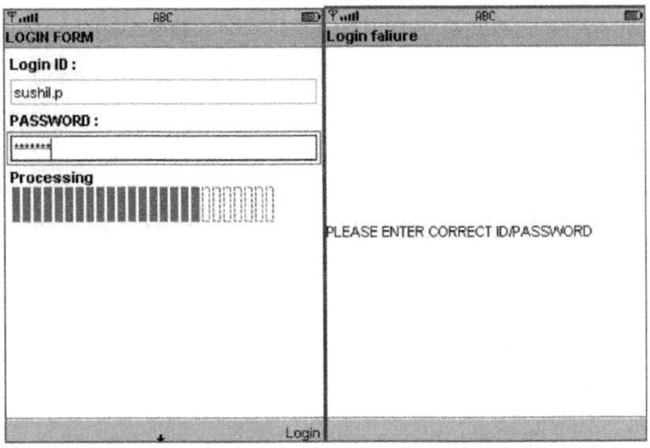

Fig. 9. Login user interface

CASE 1: Authorized User:

In this case when the user enters correct LoginID and password then the information gets logged to various log destinations and access is granted to the user.

Pseudocode:

```
AUTHORIZED_USER (A,B)
//A, B is the LoginID and password
CREATE  Logger & invoke getLogger() of LoggerFactory
CREATE appender & log outputs
SWITCH appender
CASE 1 IS FormAppender(form)
CASE 2 IS BluetoothSerialAppnder(btspp://001F3AF76C44:1)
CASE 3 IS FileAppender(filename)
CASE 4 IS SysLogAppender(169.254.0.241)
CASE 5 IS HttpAppender(http://localhost/microlog-serve/log)
END
ADD appender to log & call levels using log
CREATE obj of loginservice_stub.java // webservice
obj.verifyLogin(A,B) //call the remote function

IF AUTHORIZED
LOG INFO: Authorized Login details with LoginID/Password
END
```

Fig. 10. Authorized User Mircolog

CASE 2: Unauthorized User

In this case when the user enters wrong LoginID and password the information gets logged with incorrect ID and password which can be retrieved later.

Pseudocode:

UNAUTHORIZED_USER (A,B)
//A, B are the LoginID and password
CREATE Logger & invoke getLogger() of LoggerFactory
CREATE appender & log outputs
// Similarily logging to various destinations

ADD appender to log & call levels using log
CREATE obj of loginservice_stub.java // webservice
obj.verifyLogin(A,B) //call the remote function
IF UNAUTHORIZED
LOG INFO: Unauthorized Login detail with LoginID/Password
END

Fig. 11. Unauthorized User Microlog

CASE 3: Attempt to hack

In this case when an unauthorized user attempts to hack the application by entering wrong ID and password more than 3 times, the information gets logged with the incorrect ID and password.

Pseudocode:

UNAUTHORIZED_HACKER (A,B)
//A, B are the LoginID and password
CREATE Logger & invoke getLogger() of LoggerFactory
CREATE appender & log outputs
// Similarily logging to various destinations

IF UNAUTHORIZED
IF ATTEMPT >= 3
LOG INFO: Unauthorized Hacking details with ID/Password
END
END

Fig. 12. Attempt to hack user Microlog

4 Future Scope and Conclusion

Microlog is an important tool for security mechanism and its implementation as shown in the paper points to the fact that it can be used at much greater scale when combined with J2ME. Some of the projects which are currently using microlog are BlueWhaleMail [2], Voxtr MIDlet [2], Emergency data MIDlet [2]. In the paper we have seen when an unauthorized user tries to access the application, his details get logged with all the other information which can be retrieved later using Bluetooth printing of the log generated. In future separate library called MicroAndroid is being developed specially for logging in Android applications. The main advantage of it being small in size, yet powerful application makes it apt choice for current mobile development scenario.

References

[1] http://en.wikipedia.org/wiki/List_of_countries_by_number_of_mobile_phones_in_use
[2] Maven repository, http://microlog.sourceforge.net/site/
[3] De Joed, M.: Programming Java 2 Micro Edition on Symbian OS, A developers guide to MIDP 2.0 (2004)
[4] Yueliang, W.: Mobile Business Application based on J2ME and web services. Dongbie University of Finance and Economics, China. IEEE, Los Alamitos(2009)
[5] Sun Microsystems, http://java.sun.com/developer/technicalArticles/javame/javame-logging/
[6] Klingsheim, A.N.: J2ME bluetooth Programming, Master Theises, University of Bergen (2004)
[7] Ellis, J., Young, M.: Sun MicroSystems: J2ME web services Sun 1.0 Final Draft (2003)
[8] Hopkins, B., Antony, R.: Bluetooth for Java (2003)

[9] Zhang, X.: Design of mobile electronic commerce system based on J2ME. Shandong Economic University, China. IEEE, Los Alamitos (2009)

[10] Xianjun, Q., Changping, H., Hongping, Y.: A comparative Study of Mobile Electronic Commerce Based on the WAP and J2ME Implementation technology, Wuhan University. IEEE, Los Alamitos (2009)

[11] Nokia Forums: MIDP: Bluetooth Api Developer's Guide (2006)

Assisting Programmers Resolving Vulnerabilities in Java Web Applications

Pranjal Bathia*, Bharath Reddy Beerelli, and Marc-André Laverdière

TCS Innovation Labs Hyderabad, Tata Consultancy Services Ltd.
Deccan Park, Plot No.1, Software Units Layout
Madhapur, Hyderabad 500 081, India
{marcandre.laverdiere,bharath.beerelli}@tcs.com

Abstract. We present in this paper a new approach towards detection and correction of security vulnerabilities in Java Web applications using program slicing and transformation. Our vulnerability detector is based on an extended program slicing algorithm and handles taint propagation through strings. Our prototype is implemented as an Eclipse plug-in and leverages the WALA library to fix XSS Vulnerabilities in an interactive manner. We also show that our approach offers a good performance, both computationally and in terms of vulnerabilities found.

1 Introduction

Computer security is taking an increasingly predominant role in today's environment. The typical approach to security in the industry is the infamous find-patch-deploy cycle: a vulnerability is found in a software component, the vendor issues a patch, and end-users deploy the patch. This is often due to the developers' lack of security training and a software development process that does not take security into consideration. This is also the case with Web applications, which are increasingly used by organizations and deal with sensitive data.

A useful tool in this context is a vulnerability scanner, a tool that detects vulnerabilities in the software in an automated or semi-automated manner. A recent report shows that 49% of Web applications have high-risk vulnerabilities that can be found automatically [1]. Sadly, such tools add limited value, since 30% of vulnerabilities reported by penetration tests were not fixed, or fixed improperly [2].

According to Web Application Security Statistics [1], the most widespread vulnerability is Cross Site Scripting (XSS). XSS occurs whenever an application takes untrusted data and sends it to a web browser without proper validation and escaping. XSS allows attackers to execute scripts in the victim's browser, which can hijack user sessions, deface web sites, redirect the user to malicious sites, etc. As Java is very popular for Web Applications development, we focused

* Pranjal Bathia was involved in this research in TCS Innovation Labs Hyderabad as an intern. This research constitutes part of her M. Tech. thesis at NIT Warangal. She can now be reached at pranjal.bathia@oracle.com

N. Meghanathan et al. (Eds.): CCSIT 2011, Part III, CCIS 133, pp. 268–279, 2011.

our efforts first on finding and fixing XSS vulnerabilities in Servlet-based Java Web Applications.

Many of the approaches published are able to detect wide range of vulnerabilities and are also scalable for industrial Web Applications. However, they do not resolve these security errors. We can fill this gap by following a holistic approach while designing an application scanner. The overall idea of this project is to assist developers in detecting web application vulnerabilities and remediate them. To fix these security vulnerabilities, we integrate static analysis (for detection) with program transformation (for fixing). We made this choice because source code is the medium of work for programmers and thus where our proposal would be the most comfortable to use.

The direct consequence of these objectives would allow the experts to focus on choosing the best options to eliminate the vulnerabilities and leaving the implementation part for the non-experts to perform. It will also lower the level of study and reviews necessary to make the application robust and secure, lower the time required in order to make the necessary modifications, and enable reuse.

We show a motivating example in the Listing 1.1. This would be part of a Java Web application reading untrusted data from the servlet parameter. This example also shows some manipulation of data via string operations. In this code sample, the tainted string `t1` will get the value from the call to `getParameter` at line 4. Next, the series of string operation calls are present in the code from line 6 to 8. Method `println` is considered as XSS sink because it renders the string value of its input to the screen. Thus, the call to `println` with the argument `password` at line 9 poses a security issue. To analyze this code precisely, the analysis must track data flow, through string operation calls and the object fields all the way to `println`. To resolve this XSS vulnerability, as shown in Listing 1.2, a sanitizer like `URLEncoder.encode` is used to make the source taint free, which is then passed to the sink.

Listing 1.1. Sample Program having XSS

```
1  protected void doGet(HttpServletRequest request,
2  HttpServletResponse response) throws IOException,
3  ServletException{
4      String t1 = request.getParameter("fname");
5      PrintWriter writer = response.getWriter();
6      String preText = t1.substring(3);
7      String postText = "PUN123";
8      String password = preText.concat(postText);
9      writer.println(password);
10     super.doGet(request,response);
11 }
```

Listing 1.2. Sample Fix for XSS

```
protected void doGet(HttpServletRequest request,
HttpServletResponse response) throws IOException,
ServletException{
    String t1 = request.getParameter("fname");
```

```
    PrintWriter writer = response.getWriter();
    String preText = t1.substring(3);
    String postText = "PUN123";
    String password = preText.concat(postText);
    password = URLEncoder.encode(password,"UTF-8");
    writer.println(password);
    super.doGet(request,response);
}
```

In order to validate this approach, we implemented a proof of concept of this approach using the Eclipse Integrated Development Environment (IDE) and using the WALA libraries for static analysis.

This paper is divided as follows: in Section 2, we introduce the related work on program analysis and transformation, as well as on Web application security. Then, in Section 3, we describe our methodology, followed by our results in Section 4. Finally, we bring concluding remarks in Section 5.

2 Previous Work

There is a rich body of knowledge on the topics of program analysis and transformation. Our study of the previous work will focus on security problems at the implementation level, in the source code, and at transformations in the source code as well.

Program analysis is categorized in two types based on the time of performing the analysis. Analysis performed without the execution of a program is termed as static analysis, whereas an analysis performed during the execution of a program is termed as dynamic analysis.

Static analysis can be done at the source code, object code, and bytecode levels, which allows to verify all the control and data flow paths in the entire program, including its libraries. This is however computationally expensive. Static Analysis is known for being able to find a lot of bugs in software effectively, although it cannot detect some properties that are hard to express [3]. It remains that one of its major advantages is that it does not require modeling the proper software behavior, which would be a time-consuming activity to create for existing programs.

At a conceptual level, almost all static analysis approaches are characterized by some common properties like flow sensitivity, context sensitivity, granularity of performing analysis, etc. If the information discovered by an analysis at a program point depends on the control flow (the order in which the individual statements, instructions, or function calls of the program are executed or evaluated) paths involving the program point and could vary from one program point to another, then the analysis is *flow sensitive.* Otherwise, it is *flow insensitive.* In case of context sensitivity, if the information discovered by an inter-procedural analysis (analysis across procedures/functions) for a function varies from one calling context of a function to another then the analysis is *context sensitive.* A *context insensitive* analysis does not distinguish between different calling contexts and computes the same information for all the calling contexts of a function

[4]. Another commonality is the presence , in the tools' results, of *false positives* (errors reported that are not errors) and *false negatives* (a problem that is not reported) [5].

We introduce some tools used for static analysis that were not discussed in [6] and that are useful for analyzing Java programs. All these systems share a common weakness that they do not transform the source code with the security solution.

LAPSE [7,8] uses vulnerability specifications written in the Program Query Language (PQL) to detect various Web Application vulnerabilities. The program uses the bddbddb [9] system, which automatically translates database queries into Binary Decision Diagram (BDD) programs. The authors claim that their analysis is free of false negatives. This approach was extended [10], with integrated static analysis, optimized dynamic instrumentation, model checking and dynamic error recovery. The static analysis part is done as previously, but the parts that cannot be determined statically are augmented with dynamic monitoring code, which reduces the overhead of dynamic policy enforcement. Model checking is used to determine possible attack vectors and simulating the program execution for such vectors. Finally, dynamic error recovery replaces an offending statement by another. While this approach does code substitution, it does so at run-time. The original source code is never fixed. Further, the user is not offered any choice as to what the solution will be.

Soot[11] is another framework for analysis and transformation of Java bytecode. Internally it uses Jedd (a BDD-based Relational Extension of Java) [12], which offers a convenient way of programming with BDDs. Jedd is used to express five key interrelated whole program analysis in Soot compiler framework [13]. The transformation offered is only at the bytecode level, however.

PMD is an open source project that has been integrated with multiple Java IDEs [14]. It scans Java, JSP and JSF applications for style problems and various bugs, including some security-related checks. It is customizable with new rules (either in Java or XPath), and provides AST and Data Flow information to the rules. Its approach is mostly class-centric, but inter-class analysis can be programmed as well. While this approach has large breadth, it is not doing data flow analysis well.

The T.J. Watson Libraries for Analysis (WALA) is a project from IBM Research that offers static analysis capabilities and bytecode manipulation[15]. It operates on bytecode as well as source code and offers an abstract representation that supports other languages called CAst. It offers various kinds of intermediate representations and has been used as a foundation for TAJ – Tainted Analysis for JAVA [16]. TAJ performs static analysis of Java programs using a hybrid thin-slicing algorithm and code models to "fill in the blanks" for things like native code. While the results are interesting, the optimizations may introduce false negatives (e.g. in the case of a taint flow of more than 14 steps).

Program transformation allows to change the structure and semantics of the software in an automated or semi-automated manner. Many contributions in the field are very powerful, allowing even to convert programs from one language to another. Transformations can be done at the source code, the object code, bytecode levels, or even at run time. We will skip, for the sake of brevity, the contributions related to Refactoring and Aspect-Oriented programming. Instead, we focus on recent program transformation systems and frameworks for Java source code.

Program transformation has been used for improving the security of programs in the past, with a tool called Gemini [17]. This tool moved stack-based buffers to heap-based buffers for C programs. Security-oriented program transformations were being used to improve the security of a system's perimeter by introducing authentication, authorization and input validation components [18].

Stratego is a language for program transformations. It is implemented in the XT toolkit (and can be called Stratego/XT) [19]. It has many applications, including a Java compiler and documentation generator. In this approach, the rewriting is applied to the Abstract Syntax Tree (AST) and allows source-to-source transformation. The approach is language-independent, and uses transformation strategies and combinations. It is sadly very verbose, and the specification language can be hard to understand and develop with.

JaTS [20] uses a superset of Java in order to make transformations on Java code. It allows matching of identifiers as variables. However, its template approach requires the user to specify the whole structure of the class to modify, making the expression of the transformations verbose.

Tom [21] is another rewriting system that allows to define arbitrary grammars. It supports Java expressions embedded within its own language. Tom provides a bridge between a general purpose language and higher level specifications that use rewriting. This benefit is not however sufficient to avoid the verbosity and complexity common to program transformation systems.

The Spoon project [22] offers a framework for weaving changes into programs based on both source and compiled Java code. Spoon refines the program in its meta-model, which allows for direct access and modification of its structure at compile-time. The transformation can be reconverted into source code afterwards. Spoon also offers a template technology based on a superset of the Java language. The templates enable the creation of reusable code snippets to be added into the program. The templates are however very rigid and it would be hard to use them for a wide range of transformations.

3 Methodology

Our methodology is conceptually inspired by [23], since the vulnerability is seen as a problem where tainted information from an untrusted *source* propagates, through data and/or control flow, to a sensitive *sink* without being properly corrected by a *sanitizer* or validated by a *validator*.

A *source* is a method whose return value is considered tainted, or untrusted. A *sanitizer* is a method that manipulates its input to produce taint-free output. A *validator* is a method that ensures that the input data conforms to a specific policy or format, or will abort the execution of the operation if it is not. A *sink* is a method that performs the security sensitive computations and parameters of that method are vulnerable to the attack via tainted data.

We provide some background on program slicing in Subsection 3.1 and describe our taint propagation algorithm in Subsection 3.2. Afterwards, we describe how we added our detection algorithm and the error resolution feature in Eclipse in Subsection 3.3.

3.1 Program Slicing

Program slicing is a method which extracts parts of a program, called *slice*, that potentially affect the values computed at some point of interest, named *seed* [24]. The seed is typically a statement. Some slices are generated without making any assumptions regarding a program's input and are called *static slices*, whereas *dynamic slices* rely on some specific test case(s).

Slices are efficiently computable by reachability analysis in the program's *System Dependence Graphs* (SDG). SDGs are a collection of *Procedure Dependence Graphs* (PDGs) [25]. The nodes of a PDG represent the individual statements and predicates of the procedure and edges represent the control and data dependencies. A node is control dependent on a predicate if the predicate controls whether or not the node will be executed. A node is data dependent on an assignment, if the value assigned can be referenced in the node. There is a dependence edge from each declaration node to each of its definitions and uses (def-use chains). The PDGs are connected together to form the SDG by call edges (which represent procedure calls, and run from a call node to an entry node) and by parameter edges (which represent parameter passing and return values).

Slices can be computed by traversing the SDG in either backward or forward directions. For example, the backwards slice from the `writer.println(password);` statement in Listing 1.1, which contains all computations that affect the value printed, can be computed by traversing edges backwards in the SDG from the `println` node. The slice would contain statements from line 3 to 7.

3.2 XSS Detection Using Slicing

Program Slicing is an ideal tool for our detection algorithm, since it effectively selects a sub-graph of relevant statements for us. It is done in two phases. The first phase builds the call graph and performs a pointer analysis. The second phase runs the extended slicing algorithm to track the tainted data.

We chose to use the WALA engine for the detection of vulnerabilities over other frameworks, since it offers wide variety of static analysis and slicing algorithms and is integrated with Eclipse. The current implementation relies on WALA's context-sensitive variant of Andersen's analysis [26] with on-the-fly call graph construction. This makes our algorithm context sensitive and flow insensitive. It also includes the careful treatment of security-related Application Programming Interfaces (APIs). In particular, taint-specific APIs, such as sources and sinks,[1] are analyzed with unlimited-depth of call-string context. This is necessary due to the special role that these APIs play in taint propagation. In the example given in Listing 1.1, this context allows to disambiguate the calls to the source method `getParameter` at line 3, even though they are performed on same receiver object.

The first phase, goes through the following internal steps:

1. **Build Analysis Scope:** Sets up the analysis scope based on the target application and the exclusions defined. All Java source files along with the referred libraries in that target project are added into the scope.
2. **Build Class Hierarchy:** The hierarchy is built based on the scope of the analysis.
3. **Create Entry Points:** Defines the starting point for building the call graph. Since we only analyze servlets, we identify the entry points as the inherited methods in the servlet implementation classes.
4. **Create Call graph:** Creates the call graph based on the class hierarchy and the analysis options specified.
5. **Construct Pointer Analysis:** Provides call-backs for the pointer analysis.It establishes which pointers, or heap references, can point to which variables or storage locations. It is also known as Point-to Analysis.

Using the preliminary pointer analysis and call graph, the second phase tracks the data flow from sinks to a tainted source using backward slices. The SDG is constructed based on the call graph, pointer analysis, data dependence options and control dependence options. The slicing algorithm does not take control dependencies in consideration, and hence does not track the corresponding indirect information flow.

To find the tainted flow, we first find the sink calls in the call graph and compute the reachability in the SDG from each sink call statement s, adding necessary direct and summary edges. The nodes reachable from s represents the load, store and source statement *directly* data dependent on s. Since the basic slicing algorithm omits string operations' data dependencies from the slice, we examine the statements of the slice for string-related operations.[2] such as `String.concat()`, `String.substring()` and `StringBuilder.append()` When meeting such statements, we examine the SDG's data structure for each of its parameters and recover their related statements. These statements are then added to the slice. Figure 1 explains the basic flow of finding the XSS vulnerability. We represented start and terminal states in bold, and skipped some steps detailed for brevity. In order to avoid false negatives, we don't report as vulnerabilities the cases where a sanitizer is between the source and the sink.

3.3 Program Transformation with Eclipse

The Eclipse IDE features *markers* in the editor notably for for errors and warnings. These markers can include resolutions which participate in the workbench's

[1] We currently examine only `PrintWriter` subclasses in `Servlet` instances.

[2] Except `StringTokenizer`.

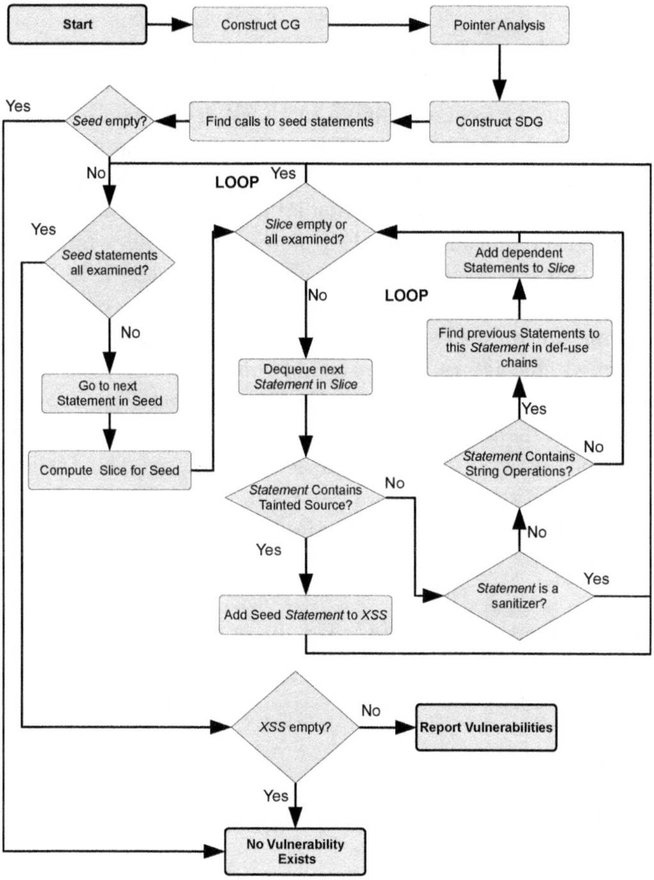

Fig. 1. Flowchart for Detecting XSS Using Slicing

Quick Fix feature. Users can select a problem marker and choose a Quick Fix from the context menu, containing the list of supplied fixes specified for the marker.

Our prototype leverages these features of the Eclipse IDE to report security errors. While building the source code, a check is automatically conducted on the target application's code. During the vulnerability detection phase, we record relevant analysis information to generate the markers. This information includes variable names, source code line number, starting offset, ending offset, etc. Once a vulnerability is found, we add a marker to the IDE on the sink's line of code that explains the vulnerability and suggests possible improvements. At the time of writing, we had defined two standard sanitizers to prevent XSS. Once the user clicks on the marker and chooses a Quick Fix, the document is modified to remove that XSS vulnerability.

4 Results

In order to verify the algorithm for fixing the vulnerability, we created an Eclipse plug-in project. It provides the functionality of Adding/Removing the vulnerability check for the projects available in the Workbench.Once the vulnerability detection is enabled, XSS vulnerabilities will be detected in the compiled source files (here, the input file is same as in Listing 1.1), as shown in Figure 2(a).

The user can view the multiple available solutions for the security error by right clicking on the marker in the Editor window, as shown in Figure 2(b). This context menu displays available solutions for fixing the XSS vulnerability. The user can choose any of the solutions. In case of doubt, the user can hover the mouse over one option and see its description. The first solution in the example escapes reserved characters.[3] The second solution uses `java.net.URLEncoder`, which internally converts unsafe characters into their byte representation using a given encoding scheme.

Once a Quick Fix is chosen, Eclipse implements the transformations using string substitution on the source code. In this example, we choose `Use URLEncode Method`, and the result is shown in Figure 2(c).

Table 1. Comparative Analysis Results on Modified Securibench Micro

Scanner	Execution	XSS Vulnerabilities	False Positives Total	False Positives Rate	Analysis
LAPSE	10 sec	142	41	28.9 %	45m
Prototype	10 sec	108	17	15.9 %	30m

We also evaluated the performance of our scanner with SecuriBench Micro [27]. WALA's slicing algorithm takes infinite time in some test cases that use `HashMap` and `StringTokenizer`. As such, we excluded some of the test files.[4] We executed the same test using LAPSE. The results are presented in Table 1. We see that our prototype executes in roughly the same time as LAPSE, has results easier to analyze, and has a lower false positive rate. The false positives were due to two factors. The first is an approximation in our algorithm, where arrays and data structures as a whole are marked as tainted the moment any tainted data is put into it. The second is because our algorithm is flow-insensitive. The false negatives were due to an incomplete analysis of the constructors. This shows the viability of our approach. Further, our approach easily transforms the source code with the solution.

[3] Reserved characters are control characters in an encoding or document format. In this case, we refer to characters part of the HTML standard. Common substitutions are: `&(&amp), <(&lt), >(&gt), "(&quot), '(&#x27), / (&#x2F).`

[4] We excluded `Basic37-39.java` and `Collections6-7.java`.

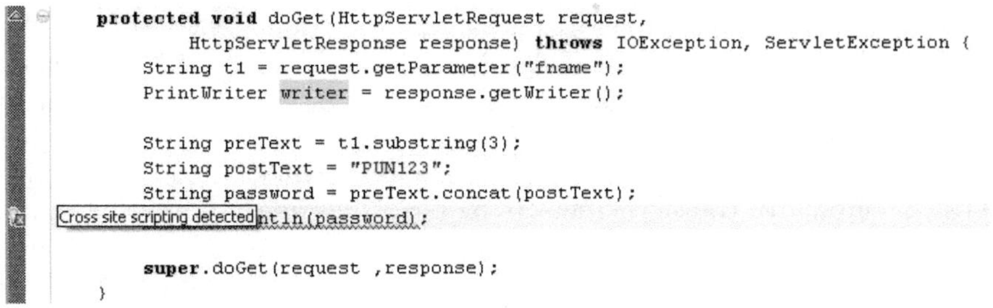

(a) Security Error for XSS

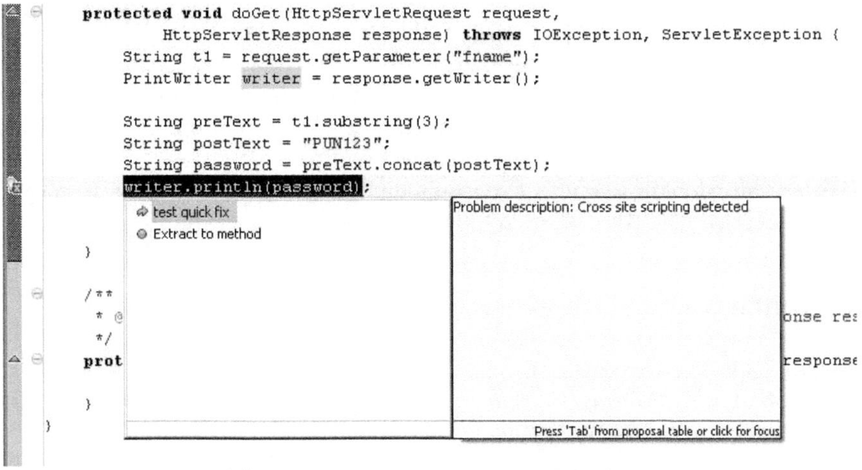

(b) Quick Fix option in Editor Window

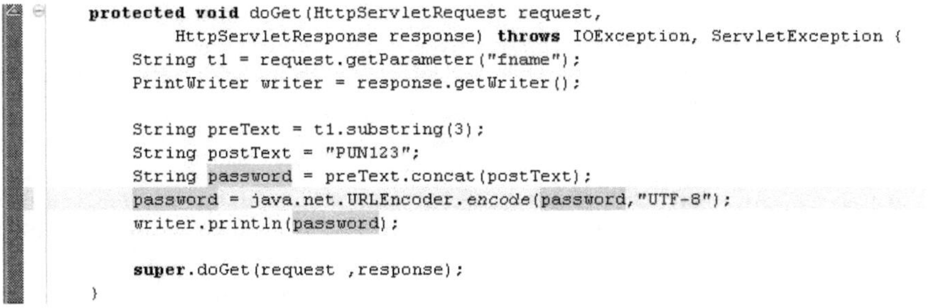

(c) After Fixing XSS Vulnerability

Fig. 2. Fixing a XSS Vulnerability in Action

5 Conclusions and Future Work

Security scanners are useful tools, but do not always yield improved security. This is because their users may not be able to fix the problems detected. This situation warrants a new approach, detailed in this paper, which integrates vulnerability detection with vulnerability correction in a simple tool integrated in an IDE. To the authors' best knowledge, no previous approach integrated static analysis and semi-automated transformations to fix security errors in Web Applications.

After surveying the existing options in program analysis and transformation, we found that no tool helped programmers fix security problems and decided to meet this need. Our detection engine is based on our proposed flow-insensitive and context-sensitive extended slicing algorithm which handles taint propagation in string operations. We first targeted XSS vulnerabilities, as they are the most common Web Application vulnerability. Our prototype reports errors as markers in the Eclipse IDE. Programmers can then choose a fix for the vulnerability. Then, our prototype changes the source code with the chosen solution.

We compared our results with the LAPSE static analyzer on the SecuriBench Micro test bench, and found that our results were comparable in terms of performance, and that we had a lower false positive rate.

We are also looking at improving our analyzer to handle all the test cases, provide no false negatives and handle more types of vulnerabilities.

References

1. Gordeychik, S., Grossman, J., Khera, M., Lantinga, M., Wysopal, C., Eng, C., Shah, S., Lee, L., Murray, C., Evteev, D.: Web application security statistics. Technical report, OWASP Foundation (2009)
2. Surf, M., Shulman, A.: How safe is it out there? Zeroing in on the vulnerabilities of application security. Technical report, Imperva™ Application Defense Center (2004)
3. Engler, D., Musuvathi, M.: Static analysis versus software model checking for bug finding. In: Steffen, B., Levi, G. (eds.) VMCAI 2004. LNCS, vol. 2937, pp. 405–427. Springer, Heidelberg (2004)
4. Khedker, U.P., Sanyal, A., Karkare, B.: Data Flow Analysis Theory and Practice. CRC Press, Boca Raton (2009)
5. Chess, B., McGraw, G.: Static analysis for security. IEEE Security and Privacy 2(6), 76–79 (2004)
6. Rutar, N., Almazan, C.B., Foster, J.S.: A comparison of bug finding tools for java. In: 15th International Symposium on Software Reliability Engineering (ISSRE 2004), pp. 245–256. IEEE Press, New York (2004)
7. Martin, M., Livshits, B., Lam, M.S.: Finding application errors and security flaws using PQL: a program query language. In: 20th Annual ACM SIGPLAN Conference on Object Oriented Programming Systems Languages and Applications (OOPSLA 2005), pp. 365–383. ACM Press, New York (2005)
8. Livshits, B., Lam, M.S.: Finding security errors in Java programs with static analysis. Technical report, Stanford University (2005)
9. bddbddb official website, `http://bddbddb.sourceforge.net/`

10. Lam, M.S., Martin, M., Livshits, B., Whaley, J.: Securing web applications with static and dynamic information flow tracking. In: 2008 ACM SIGPLAN Symposium on Partial Evaluation and Semantics-based Program Manipulation (PEPM 2008), pp. 3–12. ACM Press, New York (2008)
11. Soot official website, `http://www.sable.mcgill.ca/soot/`
12. Lhoták, O., Hendren, L.: Jedd: A BDD-based relational extension of Java. In: 2004 ACM SIGPLAN Conference on Programming Language Design and Implementation, ACM Press, New York (2004)
13. Vallée-Rai, R., Gagnon, E., Hendren, L.J., Lam, P., Pominville, P., Sundaresan, V.: Optimizing Java bytecode using the Soot framework: Is it feasible? In: Watt, D.A. (ed.) CC 2000. LNCS, vol. 1781, pp. 18–34. Springer, Heidelberg (2000)
14. PMD official website, `http://pmd.sourceforge.net/`
15. WALA: T.J. Watson Libraries for Analysis, `http://wala.sourceforge.net/`
16. Tripp, O., Pistoia, M., Fink, S.J., Sridharan, M., Weisman, O.: TAJ: effective taint analysis of web applications. In: 2009 ACM SIGPLAN Conference on Programming Language Design and Implementation, pp. 87–97. ACM Press, New York (2009)
17. Dahn, C., Mancoridis, S.: Using Program Transformation to Secure C Programs Against Buffer Overflows. In: 10th Working Conference on Reverse Engineering (WCRE 2003), p. 323. IEEE Press, New York (2003)
18. Hafiz, M., Johnson, R.E.: Improving perimeter security with security-oriented program transformations. In: 2009 ICSE Workshop on Software Engineering for Secure Systems (IWSESS 2009), pp. 61–67. IEEE Press, New York (2009)
19. Visser, E.: Program transformation with Stratego/XT: Rules, strategies, tools, and systems in Stratego/XT 0.9. In: Lengauer, C., Larson, K., Blum, A., Vetta, A. (eds.) Domain-Specific Program Generation. LNCS, vol. 3016, pp. 216–238. Springer, Heidelberg (2004)
20. JaTS official website, `http://www.cin.ufpe.br/~jats/`
21. Balland, E., Brauner, P., Kopetz, R., Moreau, P.-E., Reilles, A.: Tom: Piggybacking rewriting on java. In: Baader, F. (ed.) RTA 2007. LNCS, vol. 4533, pp. 36–47. Springer, Heidelberg (2007)
22. Pawlak, R., Noguera, C., Petitprez, N.: Spoon: Program Analysis and Transformation in Java. Research Report RR-5901, INRIA (2006)
23. LAPSE: Web Application Security Scanner for Java, `http://suif.stanford.edu/~livshits/work/lapse/pubs.html`
24. Weiser, M.: Program slicing. In: 5th international conference on Software engineering (ICSE 1981), pp. 439–449. IEEE Press, New York (1981)
25. Ferrante, J., Ottenstein, K.J., Warren, J.D.: The program dependence graph and its use in optimization. In: Paul, M., Robinet, B. (eds.) Programming 1984. LNCS, vol. 167, pp. 125–132. Springer, Heidelberg (1984)
26. Andersen, L.O.: Program Analysis and Specialization for the C Programming Language. PhD thesis, University of Copenhagen, Denmark (1994)
27. Stanford securibench micro 1.08, `http://suif.stanford.edu/~livshits/work/securibench-micro/`

Estimating Strength of a DDoS Attack Using Multiple Regression Analysis

B.B. Gupta[1], P.K. Agrawal[2], R.C. Joshi[1], and Manoj Misra[1]

[1] Department of Electronics and Computer Engineering,
Indian Institute of Technology Roorkee, Roorkee, India
{brijgdec,rcjoshfec,manojfec}@iitr.ernet.in
[2] Department of computer Engineering,
Netaji Subhas Institute of Technology, New Delhi, India
pradeep.k.agrawal84@gmail.com

Abstract. Anomaly based DDoS detection systems construct profile of the traffic normally seen in the network, and identify anomalies whenever traffic deviate from normal profile beyond a threshold. This extend of deviation is normally not utilized. This paper reports the evaluation results of proposed approach that utilizes this extend of deviation from detection threshold, to estimate strength of DDoS attack using multiple regression model. A relationship is established between strength of DDoS attacks and observed deviation in sample entropy. Various statistical performance measures, such as Coefficient of determination (R2), Coefficient of Correlation (CC), Sum of Square Error (SSE), Mean Square Error (MSE), Root Mean Square Error (RMSE), Normalized Mean square Error (NMSE), Nash–Sutcliffe Efficiency Index (η) and Mean Absolute Error (MAE) are used to measure the performance of the regression model. Internet type topologies used for simulation are generated using Transit-Stub model of GT-ITM topology generator. NS-2 network simulator on Linux platform is used as simulation test bed for launching DDoS attacks with varied attack strengths. The simulation results are promising as we are able to estimate strength of DDoS attack efficiently with very less error rate using multiple regression model.

Keywords: DDoS attack, Intrusion detection, Multiple regression, Zombies, Entropy.

1 Introduction

Denial of service (DoS) attacks and more particularly the distributed ones (DDoS) are one of the latest threat and pose a grave danger to users, organizations and infrastructures of the Internet. A DDoS attacker attempts to disrupt a target, in most cases a web server, by flooding it with illegitimate packets generated from a large number of zombies, usurping its bandwidth and overtaxing it to prevent legitimate inquiries from getting through [1,2]. Anomaly based DDoS detection systems construct profile of the traffic normally seen in the network, and identify anomalies whenever traffic deviate from normal profile beyond a threshold [3]. This extend of deviation is normally not utilized. Therefore, we use multiple regression [4,5] based approach that utilizes this extend of deviation from detection threshold to estimate strength of DDoS

N. Meghanathan et al. (Eds.): CCSIT 2011, Part III, CCIS 133, pp. 280–289, 2011.

attack. A real time estimation of strength of DDoS attack is helpful to suppress the effect of attack by choosing predicted strength of DDoS attack of most suspicious attack sources for either filtering or rate limiting. We have assumed that header information of out going packets is not spoofed. Moore et. al [6] have already made a similar kind of attempt, in which they have used backscatter analysis to estimate number of spoofed addresses involved in DDoS attack. This is an offline analysis based on unsolicited responses.

Our objective is to find the relationship between strength of DDoS attack and deviation in sample entropy. In order to estimate strength of DDoS attack, multiple regression model is used. To measure the performance of the proposed approach, we have calculated various statistical performance measures i.e. R^2, CC, SSE, MSE, RMSE, NMSE, η, MAE and residual error. Internet type topologies used for simulation are generated using Transit-Stub model of GT-ITM topology generator [7]. NS-2 network simulator [8] on Linux platform is used as simulation test bed for launching DDoS attacks with varied attack strength. In our simulation experiments, total number of zombies is fixed to 100 and attack traffic rate range between 10Mbps and 100Mbps; therefore, mean attack rate per zombie is varied from 0.1Mbps to 1Mbps.

The remainder of the paper is organized as follows. Section 2 contains overview of multiple regression model. Section 3 presents various statistical performance measures. Intended detection scheme are described in section 4. Section 5 describes experimental setup and performance analysis in details. Model development is presented in section 6. Section 7 contains simulation results and discussion. Finally, Section 8 concludes the paper.

2 Multiple Regression Model

Regression analysis [9,10] is a statistical tool for the investigation of relationships between variables. Usually, the investigator seeks to ascertain the causal effect of one variable upon another. More specifically, regression analysis helps us to understand how the typical value of the dependent variable changes when any one of the independent variables is varied, while the other independent variables are held constant. Variables which are used to 'explain', other variables are called explanatory variables. Variable which is explained is called response variable. A response variable is also called a dependent variable, and an explanatory variable is sometime called an independent variable, or a predictor, or repressor. When there is only one explanatory variable the regression model is called a simple regression, whereas if there are more than one explanatory variable the regression model is called multiple regression.

The general purpose of multiple regression [4,5] (the term was first used by Pearson, 1908) is to learn more about the relationship between several independent or predictor variables and a dependent or criterion variable. In the multivariate case, when there is more than one independent variable, the regression line cannot be visualized in the two dimensional space, but can be computed just as easily. In general form of multiple regression given in eq. 1, there are p independent variables:

$$Y_i = \hat{Y}_i + \varepsilon_i \tag{1}$$

$$\hat{Y}_i = \beta_0 + \beta_1 X_{1i} + \beta_2 X_{2i} + \ldots\ldots + \beta_p X_{pi}$$

where

- Y is dependent variable
- $X_1, X_2, \ldots\ldots, X_p$ are p independent variables
- β_0 is intercept
- $\beta_1, \beta_2, \ldots, \beta_p$ are the coefficients of p independent variables
- ε is regression residual

Input and Output
In multiple regression model, a relationship is developed between strength of DDoS attack Y (output) and observed deviation in sample volume X_1 and flow X_2 as input. Here X_1 is equal to ($X_{in}(t) - X_n^*(t)$) and X_2 is equal to ($F_{in}(t) - F_n^*(t)$). Our proposed regression based approach utilizes these deviations in volume X_1 and flow X_2 to estimate strength of DDoS attack.

3 Statistic Performance Measures

The different statistical parameters are adjusted during calibration to get the best statistical agreement between observed and simulated variables. For this purpose, various performance measures, such as Coefficient of Determination (R^2), Coefficient of Correlation (CC), Standard Error of Estimate (SSE), Mean Square Error (MSE), Root Mean Square Error (RMSE), Normalized Mean square Error (NMSE), Nash–Sutcliffe Efficiency Index (η) and Mean Absolute Error (MAE) are used to measure the performance of the proposed regression model. These measures are defined below:

i). Coefficient of Determination (R^2): Coefficient of determination (R^2) is a descriptive measure of the strength of the regression relationship, a measure how well the regression line fit to the data. R^2 is the proportion of variance in dependent variable which can be predicted from independent variable.

$$R^2 = \frac{\left(\sum_{i=1}^{N} (Y_o - \overline{Y}_o)(Y_c - \overline{Y}_c) \right)^2}{\left[\sum_{i=1}^{N} (Y_o - \overline{Y}_o)^2 \cdot \sum_{i=1}^{N} (Y_c - \overline{Y}_c)^2 \right]} \tag{2}$$

ii). Coefficient of Correlation (CC): The Coefficient of Correlation (CC) can be defined as:

$$CC = \frac{\sum_{i=1}^{N} (Y_o - \overline{Y}_o)(Y_c - \overline{Y}_c)}{\left[\sum_{i=1}^{N} (Y_o - \overline{Y}_o)^2 \cdot \sum_{i=1}^{N} (Y_c - \overline{Y}_c)^2 \right]^{1/2}} \tag{3}$$

iii). Sum of Squared Errors (SSE): The Sum of Squared Errors (SSE) can be defined as:

$$SSE = \sum_{i=1}^{N} (Y_o - Y_c)^2 \tag{4}$$

iv). Mean Square Error (MSE): The Mean Square Error (MSE) between observed and computed outputs can be defined as:

$$MSE = \frac{\sum_{i=1}^{N} (Y_c - Y_o)^2}{N} \tag{5}$$

v). Root Mean Square Error (RMSE): The Root Mean Square Error (RMSE) between observed and computed outputs can be defined as:

$$RMSE = \sqrt{\frac{\sum_{i=1}^{N} (Y_c - Y_o)^2}{N}} \tag{6}$$

vi). Normalized Mean Square Error (NMSE): The Normalized Mean Square Error (NMSE) between observed and computed outputs can be defined as:

$$NMSE = \frac{\frac{1}{N}\sum_{i=1}^{N} (Y_c - Y_o)^2}{\sigma_{obs}^2} \tag{7}$$

vii). Nash–Sutcliffe efficiency index (η): The Nash–Sutcliffe efficiency index (η) can be defined as:

$$\eta = 1 - \frac{\sum_{i=1}^{N} (Y_c - Y_o)^2}{\sum_{i=1}^{N} (Y_o - \overline{Y}_o)^2} \tag{8}$$

viii). Mean absolute error (MAE): Mean absolute error (MAE) can be defined as follows:

$$MAE = 1 - \frac{\sum_{i=1}^{N} |Y_c - Y_o|}{\sum_{i=1}^{N} |Y_o - \overline{Y}_o|} \tag{9}$$

where N represents the number of feature vectors prepared, Y_o and Y_c denote the observed and the computed/simulated values of dependent variable respectively, $\overline{Y}_o$ and σ^2_{obs} are the mean and the standard deviation of the observed dependent variable respectively.

4 Detection of Attack

Here, we will discuss proposed detection system that is part of access router or can belong to separate unit that interact with access router to detect attack traffic. A newly designed flow-volume based approach (FVBA) [11] is used to construct profile of the traffic normally seen in the network, and identify anomalies whenever traffic goes out of profile. In FVBA, two statistical measures namely volume and flow are used for profile construction. Fig. 1 depicts the FVBA architecture, where $X_{in}(t)$ represents total traffic arriving at the target machine in Δ time duration, when system is under attacks. $X_{in}(t)$ can be expressed as follows:

$$X_{in}(t) = X_n^*(t) + \hat{\dot{X}}(t), \tag{10}$$

where, $X_n^*(t)$ and $\hat{\dot{X}}(t)$ are the components of the normal and attack traffic respectively. $X_{in}(t)$ - $X_n^*(t)$ using above equation can be used for detection purpose.

To set normal profile, consider a random process $\{ X(t)\ ,\ t = \omega\, \Delta\ \ ,\omega \in N \}$, where Δ is a constant time interval, N is the set of positive integers, and for each t, X (t) is a random variable. $1 \leq \omega \leq l$, l is the number of time intervals. Here X (t) represents the total traffic volume in $\{t - \Delta, t\}$ time interval. X (t) is calculated during time interval $\{t - \Delta, t\}$ as follows:

$$X(t) = \sum_{i=1}^{Nf} n_i , i = 1, 2....N_f \tag{11}$$

where n_i represents total number of bytes arrivals for a flow i in $\{t - \Delta, t\}$ time duration and N_f represents total number of flows. We take average of X (t) and designate that as $X_n^*(t)$ normal traffic Volume. Similarly value of flow metric is calculated and designates that as $F_n^*(t)$. Here total bytes, not packets, are used to calculate volume metric, because it provides more accuracy, as different flows can contain packets of different sizes.

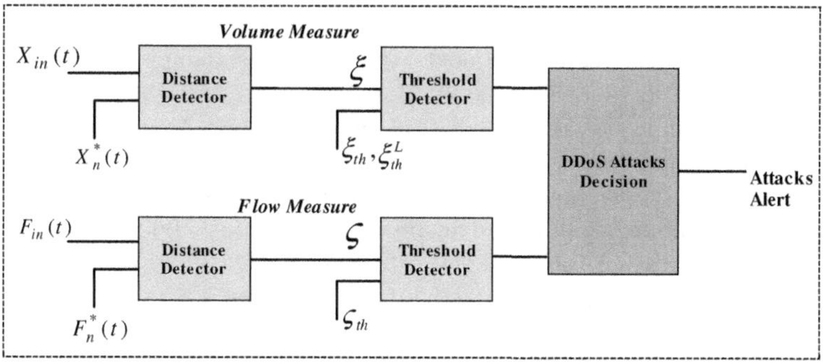

Fig. 1. FVBA architecture

To detect the attack, the value of volume metric $X_{in}(t)$ and flow metric $F_{in}(t)$ is calculated in time window Δ continuously; whenever there is appreciable deviation from $X_n^*(t)$ and $F_n^*(t)$, various types of attacks are detected. $X_{in}(t), F_{in}(t)$ and $X_n^*(t), F_n^*(t)$ gives values of volume and flow at the time of detection of attack and volume and flow values for the normal profile respectively.

5 Experimental Setup and Performance Analysis

In this section, we evaluate our proposed scheme using simulations. The simulations are carried out using NS2 network simulator [8]. We show that false positives and false negatives (or various error rates) triggered by our scheme are very less. This implies that profiles built are reasonably stable and are able to estimate strength of DDoS attack correctly.

Simulation Environment
Real-world Internet type topologies generated using Transit-Stub model of GT-ITM topology generator [7] are used to test our proposed scheme, where transit domains are treated as different Internet Service Provider (ISP) networks i.e. Autonomous Systems (AS). For simulations, we use ISP level topology, which contains four transit domains with each domain containing twelve transit nodes i.e. transit routers. All the four transit domains have two peer links at transit nodes with adjacent transit domains. Remaining ten transit nodes are connected to ten stub domain, one stub domain per transit node. Stub domains are used to connect transit domains with customer domains, as each stub domain contains a customer domain with ten legitimate client machines. So total of four hundred legitimate client machines are used to generate background traffic. Total zombie machines are fixed to 100 to generate attack traffic. Transit domain four contains the server machine to be attacked by zombie machines.

The legitimate clients are TCP agents that request files of size 1 Mbps with request inter-arrival times drawn from a Poisson distribution. The attackers are modeled by UDP agents. A UDP connection is used instead of a TCP one because in a practical attack flow, the attacker would normally never follow the basic rules of TCP, i.e. waiting for ACK packets before the next window of outstanding packets can be sent, etc. The attack traffic rate range between 10Mbps and 100Mbps; therefore, mean attack rate per zombie is varied from 0.1Mbps to 1Mbps. In our experiments, the monitoring time window was set to 200 ms, as the typical domestic Internet RTT is around 100 ms and the average global Internet RTT is 140 ms [12]. Total false positive alarms are minimum with high detection rate using this value of monitoring window. The simulations are repeated and different attack scenarios are compared by varying total attack strengths using fixed number of zombies.

Table 1. Deviation in volume and flow with DDoS attack strength

Attack Strength (Y)	Deviation in volume (X_1) ($X_{in}(t) - X_n^*(t)$)	Deviation in Flow (X_2) ($F_{in}(t) - F_n^*(t)$)
10M	90855.56	59.96
15M	109515.24	59.13
20M	133721.59	59.37
25M	143495.87	58.81
30M	146886.67	59.10
35M	144870.16	58.28
40M	156592.38	57.23
45M	160320.63	58.67
50M	213209.52	56.64
55M	178804.44	57.58
60M	181885.71	57.61
65M	187367.94	56.24
70M	199750.48	57.48
75M	209413.33	57.25
80M	219707.62	56.82
85M	227447.30	53.72
90M	227771.75	55.23
95M	249654.60	54.71
100M	269721.59	53.09

6 Model Development

In order to estimate strength of DDoS attack ($\hat{Y}$) from deviation ($X_{in}(t) - X_n^*(t)$) in volume and ($F_{in}(t) - F_n^*(t)$) in flow values, simulation experiments are done at varied attack strengths which are range between 10Mbps and 100Mbps and total number of zombies is fixed to 100; therefore, mean attack rate per zombie is varied from

0.1Mbps to 1Mbps. Table 1 represents deviation in volume and flow with actual strength of DDoS attack.

Multiple regression model is developed using DDoS attack strength (Y) and deviation ($X_{in}(t) - X_n^*(t)$) in volume and deviation ($F_{in}(t) - F_n^*(t)$) in flow values as discussed in Table 1 to fit the regression equation.

Regression equation and coefficient of correlation for multiple regression based model are as follows:

$$Y = X_1 * 0.00050 + X_2 * (-1.80) + 66.76 \qquad (12)$$
$$R^2 = 0.94$$

7 Results and Discussion

We have developed multiple regression model as discussed in section 6. Various performance measures are used to check the accuracy of this model.

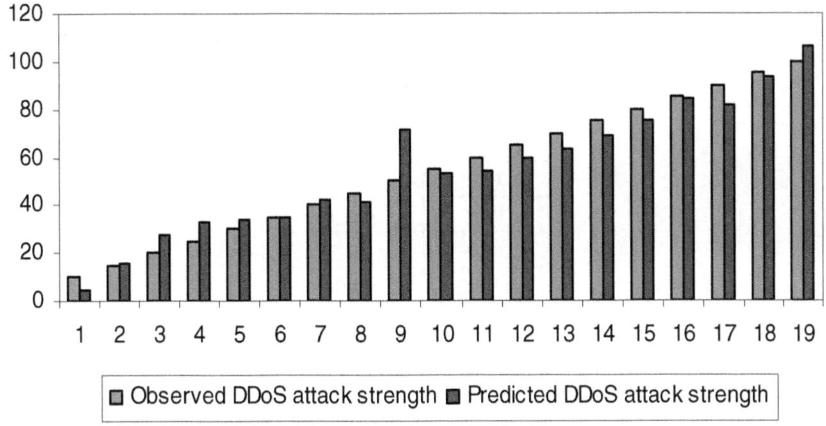

Fig. 2. Comparison between actual DDoS attack strength and predicted DDoS attack strength using multiple regression model

Constants β_0, β_1 and β_2 of various regression equations are network environment dependent. DDoS attack strength can be computed and compared with actual DDoS attack strength using multiple regression model. The comparison between actual DDoS attack strength and predicted DDoS attack strength using multiple regression model is depicted in fig. 2.

To represent false positive and false negative, we plot residual error. Positive cycle of residual error curve represents false positive, while negative cycle represents false negative. Fig. 3 represents residual error for multiple regression model.

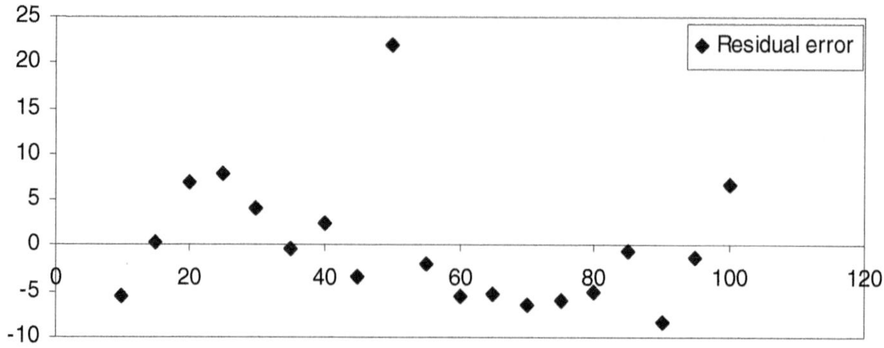

Fig. 3. Residual error in multiple regression model

Table 2 shows values of various performance measures. It can be inferred from table 2 that for multiple regression model Values of R^2, CC, SSE, MSE, RMSE, NMSE, η, MAE are 0.94, 0.97, 941.02, 49.53, 7.04, 1.76, 0.93 and 0.78 respectively. Hence strength of DDoS attack predicted by this model is closest to the observed strength of DDoS attack.

Table 2. Values of various performance measures

R^2	0.94
CC	0.97
SSE	941.02
MSE	49.53
RMSE	7.04
NMSE	1.76
η	0.93
MAE	0.78

8 Conclusion and Future Work

This paper investigates suitability of multiple regression model to predict strength of DDoS attack from deviation ($X_{in}(t)-X_n^*(t)$) in volume and deviation ($F_{in}(t)-F_n^*(t)$) in flow values. We have calculated various statistical performance measures i.e. R^2, CC, SSE, MSE, RMSE, NMSE, η, MAE and residual error and their values are 0.94, 0.97, 941.02, 49.53, 7.04, 1.76, 0.93 and 0.78 respectively. Therefore, predicted strength of DDoS attack using multiple regression model is close to actual strength of DDoS attack. However, simulation results are promising as we are able to predict strength of DDoS attack efficiently with very less error rate, experimental using a real time test bed can strongly validate our claim.

References

1. Gupta, B.B., Misra, M., Joshi, R.C.: An ISP level Solution to Combat DDoS attacks using Combined Statistical Based Approach. International Journal of Information Assurance and Security (JIAS) 3(2), 102–110 (2008)
2. Gupta, B.B., Joshi, R.C., Misra, M.: Defending against Distributed Denial of Service Attacks: Issues and Challenges. Information Security Journal: A Global Perspective 18(5), 224–247 (2009)
3. Gupta, B.B., Joshi, R.C., Misra, M.: Dynamic and Auto Responsive Solution for Distributed Denial-of-Service Attacks Detection in ISP Network. International Journal of Computer Theory and Engineering (IJCTE) 1(1), 71–80 (2009)
4. Hill, T., Lewicki, P.: STATISTICS Methods and Applications. StatSoft, Tulsa (2007)
5. Foster, D., George, E.: The risk inflation criterion for multiple regression. Annals of Statistics 22, 1947–1975 (1994)
6. Moore, D., Shannon, C., Brown, D.J., Voelker, G., Savage, S.: Inferring Internet Denial-of-Service Activity. ACM Transactions on Computer Systems 24(2), 115–139 (2006)
7. GT-ITM Traffic Generator Documentation and tool, `http://www.cc.gatech.edu/fac/EllenLegura/graphs.html`
8. NS Documentation, `http://www.isi.edu/nsnam/ns`
9. Lindley, D.V.: Regression and correlation analysis. New Palgrave: A Dictionary of Economics 4, 120–123 (1987)
10. Freedman, D.A.: Statistical Models: Theory and Practice. Cambridge University Press, Cambridge (2005)
11. Gupta, B.B., Joshi, R.C., Misra, M.: FVBA: A Combined Statistical Approach for Low Rate Degrading and High Bandwidth Disruptive DDoS Attacks Detection in ISP Domain. In: The Proceedings of 16th IEEE International Conference on Networks (ICON 2008), India (2008), doi: 10.1109/ICON.2008.4772654
12. Gibson, B.: TCP Limitations on File Transfer Performance Hamper the Global Internet. White paper (September 2006), `http://www.niwotnetworks.com/gbx/TCPLimitsFastFileTransfer.htm`

A Novel Image Encryption Algorithm Using Two Chaotic Maps for Medical Application

G.A. Sathishkumar[1,*], K. Bhoopathybagan[2], N. Sriraam[3], SP. Venkatachalam[4], and R. Vignesh[5]

[1] Assistant Professor, Department of Electronics and Communication Engineering, Sri Venkateswara College of Engineering, Sriperumbudur -602108
sathish@svce.ac.in
[2] Professor and HEAD, Department of Electronics, Madras Institute of Technology, Chrompet, Chennai-600044
kbb@mail.yahoo.com
[3] Center for Biomedical Informatics and Signal Processing, Department of Biomedical Engineering
SSN College of Engineering, Chennai 603110
[4,5] Final year student, Department of Electronics and Communication Engineering, Sri Venkateswara College of Engineering, Sriperumbudur -602108

Abstract. The advancement of information technology has provided the possibility of transmitting and retrieving medical information in a better manner in the recent years. The secured medical image transmission will help in maintaining the confidentiality of information. Such security measures are highly essential for multi media data transfer from the local place to the specialist location at the remote place. This paper devoted to provide a secured medical image encryption technique using duo chaos based circular mapping. The given original images are divided into blocks and zigzag scanning is performed .To encrypt the image, chaos based circular shift mapping procedure and scrambling based on cryptography technique are adopted. The efficiency of the proposed scheme is evaluated in terms of statistical measures such as cross correlation and peak signal –to noise ratio (PSNR). It is found that the proposed image encryption scheme yields better results, which, can be suitably tested for real time problems.

Keywords: chaotic mapping, image encryption, logistic map, Bernoulli map, scrambling, medical and tele-radiology.

1 Introduction

Secured communication [12-15],[19-22] plays a vital role in ensuring multimedia content protection which is of primary importance to military and medical applications. Although the conventional cryptography techniques introduce various data encryption schemes, (DES).The scope for better encryption scheme is still to be explored.

* Corresponding author.

N. Meghanathan et al. (Eds.): CCSIT 2011, Part III, CCIS 133, pp. 290–299, 2011.

Recently non-linear chaotic dynamic systems have drawn special attention in providing valuable security measures. This is due to the fact that the basic ideology of chaotic system matches with the fundamentals of cryptography. This paper discusses a novel chaotic mapping technique for the generation of secured key for transmission and retrieval of medical data for medical applications. The security is assured and maintained in the sense that the proposed technique adopts the combination of position permutation and value transformation DES techniques.

In recent years, the advancement of information technology in biomedicine has provided the possibility of transmitting and retrieving medical information in a better manner. For medical applications, secured medical image transmission will help in maintaining the confidentiality of information. Such security measures are highly essential for data transfer from the local place to the specialist location at the remote place. To fulfil such security and privacy needs in various applications, encryption of images and videos is very important to frustrate malicious attacks from unauthorized parties. Due to the tight relationship between chaos theory [5] and cryptography, chaotic cryptography has gain importance in designing image and video encryption schemes. This paper discusses a novel chaotic mapping technique for the generation of secret key for transmission and retrieval of medical data for medical applications. The security is assured and maintained in the sense that the proposed technique adopts the combination of both position permutation and value transformation.

2 Chaos and Cryptography

The recent research activities in the field of non-linear dynamics and especially on systems with complex (chaotic) behaviour [5][11] have showed potential applications in various fields including healthcare. The special characteristics ,such as sensitivity to initial conditions ,randomness, probability and ergodicity makes chaos mapping as a potential candidate to analyze security issues.

2.1 Choatic Maps

The chaos streams are generated by using various chaotic maps. In this paper, 1 D chaotic map is used to produce the chaotic sequence and used to control the encryption process. In this paper, 1D chaotic map is used to produce the two chaotic sequences and to control the encryption process. Among the various maps, logistic map and Bernoulli map are used specifically for generation of chaotic key. Interested readers refer [6].

3 The Proposed Image Security System

The proposed encryption algorithm belongs to the category of the combination of value transformation and position permutation. We first define two bit-circulation functions with two parameters in each function. One is used to control the shift direction and another is used to control the shifted bit-number on the data transformation. In this paper, two different types of scanning methods are used and their performances are analyzed. The images are treated as a 1D array by performing Raster scanning and Zigzag scanning [23, 24].

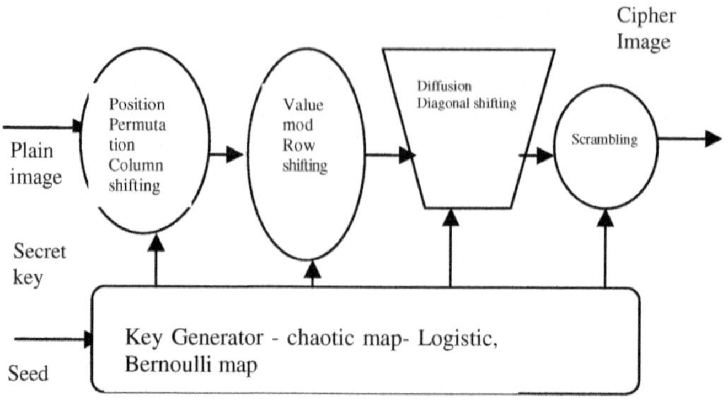

Fig. 1. Proposed Chaos based image cryptosystem

Figure 1 shows the typical schematic of the proposed method. The scanned arrays are divided into various sub blocks. Then for each sub block, position permutation and value transformation are performed and finally scramble to produce the cipher image. The sub key is generated by applying the suitable chaotic maps. Based on the initial conditions, the generated chaotic map are allowed to iterate through various orbits of chaotic maps. Hence, for each sub block various chaotic sequence patterns are applied which further increases the efficiency of the key to be determined by the brute force attack.Then, based on the chaotic system, binary sequence is generated to control the bit-circulation functions for performing the successive data transformation on the input data. Eight 8-bit data elements are regarded as a set and fed into an 8×8 binary matrix. In the successive transformation on each diagonal elements by using these two functions, we randomly determine the two parameters used in the functions according to the generated chaotic binary sequence such that the signal could be transformed into completely disorderly data.

In demonstrating the correct functionality of the proposed signal security system, we have performed the simulation on the proposed scheme. The following steps carried out for the implementation of proposed chaos based mapping technique. Interested readers refer [14] the some definitions and parameters used in this paper.

Algorithm

Step1: Covert 2-D image into 1-D array and then performs a) Raster scanning and b) Zigzag scanning.

Step2: Consider a block size of 8 x 8 and convert them in to binary values.

Step3: Sub key size is 20 bits, it is extracted from the chaos maps of Bernoulli map. The Secret key is SEED, which are the initial conditions of the each map. Based on the initial conditions the chaotic maps are allowed to iterate through various orbits. Then, based on the chaotic system, binary sequence generated to control the bit-circulation functions for performing the successive data transformation on the input data. Given pair of f and f', the combination of p, q, r, t, u and s resulting in the transformation pair may be non-unique which is the secret key.

Step4: Convert the chaotic sub key in to binary values of 20 bits.

Step5: Each 8x 8-sub block of image pixel values circularly shifted by chaos sequence generated from maps.
Step6: The Circular shifting of Diagonal as follows
Definition for Circular Shifting of Diagonal pixels:
The Mapping [14,23] $ROLR_k^{t,u}$ & $ROD_k^{t,u}$ $f \rightarrow f'$ is defined to rotate each pixel at the position (x,y) in the image such that k^{th} diagonal of f $0 \le f \le$, u bits in the up direction if t equals 1 or u bits in the down direction if t equals 0.

In different combinations of p, q, r, t, u and s, the composite mapping

$$(\Sigma_{j=0}^{7} \; ROLR_j^{q,s}) \cdot (\Sigma_{i=0}^{7} \; ROLR_i^{p,r}) . (\Sigma_{k=0}^{13} \; ROLR_k^{t,u}) \qquad (1)$$

Possesses the following three desirable features:
A binary matrix f be transformed into quite different matrixes and different matrixes can be transformed into the same matrix. Given a transformation of pair f and f' the combinations of p, q, r and s resulting in the transformation pair may be non-unique.

Since f is an 8 × 8 matrix, the result of circulating diagonal is h bits and of circulating it (kmod8) bits in the same direction. The r and s are assumed to be in the ranges of $0 \le r \le 7$ and $0 \le s \le 7$.
Step7: Perform the encryption based on the chaotic sequence key values, which is obtained from the orbits of chaos maps iteration.
Step8: Chaos Theory Based Image Scrambling [16] Transformation
For a Gray scale image I of size M x N pixels, we can have an arbitrary chaotic iteration $x_{n+1} = f(1 - x(n)) where x_i \in R$ to generate a chaotic sequence of real numbers. The initial value X_i is the secret key. The following scheme is applied to scramble and unscramble cipher image I.
Step8.1. Let an initial value X_i that is associated to the secret key. Let t = 1.
Step8.2. Iterate from 0 to N - 1 times with the chaotic iteration 8.1, get the sequence of real numbers $\{X_1, X_2, ..., X_N\}$.
Step8.3. Arrange the chaotic sequence $\{X_1, X_2, \ldots, X_N\}$ in descending order , to get the sorted sequence $\{X`_1, X`_2, \ldots, X`_N\}$.
Step8.4. Determine the set of scrambling address codes $\{t_1, t_2, \ldots, t_N\}$, where t_i € {1, 2, ..., N }. t_i is the new subscript of X_i in the sorted sequence $\{X`_1, X`_2, \ldots, X`_N\}$.
Step8.5. Permute the kth column of the cipher image *I* with permuting address code $\{t_1, t_2, \ldots, t_N\}$,namely, replace the t_i th row pixel with the ith row pixel for *i* from 1 to *N*.
Step8.6. If *k* = *M*, end of iteration. Otherwise, let $X_1 = X_N$,and *k* = *k*+1. Repeat the 8.2 to 8.5, to produce double encrypted cipher image data value in 1D form.
Step10: Transform the cipher image 1-Dimension to 2-Dimension.
Step11: Transmit the chaotic sub key via secure channel using public key algorithms.
Step12: Decrypt the cipher image using the same chaotic sub key and SEED.
Step13: Finally, performance analysis is carried out by doing correlation, histogram, loss and PSNR of the original, encrypted and decrypted image.

4 Experimental Results

An image size of 256 * 256 (example: X Ray of Chest, knee and human head etc.,) is considered as plain image and is performed with chaotic map with orbit key. The most direct method to decide the disorderly degree of the encrypted image is by the sense of sight. On the other hand, the correlation coefficient can provide the quantitative measure on the randomness of the encrypted images. General images typically have a higher degree of randomness associated with both the natural random nature of the underlying structure and the random noise superimposed on the image. In order to apply the parameters α and β must be determined according to Step 1. The selection of α and β should follow the empirical law. Based on the experimental experience, general combinations of α and β can always result in very disorderly results. In the simulation, α = 2 and β = 2 are adopted in Step 1. The initial conditions of chaotic maps used are, f(x)=0.5 for Bernoulli map . The offset values for producing various orbits are chosen to be very less than the initial conditions. The visual inspection of Fig. 2 shows the possibility of applying the algorithm successfully in both encryption and decryption. In addition, it reveals its effectiveness in hiding the information contained in them.

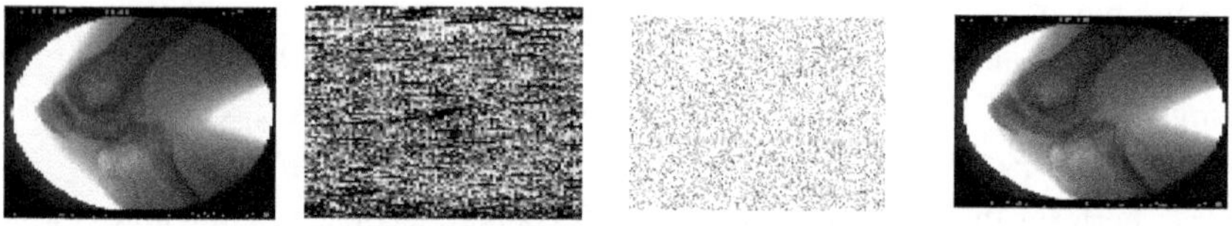

Fig. 2. (a) Original Image (b) Cipher image (c) Cipher image with Maps &Scrambling d) Decrypted image

To prevent the leakage of information to an opponent [10][15], it is also advantageous if the cipher image bears little or no statistical similarity to the plain image. An image histogram illustrates how pixels in an image are distributed by graphing the number of pixels at each intensity level. We have calculated and analyzed the histograms of the several encrypted images as well as its original images that have widely different content. One typical example among them is shown in Fig. 3(b). The histogram of a plain image contains large spikes. The histogram of the cipher image as shown in Fig. 3(d), is uniform, significantly different from that of the original image, and bears no statistical resemblance to the plain image. It is clear that the histogram of the encrypted image is uniform and significantly different from the respective histograms of the original image and hence does not provide any clue to employ any statistical attack on the proposed image encryption procedure.

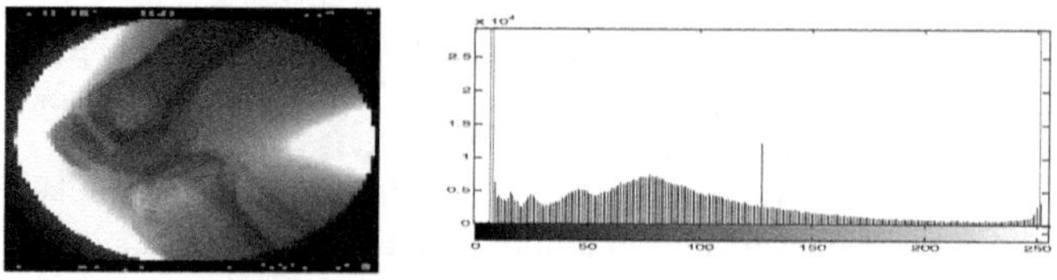

Fig. 3. a) Histogram of original image

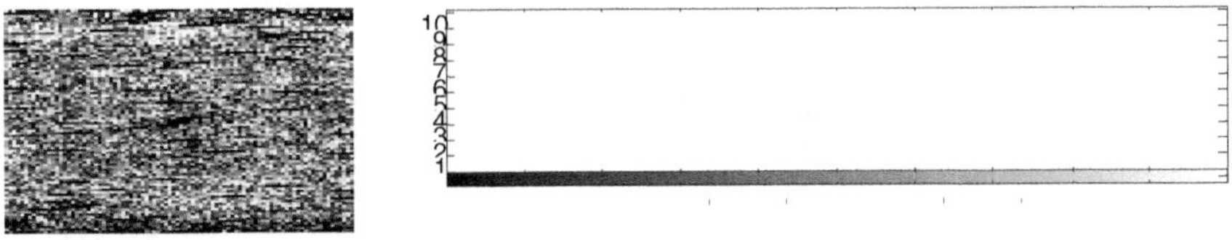

Fig. 3. b) Histogram of cipher image

In addition to the histogram analysis [16, 18, 21], we have also analyzed the correlation between two vertically adjacent pixels, two horizontally adjacent pixels and two diagonally adjacent pixels in plain image and cipher image respectively. The procedure is as follows: First, randomly select 1000 pairs of two adjacent pixels from an image. Then, calculate their correlation coefficient using the following two formulas:

$$r_{xy} = \frac{\mathrm{cov}(x, y)}{\sqrt{D(x)}\sqrt{D(y)}} \tag{2}$$

Fig. 4 shows the correlation distribution of two horizontally adjacent pixels in plain image and cipher image for the all image. The correlation coefficients are 0.9905 and 0.0308 respectively for both plain image and cipher image.

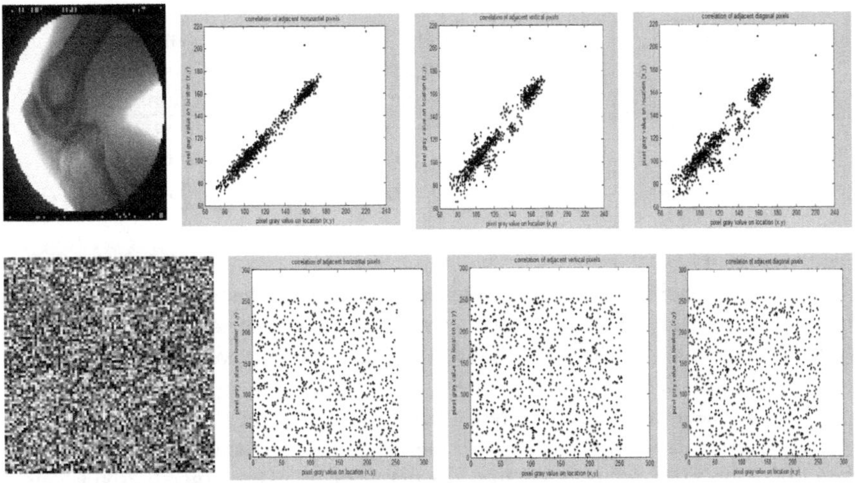

Fig. 4. Horizontal, vertical and diagonal correlation of plain and cipher image

The correlation coefficients [15, 18, and 21] of various maps are calculated and they are compared with each other. The comparison table for various plain images, various cipher images and various maps based on the correlation coefficient are given in the Tables 1-3.

Table 1. Horizontal, Vertical & Diagonal Correlation of Cipher Image

Original Image	Horizontal Correlation	Vertical correlation	Diagonal Correlation	Cipher image with Maps and scrambling
Knee	0.2254	0.4400	0.0012	-0.00070115
Chest	-0.0515	-0.0241	-0.0084	0.00010436
Human Head	0.5930	0.5759	-0.0646	-0.00094391

The correlation coefficient is found for the various directions of scanning patterns employed and the tabulated in the Table 4. The observation shows that the zigzag scanning is more efficient than the raster scanning. In addition, cipher image with multiple maps are more resistant to crypt analyst attacks.

Table 2. Horizontal Correlation Co - efficient for Raster Scanning and Zigzag Scanning

IMAGE	Raster Scanning	Zigzag Scanning
Knee	0.0539	-0.00139
Chest	-0.0535	-0.00590
Human Head	0.0174	-0.0023

Table 3. Correlation Co - efficient in Plain image and Cipher Image

Direction of Adjacent Pixels	Plain image	Cipher image using Bernoulli map	Cipher image with Maps and scrambling
Horizontal	0.9670	0.0781	0.00887
Vertical	0.9870	0.0785	0.00923
Diagonal	0.9692	0.0683	0.00893

Sensitivity Analysis

In differential attacks, to test the influence of one-pixel change on the whole image encrypted by the proposed algorithm, two common measures are used: Number of Pixels Change Rate (NPCR) [12, 13, 18, 19, 21and Unified Average Changing Intensity (UACI) [12, 18, 19, 21].

For, higher security, more difference between cipher images is expected. Number of pixel change rate (NPCR) means the number of pixels changed in the cipher image when only one pixel value is changed in plain-image. The larger the NPCR is, the higher sensitivity in the plain image has and the more difficult the system's security against differential attack. Let two ciphered images, whose corresponding plain images have only one pixel difference; be denoted by CI1 and CI2.Label the grayscale values of the pixels at grid (i,j) in CI1 and CI2 by C I(i,j) and CI(i,j), respectively. Define a bipolar array D, with the same size as images CI1 and CI2. Then, Diff(i,j)is determined by CI1(i,j) and CI2(i,j), namely, if CI1(i,j) =CI2(i,j) then Diff(i,j) = 1; otherwise, Diff(i,j) = 0.

The NPCR [12, 13, 18, 19, 21] is defined as

$$NPCR = \frac{\sum_{i,j} Diff(i,j)}{W \times H} \times 100\% \tag{3}$$

Unified average changing intensity (UACI) means changing intensity of the corresponding pixels of the plain image and cipher image. The larger the UACI is, the more resistant to the differential attack the encryption scheme.

The UACI [12, 18, 19,21] is defined by:

$$UCAI = \frac{1}{W \times H}\left[\sum_{i,j} \frac{CI1(i,j) - CI2(i,j)}{255}\right] \times 100\% \tag{4}$$

Table 4. NCPR AND UACI FOR Cipher Image

IMAGE	NPCR	UACI
Knee	99.993896	-0.000772
Chest	99.843402	-0.00546492
Human Head	98.430901	-0.00839120

PSNR [18, 21] of encrypted image and original image is computed as follows

$$PSNR = 10\log_{10} \frac{hw\left[\max_{1 < i \le m, 1 < j \le n}\{p'_{i,j}\}\right]^2}{\sum_{i=1}^{h}\sum_{j=1}^{w}(p_{i,j} - p'_{i,j})^2} \tag{5}$$

Where h and w are the width and height of original image, while $p$ij and p'ij are pixel values of encrypted image and original image respectively. In the proposed scheme, higher the visual quality of the cipher image is, the less the number of changed pixels will be, and the larger the value of PSNR will be and it is around 9.3158 for the chest image, 9.0061for the knee image and 9.2709 for the head image.

5 Conclusions and Future Scope

In this paper, a novel chaotic mapping encryption scheme for the transmission of medical images is proposed. To protect the medical information, Bernoulli and logistic chaos mapping has been used to generate the secret key. Statistical analysis such as correlation, PSNR, NPCR and UACI where used to evaluate the performance of the proposed scheme. It can be seen from the experimental that the chaos based encryption scheme provides better results and can be tested for real – time problems.

References

1. Smid, M.E., Branstad, D.K.: The data encryption standard: past and future. Proceedings of the IEEE 76(5), 550–559 (1988)
2. Yen, J.-C., Guo, J.-I.: An efficient hierarchical chaotic image encryption algorithm and its VLSI realization. IEE Proceedings—Vision, Image and Signal Processing 147(2), 167–175 (2000)

3. Kuo, C.J., Chen, M.S.: A new signal encryption technique and its attack study. In: Proc. IEEE International Carnahan Conference On Security Technology, Taipei, Taiwan, pp. 149–153 (October 1991)
4. Macq, B.M., Quisquater, J.-J.: Cryptology for digital TV broadcasting. Proceedings of the IEEE 83(6), 944–957 (1995)
5. Parker, T.S., Chua, L.O.: Chaos: a tutorial for engineers. Proceedings of the IEEE 75(8), 982–1008 (1995)
6. Wu, C.W., Rulkov, N.F.: Studying chaos via 1-Dmaps—a tutorial. IEEE Trans. on Circuits and Systems I: Fundamental Theory and Applications 40(10), 707–721 (1993)
7. Biham, E.: Cryptanalysis of the Chaotic-Map Cryptosystem Suggested at EUROCRYPT 1991. In: Davies, D.W. (ed.) EUROCRYPT 1991. LNCS, vol. 547, pp. 532–534. Springer, Heidelberg (1991)
8. Yi, X., Tan, C.H., Siew, C.K.: Fast encryption for multimedia. IEEE Transactions on Consumer Electronics 47(1), 101–107 (2001)
9. Wolter, S., Matz, H., Schubert, A., Laur, R.: On the VLSI implementation of the internal data encryption algorithm IDEA. In: Proc. IEEE Int. Symp. Circuits and Systems, Seattle, Washington, USA, vol. 1, pp. 397–400 (1995)
10. Kuo, C.J., Chen, M.S.: A new signal encryption technique and its attack study. In: Proceedings of IEEE International Conference on Security Technology, Taipei. Taiwan. DD, pp. 149–153 (1991)
11. Dachselt, F., Schwarz, W.: Chaos And Cryptography IEEE Transactions On Circuits And Systems—I. Fundamental Theory And Applications 48(12) (2001)
12. Ahmed, H.E.H., Kalash, H.M., Allah, O.S.F.: An Efficient Chaos-Based Feedback Stream Cipher (ECBFSC) for Image Encryption and Decryption. Informatica 31, 121–129 (2007)
13. Pareek, N.K., Patida, V., Sud, K.K.: Image encryption using chaotic logistic map. Elsevier Image and Vision Computing 24, 926–934 (2006)
14. Chen, H.-C.: Design and Realization of a New Signal Security System for Multimedia Data Transmission. EURASIP Journal on Applied Signal Processing 2003 13, 1291–1305 (2003)
15. El-Fishawy, N., Zaid, O.M.A.: Quality of encryption Measurement of Bitmap Images with RC6, MRC6, and Rijndael Block Cipher Algorithms. International Journal of Network Security 5(3), 241–251 (2007)
16. Xiangdong, L., Junxing, Z., Jinhai, Z., Xiqin, H.: Image Scrambling Algorithm Based on Chaos Theory and Sorting Transformation. IJCSNS International Journal of Computer Science and Network Security 8(1) (2008)
17. Wang, S., Zheng, D., Zhao, J., Tam, W.J., Speranza, F.: An Image Quality Evaluation Method Based on Digital Watermarking. Transactions Letters IEEE Transactions On Circuits And Systems For Video Technology 17(1) (2007)
18. Krishnamoorthi, R., Sheba Kezia Malarchelvi, P.D.: Selective Combinational Encryption of Gray Scale Images using Orthogonal Polynomials based Transformation. IJCSNS International Journal of Computer Science and Network Security 8(5) (May 2008)
19. Zhang, L., Liao, X., Wang, X.: An image encryption approach based on chaotic maps. Elsevier Chaos, Solitons and Fractals 24, 759–765 (2005)
20. Mao, Y., Chen, G.: Chaos-Based Image Encryption. Springer, Berlin (2003)
21. Giesl, J., Vlcek, K.: Image Encryption Based On Strange Attractor. ICGST-GVIP Journal (9) (2009), ISSN 1687-398X

22. He, X., Zhang, Q.: Image Encryption Based on Chaotic Modulation of Wavelet Coefficients. In: 2008 Congress on Image and Signal Processing, IEEE Computer Society Press, Los Alamitos (2008)
23. http://www.mathworks.com/matlabcentral/fileexchange/11362
24. http://users.ece.gatech.edu/~njayant/mmc5/sld012.htm
25. Ozturk, I.: Analysis and Comparison of Image Encryption Algorithms. Proceedings Of World Academy Of Science, Engineering And Technology 3 (2008)

Chest X-Ray Analysis for Computer-Aided Diagnostic

Kim Le

Faculty of Information Sciences and Engineering, University of Canberra
University Drive, Bruce, ACT-2601, Australia
kim.le@canberra.edu.au

Abstract. X-ray is a classical method for diagnosis of some chest diseases. The diseases are curable if they are detected in their early stages. Detection of chest diseases is mostly based on chest X-ray images (CXR). This is a time consuming process. In some cases, medical experts had overlooked the diseases in their first examinations on CXR, and when the images were re-examined, the disease signs could be detected. Furthermore, the number of CXR to examine is numerous and far beyond the capability of available medical staff, especially in developing countries.

A computer-aided diagnosis (CAD) system can mark prospected areas on CXR for careful examination by medical doctors, and can give alarm in the cases that need urgent attention.

This paper reports our continuous work on the development of a CAD system. Some preliminary results for detection of early symptoms of some chest diseases like tuberculosis, cancer, lung collapse, heart failure, etc. are presented.

Keywords: Computer aided diagnosis; Automated disease diagnosis; Chest X-ray analysis; Watershed segmentation; Cancer, tuberculosis and heart failure.

1 Introduction

Heart failure is a very serious disease, and early detection of its symptom is of vital importance. A normal heart may become serious sick just several months later. The treatment of lung cancer and tuberculosis (TB) is easier in their early stages but very difficult in the advanced stages of the diseases. The overall 5-year survival rate for lung cancer patients increases from 14 to 49% if the disease is detected in time [2, 3]. Although Computed Tomograph (CT) can be more efficient than X-ray [3], the latter is more generally available. Therefore preliminary diagnosis for TB and lung cancer, currently performed by medical doctors, is mainly based on chest X-ray images (CXR). This is a time-costly process, and the quantity of images to be examined is at an unmanageable level, especially in populous countries with scarce medical professionals.

Computerised analysis of CXR images can reveal chest diseases in their early stages. An early symptom of congestive heart failure is the increase of the cardiothoracic ratio when it is approaching the limit of 50%. Most cancer and TB cases start with the appearance of small nodules, which are hard to detect at first examinations. Our current work aims at the design and implementation of an automated X-ray image analyser to detect early signs of some chest diseases.

N. Meghanathan et al. (Eds.): CCSIT 2011, Part III, CCIS 133, pp. 300–309, 2011.

When radiologists examine a CXR image, they first need to recognise the two lungs and then find any obvious abnormality. Hence CXR segmentation is an essential process. Image segmentation is often based on the Watershed method [1] or the energy-minimization technique. The Watersnakes method [7], which uses the Watershed as a starting point, tries to make a link between the two segmentation approaches with the introduction of an adjustable energy function to change the smoothness of the boundary of a segmented area. However the Watersnakes method may be not suitable for lung segmentation on CXR.

This paper reports our continuous work on the development of a CAD system for detection of early symptoms of some chest diseases. The paper is organised as follows. Section 2 presents a brief introduction to CXR analysis in the viewpoints of radiologists. In Section 3, we propose a Watershed-based method for lung segmentation. Once lung objects have been isolated, some symptom features of some chest diseases like heart failure, lung cancer and TP, lung collapse, etc. will be identified. The paper ends with a brief discussion.

2 Chest X-Ray Analysis

CXR analysis is a basic task in medicine but it is a complex task based on careful observation, sound anatomical principles, and knowledge of physiology and pathology [9]. PA (posterior-anterior) and lateral chest X-ray images are often read together, and they complement each another. The PA exam is viewed as if the patient is standing in front of the examiner; hence the patient's right lung is on the left of a CXR. In our current work, we focus only on PA.

The basic diagnostic instance is to detect abnormality. To isolate lung objects, radiologists need to know both the structures within the mediastinum forming the mediastinal margins and the lobes of the lungs forming the margins of the lungs along the mediastinum and chest wall. Some abnormality may be recognised easily, but some may need careful examination as well as accurate measurement. For example, the detection of an early symptom of congestive heart failure needs the measure of the thoracic diameter. Lung cancer and TP start with small nodules, etc. which are hard to detect. Comparison different CXR taken in some regular examinations can be invaluable.

3 Chest X-Ray Image Processing

The first task for CXR analysis is to isolate lungs from the background. Different techniques can be used to find lung boundaries. Once the lung objects have been isolated, the CXR image is analysed to detect abnormalities.

3.1 Lung Isolation

On an X-ray image, the gray levels of pixels, ranging from 0 (black) to 255 (white), depend on both the thickness of tissues and their atomic weights, and they are clustered in the middle range of gray levels, and those of air and bone pixels are in the two extremes, black and white, respectively. In the case of a CXR image, the two lungs are darker than the background, and are easy to recognise. However the existence of ribs, shoulders and pulmonary vessels with higher gray levels makes lung boundaries harder to detect accurately (Fig. 1a).

The Watershed segmentation was originally used in topography to partition an area into regions. A Watershed segmentation process starts at some regional minima L_I, the lowest points in the area that water can flow into. The area is divided into some regions V_I (valleys) that are grown from the corresponding minima L_I by adding to V_I, iteratively, unlabelled higher points on their boundaries. The addition is repeated until no more point can be assigned to any region.

In the case of a CXR image, gray levels play the role as that of ground levels in topography. The Watershed segmentation can be used to isolate the two lungs and the dark background. However the existence of the bright region between the two lungs and the bright regions of ribs, shoulders, etc. make the original Watershed segmentation unable to be stopped accurately at the lung boundaries. We propose two modifications:

a) In addition to the minima L_I, we also find some maxima H_J, the highest points. The regions that originally consist of these maxima are called M_J (mountain). The mountain regions are grown, in concurrence with the growing of the valleys, by adding to M_J unlabelled lower points on their boundaries. The modified Watershed segmentation is carried on with the growing of all valleys V_I and mountains M_J. The segmentation is completed when there is no more point can be added to any region.
b) When the modified Watershed segmentation is complete. The boundaries between a lung and the mediastinum may be too far within the mediastinum. A drying process, starting from the maxima, will push the lung boundary back towards the lungs' centres.

The Watershed-based segmentation to find lungs' boundaries of a CXR image is summarised and is illustrated as follows.

Lung Boundary Detection Algorithm

a) Find the gray level histogram for the CXR.
b) Based on the histogram, choose six gray levels GL(i), i = 0, 1, …, 5, which are used to sort the pixels of the CXR into five regions Region (j), j = 0, …, 4, each with a specific percentage of pixels P(j), e.g. 20%, 10%, 20%, 20% and 30%, with P(0) = 20% for Region (0), P(1) = 10% for Region (1), etc., so that

$$\forall \text{pixels} \in \text{Region}(\text{j}),\ \text{j} = 0,..,4,\ \text{pixel.grayLevel} \in (GL(j), GL(j+1))$$

Where GL (0) = 0 and GL (5) = 255, the minimal and the maximal gray levels respectively.

The lung cores (valleys) including pixels with gray levels less than GL (1) then should be in Region (0) (Fig. 1b). Dark pixels on the narrow strips along the left and the right sides of the CXR image (Fig. 1c) also belong to Region (0). Brighter pixels (mountains) in a short vertical strip at the middle of the image belong to Region (3) or Region (4).

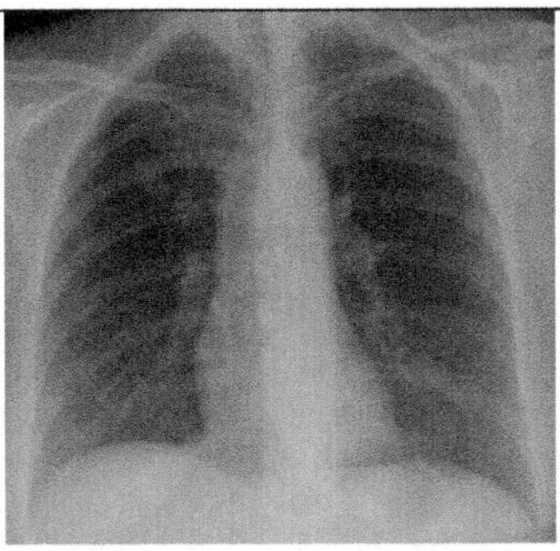

Fig. 1a. Lungs with lower gray level pixels surrounded with brighter background. Bones and pulmonary vessels make lungs' boundaries harder to detect

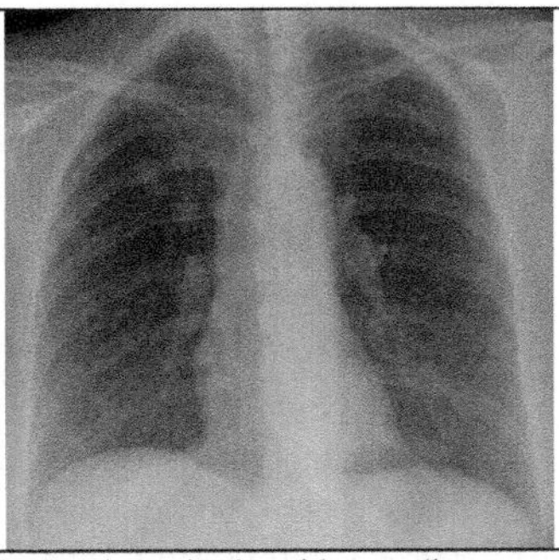

Fig. 1b. Darker pixels of lungs (lung cores) are used as starting points to find other lung pixels

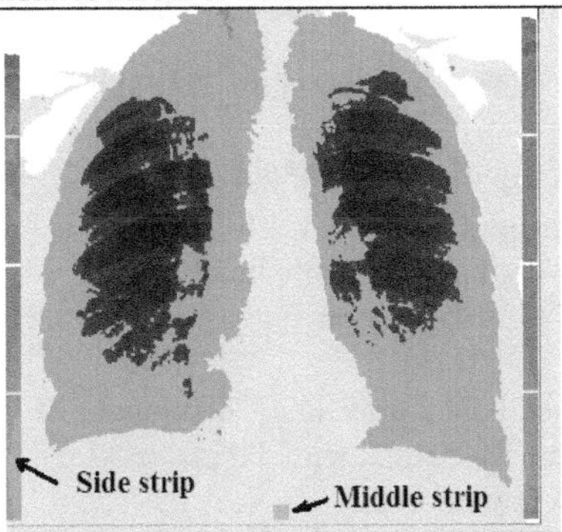

Fig. 1c. The modified Watershed segmentation classifies CXR pixels into three components: lung objects, dark background and bright background

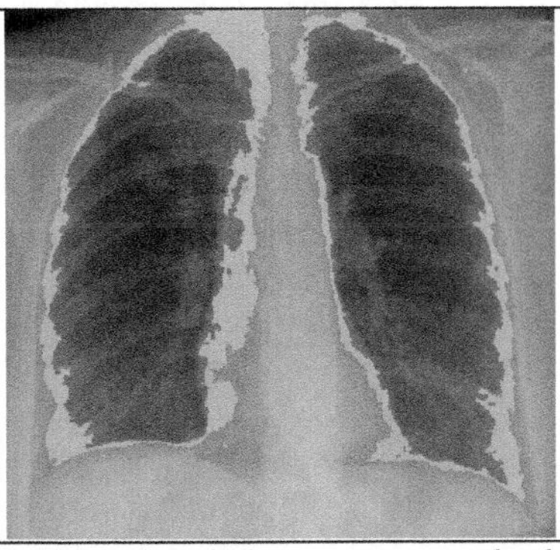

Fig. 1d. A drying process slowly pushed the lung boundaries back towards the lung cores

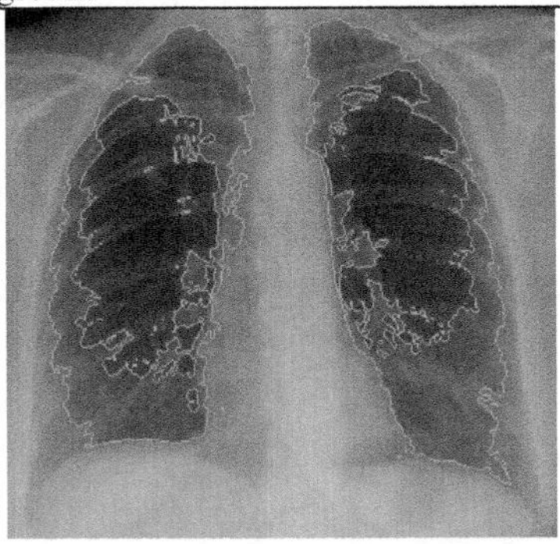

Fig. 1e. After being dried out, the lung objects have boundaries closer to those they should be

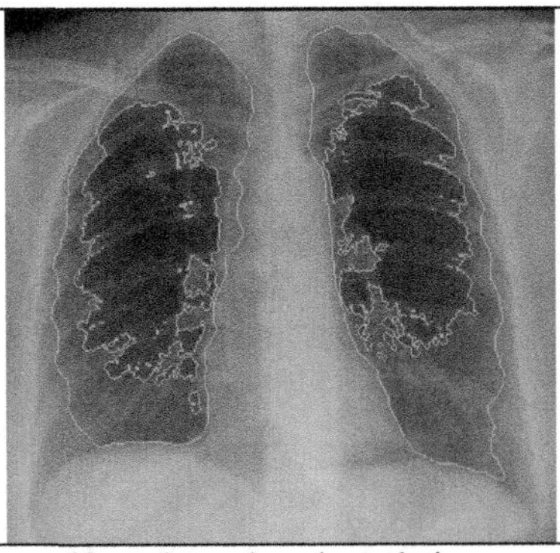

Fig. 1f. Lungs' boundaries are smoothed with some dilution and erosion processes

Fig. 1. Chest X-ray image processing with a Watershed-based segmentation

To differentiate dark pixels of lung cores from dark pixels of the background, we divide the CXR into 4x4 rectangles R (i, j), i, j = 0, 1, 2 & 3.. The dark pixels lying in the four central rectangles, i.e. R (m, n), m, n = 1, 2, should belong to lung cores, and are labelled with +1. The dark pixels on the strips along the left and the right sides of CXR should belong to the background and are labelled with –1. The bright pixels in the vertical strip mentioned above should belong to the background and are labelled with –2.

These dark and brighter pixels of the background (with labels –1 or –2), as well as dark pixels of the lung cores (with labelled +1) are used as growing seeds in the next step.

c) The modified Watershed segmentation is used to expand the lung and the background by repeating the following loop until no more pixel can be added to the lung objects or the background.
   i. Start with a dark threshold DT = GL (1) and a bright threshold BT = GL (3).
   ii. In each iterative loop, slowly increment DT (max. 255) and decrement BT (min. 0) respectively.
   iii. For all CXR pixels, conditionally mark unlabelled pixels as follows:
      - If an unlabelled pixel that has a gray level lower than DT and is within the neighbourhood of pixels with labels = +1 (i.e. lung core pixels) or with labels = +2 (i.e. new lung object pixels), mark it with +2.
      - If an unlabelled pixel that has a gray level less than DT and is within the neighbourhood of pixels with labels = –1 (i.e. dark background pixels), mark it with –1.
      - If an unlabelled pixel that has a gray level higher than BT and is within the neighbourhood of pixels with labels = –2 (i.e. bright background pixels), mark it with –2.
   iv. Label all marked pixels with the values of their marks.
   v. Repeat Steps ii, iii and iv, until no more pixel can be marked.

   As a result, the modified Watershed segmentation classifies CXR pixels into three components: lung objects, dark background and bright background as illustrated in Fig. 1c.

d) A slowly drying process, starting from a short vertical strip at the middle of the bottom part of CXR (Fig. 1c), is applied with a gray level being decremented until it equals a low threshold. The threshold is calculated based on the average value (G1Av) of gray levels of added lung pixels (labelled with +2) and the average value (G2Av) of all CXR pixels. For example,

$$GLThreshold = 0.75G1Av + 0.25G2Av$$

   Fig. 1d illustrates the parts of expanded lung area being dried. The drying gray threshold needs more tuning.

e) The boundaries of the dried lung objects (Fig. 1e) are lastly smoothed by repeating some (say 5) dilution and erosion processes. The final result is illustrated in Fig. 1f.

Once the lung objects have been detected, they can be analysed for abnormalities, some of them are presented in next sub-sections.

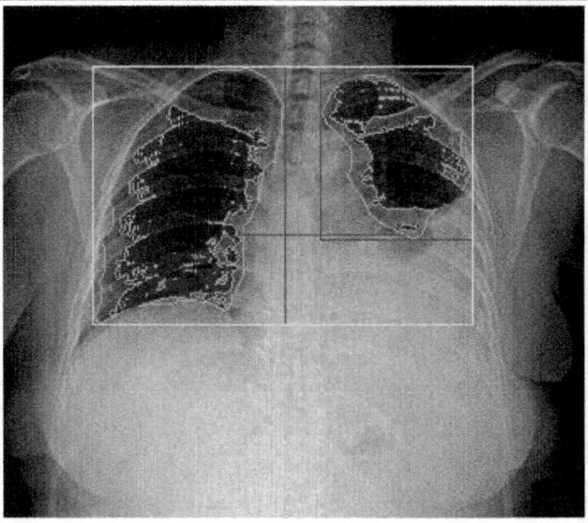

Fig. 2a. The box of the left lung in this CXR [11] has a higher bottom edge. The cardiothoracic ratio is 42%

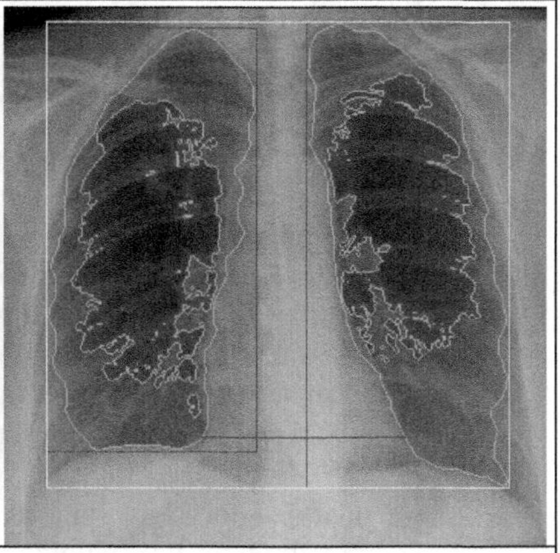

Fig. 2b. The box of the right lung has a higher bottom edge. The cardiothoracic ratio of this CXR [11] is 43%

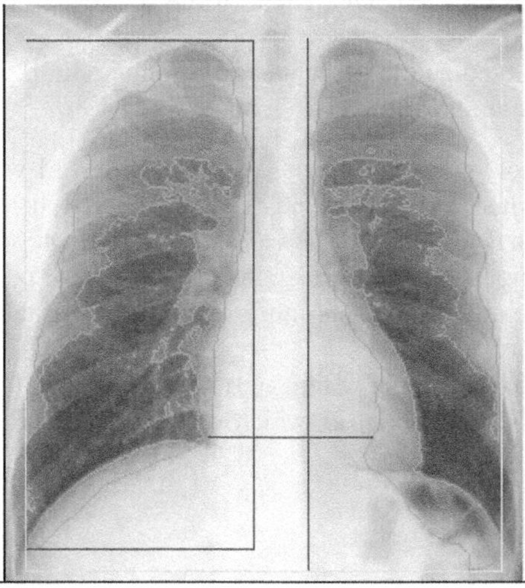

Fig. 2c. Lung with heart starting to enlarge [9] but the thoracic diameter still in normal limit (34 %)

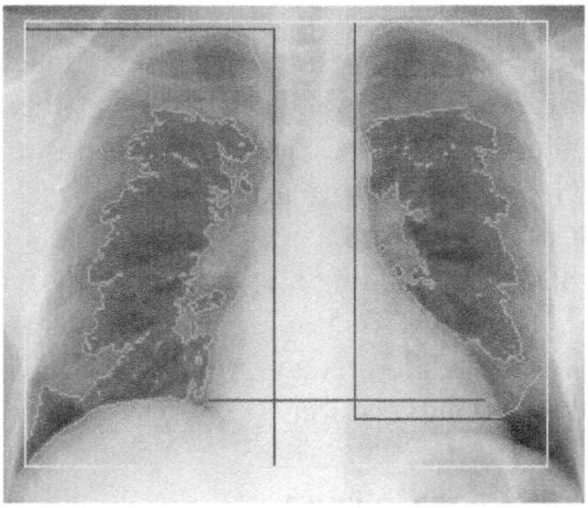

Fig. 2d. Lung with congestive heart failure when thoracic diameter equals 52 % measured on CXR took several months [9] later on the same patient

Fig. 2. Measuring cardiothoracic ratio to detect congestive heart failure

3.2 Thoracic Diameter Measure

An internal thoracic diameter is measured from the right atrial boundary of a heart to its left ventricle apex. The starting of a congestive heart failure can be detected when the cardiothoracic ratio becomes greater than 50% [9].

The thoracic diameter can be measure as follows.

Thoracic Diameter Measurement Algorithm

a) Apply the "Lung Boundary Detection" algorithm to find the boundaries of the left and the right lungs.
b) Draw a rectangle enclosing each lung (called the lung box –Fig. 2a&b).
c) Start from the bottom edge of a lung box that has the bottom edge higher than that of the other. For example in Fig. 2a, the box on the right hand side (i.e. the box of the left lung) has the bottom edge higher. Normally the box of the right lung has a higher bottom edge (Fig. 2b).
d) Detect the inner bottom corner of a lung (left lung –Fig. 2a or right lung – Fig. 2b). For example in Fig. 2b, consider several pixels (e.g. 3) on the inner boundary of the right lung at some consecutive heights above the bottom edge of the lung box. The corner is detected when there is a sharp bend on the boundary.
e) From the corner, draw a horizontal segment to the closest boundary of the other lung (e.g. of the left lung in Fig. 2b). The length of the segment is the thoracic diameter.
f) The cardiothoracic ratio is calculated as the percentage of thoracic diameter compared to the base of the common box of the two lungs.

Fig. 2c & d illustrate two CXR images of the same patient, of which, Fig. 2d was taken several months after the other when the patient heart was detected being enlarged with the cardiothoracic ratio equal to 52%. In the earlier CXR, the ratio is 34%. Most CXR images without heart congestion failure have the cardiothoracic ratio less than 45%. Hence it is necessary to examine patients more regularly when their ratios approaching a value higher than 45%.

The CXR in Fig. 2a has the cardiothoracic ratio within normal range (≤ 45%). However, there is abnormality in the CXR: lung collapse, which will be discussed in the next sub-section.

3.3 Lung Collapse

Lung collapse or atelectasis is a condition where the alveoli are deflated, as distinct from pulmonary consolidation, due to alveolar collapse or fluid consolidation. It may affect part or all of one lung.

Lung collapse can be detected by measuring the volume of each lung. With CXR, the volume is estimated by counting the number of lung pixels. For example, with the CXR in Fig. 2a, the ratio between the volumes of the right and the left lungs is 211%. For normal lungs, this ratio should be about 100%, e.g. 103% for CXR in Fig. 1. The volume ratio may be considered as a feature for diagnosis of heart failure. For example, in Fig 2d, the ratio between its two lungs is 126%.

The ratio between the numbers of pixels of a lung and its lung box is also a good feature for CXR diagnosis, and need further investigation. For example, with the lungs in Fig. 2a, the ratio for the right lung is 64% and the left lung is 59%. For the lungs in Fig. 1, the ratios are 70% and 63% respectively. However, for the lungs in Fig. 2d, the ratios are 58% and 64%.

The ratio between the number of pixels of a lung core and that of the lung is also a feature for CXR diagnosis.

3.4 Nodule Detection

Most cancer and tuberculosis cases start with the appearance of small nodules, which can be benign or malignant with malignant nodules growing up quicker. Nodule pixels are often brighter than the surrounding areas, especially calcified parts, but in some cases, the difference in gray levels is not significant. Furthermore, ribs and pulmonary arteries, which often have higher gray levels, also contribute to the complexity of lung tissue and make some nodules being undetectable. In up to 30% of cases, nodules are overlooked by radiologists on their first examinations [10], although they are visible in retrospect, especially when computer-aided diagnostic tools are used to focus radiologists' attention on suspected areas [3].

We proposed a method to detect early nodules as follows [4].

Nodule Detection Algorithm

a) Apply the "Lung Boundary Detection" algorithm to find the boundaries of the left and the right lung. Now pay attention to one lung, e.g., the right lung (Fig 3a).
b) Apply a small fixed size window –called scanning window– to every pixel inside the lung object, which has not been marked as part of suspected nodules.
c) Find the average and the maximal gray levels of the pixels within the scanning window. Select a local gray-level threshold between the average and the maximal levels.

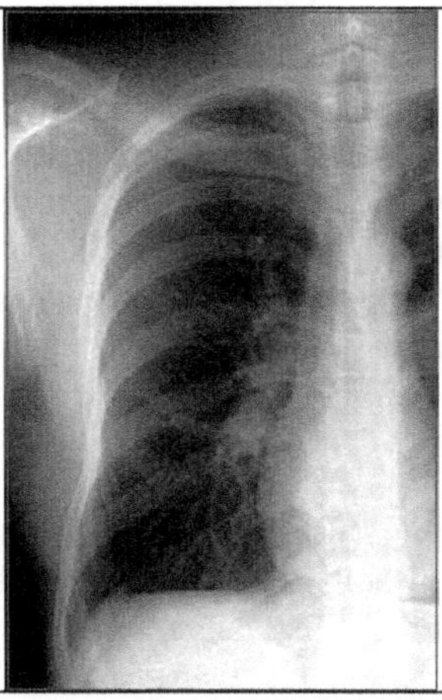

Fig. 3a. CXR image [11] with some small nodules that are hard to detect

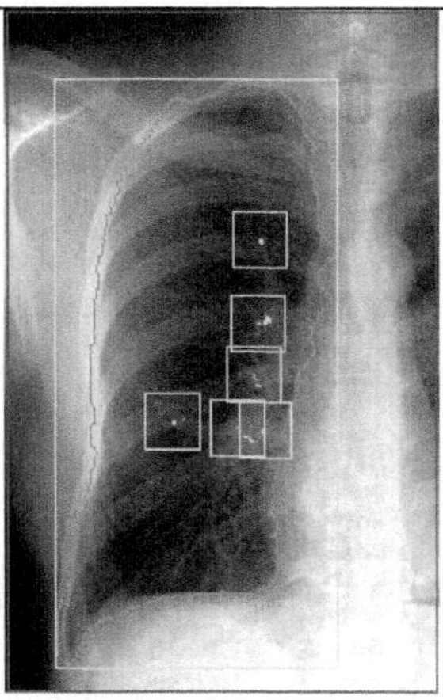

Fig. 3b. Early nodules detected by the proposed "Nodule Detection" algorithm

Fig. 3. Detection of nodules, which are difficult to detect due to the presence of ribs and pulmonary arteries

Table 1. Judgment of a medical professional on the detection of nodules obtained with the proposed algorithm on 10 lung X-rays

X-rays		Number of nodules			
Image	Quality	Detected	+ T	+ F	– F
X0	Good	4	3	1	0
X1	Good	8	5	3*	2*
X2	Hard	12	12*	*	*
X3	Blur	5	*	*	*
X4	Grain	23	*	N*	*
X5	Grain	19	*	N*	*
X6	Poor	5	3*	*	*
X7	Poor	5	*	*	*
X8	Poor	18	11*	7	1*
X9	Poor	7	5*	*	*

d) Count the number of pixels that have gray levels higher than the local threshold. If the counted number is within a specific range then mark the pixel as part of a suspected nodule.

Fig.3b shows the result obtained with the above algorithm. We also applied the algorithm on ten lung X-rays images, and the experimental result is tabulated in Table 1 with the judgement of a medical professional [8]. In the table, the column "Quality" of the "X-rays" field shows the evaluation of the examiner on the quality of the X-ray images. In the "Number of nodules" field, the column "Detected" shows the total number of nodules detected by the algorithm. The other three columns, T+ (true-positive –correctly detected nodule), F+ (false-positive –incorrectly detected nodule), and F– (false-negative –incorrectly undetected nodule), were evaluated by the medical professional. A value with (*) is probably correct. A table cell with (*) only shows that the examiner could not make any decision due to the poor quality image; an N value means "a lot". In summary, the preliminary experimental result shows that at least 50% of nodules were correctly detected, and at most 25% of nodules were overlooked.

We are tuning the algorithm with 100 CXR images collected from hospitals [5, 11].

4 Conclusion

This paper presents some basic methods for automated CXR analysis, which may be used in CAD systems. The experimental results obtained with the proposed algorithms to detect early nodules for lung cancer and TP, as well as lung collapse, congestive heart failure are very encouraging. Further tuning is in progress. Works for other chest diseases are in examination.

Acknowledgement

The work reported in this paper is a continuing work at the Faculty of Information Sciences and Engineering, University of Canberra.

The author is grateful to Dr. Peter Nickolls (Prince of Wales Medical Research Institute, New South Wales), Dr Warwick Lee (Bowral and District Hospital, New South Wales), Dr. Ngoc-Thach Tran (Tuberculosis Hospital, Saigon) and Dr. Quoc-Truc Nguyen (Ulcer and Cancer Hospital, Saigon) for their medical advice and X-ray images supply.

Medical information collected from some medical Web sites [6, 9] is also acknowledged.

References

1. Beucher, S., Meyer, F.: The Morphological Approach of Segmentation: The Watershed Transformation. In: Dougherty, E. (ed.) Mathematical Morphology in Image Processing, pp. 43–481. Marcel Dekker, New York (1992)
2. Gurcan, M.N., et al.: Lung nodule detection on thoracic computed tomography images: preliminary evaluation of a computer-aided diagnosis system. Med. Phys. 29(11), 2552–2558 (2002)
3. Kakeda, S., et al.: Improved Detection of Lung Nodules on Chest Radiographs Using a Commercial Computer-Aided Diagnosis System. American Journal of Roentgenology 182, 505–510 (2004)
4. Le, K.: Lung X-Ray Image Analysis for Automated Detection of Early Cancer and Tuberculosis. WSEAS Transactions on Information Science and Applications 3(12), 2347–2354 (2006)
5. Lee, W.: Private Correspondence. Bowral and District Hospital, New South Wales (2008)
6. MEDPIX, `http://rad.usuhs.mil/medpix/medpix.html`
7. Nguyen, H.T., et al.: Watersnakes: Energy-Driven Watershed Segmentation. IEEE Transactions On Pattern Analysis and Machine Intelligence 25(3), 330–340 (2003)
8. Nickolls, P.: Private correspondence. Prince of Wales Medical Research Institute, NSW(2006)
9. Spencer, B., et al.: Introduction to Chest Radiology, University of Virginia Health Sciences Center, Department of Radiology, `http://www.med-ed.virginia.edu/courses/rad/cxr/index.html`
10. Suzuki, K., et al.: False-positive Reduction in Computer-aided Diagnostic Scheme for Detecting Nodules in Chest Radiographs by Means of Massive Training Artificial Neural Network. Academic Radiology 12(2), 191–201 (2005)
11. Tran, N.T.: Private Correspondence. Pham Ngoc Thach Hospital, Ho-Chi-Minh City (2008)

Overcoming Social Issues in Requirements Engineering

Selvakumar Ramachandran, Sandhyarani Dodda, and Lavanya Santapoor

MSc in Software Engineering, Blekinge Institute of Technology, Sweden
rrselvakumar@gmail.com, sandhyachoudary@gmail.com,
lavanyas87@gmail.com

Abstract. Aim of this research paper is for creating awareness and consciousness of the importance about Social issues in requirements engineering by identifying those issues and analyzing it with the inputs given by several companies across the world. This paper also discusses overcoming those social issues and how currently software industry is handling those issues.

Keywords: Requirements Engineering, BESPOKE, Social issues, Elicitation.

1 Introduction

In the recent few years requirements engineering has become an important phase in software development processes. The factors that affect requirements engineering process directly or indirectly have the influence in the software development. Requirements engineering is the contiguous process of pre-study, elicitation, preparation of requirements specification document, analyzing those requirements, reviewing those requirements, prioritizing those, managing change requests, re-validating the requirements, re-negotiations. Requirements engineering tells about what the system will do without mentioning how it would do [1]. Over the period of time various studies show that requirements engineering is not only influenced by technical things and also by socially related things. Seldom requirements engineers think in line with social aspects of requirements engineering. Various factors of society such as cultural, linguistic, gender, nationality, race, and politics are also playing crucial role in requirements engineering phases started from pre-study to winding up the project. When we identify the social issues which all are common to all projects and overcoming impacts causes by those issues would take requirements engineering into next level of advancement.

2 Research Questions

This research paper answers the following research questions,

1. What are social issues meant in Software industry?
2. In general what are all the considered as social issues in requirements engineering?
   Sub. Question: What are all the potential issues in each requirement engineering phases?

N. Meghanathan et al. (Eds.): CCSIT 2011, Part III, CCIS 133, pp. 310–324, 2011.

3. What is the impact of social issues identified in the requirements engineering phases?
   Sub. Question: How much impact in elicitation phase?
4. How does industry handle the social issues in elicitation phase?
5. What are the level of negotiations and re-negotiations in all the phases of requirements engineering?
6. What is the co-ordination level between teams?
7. Do software companies need psychologist or sociologist in requirements engineering process? [2,3]
8. What are the recommendations for overcoming social issues?

In the subsequent sections, with appropriate research methodologies answers for these research questions are found out and reasons are analyzed. By analyzing answers of these research questions, mitigations for these issues are discussed and identified. The first and second questions are answered through literature review. Various papers published on these social issues requirements engineering topics had been studied and rest of the questions are formulated. For the third question it is answered with the combination of literature studies and the inputs that had been received from the companies through interviews. Fourth question is answered with the inputs from industry. Rests of the questions are answered with the inputs from company and analyzing it parallel with the literature available. For interviewing with companies a set of questionnaire is prepared and given to few selected companies across the globe.

3 Background and Related Work

In each phase of requirements engineering human interaction is inevitable. Wherever people involvement is there, inadvertently social –cultural impacts also be present. Requirements engineering also does have impacts influences caused by social issues. Very few software engineers think that social issues are relevant in requirements engineering perspective. According to Joseph A.Goguen, requirements engineering is no more a technical domain, considering social dimension is a necessity [4].

Because of global market software development had been distributed across the boundaries. To have a better software product, distributed processes had to be integrated well. For an example, "FDSA" system has to be developed and implemented in USA. Requirements for this system would be elicited by engineers from Sweden. Specifications would be written by Chinese employees of the Swedish company and development work would be outsourced to India. Finally the developed system would be tested by US engineers for implementation. In this imaginary scenario different software development processes including requirements engineering are spread across the people with different cultures, languages, belief systems, life style, and political mindset. In this long relay race when baton is passed without any issues, "FDSA" system would be implemented as expected. When we want to trace things back for example, any clarification on newly added requirement it has to be traced back to

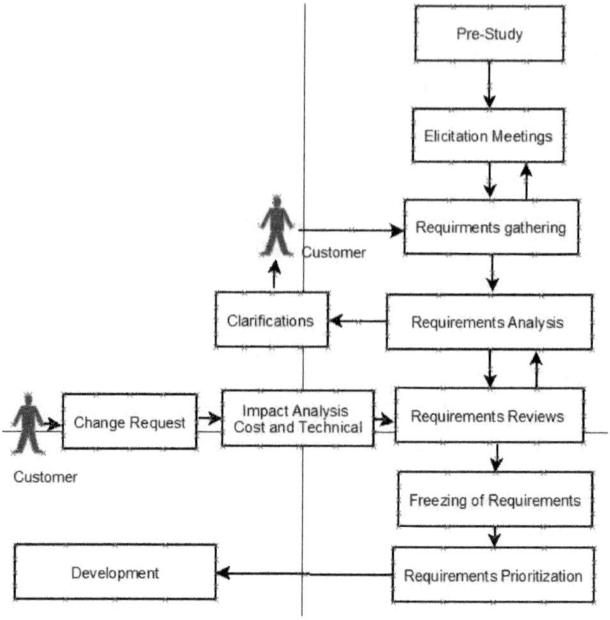

Fig. 1. Requirements engineering phases

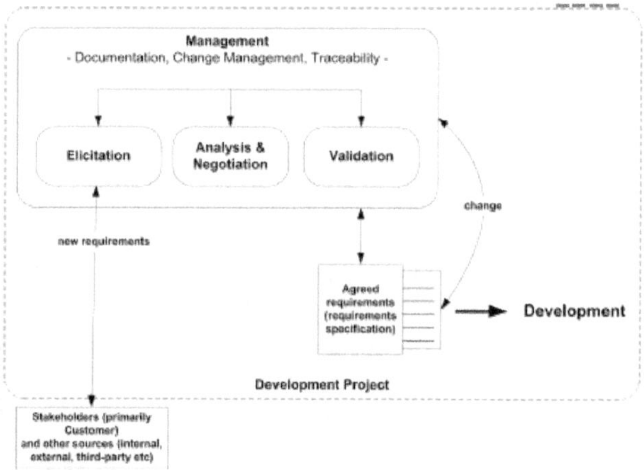

Fig. 2. BESPOKE Process [17]

specification document and to originally elicited, India-Sweden-USA. General assumption is technology is being dealt in 'English' but in real scenario there are many hidden aspects to be handled. Effective communications, level of clarity, interest towards the success of the project are varying factors from people to people, culture to culture. Software companies may practice processes, systems to regulate but at the end of the it is people who have to abide.

BESPOKE and MDRE (Market driven requirements engineering) are two main classification of requirements engineering [1]. Success of the software product in both BESPOKE and MDRE depends upon how well requirements engineering process had been done. As involvement of people in requirements engineering directly influence requirements engineering process, studying the impact of these social aspects has become important in this study. People always tend to show their culture that they have been brought in. Before elicitation meeting knowing about the political cultural scenario about the company that is going to be elicited would help in a great way to know all the requirements needed by the customer. Being biased is one of the traits of human beings. Engineers from one country may have biased opinion about other country's employees. Clashes of different culture and work styles may affect the cohesion of the relationships in turn it would affect the effectiveness of the requirements engineering process. Analyzing and evaluating social scenarios shall add an additional value to requirements engineering studies.

Social perspective in requirements engineering is one of the areas which had been explored less. J.A. Goguen "social issues are inherent to the requirements process, because the needs that drive that process are necessarily embedded in the social, cultural and political world of those who want the system, and hope to benefit once it is built"[4]. J.A.Goguen's works on Social issues in requirements engineering had been taken as the basis of this research paper [4]. Goguen's research was based upon major groups that participate in the requirements engineering process [4].

Classic example of librarian and computer scientists are discussed as two culture clashes which talks about social instincts affect the requirements process [10].

a. issues within the customer organizations
b. requirements team issues
c. issues between customer organization and requirements team [4]

Systematic review had been done extensively for writing this paper.

3.1 Systematic and Literature Review

Search string: ("Social issues" OR "Social perspectives"OR "Ethnography studies" OR "Social Analysis" OR "Social techniques") AND ("Requirements Engineering" OR "Elicitation" OR Prioritization).

With the above mentioned search string literature review was done.

The research is based upon Joseph A.Goguen's work on Social issues in Requirements engineering. This paper gives the outline of the social issues in requirements engineering [4].

Social analysis study of Viller S.Sommerville I is referred for this research [5].

Barry Boehm's how two cultures clash in requirements engineering is studied [10].

Marina Jirotka , Joseph A. Goguen's paper on social and technical issues affect the requirements engineering had added more values to the study.

Table 1. Systematic review articles list

Title	Author(s)
Social Issues in Requirements Engineering,	Joseph A.Goguen,
Social analysis in the requirements engineering process: from ethnography to method	Viller, S.; Sommerville, I.
Sociologists can be surprisingly useful in interactive systems design.	Sommerville, I., Rodden, T., Sawyer, P. and Bentley, R.,
Challenging Universal Truth of Requirements Engineering,	J. Siddiqi,
Requirements Engineering: Reconciliation of Technical and Social Issues	J. Goguen,
Requirements engineering, expectations management, and the Two Cultures,	Barry Boehm, Marwan Abi-Antoun, Dan Port, Julie Kwan, and Anne Lynch,
Techniques for requirements elicitation	Goguen, J.A. Linde, C.
Integrating ethnography into the requirements engineering process	Sommerville, I. Rodden, T. Sawyer, P. Bentley, R. Twidale, M.Dept. of Comput., Lancaster Univ.;
Human errors and system requirements	Sutcliffe, A. Galliers, J. Minocha, S.
Requirements engineering: social and technical issues	Marina Jirotka , Joseph A. Goguen,

4 Research Methodologies

Specific method for collecting data analyzing it is research method. Quantitative, Qualitative and mixed method are three kinds of approaches used in research [6] Using post positivist claims for enhancing knowledge is quantitative approach [6]. Survey and experiments which deals with statistics are used in quantitative approach [6]. Claiming on constructivist perspectives is called as qualitative approach [6]. Mixed method is using knowledge claims on practical perspectives [6].

This research topic requires information from both qualitative and quantitative approaches. From the literature review and studies social perspectives to the requirements engineering had been leant. Methods, approaches and processes taken by companies to overcome social issues are collected through interview and are compared with studies already done on social related studies on requirements engineering.

Concurrent triangulation strategy is chosen for collecting the qualitative and quantitative currently. Since this method is more familiar it had been chosen for this research topic. Reason behind for choosing this strategy is, *"concurrent triangulation helps to confirm, cross validate or corroborate findings with in single study" [6].*

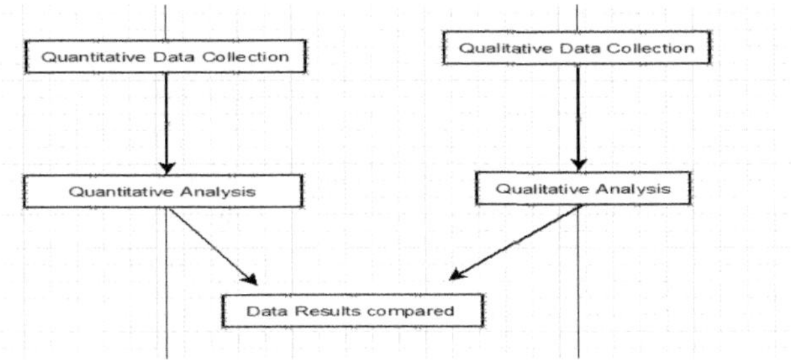

Fig. 3. Concurrent Triangulation Strategy [6]

4.2 Experiment

4.2.1 Experiment Definition

A goal is defined for having a directed way of what should be done and what are all the process to be followed for this research. Goal Question Metric [18] approach is used for defining the goal. The goal defined is divided into four parts. The goal states the purpose of the research and issue to be identified and upon which it has been detected and in whose point of view.

Table 2. Goal definition

Goal	Purpose	To evaluate and arrive recommendations
	Issue	Social issues
	Object	Requirements Engineering
	Viewpoint	From Management and project manager's point of view.

Number of Questions asked: 21
Number of Companies interviewed: 3
Number of people interviewed: 3

4.2.2 Context Selection

The experiment context is requirements engineering involves certain social issues accordance with political, geographical boundaries, race, religion, gender and language. Attributes of the experiment are how these factors are affecting requirements engineering process.

Table 3. Company details

Company Name	Number of Employees	Reason for Selection
Scope International	More than 5000	It is situated all over the globe, and they use video conferencing for elicitation
BSG Leatherlink	50	Medium Sized company
Oviam LLC	3	Small sized and situated in US and done work with customers all over the world.

The following is the list of questions that had been given to the companies.

Table 4. Questionnaire for the interview

1	How are your clients disseminated geographically?
2	Are the same proficiencies to elicit the requirements are used for all the clients?
3	During the discussion with the requirements gathering team will you include a member who belongs to clients country?
4	Do you think that the method used to gather the requirements is beneficial?? if yes justify?
5	While gathering the requirements, what are the several social issues that you face?
6	What is the impact of governmental change upon requirements engineering process?
7	How can the Requirements engineering team assure if the requirements analyst is clarified?
8	Do the requirements engineering team of your organisation have politics among the team?
9	What are the measures taken by you, when the software requirements specification is prepared at one country different from the country where development is to be done?
10	What is the impact of racism and culture while gathering the requirements?

Table 4. *(continued)*

11	Is there any case where your request for changes has been rejected?
12	During financial negotiations are there any problems?
13	What will you do in a situation when your employee is not well dealt and could not conform with the clients employment culture?
14	Do conflicts such as gender bias arise during the process?
15	Will you train the employee who is going onsite for a project regarding social issues of the client countries culture and language?
16	How can correlation be maintained among different teams when disseminated over different countries?
17	How can a situation when a member 'A' of requirement analysis team has not been given proper response by a member 'B' of requirements specification team deliberately, can be handled?
18	What prioritization technique is used in the company? In case of 100 dollar how it is ensured that people are not favouring their own requirements to go up?
19	When your client comes ï
20	Is a formative contest promoted among the substitute teams of the requirements engineering team?
21	In general, what is your opinion about social encroachments in requirements engineering process?

All the questions are close ended questions, are prepared to avoid the ambiguity.

4.2.3 Preparation

Based upon the qualitative research questions were prepared and it was reviewed in the research team meetings. Subjects are chosen according to their pioneer level in this requirements engineering field. No training was required for the subjects before the experiment.

4.2.4 Execution

After completion of preparation phase execution of the experiment was started. Three companies was chosen in three different domains of software development and located across the globe. It took about a week to complete the questionnaire and in prior to the telephonic interview, questionnaire was sent to them. Interview was conducted through Skype and Voice over IP internet telephony providers.

4.3 Hypotheses

Seeking answer for an interrogative statement is research question[6]. The predictions that a researcher wants to make is hypotheses [6]. Null hypothesis and alternative hypothesis are two hypotheses made in this research paper.

H0: Social issues never have any impact in requirements engineering. Hence social perspective to requirements engineering is not a necessity.

Here two variables are social issues and requirements engineering. According to Creswell "*null hypothesis makes a prediction in the general population no relationship or no difference exists between groups on a variable" [6]*. When expected outcome is predicted based upon the prior literature is alternative hypothesis [6].

H1: Requirements engineering has many impacts because of social issues. Hence Social perspective to requirements engineering is necessity.

In order to reject null hypothesis and for supporting the alternative hypothesis questionnaire is prepared, a survey is conducted with software companies to know the current trends in industrial practices to overcome social issues.

5 Validity Threats

5.1 Internal Validity

In order to know how well is the study, validation on threats being analyzed. Internal threats talks about relationship between cause and effect of the study. In this research paper there are no control groups hence it is single group threats[16]. *History, maturation, testing, instrumentation, statistical regression, selection, mortality,* and *ambiguity about direction of casual influence* are the eight sub categories of internal threats [15].

1. History: This is one of the valid threats as experiment (conducting interview on social issues) is only related to the contemporary time. Social issues popped up few years ago are not being discussed.
2. Maturity: This is not been considered as threat experiment is for very short time.
3. Testing: This is not a valid threat as the experiment is conducted for only one time.
4. Instrumentation: There are chances of missing out some research databases due to lack of time and awareness. As far as the questionnaire is concerned simple unambiguous questions were prepared.
5. Selection: Selection of the companies and questions influences the study. Selection of only few companies falls into this category threat.
6. Ambiguity about direct influence: This is one of the threats of our study as size of the companies, number of employees in the company , number of projects that are sourced influences the answers that been given by the companies.

Statistical regression and Mortality do not apply to this study.

5.2 External Validity

1. Interaction and selection of treatment: Software companies are selected and it can be generalized as this study can be done with any software companies. Hence this is not a threat.

2. Interaction of setting and treatment: This is a threat as one-to-one in person meeting is not possible in the short duration of time interview had been conducted.

3. Interaction History and time: The data collected from different companies through interviews in different time and date do not affect the study.

4. Time schedule is made to retain the interest of company employees to answer properly. Interview been done during the time that they have got less work load.

5.3 Construct Validity

Inadequate preoperational explication of constructs, mono-operation bias, mono-method bias, confounding constructs and levels of constructs, interaction of different treatments, interaction of testing and treatment are the construct validity threats [16]. Among these hypotheses guessing, inadequate preoperational explications of constructs are two construct validity threats for this study. In hypothesis guessing the person who has been interviewed can guess what the hypothesis is so that intentionally he can deviate the intended answers. Evaluation apprehension is, most of the industrial people may not reveal the answers for the questions asked. Inadequate pre-operational explications of constructs are having clear understanding of the subjects.

5.4 Conclusion Validity

Conclusion validity is classified into seven subcategories as following: *low statistical power, violated assumptions of statistical tests, fishing and the error rate, reliability of measures, reliability of treatment implementation, random irrelevancies in experimental setting,* and *random heterogeneity of subjects* [16].Among these only reliability measures is the applicable threat to this study. Making the appropriate questions for interview and been conducted with different people across the globe. Since the variations in the answers is one of the main themes of this search , it is made sure that questions are appropriate to social perspectives of requirements engineering.

6 Discussions

6.1 Hypothesis Testing

The problem identified is companies have impact because of social issues in requirements engineering. Null hypothesis and alternative hypothesis are formulated.

H0: Social issues never have any impact in requirements engineering. Hence social perspective to requirements engineering is not a necessity.

H1: Requirements engineering has many impacts because of social issues. Hence Social perspective to requirements engineering is necessity.

Based upon the information collected from software companies null hypothesis rejected as all the companies interviewed had mentioned that they have the influences

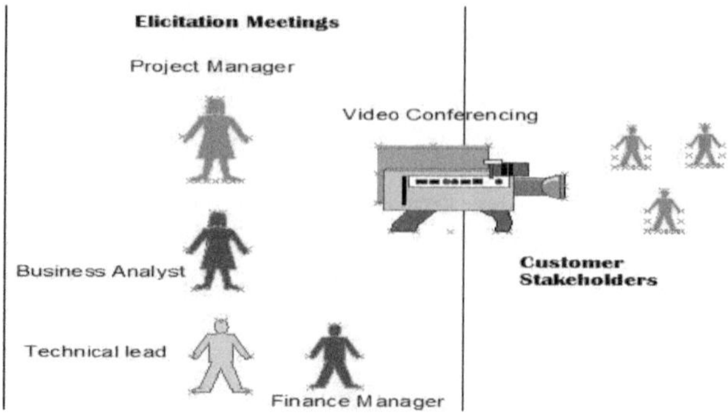

Fig. 4. Video conferencing Elicitation

of social issues in requirements engineering. Hence null hypothesis is rejected in the favor of alternative hypothesis.

6.2 Interview with Companies – Discussions

During our discussion with various companies we have gathered information that all companies have started to work on social issues which are related to requirements engineering. After our analysis among the different interviewed companies, one of the companies among them said that they will provide training on the client and country's culture and they also provide few basic linguistic knowledge of the particular country or region.

Although English is considered to be a global language and most widely spoken by all, some basic courtesy words when spoken during the discussion with the client will be an advantage and sets them into a good mood for a perfect elicitation meeting and he/she (clients) also may get impressed with the discussion and it will be an added advantage to the company

Employees are also given training who are to be interviewed in the elicitation and requirements gathering meetings.

Another company had also shared their views with us that if the time taken to train the people is too short then they will hire few people who are residing in the clients country so that this can carry away the issues on social interaction in a good manner. But this process mainly depends on the size and the cost of the project.

Dinner table discussions also play a vital role than the elicitation meetings itself so many companies are taking at most care in arranging food for the clients and the host teams. After all at the end of the day everyone works hard to fill their stomach

According to one of the Companies' managing director said that nativity linguistic skills plays a important role at crucial junctures in the elicitation process, he faced a problem that he is not able to understand the specific requirements and so he met the person and asked him for some clarification in his native language and got his problem solved though it includes a risk of groupism still it yields benefits.

When we analyzed about the internal politics among the teams in the company then they (companies) that was the only task they could not get away with.

Another company told us that politics are a part and parcel of life so they go on with these and getting rid of these can be done by getting the teams together and this reduces the drift among the teams.

When the discussion is going on about the impact of international politics on requirements engineering process we are said that during few years ago a war has occurred and the companies are not interested to give projects to them and just for no reason they have closed the head office which was located in that country.

Another great impact is the change in the government. It means that change of government in one country may affect the situation in another country

One of the companies we interviewed wanted to meet the real time users of the elicitation team so the people of the elicitation team went as if they are students so that they can know how the system is . While doing that they have come to know that there are potential problems within the employees because of this systems automation they would go on strike.

All the companies concluded that they do not have any issues related to the requirements clarification at the time of specification writing

In almost all the companies, few people from the elicitation team prepares a document and hands it over to the specification writing team after all these are confirmed by SRS team. It must be clear of all these documents as they are the people who finalize the document so they may ask for further clarification if the document cannot be understood

Among most of the companies elicitation team is kept separate from all other teams and if some person is creating any issues personally or intentionally among the teams few companies take a counseling session for him and try to get rid of his problems of why he is having so many issues.

During the company interviews it is to be said that a psychologist is required in each company to get away any mental stress of employees if they have, for example in sports having a psychologist in olden days is a weird situation but now a day's its necessary to get the players into a good form.

Mr.Karunakar Of SCOPE International said that Social consequences do not originate in their organization as they elicit the requirements by video conferencing possibly, social issues can be reduced by conducting video conferencing while gathering the requirements.

Oviam LLC, webhosting company has its customers both in India and USA.CEO of the organization said that emphasizing conflict arise when needs are specified by the client. For an instance, once if the websites design is given Americans rarely do request a change but clients who belong to India often request for a change and financial negotiations since the CEO acclaims India. Depending on the situations this has got both negative as well as positive consequences.

One of the most critical parts among the requirements engineering is the change request.

When a change request arrives it has to be evaluated, analysed revalidated and then it can be approved or rejected. This is the situation where all the members of the requirements engineering team are involved

The requirements engineering team must carefully look after that all the persons involved in the change request directly or indirectly cause any impact or not.

Many companies choose different elicitation techniques based on their companies requirement and on the locality.

Many of the companies choose the development and testing teams to be located at the same place or nearby place to get rid of miscommunication among the teams.

To get larger benefits among companies they outsource employees so that they can cut the cost of the project and can afford cheap laborers for the same work.

7 Recommendations

By nature requirements process itself social, it involves extensive interaction between engineers and clients.

1. Having social cultural training in prior to the elicitation meetings of the particular country

Motivation: Company shall get good name with the clients as they would think company is well prepared.

2. Hiring a person from customers region who can speak in line with client's management.

Motivation: Easy communication

3. A week before the elicitation meeting elicitation team may visit clients place.

Motivation: It would give them a feel 'known place'

4. Video conferencing elicitation meetings

Motivation: As no interactions in person, people shall talk to the point unnecessary diversions in the meeting shall be reduced.

5. Frequent meetings of requirements engineering team

Motivation: Documents will not say everything. Regular meetings would increase the clarity level of documents.

6. As soon as management finds rifts and drifts between teams they should immediately arrange a meeting

Motivation: Negotiation shall solve all kind of problems.

7.1 Further Studies

The various social issues pertained only with BESPOKE organizations have been discussed. Further analysis can be done by communicating with MDRE (Market Driven Requirements Engineering) organizations. With the assistance of ethnography, social issues that conform to BESPOKE organizations can be improved as MDRE.

8 Conclusion

This research paper is compliment and enhancement of J.A.Goguen's work on social issues in requirements engineering [4, 9, 11, and 12]. The components that determine social and cultural consequences are always perplexed .consequences that are caused can never be anticipated, as human behavior cannot be predicted. Answers for these social issues count on several other factors .technical, financial and domain components affect the Requirements engineering adversely along with the social consequences.

Acknowledgements

Mr. Appavu Karunakar, M.Tech(IITM) CISA CISSP cVa, Project Manager Scope International. Chennai, India Fonet # 1 390 12083, Office # 91-44-30681261 Mobile # 91-9840744409.

Mr. Ma. Sivakumar, Managing Director, BSG LeatherLink Private Limited, Plot No 18, First Floor, Jai Nagar 2nd Street, Valasaravakkam, Chennai - 600 087, India Tele: +91 44 6519 1757 / 24765181.

Mr. Ganesh Chandrasekaran, CEO,Oviam LLC, 94 Joann Ct, Monmouth JCT NJ 08852, Tele: +1 732 763 4115 gchandra@gmail.com, for giving replies on email.

References

[1] Lauesen, S.: Software Requirements Styles and Techniques. Addison-Wesley, Pearson Education Limited (2002)

[2] Sommerville, I., Rodden, T., Sawyer, P., Bentley, R.: Sociologists can be surprisingly useful in interactive systems design. In: Proc. HCI 1992, York, pp. 341–353. Cambridge University Press, Cambridge (1992)

[3] Sommerville, I., Rodden, T., Sawyer, P., Bentley, R., Twidale, M.: Integrating ethnography into the requirements engineering process. In: Proceedings of IEEE International Symposium on Requirements Engineering, January 4-6, pp. 165–173. Dept. of Computer., Lancaster Univ. (1993)

[4] Goguen, J.A.: Social Issues in Requirements Engineering. In: Proceedings of IEEE International Symposium on Requirements Engineering, January 4-6, pp. 194–195 (1993)

[5] Viller, S., Sommerville, I.: Social analysis in the requirements engineering process: from ethnography to method. In: Proceedings of IEEE International Symposium on Requirements Engineering, pp. 6–13 (1999)

[6] Creswell, W.: Research Design - Qualitative, Quantitative and Mixed Method Approaches. Sage Publications, Thousand Oaks (2002)

[7] Kitchenham, B.: Procedures for performing systematic reviews, Keele University, technical report, TR/SE-0401 (2004) ISSN:1353-7776

[8] Siddiqi, J.: Challenging Universal Truth of Requirements Engineering. IEEE Software, 18–19 (March 1994)

[9] Goguen, J.: Requirements Engineering: Reconciliation of Technical and Social Issues. Tech. report, Centre for Requirements and Foundations, Oxford University Computing Lab, Cambridge, U.K (1902)

[10] Boehm, B., Abi-Antoun, M., Port, D., Kwan, J., Lynch, A.: Requirements engineering, expectations management, and the Two Cultures. In: Proceedings of IEEE International Symposium on Requirements Engineering, pp. 14–22 (1999)

[11] Goguen, J.A., Linde, C.: Techniques for requirements elicitation. In: Proceedings of IEEE International Symposium on Requirements Engineering, pp. 152–164. Comput. Lab., Oxford Univ., January 4-6 (1993)

[12] Goguen, J.A.: Requirements Engineering as the Reconciliation of Technical and Social Issues Centre for Requirements and Foundations, Programming Research Group Oxford University Computing Lab, Oxford OX1 3QD, United Kingdom

[13] Sutcliffe, A., Galliers, J., Minocha, S.: Human errors and system requirements. In: Proceedings of IEEE International Symposium on Requirements Engineering, pp. 23–30. Centre for HCI Design, City Univ., London (1999)

[14] Jirotka, M., Goguen, J.A.: Requirements engineering: social and technical issues. Academic Press Professional, Inc., San Diego (1994)
[15] Ahl, V.: An Experimental Comparison of five Prioritization Methods- Investigating ease of Use, Accuracy and Scalability. Blekinge Institute of Technology, Thesis no: MSE-2005-11 (2005)
[16] Wohlin, C., Runeson, P.: Experimentation in Software Engineering. Kluwer Academic Publishers, Dordrecht (2000)
[17] Lecture Slides, Practical Requirements Engineering, Blekinge Institute of Technology, Ronneby, Sweden
[18] Wohlin, C., Runeson, P., Höst, M., Ohlsson, M.C., Regnell, B., Wesslen, A.: Experimentation in Software Engineering An Introduction. Kluwer Academic Publications, Dordrecht (2000)

Range-Free Localization for Air-Dropped WSNs by Filtering Neighborhood Estimation Improvements

Eva M. García, Aurelio Bermúdez, and Rafael Casado

Instituto de Investigación en Informática (I3A)
Universidad de Castilla-La Mancha
02071 Albacete, Spain
{evamaria.garcia,aurelio.bermudez,rafael.casado}@uclm.es

Abstract. Many situation management applications involve an aerial deployment of a dense sensor network over the area of interest. In this context, current range-free localization proposals, based on an iterative refinement and exchange of node estimations, are not directly applicable, due to they introduce a high traffic overhead. In this paper, we propose to control this overhead by means of avoiding the transmission of packets which do not contribute to improve the result of the localization algorithm. In particular, a node does not transmit its current position estimation if it does not significantly differ from the estimations of its neighborhood. Simulation results show that the proposed filter reduces significantly the amount of packets required by the localization process.

Keywords: wireless sensor networks, range-free localization.

1 Introduction

Situation management [1] is a novel research topic in which a wide area context awareness system provides information to make better decisions. Some examples of its application may be battlefield operations or disaster response [2], [3], and [4]. Unpredictable and dynamic scenarios like these require dense real-time sensing from a large number of distributed heterogeneous information sources. A suitable approach to quickly implement the information acquisition subsystem is to deploy a wireless sensor network from the air. *Air-dropped wireless sensor networks* (ADWSNs) consist of thousands of sensing devices which are carried in aerial –usually unmanned– vehicles, and deployed over the area of interest.

After the deployment, each network device must determine its own geographical position. This task is usually referred to as *localization process*. Unfortunately, constraints of size, energy consumption, and price make it unfeasible to equip every node in a dense ADWSN with a GPS receiver. However, it may be reasonable to incorporate a GPS only into a small subset of the sensors, and use such *beacons* to help estimate the position of the rest of the nodes. Some localization techniques consider that a sensor node is located somewhere inside the overlapping coverage area of the nodes it can hear. Then, assuming the existence of beacons, a distributed and iterative process is executed, in which each node refines its location estimation

N. Meghanathan et al. (Eds.): CCSIT 2011, Part III, CCIS 133, pp. 325–337, 2011.

starting from the information received from its neighborhood, and transmits the new estimation to the medium. This methodology is usually referred to as *range-free* localization.

By nature, ADWSNs are very dense networks composed of thousands of nodes to guarantee effective and reliable terrain coverage [1]. As it is well-known, dense networks improve the accuracy of range-free localization techniques. This behavior is shown in Fig. 1 ("Error" series). In this plot network density varies by deploying different amounts of nodes over the same area (simulation methodology is fully detailed in Section 4.1). However, density negatively affects traffic overhead, as "Loc packets" series shows.

Other specific feature of ADWSNs that we have to consider is their inherent network variability. Network topology dynamically evolves due to nodes that disappear as their battery is over, and new nodes that appear as a consequence of several sequential deployments in the same area (to extend service lifetime). Besides, although they may be static nodes, we must consider that their position changes while they are being transported and deployed, until they finally drop to the floor. To support this dynamism, we assume that nodes periodically retransmit their localization estimation, even after a stable situation has been achieved. This behavior differs from traditional statically deployed WSNs, in which the localization process finishes when each node obtains its final estimation. In Fig. 1, "Total packets" series shows that this periodic retransmission process introduces a huge additional overhead, if it is applied without any control.

In this paper, we present and evaluate a range-free localization algorithm specifically designed for dense ADWSNs. To reduce the huge traffic overhead generated by thousands of nodes executing an iterative refinement process, we propose to filter node transmissions. In particular, each time a node receives a position estimation from its neighborhood, it decides whether or not to retransmit its new estimation depending on the difference between both estimations and the distance from the sending node. In this way, as we will show in the evaluation section, an important amount of transmissions from very close nodes can be avoided. This filter will be referred to as RIF (*Received Information-based Filter*).

The rest of the paper is organized as follows. The next section introduces the general behavior of range-free localization algorithms. After that, Section 3 presents a localization scheme using the proposed filter. Then, Section 4 analyzes the behavior of this new technique by means of several simulation results. Finally, in Section 5 final conclusions and future work are given.

2 Range-Free Localization

Localization techniques for WSNs may be classified in two general groups, referred to as *range-free* and *range-based* algorithms in the literature. Range-based techniques estimate the position of a node starting from its distance to several beacon nodes. *Time difference of arrival* (TDoA) [6], *angle of arrival* (AoA)[7], and *received signal strength* (RSS) [8]are some methods to measure distances between nodes. The most popular range-based location algorithm is GPS (*global positioning system*).

On the other hand, range-free techniques are based on the next assumption: if a node A can hear the transmission of a node B, then A is located somewhere inside an area centered at B. Some authors propose to model this area by means of a square whose side length is twice the radio range of B. A seminal work is the *Bounding-Box* algorithm [9], in which each node collects the position of its neighboring beacons and then obtains the intersection of the squares centered at these locations. Obviously, the result of this simple operation is a rectangle, whose center is the final estimation that the algorithms produces.

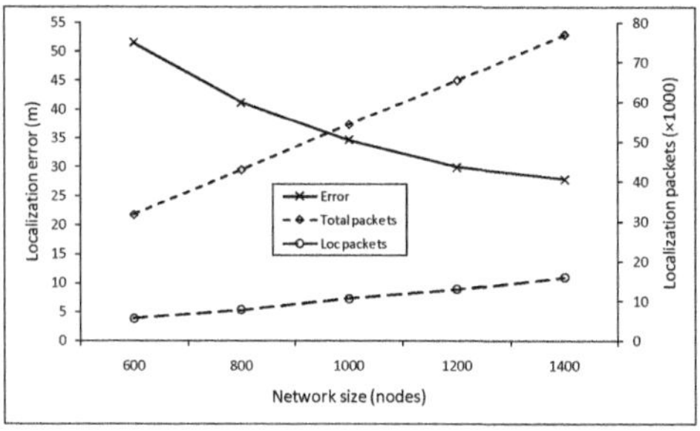

Fig. 1. Localization error and packets as a function of network size, for a generic range-free localization algorithm. "Loc packets": packets sent before the stabilization of estimations; "Total packets": packets sent after 30 minutes (retransmission period: 30 sec).

Several distributed and iterative versions of this *rectangular intersection* technique have been proposed in [10], [11], and [12]. These works consider the existence of nodes not covered by the beacons. In this case, during the activation of each device, it initializes two 2-D points determining its current localization estimation rectangle (A_C). Beacon nodes obtain their accurate position from their internal GPS receiver and, therefore, A_C becomes a point (or a very small square, if we assume a margin of error). In contrast, the rest of the nodes start from an "infinite" A_C. Then, the iterative localization process is started by the beacons, which transmit their position to the medium. From this point, each time a node receives a localization estimation (A_R), it extends the received area by using the radio range. The result of this operation will be referred to as A_{RX}. After that, the receiving node updates its current estimation (A_C), by intersecting it with A_{RX}. Finally, the new estimation is transmitted again. One of these techniques [10] is detailed in the next table:

Algorithm 1. Rectangular Intersection

1: **input**: A_R: received area, A_C: current area
2: **output**: A_C
3: compute A_{RX}: extended A_R
4: $A_C = A_{RX} \cap A_C$
5: send A_C

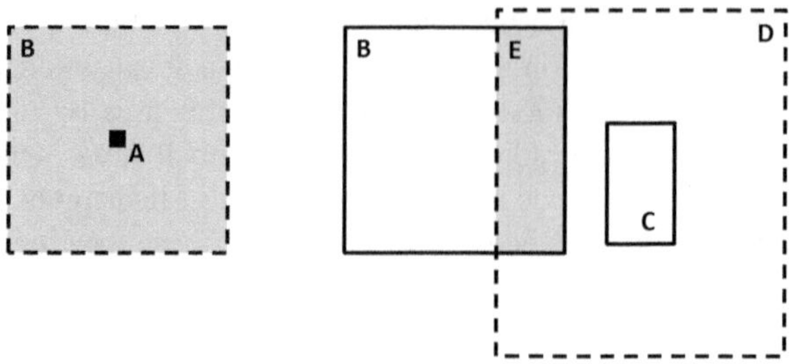

Fig. 2. Example of the iterative localization process

Fig. 2 shows an example of the previous algorithm. In (a), a beacon transmits its localization rectangle (box A). A non-located node (with an infinite A_C) under beacon coverage receives the packet containing that localization rectangle A_R (box A), and extends it by a factor equal to its radio range, obtaining A_{RX} (box B). Then, the node estimates its current position $A_C = A_{RX}$ (box B). Next, in (b), the same node receives a localization rectangle transmitted by another node (box C). Again, it extends the received area and intersects it (box D) with its own (box B), obtaining a new localization rectangle (box E).

Recently, some authors have proposed to model node coverage areas by means of hexagons [13], instead of squares, in order to reduce the additional inaccuracy introduced by this shape. In this case, the result of the area intersection operation is referred to as *pseudo-hexagon*.

Both rectangular and hexagonal intersection techniques employ fix-sized data structures to model the estimated localization areas. In particular, rectangles are represented by two points, while pseudo-hexagons can be represented by three points. Other proposals obtain more accurate estimation areas, but progressively increase the amount of data that must be transmitted. Some examples are convex polygons [14] and Bézier curves [15], represented by up to thirty two and thirty points, respectively. Obviously, the use of fix-sized data structures is more suitable for very dense network topologies, due to the additional overhead introduced by the latter proposals.

3 Filtering Localization Packets

Starting from a generic rectangular intersection technique, in this section we present our proposal to avoid irrelevant retransmissions that increment the overhead without contributing to improve the accuracy. The incorporation of the filter to the localization process has been performed decomposing the algorithm into three separate modules.

A *rectangle computation module* (RCM) is responsible of refining the node estimation in the same way that the proposals described in the previous section. That is, it updates the current rectangle (A_C) by intersecting it with the one received, previously extended by a factor equal to its radio range (A_{RX}). Also, RCM computes two values that will be used later by the filter.

$d_c \in [0\%,100\%)$: fraction of A_{RX} that A_C represents. It may be obtained directly from their respective areas, due to it is satisfied that A_{RX} contains A_C.

$r_s \in [0,R]$ (R=radio range): estimation of the distance to the sender of A_R, obtained from the packet RSS[1].

The next table details the actions performed by the RCM module:

Algorithm 2. Rectangle Computation Module (RCM)

```
input: A_R: received area, A_C: current area
output: A_C, d_C: difference between
        estimations, r_S: distance to sending node
compute A_RX: extended A_R
A_C = A_RX ∩ A_C
d_C = (|A_RX|- |A_C|) / |A_RX|
estimate r_S
```

A *decision module* (DM) is activated each time a node receives a localization packet. After refining the location estimation (by an invocation to RCM), this module decides whether or not to adopt the listened transmission as its own (i. e., as if this node were the sender). For this reason, our proposal is called *Received Information-based Filter* (RIF). The criterion is that the d_c and r_s values (obtained by RCM) simultaneously overcome two predetermined thresholds $d \in [0\%,100\%)$ and $r \in [0,R)$, respectively. Threshold d=0% will imply a non-filtered localization process. A value $r=R$ is excluded, due to it requires nodes covered by more than one beacon (otherwise, the process is stopped at the first iteration). Next, we detail the actions performed by the DM module:

Algorithm 3. *Decision Module* (DM)

```
input: A_R, A_C, d: threshold difference,
       r: threshold distance, t_C: current time
output: t_S: last packet sending time
call RCM(A_R, A_C)
if (d_C ≤ d)   (r_S ≤ r) do
        t_S = t_C
end if
```

Finally, a *sending module* (SM) is responsible of retransmitting the current estimation if it has been too long since the last transmission was performed (or adopted). The next algorithm details the actions performed by the SM module:

[1] Some range-based localization algorithms use RSS to estimate distances among nodes, and then compute node localizations by applying multilateration. Those schemes rely on the assumption that distance measurements are accurate enough. On the other hand, our proposal employs those distances to filter transmissions, instead of using them with localization purposes. As we will show in the evaluation section, the RIF filter is highly tolerant to inaccurate measurements.

Algorithm 4. *Sending Module* (SM)

```
input: tC, tS, p: transmission period, AC: current area
output: tS
if (tC ≥ tS + p) do
      send AC
      tS = tC
end if
```

4 Performance Evaluation

After describing our proposal, in this section we evaluate its behavior by simulation. First, we present the architecture of the simulator used for this purpose and the set of simulations performed. Next, we show and discuss the results obtained.

4.1 Simulation Environment and Methodology

We have used a simulation environment [16] developed for the EIDOS (Equipment Destined for Orientation and Safety) project [2], which proposes a WSN-based architecture applied to wildfire fighting operations. The environment is composed of several independent and interconnected modules, which share information by means of a global database.

The core component of the system is the sensor network simulator. This module consists of a simulation engine, developed in Python, which dynamically controls a TOSSIM [17] simulation. Before starting the simulation, the engine provides each beacon with its position, modeling in this way the real behavior of a GPS receiver. During the simulation, TOSSIM is in charge of collecting several statistics, and store them in temporal files. At the end of the simulation, the Python engine performs the storage of this information on a MySQL database.

In order to obtain realistic results, the simulator incorporates a noise and interference model and the Friis *free-space* signal propagation model. We have modeled the Crossbow's IRIS mote radio XM2110CA [18], applying a transmit power of 0 dBm and a minimum received power of -88 dBm. Under these conditions, we obtain an approximate radio range (R) of 55 meters.

Each simulation run consists on a deployment of a sensor network over a square area of 500×500 meters. For network size, we have considered 600, 800, 1000, 1200, and 1400 nodes, with an associated connectivity degree (average amount of direct neighbors) of 19.35, 25.71, 32.17, 38.91, and 45.81, respectively. Beacons represent a 2% of the network nodes. Each node is deployed in a random position over the area, in a random time during the first 10 minutes of simulation. The simulation concludes after 30 minutes, in order to guarantee that the localization process finishes. Transmission period has been set to 30 seconds.

For all the scenarios described above, we have varied the parameters of the RIF filter. In particular, we have used threshold differences (d) of 0%, 20%, 40%, 60%, 80%, and 99%; and threshold distances (r) of one quarter, one half, and three quarters of the radio range.

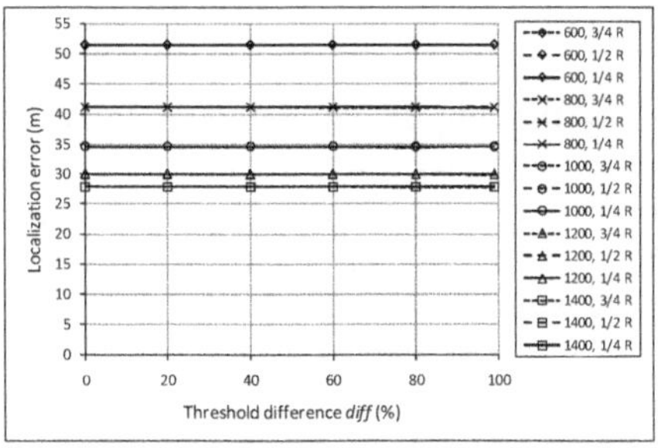

Fig. 3. Localization error as a function of the threshold difference (*d*), the threshold distance (*r*), and the network size

With the purpose of increasing the accuracy of the results, each experiment has been repeated 10 times for each configuration, and average values have been drawn from the solution set and presented graphically.

4.2 Simulation Results

First, we check that the application of the RIF filter to the localization algorithm does not degrade the accuracy of the final estimations. Fig. 3 shows the impact of the filter parameters over the absolute error (variation between real and estimated localizations). In the figure, X-axis represents the threshold (*d*) applied to the difference between A_{RX} and A_C (d_C). Series represent several network sizes and the threshold (*r*) applied to the distance to the sending node (r_S). We can see, as stated in the introduction section, that network density contributes to reduce the average localization error. Indeed, a value *d*=0% deactivates the filter, and the obtained results match with the presented in Fig. 1. On the other hand, it is shown that, for each network size, all the combinations of *d* and *r* obtain the same result.

Fig. 4(a) shows the impact of the filter over the time employed by the process to obtain the final error estimations presented in the previous figure. X-axis represents the threshold difference (*d*), and series represent the applied threshold distance (*r*). In this case, only values for 1000-node simulations are shown. In the figure, we can see

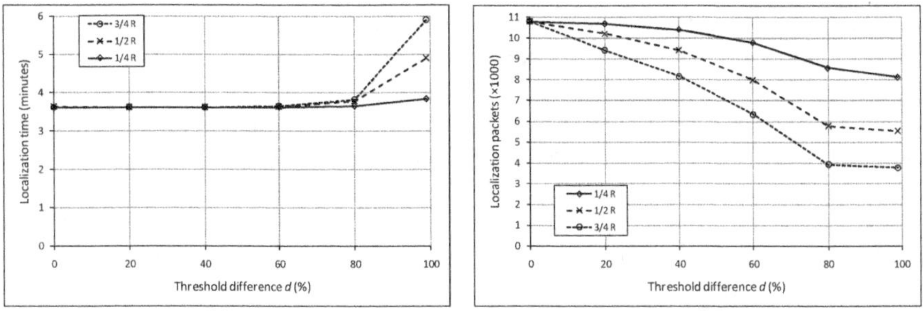

(a) (b)

Fig. 4. Localization time and localization packets as a function of the threshold difference (*d*), grouped by threshold distance (*r*) (network size: 1000 nodes) that only a very aggressive filtering (d>80% and $r \geq 1/2\ R$) is able to significantly slow down the process.

Next, Fig. 4(b) shows the impact of the RIF filter on the traffic overhead introduced by the localization processes shown in the plot (a). Again, X-axis represents the threshold difference (d), and series represent the applied threshold distance (r). Y-axis details the amount of localization packets sent by network nodes until their estimations have been stabilized.

Comparing series, we can see the expected behavior: as the range to close neighbors (under r coverage) increases, traffic overhead decreases. For each series, we can also observe the expected behavior: more restrictive values for the threshold difference (d) contribute to reduce traffic overhead. However, with very high restrictive values (d>80%), this reduction is less noticeable. A combined analysis of Fig. 4(a) and Fig. 4(b) reveals that, in this situation, relevant localization notifications are also discarded, and, therefore, the localization process is slowed down. As filtered relevant transmissions are followed by others, the global consequence is that the process execution is longer, but the traffic reduction is not effective.

A conclusion may be that a tradeoff between execution time and traffic overhead is achieved when tuning the filter with d=80% and r=3/4 R. It only increases the execution time by 5%, simultaneously reducing traffic overhead by 64%.

Fig. 5(a) shows the behavior of the filter during the localization process in function of network size. Threshold distance is fixed to 3/4 of radio range and series represent several threshold differences. A comparative analysis between series reflects the distribution of the obtained values for d_C during the simulations. We can see that the biggest traffic reduction is obtained when d varies from 60% to 80%, independently of network size.

Fig. 5(b) shows the influence of the applied threshold distance (r) on the filter's performance, in function of network size. X-axis represents πr^2 (the portion of the coverage area in which the filter is applied). The threshold difference has been fixed to 80%. We can see that as the area of application grows the relative efficacy of the filter decreases. The reason is that, although the amount of neighbors under the filter coverage increases with r, the probability to obtain higher values for d_C (different estimations) also increases. When d_C>d (fixed) transmissions are considered relevant enough to not be discarded.

On the other hand, as described in Section 3, the distance r_S to the sender is obtained from the packet RSS. For this reason, it may be highly imprecise. The obtained results show that the final accuracy (estimation error) and performance (execution time) of the localization process are not affected by imprecise RSS values that may be considered as imprecise values for r_S. Also, the contribution of the filter to reduce traffic overhead is not affected for this issue. The reason is that estimated distances shorter and longer than real distances tend to offset, canceling their effect on the filter.

Next, Fig. 6 shows the impact of the RIF filter on the traffic overhead introduced by the periodic retransmissions performed once the process has converged, which guarantee the correct localization of nodes dropped in subsequent deployments. Y-axis represents the amount of localization packets sent by all nodes during 30 minutes, assuming the situation shown in Fig. 4(a), in which estimations converge after an average period of time shorter than four minutes. We can see that the application of the filter to the post-localization period is even more efficient than during the localization

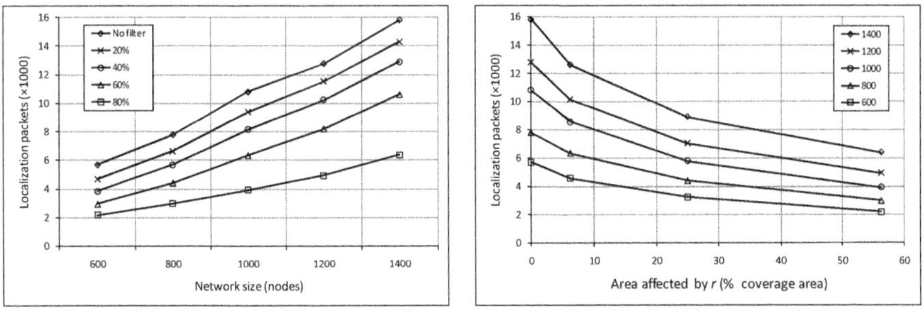

(a) Grouped by threshold difference (d) (threshold distance r = 3/4 R).

(b) Grouped by network size (threshold difference d = 80%).

Fig. 5. Localization packets as a function of the network size and the filtered area

process. Indeed, the filter works fine for very restrictive threshold differences (d>80%), achieving an overhead reduction of 83% (d=99% and r=3/4 R).

Fig. 7(a) shows the impact of network size (and density) in traffic overhead after the localization process has finished. We can see that there is not a significant traffic reduction when tuning the filter with $d \leq 60\%$. The reason is that almost all nodes are accurately located and, therefore, differences between listened estimations and the own ones are frequently substantial. The filter works fine when tuned to d=80% (as when the localization process was being executed). Indeed, it supports a very aggressive filtering (d=99%), in which only completely new information is transmitted. This minimizes traffic overhead, guaranteeing that nodes moving or being deployed will restart the localization process. Also, the filter obtains bigger reductions on traffic overhead when it is applied to very dense networks (86% for the largest simulated topology).

Fig. 7(b) shows the influence of the applied threshold distance (r) on the filter's performance once the localization process has finished. The threshold difference has been fixed to 99%. The global behavior is similar to the observed during the execution of the localization process (shown in Fig. 5(b)), but even more accentuated. The reason is that values obtained for d_C increase as estimation areas decrease, and all the nodes have achieved their respective smallest areas. The figure shows that most of

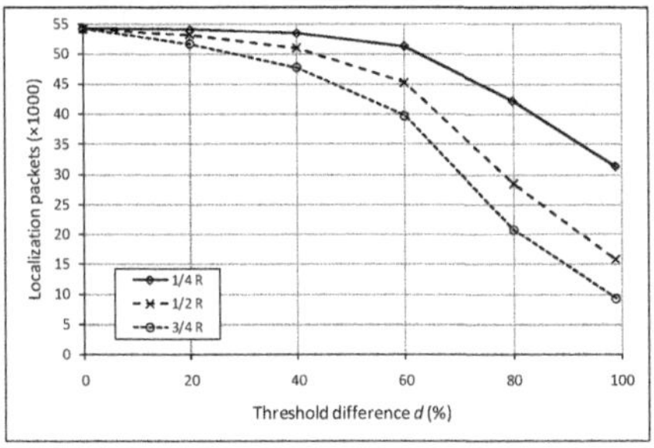

Fig. 6. Localization packets as a function of the threshold difference (d) and the threshold distance (r) (network size: 1000 nodes, execution time: 30 minutes)

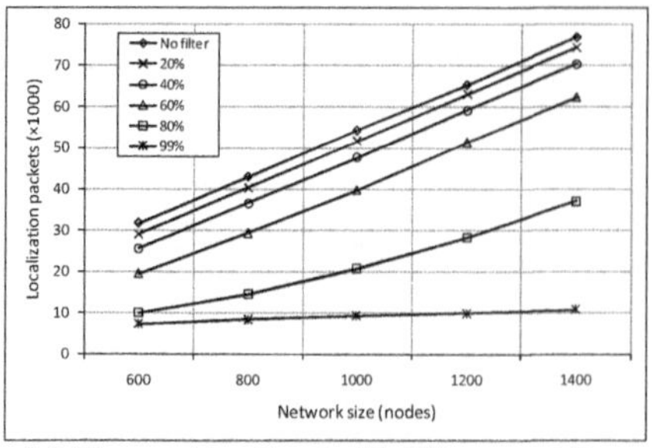

(a) Grouped by threshold difference (d) (threshold distance $r = 3/4\ R$, execution time: 30 minutes).

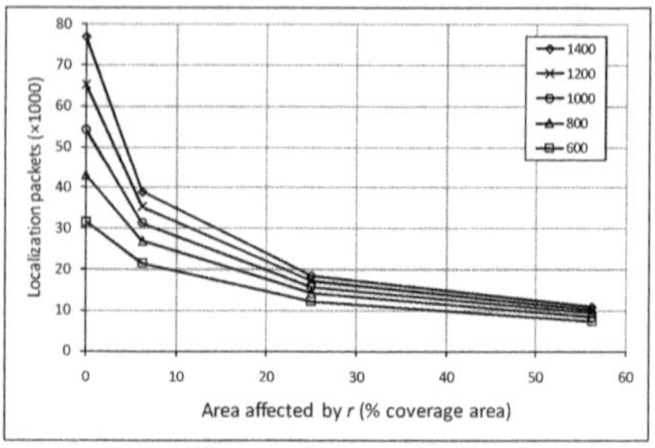

(b) Grouped by network size (threshold difference $d = 99\%$, execution time: 30 minutes).

Fig. 7. Localization packets as a function of the network size and the filtered area, grouped by threshold difference (d) (threshold distance $r = 3/4\ R$, execution time: 30 minutes)

the post-localization overhead (due to estimations periodically retransmitted) is eliminated for $r \leq 1/2\ R$.

We have shown that the RIF filter considerably reduces the global traffic overhead, maintaining the accuracy of final estimations. Now, we study the impact of the filter in their speed of convergence, by analyzing the evolution of estimation error while the process is being executed.

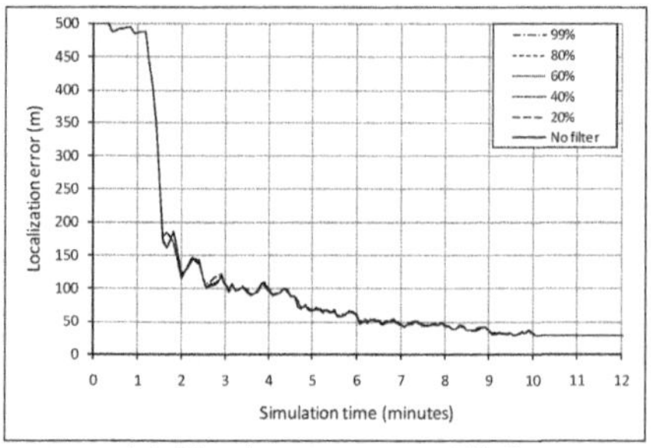

(a) Absolute error, $r = 1/4\ R$

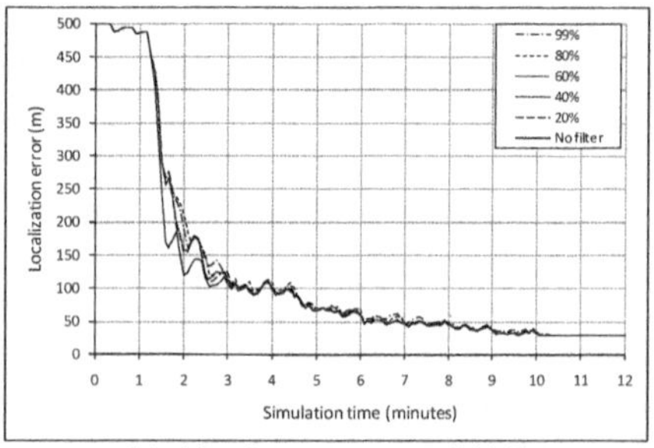

(b) Absolute error, $r = 3/4\ R$

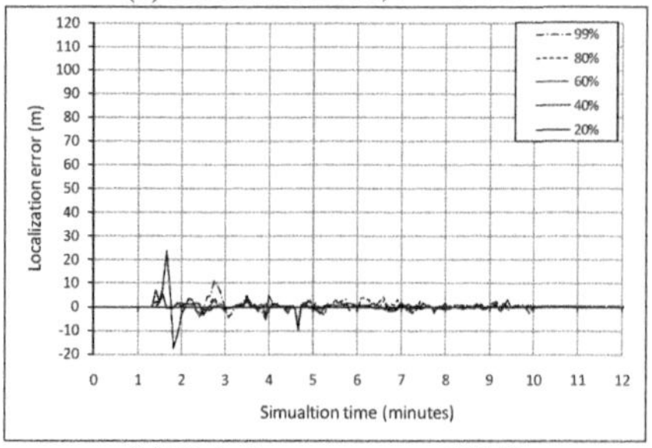

(c) Relative error, $r = 1/4\ R$

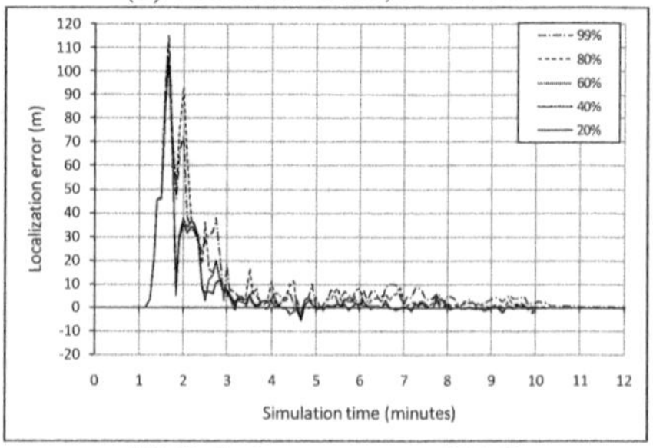

(d) Relative error, $r = 3/4\ R$

Fig. 8. Instantaneous error in function of the threshold difference (network size: 1000 nodes)

Fig. 8 and Fig. 9 show the aggregated instantaneous error versus simulation time. Although an entire simulation lasts 30 minutes, the plots only show 12 minutes, due to the network is deployed during the first 10 minutes and, after that, the aggregated error stabilizes. Each series consists on a single simulation (instead of showing average values). The same deployment, composed of 1000 nodes, has been used in all cases. 20 nodes are GPS beacons, without error in their location estimation. The other 980 nodes have an initial error equal to 500 meters.

In Fig. 8, series represent the analyzed threshold differences. Plot (a) shows the absolute error obtained with the shortest threshold distance. We can see that two beacons dropped in the first minute slightly contribute to reduce the aggregated error (due to the network is not enough connected yet). The third dropped beacon produces an important reduction in the estimation errors.

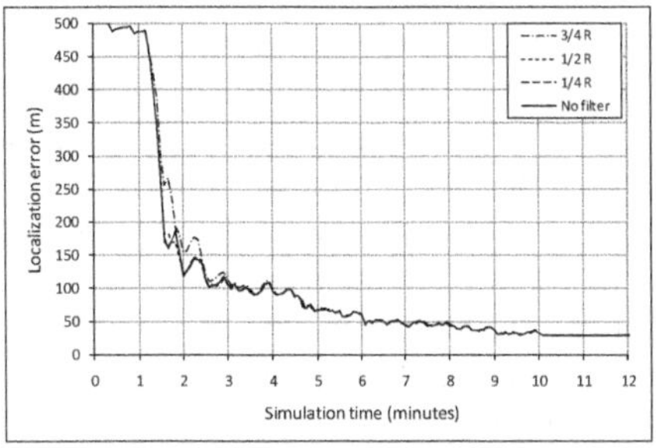

(a) Absolute error, $d = 20\%$

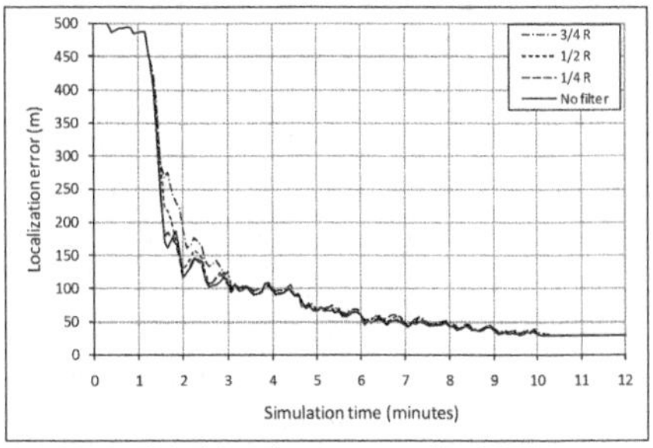

(b) Absolute error, $d = 99\%$

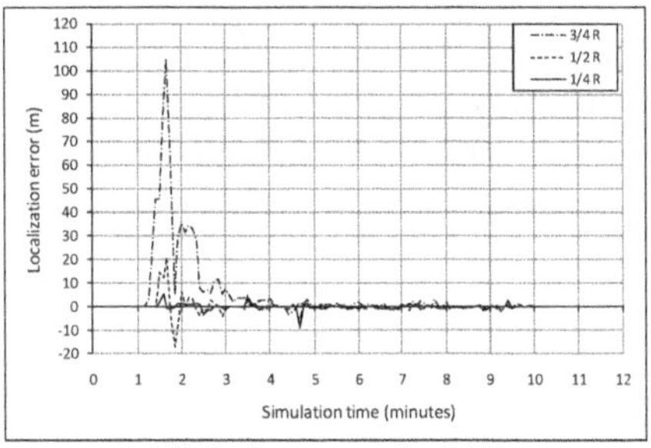

(c) Relative error, $d = 20\%$

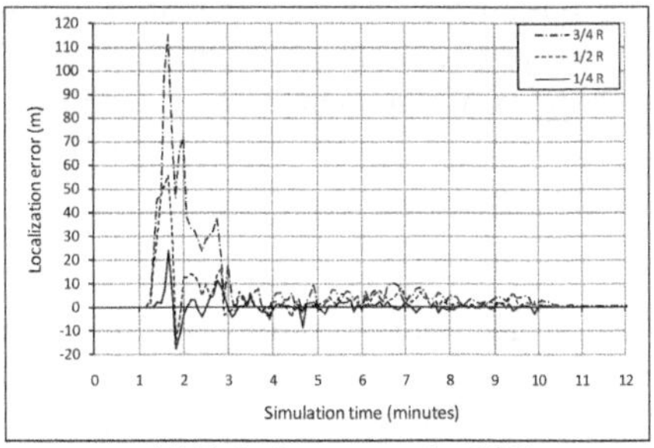

(d) Relative error, $d = 99\%$

Fig. 9. Instantaneous error in function of the threshold distance (network size: 1000 nodes)

To analyze the influence of the threshold difference in the speed of convergence, plot (c) shows the relative error between the series "No filter" and the rest of the series from plot (a). In general, we can observe that all of them present the same behavior and their relative errors are small. Even, sometimes, the relative error is negative, due to certain area reductions contribute to increase the error (for example when a big area centered in the real position lost a portion). Plots (b) and (d) show the results obtained for the largest threshold distance analyzed. Comparing them with plots (a) and (c), we can conclude that as d increases, the filter slow down the estimation updates, especially at the beginning of the process, when the network has low density. The speed of convergence is very sensible to the threshold distance applied.

Fig. 9 is similar to Fig. 8 but, in this case, series represent several threshold distances. Left plots show results obtained for the lowest threshold difference analyzed, and rights plots show the results obtained for the highest one. Upper plots show absolute errors and lower plots relative values. From the figure we may conclude that the speed of convergence of the localization process is not affected by the threshold difference applied.

5 Conclusions and Future Work

In this paper, we have proposed a range-free localization algorithm for dense wireless sensor networks, such as ADWSNs. Our contribution is to employ a *Received Information-based Filter* (RIF) to reduce the huge traffic overhead inherent to the process. In particular, a node decides whether or not to transmit its position estimation depending on if it significantly improves the estimations received from other nodes in its neighborhood. In particular, during the localization process, the filter obtains the best performance when it only transmits high differences between listened estimations and the own one ($d_C \geq 80\%$), reducing traffic overhead to one third (approximately). Once the network is stable, the filter may be more aggressive, allowing only one transmission in a neighborhood ($d_C \geq 99\%$). In this case, traffic overhead is reduced down to 14% for very dense networks. Moreover, we have seen that all these benefits are obtained without penalizing the speed of convergence of the process and the accuracy of the obtained node localization estimations.

As future work, we plan to improve the filter, by removing the distance parameter, which requires RSS radio capabilities in network devices. Other research line may be to incorporate an internal state to the filter, which allows it to make better decisions starting from a sequence of listened estimations. Also, we plan to evaluate the impact of the RIF filter on battery consumption when thousands of network devices are being transported by aerial vehicles.

Acknowledgments. This work was supported by the Spanish MEC and MICINN, as well as European Commission FEDER funds, under Grants CSD2006-00046 and TIN2009-14475-C04. It was also partly supported by the JCCM under Grants PREG-07-25, PII1C09-0101-9476, and PII2I09-0067-3628.

References

1. Jakobson, G., Buford, J.F., Lewis, L.: Situation Management. IEEE Communications Magazine: Guest Editorial 48(3) (2010)
2. García, E.M., Bermúdez, A., Casado, R., Quiles, F.J.: Collaborative Data Processing for Forest Fire Fighting. In: Adjunct poster/demo Proc. 4th European Conference on Wireless Sensor Networks, Delft (2007)
3. George, S.M., et al.: DistressNet: A Wireless Ad Hoc and Sensor Network Architecture for Situation Management in Disaster Response. IEEE Communications Magazine 48(3) (2010)
4. Song, W.-Z., LaHusen, R., Huang, R., Ma, A., Xu, M., Shirazi, B.: Air-dropped Sensor Network for Real-time High-fidelity Volcano Monitoring. In: 7th Annual International Conference on Mobile Systems, Applications and Services (MobiSys 2009), Kraków (2009)

5. Crossbow Technology, Inc., http://www.xbow.com
6. Priyantha, N.B., Chakraborty, A., Balakrishnan, H.: The cricket location-support system. In: 6th Annual International Conference on Mobile Computing and Networking (MobiCom 2000), Boston (2000)
7. Rong, P., Sichitiu, M.L.: Angle of Arrival Localization for Wireless Sensor Networks. In. 3rd IEEE Communications Society Conference on Sensor and Ad Hoc Communications and Networks (SECON 2006), Reston (2006)
8. Elnahrawy, E., Li, X., Martin, R.P.: The limits of localization using signal strength: a comparative study. In: 1st IEEE Communications Society Conference on Sensor and Ad Hoc Communications and Networks (SECON 2004), Santa Clara (2004)
9. Simić, S.N., Sastry, S.: Distributed localization in wireless ad hoc networks. University of California at Berkeley, Technical Report No. UCB/ERL M02/26 (2002)
10. Galstyan, A., Krishnamachari, B., Lerman, K., Pattem, S.: Distributed online localization in sensor networks using a moving target. In: International Symposium of Information Processing Sensor Networks (IPSN 2004), Berkeley, California (2004)
11. Savvides, A., Park, H., Srivastava, M. B.: The bits and flops of the N-hop multilateration primitive for node localization problems. In ACM International Workshop on Wireless Sensor Networks and Applications (WSNA 2002), Atlanta, Georgia (2002)
12. Sheu, J.-P., Chen, P.-C., Hsu, C.-S.: A Distributed Localization Scheme for Wireless Sensor Networks with Improved Grid-Scan and Vector-Based Refinement. IEEE Transactions on Mobile Computing 7(9), 1110–1123 (2008)
13. García, E.M., Bermúdez, A., Casado, R., Quiles, F.J.: Wireless Sensor Network Localization using Hexagonal Intersection. In: 1st IFIP International Conference on Wireless Sensor and Actor Networks (WSAN 2007), Albacete (2007)
14. Datta, S., Klinowski, C., Rudafshani, M., Khaleque, S.: Distributed localization in static and mobile sensor networks. In: IEEE International Conference on Wireless and Mobile Computing, Networking and Communications (WiMob 2006), Montreal (2006)
15. Guha, S., Murty, R.N., Sirer, E.G.: Sextant: A Unified Node and Event Localization Framework Using Non-Convex Constraints. In: ACM International Symposium on Mobile Ad Hoc Networking and Computing (MobiHoc), Urbana-Champaign (2005)
16. García, E.M., Serna, M.A., Bermúdez, A., Casado, R.: Simulating a WSN-based Wildfire Fighting Support System. In. IEEE International Workshop on Modeling, Analysis and Simulation of Sensor Networks (MASSN 2008), Sydney (2008)
17. Levis, P., Lee, N., Welsh, M., Culler, D.: TOSSIM: accurate and scalable simulation of entire TinyOS applications. In: 1st ACM Conference on Embedded Networked Sensor Systems (SenSys 2003), Los Angeles (2003)
18. Crossbow Technology, Inc., http://www.xbow.com

Evolution of Various Controlled Replication Routing Schemes for Opportunistic Networks

Hemal Shah[1,*] and Yogeshwar P. Kosta[2,**]

[1] Ganpat University
[2] Charotar University of Science & Technology, Gujarat, India
hemal.shah@ganpatuniversity.ac.in, ypkosta@gmail.com

Abstract. Opportunistic network is a recent evolution in the wireless community; they constitute basically through cooperation & coordination a special type of wireless mobile adhoc networks. These networks are formed instantaneously in a random manner, provided the basic elements of networks exist in vicinity or approachable limits. In such networks, most of the time there does not exist an end to end path, contact is opportunity based, and, could break soon after discovery. There are many realistic scenarios fitting to this situation, like wildlife tracking sensor networks, military networks, vehicular ad hoc networks to mention a few. To transmit information under such circumstances/scenarios researchers have proposed various efficient forwarding (single copy), replication routing and controlled based schemes. In this paper, we propose to explore, investigate and analyze most of the schemes [1] [2] [3] [4] [5] [6] and present the findings of the said scheme by consolidating critical parameters and issues and suggest through our study the possible future options and scopes.

Keywords: Adhoc networks, opportunistic networks, intermittent connectivity, routing, algorithms, performance.

1 Introduction

MANET is a network where the nodes are so sparse or moving in such a way that there exist at least two groups of nodes for which there is no contemporaneous path between the nodes. If the node movement is such that the inter contact times are unknown and unpredictable then the node contacts are called opportunistic. The enabler to route in opportunistic networks or delay tolerant networks (DTN) [7] is node mobility. Over time, different links come up and down due to node mobility. If the sequence of connectivity graphs over a time interval is overlapped, then an end-to-end path might exist. This implies that a message could be sent over an existing link, get buffered at the next hop until the next link in the path comes up (e.g., a new node moves in range or an existing one wakes-up), and so on and so forth, until it reaches its destination. This model of routing constitutes a significant departure from existing

* This work is carried out as partial fulfillment of Ph.D. research work at Ganpat University.
** Professor, Charotar Institute of Technology.

N. Meghanathan et al. (Eds.): CCSIT 2011, Part III, CCIS 133, pp. 338–347, 2011.

routing practices. It is usually referred to as "mobility-assisted" routing; because node mobility often needs to be exploited to deliver a message to its destination (other names include "encounter-based forwarding" or "store-carry-and-forward"). Routing here consists of independent, local forwarding decisions, based on current connectivity information and predictions of future connectivity information, and made in an opportunistic fashion. The question any routing algorithm has to answer in this context is "How to find next hop when no path to the destination currently exists and/or no other information about this destination might be available?

Despite a number of existing proposals for opportunistic routing [8] [9] [10] [11], the answer to the previous question has usually been "one" or "all". The majority of existing protocols are flooding-based that distribute duplicate copies to all nodes in the network [8] or forwarding based that forwards single copy in the network [12] [13]. Although flooding can be quite fast in some scenarios, the overhead involved in terms of bandwidth, buffer space, and energy dissipation is often prohibitive for small wireless devices (e.g., sensors). Other end, single-copy schemes that only route one copy per message can considerably reduce resource wastage [12] [14]. Yet, they can often be orders of magnitude slower than multi-copy algorithms and are inherently less reliable. These latter characteristics might make single-copy schemes very undesirable for some applications (e.g., in disaster recovery networks or tactical networks beyond enemy lines; even if communication must be intermittent, minimizing delay or message loss is a priority). Summarizing, no routing scheme for extreme environments currently exists that can achieve both small delays and prudent usage of the network and node resources.

For this reason, researchers have proposed controlled copy schemes [1] [15], also known as hybrid scheme or quota based replication or controlled replication, which can achieve both low delays and good transmissions. We have study, analyze and investigate the various controlled based replication schemes. Our objective is to present the first of its kind brief survey on these techniques and explore the problem space.

2 Related Work

Although a large number of routing protocols for wireless ad hoc networks have been proposed [16] [17] traditional routing protocols are not appropriate for networks that are sparse and disconnected. The performance of such protocols would be poor even if the network was only "slightly" disconnected. Due to the uncertainty and time-varying nature of DTNs, routing poses unique challenges. As mentioned in literature [18], some routing approaches are broadly based on forwarding approaches [10] [12] [19] [20] [21].Forwarding scheme(s) uses single message copy and thus, optimizes usage of network resources but suffers from higher delivery delay and poor message transmission ratio; Others are based on flooding or multi copy spreading approach [2] [8]. This scheme achieves better delivery ratio but, in turn, suffers from poor resource utilization and contention. Thus, researchers have proposed controlled based replication schemes [1] [2] [3] [4] [5] [6] [15] as solution to achieve better delivery ratio and optimal resource utilization. We present evolution of various controlled based replication approaches and investigate problem space as how to achieve efficient performance or improve existing scheme with limited number of message copies.

3 DTN Routing

Routing is no doubt the most challenging issue within a DTN. Many restrictions have to be taken into account and traditional network routing protocols will not satisfy the expectations. Links become available without any previous knowledge and the destination node may never be reachable immediately with a contemporaneous end-to-end path. Nodes change their routes randomly or may follow an unpredictable path, buffer and bandwidth restrictions force the protocol to send its discovery and topology information as sparingly as possible and avoid resource consuming mechanisms.

3.1 Routing Classification

Routing in opportunistic networks is broadly classify based on number of copies distributed into network namely single copy (forwarding), Multi copy (replication / flooding) and fixed number of copies (controlled replication / quota based replication/ hybrid scheme.)

3.1.1 Single Copy

There is only a single custodian for each message. When the current custodian as in fig-1 forwards the copy to an appropriate next hop, this becomes message new custodian, and so on and so forth until message reaches its destination.

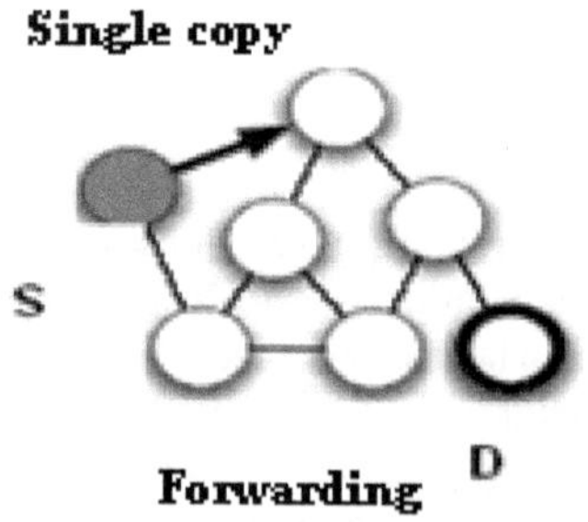

Fig. 1. Single copy routings

Each forwarding step on average should result in progress of the message towards its destination measured as reduction in distance from or expected meeting time with the destination. Question arises how to select the next node for forwarding the message?

Various forwarding strategies [17] are:

(a.) **Most forward (MFR):** Within radius r forwards packets towards the node that makes more progress towards destination.
(b.) **Nearest with forward progress (NFP):** This forwards packet towards the node that is nearest the source and closer to destination.
(c.) **Compass routing:** Selects the neighbor closest to the straight line between sender and destination.
(d.) **Random forwarding:** chooses randomly one the neighbors closer to the destination than the sender.

3.1.2 Multi Copy

Faster way of performing routing in DTN is to flood the message as shown in fig-2 throughout the network [8]. Source nodes spread copies of message to nodes in contact & not containing same copy of message.

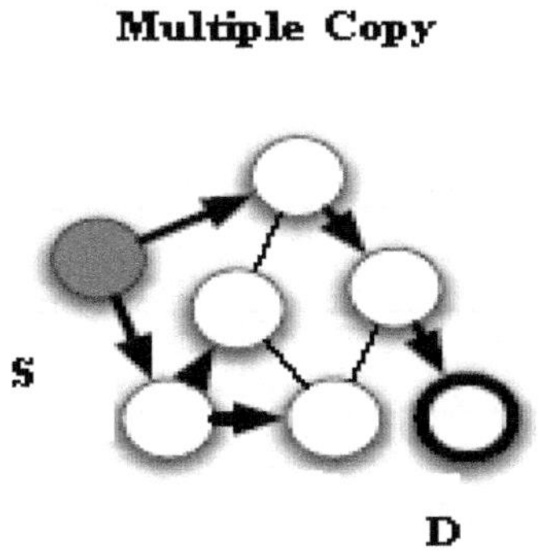

Fig. 2. Multiple copy routing

This way, each node/relay spreads same copy of messages throughout the network until messages reaches to destination. Although this scheme guaranteed to find the shortest path when no contention exists for shares resources like buffer space and bandwidth, it is extremely wasteful of such resources. In realistic scenarios where buffer, energy and bandwidth might be scarce, the performance of flooding degrades significantly due to congestion [10].

3.1.3 Controlled Copy

This hybrid scheme of single and multi copy routing is proposed by [15]. Fixed number of redundant copies is spread into network as shown in fig-3. This helps in achieving the better delivery ratio, few transmissions and lower delivery delays in presence of scarce network resources.

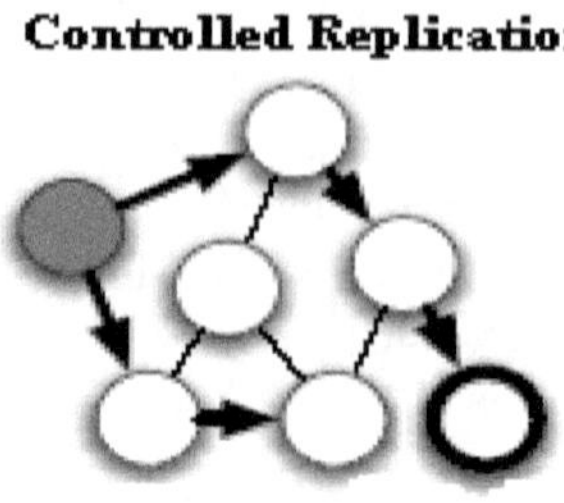

Fig. 3. Controlled Copy

Table 1. Comparative of message copy techniques

Parameters	Single copy	Multiple Copy	Controlled Copy
Reference protocol cited for comparative	Direct delivery [11] [19]	Epidemic [8]	Binary Spray and Wait [15]
Message copies	Single	Many	Fixed number
No. of transmission	Lower	Many	Lower than multiple copy
Delivery delays	Higher	Lower	Lower than single copy
Delivery ratio	Lower	Higher	Better than single copy
Contention	No	Higher	Lower
Network resource wastage	No	Higher	Lower than multi copy

4 Controlled Copy/Replication Schemes

Thrasyvoulos Spyropoulos et.al. has described controlled replication as "When a new message is generated at a source node, this node also creates L "forwarding tokens" for this message. A forwarding token implies that the node that owns it can spawn and forward an additional copy of the given message". During the spraying phase, messages get forwarded according to the following rules:

- if a node (either the source or a relay), carrying a message copy and $c > 1$ forwarding tokens for this message, encounters a node with no copy of the message1, it spawns and forwards a copy of that message to the second node; it also hands over $l(c)$ tokens to that node ($l(c)$ $[1; c\text{-}1]$) and keeps the rest c ¡ $l(c)$ for itself ("Spray" phase);
- When a node has a message copy and $c = 1$ forwarding tokens for this message, then it can only forward this message to the destination itself ("Wait" phase).

Let's look at various controlled replication schemes from its evolution to trends (latest) comprising broadly an network operating environment, algorithm, spraying schemes, message and node distribution, mobility model used, assumptions, advantages and possible extensions.

4.1 Source Spray and Wait (SNW)

For every message originating at a source node, L message copies are initially spread - forwarded by source to L distinct relay. If the destination is not found in the spraying phase, each of the L nodes carrying a message copy performs direct transmission

Algorithm+	[2]
Assumptions	No contention, Infinite bandwidth, Infinite buffer
Spraying strategy	Source node forwards L copies of same message to L first L distinct nodes
Node Movement	I.I.D.
Node Type	Homogeneous
Mobility model	Stochastic model
Advantages	Fewer transmission than epidemic, low contention under high traffic, scalable, requires little knowledge about network
Future extensions	Needs to investigate the performance in presence of real trace based mobility models, Optimal spraying strategy

4.2 Binary Spray and Wait (BSW)

Source of message starts with L copies; when a node A (Source node or relay node) that has n >1 message copies encounters node B (with no copies) it hands over to B [n/ 2] and keeps [n/2] for itself; when A has only one copy left , it switches to direct transmission and forwards the message only to its destination. When all moves in IID manner, binary spraying minimizes the expected time until all copies have been distributed.

Algorithm+	[2]
Assumptions	No contention, Infinite bandwidth, Infinite buffer
Spraying strategy	Binary
Message distribution	Random forwarding in spray phase (Greedy way)
Node Movement	I.I.D.
Node Type	Homogeneous
Mobility model	Stochastic models
Advantages	Fewer transmission than epidemic, low contention under high traffic, scalable, requires little knowledge about network
Future extensions	Needs to investigate the performance in presence of real trace based mobility models & node distribution, Explore spray strategies rather using performing random spray

+ Refer original paper for detailed algorithm.

4.3 Spray and Focus

When a new message is generated at a source node create L "forwarding tokens", with L; if a node (either the source or a relay) carries a message copy and: (i)n > 1 forwarding tokens—perform Binary Spraying ; (ii) n = 1 forwarding token — perform utility-based forwarding [12] with the last encounter timers used as the utility function.

Algorithm+	[1]
Assumptions	Infinite Buffer, Infinite Bandwidth
Spraying strategy	Binary
Message distribution	Random forwarding in spray phase and utility based direct transmission in wait phase
Node Movement	I.I.D.
Node Type	Heterogeneous
Mobility model	Stochastic Models
Advantages	Improves the performance by 20x than spray & wait
Future extensions	Finding optimal distribution strategy

4.4 Spray and Wait with Prophet

In spray phase of BSW, node A forward n/2 messages to node B as soon as A encounters B. Here, history of node encounters has not been considered for forwarding decision. So the forwarding is random and blindfold. In fact, most real users are not likely to move around randomly, but rather move in a predictable fashion based on repeating behavioral patterns such that if a node has visited a location several times before, it is likely that it will visit that location again [10]. So, to improve forwarding performance in BSW, average delivery probability is calculated using Prophet.

Algorithm+	[10] [3]
Assumptions	-
Spraying strategy	Binary with avg. delivery predictability metric
Message distribution	Delivery probability based
Node Movement	Not I.I.D.
Node Type	Heterogeneous
Mobility model	Map based mobility
Advantages	Shorter delay with small value of message copy L
Future extensions	Buffer management policies for history and messages.

4.5 Fuzzy Spray and Wait

Fuzzy-Spray uses fuzzy technique to prioritize messages in the buffer for transmission during next "contact" of the node. Two parameters were used which are simply available locally at the nodes. During transmission it is needed only to pass an extra number forward transmission count (*FTC*) along with the actual message to the peer. The fuzzy membership functions can be adaptively constructed based on known network parameters like number of nodes and range of message-lengths.

Algorithm[+]	[4]
Assumptions	Finite storage and bandwidth, Pragmatic assumption
Spraying strategy	Fuzzy
Message distribution	Based on FTC count
Node Movement	I.I.D.
Node Type	Homogeneous
Mobility model	Stochastic
Advantages	Less sensitive to chosen parameters(fuzzy membership function)
Future extensions	Needs to investigate the performance in real trace based mobility models with heterogeneous nodes

4.6 Density Aware Spray and Wait (DA-SW)

Whenever a node has a bundle to transmit, it computes its current connectivity degree and refers to the abacus to determine the exact number of copies that is expected to lead to some expected delay. Thus, the source sends more copies of a bundle when the topology is sparse and fewer copies when the topology becomes denser. Here, connectivity degree is the number of neighbors node A has within the latest 30 seconds and abacus consists in the average delay experienced by a number of SW(n) variants as a function of the average node degree observed when packets were generated.

Algorithm[+]	[5]
Assumptions	Contention free access, Infinite bandwidth, Infinite storage
Spraying strategy	Accordion phenomenon (slinky effect)
Node distribution	Not I.I.D.
Node Type	Heterogeneous
Mobility model	Roller net , trace based
Advantages	Controls communication overhead keeping delay within expected bounds
Future extensions	Investigate for good predictors for anticipating changes in mobility patterns, Study and use social communities in the roller tour. Detect the social grouping in decentralized fashion and that can be used to make good routing decisions.

4.7 Dynamic Spray and Wait

In spray phase of BSW, node A forward n/2 messages to node B as soon as A encounters B. Here, quality of node (QoN) based on differences of node activity has not been considered for forwarding decision. So the forwarding is random and blindfold. QoN indicates the activity of a node, or the number one node meets other different nodes within a given interval. In the same period of time, the more nodes that one node meets, the greater the QoN. The variation of QoN can dynamically represent the node activity in a given period of time. Ratio of QoNs to dynamically forward the number

Algorithm⁺	[6]
Assumptions	Finite buffer
Spraying strategy	Ratios of QoN
Message distribution	Based on QoN
Node movement	Not I.I.D.
Node type	Heterogeneous
Mobility model	Map based mobility
Advantages	Adapts to real dynamic network conditions, enhances delivery utility
Future extensions	Needs to make more energy efficient

of message copies is used in dynamic spray and wait.Thus, in spray phase when two nodes encounter, they will update the QoN at first and exchange QoN with each other, and then forward message copies according to the ratio of QoNs. In wait phase it performs direct transmission.

5 Conclusion and Future Work

The main contributions of this paper are twofold. First, we have presented through investigation followed by an analysis along with summary regarding controlled based replication schemes. This approach has provided us complete information starting from the evolution of the said schemes to its final stages of development as in operation and in use today. Second, we have also discussed about spraying strategies, node distribution, and node type and mobility model used. This pin points possible investigation spaces and domains fore extension of work, regarding areas pin pointed.

References

1. Thrasyvoulos, S., Konstantinos, P., Raghavendra, C.S.: Spray and Focus: Efficient Mobility-Assisted Routing for Heterogeneous and Correlated Mobility. In: Fifth Annual IEEE International Conference, Pervasive Computing and Communications Workshops, PerCom Workshop 2007, pp. 79–85. IEEE, Los Alamitos (March 2007)
2. Spyropoulos, T., Psounis, K., Raghavendra, C.S.: Efficient routing in intermittently connected mobile networks: The multiple-copy case. IEEE/ACM Trans. on Networking 16 (2008)
3. Xue, J., Fan, X., Cao, Y., Fang, J., Li, J.: Spray and Wait Routing Based on Average Delivery Probability in Delay Tolerant. In: International Conference on Networks Security, Wireless Communications and Trusted Computing. IEEE Computer Society, Los Alamitos (2009)
4. Mathurapoj, A., Pornavalai, C., Chakraborty, G.: Fuzzy Spray: Efficient Routing in Delay Tolerant Ad-hoc network based on Fuzzy Decision Mechanism. In: FUZZ-IEEE. IEEE, Korea (2009)
5. Tournoux, P.-U., Leguay, J., Benbadis, F., Conan, V., de Amorim, M.D., Whitbeck, J.: The Accordion Phenomenon: Analysis, Characterization, and Impact on DTN Routing. In: IEEE INFOCOM 2009. IEEE Communications Society (2009)

6. Wang, G., Wang, B., Gao, Y.: Dynamic Spray and Wait Routing algorithm with Quality of Node in DelayTolerant Network. In: International Conference on Communications and Mobile Computing. IEEE, Los Alamitos (2010)
7. Fall, K.: A Delay-tolerant Network Architecture for Challenged Internets. In: SIGCOMM 2003: Proceedings of the 2003 Conference on Applications, Technologies, Architectures, and Protocols for Computer Communications, pp. 27–34. ACM, NY (2003)
8. Vahdat, A., Becker, D.: Epidemic routing for partially connected ad hoc networks Technical Report CS-200006. Duke University, s.n. (2000)
9. Juang, P., Oki, H., Wang, Y., Martonosi, M., Peh, L.S., Rubenstein, D.: Energy-efficient computing for wildlife tracking: Design tradeoffs and early experiences with Zebranet. In: ASPLOS. ACM, New York (2002)
10. Lindgren, A., Doria, A., Schelen, O.: Probabilistic routing in intermittently connected networks. SIGMOBILE Mobile Computing and Communications Review 7 (2003)
11. Widmer, J., Le Boudec, J.-Y.: Network coding for efficient communication in extreme networks. In: ACM SIGCOMM Workshop on Delay-Tolerant Networking (WDTN 2005), pp. 284–291 (August 2005)
12. Spyropoulos, T., Psounis, K., Raghavendra, C.S.: Efficient routing in intermittently connected mobile networks: The single-copy case. IEEE/ACM Trans. on Networking 16 (2008)
13. Leguay, J., Friedman, T., Conan, V.: DTN Routing in mobility pattern space. In: ACM SIGCOMM Workshop on DTN (2003)
14. Shah, R.C., Roy, S., Jain, S., Brunette, W.: Data MULEs: Modeling a Three-tier Architecture for Sparse Sensor Networks. In: IEEE SNPA Workshop (May 2003)
15. Spyropoulos, T., Psounis, K., Raghavendra, C.S.: Spray and wait: an efficient routing scheme for intermittently connected mobile networks. In: SIGCOMM. ACM, USC (2005)
16. Broch, J., Maltz, D.A., Johnson, D.B., Hu, Y.-C., Jetcheva, J.: A performance comparison of multi-hop wireless ad hoc network routing protocols. In: Proc. Mobile Computing and Networking. - (1998)
17. Mave, M., Widmer, J., Hartenstein, H.: A Survey on Position-Based Routing in Mobile Ad-Hoc Networks. IEEE Network 15(6), 30–39 (2001)
18. Evan, P.C., Jones, P., Ward, A.S.: Routing Strategies for Delay-Tolerant Networks. Computer Communication Review (2006)
19. Frenkiel, R.H., Badrinath, B.R., Borres, J., Yates, R.D.: The infostations challenge: balancing cost and ubiquity in delivering wireless data. IEEE Personal Communications 7(2), 66–71 (2000)
20. Jain, S., Fall, K., Patra, R.: Routing in a Delay Tolerant Network. In: Proc. ACM SIGCOMM, pp. 145–158 (2004)
21. Wang, Y., Jain, S., Martonosi, M., Fall, K.: Erasure-coding based routing for opportunistic networks. In: ACM SIGCOMM Workshop on Delay-Tolerant Networking, pp. 229–236. ACM, New York (2005)

Collaborative Context Management and Selection in Context Aware Computing

B. Vanathi and V. Rhymend Uthariaraj

Ramanujan Computing Center, Anna University Chennai,
Chennai, Tamil Nadu, India
mbvanathi@yahoo.co.in, rhymend@annauniv.edu

Abstract. Computing and computing applications are merged into surroundings instead of having computers as discrete objects are the objective of pervasive computing. Applications must adjust their behavior to every changing surroundings. Adjustment involves proper capture, management and reasoning of context. This paper proposes representation of context in a hierarchical form, storing of context data in an object relational database rather than an ordinary database and selecting the context using heuristic pruning method. Semantic of the context is managed by Ontology and context data is handled by Object relational database. These two modeling elements are associated to each other by semantics relations build in the ontology. The separation of modeling elements loads only relevant context data into the reasoner. This influences the only limited amount of context data in the reasoning space which further improves the performance of the reasoning process.

Keywords: Context Aware Computing, Pervasive Computing, Ontology, Object Relational DataBase.

1 Introduction

Advancement in computing application is due to the evolutional growth of distributed middleware. The integration of mobile clients into a distributed environments and the ad-hoc networking of dynamic components are becoming important in all areas of applications. The continuing technical progress in computing and communication lead to an all-encompassing use of networks and computing power called ubiquitous or pervasive computing [1]. Pervasive computing system targets at constantly adapting their behavior in order to meet the needs of users within every changing physical, social, computing and communication context. Pervasive devices make ad-hoc connections among them and may be connected to different types of sensors to capture changes in the environment. In the evolution chain from centralized computing to pervasive computing as presented by [2] [3], Context awareness is at the heart of pervasive computing problems. Context can be defined as an operational term whose definition depends on the intension for which it is collected and the interpretation of the operations involved on an entity at a particular time and space rather than the inherent characteristics of the entities and the operations themselves according to Dey

N. Meghanathan et al. (Eds.): CCSIT 2011, Part III, CCIS 133, pp. 348–357, 2011.

& Winogards [4, 5]. The complexity of such problems increases in multiplicative fashion rather than additive with the addition of new components into the chain.

2 Existing Works

Data required for modeling are obtained from the applications using sensors. Sensors can be physical, virtual or logical sensors [6].Physical data are captured using physical sensors. Virtual sensors are software processes which refer to data context. Logical sensors are the hybrid of the physical and virtual sensors and are used to solve complex tasks. After collecting the data from the application, it has to be represented in a suitable way for processing. Various modeling approaches are introduced to support standardization of techniques to present context for productive reasoning in different application area. The major classifications of context management modeling approaches are *key-Value-Pair modeling, Graphical modeling, object oriented modeling, logic based modeling, Markup scheme modeling and Ontology modeling [3].* Key-Value –Pair modeling is the simplest category of the models. They are not very efficient for sophisticated and structuring purposes. It supports only exact matching and no inheritance. Graphical modeling is particularly useful for structuring. It is not used on instance level. Object oriented modeling has a strong encapsulation and reusability feature. Logic based modeling uses logic expressions to define conditions on which a concluding expression or fact may be derived from a set of other expressions or facts. Context is defined as facts, expressions and rules and has a high degree of formality. Markup schema modeling uses standard markup languages or their extensions to represent context data. Ontology based models use ontology and related tools to represent context data and its semantics. Ubiquitous computing systems make high demands on context modeling approach in terms of the *Distributed composition (dc), Partial validation(pv), Richness and quality of information (qua), Incompleteness and ambiguity (inc), Level of formality (for), Applicability to existing environments (app)* [3].Context model and its data varies with notably high dynamics in terms of time, network topology and source *(dc)*.Partial validation *(pv)* is highly desirable to be able to partially validate contextual knowledge on structure as well as on instance level against a context model in use even if there is no single place or point in time where the contextual knowledge is available on one node as a result of distributed composition. This is important because of complexity of contextual inter relationships, which make any modeling intention error-prone. The quality of information delivered by a sensor varies over time as well as the richness of information provided by different kinds of sensors. Context model must support quality (qua) and richness indications. Contextual information may be incomplete, if information is gathered from sensor networks. Context model must handle interpolation of incomplete data on the instance level *(inc)*.Contextual facts and interrelationships must be defined in a precise and traceable manner (for).A context model must be applicable within the existing infrastructure of ubiquitous computing environments (app). Summary of appropriateness of modeling approaches [3] is given in Table 1. Among all the modeling approaches, ontology based context model is more suitable for context aware computing.

Table 1. Summary of appropriateness of modeling approaches

Requirement	Approaches				
	Markup scheme	Graphical Models	OO models	Logic based	Ontology based
Distributed composition	+	-	++	++	++
Partial validation	++	-	+	-	++
Quality of information	-	+	+	-	+
Incompleteness/ ambiguity	-	-	+	-	+
Level of formality	+	+	+	++	++
Applicability	++	+	+	-	+
(Key: ++ Comprehensive + Partial - Limited or none)					

2.1 Ontology Based Context Modeling

Ontology is defined as explicit specification of a shared conceptualization [5].Context is modeled as concepts and facts using ontology. Some context aware systems that use these approaches are discussed below.

2.1.1 Context Ontology (CONtext Ontology)

CONON [7] is based on treatment of high-level implicit contexts that are derived from low-level explicit context. It supports interoperability of different devices. CONON defined generic concepts regarding context and provides extensibility for adding domain specific concepts. Logic reasoning is used to perform consistency checks and to calculate high-level context knowledge from explicitly given low-level context information. CONON consists of an upper ontology .It is extended by several domain specific ontology for intelligent environments such as home, office or vehicle. The upper ontology holds general concepts which are common to the sub domains and can therefore be extended. CONON is implemented using OWL. Context reasoning in pervasive environment is time-consuming but is feasible for non-time-critical applications. For time-critical applications like navigation systems or security systems, the data size and rule complexity must be reduced. Context reasoning is dissociated from context usage. A server does the reasoning and tiny devices like mobile phones get the pre-calculated high-level context from the server for direct use. This is an infrastructure based environment.

2.1.2 CoBrA-ONT

CoBrA-ONT [8] is a context management model that enables distributed agents to control the access to their personal information in context-aware environments. CoBrA-ONT is a collection of OWL ontology for context-aware systems. CoBrA-ONT is designed to be used as a common vocabulary in order to overcome the obstacle of proprietary context models that block the interoperability of different devices. Semantics of OWL are used for context reasoning. CoBrA-ONT is central part of CoBrA, broker-centric agent architecture in smart spaces where it supports context reasoning and interoperability. The center of this architecture is context broker agent, which is a server that runs on a resources rich stationary computer. It receives and manages context knowledge for a set of agents and devices in its vicinity, which is the smart space. Agents and devices can contact the context broker and exchange information by the FIPA Agent Communication Language. The architecture of CoBrA-ONT is based on the upper ontology and domain specific ontology that extends the upper ontology .CoBrA-ONT is defined using the Web Ontology Language (OWL) to model the counts of people, agents, places and presentation events. It also describes the properties and relationships between these concepts .CoBrA-ONT depends on the assumption that there always exists a context-broker server that is known by all the participants. CoBrA is infrastructure-centric and is not for pervasive computing whereas the platform proposed in this work is mobile device-centric, where no additional equipment for a mobile device itself is required for system operation.

2.1.3 SOUPA

SOUPA (Standard Ontology for Ubiquitous and Pervasive Applications) [9] is designed to model and support pervasive computing applications. The SOUPA ontology is expressed using the Web Ontology Language OWL and includes modular component vocabularies to represent intelligent agents with associated beliefs, desires and intension, time, space, events, user profiles, actions and policies for security and privacy. SOUPA is more comprehensive than CoBrA-ONT because it deals with more areas of pervasive computing. It also addresses CoBrA-ONT because it deals with more areas of pervasive computing and also addresses problems regarding ontology reuse. The SOUPA sub-ontology maps many of its concepts using owl: equivalent-Class to concepts of existing common ontology.

2.1.4 GAS

GAS ontology [10] is ontology designed for collaboration among ubiquitous computing devices. The basic goal of this ontology is to provide a common language to communication and collaboration among the heterogeneous devices that constitute these environments. The GAS Ontology also supports the service discovery mechanism that a ubiquitous computing environment requires.

2.1.5 Limitations

Context aware systems are based on ad-hoc models of context, which causes lack of the desired formality and expressiveness. Existing models do not separate processing of context semantics from processing and representation of context data and structure. Ontology representation tools are suitable for statically representing the knowledge in a domain. They are not designed for capturing and processing constantly changing information in dynamic environment in a scalable manner. Existing ontology languages and serialization formats are test based (xml/rdf/owl) and not designed for efficient query optimization, processing and retrieval of large context data. The main drawbacks of pure ontological approaches are low performance and data throughput.

3 Advantages of rdbms and ordbms

Relational models provide standard interfaces and query optimization tools for managing large and distributed context database or receive and send notification on context changes. Relational models are not designed for semantic interpretation of data. Relational database alone cannot be used to represent context in a pervasive environment. For semantic interpretations, ontology is used along with relational database. The table 2 below summarizes the appropriateness of both approaches in relation to the necessary features. Both approaches have strong and weak sides with respect to features for context management modeling. Best of two worlds are combined to form a hybrid context management model.From the Table 2 both relational approach and object relational approach are in the same level. Object Relational Approach is more suitable than Relational approach because of the following advantages: Object relational database supports several storage units like collection list, arrays, types and UDTs (User defined data types) and most of them are represented as objects arrays. Object relational approach ensures large storage capacity, which is an important part in web based development. The access speed is fairly quick. Object relational database have a massive scalability compared to relational approach. Object relational database boast excellent manipulation power of object databases. It supports rich data types by adding a new object-oriented layer. The systems are initially implemented by storing the inactive context to a relational database and active context to an ontology. Then the response time to get the relevant time is noted. Further system is implemented by replacing the storing of inactive context to relational database by object relational database. Then appropriate service can be provided to the user using service discovery [12].

Table 2. Advantages of rdbms and ordbms

Necessary Feature	Relational Approach	Ontology Approach	Object Relational Approach
Semantic Support	No	Yes	No
Ease of transaction (large data)	Yes	No	Yes
Query optimization	Yes	No	Yes
Reasoning support	No	Yes	No
Formality	Yes	Yes	Yes
Scalability	Yes	Yes	Yes

4 Proposed Work

The block diagram of the proposed context aware system has three layers is shown in Fig. 1. They are layers are context acquisition layer, context middleware and application layer.

Context acquisition layer gathers the context from the environment using sensors, active badges, camera, Wi-Fi devices etc. Context middleware has three components.

They are representation layer, context management layer and decision layer. Context representation layer represents context as entity relation hierarchy form. In the context management layer context is stored in the object relational database and rules are either defined or learned.

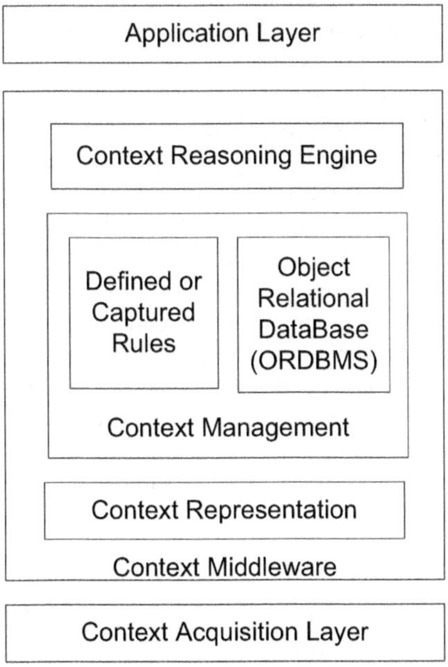

Fig. 1. Block Diagram

The pseudo code for filtering the context is shown below:

```
While (System-is_Running)
{
        newContext=null
        ContextBlock=new ContextClass()
        repeat until newContext=null
        {          newContext=ContextBlock.getNewContext()          }
        reliabilityFactor=0
        if (ContextBlock.hasRelaibleSource() { reliabilityFactor=1} else
        { reliabilityFactor=ContextBlock.estimateSourceRelaibility() }
if (reliabilityFactor>ContextBlock.reliabilityThreshold())
{ if (ContextBlock.hasStaticCategory()){ContextBlock.addContextToORDBMS()}
Else { ContextBlock.inValidContextError()}}
```

Context selector uses historic and current user information, devices availability, institutional policies etc. to select and load only part of context to reasoning space. Rules come from three different sources. They are rules defined by user, rules derived from organizational policies and rules derived from history data of past decisions using rule mining.

4.1 Context Representation

Context can be represented as Entity, Hierarchy, Relation, Axiom and Metadata [11]. Set of entities for which context is to be captured is called as Entity. Set of binary relations that form an inversely directed acyclic graph (inverted DAG) on entities is hierarchies. *Node*s of the graph represent entities and *arcs* of the graph represent hierarchical relations. The root entity at the top of the hierarchy graph is a global entity known as *ContextEntity*. Union of the sets of binary relations R_e and R_a stands for Relation. R_e is a set of binary relations having both its domain and range from the set of entity. R_a is set of binary relations defined from set of entities to set of literals representing entity attributes. Domain of the relation R_a is the set of entity while its range is set of literal values. Axiomatic relation (A) is a relation about relation. Relation can be generic or domain based. Relation can be transitive, symmetry or inverse property. Meta data (M) is a data about data. It is important in context modeling to associate quality, precision, source, time stamps and other information to the context data. Such information is important to prepare the context data for reasoning and decisions. In hierarchy representation metadata information is a relation that describes another relation instance. Hierarchy is an important structure to organize and classify context entities and relations into two layers. They are generic layer or domain layer. Layered organization is used to classify and tag context data as generic domain independent or as domain dependent. Context definition and representation is shown in Table 3.

Table 3. Generic and domain based relationship definitions

Generic level definition	Domain level definition
Person isEngagedIn Activity	Physician isEngagedIn Patient treatement
Location isLocatedIn Location	Library isLocatedIn Campus
Person isLocatedIn Location	Student isLocatedIn Library
Network hasDataRate yyy	ConnectionY hasDataRate low
Network hasDataRate yyy	ConnectionY hasDataRate low

4.2 Associating Hierarchical Context Representation to Relational Database

Relational database is a stable model that is used in a wide range of database management applications In relational database, entity relationship (ER) model is used to represent entities, attributes and relationships.A step-by-step mapping algorithm from the hierarchy components to relational schema is given as follows:

Step 1: Collect all context entities in the hierarchy model and create a relational table with attributes context entity, attributes that stores name of the entity one step above in the hierarchy (isa) and layer(generic or domain)
Step 2: Collect all non hierarchical relations (other than isa and isInstanceOf) in the hierarchy model and create a relational table with attributes Relations and Persistence (static/dynamic)
Step 3: Collect all relation instances in the hierarchy model and create a relational table with attributes Relation, Context Entity and Litral Value
Step 4: Collect all context instances in the hierarchy model and create a relational table with attribute entity instances and context entity

Step 5: Collect all relation defined on instances in the hierarchy model and creates a relational table with attribute entity instance, relation, value, timestamp, source and precision
Step 6: Collect all axioms in the hierarchy model and create a relational table with attribute relation, axiom and attribute value

4.3 Associating Hierarchical Conceptual Model to UML

Unified Modeling Language (UML) is used to formalize hierarchical as a conceptual context representation model.UML is a standard specification language for object modeling.UML is a general purpose modeling language that includes a graphical notation used to create an abstract model of a system. Entity in the hierarchical is represented as UML *Class*. The concept of hierarchical relation can be represented as *generalization* relationship in UML. Entity relations are represented using *attributes* in the UML class. Axiomatic relations are represented as *association classes* in the UML. The concept of metaclass can also be used to represent axiomatic properties like symmetric property, inverse property etc. Metadata is represented using association classes in the UML. UML is used as a tool for ordbms designing.

4.4 Purpose for Semantics

Consider the situation of staff members' (Ben ,Dan and Rita) tea break scenario in the following table, a simple query (select Subject from table.context where predicate="isLocatedIn" and Object="Room-305") select "Ben" as an output.

Table 4. Example on need for context semantics

Subject	Predicate	Object	Time
Ben	isLocatedIn	Room-305	2010022310
Dan	isLocatedIn	Room-301	2010022310
Rita	isLocatedIn	Office-305	2010022310
...	...	...	...

By common sense, terms "Office" and "Room" are synonymous in the domain of interest, the output must be "Ben" and "Rita" to the query. This example demonstrates the need for a context model that describes concepts, concepts hierarchies and their relationships. The concepts of *office* and *Room* in Table 3, *owl: sameAs* property that defines as the same concepts using OWL language as below:

```
<rdf:Description rdf:about= "#Office">
        <owl:sameAs rdf: resource = " #Room">
<rdf:Description>
```

4.5 Associating Hierarchical Conceptual Model to Ontology

Ontology provides standardization of the structure of the context representation, semantic description and relationship of entities. E with class, H with subClassOf, superClassOf, A with transitive, inverseof and meta data with reification. Using ontology, deeper knowledge analysis is performed using domain specific rules. For example, to define the similarity axiom between the concepts *ownerOf* and *owns, owl:sameAs property is used.* Similarly, the symmetric axiom on the concept of *coLocatedWith* can be defined using *owl:symmentricProperty* and the inverse relationship property between *ownerOf and OwnedBy* can be defined using *owl:inverseOf Property.* Mapping between hierarchical model and ontology is shown in Table 5.

4.6 Heuristic Selection of Context

A reasoning space is a search space from which the right set of information is extracted to perform reasoning and inferences. A search space is a set of all possible solution to a problem. Uninformed search algorithms use the intuitive method of searching through the search space, whereas informed search algorithms use heuristic functions to apply knowledge about the structure of the search space to try to reduce the amount of time spent on searching. The entire set of context data is virtually organized into the hierarchical graph. The graph consists of hierarchical tree of context entities and their corresponding relations, axioms and metadata. Pruning techniques on the hierarchical tree of context entities in the graph is used to minimize the size of the reasoning space [14].

4.7 Metrics in Selection Process

Context entities are parameters from which the contents of the reasoning space(context data) are defined.

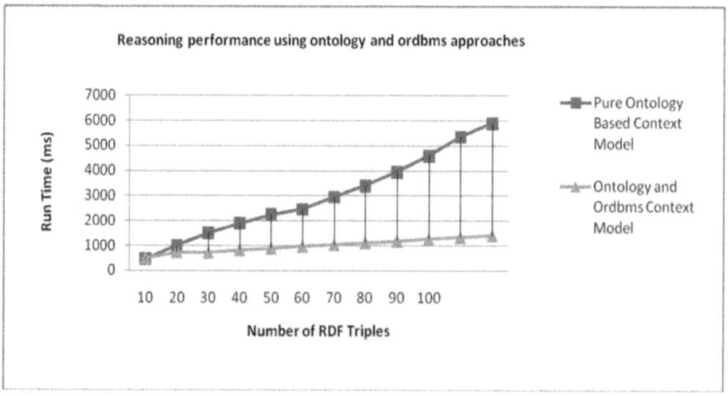

Fig. 2. Reasoning performance using ontology and ordbms approaches

Two measures of performance of the algorithm are accuracy(quality) of reasoning and the response time(speed).Context data are loaded into the reasoning space selectively by pruning the irrelevant part of the data. The context model using pure ontology and using ontology and object relational database is implemented.

5 Conclusion

Context is represented using layered and directed graph. Layered organization helps to classify and tag context data as generic domain independent or as domain dependent. A combination of context model using ontology and object relational database is proposed. This paper focuses on context representation and storage of context. Reasoning ,decision making of the context obtained from the context management are the future work.

References

1. Mattern, F., Sturn, P.: From Distributed Systems to Ubiquitous Computing- State of the Art. In: Trends and Prospects of Future Networked systems, Fachtagung Kommunication in Verteilten Systems (KiVS),Leipzig, Leipzig, pp. 3–25. Springer, Berlin (2003)
2. Satyanarayanan, M.: Pervasive Computing Vision and Challenges. IEEE Personal Communications, 10–17 (2000)
3. Strang, T., LinnhoPopien, C.: A Context Modeling Survey. In: The Proceedings of the First International Workshop on Advanced Context Modeling, Reasoning and Management, 6th International Conference on UbiComp 2004, Nottingham, England (2004)
4. Winograd, T.: Architectures for Context. Human-Computer Interaction 16(2-4), 401–419 (2001)
5. Dey, A.K., Abowd, G.D.: Towards a Better Understanding of Context and Context Awareness. In: Proceedings of the CHI Workshop on the What, Who, Where and How of Context-Awareness, The Hague, the Netherlands (2000)
6. Baldauf, M.: A survey on context aware Systems. Int. J. Ad hoc and Ubiquitous Computing 2(4), 263–277 (2007)
7. Wang, X., Zhang, D., Gu, T., Pung, H.K.: Ontology Based Context Modeling and Reasoning using OWL, Workshop on context modeling and reasoning. In: IEEE International Conference on Pervasive Computing and Communication, Orlando, Florida (2004)
8. Chen, H.: An Intelligent Broker Architecture for Pervasive Context-Aware Systems. PhD Thesis University of Maryland, Baltimore Country, USA (2004)
9. Chen, H., Perich, F., Finin, T., et al.: SOUPA: Standard Ontology for Ubiquitous and Pervasive Applications. In: International Conference on Mobile and Ubiquitous Systems: Networking And Services, Boston, USA (2004)
10. Christopoulou, E., Kameas, A.: GAS Ontology: ontology for collaboration among ubiquitous Computing devices. International Journal of Human-Computer Studies 62(5), 664–685 (2005)
11. Ejigu, D., Scuturi, M., Brunie, L.: An Ontology Based Approach to Context Modeling and Reasoning in Pervasive Computing. In: 5th IEEE International Conference on Pervasive Computing and Communications Workshops, pp. 14–19 (2007)
12. Vanathi, B., Rhymend Uthariaraj, V.: Ontology based service discovery for context aware computing. In:1st IEEE International Conference on Advanced Computing. IEEE Computer Society, Chennai (2009)
13. Vanathi, B., Rhymend Uthariaraj, V.: Context Representation and Management in a Pervasive Environmen. In: International Conference on Advances in Information and Communication Technologies, pp. 543–548. Springer, Heidelberg (2010)
14. Vanathi, B., Rhymend Uthariaraj, V.: Context Representation Using Hierarchical Method and Heuristic Based Context Selection in Context Aware Computing. In: Proceedings of the ACM-W 1st Conference of Women in Computing in India: Emerging Trends in Computer Proceedings (2010)

Privacy Preservation of Stream Data Patterns Using Offset and Trusted Third Party Computation in Retail-Shop Market Basket Analysis

Keshavamurthy B.N. and Durga Toshniwal

Department of Electronics & Compuetr Engineering
Indian Institute of Technology Roorkee,
Uttarakhand, India
{kesavdec,durgafec}@iitr.ernet.in

Abstract. Privacy preservation is widely talked in recent years, which prevents the disclosure of sensitive information during the knowledge discovery. There are many applications of distributed scenario which includes retail shops, where the stream of digital data is collected from time to time. The collaborating parties are generally interested in finding global patterns for their mutual benefits. There are few proposals which address these issues, but in the existing methods, global pattern computation is carried out by one of the source itself and uses one offset to perturb the personal data which fails in many situations such as all the patterns are not initiated at the initial participating party. Our novel approach addresses these problems for retail shops in strategic way by considering the different offsets to perturb the sensitive information and trusted third party to ensure global pattern computation.

Keywords: Privacy preservation, steam data, offset computation, trusted third party.

1 Introduction

In recent years, due to the advancement of computing and storage technology, digital data can be easily collected. It is very difficult to analyze the entire data manually. Thus a lot of work is going on for mining and analyzing such data.

In real many world applications which include retail-shops data is distributed across different sources. The distributed data base is comprised of horizontal, vertical or arbitrary fragments. In case of horizontal fragmentation, each site has the complete information on a distinct set of entities. An integrated dataset consists of the union of these datasets. In case of vertical fragments each site has partial information on the same set of entities. An integrated dataset would be produced by joining the data from the sites. Arbitrary fragmentation is a hybrid of previous two.

The key goal for privacy preserving data mining is to allow computation of aggregate statistics over an entire data set without compromising the privacy of private data of the participating data sources.

The key techniques in privacy preservation to perturb the sensitive data, includes randomization. The randomization method is a technique in which for privacy

N. Meghanathan et al. (Eds.): CCSIT 2011, Part III, CCIS 133, pp. 358–366, 2011.

preserving data mining, offset or noise is added to the sensitive data in order to mask the attribute values of records. The offset added is sufficiently large so that individual record values cannot be recovered.

Most of the methods for privacy computation use some transformation on the data in order to perform the privacy preservation. One of the methods widely used in distributed computing environment for a computation of global pattern is secure multi party computation.

The reminder of this paper is organized as follows: section 2 gives a formal definition of the problem definition of this paper and discusses the randomization and secure multiparty computation on which the proposed work is applied. In section 3, we presented proposed module for mining the stream data of retail-shop by using trusted third party and different offsets. In section 4, includes performance evaluation. We conclude our work in section 5.

2 Preliminaries

2.1 Problem Statement

A lot of research papers have discussed the privacy preserving mining across distributed databases. Major drawbacks with the existing techniques are that the global pattern computation is done at one of the data source itself which violates the privacy concern majorly. The proposed work address this issues very efficiently by using a trusted third party to alleviate privacy preservation across distributed data sources. Secondly to perturb the sensitive items uses one offset value which fails in many practical scenario of retail-market such as all the items need not be sold at a particular shop. This technical gap is resolved by taking two offsets, one which will be used for continuing items and the later used for newly initiated items at each data source to perturb the sensitive items of collaborating parties.

2.2 Background

Randomization Method

The most widely used technique in privacy preservation to perturb the sensitive attributes is randomization technique. It is described as follows: Consider a set of data denoted by $X = \{ x_1, x_2, \ldots x_N \}$. For record $x_i \in x$, we add offset component which is drawn from the probability $f_y(y)$. These offset components are drawn independently, and are denoted $y_1, y_2, \ldots y_N$ thus, the new set of distorted records are denoted by $x_1 + y_1, \ldots, x_n + y_N$. We denote this new set of records by $z_1, \ldots, z_N$. In general, it is assumed that the variance of the added offset is large enough, so that the original record values cannot be easily guessed from the distorted data. Thus, the original records cannot be recovered, but the distribution of the original records can be recovered Thus, if x be the random variable denoted the data distribution for the original record, y is the random variable describing the offset distribution, and z be the random variable denoting the final record, we have

$$Z=X+Y. \quad (1)$$

$$X=Z-Y. \quad (2)$$

Secure Multiparty Computation

A number of technologies have recently been proposed in order to perform the data mining tasks in a privacy preserving way. The most promising technique which is widely used to alleviate privacy preservation concerns in distributed database scenario includes secure multi party computation.

Generally in a distributed database environment to compute the global patterns of n data sources. In secure multiparty computation, when there are n data sources $DS_0, DS_1, \ldots, D_{n-1}$ such that each

In case of distributed environment, the most widely used technique in privacy preservation mining is secure sum computation [16]. Here when there are n data sources $DS_0, DS_1, \ldots D_{n-1}$ such that each DS_i has a private data item $d_i, i = 0,1,\ldots,n-1$ the parties want to compute $\sum_{i=0}^{n-1} d_i$ privately, without revealing their private data d_i to each other. The following method was presented:

We assume that $\sum_{i=0}^{n-1} d_i$ is in the range $[0, m-1]$ and DS_j is the protocol initiator.

Following steps were followed:

1. At the beginning DS_j chooses a uniform random number r within $[0, m-1]$.
2. Then DS_j sends the sum $d_i + r \pmod{m}$ to the data source $DS_j + 1 \pmod{n}$
3. Each remaining data sources DS_i do the following: upon receiving a value x the data source DS_i sends the sum $d_i + x \pmod{m}$ to the data source $DS_i + 1 \pmod{n}$.
4. Finally, when party DS_j receives a value from the data source $DS_{n-1} - 1 \pmod{n}$), it will be equal to the total sum $r + \sum_{i=0}^{n-1} d_i$. Since r is only known to DS_j it can find the sum $\sum_{i=0}^{n-1} d_i$ and distribute to collaborating parties.

3 Proposed Work

Our proposed work the modify the existing secure multiparty computation by introducing trusted third to enhance privacy preservation and also uses two offset values to perturb the sensitive attribute values.

3.1 Modified Secure Multiparty Computation with Two Offset Computation

Assumption

Here there are n data sources $DS_0, DS_1, ...D_{n-1}$ such that each has a private data item d_i, $i = 0,1,...n-1$, the parties want to compute $\sum_{i=0}^{n-1} d_i$ privately, without revealing their private data d_i to each other. The following method was presented: We also assume that $\sum_{i=0}^{n-1} d_i$ is in the range $[0, m-1]$ and trusted third party is the protocol initiator.

Procedure

At Trusted Third Party

1. The collaborating parties interested in global pattern computation are connecting to the trusted third party.
2. Trusted third party choose a uniform random r to select one of the N parties as an initiator (i.e., selects one of the DS_i, $i = 0,1,...,n-1$) and send the random offset to that party DS_i.
3. Trusted third party sends two offsets oldoffset and newoffset for each collaborating party except initiator. Initiator receives only newoffset.
4. Finally, when trusted third party receives a value from the data source $DS_{j-1} - 1 \pmod{n}$, it will be equal to the total sum $r + \sum_{i=0}^{n-1} d_i$ Since r is only know to trusted third party, it can find the sum $\sum_{i=0}^{n-1} d_i$ and distribute the same to collaborating data sources.

At Trusted Third Party

Collaborating party

1. If he is an initial collaborator then add its own data value D_i to newoffset value received from trusted third party.
2. For each items at DS_i following action taken at collaborator side except the last collaborator:
 a. If there are no new items in compare with the item list obtained from D_{i-1}, then sum $D_i + \text{oldoffset}$.
 Else

b. For all the new items in compare item list obtained from D_{i-1} then sum $d_i + newoffset$ at D_i.

c. Send the final list of items to the next collaborating party specified by trusted third party

3. The last collaborating party performs

a. If there are no new items in compare with the item list obtained from D_{i-1} then sum $d_i + oldoffset$.

Else

b. For all the new items in compare item list obtained from D_{i-1} then sum $d_i + newoffset$ at D_i.

c. Send the final list of items to the party trusted third party.

4 Analysis and Evaluation

This section mainly discusses the execution and performances issues of the algorithm presented in the previous section. In section A, we introduce the practical problem we considered. Section B discusses the analysis part of the algorithm.

4.1 Evaluation Environment

Experiments were conducted on the following scenario: Trusted third party with 10 data sources, each data source contains 3 records. Basically there are two tables which operate by each collaborating party, one local database table, to keep local items information and the other sendtable, to have complete information of all the items till that party.

The following table's of Fig.1 gives the complete information of first three collaborating parties followed by the analysis of the data at different data sources and trusted third party. Initially all the parties interested in global pattern computation makes a request to trusted third party. Trusted third party select one them as initiator and send random offset number i.e., offset-1 to perturb his sensitive data. At party1, adds his data with offset1 send by trusted party then result will be send to the next party which is specified by trusted third party called as party2. At party2 if there are new items in compare with the existing list which is received from party1 then he has to add offset-1 to them for rest, add offset-2 to preserve the privacy of sensitive data and send the result to next logical party which is specified by trusted third party and this will continue till the last party. At last party he adds his data with offset-1 to new items which initiated from him, for the rest add offset-2 then the final resulting table will be sent to the trusted third party for the global pattern computation.

At trusted third party he subtracts the random value from aggregate values obtained from last party. Then at third party the mining operation for the aggregate values of the collaborating party will be carried out and the mined result will be send back to the collaborating parties. In the entire process the trusted party will never gets details of the items of any of the collaborating party individually and the collaborating parties are the constituents of distributed database scenario so they can only know the party who is adjacent to him but he never knows the complete details such as what is his order which may helps in getting to know how many people are before and after him so that he can misuse the data which is receive in the course.

Table 1. Party1 local data

Item	Item Frequency	Offset-1	Perturbed Value
A	10	50	60
BC	15		65
DEF	20		70

Table 2. Party1 send data

Item	Perturbed Value
A	60
BC	65
DEF	70

Table 3. Party2 local data

Item	Item Frequency	Offset-1	Offset-2	Perturbed Value
AB	15	50	120	135
BC	5			75
DEF	75			145

Table 4. Party2 send data

Item	Perturbed Value
A	130
AB	135
BC	140
DEF	215

Table 5. Party3 local data

Item	Item Frequency	Offset-1	Offset-2	Perturbed Value
BC	10	100	220	110
A	15			115
FG	35			255

Table 6. Party3 send data

Item	Perturbed Value
A	245
AB	235
BC	250
DEF	335
FG	255

Table 7. Party10 local data

Item	Item Frequency	Offset-1	Offset-2	Perturbed Value
A	30	100	560	130
BC	20			120
DEF	25			125

Table 8. Party10 send data

Item	Perturbed Value
A	756
AB	615
AC	645
B	615
BC	645
D	670
DEF	786
FG	595
G	595
H	620

Fig. 1. Data perturbation at collaborating parties (Party1to Party 10)

4.2 Analysis of Algorithm

Table 9 gives the data items of 10 distributed data sources such as party1 to party10 along with the item frequency. The corresponding feature graph for the input data items are given in Fig.2. The integrated data of all the data sources party1 to party10 at trusted third party after deducting the integrated offset supplied to the different collaborating parties will be given by table10 and the corresponding feature graph is drawn in Fig.2. The feature graph we obtained for at the integrated data (Table 8) at the source side is same as the feature graph which we drawn at trusted party after offset subtraction at Fig. 3(Table 10).

Table 9. Items at different data sources

Party/ Item	Party1	Party2	Party3	Party4	Party5	Party6	Party7	Party8	Party9	Party10
A	10	0	15	50	10 0	0	0	0	30	0
B	0	0	0	0	0	55	0	0	0	150
AB	0	15	0	0	0	0	30	10	0	0
Ac	0	0	0	0	0	0	20	55	0	0
BC	15	5	10	15	20	0	0	0	20	0
D	0	0	0	0	0	0	40	70	0	0
DEF	20	75	0	0	35	70	0	0	25	0
FG	0	0	0	0	0	0	0	0	0	70
G	0	0	0	35	0	0	0	0	0	0
H	0	0	0	0	0	60	0	0	0	5

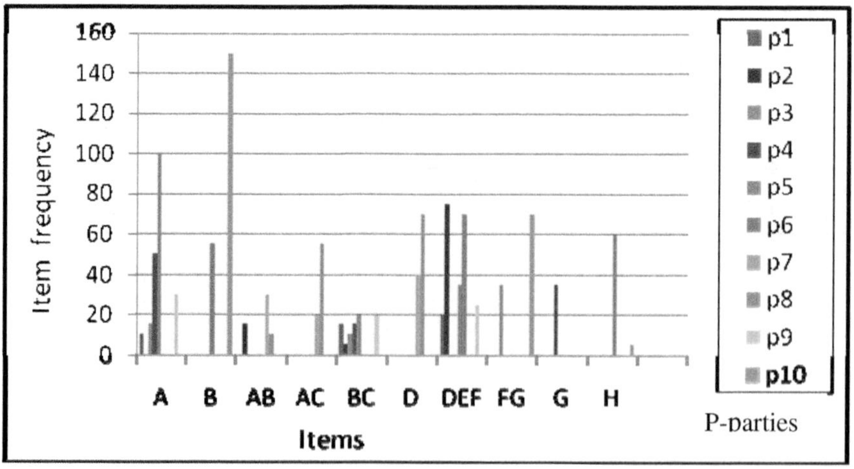

Fig. 2. Support of items at different data sources or collaborating parties

Table 10. Integrated items for collaborating parties at trusted third party

Items	Frequency
A	205
B	205
AB	55
AC	75
BC	85
D	110
DEF	225
FG	70
G	35
H	65

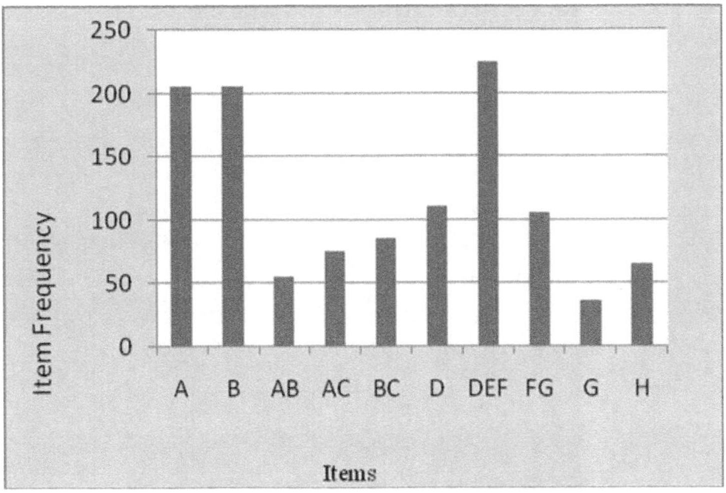

Fig. 3. Global patterns of items at trusted third party

5 Conclusion

The proposed work well suits with synthetic data and also demonstrated the efficient way of privacy preservation over distributed scenario of the retail-shop market basket analysis. The worst possibility of information misuse can take place at the second random party who can get to know the only first party details but which is always negligible in the entire crowd. The proposed model is scalable and can be used for real data set in future.

References

1. Huang, J.-W., Tseng, C.-Y., Ou, J.-C., Chen, M.-S.: A General Model for Sequential Pattern Mining with a Progressive Database. International Journal of Knowledge and Data Engineering 20, 1153–1167 (2008)

2. Mhatre, A., Verma, M., Toshniwal, D.: Privacy Preserving Sequential Pattern Mining in Progressive Databases using Noisy Data. In: International Conference on Information Visualization, pp. 456–460 (2009)
3. Agrawal, R., Srikant, R.: Privacy-preserving data mining. In: ACM SIGMOD Conference on Management of Data, New York, USA, pp. 439–450 (2000)
4. Samarati, P.: Protecting Respondents' Identities in Micro data Release. IEEE Trans. Knowledge Data Eng. 13(6), 1010–1027 (2001)
5. Fung, B., Wang, K., Yu, P.: Top-Down Specialization for Information and Privacy Preservation. In: ICDE Conference, pp. 205–216 (2005)
6. LeFevre, K., De Witt, D., Ramakrishnan, R.: Incognito: Full Domain K-Anonymity. In: ACM SIGMOD Conference, Maryland, pp. 49–60 (2005)
7. LeFevre, K., DeWitt, D., Ramakrishnan, R.: Mondrian Multidimensional K-Anonymity. In: ICDE Conference, pp. 25–25 (2006)
8. Park, H., Shim, K.: Approximate Algorithms for K-anonymity. In: ACM SIGMOD Conference, Beijing, China, pp. 67–78 (2007)
9. Wang, K., Yu, P., Chakraborty, S.: Bottom-Up Generalization: A Data Mining Solution to Privacy Protection. In: ICDM Conference, pp. 249–256 (2004)

Application of Euclidean Distance Power Graphs in Localization of Sensor Networks

G.N. Purohit[1], Seema Verma[2], and Usha Sharma[1]

[1] Centre for Mathematical Sciences,
Banasthali University, Rajasthan 304022
[2] Department of Electronics, Banasthali University
Rajasthan 30402
Usha.shama94@yahoo.com

Abstract. Localization of sensor nodes in a wireless sensor network is needed for many practical uses. If the nodes are considered as vertices of a globally rigid graph then the nodes can be uniquely localized up to translation, rotation and reflection. We have given the construction of globally rigid graph through Euclidean distance powers of Unit Disk graph.

Keywords: UD Graph, powers of a graph, vertex connectivity and henneberg sequence.

1 Introduction

Unit Disk graph [4] is an important class of graphs, which finds application in modeling a wireless sensor network. The radio coverage range of sensors is based on Euclidean distance between the nodes and we utilize this concept of Euclidean distance in graph theory. This has given rise to a new branch termed as 'geometric graph theory'. Wireless sensor network can be modeled as unit disk graph. In this modeling sensors are denoted as vertices. The sensing coverage area of a sensor is represented by a unit disk centered at the corresponding vertex. The connectivity between two sensor nodes is determined if the first sensor is within the sensing coverage area of the second sensor. Thus there is an edge between u and v iff $d(u,v) \leq R$, where d(u,v) is the Euclidean distance between u and v and R is the sensing range. Thus Unit Disk (UD) graph is a suitable model for a wireless sensor network.

Power of a graph [1] is an induced graphs which can be generated by making some additional edges to the original graphs. Square of a graph is a graph with the same vertex set in which vertices at distance 2 are connected through an edge. Cube of a graph is also the graph on the same set of vertices; however, additionally there is an edge between two vertices whenever they are at most distance 3. This concept can be applied to the UD graphs also. Powers of a UD graph as square and cube of a UD graph [1] represent the possible interfering nodes in network. Further Euclidean distance two graph [3] and Euclidean distance three graph of a UD graph also provide the information about interfering nodes in sensor network.

The nodes in a sensor network are in general deployed randomly and localization of nodes is an important issue in wireless sensor networks. Determining the geographical location of nodes in a sensor network is essential for many aspects of

N. Meghanathan et al. (Eds.): CCSIT 2011, Part III, CCIS 133, pp. 367–377, 2011.

system operation, data stamping, tracking, signal processing, querying, topology control, clustering and routing. The localization problem in the sensor networks is to determine the location of all nodes. In space R^d (d = 2,3) the location of nodes can be easily determined if initial location of 2 and 3 nodes is known in the case of d = 2 and d = 3, respectively. These initially located sensor nodes are called anchor nodes [7].

The network is said to be uniquely localizable [5] if there is a unique set of locations consistent with the given data. Uniquely localizable network in two and three dimensions can be characterized by using the results of rigid graphs. A network N is uniquely localizable if and only if the *weighted grounded graph* [5] G_N' associated with N, is a globally rigid graph [8]. The terms: globally rigid graph and weighted grounded graph are defined hereafter.

In the weighted grounded graph G_N', the vertices are the corresponding nodes of the network N and the two vertices are connected by an edge if the distance between them is known initially. Since the location of anchor nodes is known, the distance between these nodes is known (can be directly calculated). Thus these anchor node are also connected to each other in G_N'.

An intuitive definition of globally rigid graph has been considered in [5] as follows: consider a configuration graph of points in plane in which edges between some of them represents distance constraints. If there is not another configuration consisting of different points on the plane that preserves all the distance constraints on the edges, then the configuration graph is said to be globally rigid graph in the plane. As shown in figure 1 and figure 2.

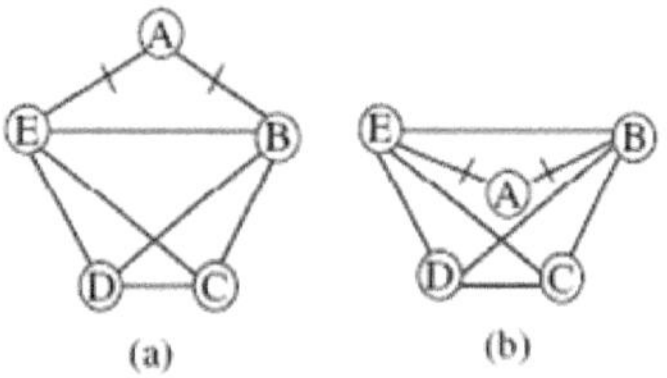

Fig. 1. Not globally rigid since distances between vertices are preserved in another configuration

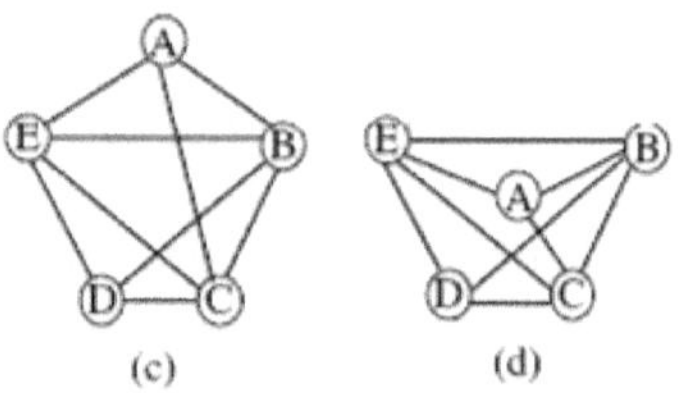

Fig. 2. Globally rigid graph since distances between vertices are not preserved in another configuration. Distance between A and C is not similar in both graphs (c) & (d).

In this paper we have provided an algorithm to construct systematically generically globally rigid graphs from those graphs which do not have these properties. This construction basically depends on adding of more edges in the graph. However, it is also important to know that how to add the extra edges in the underlying graph of a sensor network. The distance between sensor nodes and their neighbors (immediate, two hop, three hop and four hop) are involved in this construction. For a network whose graphical model is a UD graph, it corresponds to increasing the sensing radius (presumably by adjusting transmission powers) for each sensor. To determine the distance between two and three hop neighbors, the sensing radius has to be made double and triple respectively.

This paper is organized as follows: Some new terms and some other auxiliary definitions are described with examples in Section 2 for the completion of this paper. In Section 3 we have given the Condition for generically globally rigid graph and necessary definitions. In Section 4, we describe the construction of a globally rigid power graph of a UD graph. We also give the related Lemmas and Theorems for ED-2graph as well as ED-3 graph of a UD graph. The localization problem in sensor network is given in Section 4. In Section 5, we conclude the results.

2 Auxiliary Definition

2.1 Unit Disk Graph

A graph G is a Unit Disk graph if there is an assignment of unit disks centered at its vertices such two vertices are adjacent if and only if one vertex is within the unit disk centered at the other vertex. We denote a unit disk graph by G_{UD}.

2.2 Powers of a Unit Disk Graph

2.2.1 Square of a Unit Disk Graph (G_{UD}^2)

The Square G_{UD}^2 of a Unit Disk graph G_{UD} (V, E) is the graph whose vertex set is V and there is an edge between two vertices v_i and v_j if and only if their graph distance in G_{UD} is at most 2. [Figure 3 (a)].

2.2.2 Euclidean Distance Two Graph of a Unit Disk Graph (G_{UD}^{ED2})

Euclidean distance two graph of a unit disk graph G_{UD} (V, E) is the graph whose vertex set is V and there is an edge between two vertices v_i and v_j if and only if their Euclidean distance in G_{UD} is at most 2. [Figure 3 (b)].

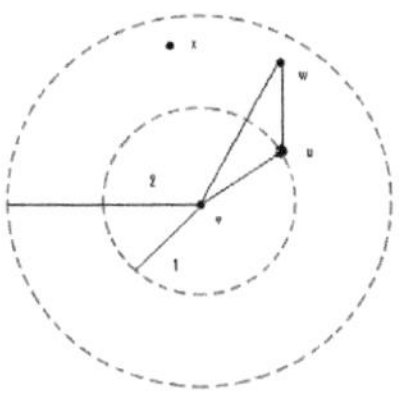

Fig. 3 (a). G_{UD}^2 Graph

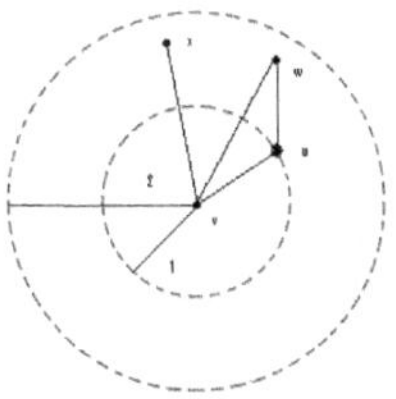

Fig. 3 (b). G_{UD}^{ED2} Graph

2.2.3 Cube of a Unit Disk Graph (G_{UD}^3)

The cube G_{UD}^3 of a Unit Disk graph G_{UD} (V, E) is the graph whose vertex set is V and there is an edge between two vertices v_i and v_j if and only if their graph distance in G_{UD} is at most 3. [Figure 4 (a)].

2.2.4 Euclidean Distance Three Graph of a Unit Disk Graph (G_{UD}^{ED3})

Euclidean distance three graph of a unit disk graph G_{UD} (V, E) is the graph whose vertex set is V and there is an edge between two vertices v_i and v_j if and only if their Euclidean distance in G_{UD} is at most 3. [Figure 4 (b)].

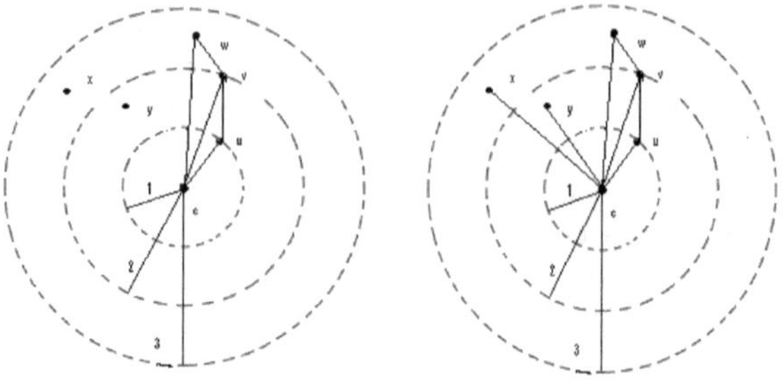

Fig. 4 (a). G_{UD}^{3} Graph **Fig. 4 (b).** G_{UD}^{ED3} Graph

2.3 Rigidity in Unit Disk Graph

2.3.1 Realization UD Frame Work

A d- dimensional UD frame work (G_{UD},p) is a unit disk graph together with a map $p{:}V \rightarrow \Re^{d}$, the framework is realization if it results in $\|p(i)\text{-}p(j)\| \leq R \ \forall i \ \& \ j \in V$ where ij $\in$ E.

2.3.2 Equivalent UD Frameworks

Two UD frameworks (G_{UD},p) and (G_{UD},q) are equivalent if $\|p(i)\text{-}p(j)\| = \|q(i)\text{-}q(j)\|$ $\forall$ i & j where ij $\in$ E. i.e. two frameworks with the same graph G are equivalent if the lengths of their edges are the same. [Figure 5].

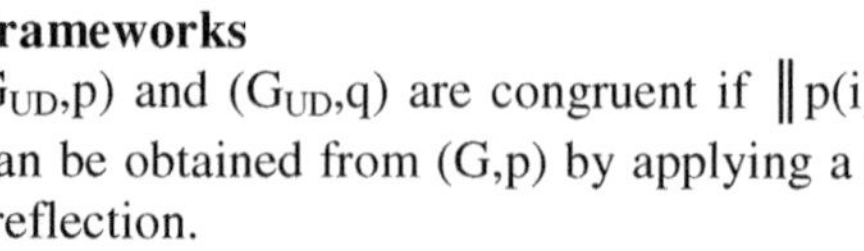

Fig. 5. Both are equivalent frameworks

2.3.3 Congruent UD Frameworks

Two UD frameworks (G_{UD},p) and (G_{UD},q) are congruent if $\|p(i)\text{-}p(j)\| = \|q(i)\text{-}q(j)\|$ $\forall$ i & j$\in$ V. i.e. (G,q) can be obtained from (G,p) by applying a set of operations of translation, rotation and reflection.

2.3.4 Rigid UD Framework

A UD framework (G_{UD},p) is rigid if there exist a sufficiently small positive ϵ such that if (G_{UD}, q) is equivalent to (G_{UD},p) and $\|p(i)\text{-}q(i)\| \leq \epsilon \ \forall i \in V$ then (G_{UD}, q) is congruent to (G_{UD},p) or we can say A framework (or graph) is rigid iff continuous motion of the points of the configuration maintaining the bar constraints comes from a family of motions of all Euclidean space which are distance-preserving. A graph that is not rigid

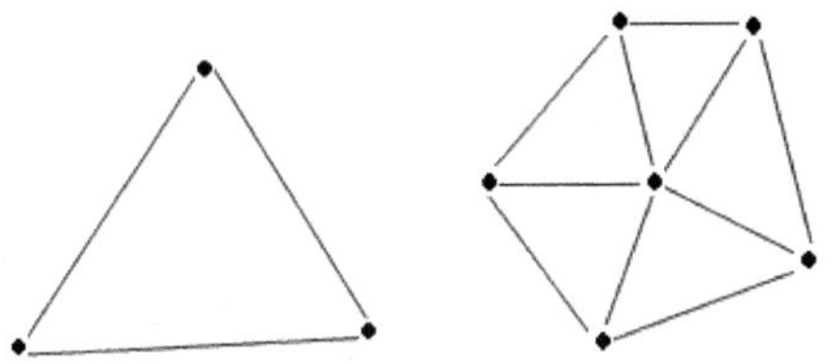

Fig. 6. Rigid Graphs

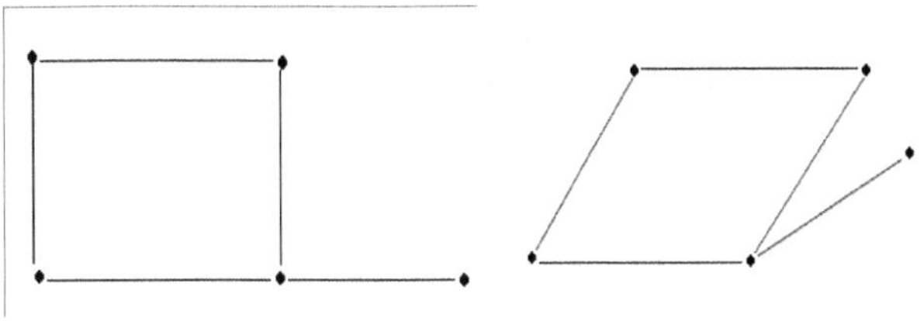

Fig. 7. Non rigid graph since it is not uniquely realizable

is said to be flexible. Figure 7 shows a non rigid graph since it is possible to rotate the pendent vertex around its neighbor and also it is possible to twist the square into parallelogram. It is causes of infinitely many configurations with respect to the edge length consistency.

2.3.5 Globally Rigid UD Framework

A UD framework (G_{UD}, p) is globally rigid if every framework which is equivalent to (G_{UD}, p) is congruent to (G_{UD}, p). i.e. it has unique realization up to rotation translation or reflection. [Figure 8].

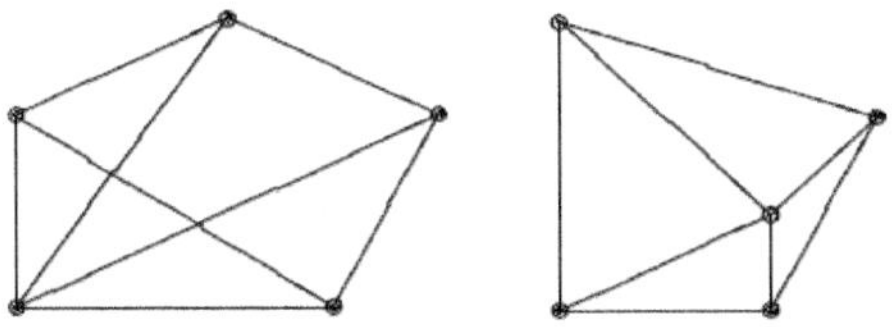

Fig. 8. Globally rigid graphs in $\Re^2$

2.3.6 Generic UD Framework

A UD framework (G_{UD}, p) is generic if the set containing the coordinates of all its point is algebraically independent over the rationals.

3 Condition for Generically Globally Rigid Graph

3.1 3-Connectivity

A graph G is said to be 3- connected if and only if it remains connected after removing any 2 vertices or we can say there are atleast three disjoint (vertex and edge disjoint) paths between every pair of vertices.

3.2 Redundantly Rigid

A graph is Redundantly Rigid if it remains rigid after removing any one of its edge. We have given a graph in figure (10). This graph is composed of two triangles connected by its vertices. It is rigid and it is 3-connected but figure 10(a) shows that there are two possible configurations for the vertices on the plane with respect to the edge length. Figure 10(b) shows that if the edge (a,f) is removed, the graph becomes non-rigid and it is possible to rotate the triangles until another position reached where the distance (a,f) is same as the previous one. In this way it is possible to find two configurations for the graph that are consistent with the edge length and therefore the graph is not uniquely realizable. So it is not a Redundantly Rigid graph.

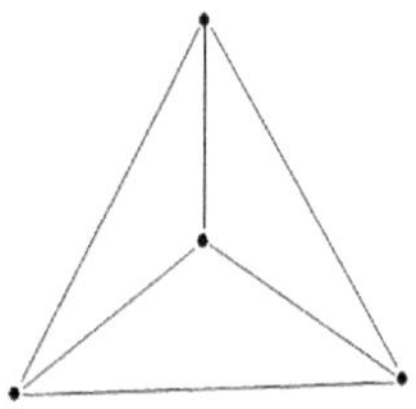

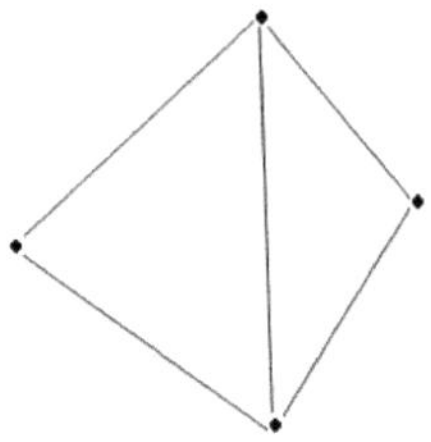

Fig. 9(a). 3-Connected Graph **Fig. 9(b).** Not 3-Connected Graph

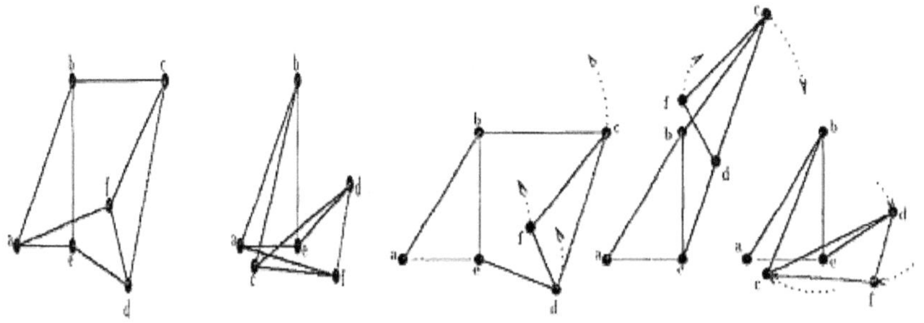

(a) Two possible configurations (b) Deforming from one configuration to another

Fig. 10. Not a Redundantly Rigid Graph

3.3 Theorem: [9] Let (G,p) be a generic framework in $\mathfrak{R}^d$. if (G,p) is globally rigid then either G is a complete graph with at most d+1 vertices or G is (d+1)-connected and redundantly rigid in $\mathfrak{R}^d$.

3.4 Theorem: [8] Let (G,p) be a generic framework in $\mathfrak{R}^2$. If (G,p) is globally rigid if and only if either G is a complete graph with 2 or 3 vertices or G is 3-connected and redundantly rigid in $\mathfrak{R}^2$.

4 Generating Globally Rigid Power Graph of a UD Graph

4.1 Theorem: If G_{UD} be a UD graph and an edge 2- connected graph then G_{UD}^{ED2} is a generically globally rigid graph.

Proof: For proving this theorem we need the following Lemmas.

Lemma 1: If a UD graph corresponding to a wireless sensor network is in the form of a cycle C_{UD} then C_{UD}^{ED2} is generically globally rigid graph.

Proof: Let S be the set of all sensor nodes $s_1, s_2, s_3, \ldots\ldots\ldots\ldots s_{n-1}, s_n$ in a sensor network. If s_n and s_{n-1} ($n \geq 2$) are in the sensing range of each other and s_n and s_1 are also in the sensing range of each other, then the corresponding UD graph will be a cycle, say C_{UD}. In this cycle $s_1, s_2, s_3, \ldots\ldots\ldots\ldots s_{n-1}, s_n$ are vertices and s_1s_2, s_2s_3, s_3s_4, $\ldots\ldots\ldots s_ns_1$ are edges. If n=3, then it will be a complete graph on three vertices and result is trivial since complete graph is generically globally rigid graph. Now consider n>3. To prove C_{UD}^{ED2} is generically globally rigid graph we first show it is three connected and then it is generically redundantly rigid.

There exist three vertex disjoint paths between every pair of vertices in C_{UD}^2 as follows:

Consider two arbitrary vertices s_i and s_j C_{UD}.

Case I: If i and j both are even or odd then,

P_1: $s_i\ s_{i-1}\ s_{i-2} \ldots\ldots s_1\ s_n\ s_{n-1}\ s_{n-2} \ldots\ldots s_{j+2}\ s_{j+1}\ s_j$, P_2: $s_i\ s_{i+2}\ s_{i+4} \ldots\ldots s_{j-4}\ s_{j-2}\ s_j$, P_3: $s_i\ s_{i+1}\ s_{i+3} \ldots\ldots s_{j-3}\ s_{j-1}\ s_j$ are three different vertex disjoint paths between s_i and s_j.

Case II: If one of i or j is even and another is odd then,

P_1': $s_i\ s_{i-1}\ s_{i-2} \ldots\ldots s_n\ s_{n-1}\ s_{n-2} \ldots\ldots s_{j+2}\ s_{j+1}\ s_j$, P_2': $s_i\ s_{i+2}\ s_{i+4} \ldots\ldots s_{j-3}\ s_{j-1}\ s_j$, P_3': $s_i\ s_{i+1}\ s_{i+3} \ldots\ldots s_{j-4}\ s_{j-2}\ s_j$ are again three vertex disjoint paths between s_i and s_j.

Therefore C_{UD}^2 is 3- connected. Also we know that C_{UD}^{ED2} is a supergraph of C_{UD}^2 with addition of more edges on same vertex set, so C_{UD}^{ED2} must be 3-connected.

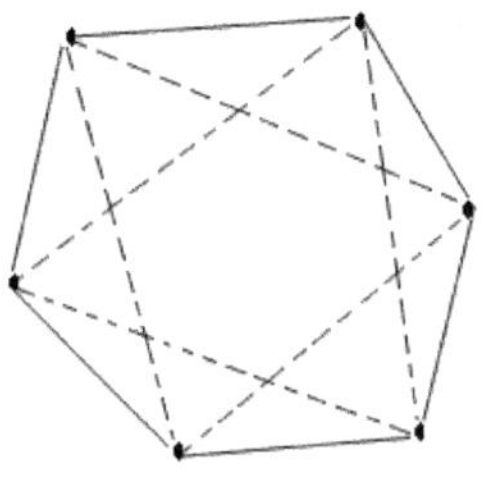

Fig. 11. C_{UD}^2

Now we prove generically redundantly rigidity of C_{UD}^{ED2}. We remove an edge from C_{UD}^{ED2} which is also an edge of C_{UD}. Let it be s_1s_n. Consider the sequence of triangles, whose all edges are in C_{UD}^{ED2}: $s_1s_2s_3$, $s_2s_3s_4, \ldots\ldots\ldots\ldots s_{n-2}s_{n-1}s_n$ and notice the corresponding subgraphs as each triangle is added.

We get a Henneberg sequence by vertex addition, in which each member of the sequence differing from the previous one by the addition of a two degree vertex. So it will be a generically globally rigid graph.

This subgraph C_{UD}^{ED2}- s_1s_n of C_{UD}^{ED2} retains all the vertices of C_{UD}^{ED2} but does not contain the edge s_1s_n. Hence C_{UD}^{ED2}- s_1s_n is a generically globally rigid graph. Thus C_{UD}^{ED2} is generically redundantly rigid.

Therefore C_{UD}^{ED2} is generically globally rigid graph.

Lemma 2: If H_0 be a generically globally rigid graph in $\mathfrak{R}^2$ with atleast three vertices and if a super graph H_1 be defined by adjoining one vertex to the vertex set of H_0 and three edges, each connecting the new vertex to three different vertices of H_0. Then H_1 is generically globally rigid.

Proof: The proof of this lemma is given in [2].

Lemma 3: if $H_1 = (V_1,E_1)$ and $H_2 = (V_2,E_2)$ be two generically globally rigid graphs in $\mathfrak{R}^2$ with atleast three vertices in common then $H_1 \bigcup H_2 = (V_1 \bigcup V_2, E_1 \bigcup E_2)$ is also generically globally rigid.

Proof: The proof of this Lemma is also given in [2].

Lemma 4: Every simple super graph of a generically globally rigid graph on same vertex set is generically globally rigid in $\mathfrak{R}^2$.

Now we provide the proof of main theorem:

Since G_{UD} is an edge 2- connected graph, it necessarily contains atleast one cycle. If it contains just one cycle then by above Lemma 1 the theorem is true. Now suppose G_{UD} contains more than one cycle. Let one of them be C_1: s_1s_2...............s_n, if the vertex set of C_1 is similar as of G_{UD} then the theorem is true by above Lemma 1.

Now suppose a vertex set of C_1 is not similar to G_{UD}. Since G_{UD} is connected, therefore every vertex in $G_{UD} \sim C_1$ is joined by a path to C_1 and hence there is a vertex of $G_{UD} \sim C_1$ joined by a single edge to a vertex of C_1. Call it s_L and let edge be s_1s_L.

Now consider $G_1 = (V_1,E_1)$ with vertex set of C_1 and edge set of C_1 together with the edge s_1s_L. Then G_1^2 has edge set with the edge set of C_1^2 and three more edges s_1s_L, s_ns_L, s_2s_L.

Using Lemma 2, if we consider C_1^2 as H_0 and G_1^2 as H_1 then G_1^2 must be generically globally rigid.

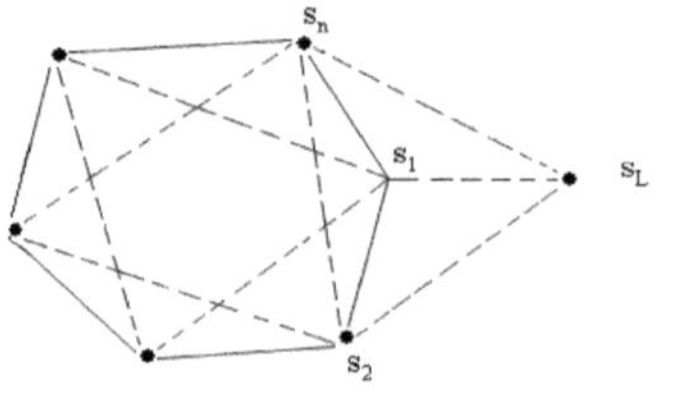

Fig. 12. G_{UD}^2

Since G_{UD} is edge 2- connected, thus there exist another path between s_l and s_L except the single edge s_ls_L. Then there will be a cycle. Call it C_2, containing s_l and s_L as adjacent vertices. Clearly this cycle can not contain both s_2 and s_n as adjacent vertices of s_l. Suppose it does not contain s_2 as an adjacent vertex of s_l. Now consider the graph $G_2 = (V_2,E_2)$ with vertex set of C_2 together with s_2 and with edge set of C_2 and also the edge s_ls_2. Then by previous argument we can say G_2^2 is generically globally rigid.

Using the Lemma 3, $G_l^2 \bigcup G_2^2$ must be generically globally rigid. It is a subgraph of $(G_l \bigcup G_2)^2$ on same vertex set and hence generically globally rigid by Lemma 4. If the vertex set of this graph is that of G_{UD}, then the theorem is proved. If not then we must find another vertex joined by a single edge to $C_l \bigcup C_2$ and by similar argument we proceed until the set of vertices of $G_l \bigcup G_2 \bigcup G_3 \bigcup \ldots\ldots\ldots\ldots \bigcup G_r = G$ (for some r) is similar to G_{UD} and G^2 is generically globally rigid. G^2 is a subgraph of G_{UD}^2 retains all the vertices of G_{UD}. Thus G_{UD}^2 must be generically globally rigid. Furthermore G_{UD}^2 is a subgraph of G_{UD}^{ED2} on same vertex set. Therefore G_{UD}^{ED2} is a generically globally rigid graph.

4.2 Theorem 2: If G_{UD} be a UD graph and an edge 2- connected graph then G_{UD}^{ED3} is a generically globally rigid graph.

Proof: For proving this theorem we need the following Lemmas:

Lemma 5: If a UD graph corresponding to a wireless sensor network is in the form of a cycle C_{UD} then C_{UD}^{ED3} is generically globally rigid graph.

Proof: The proof is straight forward as lemma 1.

Lemma 6: If H_0 be a generically globally rigid graph in $\Re^3$ with atleast four vertices and if a super graph H_l be defined by adjoining one vertex to the vertex set of H_0 and four edges, each connecting the new vertex to four different vertices of H_0. Then H_l is generically globally rigid.

Lemma 7: If $H_l = (V_l,E_l)$ and $H_2 = (V_2,E_2)$ be two generically globally rigid graphs in $\Re^3$ with atleast four vertices in common then $H_l \bigcup H_2 = (V_l \bigcup V_2, E_l \bigcup E_2)$ is also generically globally rigid.

Now we provide the proof of main theorem:

If G contains just one cycle, we have done by Lemma [5]. Now suppose G contain more than one cycle and one of them is $C_l = s_ls_2s_3\ldots\ldots\ldots.s_n$. If the vertex set of C_l is similar as of G_{UD} then also the theorem is true by Lemma [5].

Now suppose a vertex set of C_l is not similar to G_{UD}. Since G_{UD} is connected, therefore every vertex in $G_{UD} \sim C_l$ is joined by a path to C_l and hence there is a vertex of $G_{UD} \sim C_l$ by a single edge to a vertex of C_l. Call it s_L and let edge be s_ls_L. Since G_{UD} is edge 2- connected, thus there exist another path between s_l and s_L except the single edge s_ls_L. Then there will be a cycle. Call it C_2, containing s_2 and s_n as adjacent vertices of s_l. Clearly this cycle can not contain both s_2 and s_n as an adjacent vertex of s_l. Suppose it does not contain s_2 as a successor of s_l. Consider a graph $G_l = (V_l,E_l)$

with vertex set that of C_1 together with s_1s_L. Then G_1^3 has an its edge set the edge set of C_1^3 and five more edges s_1s_L, s_2s_L, s_3s_L, $s_{n-1}s_L$ and s_ns_L.

Lemma [6] Identifying C_1^3 as H_0, G_1^3 is generically globally rigid graph. Consider also the graph $G_2 = (V_2,E_2)$ with vertex set of C_2 together with s_2 and s_n if these are not in C_2 and with edge set of C_2 together with s_1s_2 and s_1s_n if s_n is not in C_2. Then arguing as in previous paragraph but applying twice to Lemma [6], we have that G_2^3 is generically globally rigid. The two graphs G_1^3 and G_2^3 are both generically globally rigid and have a common set of atleast four vertices (s_n, s_1, s_2 and s_L). Hence the graph formed from the union of the graph G_1^3 and G_2^3 is generically globally rigid by Lemma [7]. This graph is obviously a subgraph of $(G_1 \bigcup G_2)^3$ with the same vertex set. Thus $(G_1 \bigcup G_2)^3$ is generically globally rigid.

If there are any vertices of G_{UD} which are not vertices of $(G_1 \bigcup G_2)$, then above argument must br repeated by finding a vertex which is connected by a single edge to $(G_1 \bigcup G_2)$, then determining a cycle containing that edge and so on. The process must be repeated until the set of vertices of $G_1 \bigcup G_2 \bigcup G_3 \bigcup \ldots\ldots \bigcup G_r=G$ for some r is identical with the vertex set of G_{UD} and G^3 is generically globally rigid. G^3 is a subgraph of G_{UD}^3 retains all the vertices of G_{UD}. Thus G_{UD}^3 must be generically globally rigid. Furthermore G_{UD}^3 is a subgraph of G_{UD}^{ED3} on same vertex set. Therefore G_{UD}^{ED3} is a generically globally rigid graph.

5 Localization Problem in Unit Disk Graph

Let S be the set of sensor nodes. d_{ij} be the given distance between the certain pair of nodes s_i and s_j. In unit disk graph s_i and s_j are connected if $d_{ij} \leq R$ were R is the radius of the sensing circle.

Suppose the coordinates p_i of certain nodes s_i (anchor nodes) are known. The localization problem is one of finding a map $p:S \rightarrow \Re^d$ (d=2or3) which assign coordinate $p_j \in \Re^d$ to each node s_j such that $\|p(i)-p(j)\| \leq R$ holds for all pair i and j for which s_i and s_j are connected and assignment is consistent with any coordinate assignment provided in the problem statement.

The solvability of localization problem for sensor networks can be considered as follows: suppose a framework is constructed which is a realization i.e. the edge lengths corresponding to the collection of inter sensor distances. The framework may or may not be rigid and even if it is rigid there may be another and differently shaped framework which is a realization (constructible on same vertex set, edge set and length assignment). If there is a unique rigid realizing framework, up to congruence, consistent with the distances between nodes i.e. the framework is globally rigid then the sensor network can be consider as a rigid entity of known structure. Then we need only to know the Euclidian positions of several sensor nodes to locate the whole framework in two or three dimensions.

WSN localization is unique (up to rotation translation or reflection) if and only if its underlying graph is globally rigid. Thus the global rigidity of the graph ensures the unique localization of the node of a wireless sensor networks.

6 Conclusion

We have given an algorithm to construct systematically generically globally rigid graphs from those graphs which do not have these properties. This construction basically depends on adding of more edges in the graph. We have given the construction of globally rigid graph through Euclidean distance powers of Unit Disk graph. If the nodes are considered as vertices of a globally rigid graph then the nodes can be uniquely localized up to translation, rotation and reflection. In this way we can localize the nodes of a wireless sensor networks.

Acknowledgments. Ms *USHA SHARMA*, one of the authors of this paper acknowledges the grant received from Department of Science & Technology (D.S.T.), Government of India, New Delhi for carrying out this research.

References

1. Purohit, G.N., Verma, S., Sharma, U.: Powers of a Graph and Associated Graph Labeling. International Journal of Computer and Network Security (IJCNS) 2(4), 45–49 (2010)
2. Anderson, B.D.O., Belhumeur, P.N., Eren, T., Goldenberg, D.K., Stephen Morse, A., Whiteley, W., Richard Yang, Y.: Graphical properties of easily localizable sensor network"s. Wireless Networks 15(2), 177–191 (2009)
3. Ren, T., Bryan, K.L., Thoma, L.: On coloring the square of unit disk graph, University of Rhode Island Dept. of Computer Science and Statistics, Tech. Rep. (2006)
4. Bryan, K.L., Ren, T., DiPippo, L., Henry, T., Fay-Wolfe, V.: Towards Optimal TDMA Frame Size in Wireless Sensor Networks, University of Rhode Island Dept. of Computer Science and Statistics, Tech. Rep.
5. Khot, V., Hemnani, P.: Localization in wireless sensor networks, `http://www.siesgst.com/images/pdf/beyond_academics/sample_paper.pdf`
6. Alfakih, A.Y.: On The Universal Rigidity of Generic Bar Frameworks, vol. 5(1), pp. 7–17, ISSN 1715-0868, `http://cdm.ucalgary.ca/index.php/cdm/article/viewFile/103/103`
7. Priyantha, N.B., Balakrishnan, H., Demaine, E., Teller, S.: Anchor Free Distributed Localization in Sensor Networks, April 8 (2003), `http://cricket.csail.mit.edu/papers/TechReport892.pdf`
8. Connelly, R.: Generic Global rigidity, October 27 (2003), `http://www.math.cornell.edu/~connelly/global-6.pdf`
9. Hendrickson, B.: Condition for unique graph realizations. SIAM J. Comput. 21(1), 65–84 (1992)

Retracted: A New Protocol to Secure AODV in Mobile AdHoc Networks

Avinash Krishnan, Aishwarya Manjunath, and Geetha J. Reddy

Department of Computer Science and Engineering
M. S. Ramaiah Institute of Technology
{avinash.krishnan,aishwarya.m}@netapp.com, geetha.y.j@gmail.com
http://www.msrit.edu

Abstract. In this paper we propose a game theoretic approach called The New Protocol and we integrate this into the reactive Ad hoc On-demand Distance Vector (*AODV*) routing protocol to provide defense against blackhole attacks. This idea is based on the concept of non-cooperative game theory. The *AODV-NEW* outperforms *AODV* in terms of the number of dropped packets when blackhole nodes exist within a *MANET* (Mobile AdHoc Network).

Keywords: AODV, AODV-MUD, MANET, eMANET, Blackhole Attack.

1 Introduction

The nature of MANETs makes them suitable to be utilized in the context of an emergency case for various rescue teams as we depict in fig. 1. Due to their flexibility and self organizational capabilities MANETs are well suited for scenarios where certain network services such as message routing and event notification have to be provided quickly and dynamically without any centralized infrastructure. For instance we can have situations where a potentially large number of recovery workers from multiple organizations must co-operate and co-ordinate in areas where natural and man-made disasters have damaged much of the infrastructure including telecommunication services.

The inherently vulnerable characteristics of MANETs make them susceptible to attacks and counter attacks might end up being too little too late. Traditional security measures are not applicable in MANETs due to the following reasons:-

1. MANETs do not have infrastructure due to the absence of centralized authority.
2. MANETs do not have the grounds for an a priori classification due to the fact that all nodes are required to co-operate in supporting the network operations
3. Wireless attacks may come from all directions within a MANET.
4. Wireless data transmission does not provide a clear line of defense, gateways and firewalls, and

N. Meghanathan et al. (Eds.): CCSIT 2011, Part III, CCIS 133, pp. 378–389, 2011.

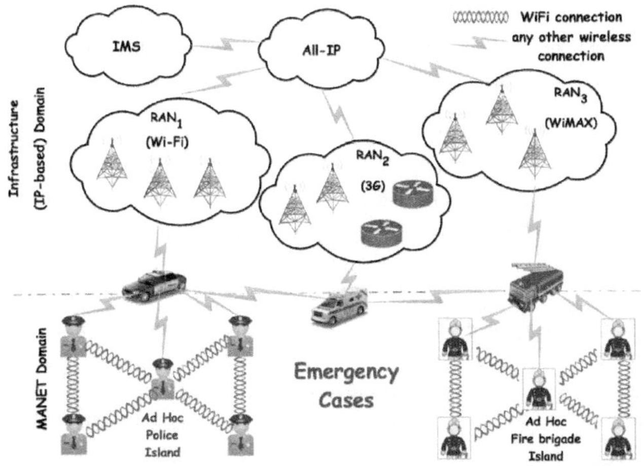

Fig. 1. An example when MANETs are deployed to support the various working teams in emergency cases such as forest fires or terrorist attacks

5. MANETs have a constantly changing topology owing to the movement of nodes in and out of the network

This paper deals with a Game Theoretic approach integrated into the AODV routing protocol to provide defense against black hole attacks.

1.1 End Users

1. Industrial and commercial end users make use of applications involving co-operative mobile data exchange.
2. Cell-based mobile network companies use mesh-based mobile networks as they can be operated as robust, inexpensive alternatives or enhancements to the traditional methods.
3. In the military networking scenario, requirements for robust, IP-compliant data services within mobile wireless communication networks are present and many of these networks consist of highly-dynamic autonomous topology segments.
4. Fabric manufacturers are developing technologies of “wearable” computing and communications which may provide applications for MANET technology.
5. Emergency response units use combination of MANETs with satellite-based information delivery to provide an extremely flexible method for establishing communications for fire/safety/rescue operations or other scenarios requiring rapidly-deployable communications with survivable, efficient dynamic networking.

1.2 General Constraints

Applications envisioned for Mobile Ad hoc networks have to be designed keeping in mind the following constraints:

- Mobility – The network topology in an Ad hoc wireless network is highly dynamic due to the movement of nodes. Hence an ongoing session suffers frequent path breaks. Disruption occurs due to the movement of the intermediate nodes in the path or due to the movement of end nodes.
- Bandwidth Constraint – In a wireless network the radio band is limited, and hence the data rates it can offer are much less than what a wired network can offer. This requires that the routing protocols use the bandwidth optimally by keeping the overhead as low as possible. The limited bandwidth availability also imposes a constraint on routing protocols in maintaining the topological information. Due to the frequent changes in topology, maintaining consistent topological information at all the nodes involves more control overhead, which, in turn results in more bandwidth wastage.
- Error-Prone Shared Broadcast Radio Channel – The broadcast nature of the radio channel poses a unique challenge in Ad hoc wireless networks. The wireless links have time-varying characteristics in terms of link capacity and link-error probability. This requires that the Ad hoc wireless network routing protocol interacts with the MAC layer to find alternate routes through better-quality links. Also, transmissions in Ad hoc wireless networks result in collisions of data and control packets. This is attributed to the hidden terminal problem described in the next section. Therefore it is required that Ad hoc wireless network routing protocols find paths with less congestion.
- Hidden and exposed terminal problems – The hidden terminal problem refers to the collision of packets at a receiving node due to the simultaneous transmission of those nodes that are not within the direct transmission range of the sender, but are within the transmission range of the receiver. Collision occurs when both nodes transmit packets at the same time without knowing about the transmission of each other.

  The exposed terminal problem refers to the inability of a node which is blocked due to transmission by a nearby transmitting node to transmit to another node.
- Resource Constraints – Two essential and limited resources that form the major constraint in an Ad hoc wireless network are battery life and processing power. Devices used in Ad hoc wireless networks in most cases require portability, and hence they also have size and weight constraints along with the restrictions on the power source. Increasing the battery power and processing ability makes the nodes bulky and less portable. Thus Ad hoc wireless network routing protocols must optimally manage these resources.

In this work we propose a methodology, for securing the reactive Ad hoc On-demand Distance Vector (AODV) routing protocol, called AODV-NEW. This approach sets up a game between a MANET and the malicious nodes, and chooses a strategy which is dominant at Nash Equilibrium.

This paper is organized as follows. In section 2, we introduce the concept of secure routing in MANETs and we discuss fundamental concepts related to our work. In Section 3, we describe the AODV-NEW. We conclude this paper and discuss our plans for future work in section 4.

2 Background

1. Routing
   Routing is an important function of any MANET given the fact that the nodes play the role of routers. Therefore, the implementation of routing protocols is an essential requirement whilst we need to guarantee that these protocols are secure.

   The disadvantage of the most ratified routing protocols forMANETs is the fact that they have been developed without considering security mechanisms in advance. The case becomes more critical when extreme emergency communications must be deployed at the ground of a rescue. In these cases adversaries could launch different kind of attacks damaging the quality of the communications.
2. AODV
   The Ad hoc On-Demand Distance Vector Algorithm assumes that, the nodes, which do not lie on active paths, neither maintain any routing information nor participate in any periodic routing table exchanges. Further, a node does not have to discover and maintain a route to another node until the two have a need to communicate, or, unless the former node is offering its services as an intermediate forwarding station to maintain connectivity between two other nodes. When the local connectivity of the mobile node is of interest, each mobile node can become aware of the other nodes in its neighborhood by the use of several techniques, including local broadcasts (not system wide) known as *hello messages*. The routing tables of the nodes within the neighborhood are organized to optimize response time to local movements and provide quick response for requests for establishment of new routes. The algorithms primary objectives are:
   - To broadcast discovery packets only when necessary
   - To distinguish between local connectivity management (neighborhood detection) and general topology maintenance
   - To disseminate information about local connectivity to those neighboring mobile nodes that are likely to need the information
3. Blackhole Attack
   A blackhole attack is a kind of Denial-of-Service (DoS) attack accomplished by dropping packets. In fig. 3, we show a case where two malicious nodes launch blackhole attacks succeeding to drop packets within the MANET. The blackhole problem in MANETs is a critical security problem given the fact that one or more malicious nodes use the routing protocol to advertise themselves as having the shortest path to the node whose packets they want to intercept. An attacker launches a blackhole attack by replying to every

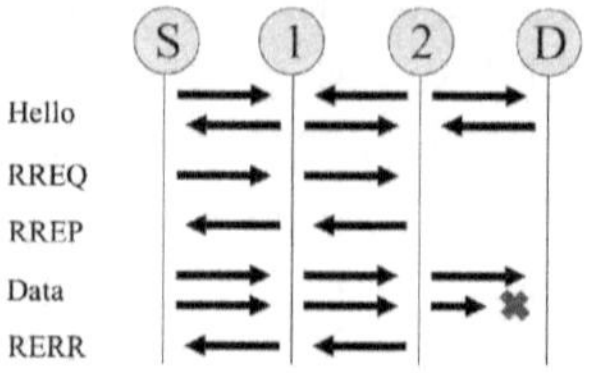

Fig. 2. Sequence Diagram of the basic AODV Protocol

routing request very fast, pretending that it has a route to the destination node. After the launching of a blackhole attack, the malicious node has the potential to drop the packets or to use its place on the route in order to launch a man-in-the-middle attack. The packet dropping may be selective affecting only a particular type of packets. The effectiveness of a blackhole attack is based on the fact that in AODV, the source node uses the first route which it receives in order to transmit its packets to the destination node. Due to the fact that a malicious node does not have to check its routing table, it is the first node that responds to the Route REQuest (RREQ) by sending a Route REPly (RREP) to the source node.

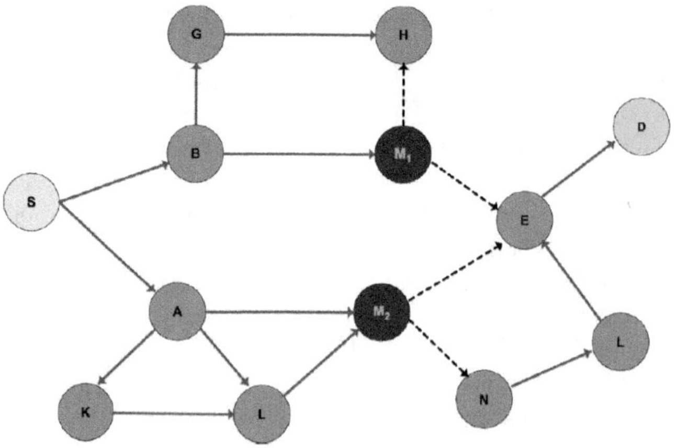

Fig. 3. An example of a MANET where blackhole nodes damage the routing function by dropping packets

4. Game Theoretic Aspects
   Game theory is a scientific area that aims to model situations in which decision makers have to take specific actions with mutual and possibly conflicting consequences. Game theory is also a branch of mathematics which has been explored fairly recently within the last century. The ideas presented in game theory are useful in outlining what the best decision making techniques are, in certain situations. The basic assumptions that underlie the theory are:

(a) the decision makers are rational and (b) they reason strategically which means they take into account their knowledge or expectations of other decision makers. The essential elements of a game are the players, the actions and the payoffs, known collectively as the rules of the game. A solution of a two-player game is a pair of strategies that a rational pair of players might use. The solution that is most widely used for game theoretic problems is the Nash equilibrium (NE). At a NE, given the strategies of other players, no user can improve its utility level by making individual changes in its strategy. In our work, we propose a non-cooperative non-zero sum game theoretic approach. In game theory a zero-sum game highlights a situation in which a players gain or loss is exactly balanced by the losses or gains of the other players. In order to find the NE in a non-zero sum game we have to consider the concept of the dominant strategy. A strategy is called dominant when it is better than any other strategy for one player, no matter how that players opponents could play.

Nash-Theorem. Every game that has a finite strategic form, with finite numbers of players and finite number of pure strategies for each player, has at least one NE involving pure or mixed strategies.

We call a strategy pure strategy when a player chooses to take one action with probability 1. A Mixed strategy is a strategy which chooses randomly between possible moves. In other words this strategy is a probability distribution over all the possible pure strategy profiles. The game we examine satisfies the assumptions of the Nash theorem which means that a NE exists in that game.

3 Proposed Methodology

In this section, we define the emerging non-cooperative game between the MANET and potential blackhole nodes and we describe our proposed methodology called AODV-NEW. About the former, we study a two-player non-cooperative nonzero sum route selection game in order to forward the packets of the legitimate nodes across the MANET. Furthermore, we describe the potential non-cooperative strategies of each player. In fig. 3 we show a MANET scenario where two malicious nodes M1, M2 are trying to launch blackhole attacks. Specifically, the adversaries have the potential to advertise shorter routes to a destination node. As a result the source nodes believe that their packets should be passed through the nodes M1, M2. In this case, the function of the routing protocol has been disrupted. Later on, the malicious nodes succeed in dropping a significant number of packets.

In accordance with our methodology, we will formulate the described situation using a game theoretic framework. The players of the game are 1. the MANET and 2. a blackhole node. Thus, the two-player game is emerging. The game reaches a NE as we will show later on. The concept could be generalized for n blackhole nodes assuming all the two-player games between the MANET and each malicious node.

1. *Formulation of the Game theoretic framework*
   In our work we examine especially the case of a non-cooperative game where the MANET tries to defend the most critical route among all the routes that are delivered to the source node by the AODV protocol. On the other hand, malicious nodes try to launch blackhole attacks on these routes. Towards the formulation of our game we define the strategy space for each player.
   - strategy space of the MANET:
     - D_i: the MANET defends a route i
     - D_{-i}: the MANET defends a route -i
   - strategy space of a blackhole node:
     - m_i: the blackhole node attacks a route i
     - m_0: the blackhole node does not attack the MANET
     - m_h: the blackhole node attacks a route h

   Therefore, the MANET has the potential to play:

$$D = (d_i, d_i, d_{-i}) \ . \tag{1}$$

   And each malicious node,

$$M = \begin{pmatrix} m_i \\ m_0 \\ m_h \end{pmatrix} \tag{2}$$

Our idea is to choose a strategy for the MANET such that, no matter what strategy a malicious node chooses, the MANET always remains at an advantage.

In our work we assume that a malicious node (Blackhole Node) can attack a MANET by

(a) Placing itself in a dense region of the MANET
    AND
(b) Sending False RREPs with shortest path to destination

Note: The metric for choosing a route is assumed to be the Hop Count obtained from the RREP

Assumption 1 can be justified as follows:

This proposal revolves around the fact that any blackhole node prefers to choose a dense region in the network to place itself due to the following reasons:

(a) The payoff of the malicious node is high only if it is in a dense region
(b) The payoff of the malicious node is not satisfactorily high (lesser than the payoff of the MANET) if it resides in a sparse region

We offer to present a solution which

(a) Does not choose a route which is most likely to have a malicious node (dense region)
(b) Does not choose which apparently has the least hop count (it might be a blackhole)

We develop a probability function which reflects the above points in our solution.

If **p** is the probability of not choosing a route R with hop count **h** and average density $\boldsymbol{\rho}$, then

$$\mathbf{p} = e^{1-h} + \varphi e^{\frac{-\rho_t}{\rho}} \tag{3}$$

Here, φ is the security factor of the network which is proportional to the degree of security needed. As φ increases, p increases and a less optimal route is selected in terms of hop count. ρ_t is the threshold density of the network, the maximum density which a given network can support.

After finding p, the procedure is repeated recursively with a lesser security factor each time. Hence, this protocol provides a reasonable amount of security even in case of a multiple coordinated attack in which case a legitimate node is surrounded by only blackhole nodes.

The behavior of the probability function with different values of **h** and ρ are shown in the graphs in fig. 4 and fig. 5.

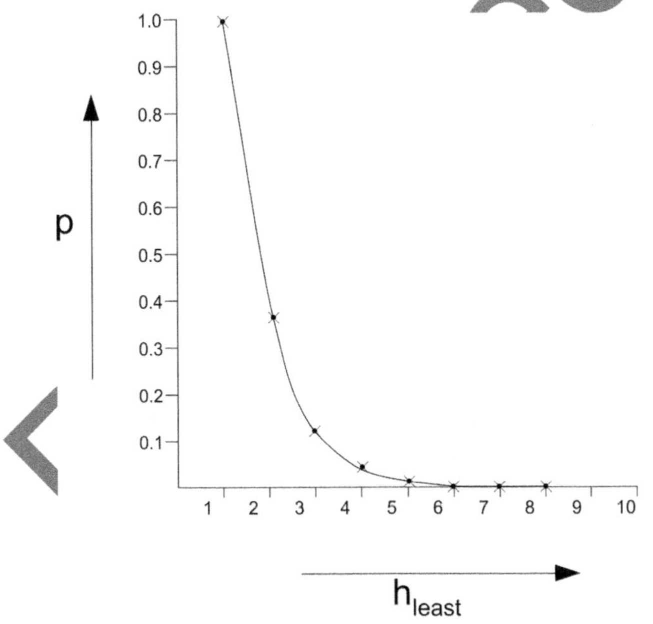

Fig. 4.

It is evident from the graphs that there is an exponential decrease in p with the increase of ρ and an exponential increase in p with the decrease of h.

In other words, Higher the Density, Higher the suspicion; Lower the Hop Count, Higher the suspicion.

It is worth mentioning why our game is a non-zero sum game. Due to the fact that even if the attacker does not attack the MANET is defending,

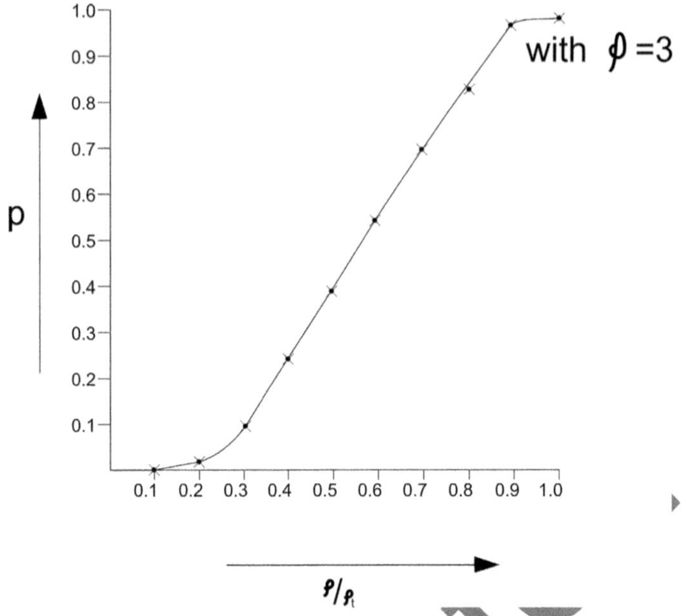

Fig. 5.

the payoff of the latter decreases while the payoff of the malicious node is steady. The above assumption contradicts with the zero-sum assumption which means that our game is a non-zero sum game. In this kind of games the NE has to be found considering the concept of the dominant strategy as shown.

2. *Integration of AODV-NEW into AODV*
   In this section, we describe how AODV-NEW is integrated into the AODV protocol. We assume that a node S wants to find out a route to a node D. According to AODV, if S does not have a route to D, it has to send a RREQ message to its one-hop neighbors. Every node A which receives a RREQ checks its routing table. If A does not have a route to D it forwards the packet according to AODV. On the other hand, if A has a route to D, first, it adds the number of cumulative neighbors from A to D, CNN_{AD} to CNN_{SD} (cumulative number of neighbors of S to D) in the RREP packet which A generates. Also RREP packet contains a field to hold the number of maximum neighbors any node in the route has (nb_{max}), which is initialized from the routing table. After the RREP packet is sent through the reverse route established by AODV, at every intermediate node I in the reverse route,
   (a) Hop Count H is incremented
   (b) CNN_{SD} += nn_I
       where nn_I is the number of neighbors of I.
   (c) Update nb_{max}

If A itself is the destination, A generates a reply packet with the following parameters:

(a) Hop Count H = 0
(b) $CNN_{SD} = nb_{max} = nn_A$

Again, at every intermediate node I in the reverse route,

(a) Hop Count H is incremented
(b) CNN_{SD} += nn_I
where nn_I is the number of neighbors of I.
(c) Update nb_{max}

According to AODV, S sends its packets to D using the route which it receives first. In other words, S saves only one route to D. According to AODV-NEW, S has to save all the routes which it receives. For this purpose, S waits for a timeout to receive all the potential routes. We set the value of timeout equal to Net Traversal Time (NetTT). This is the maximum time in milliseconds waiting for the receiving of a RREP after the sending of a RREQ. In the next step, S derives the density ρ_i of each route i which has cached using the following equation:

$$\rho = \frac{CNN_{SD}}{h_i} \tag{4}$$

S then derives the average density of the region using the formula:

$$\rho_{avg} = \frac{\Sigma \rho_i}{Number\ of\ Replies} \tag{5}$$

S then sorts all the replies on increasing h and calculates the probability p given by the equation,

$$p = e^{1-h} + \varphi e^{\frac{-\rho_t}{\rho}} \tag{6}$$

After finding p, we repeat the following steps till a route with hop count hleast is selected:

(a) Generate a random number R
(b) If $0 \leq R \leq P$, remove the route with hop count h from consideration
(c) For the remaining candidate routes, calculate p again with $\varphi = \frac{\varphi}{2}$
(d) Return to step (a)

This solution is elegant for the following reasons:

- The malicious node can never guess the hop count it needs to advertize to stand selected by the source.
- The malicious node can never guess when it needs to send the RREP to stand selected by the source.
- Optimality is not compromised.
- This protocol works reasonably well even in case of a multiple coordinated attack.
- Number of false positives generated is negligible.
- The security factor φ provides flexibility to the end user who can make a suitable tradeoff between security and optimality

We integrate within the AODV protocol our proposed methodology as we show in algorithms 1 and 2.

Algorithm 1. – Node S sends RREQ

If a node A receives RREQ then,
    If A does not have a route to D then,
        A adds itself to the source route
        Forwards the packet according to AODV
    Else if A has a route to D, generate RREP with
        Initialize h = h_{AD}
        Initialize CNN_{SD} = CNN_{AD} + nn_A
        Initialize nb_{max} from the routing table
        Send RREP to S
      At every intermediate node I from A to S
            Increment h
            CNN_{SD} += nn$I$
            Update nb_{max}
Else if A is D, generate RREP with
        Hop Count H = 0
        CNN_{SD} = nb_{max} = nn_A
  At every intermediate node I from D to S
        Increment h
        CNN_{SD} += nn_I
        Update nb_{max}

Algorithm 2. – Node S receives RREP

While (! ReplyTimeout)
    Receive RREPs
Calculate $\rho_i = \frac{CNN_{SD}}{h_i}$
Calculate $\rho_{avg} = \frac{\Sigma\rho_i}{NumberofReplies}$
Sort the RREPs on increasing h
Calculate p = $e^{1-h} + \varphi e^{\frac{-\rho_t}{\rho}}$
While route with hop count h_{least} is not selected
    Generate a random number R
    If (0 $\leq$ R $\leq$ P)
        remove the route with hop count h_{least} from consideration
        For the remaining candidate routes,
        calculate p again with $\varphi = \frac{\varphi}{2}$

4 Conclusion and Future Work

In this paper we proposed a game theoretic approach called AODV-NEW and we integrated it into the AODV protocol for securing AODV in Mobile Ad hoc NETworks (MANETs) against blackhole attacks. Theoretically it has been proved that AODV-NEW outperforms AODV in terms of number of packets dropped within a MANET. To this end, we formulated a game between the MANET and each potential blackhole node. We found the NE and we showed that the most effective route to forward the packets according to AODV-NEW is the least possible route to be attacked.

Our future work includes integration of detection, identification and removal of blackhole nodes in a MANET into the same protocol.

Also, we plan to integrate a criticality factor into equation for p to provide protection of critical nodes in sparse regions of the network. After that, we plan to extend the solution to other protocols apart from AODV – both reactive and proactive.

References

1. Emmanouil, A., Panaousis, E.A., Christos, P.: A Game Theoretic Approach for Securing AODV in Emergency Mobile Ad Hoc Networks. In: The 9th IEEE International Workshop on Wireless Local Networks (WLN 2009), Zrich, Switzerland, October 20-23 (2009)
2. Emmanouil, A., Panaousis, E.A., Christos, P.: Securing ad hoc networks in extreme emergency cases. In: WWRF, Paris, France (2009)
3. Panaousis, E.A., Ramrekha, A.T.R., Birkos, K., Papageorgiou, C., Talooki, V., Matthew, G., Nguyen, C., Sieux, C., Politis, C., Dagiuklas, T., Rodriguez, J.: A framework supporting extreme emergency services. In: ICT-MobileSummit, Santanter, Spain (2009)
4. Perkins, C., Royer, E.: Ad-hoc on-demand distance vector routing. In: Proceedings of the 2nd IEEE Workshop on Mobile Computing Systems and Applications, pp. 90–100 (1997)

Spelling Corrector for Indian Languages

K.V.N. Sunitha and A. Sharada

CSE Dept, G.Narayanamma Institute of Technology and Science,
Shaikpet, Hyderabad, India
k.v.n.sunitha@gmail.com,
sharada.nirmal@gmail.com

Abstract. With the advancements in computational linguistic processing, the paper work is replaced by documents in the form of soft copies. Though there are many software and keyboards available to produce such documents, the accuracy is not always acceptable. The chance of getting errors is more. This paper proposes a model which can be used to correct spellings of Indian languages in general and Telugu in particular. This paper also discusses the experimental setup and results of implementation. There are few spell checkers and correctors which were developed earlier. The spelling corrector proposed in this paper is different from that in terms of the approach used. Main claim of the paper is implementation of the correction algorithm and proposal of architecture.

Keywords: Indian Languages, Spelling Corrector, Edit distance, Validation, Samdhi Formation.

1 Introduction

Documents prepared in local language reach large number of people. A lot of research is carried out throughout India over the decade and most of the documents are being prepared in local language through software available for the purpose. Though there are many software's and keyboards available to produce such documents, the accuracy is not always acceptable, the chance of getting errors is more.' particularly for Indian language most of which are highly inflecting.

Indian language has close tie with Sanskrit and is characterized by a rich system of inflectional morphology and a productive system of derivation, saMdhi (conation of full words) and compounding. This means that the number of surface words will be very large and so will be the raw feature space, leading to data scarcity [1].

The main reason for richness in morphology of Indian languages is a significant part of grammar that is handled by syntax in English (and other similar languages) is handled within morphology. Phrases including several words in English would be mapped on to a single word in Telugu.

In highly inflecting language, such as Telugu, there may be thousands of word forms of the same root, which makes the construction of a fixed lexicon for any reasonable coverage hardly feasible. Also in compounding languages, complex concepts can be expressed in a single word, which considerably increases the number of possible word forms.

N. Meghanathan et al. (Eds.): CCSIT 2011, Part III, CCIS 133, pp. 390–399, 2011.

2 Literature Survey

There are few spell checkers and correctors which were developed earlier [8]. This spelling corrector is different from that in terms of the approach used. Many spell checkers store a list of valid words in the language. A given word is assumed to be free of spelling errors if that word is found in this stored list. But, as discussed in the above section, it is very difficult, if not impossible, to cover all the words of any Indian language, where each word may have thousands and millions of word forms. Such languages have a disadvantage with word-based approaches, thus leading to data scarcity problem in n-gram language modeling.

Factored language models have recently been proposed for incorporating morphological knowledge in the modeling of inflecting language. As suffix and compound words are the cause of the growth of the vocabulary in many languages, a logical idea is to split the words into shorter units [2].

2.1 Our Earlier Work in NLP

Details of our work in NLP can be found in papers [3] [4]. The necessity of designing this architecture can be found in [3] and details of ***notation used for transliteration*** and ***corpus*** on which we are working can be found in paper [4].

3 Proposed Model

The design of Spelling Corrector for Telugu, basically involves the interface architecture, Trie Creation, and Spelling Corrector module architecture. The user need to enter the input provided through the GUI. Then the input is syllabified and analyzed based on the rules to display the root word, inflection and correct word.

3.1 Trie Data Structure

In computer science, a trie, or prefix tree, is an ordered tree data structure that is used to store an associative array where the keys are usually strings. Unlike a binary search tree, no node in the tree stores the key associated with that node; A Trie is a multi-way tree structure useful for storing strings over an alphabet.

Trie Creation

The *trie* considered here is different from standard trie in two ways:

1) A standard trie does not allow a word to be prefix of another, but the trie we used here allows a word to be prefix of another word. The node structure and search algorithm also is given according to this new property.

2) Each word in a standard trie ends at an external node, where as in our trie a word may end at either an external node, or the internal node. Irrespective of whether the word ends at internal node or external node, the node stores the index of the associated word in the occurrence list.

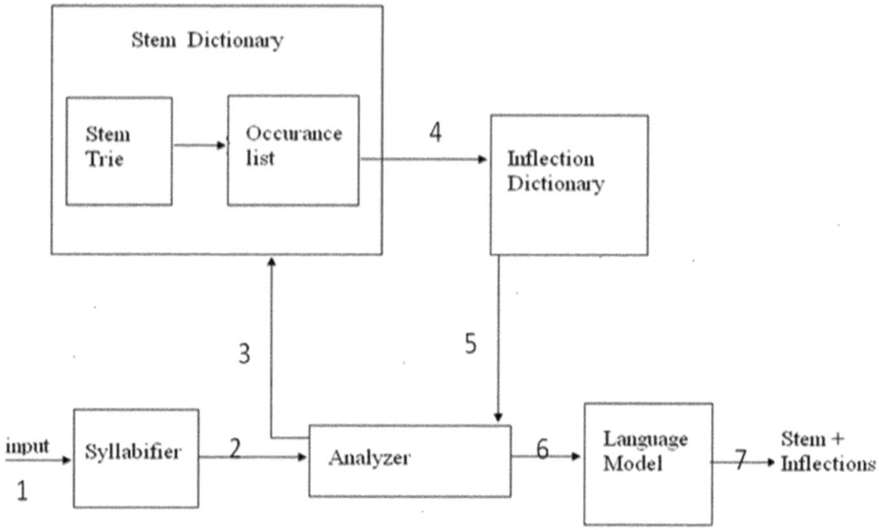

Fig. 1. Search process in a Trie

The node structure is changed such that, each node of the trie is represented by a triplet **<C,R,Ind>**.

C represents character stored at that node.

R represents whether the concatenation of characters from root till that node forms a meaningful stem word. Its value is 1, if characters from root node to that node form a stem, 0 otherwise.

Ind represents index of the occurrence list. Its value depends on the value of R. Its value is -1 (negative 1), if R=0, indicating it is not a valid stem. So no index of occurrence list matches with it. If R=1, its value is index of occurrence list of associated stem.

Advantages Relative to Binary Search Tree

The following are the main advantages of tries over binary search trees (BSTs):

- Looking up keys is faster. Looking up a key of length m takes worst case O(m) time. A BST performs O(log(n)) comparisons of keys, where n is the number of elements in the tree, because lookups depend on the depth of the tree, which is logarithmic in the number of keys if the tree is balanced. Hence in the worst case, a BST takes O(m log n) time. Moreover, in the worst case log(n) will approach m. Also, the simple operations tries use during lookup, such as array indexing using a character, are fast on real machines.
- Tries can require less space when they contain a large number of short strings, because the keys are not stored explicitly and nodes are shared between keys with common initial subsequences.
- Tries facilitating longest-prefix matching, helping to find the key sharing the longest possible prefix of characters all unique.

3.2 Architecture of the Proposed System

3.2.1 Dictionary Design

Dictionary design here involves creating stem words dictionary and inflections dictionary. Main claim of this work is the design of stem word dictionary which is implemented as an **Inverted Index** for better efficiency. The Inverted index will have the following 2 data structures in it:

a) *Occurrence list*, which is an array of pairs, <stem word, list of inflection indexes>
b) Variation of *trie* consisting of stem words

Occurrence list is constructed based on the grammar of the language, where each entry of the list contains the pair <stem word, index list of possible inflections>

3.2.2 Stem Dictionary

A Stem dictionary is maintained, which contains all the root words. As shown in the Table 1, each stem also contains a list of indices of Inflection dictionary indicating inflections possible with that word.

Table 1. Stem Dictionary

Word	Inflection Indices
amma (అమ్మ)	1, 2, 4, 6,7,8
anubhUti (అనుభూతి)	1,7
ataDu (అతడు)	....
Ame (ఆమె)	
AlOcana (ఆలోచన)	
AlApana (ఆలాపన)	
.....	

Table 2. Inflection dictionary

Sl.No	Inflection
1	ki (కి)
2	tO (తో)
3	lO (లో)
4	guriMci (గురించి)
5	lu (లు)
6	yokka (యొక్క)
7	ni (ని)
8	valana (వలన)
....	....

Inflections Dictionary

All the possible inflections of the language are stored in the Inflection dictionary. Table 2 gives structure of Inflection Dictionary.

4 Spelling Corrector

A spelling corrector detects the spelling errors and gives the correct form of word. When a mis-spelled word is detected, a quantitative measure of the closeness of spelling is used to select the probable words list.

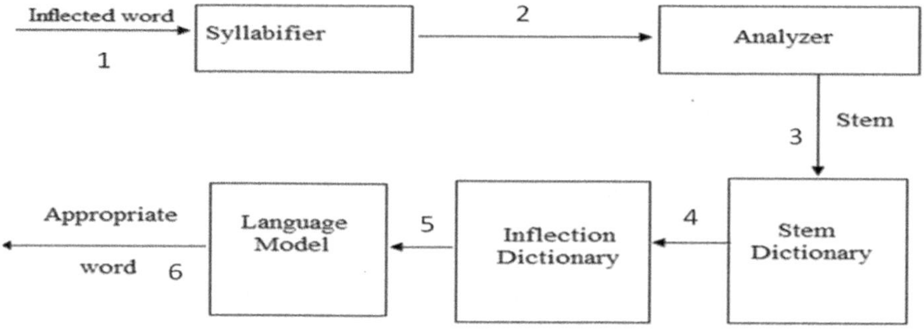

Fig. 2. Block Diagram for Spelling Corrector

4.1 Block Diagram for Spelling Corrector

Input the spelling corrector is an Inflected word. Syllabifier takes this word and divides the word into syllables and identifies if the letter is a vowel or a consonant. After applying the rules syllabified form of the input will be obtained. Once the process of syllabification is done, this will be taken up by the analyzer. Analyzer separates the stem and inflection part of the given word. This stem word will be validated by comparing it with the stem words present in stem dictionary. If the stem word is present, then the inflection of the input word will be compared with the inflections present in inflection dictionary of the given stem word. If both the inflections get matched then it will directly displays the output otherwise it takes the appropriate inflection(s) through comparison and then displays.

4.2 Steps for Spelling Correction

- Receiving the inflected word as an input from the user.
- Syllabifying the input
- Analyzing the input and validating the stem word.
- Identifying the appropriate inflection for the given stem word by comparing the inflection of given word with the inflections present in inflection dictionary of the stem word.
- Displaying the appropriate inflected word.

4.3 Rules for Implementing Spelling Corrector

Telugu is a syllabic language. Similar to most languages of India, each symbol in Telugu script represents a complete syllable. Syllabification is the separation of the words into syllables, where syllables are considered as phonological building blocks of words. It is dividing the word in the way of our pronunciation. The separation is marked by hyphen.

In the morphological analyzer, the main objective is to divide the root word and the inflection. For this, we divide the given input word into syllables and we compare the syllables with the root words and inflections to get the root word and appropriate inflection.

The Roman transliteration format has been considered for the representation of Vowels and Consonants in Telugu in this software.

The user input, the inflected word is taken as the input to the syllabification module and it divides the word into lexemes and decides whether each lexeme is a vowel(V) or a consonant(C), type of the lexeme is stored in a different array and it is processed by applying the Syllabification rules defined below in this section.

For example, considering the word **"nAnnacAriku"** (నాన్నచారికు) which is misspelled form of **"nAnnagariki"** (నాన్నగారికి) meaning **"to father"**, the input is given the user in Roman transliteration format. This input is basically divided into lexemes as:

nAnnacAriku

⇩

n – A – n – n – a – c – A – r – i – k – u

⇩

c – v – c – c – v – c – v – c – v – c – v

Now, the array is processed which gives the type of lexeme by applying the rules of syllabification one by one.

- **Applying Rule 1**

" No two vowels come together in Telugu literature."

The given user input does not have two vowels together. Hence this rule is satisfied by the given user input. The output after applying this rule is same as above. If the rule is not satisfied, an error message is displayed that the given input is incorrect. Now the array is:

- **Applying Rule 2**

" Initial and final consonants in a word go with the first and last vowel respectively."

Telugu literature rarely has the words which end up with a consonant. Mostly all the Telugu words end with a vowel. So this rule does not mean the consonant that ends up with the string, but it means the last consonant in string. The application of this rule2 changes the array as following:

c – v – c – c– v – c – v – c – v – c – v

⇩

cv – c – c – v – c – v – c – v – cv

This generated output is further processed by applying the other rules.

- **Applying Rule 3**

" **VCV**: The C goes with the right vowel."

The string wherever has the form of VCV, then this rule is applied by dividing it as V – CV. In the above rule the consonant is combined with the vowel, but here in this rule the consonant is combined with the right vowel and separated from the left vowel. To the output generated by the application of rule2, this rule is applied and the output will be as:

cv – c – c – v – c – v – c – v – cv

⇩

cv – c – c – v – cv – cv – cv

This output is not yet completely syllabified, one more rule is to be applied which finishes the syllabification of the given user input word.

- **Applying Rule 4**

" Two or more Cs between Vs - First C goes to the left and the rest to right."

It is the string which is in the form of VCCC*V, then according to this rule it is split as VC – CC*V. In the above output VCCV in the string can be syllabified as VC – CV. Then the output becomes as:

cv – c – c – v – cv – cv – cv

⇩

cvc– cv – cv – cv – cv

Now that this output is converted to the respective consonants and vowels. Thus giving the complete syllabified form of the given user input.

nAn – na –cA – ri – ku

⇩

cvc – cv – cv – cv – cv

Hence, for the given user input, **"nAnnacAriku",** the generated syllabified form is,

"nAn – na – cA – ri – ku".

4.4 Spelling Correction Process

Using the rules the possible set of root words are combined with possible set of inflections and the obtained results are compared with the given user input and the nearest possible root word and inflection are displayed if the given input is *correct.*

If the given input is *not correct* then the inflection part of the given input word is compared with the inflections of that particular root word and identifies the nearest possible inflection and combines the root word with those identified inflections, applies sandhi rules and displays the output.

The user input is syllabified and this would be the input to the analyzer module. Matching the syllabified input from starting with the root words stored in dictionary module a possible set of root words is obtained.

For eg: ***nAnnacAriku*** ← user input

⇩ (After syllabification)

nAn-na-cA-ri-ku

Now, scanning the syllabified input from starting and matching it with the set of root words stored in dictionary module.

⟹ ***nAn-na-cA-ri-ku*** (matching from starting)

This process will identify the possible set of root words from the Stem dictionary using the procedure mentioned in [3].

....
nAnna (నాన్న)
nANemu (నాణెము)
....

Once possible root words identified the given word is segmented into two parts, first being the root word and second part inflection. Now the inflection part is compared in the reverse direction for a match in the inflection dictionary. It will consider only the inflections that are mentioned against the possible root words, thus reducing the search space and making the algorithm faster.

nAn-na-cA-ri-ku ⟸ (matching from reverse)

Possible set of inflections in inflections dictionary

ki (కి)
ni (ని)
gAriki (గారికి)

After getting the possible set of root words and possible set of inflections they are combined with the help of SaMdhi formation rules. Here in this example ***cA-ri-ku*** is compared with the inflections of the root word ***nAnna***

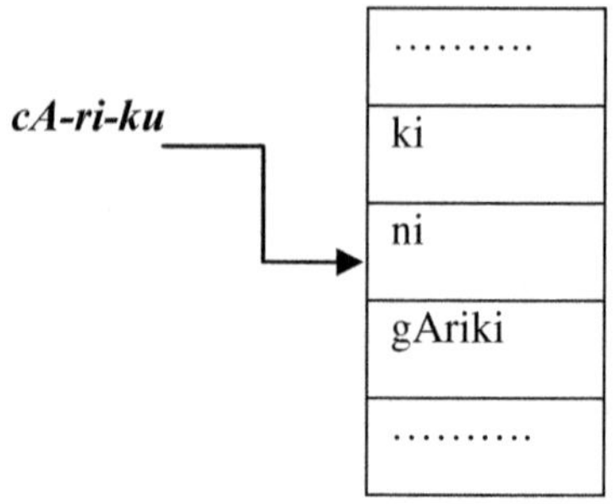

After comparing it identifies ***gAriki*** as the nearest possible inflection and combines the root word with the inflection and displays the output as ***"nAnnagAriki"***.

5 Results and Experimental Setup

This model is implemented using PERL. We have used a corpus of 5 Million words, including 2 Million words GNITS Corpus developed in our institute and CIIL corpus.

Table 3. Sample Results

Input word	Nearest Root word	Nearest Inflection	Is Correct	Corrected form
pustakAlu (పుస్తకాలు)	pustakaM	lu	yes	---
pustakAdu (పుస్తకాడు)	pustakaM	du	no	pustakAlu (పుస్తకాలు)
pustakaMdO (పుస్తకండో)	pustakaM	lO tO	no	pustakaMlO (పుస్తకంలో) pustakaMtO (పుస్తకంతో)
putakaM (పుతకం)	patakaM (పతకం) pustakaM	---	no	patakaM (పతకం) pustakaM (పుస్తకం)

When there is more than one root word or more than one inflection has minimum edit distance then the model will display all the possible options. User can choose the correct one from that. E.g., when the given word is ***pustakaMdO*** (పుస్తకండో), the inflections ***tO*** making it ***pustakaMtO*** (పుస్తకంతో) meaning 'with the book' and ***lO*** making it ***pustakaMlO*** (పుస్తకంలో) meaning 'in the book') mis are possible. Present work will list both the words and user is given the option. We are working on improving this by selecting the appropriate word based on the context. Sample results are shown in Table 3.

6 Conclusion

The model proposed is useful for the spelling correction of native language documents and it could be a base work for accelerating the researches on speech recognition software and NLP. This tool will be a big boon for the researchers working on Natural Language Processing for Telugu. This tool also helps in knowing all the words that can be derived from a single root. The tool will help the beginners to learn new words and the specialists to create new terminology.

With the advancements in computational linguistic processing, although the paper work or the manual effort is replaced by documents and soft copies the chance of getting errors is more. Hope our *Spelling Corrector* improves this situation.

References

1. Uma Maheshwara Rao, G.: Morphological complexity of Telugu. In: ICOSAL-2 (2000)
2. Lovins, J.: Development of stemming algorithm. Journal of mechanical translation and computational linguistics 11, 22–31 (1968)
3. Sunitha, K.V.N., Sharada, A.: Building an Efficient Language Model based on Morphology for Telugu ASR. In: KSE-1, CIIL, Mysore (March 2010)
4. Sunitha, K.V.N., Sharada, A.: Telugu Text Corpora Analysis for Creating Speech Database. IJEIT 1(2) (December 2009), ISSN 0975-5292
5. Paice, C., Husk, G.: Another Stemmer. ACM SIGIR Forum 24(3), 566 (1990)
6. Porter, M.F.: An algorithm for suffix stripping. In: Readings in Information Retrieval, pp. 313–316. Morgan Kaufmann Publishers Inc., San Francisco (1997)
7. Xu, J., Croft, W.B.: Corpus based stemming using co-occurrence of word variants. ACM Trans. Inf. Syst. 16(1), 61–81 (1998)
8. Dawson, J.L.: Suffix removal for word conflation. Bulletin of the Association for Literary and Linguistic Computing 2(3), 33–46 (1974)
9. Krovetz, R.: Viewing morphology as an inference process. In: Proceedings of Sixteenth Annual International ACM SIGIR Conference on Research and Development in Information Retrieval, pp. 191–203 (1993)
10. vishwabharat@tdil
11. Emerald Group Publishing Ltd., Issues in Indian languages computing in particular reference to search and retrieval in Telugu Language
12. LANGUAGE IN INDIA Strength for Today and Bright Hope for Tomorrow, August 2006, vol. 6 (2006)

Voltage Collapse Based Critical Bus Ranking

Shobha Shankar[1] and T. Ananthapadmanabha[2]

[1] Research Scholar and Assistant Professor,
Department of Electrical and Electronics Engineering,
Vidyavardhaka College of Engineering, Mysore, India
shobha.prathi@gmail.com
[2] Professor and Head,
Department of Electrical and Electronics Engineering,
The National Institute of Engineering, Mysore, India
drapn2008@yahoo.co.in

Abstract. Identification of critical or weak buses for a given operating condition is an important task in the load dispatch centre. It has become more vital in view of the threat of voltage instability leading to voltage collapse. This paper presents a fuzzy approach for ranking critical buses in a power system based on line flow index and voltage profiles at load buses. The line flow index determines the maximum load that is possible to be connected to a bus in order to maintain stability before the system reaches its bifurcation point. Line flow index (LF index) along with voltage profiles at the load buses are represented in fuzzy set notation. Further they are evaluated using fuzzy rules to compute composite index. Based on this index, critical buses are ranked. The bus with highest rank is the weakest bus as it can withstand a small amount of load before causing voltage collapse. The proposed method is tested on five bus test system.

Keywords: Composite index, critical bus ranking, fuzzy set notation, Line flow index.

1 Introduction

Voltage stability and system security are emerging as major problems in the operation of stressed power system The main cause for voltage collapse is the inability of the system to supply reactive power to cope up with the increasing load growth. The increase in load of a bus beyond a critical limit pushes the system to the verge of voltage collapse, if the system is not compensated adequately. This critical limit of the bus load is defined as the voltage stability margin. The voltage stability margin estimates the criticality of a bus. Hence, the identification of the critical buses in a system is useful in determining the location of additional voltage support devices to prevent possible voltage instability.

The occurrence of voltage collapse is very much dependent upon the maximum load that can be supported at a particular load bus. Any attempt to increase the load beyond this point could force the entire system into instability, leading to voltage

N. Meghanathan et al. (Eds.): CCSIT 2011, Part III, CCIS 133, pp. 400–409, 2011.

collapse. This would indicate that the power system physically could not support the amount of the connected load. Line flow index (LF index) is used to estimate maximum loadability of a particular load bus in the system. The load buses are ranked according to their maximum loadability, where the load bus having the smallest maximum loadability is ranked highest. Hence this bus is identified as the weakest bus because it can withstand only a small amount of load increase before causing voltage collapse. This information is useful to planning or operation engineers in ensuring that any increment in the system will not exceed the maximum loadability, hence violating the voltage stability limit.

A fuzzy set theory based algorithm is used to identify the weak buses in a power system. Bus voltage and reactive power loss at that bus are represented by membership functions for voltage stability study [1]. Newton optimal power flow is used to identify the weakest bus / area, which is likely to cause voltage collapse. The complex power – voltage curve is examined through Newton optimal power flow. The indicator, which identifies the weakest bus, was obtained by integrating all the marginal costs via Kuhn-Tucker theorem [2]. A fast voltage stability indicator (FVSI) is used to estimate the maximum loadability for identification of weak bus. The indicator is derived from the voltage quadratic equation at the receiving bus in a two bus system. The load of a bus, which is to be ranked is increased till maximum value of FVSI is reached and this load value is used as an indicator for ranking the bus [3]. A weak bus-oriented criterion is used to determine the candidate buses for installing new VAR sources in VAR planning problem. Two indices are used to identify weak buses based on power flow Jacobian matrix calculated at the current operating point of the system [4]. A neural network based method for the identification of voltage-weak buses/areas uses power flow analysis and singular value decomposition method. Kohonen neural network is trained to cluster/rank buses in terms of voltage stability [5]. Voltage Stability Margin Index (VSMI) is developed based on the relationship of voltage stability and angle difference between sending and receiving end buses. VSMI is used to estimate voltage stability margin and identify weak transmission lines and buses at any given operating condition [6]. The weakest bus, most loaded transmission path for that bus from voltage security point of view is identified using nodal voltage security assessment. Control actions are taken to alleviate power flows across that branch to enhance voltage security condition [7]. The Singular Value Decomposition method is used in identifying weak boundaries with respect to voltage instabilities well as in the assessment of the effects of possible disturbances and their corrective actions [8]. The existing techniques [1] - [8] are basically to identify weak buses for a pre contingency system. But for secured operation of the stressed power system, it is essential to know the criticality of a bus at the verge of voltage collapse.

This paper presents a fuzzy approach to rank critical buses in a power system. Voltage stability margin expressed in terms of static voltage collapse proximity indicator at critical load of a selected load bus accurately estimates the criticality of that bus from the voltage collapse point of view. Hence the line flow index is used as a static voltage collapse proximity indicator. The line flow index and bus voltage profiles of the load buses are expressed in fuzzy set notation. Further, they are evaluated using fuzzy rules to compute composite severity index. Critical buses are ranked based on decreasing order of composite index. The proposed approach is tested on 5 bus test system.

2 Formulation of Line Flow Index

Consider a typical transmission line of an interconnected power system shown in fig.1. Optimal impedance concept used in [9] to develop a simple criterion for voltage stability is as follows;

Load impedance $Z_L \angle \theta$ fed by constant voltage source Vs with internal impedance $Z_S \angle \Phi$ as shown in fig.2. Application of maximum power transfer theorem to the equivalent circuit shown in fig.2 results in $Z_L / Z_S = 1$ for maximum power to be flown to the load from the source. Z_L/Z_S is used as the VCPI voltage collapse proximity indicator. The system is considered to be voltage stable if this ratio is less than 1, other- wise voltage collapse occurs in the system.

The single line model shown in [9] is used, but the system is represented by the admittance model. It is assumed that the load at the bus is total power flow in the represented line. Equivalent admittance model is shown in fig. 3 where $Y_L \angle \theta$ is the line admittance and the $Y_R \angle \Phi$ is the load admittance and

$$\Phi = \tan^{-1}[\, Q_r / P_r]$$

The indicator is developed with an assumption that only the modulus of the load admittance changes with the change in the system load i.e., it is assumed that always efforts will be made in the system to maintain the constant power factor for the changes in the bus load. Increase in load results in increase in admittance and there by increase in current and the line drop and hence decrease in the voltage at the receiving end.

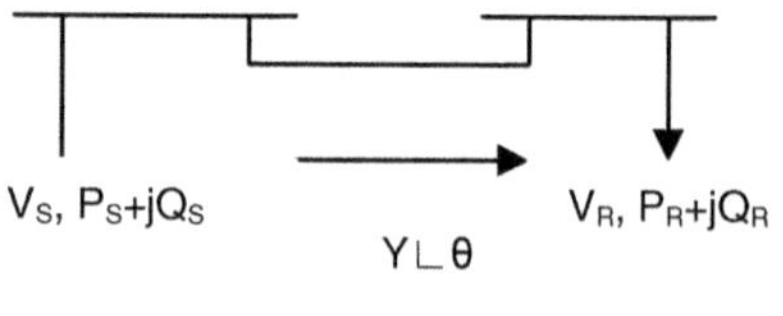

Fig. 1. Typical transmission line of a power system network

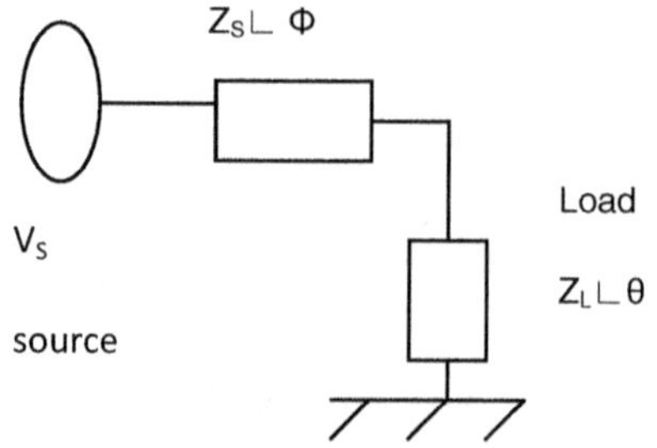

Fig. 2. Thevenin's equivalent of a network

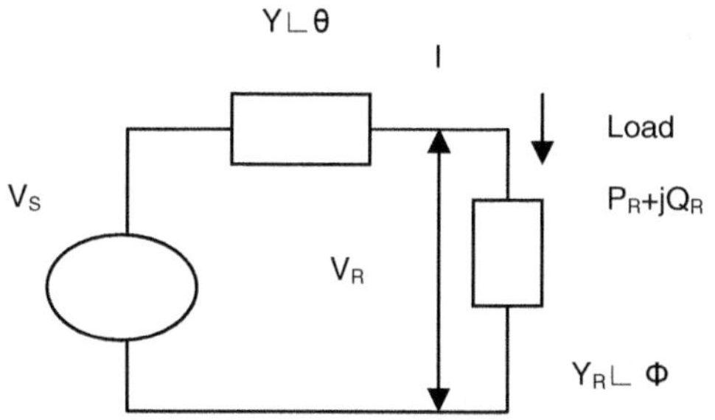

Fig. 3. Transmission line modeled with admittance

$$I = V_s Y_{eq} \tag{1}$$

$$Yeq = \frac{Y_L Y_R}{\left[\sqrt{Y_L^2 + Y_R^2 + 2Y_L Y_R \cos(\theta - \Phi)}\right]}$$

$$V_R = I / Y_R \tag{2}$$

$$\frac{V_S}{Y_R}\left(\frac{Y_L Y_R}{\left[\sqrt{Y_L^2 + Y_R^2 + 2Y_L Y_R \cos(\theta - \Phi)}\right]}\right)$$

Now the active power at the receiving end is given by

$$P_R = V_R I \cos\emptyset$$

$$P_R = \frac{V_S^2 Y_L^2 Y_R}{\left[\sqrt{Y_L^2 + Y_R^2 + 2Y_L Y_R \cos(\theta - \Phi)}\right]} \tag{3}$$

The maximum real power transfer to the bus is obtained by applying the condition $\delta P_R / \delta Y_R = 0$ which leads to a criterion of $|Y_L| = |Y_R|$

Substituting $|Y_L| = |Y_R|$ in equation (3), we get

$$P_{R(max)} = \frac{V_S^2 Y_L \cos\emptyset}{[2(1 + \cos(\theta - \Phi)]} \tag{4}$$

Equation (4) gives the maximum real power that can be transferred through a given line safely without any voltage instability threat. The actual line flow is compared with this maximum power transfer and the stability margin for that line is defined as,

$$LF\ index = \frac{Actual\ real\ power\ flow\ in\ the\ line\ (P_R)}{Maximum\ real\ power\ that\ can\ be\ transferred\ P_{R(max)}}$$

$$LF\ index = \frac{2P_R\left(1 + \cos\left(\theta - \Phi\right)\right)}{V_S^2 Y_L \cos\emptyset} \tag{5}$$

P_R values can be obtained from the load flow solution.

The main cause for the problem of voltage instability leading to voltage collapse is stressed power system characterized by excessive line loading. As the maximum power transfer theory restricts the amount of load that can be transferred through a line, the LF index precisely indicate the voltage stability margin for a selected operating condition.

3 Methodology

Voltage stability margin expressed in terms of static voltage collapse proximity indicators at a given load of a selected load bus accurately estimates the criticality of that bus from the voltage collapse point of view. Hence computation of these indicators along with voltage profiles at load buses can serve as a very good measure in assessing the criticality of a bus. In addition to line flow index, bus voltage profiles are used to identify weak buses under varying load condition. The point at which LF index is close to unity indicates the maximum possible connected load called as maximum loadability at the point of bifurcation. The line flow indices and bus voltage profiles are divided into different categories and are expressed in fuzzy set notation. The severity indices are also divided into different categories. The fuzzy rules are used to evaluate the severity of load buses. Composite index is computed based on severity of LF index and voltage profiles at different load buses. Based on this index the critical buses are ranked. The ranking obtained using fuzzy approach is verified with fast voltage stability index (FVSI) [3].

3.1 Bus Voltage Profiles

The bus voltage profiles are divided into three categories using fuzzy set notations: low voltage (LV), normal voltage (NV) and over voltage (OV). Figure 4 shows the correspondence between bus voltage profiles and the three linguistic variables.

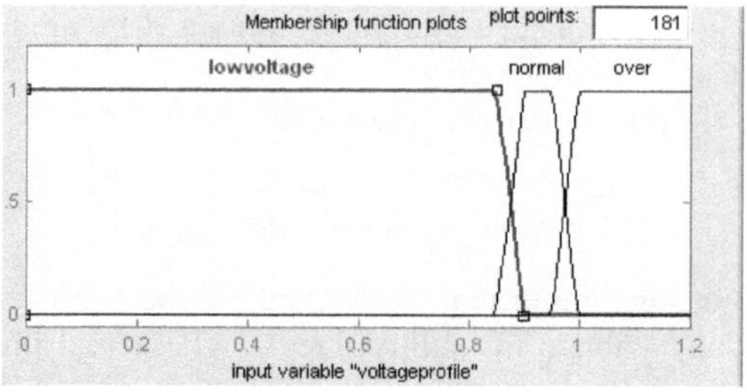

Fig. 4. Voltage profiles and the corresponding linguistic variables

3.2 Line Flow Index

The line flow indices are divided into five categories using fuzzy set notations: very small index (VS), small index (S), medium index (M), high index (H), and very high index (VH). Fig. 5 shows the correspondence between the line flow index and the five linguistic variables. Fig. 6 shows the severity index for voltage profile and line flow index.

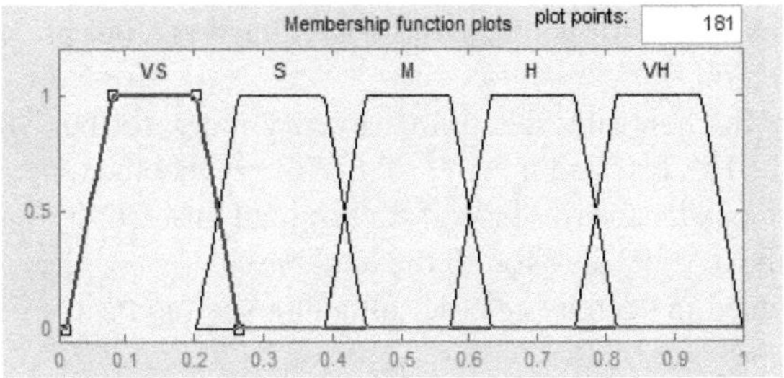

Fig. 5. Line flow index and the corresponding linguistic variables

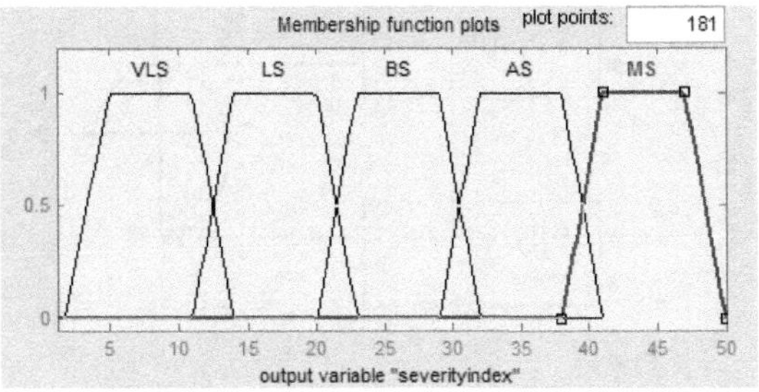

Fig. 6. Severity index for voltage profile and line flow index

The fuzzy rules, which are used for evaluation of severity indices of bus voltage profiles and line flow indices, are given in Table 1.

Table 1. Fuzzy rules

Quantity	Severity
LV NV OV	MS BS MS
VS S M H VH	VLS LS BS AS MS

Note: VLS - very less severe; LS - less severe BS - below severe; AS - above severe; MS - more severe.

The composite index is obtained by adding the two severity indices as shown in Fig. 7. The composite index is obtained at critical load for all the load buses. The buses are ranked in decreasing order of composite index.

The following are the steps involved in the approach:

1. Perform the load flow analysis at base case load to determine bus voltage profiles.
2. For each line, determine the line flow index using equation (5).
3. For a chosen load bus, increase the reactive power loading until the load flow solution fails to converge. The load prior to divergence is critical load for that bus.
4. At critical load, determine bus voltage profiles at load buses and line flow index for each line.
5. Express bus voltage profiles and line flow index in fuzzy set notation.

6. Severity index of line flow index and bus voltage profiles are also represented in fuzzy set notation.
7. Using Fuzzy-If-Then rules determine severity index for bus voltage profiles and LF-index. The FIS is tested in MATLAB 7 Fuzzy Toolbox.
8. Compute composite severity index for each load bus, $CI = \sum SI_{VP} + \sum SI_{LF}$.
9. Repeat the above procedure for all the load buses.
10. Buses are ranked in decreasing order of composite index.

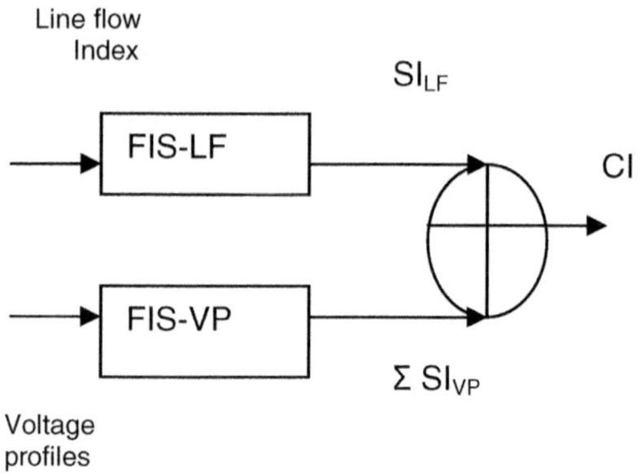

Fig. 7. Parallel Operated Fuzzy Inference System

4 Test Results

The proposed approach is tested on 5-bus test system. It consists of 2 generators, 3 load buses and 7 transmission lines. Table 2 shows the voltage profile of load buses at base load and critical load at respective load buses. Critical load of a bus is determined by increasing reactive load at that bus until load flow fails to converge. Table 3 shows line flow index for each at base load and critical load at load buses. Table 4 and 5 shows severity index for voltage profiles and line flow index calculated using fuzzy rules shown in Table 1. Table 6 provides the composite index along with rank obtained from fuzzy approach.

Table 2. Load bus voltage profile at base case load and critical load

Load bus no.	Voltage in p. u. at base case load	Voltage in p. u. (critical load at bus 3)	Voltage in p. u. (critical load at bus 4)	Voltage in p. u. (critical load at bus 5)
3	0.987	0.7	0.8078	0.889
4	0.984	0.752	0.7543	0.748
5	0.972	0.892	0.8926	0.751

Table 3. Line flow index for each line at base case load and critical load

lines	LF index at base case load	LF index critical load at bus 3	LF index critical load at bus 4	LF index critical load at bus 5
1-2	0.083	0.135	0.115	0.15
1-3	0.187	0.155	0.146	0.189
2-3	0.128	0.092	0.075	0.061
2-4	0.141	0.096	0.086	0.059
2-5	0.168	0.125	0.120	0.133
3-4	0.015	0.325	0.015	0.006
4-5	0.038	0.784	0.770	0.571

Table 4. Severity indices for voltage profiles at critical load

Load bus no.	Severity Index for voltage profiles(SI_{VP})		
	Critical load at bus 3	Critical load at bus 4	Critical load at bus 5
3	46.2	34.8	15.4
4	42.3	42.7	40.2
5	23.5	23	42.0
$\sum SI_{VP}$	112	100.5	97.6

Table 5. Severity Indices for LF index at critical load

Lines	Severity Index for LF index(SI_{LF})		
	Critical load at bus 3	Critical load at bus 4	Critical load at bus 5
1-2	4.71	4.71	7.61
1-3	8.75	6.56	12.8
2-3	4.71	4.71	4.71
2-4	4.71	4.71	4.71
2-5	4.71	4.71	4.71
3-4	13.5	4.71	4.71
4-5	41.9	39.6	29.4
$\sum SI_{LF}$	82.99	69.71	68.65

Table 6. Composite Index and Rank using fuzzy approach and FVSI

Bus no.	$CI==\sum SI_{VP} + \sum SI_{LF}$	Rank	FVSI	Rank
3	194.99	I	0.966	I
4	170.21	II	0.964	II
5	166.25	III	0.679	III

From the results, it can be observed that bus number 3 is the most critical bus and bus number 5 is less critical. This indicates that at the verge of voltage instability or voltage collapse, it is the load at bus no. 3 to be monitored and controlled at the earliest. Further additional voltage support devices can be installed to improve system stability. The result obtained from fuzzy approach is compared with Fast Voltage Stability Index (FVSI). The ranking from both the methods agree with each other. The fuzzy approach effectively ranks the critical buses eliminating the masking effect.

5 Conclusion

A fuzzy based composite severity index is developed in this paper to rank critical or weak buses in a power system. Line flow index and voltage profiles at load buses are evaluated using fuzzy rules to compute the severity index, which is further used to rank the critical buses. The identification of a critical bus in a power system is useful in determining the location of additional voltage support devices to prevent possible voltage instability. The proposed method is tested on 5 bus test system.

References

1. Alammari, R.A.: Fuzzy System Applications for Identification of Weak Buses in Power Systems. The Arabian Journal for Science and Engineering 27(2B) (October 2002)
2. Hong, Y.Y., Gau, C.H.: Voltage Stability Indicator for Identification of the Weakest Bus /Area in Power Systems. IEE Proceedings Generation Transmission Distribution 144(4) (July 1994)
3. Musirin, I., Abdul Rahman, T.K.: Estimating maximum loadability of weak bus identification using FVSI. In: IEEE Power Engineering Review (November 2002)
4. Chen, Y.L.: Weak Bus-Oriented Optimal Multi-objective VAR Planning. IEEE Transactions on Power Systems 11(4) (November 1996)
5. Song, Y.H., Wan, H.B., Johns, A.T.: Kohonen neural network based approach to voltage weak buses/areas identification. IEE Proceedings Generation Transmission Distribution 144(3) (May 1997)
6. He, T., Kolluri, S., Mandal, S., Galvan, F., Rastgoufard, P.: Identification of Weak Locations in Bulk Transmission Systems Using Voltage Stability margin Index. In: IEEE Power Engineering Society General Meeting (2004)
7. Prada, R.B., Palomino, E.G.C., Pilotto, L.A.S., Bianco, A.: weakest bus, most loaded transmission path and critical branch identification for voltage security reinforcement. Electrical Power Systems Research (73), 217–226 (2005)

8. Ekwue, A.O., Wan, H.B., Cheng, D.T.Y., Song, Y.H.: Singular Value Decomposition method for voltage stability analysis on the National Grid System(NGC). Electrical Power and Energy Systems (21), 425–532 (1999)
9. Chebbo, A.M., Irving, M.R., Sterling, M.J.H.: Voltage Collapse Proximity Indicator: Behaviour and Implications. IEE Proceedings-C 139 (May 1992)

Biographies

Shobha Shankar received the B.E. degree in Electrical Engineering in 1994, M.Tech degree in Power Systems in 1997 from the University of Mysore, Mysore. She is working as Asst. Professor in the department of Electrical and Electronics Engineering, Vidyavardhaka College of Engineering, Mysore. She is pursing her Doctoral degree from Visvesvaraya Technological University, India in the field of Power Systems.

T. Ananthapadmanabha received the B.E. degree in Electrical Engineering in 1980, M.Tech degree in Power Systems in 1984 and Ph.D. degree in 1997 from University of Mysore, Mysore. He is working as Professor and Head, Department of Electrical and Electronics Engineering, The National Institute of Engineering, Mysore. His research interest includes reactive power optimization, voltage stability, distribution automation and AI applications to power systems.

Multiplexer Based Circuit Synthesis with Area-Power Trade-Off

Sambhu Nath Pradhan[1] and Santanu Chattopadhyay[2]

[1] Dept. of ECE NIT-Agartala, and [2] Dept. of Electronics & ECE, IIT-Kharagpur, India
sambhu.pradhan@gmail.com, santanu@ece.iitkgp.ernet.in

Abstract. Due to the regularity of implementation, multiplexers are widely used in VLSI circuit synthesis. This paper proposes a technique for decomposing a function into 2-to-1 multiplexers performing area-power tradeoff. To the best of our knowledge this is the first ever effort to incorporate leakage into power calculation for multiplexer based decomposition. With respect to an initial ROBDD (Reduced Ordered Binary Decision Diagram) based representation of the function, the scheme shows more than 30% reduction in area, leakage and switching for the LGSynth91 benchmarks without performance degradation. It also enumerates the trade-offs present in the solution space for different weights associated with these three quantities.

Keywords: Power minimization, area-power trade off, multiplexer synthesis, ROBDD.

1 Introduction

Multiplexers have long drawn the attention of VLSI design and research community for circuit realization. This is mainly due to the high regularity of multiplexers that make the structure particularly suitable for VLSI implementation. Introduction of low-power regime has brought with it further challenges due to the increased usage of portable, handheld, battery-operated, plastic-packaged devices. This type of devices necessitate low-power consumption for increased battery life, low-cost etc. Due to this, researchers have been motivated to look into the multiplexer decomposition problems [3 - 7]. In these works, a large multiplexer is decomposed into a tree of 2-to-1 multiplexers. The problem of power-efficient decomposition has been handled in [3]. Here, given an arbitrary *n*-to-1 multiplexer with a fixed encoding for the data signal, minimum power balanced decomposition into a multiplexer tree consisting of 2-to-1 multiplexers has been done. Both uniform and nonuniform low power decompositions have been studied. Power dissipation of all the multiplexers in the tree is calculated from the ON probabilities of their outputs. In this work only single output functions have been considered. References [4] and [6] dealt with delay minimal decomposition of multiplexers. The main objective of [4] and [6] is to minimize the depth of the 2-to-1 multiplexer decomposed tree. Here, multi-output functions and power reduction issues are not considered. In [7] a method of estimating the signal

N. Meghanathan et al. (Eds.): CCSIT 2011, Part III, CCIS 133, pp. 410–420, 2011.

transition number in multiplexer tree has been proposed. It also describes a low power decomposition method based on signal transitions. In this work, the transition number or transition probability of input data signal is measured in advance. The drawback in this approach is that when the circuit is in working condition, we cannot say the exact transition probability or transition number of the data signal. It may be noted further that in [7] the authors have used a test vector generator to get an estimation of signal transitions. This is not very suitable since the input patterns fed to a circuit during its normal operation are generally substantially different from the test patterns. In normal operation, inputs are highly correlated, whereas, to maximize fault coverage, successive test patterns are made uncorrelated. Thus, until and unless the exact environment in which the circuit is going to be placed is known, it is not possible to predict the signal transitions.

Moreover, none of these techniques handled multi-output functions which are the most common structures in any digital system. The decomposition obtained in all the above works is in the form of tree only. Sharing of subfunctions at various levels of decomposition has not been considered. For multi-output functions, there exists a high chance of common subfunctions being shared by number of outputs. Authors in [12] have proposed a methodology to synthesize multi-output function using 2-1 multiplexers. The work also performed a trade-off between the area of the resulting circuit (in terms of number of 2-1 multiplexers) and the dynamic power consumed (measured as estimated switching activity over all multiplexers). However, the work ignored the leakage power consumed by the circuit under the premises that leakage power is quite insignificant as compared to the dynamic power. The International Technology Roadmap for Semiconductors (ITRS) projects an exponential increase in the leakage power with minimization of devices [2]. As the technology drops below 65 nm feature sizes, subthreshold leakage is expected to exceed the total dynamic power. As leakage current becomes the major contributor to power consumption, the industry must reconsider the power equation that limits system performances, chip sizes and cost.

In this paper we have presented a multiplexer targeted circuit synthesis scheme that thrives to attain the minimization of both dynamic and leakage power. To the best of our knowledge this is the first ever work that handles leakage power in multiplexer synthesis process. A trade-off has also been performed between the area of the resulting circuit and its estimated dynamic and leakage power consumptions.

Binary Decision Diagrams (BDDs) [1] are the natural representation of functions implemented using multiplexers. Each BDD node corresponds to a multiplexer. Figure 1(a) shows the BDD representation of a 2-output Boolean function, whereas, Figure 1(b) shows the corresponding multiplexer realization. Due to this natural correspondence, we have used Reduced Ordered BDD (ROBDD) representation of function to arrive at the area and power optimized multiplexer-based realization of the function.

The rest of the paper is organized as follows. In Section 2, different sources of power dissipation of CMOS circuits, estimation of switching activity and leakage power are given. Section 3 of this paper illustrates the multiplexer based circuit synthesis strategy. Section 4 shows the experimental result of our decomposition method.

2 Sources of Power Dissipation

In order to develop techniques for minimization of power dissipation, it is essential to identify various sources of power dissipation and different parameters involved in each of them. CMOS has emerged as the technology of choice for low power applications and is likely to remain so in the near future. The power dissipated in CMOS circuits is classified into dynamic power and leakage power.

2.1 Dynamic Power Dissipation

Dynamic power dissipation in CMOS circuit occurs when the circuit is in working condition or active mode. Following are the two major constituents of dynamic power dissipation [10]: Switching power, Short-circuit power.

Amongst these, the switching power is the dominating contributor. This occurs due to the charging and discharging of load and parasitic capacitors.

$P_{dynamic} = \alpha_L . C_L V_{DD}^2 . f + \sum_i \alpha_i . C_i . V_{DD} . (V_{DD} - V_T)$ here, α_L and α_i are the switching activity at the load and at the internal node of the circuit respectively. V_{DD} is the supply voltage, f is the frequency of operation, C_L and C_i are the load and internal gate capacitances respectively, V_T is the threshold voltage.

Switching activity estimation strategy

To compute the total switching activity in a BDD, we need to first find the switching activities at individual nodes and then sum them up to get the overall quantity. In the following, the process has been enumerated.

A Boolean function f can be expanded around one of its variable, say x, using Shannon Expansion [4] as follows.

$$f = x \cdot f_1 + x' \cdot f_0$$

where, f_1 and f_0 are the functions resulting from f, setting $x = 1$ and $x = 0$ respectively.

If $P_{on}[f]$ be the probability of the function f being ON, then,

$$P_{ON}[f] = P_{ON}[x].P_{ON}[f_1] + P_{ON}[x'].P_{ON}[f_0] = P_{ON}[x].P_{ON}[f_1] + (1-P_{ON}[x]).P_{ON}[f_0].$$

Similarly, if $P_{OFF}[f]$ be the probability of f being OFF, then,

$$P_{OFF}[f] = P_{OFF}[x].P_{OFF}[f_0] + P_{ON}[x].P_{OFF}[f_1] = (1-P_{ON}[x]).(1-P_{ON}[f_0]) + P_{ON}[x].(1-P_{ON}[f_1]).$$

Now, a switching of f implies either of the following:

Case I : f was ON at time t and is OFF at its successive time instant.
Case II: f was OFF at time t and is ON at its successive time instant.

Thus, if $P_{switching}[f]$ denotes the transition probability of f, then,

$$P_{switching}[f] = P_{ON}[f].P_{OFF}[f] + P_{OFF}[f].P_{ON}[f] = 2.\,P_{ON}[f].P_{OFF}[f] = 2.\,P_{ON}[f].\,(1-P_{ON}[f]) \quad (1)$$

Assuming uniform input probabilities, that is ON and OFF probabilities of inputs like x to be 0.5, $P_{ON}[f]$ can further be simplified to

$$P_{ON}[f] = 0.5\, P_{ON}[f_1] + 0.5\, P_{ON}[f_0] \quad (2)$$

ON probability of any ROBDD node with variable x can be computed by recursively descending down the tree and using Equation 2. The recursion is terminated when a trivial ROBDD node, i.e., a constant node is reached. At a trivial ROBDD node $P_{ON}[0] = 0$ and $P_{ON}[1] = 1$. After calculating ON probability of a ROBDD node we can calculate the switching probability using Equation 1. Switching probabilities of all nodes are then summed up to get the overall switching activity.

2.2 Leakage Power Dissipation

Static power dissipation occurs due to various leakage mechanisms. A good review of leakage current is given in [9]. Among the various leakage components, two main leakage current components are sub-threshold leakage current and gate oxide tunneling current.

Leakage power estimation

In this section, leakage power calculation at each of the ROBDD nodes has been illustrated. Each ROBDD node can be implemented using two transmission gates connected to form a multiplexer. To calculate the leakage of such a structure, we have used the runtime mode leakage [15] considering all input probabilities. It may be noted that input probabilities are already computed in the switching activity estimation process in Section 2.1. Figure 2 shows the realization of a multiplexer using transmission gates. Table 1 gives input dependent leakage current values. It may be noted that due to the symmetrical structure of the transmission gate multiplexer, leakage current values for the patterns '000' and '100' are same. Similarly, for the patterns '011' and '111', leakages are same. Leakage current dissipation for each of the other patterns is also same for this symmetrical structure. Simulation for leakage power has been carried out using Cadence Spectre at 90 nm UMC technology. Length and width of PMOS and NMOS transistors are 90 nm and 180 nm respectively. The supply is 1 voltage. We have calculated the leakage current and hence leakage power of multiplexer using the state probabilities of the multiplexer inputs. As we know the state probabilities of the individual input nodes of the multiplexer, we can compute the probability of each input state of the multiplexer. The estimated leakage power after calculating the probability of each state would thus be given by,

$$P_{leakage} = V_{dd} \textstyle\sum_k S_k * I_k \quad (3)$$

k is over all the possible eight input states of the multiplexer. S_k is the probability of state k and I_k is the leakage current in state k. V_{dd} is the supply voltage.

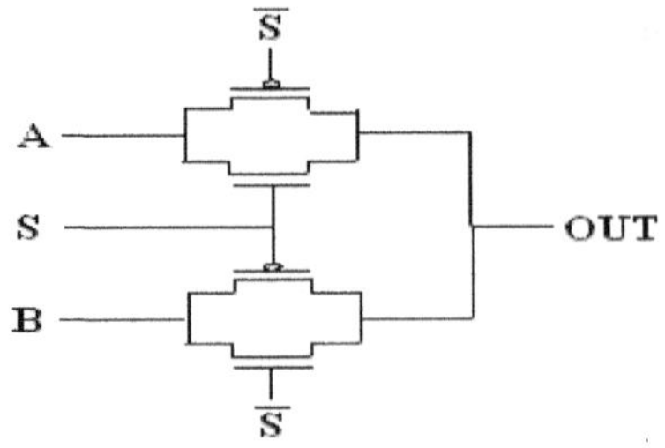

Fig. 2. Schematic of multiplexer

Table 1. Leakage current for different input values

S	A	B	Leakage current
0	0	0	0.01fA
0	0	1	2.44nA
0	1	0	2.44nA
0	1	1	0.02fA
1	0	0	0.01fA
1	0	1	2.44nA
1	1	0	2.44nA
1	1	1	0.02fA

3 Multiplexer Circuit Synthesis

In our approach, we have used a top-down heuristic [3] to decompose a given multi-output combinational function into 2-to-1 multiplexers. The heuristic has three objectives — minimize the area of the resulting circuit (in terms of number of 2-to-1 multiplexers needed), minimize the estimated switching activity at all multiplexers, and minimize leakage. The algorithm starts with a Reduced Ordered Binary Decision Diagram (ROBDD) based representation of the function using the BDD package *BuDDy* [13]. It then selects one of the variables around which the individual component functions of the multi output function are decomposed using Shanon expansion. This generates a set of next-level functions. These next-level functions are again decomposed using one of the remaining primary input variables. The process continues till we have trivial subfunctions (constant 0, 1, or a single variable).

The major decision in the process outlined above is to select a variable around which decomposition is to be carried out at a level. Ideally, for each variable choice, we should decompose the resulting subfunctions using all possible sequences of remaining variables to get the minimum. However, the process is of exponential complexity. To simplify the process, to compare between two contending variables at any level of decomposition we do the following.

(i) Area complexities are compared by looking into the number of unique subfunctions generated at next level due to decomposition through each of the variables.
(ii) Dynamic and leakage powers are estimated as shown in Section 2.1 and 2.2 respectively.

Since we are targeting a power-area trade-off, we associate a cost function with each of the variables to evaluate their fitness to be used for decomposition. For variable x, its cost is given by,

$$cost(x) = w_1 \frac{area}{max\_area} + w_2 \frac{Switching}{max\_switching} + w_3 \frac{leakage}{max\_leakage}$$

Here, *"area"* is the number of next level unique subfunctions and *"max-area"* is the maximum number of next level unique functions amongst all the variables. Similarly, *"max-switching"* is the maximum of total switching activities in the set of next level subfunctions generated through decomposition around each of the contending variables, and "max-leakage" is the maximum leakage value. The weights w_1 , w_2 , w_3 can be set by the designer with $w_1 + w_2 + w_3$ being equal to 1. Next the algorithm for decomposition is given formally.

Algorithm Mux-Decomposition

Input : A multi output Boolean function
Output : A multiplexer based graph representation of the input function
1. Obtain the ROBDD representation of the given circuit
2. While(no_variable>1 and no_function>0)
i) For(k=1 to no_variable) do
*restricted_function[k]=restrict_function_by_variable(k)/*Shannon expansion around k */*
check for possible sharing.
mux_count_function[k] = find_no_of_nextlevel_function(restricted_function[k])
switching_activity[k] = total_switching_of_nextlevel_function(restricted_function[k])
leakage_power[k]=tatal_leakage_power_of_nextlevel_function(restricted_function[k])
cost_function[k]=weighted_average(mux_count_function[k],switching_activity[k],leakage_power[k])
end for
ii) variable_selected = find_variable_resulting_minimum_cost()
iii) no_variable =no_variable -1
iv) no_function = update_function(restricted_function(variable_selected))
end while
3. Find multiplexer based graph representation

4 Experimental Results

In this section we present the results of our multiplexer based circuit synthesis heuristic. The decomposition procedure explained in Section 3 has been implemented using ROBDDs. The construction and manipulation of the ROBDDs for implementation are performed using BDD package *BuDDy* [13]. For the experiment, a set of LGSynth91 benchmark circuits [14] has been used. The experimentation of the algorithm has been done on these circuits on a Linux based platform with Pentium-IV processor having 3GHz clock frequency and 1 GB main memory. Simulation of multiplexer circuit has been carried out at 90 nm technology to get leakage power values.

First, we present a comparison of our multiplexer synthesis approach with the initial ROBDD results given by *BuDDy*. Here, BDD package, *BuDDy* tries to represent a Boolean function using the specified variable ordering, which, in the default case, is the order in which the inputs are specified. The package performs some reordering in the case of increase in the number of nodes beyond certain limit. It is never the area-optimized realization. Henceforth, initial area, switching and leakage obtained from this initial ROBDD will be termed as *initial_area*, *initial_switching* and *initial_leakage*. We also have compared our synthesis results with the inorder results obtained using *BuDDy*. To obtain *inorder* results we have followed the same algorithm described in Section 3 but in this case variable selection is not based on the minimum cost. Here, variable ordering is the same as the sequence in which inputs are specified in the circuit. Table 2 shows the area (in terms of no. of multiplexers), switching (switching activity) and leakage (nw) comparisons. As it can be seen from the table, our approach requires much lesser number of multiplexers compared to the initial and inorder approaches. Column 2 of Table 2 gives the number of multiplexers of the initial ROBDD. Column 3 shows the number of multiplexers needed for inorder decomposition. Saving of area in approach *(w_1=1 w_2=0 w_3 =0)* compared to

Table 2. Area, switching and leakage comparison

Circuit	area			Switching			Leakage (nw)		
	Initial ROBDD	Inorder ROBDD	Our approach (w_1=1 w_2=0 w_3=0)	Initial ROBDD	Inorder ROBDD	Our approach (w_1=0 w_2=1 w_3=0)	Initial ROBDD	Inorder ROBDD	Our approach (w_1=0 w_2=0 w_3=1)
alu2	257	252	200	108.82	106.32	90.39	289.57	277.52	288.47
alu4	1352	1342	718	543.31	538.31	281.41	1369.8	1345.67	1231.58
apex4	1021	1015	964	418.70	415.70	398.00	1104.8	1090.38	1143.83
apex5	2705	2611	1854	1242.74	1195.74	451.55	3263.5	3036.96	1851.82
aralis	229	222	166	45.22	41.72	29.79	132.47	115.59	115.59
bw	114	109	108	43.69	41.19	40.12	126.12	114.07	108.27
b12	91	76	67	30.55	23.05	25.03	103.09	66.92	70.27
cc	105	93	48	37.81	31.81	12.59	2270.0	91.57	42.40
cht	149	112	83	60.78	42.28	37.37	208.50	119.31	108.53
clip	254	247	94	109.25	105.75	38.46	8968.7	281.55	283.63
cm138a	17	16	16	1.82	1.32	1.32	6.03	3.62	3.62
count	219	184	168	91.00	73.50	88.81	282.78	198.39	241.17
cps	2329	2316	1923	421.65	415.15	280.60	1212.3	1180.96	1438.22
c8	145	125	100	64.92	54.92	43.43	4864.0	147.06	132.60
decode	118	94	66	42.30	30.30	25.55	147.07	89.21	77.30
duke2	976	969	398	143.51	140.01	88.91	372.34	355.47	247.39
ex1010	1079	1074	1072	306.55	304.05	297.85	789.39	777.34	767.60
ex4	1301	1235	563	484.67	451.67	214.10	1548.4	1389.26	1192.47
f51m	70	66	61	30.90	28.90	27.13	97.05	87.40	87.40
frg2	6520	6462	1238	2795.41	2766.42	229.24	7129.6	6990.10	1215.99
k2	2985	2951	1995	902.95	885.95	630.09	2450.2	2368.26	3461.43
lal	182	157	91	69.39	56.89	24.71	7390.5	162.89	137.11
maskmx	85	82	57	35.50	34.00	12.64	3565.3	94.74	54.74
misex1	47	37	36	19.37	14.37	13.87	65.34	41.23	46.55
misex2	140	127	111	24.74	18.24	13.19	1311.9	52.48	45.23
misex3c	847	838	484	326.07	321.67	159.05	852.8	831.07	1042.06
pbo2	226	215	187	76.11	70.61	61.48	6902.6	202.24	191.89
pbonew	326	315	284	111.09	105.60	88.07	329.8	303.28	258.76
pcle	93	78	62	35.39	27.89	8.35	2295	80.61	83.78
pcler8	145	129	85	60.02	52.02	23.56	186.78	148.20	164.69
pdc	705	683	667	139.89	128.89	67.15	424.07	371.04	307.09
pm1	50	43	43	14.01	10.57	8.34	1781.1	29.27	28.25
sao2	154	153	87	38.76	38.26	23.26	2032.9	97.30	111.36
sct	169	146	54	63.76	52.26	18.61	193.95	138.49	115.13
seq	142321	*	2000	27967.20	*	649.92	71608.13	*	5829.20
shiftc	102	90	79	39.16	33.16	32.16	3601.6	96.25	79.22
sp	625	605	585	136.94	126.94	126.82	406.60	358.35	678.06
spla	681	661	659	135.74	125.74	78.33	402.86	354.64	642.80
table3	941	934	1349	109.3	105.80	115.33	287.85	270.98	548.28
table5	873	866	742	147.59	143.62	118.21	398.77	379.56	600.51
term1	586	572	162	154.15	147.15	76.51	11059.7	359.44	648.43
ttt2	248	223	139	108.26	95.76	52.92	309.66	249.38	223.52
vda	4421	4417	752	1854.20	1852.02	282.48	4619.1	4604.70	4606.70
vg2	1059	1049	96	362.39	357.39	25.36	959.08	934.97	1211.21
x1	1583	1549	578	341.03	324.03	178.71	955.20	873.23	765.42
x2	73	70	30	28.57	27.07	10.09	82.21	74.98	59.62
x4	916	846	388	369.24	334.24	139.81	1063.7	894.9	754.71
Average % saving of our approach	**34.17**	**29.22**		**41.35**	**34.07**		**31.18**	**-03.05**	

initial and inorder ROBDD are *34%* and *29%* respectively. As inorder approach considers possible sharing at each level of decomposition, saving is lower than the initial approach. Switchings of initial, inorder and our approach (w_1=0 w_2=1 w_3=0) are noted in Coulumn 5, 6 and 7 respectively. From Table 2, it is seen that average savings in switching of our approach compared to initial and inorder are *41%* and *34%*. Average leakage saving compared to initial ROBDD is *31%* but on the average we cannot get leakage saving compared to inorder approach. In some circuits like, *apex5(39%),cc(54%),decode(13%), duke2(30%), ex4(14%), frg2(83%), maskmx(42%), misex2 (14%), pbonew(15%),pdc(17%), x2(20%), x4(16%),* leakage saving is there. The reason for not getting leakage saving for other circuits is, for only leakage based decomposition (w_1=0 w_2=0 w_3=1) area obtained is quite high and leakage power dissipation increases as area increases. So, in our leakage based decomposition, giving full weight to leakage only, leakage power is high (given in Table 4). It may be noted that for the large circuits like *seq*, BuDDy is unable to find the ROBDD when inputs are taken in the order specified in the circuit.

Next, we present the result of area-power trade-offs achievable in our approach. For this purpose we have varied w_1(area weight), w_2(dynamic power weight) and w_3(leakage power weight) in a range of 0 to 1. Table 3 and 4 present some of the example cases for the values of w_1, w_2 and w_3. In particular we have presented the results for w_1, w_2, w_3 values of *(1,0,0)*, *(0.5,0.5,0)*, *(0,1,0)*, *(0,0.5,0.5)*, *(0,0,1)*, *(0.5,0.25,0.25)*, *(0.5,0,0.5)*. Last column in Table 4 shows the maximum CPU time required among all these decompositions. To summarize the results, we have computed the number of circuits having minimum area, switching and leakage value for each weighted decomposition. For example, out of 47 circuits, 23 circuits give minimum area value for the weight *(1,0,0)*. Though, average saving in area with respect to initial ROBDD for all 47 circuits for the weight *(0.5,0.5,0)* is also the minimum, number of circuits having minimum area value, in this case, is 16. For other cases, number of circuits having minimum area is further lesser. So, for only area based decomposition, area weight should be 1 and the maximum area saving can be achieved. But switching and leakage power are high in this case. In fact, switching is *16%* higher than its minimum value and leakage is 14% higher than the minimum leakage value. We have also computed some ratios. For getting area ratios, the area value has been divided by the initial area value of the initial ROBDD of each circuit. Similarly, for all the decompositions, area, switching and leakage ratios have been obtained with respect to initial area, switching and leakage of the initial ROBDD. Average of all these ratios have been noted in the second last row of Tables 3 and 4. Also, for clear understanding, average ratios for all the decompositions have been noted in Table 5. From Table 5, it is observed that minimum switching is obtained for the decomposition *(0,1,0)*. So, maximum number of circuits results in minimum switching for full weight to switching activity and in this case, area value is only *3%* higher compared to their minimum values. Saving in switching activity for this weight *(0,1,0)* is *43%*. It is interesting to note that for this decomposition, leakage value is also at its minimum. Though it is expected that leakage power dissipation be at its minimum for the weight *(0,0,1)* (decomposition is only leakage based), this is not true. Decomposition for the weight *(0,0,1)* results in maximum increase in area. In fact, with respect to initial ROBDD it requires *1%* more area. Average leakage saving for the weight *(0,0,1)* is *33%* which is not the minimum among all other decompositions. This happens because, as area increases, leakage power also increases, so we cannot get maximum leakage saving for the decomposition *(0,0,1)*. As observed from Tables 3and 4, the best results are obtained for the weight *(0, 1, 0)* for which switching and leakage both are at minimum and area is only *3%* higher compared to its minimum value. So, one can choose this weight, where total power dissipation becomes the critical factor.

It may also be noted that for the weight *(0.5, 0.5, 0)* average area is at minimum, switching and leakage results are also good. In this case, switching and leakage values are *9%* and *12%* higher compared to their respective minimum results. So, we can decompose the circuits for weight *(0, 1, 0)* or *(0.5,0.5,0)* for which area, switching and leakage values are within acceptable limits.

However, it must be mentioned that these weight can best be adjusted by the designer based upon the target technology, design constraints, and optimization criterions.

Comparison of area and switching results of our approach with the previous reported work [16] is shown in Table 5. In [16] experiment has been carried out using few circuits, noted in first column of the table. The nodes of a BDD are mapped to adiabatic multiplexers. As a pair of complementary nodes in the BDD have been replaced by single adiabatic multiplexer, number of nodes in the mapped BDD is reduced. Power improvement is due to the usage of adiabatic logic. It may be noted

Table 3. Weighted decomposition results

Circuit	w_1=1.0 w_2=0.0 w_3=0.0			w_1=0.5 w_2=0.5 w_3=0.0			w_1=0.0 w_2=1.0 w_3=0.0			w_1=0.0 w_2=0.5 w_3=0.5		
	Mux	Switching	leakage (nw)	mux	switching	leakage (nw)	mux	Switching	leakage (nw)	mux	switching	leakage (nw)
alu2	200	90.04	241.68	202	90.39	241.91	202	90.39	241.91	203	89.82	240.19
alu4	718	183.49	751.78	718	183.5	751.78	727	281.41	756.21	1255	454.04	1248.3
apex4	964	398.00	1038.9	964	398.0	1038.95	964	398.00	1038.95	1079	445.03	1135.3
apex5	1854	626.47	1662.4	1919	460.6	1251.39	2596	451.55	1250.28	2249	297.89	911.77
aralis	166	32.01	85.74	179	29.34	83.24	188	29.79	85.54	188	29.79	85.54
bw	108	40.72	112.68	109	40.12	115.84	109	40.12	115.84	114	42.19	117.01
b12	67	24.50	72.74	70	25.03	71.78	70	25.03	71.78	77	25.24	70.96
cc	48	18.50	54.08	45	16.95	46.99	42	12.59	38.23	45	13.09	39.64
cht	83	36.75	100.36	90	38.44	105.10	92	37.37	102.77	109	39.73	109.64
clip	94	38.95	110.74	94	38.46	108.96	94	38.46	108.96	165	65.51	175.93
cm138a	16	1.32	3.62	16	1.32	3.62	16	1.32	3.62	16	1.32	3.62
count	168	82.00	202.52	192	88.50	222.41	193	88.81	223.09	142	48.17	125.48
cps	1923	348.55	972.38	1500	208.9	601.06	1973	280.60	691.15	1999	284.28	700.10
c8	100	43.43	113.31	100	43.43	113.31	100	43.43	113.31	106	46.43	123.56
decode	66	24.55	72.18	68	24.61	72.33	78	25.55	74.74	76	26.77	75.64
duke2	398	89.41	251.64	621	84.97	228.54	657	88.91	234.59	786	109.09	292.49
ex1010	1072	302.87	772.97	1072	302.7	772.33	1059	297.85	756.64	1051	293.82	747.69
ex4	563	171.21	487.83	586	214.1	607.36	586	214.10	607.36	590	198.59	564.61
f51m	61	27.13	74.97	61	27.13	74.97	61	27.13	74.97	61	27.13	74.97
frg2	1238	438.39	1261.9	1086	236.5	600.18	1161	229.24	581.36	1304	250.56	631.89
k2	1995	642.35	1697.8	1964	627.7	1658.71	2013	630.09	1668.07	2500	781.17	2019.4
lal	91	29.93	95.49	85	25.08	78.93	94	24.71	72.25	84	23.37	64.77
maskmx	57	23.37	64.43	41	14.97	42.97	37	12.64	36.86	62	18.72	53.59
misex1	36	13.99	37.92	36	13.87	38.22	36	13.87	38.22	40	15.05	40.84
misex2	111	17.55	50.38	92	13.19	38.07	92	13.19	38.07	95	14.12	40.32
misex3c	484	165.71	448.90	491	167.9	454.4	479	159.05	438.01	870	315.92	855.34
pbo2	187	64.46	187.40	187	61.58	179.49	190	61.48	173.91	190	48.55	142.4
pbonew	284	97.84	278.26	284	97.84	278.26	267	88.07	255.74	290	84.85	245.58
pcle	62	23.02	60.27	33	8.35	22.41	33	8.35	22.41	45	9.96	26.39
pcler8	85	33.15	94.70	90	23.56	62.25	90	23.56	62.25	101	24.71	64.74
pdc	667	126.85	359.32	657	117.9	326.22	718	67.15	180.10	948	76.01	191.46
pm1	43	12.43	35.72	43	11.45	36.72	41	8.34	24.17	39	8.04	22.26
sao2	87	23.26	64.57	97	25.98	73.07	97	23.26	65.44	97	23.26	65.44
sct	54	18.75	54.13	59	17.28	49.46	70	18.61	52.11	124	34.35	95.99
seq	2000	569.99	1557.6	2451	665.5	1810.77	3217	649.92	1623.85	3691	567.19	1414.2
shiftc	79	29.96	86.46	79	29.96	86.46	87	32.16	91.94	73	26.39	80.72
sp	585	121.8	336.22	572	108.7	299.85	667	126.82	351.52	720	120.96	330.88
spla	659	128.39	360.05	636	106.55	295.51	621	78.33	213.5	991	84.23	213.73
table3	1349	277.18	724.91	1479	323.4	826.89	810	115.33	314.96	1318	178.4	459.14
table5	742	120.68	331.14	746	118.36	329.16	749	118.21	328.67	1156	215.18	568.41
term1	162	47.03	133.22	138	39.95	112.64	434	76.51	207.43	779	144.73	367.16
ttt2	139	56.87	154.21	131	48.24	139.36	141	52.92	152.31	132	45.57	129.56
vda	752	286.35	766.28	748	278.99	749.79	770	282.48	765.33	1933	779.42	1943.0
vg2	96	28.22	74.66	87	25.36	67.44	87	25.36	67.44	591	176.6	468.48
x1	578	168.94	482.82	588	164.6	471.19	662	178.71	508.53	704	165.59	460.05
x2	30	10.15	29.69	30	10.15	29.69	31	10.09	29.92	38	12.46	37.50
x4	388	141.16	435.55	399	138.08	422.58	437	139.81	395.43	613	190.89	509.32
Average wrt initial	**0.64**	**0.66**	**0.48**	**0.64**	**0.62**	**0.47**	**0.66**	**0.57**	**0.42**	**0.78**	**0.65**	**0.48**
No. of circuits having min. value	**23**	**9**	**11**	**16**	**19**	**16**	**15**	**19**	**17**	**5**	**12**	**9**

that power saving in adiabatic logic can be achieved only during low-frequency operation. However, it should be noted that, experiments in [16] has been carried out using 180 nm technology library. Thus, a direct comparison with our approach is not possible. We have noted the % improvement values reported in [16]. The average percentage saving in area achieved there [16] is much lower than our result. Though the average switching power result in [16] is good, most of the circuits like pcle(76.40%), ttt2(51.12%), vda(84.78%) and x2(64.68%) show higher saving in our approach compared to [16]. Unfortunately, there is no leakage power result available in [16]. So, we are unable to compare leakage result.

Effect on performance: To see the effect on performance maximum levels of *initial*, *inorder* and *weigted* decomposed BDD have been considered. This maximum level depicts the critical path delay of the circuit, as in each level the decomposition is performed around one input variable. The number of levels is same for *initial* and *inorder* decomposed BDD. In our decomposition approach, at each level a suitable variable is selected and after checking the sharing, decomposition is carried out. Hence, critical path delay corresponds to the number of input variables used to decompose the full function. As there is no change in the number of variables, the critical path delay remains unaltered.

Table 4. Weighted decomposition results

Circuit	w_1=0.0 w_2=0.0 w_3=1.0			w_1=0.50 w_2=0.250 w_3=0.250			w_1=0.5 w_2=0.0 w_3=0.5			CPU time (micro Second)
	mux	switching	leakage (nw)	mux	switch ing	leakage (nw)	mux	switching	leakage (nw)	Max-time among all the decompositions
alu2	263	110.17	288.47	202	90.39	241.91	203	89.99	240.79	7.0
alu4	1300	469.15	1231.58	888	331.33	883.70	1142	425.57	1126.93	85.0
apex4	1071	446.89	1143.83	1079	445.03	1135.34	1079	445.03	1135.34	29.0
apex5	2151	740.76	1851.82	1870	372.61	1065.05	1799	528.59	1456.98	2973.0
aralis	255	41.72	115.59	179	29.34	83.24	180	36.34	101.36	2.0
bw	109	40.19	108.27	109	39.85	106.31	109	40.19	108.27	0.001
b12	76	24.94	70.27	73	23.97	70.29	75	26.96	77.07	3.0
cc	47	15.20	42.40	49	17.05	48.73	49	16.55	47.90	3.0
cht	112	39.84	108.53	100	39.59	110.79	116	42.25	120.62	17.0
clip	258	105.43	283.63	113	46.39	128.38	168	68.70	186.80	4.0
cm138a	16	1.32	3.62	16	1.32	3.62	16	1.32	3.62	0.01
count	268	96.81	241.17	121	42.15	112.63	142	48.20	125.48	51.0
cps	2464	500.99	1438.22	1527	209.98	603.62	1470	310.40	830.42	29.4
c8	112	49.43	132.60	106	46.43	121.75	107	46.93	125.06	10.0
decode	74	27.52	77.30	74	26.65	76.55	74	27.52	77.30	1.0
duke2	633	93.40	247.39	626	114.27	308.53	584	76.57	200.31	39.0
ex1010	1076	300.8	767.60	1051	293.82	747.69	1063	297.31	759.40	42.0
ex4	1115	394.53	1192.47	596	198.91	564.76	593	179.7	503.63	1830.0
f51m	66	28.90	87.40	61	27.13	74.97	61	27.13	74.97	1.0
frg2	2292	481.35	1215.99	1138	249.14	631.06	1242	277.01	710.62	30407.0
k2	3991	1386.202	3461.43	2230	689.27	1813.36	2387	753.66	1946.73	4180.0
lal	161	46.80	137.11	93	27.37	79.26	84	23.37	64.80	10.0
maskmx	71	19.77	54.74	42	14.57	42.54	62	19.85	56.38	4.0
misex1	45	17.01	46.55	40	15.05	40.84	43	16.26	42.37	0.01
misex2	119	16.23	45.23	94	13.58	37.79	118	16.74	48.19	7.0
misex3c	1063	396.65	1042.06	547	180.59	495.53	878	319.36	861.80	32.0
pbo2	271	68.55	191.89	190	62.38	184.32	185	47.75	138.96	7.0
pbonew	335	89.65	258.76	275	86.40	250.63	290	86.43	250.76	0.01
pcle	108	32.01	83.78	33	8.35	22.41	76	22.01	58.85	3.0
pcler8	208	64.48	164.69	86	21.73	57.57	101	24.71	64.74	21.0
pdc	1085	118.86	307.09	674	80.34	215.71	935	102.71	272.43	177.0
pm1	44	10.07	28.25	41	10.365	32.34	40	8.45	23.36	2.0
sao2	154	40.35	111.36	110	28.23	80.42	110	28.23	80.42	3.0
sct	147	43.04	115.13	68	18.86	53.97	99	25.55	70.67	5.0
seq	1139	2239.45	5829.20	2920	618.94	1566.13	4337	970.38	2556.73	2225.0
shiftc	79	27.26	79.22	73	26.39	80.72	73	26.39	80.72	1.0
sp	1102	241.92	678.06	597	122.11	335.99	863	159.06	417.76	43.0
spla	1314	228.69	642.8	706	126.79	356.92	867	95.73	246.54	232.0
table3	1391	215.93	548.28	1455	273.66	710.48	1249	171.16	441.64	56.0
table5	1339	233.94	600.51	1295	279.64	742.42	1624	356.69	927.36	186.0
term1	1048	250.23	648.43	245	58.44	158.56	415	106.25	288.04	123.0
ttt2	238	85.55	223.52	149	53.98	151.38	123	44.33	121.77	16.0
vda	4417	1852.02	4606.70	1077	421.38	1088.92	1903	764.48	1910.30	116.0
vg2	1419	459.46	1211.21	87	25.36	67.44	94	27.05	73.67	93.0
x1	1119	277.43	765.42	663	161.55	447.48	672	192.08	532.61	686.0
x2	61	22.37	59.62	32	10.49	30.41	38	12.46	37.58	0.1
x4	809	285.8	754.71	428	144.95	408.38	562	188.20	519.76	1147.0
Average wrt initial	**1.01**	**0.92**	**0.67**	**0.68**	**0.64**	**0.48**	**0.76**	**0.69**	**0.51**	
No. of circuits having min. value	**1**	**1**	**3**	**9**	**12**	**11**	**8**	**5**	**5**	

Table 5. Comparison of our approach to the approach [16]

Circuit	area				switching			
	Initial ROBDD	Our approach (w_1=1 w_2=0 w_3=0)	% saving of our approach	% saving in [181]	Initial ROBDD	Our approach (w_1=0 w_2=1 w_3=0)	% saving of our approach	% saving in [181]
count	219	168	23.29	32.65	91	73.5	2.41	57.22
f51m	70	61	12.86	28.57	30.9	28.9	12.20	54.62
k2	2985	1995	33.16	19.06	902.95	885.95	30.22	48.58
pcle	93	62	33.33	18.6	35.39	27.89	76.40	48.29
ttt2	248	139	43.95	19.35	108.26	95.76	51.12	48.77
vda	4421	752	82.99	17.8	1854.2	1852.02	84.76	47.78
x2	73	30	58.90	17.5	28.57	27.07	64.68	40.59
Averag e % saving			**41.21**	**21.93**			**45.97**	**49.41**

5 Conclusion

The approach described in this paper performs an area-power trade-off in multiplexer based circuit synthesis. It takes both the dynamic and leakage power into consideration, which, to the best of our knowledge is the first ever approach in multiplexer-based realization of multi-output Boolean functions. As the leakage power is much significant at 90 nm or lower technology, the proposed method can be well applied for the leakage aware multiplexer-based realization of Boolean functions in these technologies.

References

[1] Akers, S.B.: Binary decision diagrams. IEEE Trans on Computers C-27(6), 509–516 (1978)
[2] Thompson, Packan, P., Bohr, M.: MOS Scaling: Transistor Challenges for the 21st Century. Intel Technology Journal, Q3 (1998)
[3] Narayanan, U., Leong, H.W., Chung, K., Liu, C.L.: Low Power Multiplexer Decomposition. In: International Symposium on Low Power Electronics and Design, pp. 269–274 (1997)
[4] Thakur, S., Wong, D.F., Krishnamoorthy, S.: Delay Minimal Decomposition of Multiplexers in Technology Mapping. In: Design Automation Conference, pp. 254–257 (1996)
[5] Murgai, R., Brayton, R.K., Sangiovanni- Vincentelli, A.: An improved Synthesis Algorithm for Multiplexer-based PGA's. In: Design Automation Conference, pp. 404–410 (1995)
[6] Rudell, R.: Logic Synthesis for VLSI Design, PhD Thesis, U.C. Berkley (April 1989)
[7] Kim, K., Ahn, T., Han, S.Y., Kim, C.S., Kim, K.H.: Low-power multiplexer decomposition by suppressing propagation of signal transitions. In: IEEE International Symposium on Circuits and Systems, vol. 5, pp. 85–88 (2001)
[8] Anis, M., Elmasry, M.: Multi-Threshold CMOS Digital Circuits Managing Leakage Power, p. 14. Kluwer academic publishers, Dordrecht (2003)
[9] Roy, K., Mukhopadhyay, S., Mahmoodi-Meimand, H.: Leakage Current Mechanisms and Leakage Reduction Techniques in Deep-Submicrometer CMOS Circuits. Proceedings of the IEEE 91(2), 305–327 (2003)
[10] Roy, K., Prasad, S.C.: Low-Power CMOS VLSI Circuit Design. John Wiley & Sons, Inc., Chichester (2000)
[11] Lindgren, P., Kerttu, M., Thornton, M., Drechsler, R.: Low Power Optimization Technique for BDD Mapped Circuits. In: Asia South Pacific Design Automation Conference, pp. 615–621 (2001)
[12] Satyanarayana, D., Chattopadhyay, S., Sasidhar, J.: Low Power Combinational Circuit Synthesis targeting Multiplexer based FPGAs. In: Proceedings of 17th International Conference on VLSI Design (2004)
[13] BDD packages BuDDY, `http://www.itu.dk/research/buddy`
[14] Computer-Aided benchmarking Laboratory, `http://www.cbl.ncsu.edu/benchmarks`
[15] Lee, D., Blaauw, D., Sylvester, D.: Runtime Leakage Minimization through probability-Aware Dual Vt or Dual-Tox Assignment. In: Asia-Pacific Desig Automation Conference, pp. 399–404 (2005)
[16] Paul, G., Pradhan, S.N., Bhattacharya, B.B., Pal, A., Das, A.: BDD-based synthesis of logic functions using adiabatic multiplexers. International Journal on Systemics, Cybernetics, and Informatics (IJSCI) 1, 44–49 (2006)

Exergaming – New Age Gaming for Health, Rehabilitation and Education

Ankit Kamal

Department of Information Technology, Pune Institute of Computer Technology, Pune, India
anktkml@gmail.com

Abstract. The urban lifestyle is hectic and information rich. A busy work pace and digital entertainment take time away from real world physical exercise, while lifestyle diseases increase globally. Exergaming, which is a term combining "exercise" and "gaming", has a lot of potential to provide various new service business opportunities for the entertainment and recreation as well as the healthcare sectors. In this paper, I review some new exergaming prototypes. Also I present current rehabilitation schemes, especially the PS3 based rehabilitation of children with hemiplegia. The Nintendo Wii is also an emerging contender in the health field. I discuss Wii based balance and wrist therapies that are becoming widespread. The Wii fit and Wii sports are becoming a hit among health conscious people. Also researchers from the the University of Ulster have made some new webgames for upper limb rehabilitation. The use of PSPs in English lab classes is also shown. Together the gaming industry contributes a lot today.

Keywords: Exergame; Fitness adventure; Figuremeter, Nintendo Wii, PS3, PSP, xbox360, rehabilitation, hemiplegia, stroke, Wii remote, webcam.

1 Introduction

The lifestyle is changing and formulating new needs and new augmented solutions will become more important. Focus in healthcare is moving from the treatment to the prevention of illness. Widespread clinical acceptance of virtual rehabilitation is slowed in part by the relatively high cost of current commercially- available systems (such as the $10,000 IREX, or the $52,000 Armeo), the lack of sufficient training of physical therapists in the new technology, lack of large scale clinical data to show medical efficacy, and clinician technophobia [1].

Nowadays, postural instability and balance disorders affect millions of people. Postural instability and balance disorders can be a consequence of stroke, ageing, positional dizziness and many other disorders. Although mortality from these disorders is very low, their influence in the decrement in a patient's quality of life is very high. The treatment for these disorders depends on the cause; but most types of balance disorders require balance rehabilitation and training, prescribed by a physiotherapist. This rehabilitation is usually an expensive and time-consuming process. Moreover, the success of this process depends on a patient's motivation and on the continuity of

N. Meghanathan et al. (Eds.): CCSIT 2011, Part III, CCIS 133, pp. 421–430, 2011.

the procedure. Therefore, it is essential that the rehabilitation use a system that is attractive to the patient. Also, if the system allows the user to do the rehabilitation exercises at home, the continuity of the rehabilitation process is increased greatly. An ideal rehabilitation system oriented for use by the patient at home must be robust and simple, with an easy setup. Moreover, if the system is inexpensive it can be used widely. A few of such systems are discussed as follows.

2 Fitness Adventure Prototype

The Fitness Adventure prototype is an application platform supporting physical outdoor exercise. It utilizes location information and a mobile phone acts as a terminal device for the game. The aim of the prototype is to combine a mobile game and fitness exercise and thus create new opportunities for the mobile phone to enhance the efficiency of lifestyle improvement and management. The concept is supposed to offer a proactive, location-aware solution that would motivate people to move from place to place with the help of GPS location technology. The person uses the service with his/her own mobile phone. The application allures the person to go out for a walk or a run. It is meant to entertain the user with an interesting fictional story, spiced up with additional information on different sites along the route that the person walks or runs. The concept takes advantage of architecturally interesting buildings, tourist attractions, sights and nature trails around the selected area. Fitness Adventure application supports also various tags, which can be used to spice the story in the adventure. Visual tags can be read with a normal camera of a mobile phone, which makes them usable with most of the mobile phone models.

3 Figuremeter Protype Concept

The Figuremeter concept prototype combines casual exercise and online communities. Figuremeter consists of a mobile device that measures the physical activity of a user, and software that transfers measured data to a computer and an online community or a game. The aim of Figuremeter is to motivate people to exercise by giving advantages and special abilities in online games and communities according to their real life exercising. Figuremeter device is a combination of a pedometer and cyclometer with wired or wireless connectivity [2].

4 PS3 Based Rehabilitation of Children with Hemiplegia

Children can develop hemiplegia from a prenatal or a later brain injury that affects only one side of their brain or one side far more than the other. Hand dysfunction is probably one of the most disabling aspects of hemiplegia. Most tasks of everyday living use both hands (getting dressed, self-grooming, picking up and handling objects from food to books to toys). Children with hemiplegia struggle with the activities of daily living (ADL) from the time they get up in the morning to the time they go to bed. The novel virtual rehabilitation system presented here is a therapy likely to be better tolerated by children; instead of forcing use of their hemiplegic hand by constraining the other hand, it encourages use of the plegic hand by fitting a sensing glove to the plegic hand to connect to the videogame system. The children are given an enjoyable activity to perform (videogames and game-type exercises) with the plegic hand. Many families cannot afford to provide additional therapy, and are further limited by the working schedules of both parents. This provides in-home remotely monitored therapy to children who otherwise would not be able to access it.

The experimental system described here is built around a PlayStation 3, owing to its ability to run Linux OS. Other reasons to choose the PlayStation 3 are its input/output characteristics, its high performance multi-core computation power and the large existing home base of such consoles. The PlayStation 3 is familiar and easy to be used by children, the targeted age group of the study. Since the purpose of training is hand rehabilitation, a number of commercially-available sensing gloves are considered. The 5DT 5 Ultra (five sensor) glove was selected due to its lower cost, and the willingness of the manufacturer to build custom child-size gloves.

Each home tele-rehabilitation system [3] consists of a PlayStation 3, a right-hand 5DT Ultra glove, computer keyboard, optical mouse, and a flat panel TV monitor (Figure 1). The TV connects through a High Definition Monitor Interface (HDMI) cable to the HDMI port of the PS3. The PS3 has six USB ports, two of which are used to plug a keyboard and a mouse. The 5DT 5 Ultra glove has one fiber optical sensor per finger, thus measuring the "total" flexion or extension of each finger. Each sensor reading represents an integer from 0 to 4095 due to the 12 bit analog/digital converter electronics embedded in the glove wrist unit. A glove calibration is needed to map this range to a % of finger flexion/extension. The 5DT 5 Ultra glove wrist unit has a USB connection.

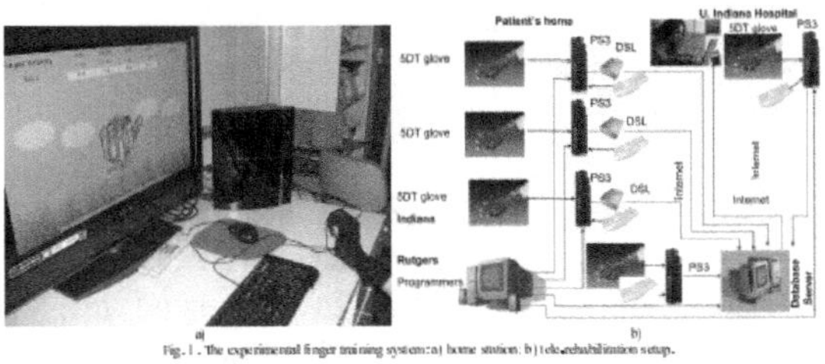

Fig. 1. The Experimental finger training system

In order to implement the tele-rehabilitation setting, the PS3 uses a DSL modem/router in the home. The router is connected to the local area network (LAN) port of the PS3 and to the wall phone jack as illustrated in Figure 1. Under tele-rehabilitation conditions data stored in each home session is uploaded to a clinical database server. A database Oracle module allows one to remotely monitor patient progress, as well as compliance with the established therapeutic protocol. This is done using a password-protected web page and graphing environment that allows the clinicians to select variables to be graphed for a specific subject, over the duration of therapy. The infrastructure developed here makes the system a multiplexed tele-rehabilitation set up, since a single physician can monitor several patients remotely.

First in this category of games is the "butterfly" exercise which asks patients to initially make a fist (if extension is trained) or open their hand as much as possible (if flexion is trained) (see Figure 2). Subsequently virtual butterflies appear from the side of the screen and need to be “scared away” by moving the fingers or the thumb fast. As long as the patient achieves the set flexion/extension goals before the butterfly reaches the hand avatar, it will fly away, and a virtual flower appears on the screen. If the patient did not move the fingers fast enough, the butterfly comes back and needs to be scared away again. After a number of butterflies have flown away from the hand avatar, a mosquito attempts to sting it. The patient has to move the fingers fast enough to scare the mosquito away, or else the hand is stung (it flashes red and a corresponding unpleasant sound is produced). The difficulty of the game is increased by making the butterflies or the mosquitoes fly faster. This in turn requires faster reaction time from the patient.

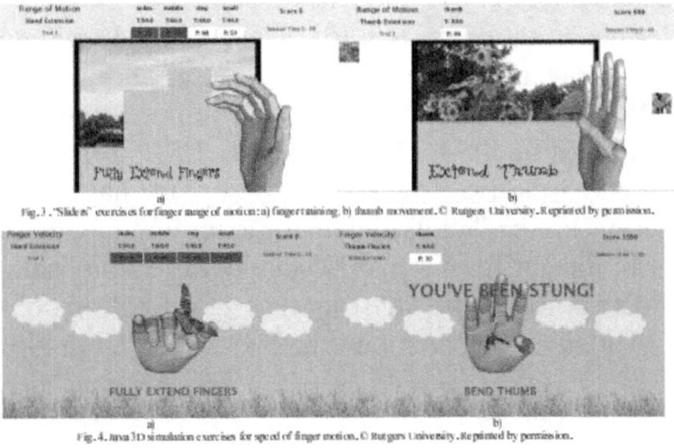

Fig. 2. Slider Exercises for finger range of motion (upper panel) and Java 3D simulation exercise for finger motion (lower panel)

A more recent addition to the finger velocity training game category is the UFO game (Figure 3). Butterflies are replaced by various UFO models (depending on the level of difficulty). In the “bonus” round, the UFO beams a “shrink ray” if the patients had not opened/closed the hand fast enough. The hand avatar then turns green and shrinks. If however, the patient is moving the fingers fast, the UFO flies away and crashes (with corresponding explosion sounds). An integral part of the system is the clinical database. It stores the computerized data generated from the games, and online periodic subjective evaluation surveys. The database module consists of six components. A Java program installed on the PlayStation 3 uploads the data collected from the different games to a clinical server using HTTPS.

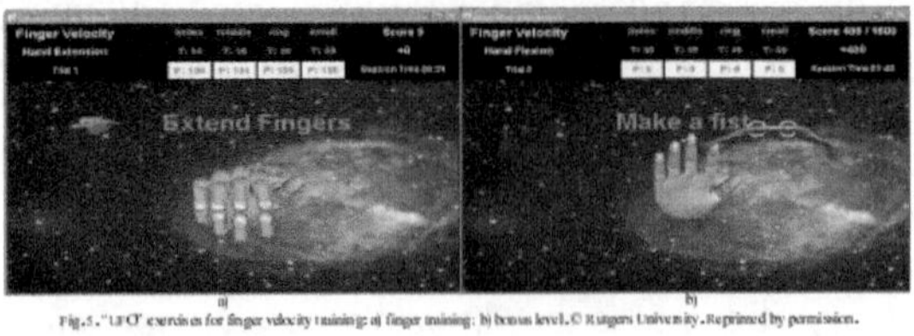

Fig. 3. UFO exercise for finger velocity training

A Java program installed on the clinical server then receives these files. Once received another Java program runs to parse these files and extract clinical data and store them on the local database (to ensure security of the data), and saves a copy of the files in an archived folder. The Oracle database module contains the raw data, namely session date and duration, exercise-specific performance, as well as the performance data (averages for finger range of motion and finger velocity). A web portal (also running on the clinical server) allows authorized users to log in, and graph relevant variables showing each patient's progress over the duration of the home therapy. The last component of the clinical database program makes sure that patients practice according to the schedule given by the physical therapist. If they fail to practice on a day they were supposed to, or practiced more than they were supposed to, the program automatically notifies the physical therapist about this discrepancy in practice.

Three children were recruited for this pilot study[3]. They are teenagers with severe hemiplegic cerebral palsy, have difficulty opening and closing their plegic hand, and struggle to pick up objects with that hand. During the study, none of the subjects received other rehabilitation of any kind. It is necessary to stress that patient selection for the pilot study was extremely important. The three teenage subjects were chosen because they have good cognitive function and the ability to understand that "pilot study means things will go wrong."

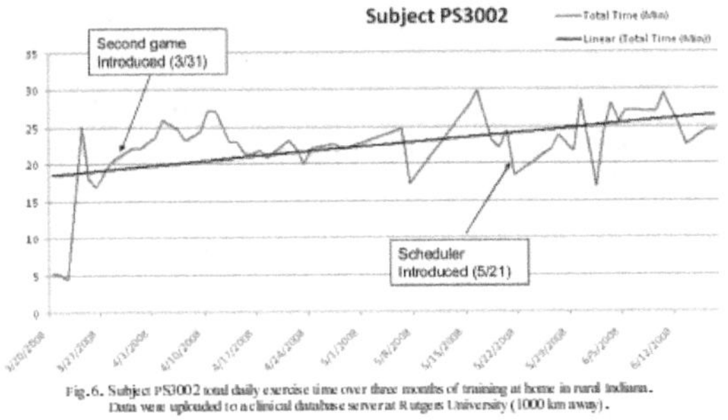

Fig. 4. Subject PS3002 total daily exercise timeover three months of training at home in rural Indiana. Data were uploaded to a clinical database server 100 km away [3].

All subjects were told to attempt to practice 30 minutes daily (including rest time between exercises). Figure 4 plots the variation in actual exercise time (exclusive of rest periods) for subject PS3002. Looking at this subject's daily practice over the three months of training is informative of the impact game characteristics and the control patients have on training intensity. At the start of therapy this subject (and the others) had difficulty donning their 5DT Ultra gloves, and practiced less. Once the second game (butterflies) was introduced, the subject's exercise time increased. Subjects were frustrated by the need to do repeated calibrations in a session, and by the fixed number of trials they had to do for each game. These issues were addressed once the scheduler was introduced to them. From then on, they only needed one calibration/baseline per session, and had control on the games they wanted to play. This had the positive effect on addressing boredom, and the subjects continued to exercise more and more. Three months of testing of the three in-home systems have showed that playing therapeutic games on the PlayStation 3 can improve hand function in children with hemiplegia.

5 Nintendo WII Based Rehabilitation

The Nintendo Wii Remote (aka the Wiimote) was introduced with considerable fanfare with the Nintendo Wii in the fall of 2006 to North America. While the controls of the remote itself were largely unremarkable, the intuitive nature of the motion capture control was unparalleled in consumer-level electronics. The free inclusion of the Wii Sports game was an instant hit, notably due to the mass appeal afforded by the unique interface. Video games that in the past had required esoteric key combinations could now be played by mimicking the actions of the actual activity, whether that activity was golf, baseball, tennis, or bowling. In short, one's life experience in those particular activities were the only knowledge required (also available in game through on-screen instructions) with feedback through visual cues being instantaneous and often immensely gratifying.

The inclusion of motion capture in large part bridged a tremendous generational gap no longer requiring extensive manuals nor training to use the device. The cross-generational appeal was not lost on the manufacturer (Nintendo) which frequently employed ads showing senior citizens or entire families enjoying video games that were once the near exclusive domain of younger, more technology savvy individuals.

The release of the Wii Fit (software) and the Wii Balance Board (platform) for the Nintendo Wii presented an important question in the field of rehabilitation: is the Wii Fit a real option for physical rehabilitation exercises? Several authors have tested and given their opinion on the system and the general opinion is that the Wii Fit (with the Wii Balance Board) is a good tool for physical rehabilitation exercises, especially for stability training. Following this direction reserchers have developed a rehabilitation system –easy Balance Virtual Rehabilitation System (eBaViR System) that utilizes the Wii Balance Board as the platform, but instead of using the Wii Fit, it utilizes exercises that have developed specifically for the rehabilitation of balance disorders.

The eBaViR System has huge potential as an "at home" rehabilitation system because the required elements are affordable (a Personal Computer with no special features, and a Wii Balance Board –costing less than 90 €-), the setup is very easy (no initial calibration is needed) and the software is designed to be utilized by non-technical users. For clinical specialists the system also offers high added-value for the rehabilitation process, not only because of the features previously described, but also because of the capabilities of the system: the games can be customized to adapt to the patient's limitations and the results attained by the patients in each session are recorded for later clinical evaluation. Figure 5 also shows how wii is used for wrist therapy.

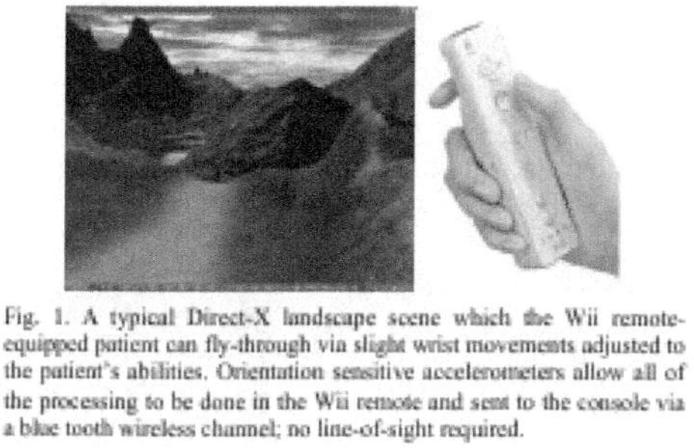

Fig. 5. A typical DirectX landscape scene which the Wiimote equipped patient can fly through with slight wrist movement

6 Webcam Games for Rehabilitation

Two games have been developed by researchers of University of Ulster, North Ireland which use standard webcam technology to capture video data of user movement. The games were built in Microsoft's XNA platform for Windows, using the C# .NET framework. DirectShow libraries are used in order to allow the games to communicate and interface with any USB web camera. The games are designed to promote gross arm movements in order to aid upper limb rehabilitation. The first game, "Rabbit Chase", was developed for single arm rehabilitation (either right or left arm). The second game, "Arrow Attack", was developed for bimanual rehabilitation (both arms). These games are controlled by the player moving his or her hands. In order that the hands can be tracked, the player either wears a glove or holds an object of a single consistent colour, such as a piece of card (the marker). The colour of the glove or card is chosen so as not to conflict with the background colour. Prior to the games commencing, a short calibration process takes place whereby the user covers a small square area on the screen with the marker in order for the game to identify the marker's colour. The position of the marker can then be tracked in 2D space using an RGB colour segmentation algorithm on the image feed from the webcam. There is also an option to unable an adaptive difficulty mechanism. When this option is selected, the game automatically speeds up or slows down depending on the user's performance. This is achieved by altering the speed of the rabbit (in Rabbit Chase) or the arrows (in Arrow Attack). This can help maintain an appropriate level of challenge which alters accordingly as the user's level of skill improves or deteriorates as the game progresses.

"Rabbit Chase" is played using one marker on either the left or right hand as appropriate, with the goal of catching a rabbit as it peers out of one of 4 holes displayed on screen (Figure 6). The rabbit stays at a hole for a short amount of time (depending on the current pace of the game) before running to the next hole (chosen at random). The player can see the rabbit as it runs between holes and so can anticipate its next location. The webcam's image feed is displayed in the background so that the player can see themselves and is aware of their position in relation to the game. The goal is to touch the correct hole at the same time as the rabbit peers out of it. If the player touches the target at the right time, the hole and the rabbit both change colour and a buzzer sound is played. There is no penalty for touching the wrong hole; however the player's score will not increase unless the correct hole is touched. The player's current score and time remaining are also displayed on the screen. The aim of the game is for the player to score as highly as possible before the time runs out.

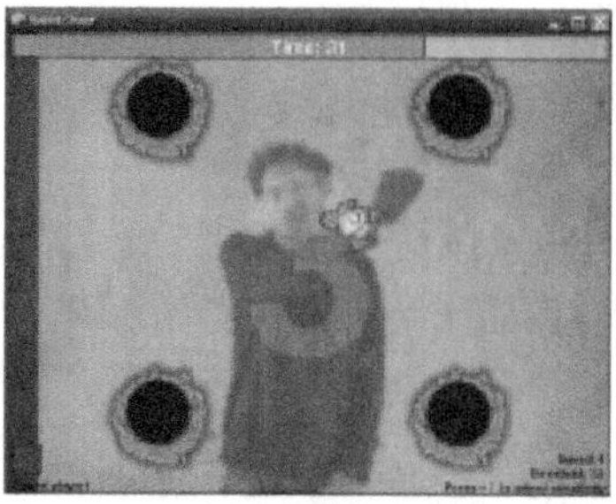

Figure 4: Rabbit Chase game

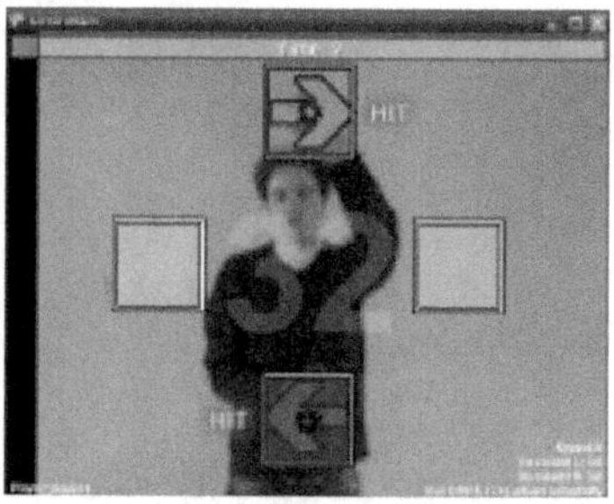

Figure 5: Arrow Attack game

Fig. 6. Rabbit Chase game and Arrow Attack Game

"Arrow Attack" (Fig. 6) requires the player to track two arrows, one pointing left and one pointing right, and touch the arrows as they reach each box using the correct hand. Since the game requires differentiation between the left and right hand marker, the player uses two markers of differing colour. The arrows are also coloured according to the colour of the markers in order to aid the player in distinguishing which arm to use. The game's concept is similar to that of "Rabbit Chase" whereby the arrows will move between the boxes, with the next box chosen at random; however the box selection is limited so that the game will never require the user to fully cross their arms as this could cause unnecessary complications and stress for more impaired players, as well as causing the game to become too difficult. The interface is also similar to "Rabbit Chase", with the player's score and time remaining displayed on-screen, as well as a buzzer sounding and the box changing colour to indicate a point scored.

7 Improving English Lab Classes Using PSP

There has been a new method for improving English lab classes using Sony PSP handheld game consoles especially for Iranian schools. English lab classes usually consist of some chairs which are equipped with microphone and headphone. But they don't have any monitor or display screen, because it needs a high costs to implement above system. In Iran the PSP game console is popular among young children and many of them have PSP console game. Almost all of the PSP game consoles are enabled to execute homebrew software. The aim of the project is showing the English lessons in English lab classes – in addition to playing sounds through the headphones – for the students. For this purpose we use the PSP game console. In this, a computer with Wi-Fi card is provided. Then the lesson videos converted to PMP format and putted on the PC computer. There are many programs which can convert other video files formats to PMP format. We use XviD4PSP [4]. It is a PC-based homebrew application for converting videos for PSP, PS3, Xbox 360, iPod, iPhone, BlackBerry, Hardware DVD and PC. Also NethostFS program is running on the PC computer. NethostFS allows you to view and execute applications using files from your PC via Wi-Fi. Each student installs PMPlayer AdVanCe program on his/her PSP. PMPlayer AdVanCe media player application is a homebrew application which enables users to play PMP format files on their PSP. Also this program allows users to play PMP movies from their PC remotely using NethostFS program. Now the students are connecting to the PC computer through Wi-Fi and viewing lesson movies on their PSP by using PMPlayer AdVanCe program. However it is possible that some students do not have PSP. Therefore we also connect a video projector to the computer and play the videos on the wall for the students. The cost of implementing this project is not high, because we only need an average PC computer with Wi-Fi card – and a projector if some students do not have a PSP. Because the PSP is popular with children and they like it, so using it for learning attract them to the courses. Similar to this method, we can also use other homebrew applications for educating the students. For example AcademicAid is a homebrew application built specifically to help students in the fields of Algebra I, Algebra II, Calculus, Trigonometry, Physics I, and Physics AP in high school and college.

8 Future Advancements

8.1 Xbox360's Project Natal

The **Project Natal** is the code name for a "controller-free gaming and entertainment experience" byMicrosoft for theXbox 360 video game platform. Based on an add-on peripheral for the Xbox 360 console, project Natal enables users to control and interact with the Xbox 360 without the need to touch a game controller through a natural user interface using gestures, spoken commands, or presented objects and images. The project is aimed at broadening the Xbox 360's audience beyond its typically hardcore base.

Fig. 7. Project Natal

8.2 PS3 Motion Controller

The Play station Motion Controller (tentative name) is a motion-sensing game controller in development for the PS3 video game console by Consisting of a handheld wand, the controller uses the Playstation eye webcam to track the wand's position, and inertial sensors to detect its motion.

9 Conclusion

In this paper, I have discussed about all the recent gaming technologies and consoles that are being used not only for the gaming purpose, but also for human health and rehabilitation of stroke affected people. Also the Exergame concept is becoming very popular with new prototypes. In this run, the PS3, Nintendo Wii have been very significant. PS3 based rehab for children with hemiplegia is fastcoming. To support it, some research data is also pesented. The Nintendo Wii is a lot popular too with its Wii fit and Wii sports games. It is also being used for wrist and balance therapy (using balance board). The PSP is being used for educational purpose too, especially where it is quite popular (like Iran). Thus in a nutshell, the future will fuse heath matters and gaming fun together, leading to more participation.

References

1. Laikari, A.: Exergaming – gaming for health-A bridge between real world and virtual communities. In: The 13th IEEE International Symposium on Consumer Electronics (ISCE 2009), pp. 665–668 (2009)
2. Burke, J.W., McNeill, M.D.J., Charles, D.K., Morrow, P.J., Crosbie, J.H., McDonough, S.M.: Serious Games for Upper Limb Rehabilitation Following Stroke. In: Conference in Games and Virtual Worlds for Serious Applications, pp. 103–110 (2009)
3. Huber, M., Rabin, B., Docan, C., Burdea, G., Nosu, M.E., Abdelbaky, M., Golomb, M.R.: PlayStation 3-based Tele-rehabilitation for Children with Hemiplegia. In: Eighth IEEE International Conference on Advanced Learning Technologies, ICALT 2008, pp. 105–112 (2008)
4. Shirali-Shahreza: Improving English Lab Classes Using Sony PSP (PlayStation Portable). In: Eighth IEEE International Conference on Advanced Learning Technologies, ICALT 2008, pp. 489–490 (2008)

Inclusion/Exclusion Protocol for RFID Tags

Selwyn Piramuthu

RFID European Lab, Paris, France &
Information Systems and Operations Management, University of Florida
Gainesville, Florida 32611-7169, USA
selwyn@ufl.edu

Abstract. It is not uncommon to encounter objects with several RFID tags. However, the tags on these objects are generally mobile and move from or to (or, both) the object. No existing RFID authentication protocol considers this scenario. Moreover, an authentication protocol in such a scenario has the potential to be vulnerable to relay attacks where a tag that is not present on the object may pretend to be present. We present an authentication protocol that facilitates inclusion as well as exclusion of RFID tags on an object while simultaneously providing immunity to relay attacks.

Keywords: RFID, tag inclusion/exclusion, authentication protocol.

1 Introduction

Objects with multiple RFID tags are not uncommon. An example scenario that illustrates this include a primary object (e.g., car chasis) with several attached parts (e.g., car door, wheels) each with its own RFID tag. In such scenarios, both the number of tags as well as the individual tags themselves may vary over time. I.e., when a tire is replaced, the new tire may come with its own embedded RFID tag; when the owner decides to add a GPS system, it may come with its own RFID tag; when the spare tire is removed from the car, there would be one less RFID tag on the car. To our knowledge, no existing RFID authentication protocol addresses this scenario, and there is a clear need for such protocols.

RFID tags broadcast information about tagged object to any reader with appropriate credentials without physical verification of the reader. Given security and privacy concerns, lightweight cryptographic protocols have been proposed that restrict when, how, and what communication occurs between RFID tags and reader. Although these protocols prevent most problems that are associated with secure and privacy concerns associated with communication between RFID tag and reader, relay attacks pose a dire threat.

Relay attacks occur when an adversary simply relays signals between honest reader and tag without modifying it in any way. Since the signal content is not modified by the adversary, almost all of the extant RFID cryptographic protocols are immune to such attacks. There have been several proposed protocols that purport to alleviate this problem for a single tag. We propose an authentication

N. Meghanathan et al. (Eds.): CCSIT 2011, Part III, CCIS 133, pp. 431–437, 2011.

protocol for inclusion/exclusion of RFID tags that also resists relay attacks. This protocol is an extension of those presented in Kapoor and Piramuthu (2008) and Piramuthu (2010) addressing some identified vulnerabilities.

This paper is organized as follows: The next section discusses relay attacks and their variants known as mafia attack and terrorist attack. Section 3 provides a sketch of the proposed protocol for multiple tags on an object. Section 4 provides a brief security analysis of the proposed protocol. Section 5 concludes the paper with a brief discussion.

2 Relay Attacks

The ISO air-interface protocol (e.g., ISO 14443) requires the tags to be within about 4 inches from the reader. This, in principle, would deter adversaries operating in-between a tag and a reader. However, exploiting or circumventing a weakness in authentication protocols is not the only means to compromise an RFID tag enabled system. Relay attacks are one such attack that does not require physical proximity of a valid tag and reader. An adversary places two devices - a ghost (or proxy) and a leech (or mole) - between a tag and a reader. The ghost relays the reader's signal to the leech, which is in physical proximity to the tag. To the tag, the leech is a valid reader. The adversary then relays messages between the tag and reader without necessarily exploiting any weakness in the authentication protocol. Examples of scenarios that could fall prey to this type of vulnerability include RFID-enabled credit card, building access card, passport, etc.

Pervasive computing has motivated interest in systems that can precisely determine the location of a mobile device. The integrity and privacy of a location-proving system are important to prevent dishonest provers from falsifying location as well as to prevent adversaries from learning or mimicking privileged location information. Although one could verify location through use of GPS coordinates (e.g., Denning and MacDoran, 1996), RFID tags do not lend themselves to such applications. Distance bounding protocols to prevent such distance fraud attacks can be broadly classified as two types, one based on measuring the signal strength and the other based on measuring the round-trip time between prover and verifier.

The proof based on measuring signal strength is not secure. An adversary can easily amplify signal strength as desired or use stronger signals to read from afar. For example, the maximum range of a Bluetooth device is about 10 meters which can be increased to about 100 meters (328 feet) by increasing the power. John Hering (2004) and his colleagues at Flexilis created the BlueSniper 'rifle' and used it to grab the phone book and text messages from a Nokia 6310i phone that was 1.1 miles away. This example illustrates that measuring signal strength does not prevent distance-based attacks. It has been shown that using only electronics hobbyist supplies and tools, a cheap (for about $100) skimmer can be built that can read RFID tags from a distance longer than their typical range (e.g., Kirschenbaum and Wool, 2006; Kfir and Wool, 2005).

The proof based on measuring the round-trip time relies on the fact that no information can propagate faster through space-time than light (Hancke and Kuhn, 2005). The adversary under such a scenario can claim only to be farther away from its current location by delaying the response. Since we are dealing with very small numbers, the verifier must be capable of precisely measuring the round-trip time. For most practical purposes, this also implies that processing delay at the prover's end must be negligible compared to propagation delay between prover and verifier. In addition to simple distance fraud attacks, two other types of attacks have been identified under such scenarios: mafia (man-in-the-middle) fraud, and terrorist fraud attacks (Desmedt, 1988).

The mafia fraud attack is where the adversary consists of a cooperating rogue prover ($\bar{T}$) and rogue verifier ($\bar{R}$) where ($\bar{T}$) interacts with the honest verifier (R) and ($\bar{R}$) interacts with the honest prover (T) as follows: $R - \bar{T} - \bar{R} - T$. I.e., the adversary relays signals between the verifier and prover as if they were in close proximity to each other. Since the adversary does not modify any of the signal it receives, no amount of secure encryption could prevent these types of attacks. Brands and Chaum (1994) presented a distance bounding protocol based on a series of rapid bit challenge-response iterations to determine the distance between the prover and the verifier based on round-trip times. The authenticity of the prover and verifier still needs to be done. Clearly, the prover needs additional hardware (e.g., gates, etc.) dedicated to this protocol.

The terrorist fraud attack is where a dishonest prover collaborates with the adversary to convince the honest verifier of its proximity. Here, although the prover and adversary cooperate, the adversary does not know the secret key of the prover. Clearly, if the adversary knows the secret key, it would be hard to distinguish it from the prover.

3 Protocol for Multi-tagged Object

The following notations are used throughout the paper:

- $N_T, N_R, N_R^{'}, N_P, N_T, r_A, r_B$: random l-bit nonce
- s_c, s_{c+1}: Tag's current and subsequent keys
- $f_k^{\prime}, f_k$: keyed (with key k) encryption function
- H_k: keyed (with key k) one-way hash function
- t_j: shared secret between tag$_i$ and TTP, Reader
- r_i: shared secret between Reader R_i and TTP

3.1 Inclusion/Exclusion of Tag(s)

This protocol (Figure 1) can be used for inclusion and exclusion of tags in a multiple-tagged object. We assume that a TTP mediates between the reader and tags in accomplishing this change in shared secret key. The actors involved in this protocol include the reader, the TTP, and every tag that is a part of the object of interest either before or after components (tags) were added or removed.

We assume that every component (tag) that is a part of the object of interest share a common secret key (s_c). This key is updated every time the object of interest experiences addition or removal of a component or group of components. The primary purpose here is to ensure that the updated key is known only to the reader, the TTP, and the tags that are currently attached to the object. The components (tags) that were dropped from this object should not have knowledge of this new shared key. This is a single round protocol that has three main "loops." This protocol is repeated for each tag that is associated with the object including those that are present on the object and those that were just removed from the object.

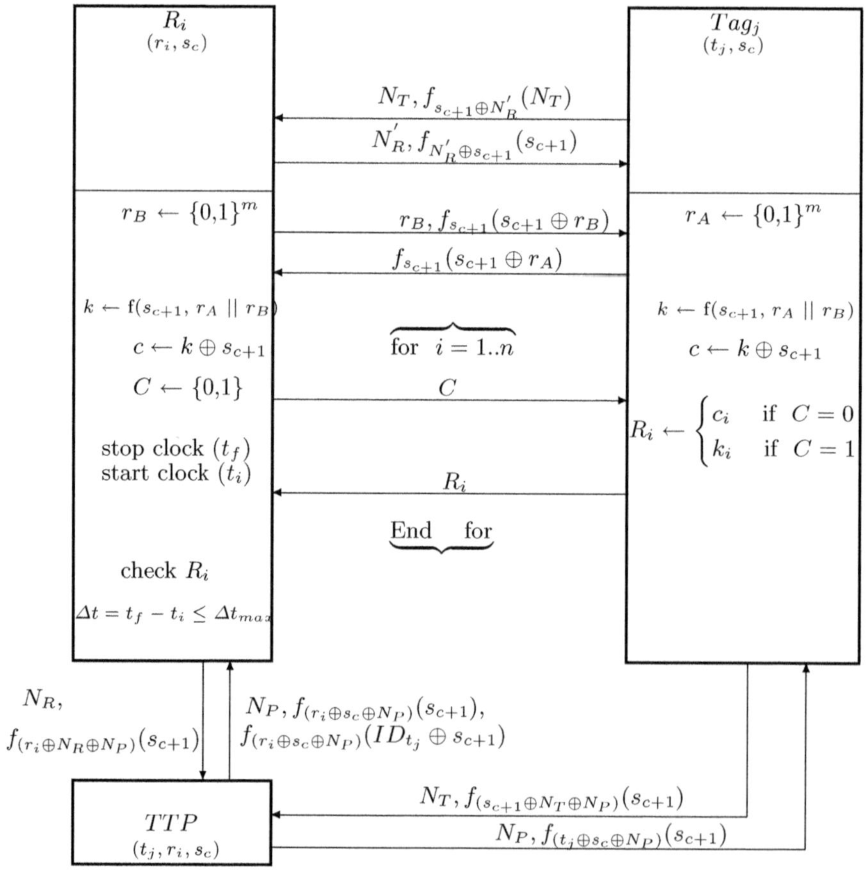

Fig. 1. Tag Inclusion/Exclusion Protocol

The first loop between the TTP and tag begins the shared key change process when the TTP generates a new shared secret for the tags and distributes this secret to each tag currently attached to the object. The TTP waits for response from the tag for a predetermined amount of time. If the TTP does not hear back from the tag during this time, it generates a fresh random nonce (N_P) and the forward part of the loop is repeated. This process continues until this loop is completed. After completion of the first loop, the tag attached to the object knows the new shared secret (s_{c+1}). For those tags that are no longer a part of the object of interest, the same process is followed but with s_{c+1} set to some predetermined string (e.g., null bits). The second loop is between the TTP and the reader. Here, the TTP shares the new shared secret key with the reader. This process is repeated for all relevant readers. The first term ($N_P, f_{(r_i \oplus s_c \oplus N_P)}(s_{c+1})$) is used to transfer the new shared key. The second term ($f_{(r_i \oplus s_c \oplus N_P)}(ID_{t_j} \oplus s_{c+1})$) conveys the unique ID value of the tag to the reader so that the reader can associate the ID value with its corresponding shared secret key value. This process is repeated until the TTP hears back from the reader. Once ID and s_{c+1} values are retrieved, the reader verifies the new common shared secret directly with the tag in the final loop. The third loop is between the reader and the tag. The third "loop" accomplishes two goals: mutually authenticating the tag using the new key (i.e., s_{c+1}) and then ensuring that this tag does indeed exist in the field of the reader. The former is initiated by the reader. The latter (distance bounding part) addresses issues related to relay attacks, and is adapted from Reid, et al. (2006).

The distance bounding part of the protocol operates through measuring the round-trip taken by the signal between reader and tag. In the proposed protocol, there is a need for the distance bounding part only between the reader and tags and not between the other two pairs of entities. The reader and TTP are generally assumed to be linked through a secure connection and, moreover, the distance between these are not of concern in most systems. Communication between the TTP and tags primarily involves generating and transferring the updated shared key from TTP to tags and the physical distance between TTP and tags is really not of concern for security/privacy purposes. However, the physical proximity of reader and tags is of concern since an adversary can initiate a relay attack to modify the physical distance between reader and tag(s) while still ensuring that the reader gets what it needs from the tag(s) for authentication purposes.

4 Security Analysis

1. Secrecy/Data Integrity and Authenticity:
   The cryptographic methods used (e.g., the function ensemble f_{s_i}) reasonably guarantees the secrecy of the message.
2. DoS/Synchronization problem:
   The DoS problem is addressed in the following way: Consider a situation where an adversary blocks a message. Since acknowledgements are expected for the key change and first post-key change communique between two entities, blocking any message creates no breach in the system.

3. Prevention of Mafia attack:
   Mafia attacks are prevented by using both timed and untimed phases, where the timed phase is used to verify distance between the tag and the reader and the un-timed phase is used to authenticate tag and reader. Thus, an adversary cannot respond to the reader in time, if the tag is farther away from the reader. The round trip times (Δt) are used to verify the distance between tag and reader.
4. Prevention of Replay attack:
   Replay attacks are prevented by generating fresh random nonce for every round of the protocol. Using freshly generated random nonce on both ends makes it hard to impersonate either the tag or the reader. In addition, the nonce is XORed with the secret keys to avoid revealing them to outside entities. Using a random nonce with every message in the protocol renders it difficult for an adversary to track the tag. Moreover, during the timed phase, the fast bit exchanges between the reader and tags are dependent on one another and therefore cannot be successfully recorded and replayed.
5. Prevention of Terrorist attack:
   Adapted from Reid et al. (2006), generating c (similarly, c') from both x and k prevents terrorist attacks by ensuring that the colluding tag does not share its secrets with an adversary. The secret (x) can be retrieved from simultaneous knowledge of both c and k.
6. Forward Security:
   This signifies that when the current key of a tag is known, it can be used to extract previous messages (assuming that *all* its past conversations are recorded). Most messages between any two entities are hashed or encrypted with freshly generated nonce in the ensemble. In the distance bounding part, to prevent a malicious reader from obtaining the c (or, c_i') or k (or, k_i') values by repeatedly sending the same R_i (or, R_i') to a tag, the key update uses the complement of R_i (or, R_i') that was transmitted to the reader or malicious adversary as the case may be.

5 Discussion

Inclusion/exclusion of RFID tags on any given (composite) object is not uncommon and there is an urgent need for authentication protocols that consider this scenario. The protocol presented in this paper purports to fill this gap, and is only a first attempt.

Relay attacks are difficult to prevent since these attacks do not depend on cryptography. Moreover, these attacks are passive, and occur without the knowledge of the tag as well as the reader involved. Of the means that have been proposed in the literature thus far, the ones that seem promising are based on measuring the round-trip distance traveled by signals between tag and reader. We use one such method and seamlessly incorporate the same in developing the proposed inclusion/exclusion protocol.

References

1. Brands, S., Chaum, D.: Distance-Bounding Protocols. In: Helleseth, T. (ed.) EUROCRYPT 1993. LNCS, vol. 765, pp. 344–359. Springer, Heidelberg (1994)
2. Denning, D.E., MacDoran, P.F.: Location-Based Authentication: Grounding Cyberspace for Better Security. In: Computer Fraud & Security, pp. 12-16 (February 1996)
3. Desmedt, Y.: Major Security Problems with the 'Unforgeable' (Feige)-Fiat-Shamir Proofs of Identity and How to Overcome Them. In: Proceedings of the Securicom 88, 6th Worldwide Congress on Computer and Communications Security and Protection, pp. 147–159 (1988)
4. Hancke, G.P., Kuhn, M.G.: An RFID Distance Bounding Protocol. In: Proceedings of the IEEE/Create-Net SecureComm, pp. 67–73 (2005)
5. Hering, J.: The BlueSniper 'rifle.' presented at 12th DEFCON. Las Vegas (2004)
6. Kapoor, G., Piramuthu, S.: Protocols for Objects with Multiple RFID Tags. In: Proceedings of the Sixteenth International Conference on Advanced Computing and Communications (ADCOM), pp. 208–213 (2008)
7. Kfir, Z., Wool, A.: Picking Virtual Pockets using Relay Attacks on Contactless Smartcard Systems. In: Proceedings of the 1st International Conference on Security and Privacy for Emerging Areas in Communication Networks (SecureComm), pp. 47–58 (2005)
8. Kirschenbaum, I., Wool, A.: How to Build a Low-Cost, Extended-Range RFID Skimmer. Cryptology ePrint Archive: Report 2006/054 (2006)
9. Piramuthu, S.: Relay Attack-Resisting Inclusion/Exclusion Protocol for RFID. In: 2nd International Workshop on DYnamic Networks: Algorithms and Security (DYNAS), Bordeaux (2010)
10. Reid, J., Gonzalez Nieto, J.M., Tang, T., Senadji, B.: Detecting Relay Attacks with Timing-Based Protocols. Queensland University of Technology ePrint (2006), `http://eprints.qut.edu.au/view/year/2006.html`

Min Max Threshold Range (MMTR) Approach in Palmprint Recognition

Jyoti Malik[1], G. Sainarayanan[2], and Ratna Dahiya[3]

[1] Electrical engineering Department, National Institute of Technology, Kurukshetra
jyoti_reck@yahoo.com
[2] ICT Academy of Tamil Nadu, Chennai, India
sainarayanan@ictact.in
[3] Electrical engineering Department, National Institute of Technology, Kurukshetra
ratna_dahiya@yahoo.co.in

Abstract. Palmprint recognition is an effective biometric authentication method to automatically identify a person's identity. The features in a palmprint include principal lines, wrinkles and ridges etc. All these features are of different length and thickness. It is not possible to analyse them in single resolution, so multi-resolution analysis technique is required. Here, Wavelet transform is proposed as a multi-resolution technique to extract these features. Euclidian distance is used for similarity measurement. In addition, a Min Max Threshold Range (MMTR) method is proposed that helps in increasing overall system accuracy by matching a person with multiple threshold values. In this technique, firstly the person is authenticated at global level using Reference threshold. Secondly, the person is authenticated at local level using range of Minimum and Maximum thresholds defined for a person. Generally, personal authentication is done using reference threshold but there are chances of false acceptance. So, by using the Minimum and Maximum Thresholds range of false accepted persons at personal level, a person is identified to be false accepted or genuinely accepted. MMTR is an effective technique to increase the accuracy of the palmprint authentication system by reducing the False Acceptance Rate (FAR). Experimental results indicate that the proposed method improves the False Acceptance Rate drastically.

Keywords: Multi-resolution analysis, Wavelet transform, Min Max Threshold Range, False Acceptance Rate.

1 Introduction

Personal identification using biometric methods is becoming popular in today's automated world. Biometric authentication methods utilize automated techniques to authenticate a person's identity based on his/her behavioural/physiological characteristics. The physiological characteristics consist of individual body parts like iris, face, hand, palmprint and fingerprint etc. [1, 2, 3, 4, 5]. The behavioural characteristics are the actions performed by person such as signature, gait and voice print. Behavioural characteristics are more prone to change with time than physiological characteristics.

N. Meghanathan et al. (Eds.): CCSIT 2011, Part III, CCIS 133, pp. 438–449, 2011.

For example, the signature varies every time an individual sign, but human body parts are subject minimal changed over time.

Palmprint is universal, unique, permanent, collectible, consistent, comparable, inimitable and tamper-resistant biometric method. Palmprint has several features like geometry features, line features, point features, texture features etc [6, 7, 8, 9, 10]. In this paper, line feature is analysed for palmprint recognition. Line feature includes principal lines, wrinkles and ridges. All these line features are of different thickness, length and direction. Principal lines are thicker than wrinkles, so they can be analysed in low resolution whereas wrinkles in medium resolution. Ridges are thinner than wrinkles, so they can be analysed in high resolution. It is not easy to analyse these lines because different thickness need analysis in different resolutions [11, 12, 13]. In this paper the Wavelet transform, a multi-resolution method is proposed for line feature analysis. Euclidian distance method is used for similarity measurement. Min Max Threshold Range (MMTR) method is defined that can reduce FAR and makes the authentication system more reliable.

The following section of the paper is organised as follows: In section 2, Palmprint authentication system is briefed. Section 3 describes palm image pre-processing. Section 4 and section 5 describes feature extraction by wavelet transform and feature matching method. Section 6 includes Min Max Threshold Range (MMTR) approach. Section 7 describes experimental results and section 8 gives the conclusion.

2 Palmprint Authentication System

The palmprint authentication system has following four stages as mentioned in figure 1:

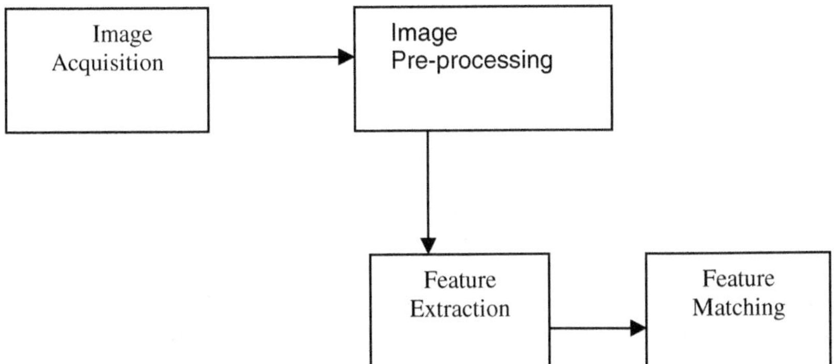

Fig. 1. Palmprint authentication system

In image acquisition the hand image can be captured by using scanner, CCD camera or digital camera.

In image pre-processing, image is first enhanced using low pass filter to remove noise. The portion of the enhanced image is cropped out that contains desired features of the palm and the cropped area is known as Region Of Interest (ROI). The shape of ROI can be square, circle etc.

The feature extraction is a main step to extract the desired features from ROI. The features can be of different types, line feature, geometry feature, point features etc.

Feature matching is the stage where similarity between features is calculated. The person is authenticated based on the similarity measurement value. Several methods like Hamming Distance, Euclidian Distance or Neural Network can be used for similarity measurement.

3 Palm Image Pre-processing

The purpose of image pre-processing is to enhance the image and to get ROI (Region Of Interest) for feature extraction. It is important to define a coordinate system that is used to extract the central part of a palmprint ie. ROI. The valley points between little finger, ring finger (V1) and index finger, center finger (V3) are used as reference points to determine a coordinate system as shown in Figure 2. The basic steps in pre-processing stage are:

Step 1: Apply low-pass filter to enhance the palm image from the effects of noise and poor illumination. Convert the palm image into grayscale image if it is other than grayscale.
Step 2: Apply threshold, T_h to convert the gray image to binary image using the below transformation functions:

$$B_i(x, y) = 1, \text{ if } P_e(x, y) \geq T_h \tag{1}$$

$$B_i(x, y) = 0, \text{ if } P_e(x, y) < T_h \tag{2}$$

Where $B_i(x, y)$ is a binary image,

$P_e(x, y)$ is the enhanced greyscale palm image,

T_h is threshold value used to convert gray image to binary image.
Step 3: Find the boundary of the palm image using boundary tracing method taking two points on the wrist as the starting and last point.
Step 4: Track boundary of the binarized palm image to find out the valleys and tips of the fingers. Our main aim is to calculate the valleys so as to find out the reference points between ring finger and little finger (V1) and index finger and center finger (V3).
Step 5: Join valley points V_1 and V_3 by a line.
Step 6: Make a line parallel to the line joining V_1 and V_3 by a distance d. Distance d is decided on the basis that required palmprint should have all the unique features of a palm.

All the image pre-processing steps are described in the figure 2 below:

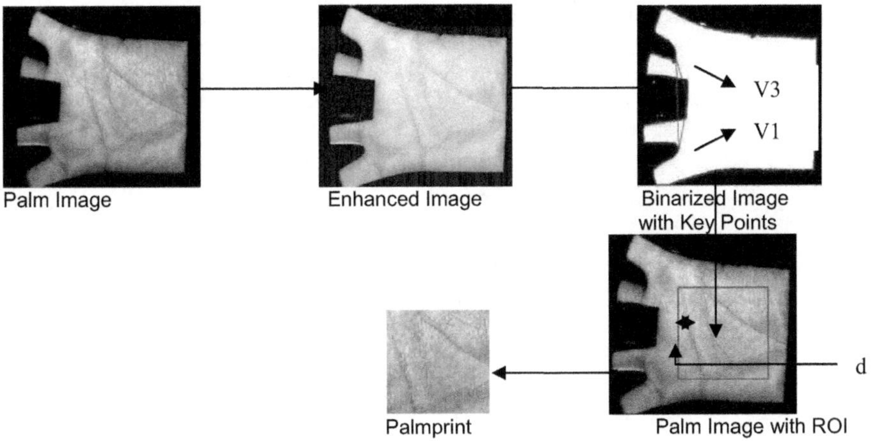

Fig. 2. Stages of Image Pre-processing

4 Feature Extraction by Wavelet Transform

The main aim of feature extraction is to get the desired features, here line feature from the palmprint. Line feature includes principal lines, wrinkles and ridges. All these features are of different thickness, length and direction. It is difficult to analyse these lines in single resolution because of different thickness and length of lines. Wavelet transform is one of the promising tool to analyse the image in different resolutions. Here, Wavelet transform, a multi-resolution analysis method is proposed for line features extraction.

A 2-D wavelet transform decomposes the image in approximation and detail coefficients as shown in following figure 3.

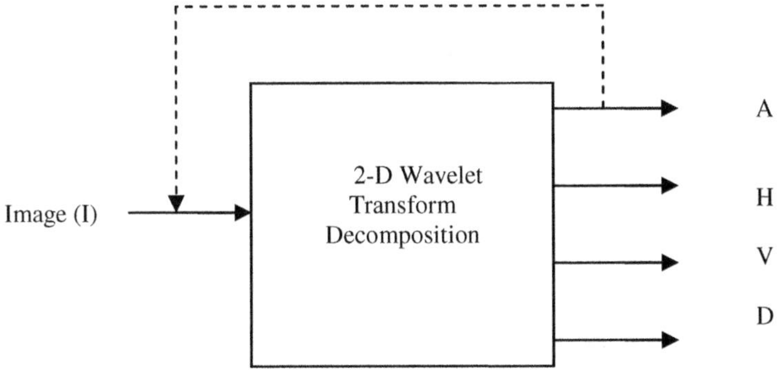

Fig. 3. 2-D Wavelet Decomposition

In figure 3 Image (I) is decomposed to approximation coefficients (A) and Horizontal (H), Vertical (V) and Diagonal (D) detail coefficients. Approximation coefficients can be further decomposed similar to original image for further details. Multi-level decomposition of approximation coefficients gives detail of all lines, wrinkles and ridges. Detail coefficients are transformed to wavelet energy to represent palmprint features.

The wavelet energy is defined as:-

$$E_i^h = \sum_{x=1}^{M}\sum_{y=1}^{N}\left(H_i(x,y)\right)^2 \tag{3}$$

$$E_i^v = \sum_{x=1}^{M}\sum_{y=1}^{N}\left(V_i(x,y)\right)^2 \tag{4}$$

$$E_i^d = \sum_{x=1}^{M}\sum_{y=1}^{N}\left(D_i(x,y)\right)^2 \tag{5}$$

where equations (3) - (5) denote wavelet energies in Horizontal (H), Vertical (V), Diagonal (D) directions respectively. (M, N) is the size of the detail coefficient image. The wavelet energies in different decomposition levels are arranged in the form of feature vector as below.

$$\left(E_i^h, E_i^v, E_i^d\right)_{i=1,2,\dots\dots,K} \tag{6}$$

where K is the level of decomposition.

5 Feature Matching

A matching algorithm describes the degree of similarity between two feature vectors. In this paper, Euclidean Distance similarity measurement method is used. Euclidean distance involves computation of square root of the sum of the squares of the differences between two feature vectors.

$$ED = \sqrt{\sum_{k=1}^{m}\left(FV_{i,k} - FV_{j,k}\right)^2} \tag{7}$$

where $FV_{i,k}$, $FV_{j,k}$ are feature vectors with length 'm'. 'i', 'j' are the iterators on the feature vector database.

Euclidean Distance value "0" signifies both feature vectors are exactly same and a value approaching "0" signifies both feature vectors belongs to same hand.

6 Min Max Threshold Range (MMTR) Approach

In the last section it is discussed that Euclidean Distance value approaching "0" signifies both feature vectors belongs to same palm image. A value near to "0" is identified that is known as reference threshold. If matching score (or Euclidean distance) of two feature vectors is less than reference threshold value, feature vectors are considered to be from same hands otherwise different hands. In this paper, a unique and effective way to identify reference threshold and threshold range for each hand is proposed. The proposed approach can improve overall system accuracy. The accuracy of the biometric authentication can be defined by following equation:

$$Accuracy(\%) = \left(100 - \left(FAR(\%) + FRR(\%)\right)/2\right) \tag{8}$$

Where, FAR is False Acceptance Rate, FRR is False Rejection Rate.

If either FAR or FRR is decreased, overall system accuracy is increased. The MMTR method can extremely decrease FAR that can result in stable authentication system.

In MMTR method, multiple hand image samples are required to find out reference threshold and min max threshold range of each hand. The hand image samples are divided into two groups G1 and G2.

G_1 group

$$P_1 = \lfloor I_1, I_2, \ldots\ldots I_{(M-1)} \rfloor, P_2 = \lfloor I_1, I_2, \ldots\ldots I_{(M-1)} \rfloor, \ldots\ldots\ldots P_N = \lfloor I_1, I_2, \ldots\ldots I_{(M-1)} \rfloor \tag{9}$$

G_2 group

$$P_1 = [I_M], \quad P_2 = [I_M], \ldots\ldots\ldots\ldots\ldots P_N = [I_M] \tag{10}$$

Where P_i denotes i^{th} person in group G_1, G_2, I_j denotes the jth palm image in group G_1, G_2.

Table 1. Matching in group G_1 among person P_1

j \ i	1	2	3		M-1
1	X	ED_{12}	ED_{13}	....	$ED_{1(M-1)}$
2	ED_{21}	X	ED_{23}	....	$ED_{2(M-1)}$
:	:	:	:	:	:
:	:	:	:	:	:
M-1	$ED_{(M-1)1}$	$ED_{(M-1)2}$	$ED_{(M-1)3}$		X

In group G1, each hand feature vector in P_1 is matched with all other (m-1) hands feature vector by Euclidian distance measurement method. The matching values are approaching "0" and are stored in threshold array.

$$TA_1 = \lfloor ED_{12}, ED_{13}, \ldots ED_{1M-1}, ED_{21}, ED_{23}, \ldots ED_{2M-1}, \ldots ED_{(M-1)1}, ED_{(M-1)2}, \ldots ED_{(M-1)(M-2)} \rfloor \tag{11}$$

Similarly, all N hand image samples matching results are stored in Threshold array (TA).

$$T_A = TA_1 + TA_2 + \ldots\ldots + TA_N \tag{12}$$

$$\left.\begin{aligned} T_{AiMIN} &= \min(T_{Ai}) \\ T_{AiMAX} &= \max(T_{Ai}) \end{aligned}\right\}_{i=1,\ldots,N} \tag{13}$$

The accuracy of the system is identified by matching group G_2 samples with group G_1 samples using threshold values stored in threshold array. Finally, a threshold value is chosen where FAR and FRR is minimum, this value is called Reference threshold.

In real time authentication system, if a person's hand is compared with the samples present in the database, the authenticity depends on the matching score. If matching score (Euclidean Distance value) is less than reference threshold, the person is considered to be genuine otherwise imposter. It is possible that some wrong hand can be accepted as genuine if matching score fulfils the reference threshold criteria. Here, a second level of verification by min-max threshold range (MMTR) at hand level is proposed. For successful authentication matching score must be less than reference threshold and within the min-max threshold range of the person. MMTR method is explained in detail as follows:

Each hand feature vector is matched with all other hands feature vector of the same person by Euclidian distance measurement method and the matching values are stored in threshold array as shown in equation 1 and 2. The min and max threshold values are identified from threshold array in equation 3 and stored in database. It is observed that different hands have different min and max range of threshold. So, the second level of verification within min and max range of threshold can reduce the chances of false acceptance.

7 Experimental Results and Analysis

A database of 600 palmprint images from 100 palms with 6 samples for each palm is taken from PolyU palmprint database [14]. The palmprint database is divided into two groups, first group (G_1) consists of 100 persons with each person having 5 palm sample images to train the system, and second group (G_2) contains 100 persons with each person having one palm image different from the first group images. Second group is used as testing sample. The image size is 284×384 pixels.

G_1 group

$$P_1 = [I_1, I_2, I_3, I_4, I_5],\ P_2 = [I_1, I_2, I_3, I_4, I_5], \ldots\ P_{100} = [I_1, I_2, I_3, I_4, I_5] \quad (14)$$

In G_1 group each hand P_i contains 5 sample image $I_{1\text{-}5}$.

G_2 group

$$P_1 = [I_6],\ P_2 = [I_6], \ldots\ldots P_{100} = [I_6] \quad (15)$$

In G_2 group each hand P_i contains only sample image I_6.

Image is pre-processed to get the region of interest. Pre-processing includes image enhancement, image binarization, boundary extraction, cropping of palmprint/ROI. The ROI size is 64×64 pixels. Sample of ROI is shown in figure 2.

Feature extraction is done by wavelet transform to get the wavelet energies of various details coefficients. Wavelet transform with 6-level decomposition using Haar wavelet is applied. The feature vector contains 18 wavelet energy elements for each hand. Feature vector of all hand images samples is calculated and stored in database. Feature vector matrix is $\left(E_i^h, E_i^v, E_i^d\right)_{i=1,2,\ldots,K}$. K is the level of decomposition.

Euclidian distance is used as a similarity measurement method for feature matching.

In group G1, each hand feature vector in P_1 is matched with all other 4 hands feature vector by Euclidian distance measurement method. The matching values are approaching "0" and are stored in threshold array as shown in table 2.

Table 2. FAR, FRR, Accuracy values with and without MMTR

Wavelet Type	Decomo p--osition Level	Reference Threshold	FAR	FRR	Accu-racy	FAR with MMTR	FRR with MMTR	Accuracy with MMTR	Accuracy Improve-ment	Compari-son Time
haar	1	0.00003	0	1	99.5	0	0.29	99.9	0.355	0.0348
haar	1	0.000328	7.88	0.6	95.8	6.81	0.2	96.5	0.735	0.0348
haar	1	0.000653	16.2	0.29	91.8	12.3	0.14	93.8	2.00	0.0348
haar	1	0.000978	23.5	0.19	88.2	14.5	0.07	92.7	4.57	0.0348
haar	1	0.0013	29.7	0.08	85.1	15.6	0.03	92.2	7.04	0.0348
haar	1	0.00163	35	0.07	82.4	16.4	0.02	91.8	9.37	0.0348
haar	1	0.00195	39	0.05	80.5	16.9	0.02	91.6	11.1	0.0348
haar	1	0.00228	42.8	0.04	78.6	17.3	0.02	91.4	12.8	0.0348
haar	1	0.00260	46	0.03	77	17.6	0.02	91.2	14.2	0.0348
haar	1	0.00293	48.7	0.02	75.6	17.6	0.01	91.2	15.6	0.0348
haar	1	0.00325	51.4	0.01	74.3	17.8	0.01	91.1	16.8	0.0348
haar	1	0.00358	53.6	0.01	73.2	17.8	0.01	91.1	17.9	0.0348
haar	1	0.00390	55.8	0.01	72.1	17.9	0.01	91.1	19	0.0348
haar	1	0.00423	58	0.01	71	17.9	0.01	91	20	0.0348
haar	1	0.00455	59.9	0	70	18	0	91	21	0.0348
haar	1	0.00488	61.7	0	69.2	18	0	91	21.8	0.0348
haar	1	0.00520	63.2	0	68.4	18.1	0	91	22.6	0.0348
haar	1	0.00553	64.7	0	67.7	18.1	0	91	23.3	0.0348
haar	1	0.00585	66	0	67	18.1	0	91	24	0.0348
haar	1	0.00617	67.3	0	66.3	18.1	0	90.9	24.6	0.0348
haar	1	0.00650	68.4	0	65.8	18.1	0	90.9	25.1	0.0348
haar	1	0.00682	69.5	0	65.3	18.1	0	90.9	25.7	0.0348
haar	1	0.00715	70.6	0	64.7	18.2	0	90.9	26.2	0.0348
haar	1	0.00747	71.5	0	64.2	18.2	0	90.9	26.7	0.0348
haar	1	0.00780	72.4	0	63.8	18.2	0	90.9	27.1	0.0348

Min and Max threshold value of person P_i is calculated and stored in database. These values are used later in second level of authentication.

Similarly, all 100 hand image samples 2000 matching values are stored in Threshold array (TA).

$$T_A = TA_1 + TA_2 + \dots\dots + TA_{100}$$

$$\left.\begin{aligned} T_{AiMIN} &= \min(T_{Ai}) \\ T_{AiMAX} &= \max(T_{Ai}) \end{aligned}\right\}_{i=1,\dots,100}$$

The maximum and minimum values are found out from threshold array.

$$T_{AMIN} = 0.0195$$

$$T_{AMAX} = 0.8627$$

These minimum and maximum values of threshold array are divided into 25 threshold values.

$$\Delta = (T_{AMAX} - T_{AMIN})/25$$
$$= (0.8627 - 0.0195)/25$$
$$= 0.0337$$
$$\Delta 1 = T_{AMIN} + \Delta$$
$$= 0.0195 + 0.0337$$
$$= 0.0533$$
$$\Delta 2 = T_{AMIN} + 2\Delta$$

Similarly, $\Delta 25 = T_{AMIN} + 25\Delta$

These 25 threshold values are tested with group G_2 and group G_1 images. The 25 threshold values and the respective FAR and FRR values are shown in table 2.

The FAR and FRR are values are plotted with respect to 25 threshold range values in Figure 4. From the graph the value of reference threshold is chosen where FAR and FRR are minimum.

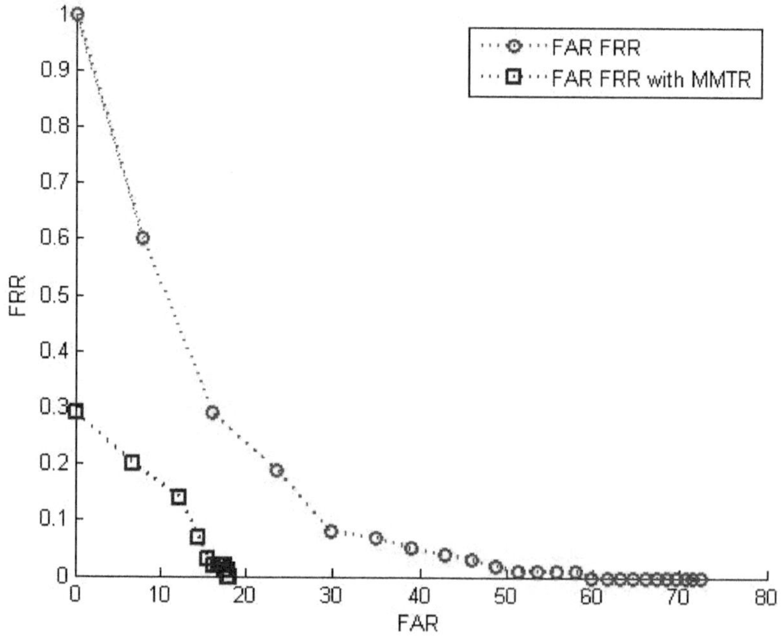

Fig. 4. Graph between Threshold Range and FAR/FRR

Accuracy improvement is plotted in Fig. 5.

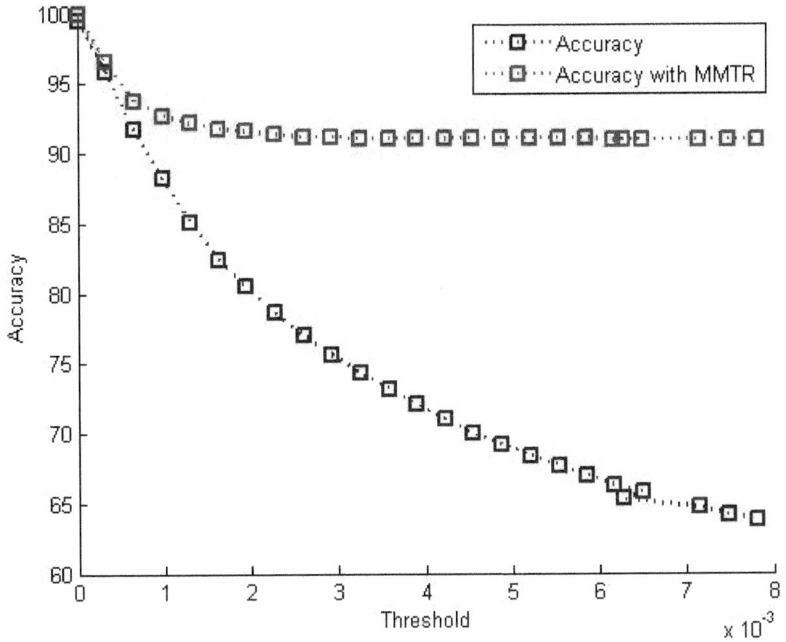

Fig. 5. Accuracy Vs Threshold

The relation of decomposition level with comparison time is tabulated in table 3 and plotted in Fig. 6.

Table 3. Decomposition level and Comparison time

Decomposition Level	Comparison Time
1	0.0348
2	0.0326
3	0.0378
4	0.0509
5	0.0558
6	0.0505

The min max threshold range approach came into picture once the reference threshold value is found out. Here, if the person matching score (Euclidean distance) is below the reference threshold value, the person is considered as genuine. But there are chances of person getting false accepted. So, the Euclidean distance value of the person is compared within the maximum and minimum range values of person with whom the person is claimed to be identified. The min and max threshold values are already stored in the database. Here, by introducing second level of authentication

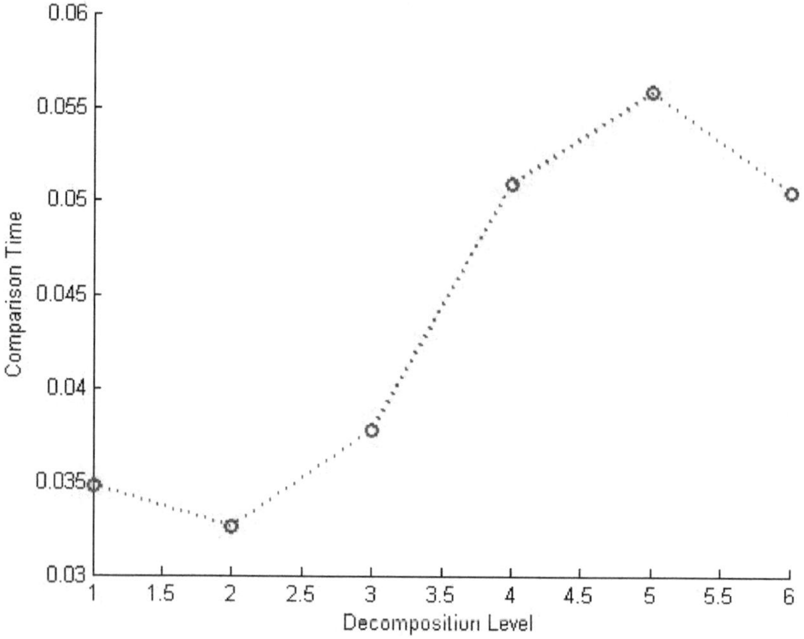

Fig. 6. Comparison time Vs Decomposition level

criteria to check the authenticity of a person, FAR values are improved, that further increase the accuracy.

It can be seen in the graphs of accuracy and FAR, FRR, that with the proposed approach of MMTR, results got improved.

8 Conclusion

In a palmprint image different features have different resolutions. The wavelet transform using Haar wavelet is applied to each palmprint image in the database to get sub-images of different resolutions. The wavelet energy computed from the wavelet detail coefficients has the ability to discriminate similar palmprints. Experimental results clearly show that our proposed Min Max Threshold Range (MMTR) methodology can effectively improve the recognition rate.

References

1. Jonathon Phillips, P., Martin, A., Wilson, C.L., Przybocki, M.: An Introduction to Evaluating Biometric Systems. In: IEEE, Proceedings of Computer society (February 2000)
2. Pankanti, S., Bolle, R.M., Jain, A.: Biometrics: The Future of Identification. In: IEEE, Proceedings of Computer society (February 2000)
3. Zhang, D.: Automated Biometrics—Technologies and Systems. Kluwer Academic, Boston (2000)

4. Pankrmti, S., Bolle, R., Jain, A.K.: Biometrics-The Future of identification. IEEE Computer 33, 46–49 (2000)
5. Jain, A., Bolle, R., Pankanti, S.: Biometrics: Personal Identification in Networked Society. Kluwer Academic, Boston (1999)
6. Zhang, D., Kong, W., You, J., Wong, M.: Online palmprint identification. IEEE Transactions on Pattern Analysis and Machine Intelligence 25(9), 1041–1050 (2003)
7. Han, C.-C., Cheng, H.-L., Lin, C.-L., Fan, K.-C.: Personal authentication using palm-print features. Pattern Recognition and Machine Intelligence 36, 371–381 (2003)
8. Wu, X., Zhang, D., Wang, K., Huang, B.: Palmprint classification using principal lines. Pattern Recognition 37(37), 1987–1998 (2004)
9. Shu, W., Rong, G., Bian, Z., Zhang, D.: Automatic palmprint verification. Int'l J. Image and Graphics 1, 135–151 (2001)
10. Kwnar, A., Wong, D.C.M., Shen, H.C., lain, A.K.: Personal verification using palmprint and hand geometry biometric. In: Kittler, J., Nixon, M.S. (eds.) AVBPA 2003. LNCS, vol. 2688, pp. 668–678. Springer, Heidelberg (2003)
11. Wu, X.-Q., Wang, K.-Q., Zhang, D.: Wavelet Based Palmprint Recognition. In: IEEE, Proceedings of the First International Conference on Machine Learning and Cybernetics, November 4-5, vol. 3, pp. 1253–1257 (2002)
12. Graps, A.: An Introduction to Wavelets. IEEE Computer Society, Computational Science and Engineering 2(2), 50–61 (1995)
13. Mallat, S.: A wavelet tour of Signal Processing, pp. 119–132
14. PolyU Palmprint Database, `http://www.comp.polyu.edu.hk/~biometrics/`
15. Gonzalez, R.C., Woods, R.E., Eddins, S.L.: Digital Image Processing using MATLAB, pp. 256–295
16. Gonzalez, R.C., Woods, R.E., Eddins, S.L.: Digital Image Processing, pp. 371–426
17. Misiti, M., Misiti, Y., Oppenheim, G., Poggi, J.-M.: Wavelet Toolbox™ 4 User's Guide, pp. 47–50
18. Li, W., Zhang, D., Xu, Z.: Palmprint Identification by Fourier Transform. Int'l J. Pattern Recognition and Artificial Intelligence 16(4), 417–432 (2002)
19. Wu, X.Q., Wang, K.Q., Zhang, D.: Wavelet Based Palm print Recognition. In: Proceedings of First International Conference on Machine Learning and Cybernetics, vol. 3, pp. 1253–1257 (2002)
20. Jain, A.K., Ross, A.: A Prototype hand geometry-based verification system. In: Proc. 2nd Inl'l Conference on Audio- and Video-based Biometric Personal Authentication (AVBPA), pp. 166–171 (1999)
21. You, J., Li, W., Zhang, D.: Hierarchical palmprint identification via multiple feature extraction. Pattern Recognition 35, 847–859 (2002)
22. Lu, G., Wang, K.: Wavelet Based Independent Component Analysis for Palmprint Identification. In: Proceedings of the Third International Conference on Machine Learning and Cybernetics, pp. 3547–3550 (2004)
23. Zhang, L., Zhang, D.: Characterization of palmprints by wavelet signatures via directional context modeling. IEEE Trans. Syst., Man, Cybern. B, Cybern. 34(3), 1335–1347 (2004)

Power and Buffer Overflow Optimization in Wireless Sensor Nodes

Gauri Joshi, Sudhanshu Dwivedi, Anshul Goel,
Jaideep Mulherkar, and Prabhat Ranjan

DAIICT, Gandhinagar, India
{gauri_joshi,sudhanshu_dwivedi,anshul_goel,
jaideep_mulherkar,prabhat_ranjan}@daiict.ac.in

Abstract. Prolonging the life span of the network is the prime focus in highly energy constrained wireless sensor networks. Sufficient number of active nodes can only ensure proper coverage of the sensing field and connectivity of the network. If most of the nodes get their batteries depleted then it is not possible to maintain the network. In order to have long lived network it is mandatory to have long lived sensor nodes and hence power optimization at node level becomes equally important as power optimization at network level. In this paper need for a dynamically adaptive sensor node is signified in order to optimize power at individual nodes.

We have analyzed a wireless sensor node using queuing theory. A sensor node is looked upon as a tandem queue in which first server is the processor or micro controller and the second server in series is the transmitter. Both the servers have finite and very small buffers associated with them as the sensor nodes are tiny devices and have very limited hardware.

In this paper we have analyzed and simulated sensor node models. First we have considered a sensor node working with fixed service rate (processing rate and transmission rate). Secondly we have considered an adaptive sensor node which is capable of varying its service rates as per the requirement and ensure the quality of service. We have simulated both the models using MATLAB and compared their performances like life time, power consumption, buffer overflow probability and idle time etc.

We have compared the performances of both the models under normal work loads as well as when the catastrophe (heavy wok load) occurs. In both the situations an adaptive service model out performs the fixed service model as it saves the power during normal period and increases the lifetime and during catastrophe period it consumes more power but ensures the QoS (Quality of Service) by reducing the overflow probability.

Keywords: wireless sensor nodes, power optimization, buffer overflow, MATLAB simulation, queuing model.

1 Introduction

Our focus is on the power optimization at sensor node level with ultimate aim to increase the lifetime of the Wireless Sensor Network. In a wireless sensor node maximum power is consumed for wireless communication and data processing also

N. Meghanathan et al. (Eds.): CCSIT 2011, Part III, CCIS 133, pp. 450–458, 2011.

consumes moderate amount of power. We are trying to optimize the power consumption of processor and radio unit dynamically by adopting the optimized service rates (processing rate and transmission rate respectively) with respect to the instantaneous workload requirements.

For a long-lived Wireless Sensor Network, low power hardware is the basic requirement and low duty cycling applied on these hardware further increases the lifetime of the sensor nodes and long lived sensor nodes support to work the network over longer period. We have considered rotational sleep schedule (time triggered wake up) as it do provide better network coverage and connectivity till sufficient number of nodes fail. As sensor networks are mainly deployed to sense some rare events, most of the times there is no much traffic in the network and no much work for the sensor nodes to carry. The problem arises when a node is turned ON but there is no much work to carry and hence remain idle for a longer duration. This idle state power consumption is the power wastage as power is consumed for doing nothing. More the idle period more is the more wastage. So it is important to control the power consumption during ON state by reducing the idle time periods. Here we have classified the time period over which sensor nodes are alive in the two categories- normal period and catastrophic period. Normal period is the time interval when event of interest has not occurred and everything is normal. It results in small data arrival rates in the input buffer of sensor nodes. Catastrophic period is the time duration when the event occurs. Lot of information is sensed by the nodes as well as lot of data received from the neighbouring nodes results in the peak data arrival rate.

In order to reduce the idle power consumption during normal period if the service rates of sensor nodes are kept smaller, then large amount of data arriving at the sensor node can not be handled during the catastrophic period . Sensor nodes being very small sized devices have very small buffers to store the data and if not served with proper service rate then result in the buffer overflow and data gets lost. Hence wireless sensor nodes with longer life time but providing desired QoS are required. ***Reducing the idle power consumption during the normal period and reducing the buffer overflow during the catastrophic period are equally important.*** A sensor node capable of variable service rates can handle both the issues. Working with the smaller service rates consumes less power and reduction in idle power consumption increases the life time during normal period while offering higher service rates during the catastrophic period consumes more power but reduces the data loss because of buffer overflow.

We have modeled a sensor node with fixed service rates as well as a sensor node with variable service rates and compared their performances.

Fig.1 shows the basic block schematic of a wireless sensor node and Fig.2 shows the tandem queue model of a sensor node with fixed service rate.

Data arrives in the input buffer from two sources- data sensed by its own sensors and the data received from the neighboring nodes. The processor processes this data and the processed data comes in the output buffer. Transmitter transmits this data. Here processing rate and the transmission rate are fixed. Sensor nodes with fixed service rates are designed to handle moderate data arrival rates otherwise if designed to handle low data rates will result in data loss due to buffer overflow during catastrophic period or if designed to handle peak data rates then will remain idle over a longer period and power wastage will be more which reduces the lifetime of the sensor nodes.

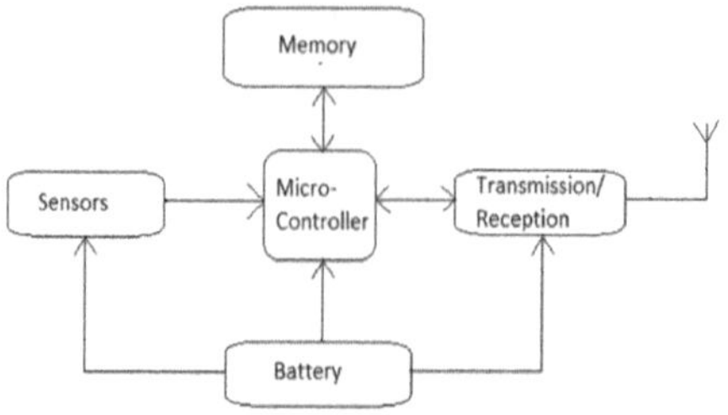

Fig. 1. Basic architecture of wireless sensor node

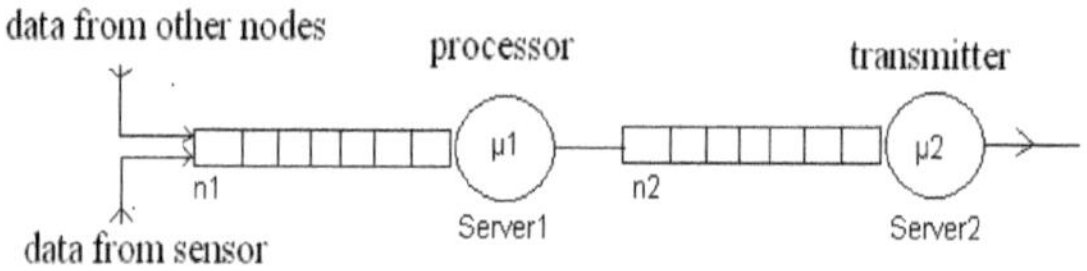

Fig. 2. Tandem queue model of wireless sensor node (fixed service rate)

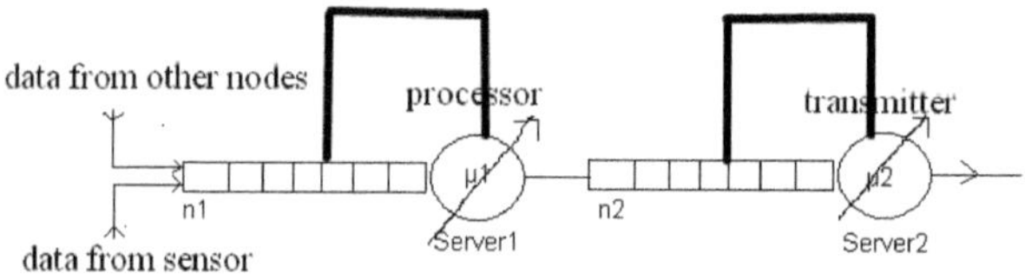

Fig. 3. A sensor node with variable service rates

Fig. 3 shows the sensor node architecture with variable processing rate and variable transmission rate. Here a monitor checks the queue length and the probability of buffer overflow. Processing rate of the processor is varied as per the principle of dynamic voltage / frequency scaling (DVFS) and the data transmission rate is varied using dynamic modulation scaling (DMS). The concept of dynamic voltage scaling is nicely elaborated by Amit Sinha, Anantha Chandrakasan et al [1],[2]. Dynamic modulation scaling (DMS) concept is elaborated by Schurgers, et al [3]. It seems better to reduce the transmission time Ton in order to reduce the energy consumption, so generally it is better to transmit as fast as possible and then turn to OFF state. Hence it is desirable to transmit multiple bits per symbol (M-ary modulation) in order to reduce Ton. But unfortunately for today's available transceivers start up time is much higher hundreds of microseconds) and it increases the power consumed by electronic hardware of the transmitter very aggressively as compared to output power transmitted. So switching transmitter ON and OFF frequently is not a wise decision and may not result in significant energy saving. In case of M-ary modulation ($M = 2^b$) as the constellation size b (number of bits per symbol) increases, power consumed by hardware as well as output power increases so for a particular transmission system value of b should be optimized for specific symbol rate. The energy consumption in data transmission is proportional to the transmission data rate [4], [5]. Increasing the constellation size b, energy consumed for transmission of each bit increases while associated transmission delay is decreased. Dynamic modulation scaling is useful to achieve multiple data rate and dynamic power scaling to provide energy savings.

2 System Specifications

From the architecture of a sensor node it can be viewed as two systems connected in tandem (output of first system is input for the second system). We have assumed that the arrival of data packets follows Poisson distribution. During normal conditions the arrival rate is assumed to be λ1 while during catastrophe it is assumed to be λ2. Both the system queues are of fixed lengths len1 and len2 respectively. When there is a sudden change in the surroundings the data flow increases to a comparatively higher rate and that is why there is a need for higher value of service rate during catastrophe period.

The node is designed in such a way that it analyses the overflow probability for both the servers after every 20 time units. During this period if the overflow of packets in any of the queues has reached above a threshold level then their respective service rates will increase, so that the higher traffic of data could be managed with less overflow.

As soon as the condition is back to normal the service rates will be changed back to the initial values.

Using the lower values of service rates during normal conditions (because there is less data traffic in the system during normal conditions) we are trying to save the battery power since power consumption increases with the increase in service rate. And by increasing the value of service rates during catastrophe we are reducing the overflow of packets since during catastrophe data traffic in the system increases to a great extent.

Since most of the time the system is in normal condition so the energy is saved by using lower value of service rates during this condition, and so the lifetime of the system is increased. Also there is timer set inside the system which causes the node to sleep after every fixed intervals of time. This also adds up to the lifetime of the node. A wireless sensor node with two ON states is considered and low duty cycling is applied using rotational sleep schedule. Sensor node remains OFF for a duration of T1 then turns on for a duration of T2 and so on.

3 Theoretical Analysis

Given the time duration of catastrophe period (T_C), formulae for Average Power consumed by any server during catastrophe can be derived as [6]:

$$P_{avg\_cat} = ((1 - P_0)\, T_C .\, P_{high} + P_0 .\, T_C .\, P_{idle}) / T_C$$
$$= (1 - P_0)\, P_{high} + P_0 .\, P_{idle}$$

Similarly, given the time duration of Normal period (T_N), formulae for Average Power during Normal period can be derived as:

$$P_{avg\_nor} = ((1 - P_0)\, T_N .\, P_{low} + P_0 .\, T_N .\, P_{idle}) / T_N$$
$$= (1 - P_0)\, P_{low} + P_0 .\, P_{idle}$$

Here (1- P_0) represents the probability of time when the server is not idle i.e. it is busy and servicing some request and P_0 represents the probability of time when there is no request to be serviced and the server is idle.

P_0, P_{high} and P_{low} can be given as:

$$P_0 = (1 - (\lambda/\mu))/ (1 - (\lambda/\mu)^{(len+1)})$$

Here it is to be noted that values of λ and μ will be different for catastrophe and normal period, and so the values of P_0 will also be different in both the cases.

For both the models the Arrival rate (λ) is kept to be same.

As in [7] P_{high}, $P_{low} = \mu^3$ for processor, during normal period the lower value of μ will give P_{low} and during catastrophe the higher value of μ will give P_{high}. For transmitter power consumed is proportional to the square of M [4].

We can also calculate the overflow probabilities of the models theoretically, which is given by Plen. Plen is the probability of the server for being in the state when the server queue is full up to the total length and in this proportion of time the overflow will occur. So for each server the overflow probability can be measured as:

$$P_{len} = (\lambda / \mu)^{len} (1 - (\lambda / \mu) / (1 - (\lambda / \mu)^{(len+1)})$$

Where:

λ: Arrival rate for the server
μ: Service rate of the server
len: maximum queue length possible

We have simulated sensor node in MATLAB 6.1. For the purpose of simulation a senor node is considered as a tandem queue model with both servers with finite capacity buffers. In order to have longer life time sensor nodes are allowed to go to the sleep mode for a fixed predetermined time and again wake up after some fixed time. This rotational sleep scheduling is used in order to have low duty cycled sensor nodes.

4 Simulations and Observations

We have considered for normal period arrival rate = λ1 = 0.2 and for catastrophic period arrival rate = λ2 = 0.9, Total battery energy = 1000 units, Catastrophe occurs during 200 to 600 time units. Following results (Table1) were observed by MATLAB simulation.

Table 1. Simulation Results

μ 1, μ 2 (Normal)	**μ 11, μ 22 (Cat.)**	**Ov1,Ov2 (Cat.)**	**Ov1,Ov2 (Normal)**	**P1,P2 (Cat.)**	**P1,P2 (Normal)**
0.55,0.45	**0.55,0.45**	**0.40,0.23**	**0.001,0.004**	**0.16,0.08**	**0.07,0.05**
0.3,0.3	1,1	**0.1,0.06**	0.03,0.02	0.81,0.75	**0.024,0.024**
0.35,0.35	1,1	**0.1,0.06**	0.01,0.01	0.81,0. 75	**0.032,0.032**

Table 2. Theoretical Results

μ 1, μ 2 (Normal)	μ 11, μ 22 (Cat.)	Ov1,Ov2 (Cat.)	Ov1,Ov2 (Normal)	P1,P2 (Cat.)	P1,P2 (Normal)
0.55, 0.45	**0.55,0.45**	0.40 , 0.22	**0.002,0.007**	**0.16,0.08**	0.07,0.05
0.3, 0.3	1, 1	**0.1, 0.06**	0.03, 0.02	0.81, 0.75	**0.028,0.028**
0.35, 0.35	1, 1	**0.1, 0.06**	0.01, 0.01	0.81,0. 75	**0.036,0.036**

From the above tables simulation results are seen in close approximation with the theoretical results.

Here –

μ 1- service rate of the processor under normal conditions
μ 2- service rate of the transmitter under normal conditions
μ 11- service rate of the processor under catastrophe
μ 22- service rate of the transmitter under catastrophe
Ov1- average overflow probability of the input buffer
Ov2- average overflow probability of the output buffer
P1- power consumption of the processor
P2- power consumption of the transmitter

First row in above tables shows the results for a sensor node with fixed service rate. Here we have considered a fixed wake up energy cost whenever a sensor node is turned ON from OFF state. Also a switching energy overhead is considered while switching from one ON state to other.

Simulation graphs of sensor node behaviour during normal period as well as during catastrophic period are shown in Figure 4 and Figure 5. Graphs for a sensor node with fixed service rate and with variable service rates have been shown and can be easily compared. During normal period packet arrival rate is smaller (0.2) and during catastrophe peak arrival rate occurs (0.9).

A sensor node with fixed service rate is designed to handle the moderate traffic (0.5). Mehdi Kargahi, Ali Movaghar [8] have analysed a multi variable service rate processor. Whenever the value of service rate is at least equal to the value of arrival rate, buffer over flow probability is negligible. It can be clearly seen from the graphs during normal period. We can consider the tolerable buffer overflow limit as 2%. From the graph it is seen that a sensor node with fixed service rate remains idle more during normal period and consume more power.

A sensor node with variable service rates works with lower service rates during normal periods and consumes less power compared to that of fixed service rate sensor node. Also working with lower service rate reduces the idle time periods and the power wastage during that time.

In the graphs curve for queue length is shown. Whenever queue length becomes zero (no packets in the buffer), server becomes idle. During the period of catastrophe the packet arrival rate increases and may exceed the service rate in case of fixed service rate sensor node. As the buffer length is very small, the probability of buffer overflows increases and results in the data loss before the transmission. In order to have better QoS, probability of buffer overflow should remain within the tolerance limit.

From the graphs shown for catastrophic period it is observed that the buffer overflow becomes very high in case of a sensor node with fixed service rate as most of the time queue length reaches its full value. A sensor node with variable service rate can manage this situation by increasing the service rate. For increased service rate it consumes more power but results in less buffer overflow.

Similar graphs can be seen for transmitter with output buffer. In Table 3 all the performance parameters observed in both the models under normal as well as under catastrophe conditions are listed for the purpose of comparison.

Table 3. Performance parameters observed by simulation

Service Rate	μ1, μ2 (Normal)	μ11, μ22 (Catastrophe)	Ov1,Ov2 (Catastrophe)	Ov1,Ov2 (Normal)	P1,P2 (Catastrophe)	P1,P2 (Normal)	Idle time Probability	Lifetime
Fixed→	**0.55,0.45**	**0.55,0.45**	0.44 ,0.24	**0.002,0.002**	**0.16,0.08**	0.06,0.03	0.64,0.58	34620
Variable	0.3,0.3	0.8,0.8	0.32, 0.14	0.03, 0.02	0.41, 0.35	0.032, 0.032	0.37, 0.40	48260
	0.3,0. 3	0.9,0. 9	0.30, 0.17	0.02, 0.01	0.44,0. 33	0.032,0.0 29	0.36, 0.40	44083
	0.3,0.3	1,0.8	0.24, 0.13	0.02, 0.02	0.61, 0.33	0.033,0.027	0.36, 0.40	39483
	0.35,0.35	0.85, 0.85	0.28, 0.16	0.01, 0.01	0.39,0. 35	0.032, 0.030	0.45, 0.47	44044
	0.4,0.4	0.9,0.9	0.23, 0.16	0.01, 0.04	0.43, 0.42	0.034, 0.035	0.48, 0.50	38504
	0.4,0.4	1,0.9	0.21, 0.13	0.01, 0.00	0.66, 0.46	0.037, 0.037	0.48, 0.50	31401

The first row depicts parameters obtained for the fixed service rate model. The rest of the rows depict parameters obtained for varying service rate model. Note that the values of varying service rate model show better results.; (μ_1- μ_{11}: service rates during normal (μ_1) and catastrophic (μ_{11}) period in server1; μ_2- μ_{22}: service rates during normal(μ_1) and catastrophic(μ_{11}) period in server2; Ov1-Ov2: Overflow probabilities in server1(Ov1) and server2(Ov2); P1-P2: Average power of server1(P1) and server2(P2); Idle time Probability: Probability that server1 and server2 are in idle state; Lifetime: Total lifetime of the node for the given energy.

4.1 Simulation Results

Fig.4 and Fig.5 shows the graphs of power consumed, queue length and buffer overflow probability of a sensor node with fixed service rate and that of a sensor node with variable service rate. Fig.4 compares both type of sensor nodes under normal condition while Fig.5 shows comparison under catastrophic conditions.

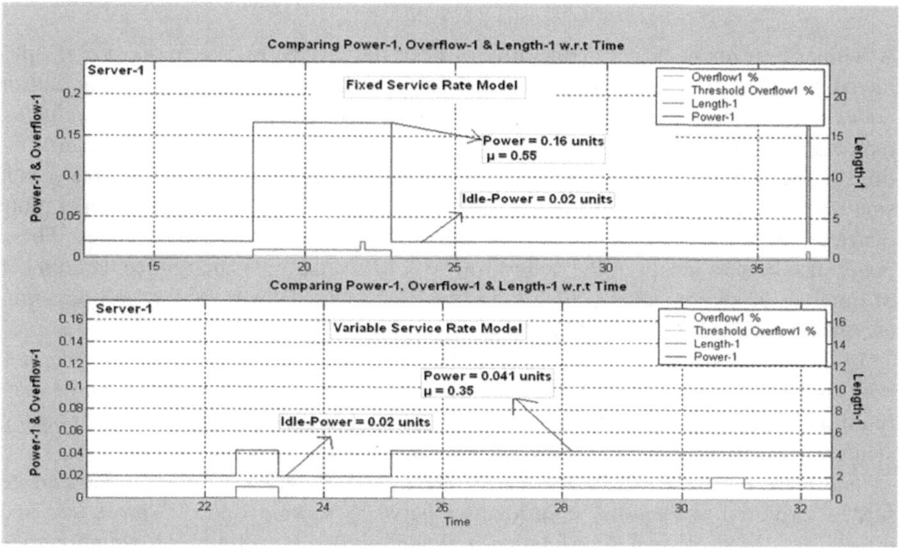

Fig. 4. Performance graphs of processor with input buffer with fixed service rate and with variable service rates under normal condition

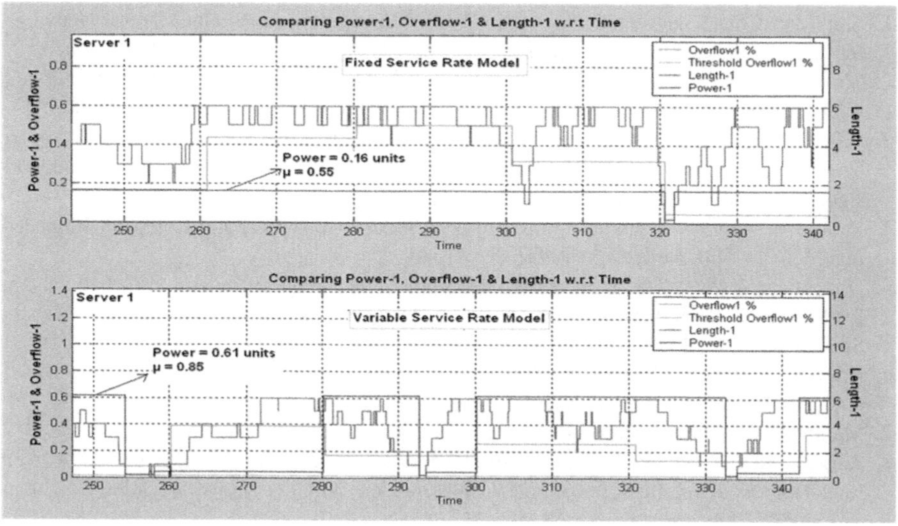

Fig. 5. Performance graphs of processor with input buffer with fixed service rate and with variable service rates under catastrophe

5 Conclusion and Future Work

A wireless sensor node with capability of adaptive service rates is more power optimized as compared with the sensor node with fixed service rate. Adaptive sensor nodes not only result in longer lifetime but also provide the better QoS by reducing the data loss due to the buffer overflow during the period of catastrophe. Longer lifetime is achieved by reducing the idle time periods and keeping sensor node busy with small service rates and consuming less power during normal period of operation. Service rate adaptive sensor nodes are actually power adaptive sensor nodes. These nodes also help to meet out the node-to-node delay constraints and reduce the number of time out dropped packets. Such long lived sensor nodes with better QoS performance will be helpful in making Wireless Sensor Networks more feasible.

In this paper we have considered only two ON states of a sensor node for the purpose of analysis. Similarly a sensor node with multiple number of states can be analysed and will result in better performance as switching between two neighbouring states will take less switching time and will consume less switching energy.

This tandem queue, variable service rate model of wireless sensor node can be further explored with some coordination between service rates of processor and transmitter. Idea of such coordination is floated in [9]. It will give us a sensor node with coordinated DVFS and DMS techniques which may result in better power optimisation.

References

1. Sinha, A., Chandrakasan, A.: 'Dynamic Power Management in Wireless Sensor Networks. In: IEEE Design & Test of Computers. IEEE, Los Alamitos (2001), 0740-7475/01
2. Min, R., Furrer, T., Chandrakasan, A.: Dynamic Voltage Scaling Techniques for Distributed Micro sensor Networks. In: Workshop on VLSI (WVLSI 2000), pp. 43–46 (April 2000)
3. Schurgers, C., Aberthorne, O., Srivastava, M.B.: Modulation Scaling for Energy Aware Communication Systems. In: International Symposium on Low Power Electronics and Design, August 6-7, Huntington Beach, California (2001)
4. Proakis, J.: Digital Communications, 3rd edn. Series in Electrical and Computer Engineering. McGraw-Hill, New York (1995)
5. Dongming, W.W., Wang, P.H., Sharif, H.: Study of an Energy Efficient Multi Rate Scheme for Wireless Sensor Network MAC Protocol. In: Q2SWinet 2006, Torremolinos, Malaga, Spain, October 2 (2006)
6. Ross, S.: "Queueing Theory" in Introduction to Probability models, 8th edn., San Diego, CA, pp. 475–501. Elsevier, Amsterdam (2003)
7. Mobile AMD Athlon 4, Processor Model 6 CPGA data sheet, http://www.amd.com
8. Kargahi, M., Movaghar, A.: A Stochastic DVS-Based Dynamic Power Management for Soft Real-Time Systems. In: International Conference on Wireless Networls, Communications and Mobile Computing, pp. 63–68 (2005)
9. Raghunathan, V., Schurgers, C., Park, S., Srivatava, M.B.: Energy-Aware Wireless Microsensor Networks. IEEE Signal Processing Magazine (March 2002)

Web Log Data Analysis and Mining

L.K. Joshila Grace[1,3], V. Maheswari[2,3], and Dhinaharan Nagamalai[4]

[1] Research Scholar, Department of Computer Science and Engineering
[2] Professor and Head, Department of Computer Applications
[3] Sathyabama University, Chennai, India
[4] Wireilla Net Solutions PTY Ltd, Australia

Abstract. Log files contain information about User Name, IP Address, Time Stamp, Access Request, number of Bytes Transferred, Result Status, URL that Referred and User Agent. The log files are maintained by the web servers. By analysing these log files gives a neat idea about the user. This paper gives a detailed discussion about these log files, their formats, their creation, access procedures, their uses, various algorithms used and the additional parameters that can be used in the log files which in turn gives way to an effective mining. It also provides the idea of creating an extended log file.

Keywords: Web Log file, Web usage mining, Web servers, Log data, Log Level directive.

1 Introduction

Log files are files that list the actions that have been occurred. These log files reside in the web server. Computers that deliver the web pages are called as web servers. The Web server stores all of the files necessary to display the Web pages on the users computer. All the individual web pages combines together to form the completeness of a Web site. Images/graphic files and any scripts that make dynamic elements of the site function. The browser requests the data from the Web server, and using HTTP, the server delivers the data back to the browser that had requested the web page. The browser in turn converts, or formats, the files into a user viewable page. This gets displayed in the browser. In the same way the server can send the files to many client computers at the same time, allowing multiple clients to view the same page simultaneously.

2 Contents of a Log File

The Log files in different web servers maintain different types of information. [6]The basic information present in the log file are

- User name: This identifies who had visited the web site. The identification of the user mostly would be the IP address that is assigned by the Internet Service provider (ISP). This may be a temporary address that has been assigned. There fore here the unique identification of the user is lagging. In some web sites the

N. Meghanathan et al. (Eds.): CCSIT 2011, Part III, CCIS 133, pp. 459–469, 2011.

user identification is made by getting the user profile and allows them to access the web site by using a user name and password. In this kind of access the user is being identified uniquely so that the revisit of the user can also be identified.

- Visiting Path: The path taken by the user while visiting the web site. This may be by using the URL directly or by clicking on a link or trough a search engine.
- Path Traversed: This identifies the path taken by the user with in the web site using the various links.
- Time stamp: The time spent by the user in each web page while surfing through the web site. This is identified as the session.
- Page last visited: The page that was visited by the user before he or she leaves the web site.
- Success rate: The success rate of the web site can be determined by the number of downloads made and the number copying activity under gone by the user. If any purchase of things or software made, this would also add up the success rate.
- User Agent: This is nothing but the browser from where the user sends the request to the web server. It's just a string describing the type and version of browser software being used.
- URL: The resource accessed by the user. It may be an HTML page, a CGI program, or a script.
- Request type: The method used for information transfer is noted. The methods like GET, POST.

These are the contents present in the log file. This log file details are used in case of web usage mining process. According to web usage mining it mines the highly utilized web site. The utilisation would be the frequently visited web site or the web site being utilized for longer time duration. There fore the quantitative usage of the web site can be analysed if the log file is analysed.

3 Location of a Log File

A Web log is a file to which the Web server writes information each time a user requests a web site from that particular server. [7]A log file can be located in three different places:

- Web Servers
- Web proxy Servers
- Client browsers

3.1 Web Server Log Files

The log file that resides in the web server notes the activity of the client who accesses the web server for a web site through the browser. The contents of the file will be the same as it is discussed in the previous topic. In the server which collects the personal information of the user must have a secured transfer.

3.2 Web Proxy Server Log Files

A Proxy server is said to be an intermediate server that exist between the client and the Web server. There fore if the Web server gets a request of the client via the proxy server then the entries to the log file will be the information of the proxy server and not of the original user. These web proxy servers maintain a separate log file for gathering the information of the user.

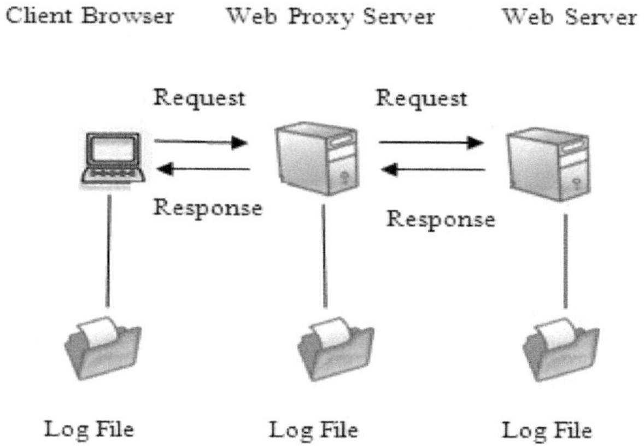

Fig. 1. Web Proxy Server Log files

3.3 Client Browsers Log Files

This kind of log files can be made to reside in the client's browser window itself. Special types of software exist which can be downloaded by the user to their browser window. Even though the log file is present in the client's browser window the entries to the log file is done only by the Web server.

4 Types of Web Server Logs

Web Server logs are plain text (ASCII) files and are Independent from the server. [10]There are some Distinctions between server software, but traditionally there are four types of server logs:

- Transfer Log
- Agent Log
- Error Log
- Referrer Log

The first two types of log files are standard. The referrer and agent logs may or may not be "turned on" at the server or may be added to the transfer log file to create an "extended" log file format. [11]The log file entries of Apache HTTP Server Version 1.3 are discussed below:

4.1 Error Log

When ever an error is occurred while the page is being requested by the client to the web server the entry is made in the error log. The information that is contained in most error log entries is the message given below

[Wed Oct 11 14:32:52 2000] [error] [client 127.0.0.1] client denied by server configuration: /export/home/live/ap/htdocs/test

The first set of item present in the log entry is the date and time of the message. The second entry lists the severity of the error being reported. The Log Level directive is used to control the types of errors that are sent to the error log by restricting the severity level. The third entry gives the IP address of the client that generated the error. Next is the message itself, which in this case indicates that the server has been configured to deny the client access. The server reports the file-system path of the requested document.

4.2 Access Log

The server access log records all requests that are processed by the server. The location and content of the access log are controlled by the Custom Log directive. The Custom Log directive is used to log requests to the server. A log format is specified, and the logging can optionally be made conditional on request characteristics using environment variables.The Log Format directive can be used to simplify the selection of the contents of the logs. This section describes how to configure the server to record information in the access log. here are three log formats considered for access log entries in the case of Apache HTTP Server Version 1.3.They are briefly discussed below:

Common Log Format (CLF)
The configuration of the common log format is given below

LogFormat "%h %l %u %t \"%r\" %>s %b" common
CustomLog logs/access_log common

The log file entries produced in CLF will look something like this:

127.0.0.1 - frank [10/Oct/2000:13:55:36 -0700] "GET /apache_pb.gif HTTP/1.0" 200 2326

The entries give details about the client who had requested for the web site to the web server

- 127.0.0.1 (%h) - This is the IP address of the client which made the request to the server.
- - (%l) - The hyphen present in the log file entry next to the IP address indicates that the requested information is not available.
- frank (%u) - The user id of the person requesting the document as determined by HTTP authentication.
- [10/Oct/2000:13:55:36 -0700] (%t) -The time format resembles like [day/month/year: hour: minute: second zone]
- "GET /apache_pb.gif HTTP/1.0" (\"%r\") - The request sent from the client is given in double quotes. GET is the method used. apache_pb.gif is the information requested by the client. The protocol used by the client is given as HTTP/1.0.
- 200 (%>s) - This is the status code sent by the server. The codes beginning with 2 for successful response, 3 for redirection, 4 for error caused by the client, 5 for error in the server.

- 2326 (%b) - The last entry indicates the size of the object returned to the client by the server, not including the response headers. If there is no content returned to the client, this value will be "-".

Combined Log Format
The configuration of the combined log format is given below

LogFormat "%h %l %u %t \"%r\" %>s %b \"%{Referer}i\" \"%{User-agent}i\"" combined
CustomLog log/acces_log combined

The log file entries produced in combined log format will look something like this:

127.0.0.1 - frank [10/Oct/2000:13:55:36 -0700] "GET /apache_pb.gif HTTP/1.0" 200 2326 "http://www.example.com/start.html" "Mozilla/4.08 [en] (Win98; I ;Nav)"

The additional parameters that are present in the combined log format are discussed below

- *"http://www.example.com/start.html" (\"%{Referer}i\")* - This gives the site that the client reports having been referred from. (This should be the page that links to or includes /apache_pb.gif).
- *"Mozilla/4.08 [en] (Win98; I ;Nav)" (\"%{User-agent}i\")* - This is the information that the client browser reports about itself to the server.

These entries are made in the log file for a combined log format entry.

Multiple Access Logs
Multiple access logs can be created simply by specifying multiple Custom Log directives in the configuration file. In this type of log file there are three files created as access log files containing the details about the client. It is said to be a combination of common log format and combined log format.

The configuration of the multiple access log is given below:

LogFormat "%h %l %u %t \"%r\" %>s %b" common
CustomLog logs/access_log common
CustomLog logs/referer_log "%{Referer}i -> %U"
CustomLog logs/agent_log "%{User-agent}i"

The first line contains the basic CLF information, while the second and third line contains referrer and browser information.

Most of the web servers have the same formats being followed for the log file entry.

5 Status Codes Sent by the Server

After processing the request of the client in the web server the status code is sent by the web server. There are various status that are exhibited by Apache HTTP Server Version 1.3 is given below:

1xx Info
HTTP_INFO – Request received, continuing process

- 100 Continue – HTTP_CONTINUE
- 101 Switching Protocols -HTTP_SWITCHING_PROTOCOLS
- 102 Processing – HTTP_PROCESSING

2xx Success
HTTP_SUCCESS – action successfully received, understood, accepted

- 200 OK – HTTP_OK
- 201 Created – HTTP_CREATED
- 202 Accepted – HTTP_ACCEPTED

3xx Redirect
HTTP_REDIRECT – The client must take additional action to complete the request xx Info

- 301 Moved Permanently – HTTP_MOVED_PERMANENTLY
- 302 Found – HTTP_MOVED_TEMPORARILY
- 304 Not Modified – HTTP_NOT_MODIFIED

4xx Client Error
HTTP_CLIENT_ERROR – The request contains bad syntax or cannot be fulfilled

- 400 Bad Request – HTTP_BAD_REQUEST
- 401 Authorization Required –HTTP_UNAUTHORIZED
- 402 Payment Required – HTTP_PAYMENT_REQUIRED
- 404 Not Found – HTTP_NOT_FOUND
- 405 Method Not Allowed – HTTP_METHOD_NOT_ALLOWED

5xx Server Error
HTTP_SERVER_ERROR – The server failed to fulfill an apparently valid request.

- 500 Internal Server Error – HTTP_INTERNAL_SERVER_ERROR
- 501 Method Not Implemented – HTTP_NOT_IMPLEMENTED
- 503 ServiceTemporarily Unavailable – HTTP_SERVICE_UNAVAILABLE
- 505 HTTP Version Not Supported – HTTP_VERSION_NOT_SUPPORTED

Due to space constraints only few status codes are discussed above. These status codes that are sent along with the response data is also entered in the log file.

6 Overview of Web Mining

Web mining employs the technique of data mining into the documents on the World Wide Web. The overall process of web mining includes extraction of information from the World Wide Web through the conventional practices of the data mining and putting the same into the website features.

In the web mining process there are three types of mining they are web content mining, Web structure mining, Web usage mining.

Web Structure mining
This involves the usage of graph theory for analyzing the connections and node structure of the website. According to the type and nature of the data of the web structure, it is again divided into two kinds

- Extraction of patterns from the hyperlink on the net: The hyperlink is structural form of web address connecting a web page to some other locations.
- Mining of the structure of the document: The tree like structure gets used for analyzing and describing the XHTML or the HTML tags in the web page.

Web Content mining

In this kind of mining process attempts to discover all links of the hyperlinks in a document so as to generate the structural report on a web page. There are two groups of web content mining strategies. First strategy is to directly mine the content of documents and the second one are those that improve on the content search of other tools like search engines.

Web Usage mining

In the web usage mining process, the techniques of data mining are applied so as to discover the trends and the patterns in the browsing nature of the visitors of the website. There is extraction of the navigation patterns as the browsing patterns could be traced and the structure of the website can be designed accordingly. When it is talked about the browsing nature of the user it deals with frequent access of the web site or the duration of using the web site. This information can be extracted from the log file. Only these log files record the session information about the web pages. [5][8] The fig 2 shows the step wise procedure for web usage mining process.

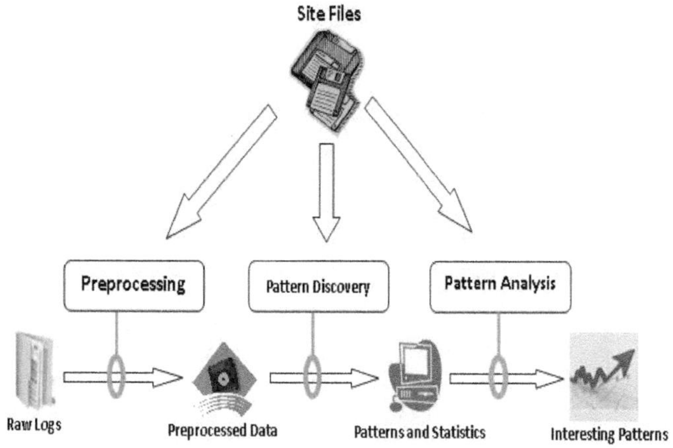

Fig. 2. One High level web usage mining process

7 Using Log File Data in Web Usage Mining

The contents of the Log files are used in this type of mining. Web usage mining also consists of three main steps:

Preprocessing: The data present in the log file cannot be used as it is for the mining process. [9]There fore the contents of the log file should be cleaned in this preprocessing step. The unwanted data are removed and a minimized lo file is obtained.

- *Data cleaning:* In this process the entries made in the log file for the unwanted view of images, graphics, Multi media etc., made by the users are removed. Once these data are removed the size of the file is minimized to a greater extent.

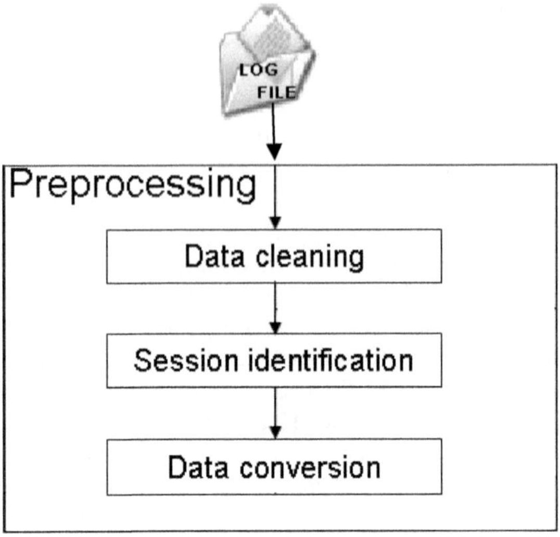

Fig. 3. Pre-processing of Log File

- *Session Identification:* This done by using the time stamp details of the web pages. The total time used by each user of each web page. This can also be done by noting down the user id those who have visited the web page and had traversed through the links of the web page. Session is the time duration spent in the web page.
- *Data conversion:* This is conversion of the log file data into the format needed by the mining algorithms.

Pattern discovery: After the conversion of the data in the log file into a formatted data the pattern discovery process is under gone. [8]With the existing data of the log files many useful patterns are discovered either with user id's, session details, time outs etc.,

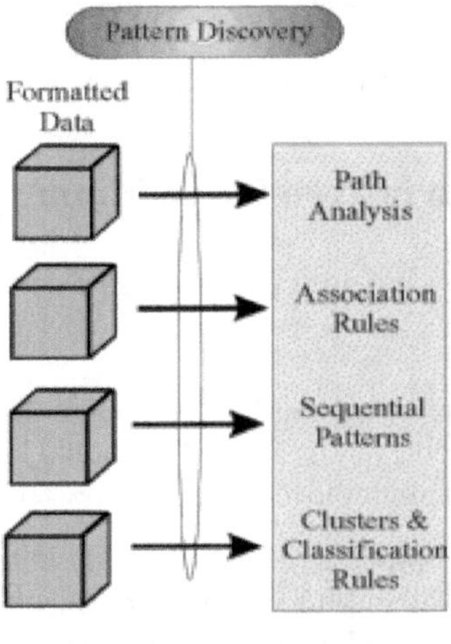

Fig. 4. Pattern Discovery

- *Path analysis:* Graph models are most commonly used for Path Analysis. A graph represents some relation defined on Web pages and each tree of the graph represents a web site. Each node in the tree represents a web page (html document), and edges between trees represent the links between web sites, while the edges between nodes inside a same tree represent links between documents at a web site.

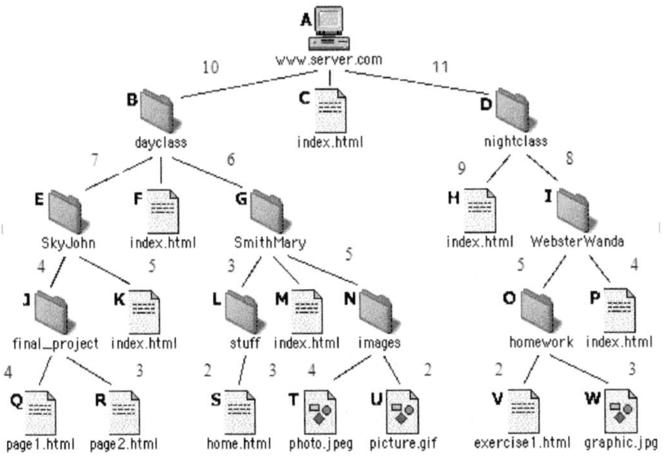

Fig. 5. Path analysis

The Fig 5 shows the access made to a single website. Each node represents the web page within the same web site. Links made is connected to the corresponding nodes and the number of users used each link is also noted with values given between their edges.

- *Association Rules:* This technique is used to predict the correlation of items where the presence of one set of items in a transaction implies the presence of other items. The fig 6 gives the idea of correlation of the same item sets that is with same customer ID or session ID. The example is considered for two different log file details.
- *Sequential Patterns:* sequential patterns discover the user's navigation behaviour. The sequence of items occurring in one transaction has a particular order between the items or the events. The same sequence of item may re-occur in the same order. For example 30% of the user may under go link in this order "A=>B=>C=>D=>E" where ABCDE corresponds to each web page.
- *Clusters and Classification rule:* This process groups profiles of items with similar characteristics. This ability enhances the discovery of relationships. The classification of Web access logs allows a company to discover the average age of customers who order a certain product. This information can be valuable when developing advertising strategies. But these kind of information involves personal information about the user.

Session ID	Page URL
123	Condition_home.htm
123	See_doctor.ht
134	Side_effects.htm
134	See_doctor.htm
134	Screening.htm
245	See_doctor.htm
245	Condition_home.htm

Customer ID	Product
123	Cola
123	Pretzels
123	Chips
134	Diapers
134	Cola
134	Bandaids
134	Apples
245	Cola
245	Pretzels

Fig. 6. Association rules exhibited by using session ID and Customer ID

Pattern analysis: This analysis process would eliminate the irrelevant rules or patterns that were generated. They tend to extract the interesting rules or patterns from the output of the pattern discovery process. [4]The most common form of pattern analysis consists of a knowledge query mechanism such as SQL (Structured Query Language) or loads the usage data into a data cube in order to perform OLAP (Online analytical processing) operations. Visualization techniques, such as graphing patterns or assigning colors to different values, can often highlight overall patterns or trends in the data. Various other mechanisms used for mining these patterns are

- *Site Filter:* This technique is used in WEBMINER system. [5]The site filter uses the site topology to filter out rules and patterns that are not interesting. Any rule that confirms direct hypertext links between pages is filtered out.
- *mWAP(Modified Web Access Pattern):* [3]This technique totally eliminates the need to engage the numerous reconstruction of intermediate WAP-trees during mining and considerably reduces execution time.
- *EXT-Prefixspan:* [1]This method mines the complete set of patterns but greatly reduces the efforts of candidate subsequence generation. Prefix –projection process involved in this method substantially reduces the size of projected database.
- *BC-WAPT (Binary coded Web Access pattern Tree):* [2]eliminates recursive reconstruction of intermediate WAP tree during the mining by assigning the binary codes to each node in the WAP Tree

8 Creation of an Extended Log File

The log file contents would be even more efficient if it provides the details of the clicks made by the user while visiting the web site. If the user opens a particular web site and does some other work outside the system then it may also be considered as the usage of the web site. The details regarding the clicks made by the user and the time he or she scrolled or did any other operation can also be noted for effective mining of the web usage data.

We shall consider one more situation were the user clicks to open a web site and also works with some other web site in a different browser window. In this situation we can analyze that the user can only read details of only one web site at a time. Then it is understood that the other web site is said to be ideal. But even in this situation the details in the log file would note the input as the web page is being used.

By taking these small differences in the time or the session of the web page being used, still an efficient web mining can be done.

9 Conclusions

The Paper gives a detailed look about the web log file, its contents, its types, its location etc., Added to these information it also gives a detailed description of how the file is being processed in the case of web usage mining process. The various mechanisms that performs each step in mining the log file is being discussed along with their disadvantages. The additional parameters that can be considered for Log file entries and the idea in creating the extended log file is also discussed briefly.

References

1. Vijayalakshmi, S., Mohan, V., Suresh Raja, S.: Mining Constraint-based Multidimensional Frequent Sequential Pattern in Web Logs. European Journal of Scientific Research 36, 480–490 (2009)
2. Vasumathi, D., Govardan, A.: BC-WASPT: Web Acess Sequential Pattern Tree Mining. IJCSNS International Journal of Computer Science and Network Security 9, 569–571 (2009)
3. Parmar, J.D., Garg, S.: Modified web access pattern (mWAP) approach for sequential pattern mining. INFOCOMP Journal of Computer Science, 46–54 (June 2007)
4. Cooley, R., Mobasher, B., Srivastava, J.: Web Mining: Information and Pattern Discovery on the World Wide Web. IEEE Computer Society, 558 (1997)
5. Cooley, R., Mobasher, B., Srivastava, J.: Data Preparation for Mining World Wide Web Browsing Patterns. KNOWLEDGE AND INFORMATION SYSTEMS 1 (1999)
6. Jain, R.K., Kasanal, D.R.S., Suresh Jain, D.: Efficient Web Log Mining using Doubly Linked Tree. International Journal of Computer Science and Information Security, IJCSIS 3 (July 2009)
7. Suneetha, K.R., Krishnamoorthi, R.: Identifying User Behavior by Analyzing Web Server Access Log File. IJCSNS International Journal of Computer Science and Network Security 9, 327–332 (2009)
8. Etminani, K., Mohammad, R., Akbarzadeh, T., Yanehsari, N.R.: Web Usage Mining: users' navigational patterns extraction from web logs using Ant-based Clustering Method. In: Proc. IFSA-EUSFLAT 2009 (2009)
9. Ivántcsy, R., Vajk, I.: Frequent Pattern Mining in Web Log Data. Acta Polytechnica Hungarica 3(1) (2006)
10. Wahab, M.H.A., Mohd, M.N.H., Hanafi, H.F., Mohsin, M.F.M.: Data Pre-processing on Web Server Logs for Generalized Association Rules Mining Algorithm. World Academy of Science, Engineering and Technology 48 (2008)
11. Apache HTTP Server Version 1.3, `http://httpd.apache.org/docs/1.3/logs.html`

Steganography Using Version Control System

Vaishali S. Tidake and Sopan A. Talekar

Department of Computer Engineering,
NDMVP COE, Nashik, India
vaishalitidake@yahoo.co.in, sopan_talekar@yahoo.co.in

Abstract. In this paper two different techniques of steganography using change tracking are discussed. First method, steganography using change tracking technique uses change tracking feature of MS Word for data hiding. Message embedding and extraction in MS Word document is discussed briefly along with the example. Second method, steganography using version control system is also proposed in this paper. It elaborates the idea of using the version control system for data hiding. One of the most important features provided by version control systems is version control. It helps to keep track of changes by maintaining multiple versions of the project depending on the requirements. One of the versions of this project can be utilized as a cover medium for data hiding. Generally a project consists of many files. Hence long message can be fragmented and one message fragment can be embedded in one file of the project. Experimentation is carried out using Microsoft Visual SourceSafe as the version control system and C# sample project as the cover project.

Keywords: change tracking, cover project, message embedding, stego project, message extraction, version control system.

1 Introduction

Steganography is an art of hiding information using the techniques that prevent its detection [1]. Computer-based steganographic techniques allow faster ways of message embedding and extraction. They use digital covers to embed information.

The main purpose of steganography is that information should be hidden in the cover in such a way that it should be unnoticeable to the user. It can be achieved by taking advantage of human weaknesses in auditory and visual system [6].

Steganography can be broadly classified as visual steganography and text steganography. Visual steganography uses multimedia objects such as images, audio and video files for data hiding. For example, changing the low bits of an image is the most general technique to hide data in an image. Text steganography uses text as the cover medium. For example, using the redundant spaces in the document, inserting extra white spaces in the document, changing the formatting of text are general techniques used to hide data in the text cover [7].

Text steganography can be done using different techniques [3]. Semantic substitution is frequently used method for text steganography [8]. In this method, the synonyms of certain words are used for hiding information in the text. For example,

N. Meghanathan et al. (Eds.): CCSIT 2011, Part III, CCIS 133, pp. 470–480, 2011.

consider the sentence: "It is nice". The word "nice" has synonym "good". Let the words "nice" and "good" represent bits 0 and 1 respectively. So the result "It is nice" hides bit 0 and "It is good" hides bit 1. So if a word has two synonyms, it can hide one bit. If a word has four synonyms, it can hide two bits. In general, if a word has 2^k synonyms, it can hide k bits of information. However, this method may alter the meaning of the text.

Section 2 gives introduction to track changes feature of MS Word. Section 3 explains steganography using change tracking technique. Section IV gives introduction to version control system. Section V explains steganography using version control system. Section VI and VII discusses about implementation, results, and security considerations. Finally section VIII tells conclusion.

2 Track Changes Feature of MS Word

"Track Changes" is a feature of Microsoft Word to keep track of the changes made to a document. These changes can be accepted or rejected. Using this feature, the owner of MS Word document can enable others to edit or add comments to his document without original text being changed. When the document is returned to the owner, he can accept or reject any editing changes that have been made. Track Changes is also known as redline, or redlining. This is because some industries traditionally draw a vertical red line in the margin to show that some text has changed. Few important points about track changes are as given below:

- "Track changes" submenu on the Tools menu helps to use the change tracking feature of MS word. It can also be enabled by double clicking TRK in the status bar.
- "Track Changes Options" can be set to specify the way in which editing changes will appear in the document.
- Those who edit a document will need to set the user information before editing so that the person who created the original document will be able to determine who edited which part of the document.
- After enabling track changes feature, any change, insertion, deletion, formatting to the original text will be marked. A black bar will appear in the margin to the left of any text that has been edited, as shown in fig. 1.

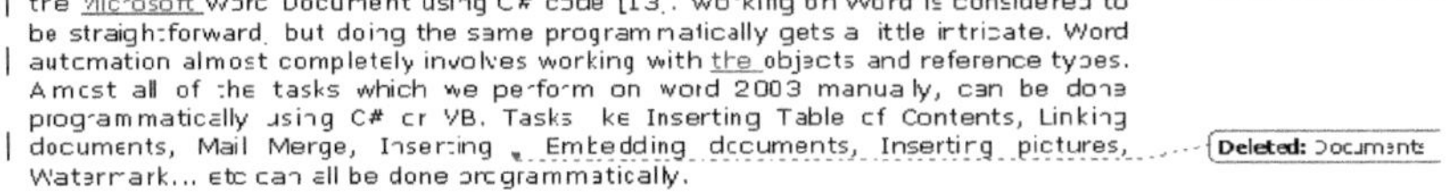
Word Automation through C# is all about programmatically generating or updating the Microsoft Word Document using C# code [13]. Working on Word is considered to be straightforward, but doing the same programmatically gets a little intricate. Word automation almost completely involves working with the objects and reference types. Almost all of the tasks which we perform on word 2003 manually, can be done programmatically using C# or VB. Tasks like Inserting Table of Contents, Linking documents, Mail Merge, Inserting, Embedding documents, Inserting pictures, Watermark... etc can all be done programmatically.

Deleted: modifying

Deleted: Documents

Fig. 1. Change Tracking Feature in MS Word

3 Steganography Using Change Tracking Technique

In this section, a new approach of steganography in MS Word document using change tracking technique is introduced [2]. It's a text steganography technique which uses semantic substitution method. In this technique, a secret message M is embedded inside a cover document D to obtain a stegodocument S.

3.1 Message Embedding and Extraction

Embedding of message in cover document and extraction of message from stegodocument is explained in this section.

3.1.1 Message Embedding

Before embedding, the secret message is converted to the following form:

<Header> <Binary Message><Padding>

Header consists of length of the message. Padding bits are attached randomly as per the need. The embedding process is divided into two stages:

1 **The degeneration stage**
The cover document D is partitioned into text segments $d_1, d_2 \ldots d_n$. Each segment d_i is either kept unchanged or degenerated into a new version d'_i during the degeneration stage. In each segment, an embedding place is selected using secret key K and the position of next embedding bits in secret message M. Synonyms are computed for the word at selected embedding place and the degeneration set is constructed. Then Huffman codes are constructed for all the words in the degeneration set. The data to embed tells which synonym should be used for degeneration. Thus the secret message is embedded during the degeneration process, which produces a degenerated document D'.

2 **The revision stage**
Each previously degenerated text segment is revised back. The revisions are tracked by using the "Track Changes" feature of MS Word. The result is a stegodocument S. It consists of revised text segments $s_1, s_2 \ldots s_n$. Here, each s_i includes its original text segment d_i and the associated change tracking information.

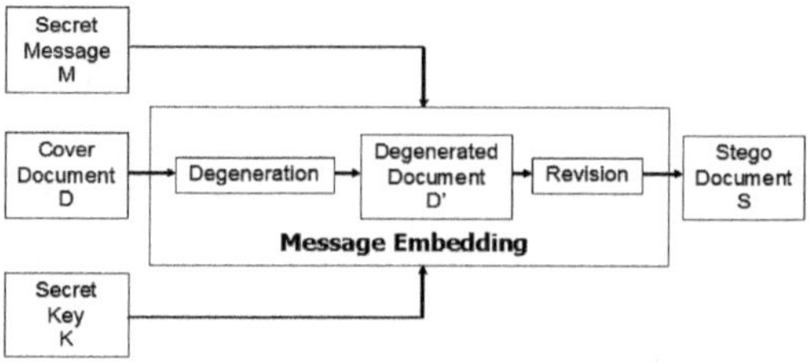

Fig. 2. Message embedding for Steganography using Change Tracking Technique

3.1.2 Message Extraction

Message extraction from the stegodocument S is basically reverse of the message embedding process. Using the stegodocument S, the original text segments D and the degenerated text segments D' are recovered. While processing each tracked change, choice of degeneration is computed using the synonym set of D, which also includes D'. Huffman tree is constructed for the synonym set and the data embedded at that position is decoded.

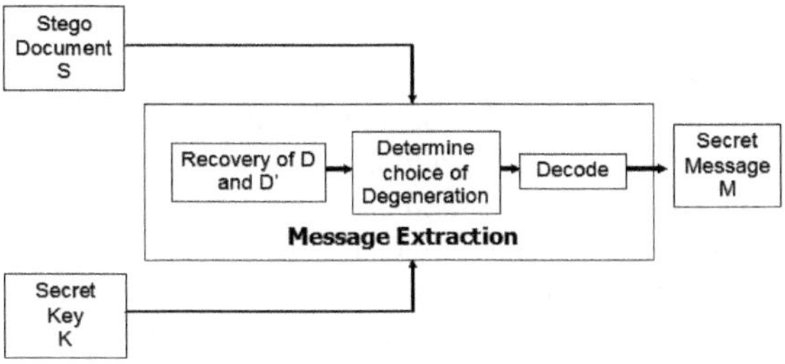

Fig. 3. Message extraction for Steganography using Change Tracking Technique

3.2 Illustration with Example

Working of message embedding and message extraction is illustrated with an example as given below.

- Message embedding

Let the text segment to be degenerated is d= "Scheme". To construct the degeneration set, synonyms of word "Scheme" should be computed. The synonym database is available from different resources like WordNet database [4]. But we have carried the experimentation with the synonym set constructed from thesaurus available in MS Word itself. Suppose the degeneration set of "Scheme" contains the eight entries Scheme, System, Plan, Method, Format, Idea, Proposal and Design. Probabilities of occurrences for these synonyms are calculated from related databases and Huffman tree T is constructed using these probabilities as weights. By labeling left branch as 0 and right branch as 1, Huffman codes for synonyms of word "Scheme" are constructed as shown in Table 1.

Table 1. Huffman Codes for Synonyms of "Scheme"

Sr. No.	Synonym	Huffman Code
1	Scheme	011
2	System	00
3	Plan	01001
4	Method	10
5	Format	110
6	Idea	0101
7	Proposal	01000
8	Design	111

Let the message bits to be embedded at this position are 110. So when the Huffman tree T is traversed from its root visiting the branches 1, 1, 0 respectively, we will reach at a leaf node of "Format". Hence the text segment

d_i= "Scheme" is degenerated to text segment d'_i = "Format". Then track changes feature of MS Word is turned on and d'_i = "Format" is revised back to d_i = "Scheme". It will be shown by stegotext as S = "~~Format~~Scheme". The process is repeated using next text segments until whole message is embedded.

- Message extraction

Given a stegotext segment S = "~~Format~~Scheme", the original and the degenerated text segments namely d_i = "Scheme" and d'_i = "Format" are recovered. To determine the choice of degeneration, again the Huffman tree T is constructed for d_i using the same synonyms and same probabilities to get the same Huffman codes as in message embedding. Since the degenerated text segment is "Format", the Huffman tree is traversed from the root to a leaf node "Format". The path traveled is analyzed to decode bits "110". It means that the bits "110" were embedded at that position. The process is repeated with all the text segments in which message bits are embedded.

3.3 Implementation and Results

The system is implemented using Microsoft Word 2003 and C#. The automation techniques of Microsoft Word are used for implementation. The degeneration database is constructed using the thesaurus available in Microsoft Word 2003.

The System is evaluated by comparing the results obtained using the three coding techniques, namely Huffman, block and arithmetic coding. The results obtained from these three techniques are compared with each other as shown in fig. 4. Results show that embedding capacity of block encoding is better than Huffman coding. Embedding capacity of arithmetic coding is better than block encoding. The embedding capacity of system is improved when the message is compressed before embedding using the arithmetic coding.

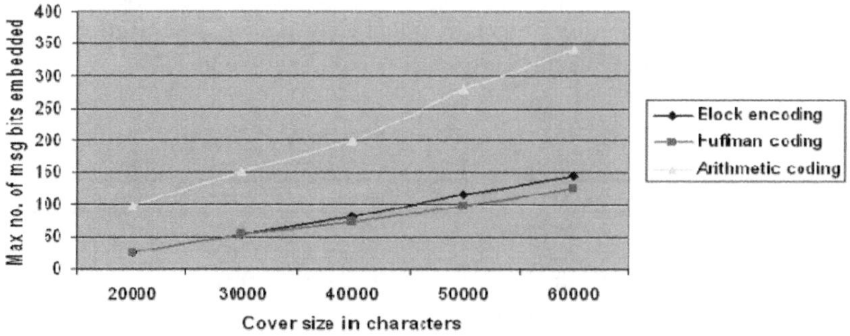

Fig. 4. Embedding capacity of different coding techniques

4 Version Control System

Version Control System is sometimes called as source code control system. It is the system which is used to maintain multiple versions of the same information. It is beneficial in many cases. For example, in a software development industry it is very difficult to manage critical information of an ongoing project as whole team works on development of a same software. Version control system is useful for it. It associates with each document a version number as well as name of the person making the changes. The version number is increased with each major change.

Few of the source code version control systems are:

- VSS (Microsoft Visual SourceSafe)
- CVS (Concurrent Versions System)
- RCS (Revision Control System)
- PRCS (Project Revision Control System)
- Aegis

4.1 Visual SourceSafe

Visual SourceSafe is generally termed as `VSS'. It is the source control system from Microsoft [9]. VSS provides many features. The two most important features provided by VSS are the version control and parallel development. Version control is also called as source control. This feature helps to keep track of changes by maintaining different versions of the source code. In a software development company, whole team works on development of particular software. Many persons have to work simultaneously on the same file. When the team size is large, it becomes more difficult to manage who will work on which file at what time. The parallel development feature of VSS provides solution to this problem. The project manager creates a VSS database and adds his project in this database. All the team members working on the project are given access rights to this database. Whenever any user wants to work on some file of the project, he first performs check out on that file, do modifications and check in the file. So many users can work on different parts of the same file simultaneously. In case of any problem, the project manager can recover from the previous working version of project stored in the VSS database.

5 Steganography Using Version Control System

The version control feature of VSS can be used for steganographic purpose. When a project is stored in VSS database, different versions of that project exist. One of its versions can be used as a cover medium for steganographic purpose.

The message M to be embedded is assumed to be in the character form. Fragment size is fixed initially to a suitable value. If input message is larger than fragment size, then it is divided into smaller fragments. Each fragment of a message is processed individually. One message fragment is embedded in one file of a project. We are using C# project as a cover project and the data is embedded only in .cs files of the project. The algorithms for message embedding and message extraction are described below.

5.1 Message Embedding Algorithm

Block diagram for the message embedding algorithm using version control system is shown in fig. 5.

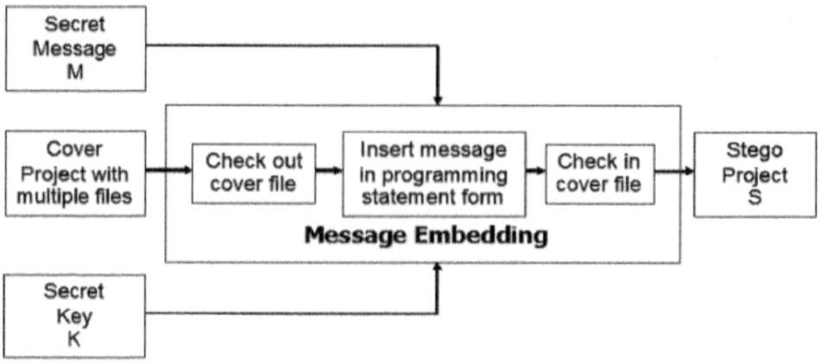

Fig. 5. Message embedding for Steganography Using Version Control System

Working of the message embedding algorithm is described next.

Input: version of project added to VSS DB as a cover project, a secret key K, and a message to be embedded M
Output: stego project S
Steps:

1. Divide input message M in F fragments F_1, F_2...F_F of fixed size where F should be less than number of .cs files in the cover project. Size of each fragment is dependent on the secret key K.
2. For each message fragment F_i, do the following:
   a. Select the .cs file in which we are going to embed fragment F_i. Let us call this file as cover file.
   b. Check out the cover file.
   c. Find a position P_i in the cover file where message fragment F_i is to be embedded.
   d. Depending on the data in message F_i, construct variable names, form declaration statements and generate arithmetic statements from the constructed variables.
   e. Insert the newly constructed program statements in the cover file at position P_i computed in step 2b.
   f. Check in the cover file.
3. Repeat step 2 for all fragments F_1, F_2...F_F of the message.

This algorithm gives an abstract idea of message embedding in the cover file. All the generated code is placed in comments so that it will not affect running status of the cover project. Now let us see construction of variable names from the message, creation of declaration statements and generation of arithmetic statements from the constructed variables.

- Generation of declaration statements

Before generating declaration statements, we have to construct variable names from the data in message fragment F_i. First decide the data type to be used for declaring variables. Number of variables to be generated is a function of fragment size. Let V denotes number of variables generated. Let V_1, V_2...V_V denotes set of variables generated.

$$V = f\text{ (size of message fragment } F_i)$$

1. For each variable V_i, compute $G = f(i)$. This value G guides us to decide which characters from message fragment F_i should be used to form that variable name.
2. Once a variable is formed, use value of G to initialize variable V_i in the declaration statement. Value of G helps for decoding variable name V_i during message extraction.

- Generation of arithmetic statements

Once declaration statements are formed, we have various options to generate arithmetic statements using those variables. Out of V variables, first V-1 variable names are used to form arithmetic statements and last one is used to store result of arithmetic expression. For example, depending on the first character in F_i, we can decide which construct should be used: if, if-else, while, etc. Once the construct is decided, we can form the condition clause using our variable names.

5.2 Message Extraction Algorithm

Block diagram for the message extraction algorithm using version control system is shown in fig. 6.

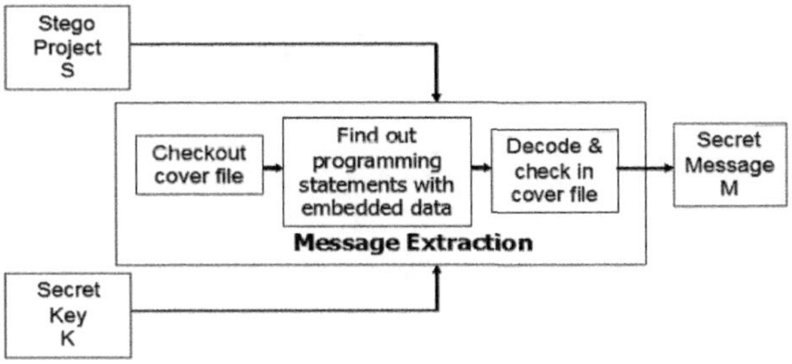

Fig. 6. Message extraction for Steganography Using Version Control System

Working of the message extraction algorithm is described next.

Input: stego project S, secret key K
Output: extracted message M
Steps:

1. From the stego project S, find out comments of all the stego files in which data is hidden.
2. For each stego file, do the following:
   a. Check out the stego file.
   b. Find out the position in the stego file where the message fragment F_i is embedded.
   c. Process variable names, declaration statements and arithmetic statements in the embedded code. Each declaration statement has the following form:

<data type> <var V_i name> = G

Put each character in the name of V_i at proper place P_j in extracted message fragment F_i, where $P_j = f(i, G)$. Similarly the construct used in the arithmetic statement tells us start of message fragment F_i and the condition of the construct used helps for extracting remaining characters in F_i.

d. Check in the stego file.

3. Combine all message fragments $F_1, F_2 \ldots F_F$ obtained from each stego file to obtain the original message M.

6 Implementation and Results

The system is implemented in C# language and Microsoft Visual SourceSafe is used as a version control system. The results obtained after embedding different messages in the cover project are shown in fig. 7. The analysis of these results shows that space required for embedding is totally message dependent. Because how many statements are generated and which statements are generated is totally decided using characters in the message. Hence difference in the size of cover project and the stego project may be more for smaller message and less for comparatively bigger message.

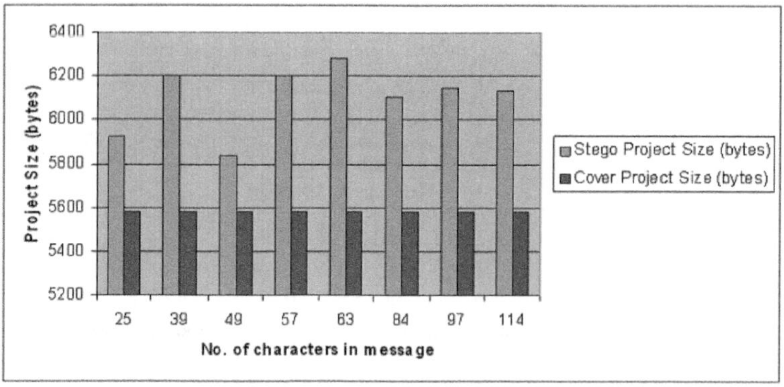

Fig. 7. Results of Steganography using Version Control System

7 Security Consideration

Security and robustness are the most important features of any system. Let us focus on the security aspects first. The variable names are formed using the message characters. So we have to take care that variable names are constructed according to rules. We can use various ways to construct variable names according to their construction rules. Simplest way is mapping of our variable name to some proper variable name. But obviously this mapping should be such that mapped variable helps for decoding at the time of message extraction.

We can assign some value to each variable which helps us for decoding of that variable. Suppose we restrict the message to lowercase letters only. So we can represent ‘a’ to ‘z’ by 1 to 26 respectively. Now if we want to map variable name “adfh”.

Then we can do the following. Each of a, d, f, h denotes numbers 1, 4, 6, 8 respectively. So according to position of letters in variable name, we can construct a number as

$$(1 \times 1000) + (4 \times 100) + (6 \times 10) + 8 = 1468$$

So generated declaration statement looks like this:

$$< \text{data type} > a = 1468$$

Obviously we can decode the number 1468 to "adfh" easily. And also it makes constructed variable name look natural as used in practice. So it helps to make appearance of newly inserted code similar to that of original code in cover file and hence it will not be under close scrutiny by adversary. Alternate option for this method is mapping of constructed variable names to those used in cover file. We can do this by analyzing the cover file first, collecting information about all existing variables and their data types, using only those variables of required data type. Thus it makes newly inserted code compatible to cover file.

Now let us focus on robustness. If anything from the newly inserted code is deleted, then we can't extract the message completely and correctly. We can avoid this problem by inserting more than once replicas of newly generated code at different places in one file, or different files in same project or files of different projects. So even if our data is destroyed at one place, we can recover by using data at other place. In other words, robustness of the system can be increased using multiple versions maintained in VSS database.

Compression and/or encryption can also be used to increase security of the system. We can apply these techniques to the input message before embedding it. Compression reduces the size of input message. Encryption increases randomness in the input message.

8 Conclusion

In this paper, different techniques of steganography using change tracking are discussed. The first approach of text steganography uses change track feature of MS Word for data hiding. The experimentation is carried out using three coding techniques, namely Huffman , block and arithmetic.

One more approach of steganography using version control system is proposed in this paper. It uses Microsoft Visual SourceSafe (VSS) as a version control system. It helps to keep track of changes by maintaining multiple versions of the project depending on the requirements. From the experimentation carried out, it is observed that one of the versions maintained using version control system can be used as a cover medium for data hiding. Message can be used to construct program statements which are then inserted in the cover project files. Obviously newly inserted statements should be compatible to the existing statements in the cover medium, so that they will not attract attention. The proposed system is implemented using C# project as cover medium, hence message is embedded in the form of C# statements. Also the system inserts the statements as comments. Hence the running status of the cover project is not affected even after message embedding. Also the changes in the cover project are ignored by compiler and hence will not be focused immediately.

As the cover medium chosen here consists of programming statements, there is a lot of scope to hide data within it in various ways. The simplest approach of embedding programming statements is discussed in this paper. Multiple versions maintained by version control system can be used to increase robustness of the system.

References

1. Johnson, N.F., Jajodia, S.: Steganography: Seeing the Unseen. IEEE Computer, 26–34 (February 1998)
2. Liu, T.-Y., Tsai, W.-H.: A New Steganographic Method for Data Hiding in Microsoft Word Documents by a Change Tracking Technique. IEEE Transactions On Information Forensics And Security 2(1) (March 2007)
3. Hassan Shirali-Shahreza, M., Shirali-Shahreza, M.: A New Approach to Persian/Arabic Text Steganography. In: Proc. of the 5th IEEE/ACIS International Conference on Computer and Information Science and 1st IEEE/ACIS International Workshop on Component-Based Software Engineering, Software Architecture and Reuse (ICIS-COMSAR 2006). IEEE, Los Alamitos (2006)
4. WordNet v2.1, a lexical database for the English language. Princeton Univ., Princeton (2005), `http://wordnet.princeton.edu/`
5. Chapman, M., George, I.D., Marc, R.: A practical and effective approach to large-scale automated linguistic steganography. In: Proc. Information Security Conf., Malaga, Spain, pp. 156–165 (October 2001)
6. Bender, W., Gruhl, D., Morimoto, N., Lu, A.: Techniques for data hiding. IBM Syst. J. 35(3-4), 313–336 (1996)
7. Petitcolas, F.A.P., Anderson, R.J., Kuhn, M.G.: Information hiding-A survey. Proc. IEEE 87(7), 1062–1078 (1999)
8. Bennett, K.: Linguistic steganography: Survey, analysis, and robustness concerns for hiding information in text, Purdue Univ., West Lafayette, IN, CERIAS Tech. Rep. 2004-13 (May 2004)
9. `http://msdn.microsoft.com`
10. Stutsman, R., Grothoff, C., Attallah, M., Grothoff, K.: Lost in just the translation. In: Proc. ACM Symp. Applied Computing, pp. 338–345 (2006)
11. Spinellis, D.: Version Control Systems. In: IEEE SOFTWARE. IEEE Computer Society, Los Alamitos (2005)

Erratum: A New Protocol to Secure AODV in Mobile AdHoc Networks

Avinash Krishnan, Aishwarya Manjunath, and Geetha J. Reddy

Department of Computer Science and Engineering
M. S. Ramaiah Institute of Technology
{avinash.krishnan,aishwarya.m}@netapp.com, geetha.y.j@gmail.com
http://www.msrit.edu

N. Meghanathan et al. (Eds.): CCSIT 2011, Part III, CCIS 133, pp. 378–389, 2011.

DOI 10.1007/ 978-3-642-17881-8_46

The paper "A New Protocol to Secure AODV in Mobile AdHoc Networks" appearing on pages 378-389 of this publication has been retracted due to a severe case of plagiarism.

The original online version for this chapter can be found at
http://dx.doi.org/10.1007/978-3-642-17881-8_36

Author Index

GPSR Compliance

The European Union's (EU) General Product Safety Regulation (GPSR) is a set of rules that requires consumer products to be safe and our obligations to ensure this.

If you have any concerns about our products, you can contact us on ProductSafety@springernature.com

In case Publisher is established outside the EU, the EU authorized representative is:

Springer Nature Customer Service Center GmbH
Europaplatz 3
69115 Heidelberg, Germany

Batch number: 10844619

Printed by Printforce, the Netherlands